UNCLE TOBY.

THE WORKS OF LAURENCE STERNE,

IN ONE VOLUME:

WITH

A LIFE OF THE AUTHOR,

WRITTEN BY HIMSELF.

BEAUTIFULLY ILLUSTRATED BY DARLEY.

PHILADELPHIA:
LIPPINCOTT, GRAMBO & CO.
1855.

Memoirs

OF THE

LIFE AND FAMILY

OF THE LATE

REVEREND MR. LAURENCE STERNE,

WRITTEN BY HIMSELF.

ROGER STERNE* (grandson to Archbishop Sterne) Lieutenant in Handaside's regiment, was married to Agnes Hebert, widow of a Captain of good family. Her family name was (I believe) Nuttle, though upon recollection, that was the name of her father-in-law, who was a noted sutler in Flanders, in Queen Anne's wars, where my father married his wife's daughter, (N. B. he was in debt to him), which was on September 25, 1711, old style.—This Nuttle had a son by my grandmother,—a fine person of a man, but a graceless whelp!—what became of him I know not.—The family (if any left) live now at Clonmel, in the south of Ireland; at which town I was born, November 24, 1713, a few days after my mother arrived from Dunkirk.—My birth-day was ominous to my poor father, who was, the day of our arrival, with many other brave officers, broke, and sent adrift into the wide world, with a wife and two children;—the elder of which was Mary. She was born at Lisle, in French Flanders, July 10, 1712, new style.—This child was the most unfortunate:—She married one Weemans, in Dublin,—who used her most unmercifully;—spent his substance, became a bankrupt, and left my poor sister to shift for herself; which she was able to do but for a few months, for she went to a friend's house in the country, and died of a broken heart. She was a most beautiful woman,—of a fine figure, and deserved a better fate.—The regiment in which my father served being broke, he left Ireland as soon as I was able to be carried with the rest of his family, and came to the family seat at Elvington, near York, where his mother lived. She was daughter to Sir Roger Jaques, and an heiress. There we sojourned for about ten months, when the regiment was established, and our household decamped with bag and baggage for Dublin.—Within a month of our arrival, my father left us, being ordered to Exeter; where, in a sad winter, my mother and her two children followed him, travelling from Liverpool, by land, to Plymouth.—(Melancholy description of this journey, not necessary to be transmitted here.)—In twelve months we were all sent back to Dublin.—My mother, with three of us (for she lay-in at Plymouth of a boy, Joram) took ship at Bristol, for Ireland, and had a narrow escape from being cast away, by a leak springing up in the vessel.—At length after many perils and struggles we got to Dublin. There my father took a large house, furnished it, and in a year and a-half's

---

* Mr. Sterne was descended from a family of that name in Suffolk, one of which settled in Nottinghamshire. The following genealogy is extracted from Thoresby's Ducatus Leodinensis, p. 215.

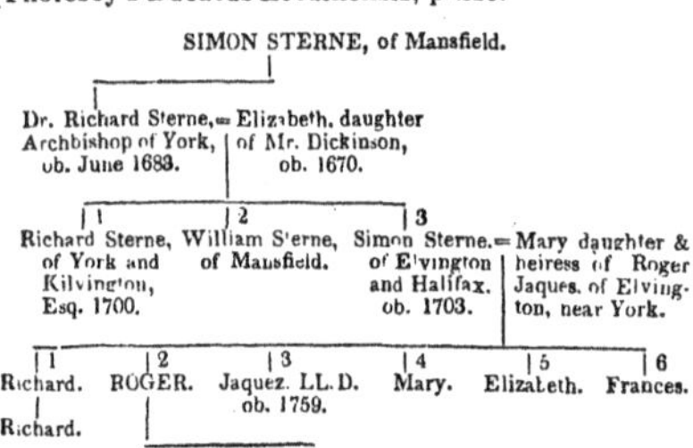

The arms of the family, says Guillam, in his book of Heraldry, p. 77, are, Or, a chevron between three crosses flory, sable. The crest, on a wreath of his colors, *a starling proper.*

Trifling circumstances are worthy of notice, when connected with distinguished characters. The arms of Mr. Sterne's family are no otherwise important than on account of the crest having afforded a hint for one of the finest stories in "The Sentimental Journey."

time spent a great deal of money.—In the year one thousand seven hundred and nineteen, all unhinged again; the regiment was ordered, with many others, to the Isle of Wight, in order to embark for Spain in the Vigo expedition. We accompanied the regiment, and were driven into Milford-Haven, but landed at Bristol; from thence, by land, to Plymouth again, and to the Isle of Wight;—where, I remember, we staid encamped some time before the embarkation of the troops—(in this expedition, from Bristol to Hampshire, we lost poor Joram,—a pretty boy, four years old, of the small-pox) my mother, sister, and myself, remained at the Isle of Wight during the Vigo expedition, and until the regiment had got back to Wicklow, in Ireland; from whence my father sent for us.—We had poor Joram's loss supplied, during our stay in the Isle of Wight, by the birth of a girl, Anne, born September the twenty-third, one thousand seven hundred and nineteen.—This pretty blossom fell at the age of three years, in the barracks of Dublin:—She was, as I well remember, of a fine delicate frame, not made to last long,—as were most of my father's babes.—We embarked for Dublin, and had all been cast away by a most violent storm; but through the intercessions of my mother, the captain was prevailed upon to turn back into Wales, where we staid a month, and at length got into Dublin, and travelled by land to Wicklow; where my father had for some weeks given us over for lost.—We lived in the barracks at Wicklow, one year—(one thousand seven hundred and twenty) when Devijeher (so called after Colonel Devijeher) was born; from thence we decamped to stay half a year with Mr. Fetherston, a clergyman, about seven miles from Wicklow; who being a relation of my mother's, invited us to his parsonage at Animo.—It was in this parish, during our stay, that I had that wonderful escape in falling through a mill-race whilst the mill was going, and of being taken up unhurt: the story is incredible, but known for truth in all that part of Ireland, where hundreds of the common people flocked to see me. From hence we followed the regiment to Dublin, where we lay in the barracks a year. In this year (one thousand seven hundred and twenty-one) I learnt to write, &c.—The regiment ordered in twenty-two to Carrickfergus, in the north of Ireland. We all decamped; but got no further than Drogheda;—thence ordered to Mullengar, forty miles west, where, by Providence, we stumbled upon a kind relation, a collateral descendant from Archbishop Sterne, who took us all to his castle, and kindly entertained us for a year, and sent us to the regiment at Carrickfergus, loaded with kindnesses, &c. A most rueful and tedious journey had we all (in March) to Carrickfergus, where we arrived in six or seven days.—Little Devijeher here died; he was three years old: he had been left behind at nurse at a farm-house near Wicklow, but was fetch'd to us by my father the summer after:—another child sent to fill his place, Susan. This babe too left us behind in this weary journey. The autumn of that year, or the spring afterwards (I forget which) my father got leave of his colonel to fix me at school,—which he did near Halifax, with an able master; with whom I staid some time, till by God's care of me, my cousin Sterne, of Elvington, became a father to me, and sent me to the university, &c. &c.—To pursue the thread of our story, my father's regiment was the year after ordered to Londonderry, where another sister was brought forth, Catherine, still living; but most unhappily estranged from me by my uncle's wickedness and her own folly. From this station the regiment was sent to defend Gibraltar, at the siege, where my father was run through the body by Captain Phillips, in a duel (the quarrel began about a goose!) with much difficulty, he survived, though with an impaired constitution, which was not able to withstand the hardships it was put to; for he was sent to Jamaica, where he soon fell by the country fever, which took away his senses first, and made a child of him; and then, in a month or two, walking about continually without complaining, till the moment he sat down in an arm-chair, and breathed his last, which was at Port Antonio, on the north of the island. My father was a little smart man, active to the last degree in all exercises, most patient of fatigue and disappointments, of which it pleased God to give him full measure. He was, in his temper, some what rapid and hasty, but of a kindly sweet disposition, void of all design; and so innocent in his own intentions, that he suspected no one; so that you might have cheated him ten times in a day, if nine had not been sufficient for your purpose. My poor father died in March 1731. I remained at Halifax till about the latter end of that year, and cannot omit mentioning this anecdote of myself and schoolmaster.—He had the ceiling of the room new white-washed; the ladder remained there: I one unlucky day mounted it, and wrote with a brush in large capital letters, LAU. STERNE, for which the usher severely whipped me. My master was very much hurt at this, and said before me, that never should that name be effaced, for I was a boy of genius, and he was sure I should come to preferment.—This expression made me forget the stripes I had received.—In the year thirty-two* my cousin sent me to the university, where I staid some time. 'Twas there that I commenced a friendship with Mr. H—, which has been lasting on both sides.—I then came to York, and my uncle got me the living of Sutton: and at York, I became acquainted with your mother, and courted her for two years:—she owned she liked me; but thought herself not rich enough, or me too poor, to be joined together.—She went to her sister's in S—; and I wrote to her often.—I believe then she was partly determined to have me, but would not say so.—At her return she fell into a consumption;—and one evening that I was sitting by her, with an almost broken heart to see her so ill, she said, "My dear Laurey, "I never "can be yours, for I verily believe I have "not long to live! but I have left you every "shilling of my fortune." Upon that she showed me her will.—This generosity overpowered me.—It pleased God that she recovered, and I married her in the year 1741. My uncle† and myself were then upon very good terms; for he soon got me the Prebend of York; but he quarrelled with me afterwards because I would not write paragraphs in the newspapers:—though he was a party-man, I was not, and detested such dirty work: thinking it beneath me. From that period he became my bitterest enemy.*—By my wife's means I got the living of Stillington: a friend of hers in the south had promised her, that if she married a clergyman in Yorkshire,—when the living became vacant, he would make her a compliment of it. I remained near twenty years at Sutton, doing duty at both places. I had then very good health. Books,† painting, fiddling, and shooting, were my amusements. As to the Squire of the parish, I cannot say we were upon a very friendly footing: but at Stillington, the family of the C—s showed us every kindness: 'twas most truly agreeable to be within a mile and a half of an amiable family, who were ever cordial friends.—In the year 1760 I took a house at York for your mother and yourself, and went up to London to publish ‡ my two first volumes of Shandy.§ In that year Lord Falconbridge presented me with the curacy of Coxwold; a sweet retirement in comparison of Sutton. In sixty-two I went

---

* He was admitted of Jesus' College, in the university of Cambridge, 6th July 1733, under the tuition of Mr. Cannon.

Matriculated 29th March 1735.

Admitted to the degree of B. A. in January 1736.

Admitted M. A. at the commencement of 1740.

† Jaques Sterne, LL. D. He was Prebendary of Durham, Canon Residentiary, Precentor and Prebendary of York, Rector of Rise, and Rector of Hornsea cum Riston both in the East Riding of the county of York. He died June 9th, 1759.

* It hath, however, been insinuated, that he for some time wrote a periodical electioneering paper at York, in defence of the Whig interest.—*Monthly Review*, vol. 53, p. 344.

† A specimen of Mr. Sterne's abilities in the art of designing, may be seen in Mr. Wodhul's poems, 8vo. 1772.

‡ The first edition was printed in the preceding year at York.

§ The following is the order in which Mr. Sterne's publications appeared:

1747. The Case of Elijah and the Widow of Zerephath considered, a Charity Sermon preached on Good-Friday, April 17, 1747, for the support of two charity-schools in York.

1750. The Abuses of Conscience. Set forth in a Sermon preached in the cathedral church of St. Peter, York, at the summer assizes, before the Hon. Mr. Baron Clive, and the Hon. Mr. Baron Smith; on Sunday, July 29, 1750.

1759. Vol. 1 and 2 of Tristram Shandy.
1760. Vol. 1 and 2 of Sermons.
1761. Vol. 3 and 4 of Tristram Shandy.
1762. Vol. 5 and 6 of Tristram Shandy.
1765. Vol. 7 and 8 of Tristram Shandy.
1766. Vol. 3, 4, 5, and 6 of Sermons.
1767. Vol. 9 of Tristram Shandy.
1768. The Sentimental Journey.

The remainder of his works were published after his death.

to France before the peace was concluded; and you both followed me. I left you both in France, and in two years after, I went to Italy for the recovery of my health; and, when I called upon you, I tried to engage your mother to return to England with me:* she and yourself are at length come, and I have had the inexpressible joy of seeing my girl every thing I wished her.

I have set down these particulars relating to my family and self for my Lydia, in case hereafter she might have a curiosity, or a kinder motive to know them.

As Mr. Sterne, in the foregoing narrative, hath brought down the account of himself until within a few months of his death, it remains only to mention that he left York about the end of the year 1767, and came to London, in order to publish *The Sentimental Journey*, which he had written during the preceding summer at his favourite living of Coxwold. His health had been for some time declining; but he continued to visit his friends, and retained his usual flow of spirits. In February, 1768, he began to perceive the approaches of death; and with the concern of a good man, and the solicitude of an affectionate parent, devoted his attention to the future welfare of his daughter. His letters, at this period, reflect so much credit on his character, that it is to be lamented some others in the collection were permitted to see the light. After a short struggle with his disorder, his debilitated and worn-out frame submitted to fate on the eighteenth day of March, 1768, at his lodgings in Bond-street. He was buried at the new burying-ground belonging to the parish of St. George, Hanover-square, on the 22d of the same month, in the most private manner; and hath since been indebted to strangers for a monument very unworthy of his memory, on which the following lines are inscribed:—

"Near to this Place
Lies the Body of
The Reverend LAURENCE STERNE, A. M
Died September 13th, 1768,*
Aged 53 Years.

Ah! molliter ossa quiescant

If a sound Head, warm Heart, and Breast humane,
Unsullied Worth, and Soul without a Stain;
If Mental Pow'rs could ever justly claim
The well-won Tribute of immortal Fame,
Sterne was *the man*, who, with gigantic Stride,
Mow'd down luxuriant Follies far and wide.
Yet what tho' keenest Knowledge of Mankind
Unseal'd to him the springs that move the Mind
What did it cost him?—Ridicul'd, abus'd,
By Fools insulted, and by Prudes accus'd!
In his, mild Reader, view thy future fate;
Like him despise what 'twere a Sin to hate.

This monumental Stone was erected by two brother masons; for though he did not live to be a member of their society, yet, as his all-incomparable performances evidently prove him to have acted by rule and square, they rejoice in this opportunity of perpetuating his high and irreproachable character to after-ages. W. & S."

---

* From this passage it appears that the present account of Mr. Sterne's Life and Family was written about six months only before his death.

* It is scarcely necessary to observe, that this date is erroneous.

THE

LIFE AND OPINIONS

OF

Tristram Shandy,

GENTLEMAN.

CHAP. I.

I WISH either my father or my mother, or indeed both of them, as they were in duty both equally bound to it, had minded what they were about when they begot me: had they duly considered how much depended upon what they were then doing;—that not only the production of a rational being was concerned in it, but that possibly the happy formation and temperature of his body, perhaps his genius, and the very cast of his mind; and, for aught they knew to the contrary, even the fortunes of his whole house, might take their turn from the humors and dispositions which were then uppermost;—had they duly weighed and considered all this, and proceeded accordingly,—I am verily persuaded I should have made a quite different figure in the world from that in which the reader is likely to see me.—Believe me, good folks, this is not so inconsiderable a thing as many of you may think it;—you have all, I dare say, heard of the animal spirits, as how they are transfused from father to son, &c. &c.—and a great deal to that purpose:—well, you may take my word, that nine parts in ten of a man's sense, or his nonsense, his successes and miscarriages in this world, depend upon their motions and activity, and the different tracks and trains you put them into; so that when they are once set a-going, whether right or wrong, 'tis not a halfpenny matter,—away they go cluttering like hey-go mad; and by treading the same steps over and over again, they presently make a road of it, as plain and as smooth as a garden-walk, which when they are once used to, the devil himself sometimes shall not be able to drive them off it.

Pray, my dear, quoth my mother, *have you not forgot to wind up the clock?*——*Good G—d!* cried my father, making an exclamation, but taking care to moderate his voice at the same time,——*Did ever woman, since the creation of the world, interrupt a man with such a silly question?* Pray, what was your father saying?——Nothing.

CHAP. II.

——Then, positively, there is nothing in the question that I can see, either good or bad.——Then, let me tell you, Sir, it was a very unseasonable question at least,—because it scattered and dispersed the animal spirits, whose business it was to have escorted, and gone hand in hand with the *Homunculus*, and conducted him safe to the place destined for his reception.

The *Homunculus*, Sir, in however low and ludicrous a light he may appear, in this age of levity, to the eye of folly or prejudice;—to the eye of reason in scientific research, he stands confessed—a *being* guarded and circumscribed with rights.——The minutest philosophers, who, by the bye, have the most enlarged understandings (their souls being inversely as their inquiries) show us incontestably that the *Homunculus* is created by the same hand,—engendered in the same course of nature,—endowed with the same locomotive powers and faculties with us:—that he consists, as we do, of skin, hair, fat, flesh, veins, arteries, ligaments, nerves, cartilages, bones, marrow, brains, glands, genitals, humors, and articulations;—is a being of as much activity,—and, in all senses of the word, as much and as truly our fellow-creature as my Lord Chancellor of England.—He may be benefited,—he may be injured, he may obtain redress; in a word, he has all the claims and rights of humanity which Tully, Puffendorf, or the best ethic writers, allow to arise out of that state and relation.

Now, dear Sir, what if any accident had befallen him in his way alone!—or that, through terror of it, natural to so young a traveller, my little gentleman had got to his journey's end miserably spent;—his muscular strength and virility worn down to a thread;—his own animal spirits ruffled beyond description,—and that in this sad disordered state of nerves, he had lain down a prey to sudden starts, or a series of melancholy dreams and fancies, for nine long, long months together,—I tremble to think what a foundation had been laid for a thousand weaknesses both of body and mind, which no skill of the physician or the philosopher could ever afterwards have set thoroughly to rights.

CHAP. III.

To my uncle, Mr. Toby Shandy, do I stand indebted for the preceding anecdote, to whom my father, who was an excellent natural philosopher, and much given to close reasoning upon the smallest matters, had oft and heavily complained of the injury; but once more particularly, as my uncle Toby well remembered, upon his observing a most unaccountable obliquity (as he called it) in my manner of setting up my top; and justifying the principles upon which I had done it,—the old gentleman shook his head, and in a tone more expressive by half of sorrow than reproach, he said his heart all along foreboded, and he saw it verified in this, and from a thousand other observations he had made upon me, that I should neither think nor act like any other man's child:—*But alas!* continued he, shaking his head a second time, and wiping away a tear which was trickling down his cheeks, *My Tristram's misfortunes began nine months before ever he came into the world!*

—My mother, who was sitting by, looked up; but she knew no more than her backside what my father meant;—but my uncle, Mr. Toby Shandy, who had been often informed of the affair,—understood him very well.

CHAP. IV.

I KNOW there are readers in the world, as well as many other good people in it, who are no readers at all,—who find themselves ill at ease, unless they are let into the whole secret, from first to last, of every thing which concerns you.

It is in pure compliance with this humor of theirs, and from a backwardness in my nature to disappoint any one soul living, that I have been so very particular already. As my life and opinions are likely to make some noise in the world, and, if I conjecture right, will take in all ranks, professions, and denominations of men whatever,—be no less read than the Pilgrim's Progress itself,—and, in the end, prove the very thing which Montaigne dreaded his Essays should turn out, that is, a book for a parlor-window;—I find it necessary to consult every one a little in his turn; and therefore must beg pardon for going on a little farther in the same way: for which cause right glad I am that I have begun the history of myself in the way I have done; and that I am able to go on, tracing every thing in it, as Horace says, *ab ovo.*

Horace, I know, does not recommend this fashion altogether: but that gentleman is speaking only of an epic poem, or a tragedy —(I forgot which;)—besides, if it was not so, I should beg Mr. Horace's pardon;—for in writing what I have set about, I shall confine myself neither to his rules, nor to any man's rules that ever lived.

To such, however, as do not choose to go so far back into these things, I can give no better advice than that they skip over the remaining part of this chapter; for I declare beforehand, 'tis wrote only for the curious and inquisitive.

———Shut the door.———I was begot in the night betwixt the first Sunday and the first Monday in the month of March, in the year of our Lord one thousand seven hundred and eighteen. I am positive I was.—But how I came to be so very particular in my account of a thing which happened before I was born, is owing to another small anecdote known only in our own family; but now made public for the better clearing up of this point.

My father, you must know, who was

originally a Turkey merchant, but had left off business for some years, in order to retire to and die upon his paternal estate in the county of ——, was, I believe, one of the most regular men in every thing he did, whether it was matter of business or matter of amusement, that ever lived. As a small specimen of this extreme exactness of his, to which he was in truth a slave, he had made it a rule for many years of his life,—on the first Sunday night of every month throughout the whole year, as certain as ever the Sunday night came,—to wind up a large house-clock, which we had standing on the back-stairs head, with his own hands: and being somewhere between fifty and sixty years of age at the time I have been speaking of, he had likewise gradually brought some other little family concerns to the same period, in order, as he would often say to my uncle Toby, to get them all out of the way at one time, and be no more plagued and pestered with them the rest of the month.

It was attended but with one misfortune, which, in a great measure, fell upon myself, and the effects of which, I fear, I shall carry with me to my grave; namely, that from an unhappy association of ideas, which have no connexion in nature, it so fell out at length, that my poor mother could never hear the said clock wound up, but the thoughts of some other things unavoidably popped into her head—*et vice versa*:—— which strange combination of ideas, the sagacious Locke, who certainly understood the nature of these things better than most men, affirms to have produced more wry actions than all other sources of prejudice whatsoever.

But this by the bye

Now it appears by a memorandum in my father's pocket-book, which now lies upon the table, "That on Lady-day, which was on the 25th of the same month in which I date my geniture,——my father set out upon his journey to London, with my eldest brother Bobby, to fix him at Westminster school;" and, as it appears from the same authority, "That he did not get down to his wife and family till the *second week* in May, following,"—it brings the thing almost to a certainty. However, what follows in the beginning of the next chapter puts it beyond all possibility of doubt.

———But pray, Sir, what was your father doing all December, January, and February?——Why, Madam,—he was all that time afflicted with a Sciatica.

CHAP. V.

On the fifth day of November, 1718, which, to the era fixed on, was as near nine calendar months as any husband could in reason have expected,—was I, Tristram Shandy, gentleman, brought forth into this scurvy and disastrous world of ours.——I wish I had been born in the moon, or in any of the planets, (except Jupiter or Saturn, because I never could bear cold weather,) for it could not well have fared worse with me in any of them (though I will not answer for Venus) than it has in this vile, dirty planet of ours,—which, o' my conscience, with reverence be it spoken, I take to be made up of the shreds and clippings of the rest;——not but the planet is well enough, provided a man could be born in it to a great title, or to a great estate; or could any how contrive to be called up to public charges and employments of dignity or power;——but that is not my case;—— and therefore every man will speak of the fair as his own market has gone in it;——— for which cause, I affirm it over again to be one of the vilest worlds that ever was made;—for I can truly say, that from the first hour I drew my breath in it, to this, that I can now scarce draw it at all, for an asthma I got in skating against the wind in Flanders,—I have been the continual sport of what the world calls Fortune; and though I will not wrong her by saying, She has ever made me feel the weight of any great or signal evil;——yet, with all the good temper in the world, I affirm it of her, that in every stage of my life, and at every turn and corner where she could get fairly at me, the ungracious duchess has pelted me with a set of as pitiful misadventures and cross-accidents as ever small *Hero* sustained

CHAP. VI.

In the beginning of the last chapter, I informed you exactly *when* I was born; but I did not inform you *how*. No; that particular was reserved entirely for a chapter by itself;—besides, Sir, as you and I are in a manner perfect strangers to each other, it would not have been proper to have let you into too many circumstances relating to myself all at once.—You must have a little patience. I have undertaken, you see, to write not only my life, but my opinions also; hoping and expecting that your knowledge of my character, and of what kind of a mortal I am, by the one, would give you a better relish for the other. As you proceed farther with me, the slight acquaintance, which is now beginning betwixt us, will grow into familiarity; and that, unless one of us is in fault, will terminate in friendship.—*O diem præclarum!*—then nothing which has touched me will be thought trifling in its nature, or tedious in its telling. Therefore, my dear friend and companion, if you should think me somewhat sparing of my narrative on my first setting out—bear with me—and let me go on and tell my story my own way:—or, if I should seem now and then to trifle upon the road,—or should sometimes put on a fool's cap, with a bell to it, for a moment or two as we pass along,—don't fly off,—but rather courteously give me credit for a little more wisdom than appears upon my outside;—and, as we jog on, either laugh with me, or at me, or, in short, do any thing,—only keep your temper.

CHAP. VII.

In the same village where my father and my mother dwelt, dwelt also a thin, upright, motherly, notable, good old body of a midwife, who, with the help of a little plain good sense, and some years' full employment in her business, in which she had all along trusted little to her own efforts, and a great deal to those of dame Nature,—had acquired, in her way, no small degree of reputation in the world:—by which word *world*, need I in this place inform your worship that I would be understood to mean no more of it than a small circle described upon the circle of the great world, of four English miles diameter, or thereabouts, of which the cottage where the good old woman lived is supposed to be the centre?—She had been left, it seems, a widow in great distress, with three or four small children, in her forty-seventh year; and as she was at that time a person of decent carriage,—grave deportment,—a woman moreover of few words, and withal an object of compassion, whose distress, and silence under it, called out the louder for a friendly lift,—the wife of the parson of the parish was touched with pity; and having often lamented an inconvenience to which her husband's flock had for many years been exposed, inasmuch as there was no such thing as a midwife, of any kind or degree, to be got at, let the case have been ever so urgent, within less than six or seven long miles' riding; which said seven long miles in dark nights and dismal roads, the country thereabouts being nothing but a deep clay, was almost equal to fourteen; and that in effect was sometimes next to having no midwife at all, it came into her head that it would be doing as seasonable a kindness to the whole parish as to the poor creature herself, to get her a little instructed in some of the plain principles of the business, in order to set her up in it. As no woman thereabouts was better qualified to execute the plan she had formed than herself, the gentlewoman very charitably undertook it; and having great influence over the female part of the parish, she found no difficulty in effecting it to the utmost of her wishes. In truth, the parson joined his interest with his wife's in the whole affair; and, in order to do things as they should be, and give the poor soul as good a title by law to practise, as his wife had given by institution,—he cheerfully paid the fees for the ordinary's license himself, amounting in the whole to the sum of eighteen shillings and fourpence; so that, betwixt them both, the good woman was fully invested in the real and corporal possession of her office, together with all its *rights, members, and appurtenances whatsoever.*

These last words, you must know, were not according to the old form in which such licenses, faculties and powers usually ran, which, in like cases, had heretofore been granted to the sisterhood; but it was according to a neat formula of Didius his own devising, who having a particular turn for taking to pieces and new-framing over again all kinds of instruments in that way, not only hit upon this dainty amendment, but coaxed many of the old licensed matrons in the neighborhood to open their faculties afresh, in order to have this whimwham of his inserted.

I own I never could envy Didius in these kinds of fancies of his:—but every man to his own taste.—Did not Dr. Kunastrokius, that great man, at his leisure hours, take the greatest delight imaginable in combing of asses' tails, and plucking the dead hairs out with his teeth, though he had tweezers always in his pocket? Nay, if you come to that, Sir, have not the wisest of men in all ages, not excepting Solomon himself,—have they not had their Hobby-Horses,—their running horses,—their coins and their cockle-shells, their drums and their trumpets, their fiddles, their pallets, their maggots, and their butterflies?—and so long as a man rides his Hobby-Horse peaceably and quietly along the King's highway, and neither compels you nor me to get up behind him,—pray, Sir, what have either you or I to do with it?

CHAP. VIII.

—*De gustibus non est disputandum*;—that is, there is no disputing against Hobby-Horses; and for my part I seldom do; nor could I with any sort of grace, had I been an enemy to them at the bottom; for happening, at certain intervals and changes of the moon, to be both fiddler and painter, according as the fly stings,—be it known to you, that I keep a couple of pads myself, upon which, in their turns, (nor do I care who knows it,) I frequently ride out and take the air; though sometimes, to my shame be it spoken, I take somewhat longer journeys than what a wise man would think altogether right.—But the truth is,—I am not a wise man;—and besides, am a mortal of so little consequence in the world, it is not much matter what I do: so I seldom fret or fume at all about it: nor does it much disturb my rest, when I see such great lords and tall personages as hereafter follow;—such, for instance, as my lord A, B, C, D, E, F, G, H, I, K, L, M, N, O, P, Q, and so on, all of a row, mounted upon their several horses;—some with large stirrups, getting on with a more grave and sober pace;———others, on the contrary, tucked up to their very chins, with whips across their mouths, scouring and scampering away like so many little party-colored devils astride a mortgage,—and as if some of them were resolved to break their necks.—So much the better,—say I to myself;—for, in case the worst should happen, the world will make a shift to do excellently well without them; and for the rest,—why,—God speed them,—e'en let them ride on without opposition from me; for, were their lordships unhorsed this very night—'tis ten to one but that many of them would be worse mounted by one half before to-morrow morning.

Not one of these instances therefore can be said to break in upon my rest.—But there is an instance, which I own puts me off my guard, and that is, when I see one born for great actions, and, what is still more for his honor, whose nature ever inclines him to good ones;—when I behold such a one, my Lord, like yourself, whose principles and conduct are as generous and noble as his blood, and whom, for that reason, a corrupt world cannot spare one moment;—when I see such a one, my Lord, mounted, though it is but for a minute beyond the time which my love to my country has prescribed to him, and my zeal for his glory wishes,—then, my Lord, I cease to be a philosopher, and in the first transport of an honest impatience, I wish the Hobby-Horse, with all its fraternity, at the Devil.

"My Lord,

"I maintain this to be a dedication, "notwithstanding its singularity in the "three great essentials of matter, form, and "place: I beg, therefore, you will accept it "as such, and that you will permit me to "lay it, with the most respectful humility. "at your Lordship's feet,—when you are "upon them,—which you can be when you "please;—and that is, my Lord, whenever "there is occasion for it; and I will add, to "the best purposes too.

"I have the honor to be,

"My Lord,

"Your Lordship's most obedient,

"and most devoted,

"and most humble servant,

"TRISTRAM SHANDY."

CHAP. IX.

I SOLEMNLY declare to all mankind, that the above dedication was made for no one Prince, Prelate, Pope, or Potentate,—Duke, Marquis, Earl, Viscount, or Baron, of this, or any other realm in Christendom;—nor has it yet been hawked about, or offered publicly or privately, directly or indirectly, to any one person or personage, great or small; but is honestly a true virgin-Dedication untried on, upon any soul living.

I labor this point so particularly, merely to remove any offence or objection which might arise against it from the manner in which I propose to make the most of it;—which is the putting it up fairly to public sale; which I now do.

—Every author has a way of his own in bringing his points to bear;—for my own part, as I hate chaffering and higgling for a few guineas in a dark entry, I resolved within myself, from the very beginning, to deal squarely and openly with your Great Folks in this affair, and try whether I should not come off the better by it.

If therefore there is any one Duke, Marquis, Earl, Viscount, or Baron, in these His Majesty's dominions, who stands in need of a tight, genteel dedication, and whom the above will suit, (for, by the bye, unless it suits in some degree, I will not part with it,)—it is much at his service for fifty guineas; which I am positive is twenty guineas less than it ought to be afforded for, by any man of genius.

My Lord, if you examine it over again, it is far from being a gross piece of daubing, as some dedications are. The design, your Lordship sees, is good, the coloring transparent,—the drawing not amiss;—or, to speak more like a man of science, and measure my piece in the painter's scale, divided into 20,—I believe, my Lord, the outlines will turn out as 12,—the composition as 9,—the coloring as 7,—the expression 13 and a half,—and the design, if I may be allowed, my Lord, to understand my own *design*, and supposing absolute perfection in designing, to be as 20,—I think it cannot well fall short of 19. Besides all this,—there is keeping in it; and the dark strokes in the HOBBY-HORSE (which is a secondary figure, and a kind of back-ground to the whole,) give great force to the principal lights in your own figure, and make it come off wonderfully;—and besides, there is an air of originality in the *tout ensemble.*

Be pleased, my good Lord, to order the sum to be paid into the hands of Mr. Dodsley, for the benefit of the author; and in the next edition care shall be taken that this chapter be expunged, and your Lordship's titles, distinctions, arms, and good actions, be placed at the front of the preceding chapter: all which, from the words *De gustibus non est disputandum*, and whatever else in this book relates to HOBBY-HORSES, but no more, shall stand dedicated to your Lordship.—The rest I dedicate to the MOON, who, by the bye, of all the Patrons or Matrons I can think of, has most power to set my book a-going, and make the world run mad after it.

Bright Goddess,

If thou art not too busy with CANDID and Miss CUNEGUND'S affairs,—take Tristram Shandy's under thy protection also.

CHAP. X.

WHATEVER degree of small merit the act of benignity in favor of the midwife might justly claim, or in whom that claim truly rested,—at first sight seems not very material to this history; certain, however, it was, that the gentlewoman, the parson's wife, did run away at that time with the whole of it: and yet, for my life, I cannot help thinking but that the parson himself, though he had not the good fortune to hit upon the design first,—yet, as he heartily concurred in it the moment it was laid before him, and as heartily parted with his money to carry it into execution, had a claim to some share of it,—if not a full half of whatever honor was due to it.

The world at that time was pleased to determine the matter otherwise.

Lay down the book, and I will allow you half a day to give a probable guess at the grounds of this procedure.

Be it known then, that, for about five years before the date of the midwife's license, of which you have had so circumstantial an account,—the parson we have to do with, had made himself a country-talk by a breach of all decorum, which he had committed against himself, his station, and his office:—and that was in never appearing better, or otherwise mounted, than upon a lean, sorry, jack-ass of a horse, value about one pound fifteen shillings; who, to shorten all description of him, was full brother to Rosinante, as far as similitude congenial could make him; for he answered his description to a hairbreadth in every thing,—except that I do not remember 'tis anywhere said that Rosinante was brokenwinded; and that, moreover, Rosinante, as it is the happiness of most Spanish horses, fat or lean,—was undoubtedly a horse at all points.

I know very well that the Hero's horse was a horse of chaste deportment, which may have given grounds for the contrary opinion: but it is as certain, at the same time, that Rosinante's continency (as may be demonstrated from the adventure of the Yanguesian carriers) proceeded from no bodily defect or cause whatsoever, but from the temperance and orderly current of his blood.—And let me tell you, Madam, there is a great deal of very good chastity in the world, in behalf of which you could not say more for your life.

Let that be as it may, as my purpose is to do exact justice to every creature brought upon the stage of this dramatic work,—I could not stifle this distinction in favor of Don Quixote's horse;—in all other points, the parson's horse, I say, was just such another: for he was as lean, and as lank, and as sorry a jade, as Humility herself could have bestrided.

In the estimation of here and there a man of weak judgment, it was greatly in the parson's power to have helped the figure of this horse of his,—for he was master of a very handsome demi-peak'd saddle, quilted on the seat with green plush, garnished with a double row of silver-headed studs, and a noble pair of shining brass stirrups, with a housing altogether suitable, of grey superfine cloth, with an edging of black lace, terminating in a deep, black, silk fringe, *poudré d'or*:—all which he had purchased in the pride and prime of his life, together with a grand embossed bridle, ornamented at all points as it should be.——But not caring to banter his beast, he had hung all these up behind his study-door; and, in lieu of them, had seriously befitted him with just such a bridle and such a saddle as the figure and value of such a steed might well and truly deserve.

In the several sallies about his parish, and in the neighboring visits to the gentry who lived around him,—you will easily comprehend, that the parson, so appointed, would both hear and see enough to keep his philosophy from rusting. To speak the truth, he never could enter a village, but he caught the attention of both old and young.——Labor stood still as he passed,—the bucket hung suspended in the middle of the well —the spinning-wheel forgot its round,—even chuck-farthing and shuffle-cap themselves stood gaping till he had got out of sight; and as his movement was not of the quickest, he had generally time enough upon his hands to make his observations,—to hear the groans of the serious,—and the laughter of the light-hearted: all which he bore with excellent tranquillity.—His character was,—he loved a jest in his heart,—and as he saw himself in the true point of ridicule, he would say he could not be angry with others for seeing him in a light in which he so strongly saw himself;—so that to his friends, who knew his foible was not the love of money, and who therefore made the less scruple in bantering the extravagance of his humor,—instead of giving the true cause,—he chose rather to join in the laugh against himself; and as he never carried one single ounce of flesh upon his own bones, being altogether as spare a figure as his beast,—he would sometimes insist upon it, that the horse was as good as the rider deserved;—that they were, centaur-like, both of a piece. At other times, and in other moods, when his spirits were above the temptation of false wit.—he would say, he found himself going off fast in a consumption; and, with great gravity, would pretend, he could not bear the sight of a fat horse, without a dejection of heart, and a sensible alteration in his pulse; and that he had made choice of the lean one he rode upon, not only to keep himself in countenance, but in spirits.

At different times he would give fifty humorous and apposite reasons for riding a meek-spirited jade of a brokenwinded horse, preferably to one of mettle;—for on such a one he could sit mechanically, and meditate as delightfully *de vanitate mundi et fugâ sæculi*, as with the advantage of a death's-head before him;—that, in all other exercitations, he could spend his time, as he rode slowly along,—to as much account as in his study;—that he could draw up an argument in his sermon,—or a hole in his breeches, as steadily on the one as in the other;—that brisk trotting and slow argumentation, like wit and judgment, were two incompatible movements.—But that upon his steed, he could unite and reconcile every thing;—he could compose his sermon,—he could compose his cough,—and, in case nature gave a call that way, he could likewise compose himself to sleep.—In short, the parson upon such encounters would assign any cause but the true cause;—and he withheld the true one, only out of a nicety of temper, because he thought it did honour to him.

But the truth of the story was as follows:—In the first years of this gentleman's life, and about the time when the superb saddle and bridle were purchased by him, it had been his manner, or vanity, or call it what you will,—to run into the opposite extreme.—In the language of the country where he dwelt, he was said to have loved a good horse, and generally had one of the best in the whole parish standing in his stable always ready for saddling; and as the nearest midwife, as I told you, did not live nearer to the village than seven miles, and in a vile country, it so fell out that the poor gentleman was scarce a whole week together without some piteous application for his beast · and as he was not an unkind-hearted man, and every case was more pressing and more distressful than the last,—as much as he loved his beast, he had never a heart to refuse him; the upshot of which was generally this, that his horse was either clapped, or spavined, or greazed; or he was twitter-boned, or brokenwinded, or something, in short, or other had befallen him, which would let him carry no flesh;—so that he had every nine or ten months a bad horse to get rid of,—and a good horse to purchase in his stead.

What the loss in such a balance might amount to, *communibus annis*, I would leave to a special jury of sufferers in the same traffic, to determine;—but let it be what it would, the honest gentleman bore it for many years without a murmur, till at length, by repeated ill accidents of the kind, he found it necessary to take the thing under consideration; and, upon weighing the whole, and summing it up in his mind, he found it not only disproportioned to his other expenses, but withal so heavy an article in itself as to disable him from any other act of generosity in his parish; besides this, he considered that with half the sum thus galloped away, he could do ten times as much good;—and what still weighed more with him than all other considerations put together, was this, that it confined all his charity into one particular channel, and where, as he fancied, it was the least wanted; namely, to the child-bearing and child-getting part of his parish; reserving nothing for the impotent,—nothing for the aged,—nothing for the many comfortless scenes he was hourly called forth to visit, where poverty, and sickness, and affliction dwelt together.

For these reasons he resolved to discontinue the expense; and there appeared but two possible ways to extricate him clearly out of it; and these were, either to make it an irrevocable law never more to lend his steed upon any application whatever,—or else be content to ride the last poor devil, such as they had made him, with all his aches and infirmities, to the very end of the chapter.

As he dreaded his own constancy in the first,—he very cheerfully betook himself to the second; and though he could very well have explained it, as I said, to his honour,—yet, for that very reason, he had a spirit above it; choosing rather to bear the contempt of his enemies and the laughter of his friends, than undergo the pain of telling a story which might seem a panegyric upon himself.

I have the highest idea of the spiritual and refined sentiments of this reverend gentleman, from this single stroke in his character, which I think comes up to any of the honest refinements of the peerless knight of La Mancha, whom, by the bye, with all his follies, I love more, and would actually have gone farther to have paid a visit to, than the greatest hero of antiquity.

But this is not the moral of my story: the thing I had in view was to show the temper of the world in the whole of this affair.— For you must know, that so long as this explanation would have done the parson credit,—the devil a soul could find it out:— I suppose his enemies would not, and that his friends could not.———But no sooner did he bestir himself in behalf of the midwife, and pay the expenses of the ordinary's license to set her up,—but the whole secret came out; every horse he had lost, and two horses more than ever he had lost, with all the circumstances of their destruction, were known and distinctly remembered.—The story ran like wildfire;—"The parson had "a returning fit of pride which had just "seized him, and he was going to be well "mounted once again in his life; and if it "was so, 'twas plain as the sun at noon-day, "he would pocket the expense of the li-"cense ten times told, the very first year:— "so that every body was left to judge what "were his views in this act of charity."

What were his views in this, and in every other action of his life,—or rather what were the opinions which floated in the brains of other people concerning it, was a thought which too much floated in his own, and too often broke in upon his rest, when he should have been sound asleep.

About ten years ago, this gentleman had the good fortune to be made entirely easy upon that score,—it being just so long since he left his parish,—and the whole world at the same time, behind him;—and stands accountable to a Judge of whom he will have no cause to complain.

But there is a fatality attends the actions of some men: order them as they will, they pass through a certain medium, which so twists and refracts them from their true directions, that, with all the titles to praise which a rectitude of heart can give, the doers of them are nevertheless forced to live and die without it.

Of the truth of which, this gentleman was a painful example.———But to know by what means this came to pass,—and to make that knowledge of use to you, I insist upon it that you read the two following chapters, which contain such a sketch of his life and conversation, as will carry its moral along with it.—When this is done, if nothing stops us in our way, we shall go on with the midwife.

CHAP. XI.

Yorick was this parson's name, and, what is very remarkable in it (as appears from a most ancient account of the family, wrote upon strong vellum, and now in perfect preservation,) it had been exactly so spelt for near,———I was within an ace of saying nine hundred years;—but I would not shake my credit in telling an improbable truth, however indisputable in itself;—and therefore I shall content myself with only saying,———it had been exactly so spelt, without the least variation or transposition of a single letter, for I do not know how long; which is more than I would venture to say of one half of the best surnames in the kingdom: which, in a course of years, have generally undergone as many chops and changes as their owners.—Has this been owing to the pride, or to the shame of the respective proprietors?—In honest truth, I think sometimes to the one, and sometimes to the other, just as the temptation has wrought. But a villanous affair it is, and will one day so blend and confound us all together, that no one shall be able to stand up and swear, "That his own great-"grandfather was the man who did either "this or that."

This evil had been sufficiently fenced against by the prudent care of the Yorick family;—and their religious preservation of these records I quote, which do farther inform us, That the family was originally of Danish extraction, and had been transplanted into England as early as in the reign of Horwendillus, king of Denmark, in whose court, it seems, an ancestor of this Mr. Yorick, and from whom he was lineally descended, held a considerable post to the day of his death. Of what nature this considerable post was, this record saith not;—it only adds, That for near two centuries, it had been totally abolished, as altogether unnecessary not only in that court, but in every other court of the Christian world.

It has often come into my head, that this post could be no other than that of the king's chief jester,—and that Hamlet's Yorick, in our Shakspeare, many of whose plays, you know, are founded upon authenticated facts, was certainly the very man.

I have not the time to look into Saxo-Grammaticus's Danish History, to know the certainty of this,—but if you have leisure and can easily get at the book, you may do it full as well yourself.

I had just time in my travels through Denmark, with Mr. Noddy's eldest son, whom, in the year 1741, I accompanied as governor, riding along with him at a prodigious rate through most parts of Europe, and of which original journey performed by us two, a most delectable narrative will be given in the progress of this work;—I had just time, I say, and that was all, to prove the truth of an observation made by a long sojourner in that country;——namely, "That Nature was neither very "lavish, nor was she very stingy in her "gifts of genius and capacity to its inhab-"itants;—but, like a discreet parent, was "moderately kind to them all; observing "such an equal tenor in the distribution of "her favors, as to bring them, in those "points, pretty nearly to a level with each "other; so that you will meet with few "instances in that kingdom of refined parts; "but a great deal of good plain household "understanding amongst all ranks of people, "of which every body has a share;" which is, I think, very right.

With us, you see, the case is quite different:—we are all ups and downs in this matter;—you are a great genius;—or 'tis fifty to one, Sir, you are a great dunce and a blockhead;—not that there is a total want of intermediate steps;—no, we are not so irregular as that comes to;—but the two extremes are more common, and in a greater degree in this unsettled island, where Nature, in her gifts and dispositions of this kind, is most whimsical and capricious Fortune herself not being more so in the bequest of her goods and chattels than she.

This is all that ever staggered my faith in regard to Yorick's extraction, who, by what I can remember of him, and by all the accounts I could ever get of him, seemed not to have had one single drop of Danish blood in his whole crasis: in nine hundred years, it might possibly have all run out;——I will not philosophize one moment with you about it: for happen how it would, the fact was this:—That instead of that cold phlegm and exact regularity of sense and humors you would have looked for in one so extracted,—he was, on the contrary, as mercurial and sublimated a composition,—as heteroclite a creature in all his declensions,——with as much life and whim, and *gaité de cœur* about him, as the kindliest climate could have engendered and put together. With all this sail, poor Yorick carried not one ounce of ballast; he was utterly unpractised in the world; and, at the age of twenty-six, knew just about as well how to steer his course in it as a romping unsuspicious girl of thirteen; so that upon his first setting out, the brisk gale of his spirits, as you will imagine, ran him foul ten times in a day of somebody's tackling; and as the grave and more slow-paced were oftenest in his way,——you may likewise imagine, 'twas with such he had generally the ill luck to get the most entangled. For aught I know, there might be some mixture of unlucky wit at the bottom of such *fracas*:——for, to speak the truth, Yorick had an invincible dislike and opposition in his nature to gravity;—not to gravity as such;—for where gravity was wanted, he would be the most grave or serious of mortal men for days and weeks together; but he was an enemy to the affectation of it, and declared open war against it, only as it appeared a cloak for ignorance, or for folly: and then, whenever it fell in his way, however sheltered and protected, he seldom gave it much quarter.

Sometimes, in his wild way of talking, he would say, that Gravity was an errant scoundrel, and, he would add,—of the most dangerous kind too,—because a sly one and that he verily believed, more honest well-meaning people were bubbled out of their goods and money by it in one twelvemonth, than by pocket-picking and shop-lifting in seven. In the naked temper which a merry heart discovered, he would say there was no danger,—but to itself:—whereas the very essence of gravity was design, and consequently deceit;—'twas a taught trick, to gain credit of the world for more sense and knowledge than a man was worth; and that, with all his pretensions,—it was no better, but often worse, than what a French wit had long ago defined it, *viz.* *A mysterious carriage of the body, to cover the defects of the mind:*—which definition of gravity, Yorick, with great imprudence, would say, deserved to be wrote in letters of gold.

But, in plain truth, he was a man unhackneyed and unpractised in the world; and was altogether as indiscreet and foolish on every other subject of discourse where policy is wont to impress restraint. Yorick had no impression but one, and that was what arose from the nature of the deed spoken of; which impression he would usually translate into plain English, without any periphrasis;—and too oft without much distinction of either person, time, or place;—so that when mention was made of a pitiful or an ungenerous proceeding,——he never gave himself a moment's time to reflect who was the hero of the piece,——what his station, or how far he had power to hurt him hereafter;——but, if it was a dirty action,—without more ado,—The man was a dirty fellow;—and so on.—And as his comments had usually the ill fate to be terminated either in a *bon mot*, or to be enlivened throughout with some drollery or humor of expression, it gave wings to Yorick's indiscretion. In a word, though he never sought, yet, at the same time, as he seldom shunned, occasions of saying what came uppermost, and without much ceremony,——he had but too many temptations in life, of scattering his wit and his humor,—his gibes and his jests, about him.——They were not lost for want of gathering.

What were the consequences, and what was Yorick's catastrophe thereupon, you will read in the next chapter.

CHAP XII.

The Mortgager and Mortgagee differ the one from the other not more in length of purse, than the Jester and Jestee do in that of memory. But in this the comparison between them runs, as the scholiasts call it, upon all-four; which, by the bye, is upon one or two legs more than some of the best of Homer's can pretend to;—namely, That the one raises a sum, and the other a laugh at your expense, and thinks no more about it. Interest, however, still runs on in both cases;—the periodical or accidental payments of it, just serving to keep the memory of the affair alive; till, at length, in some evil hour,—pop comes the creditor upon each, and by demanding principal upon the spot, together with full interest to the very day, makes them both feel the full extent of their obligations.

As the reader (for I hate your *ifs*) has a thorough knowledge of human nature, I need not say more to satisfy him, that my Hero could not go on at this rate without some slight experience of these incidental mementoes. To speak the truth, he had wantonly involved himself in a multitude of small book-debts of this stamp, which, notwithstanding Eugenius's frequent advice, he too much disregarded; thinking, that as not one of them was contracted through any malignancy;—but, on the contrary, from an honesty of mind, and a mere jocundity of humor, they would all of them be crossed out in course.

Eugenius would never admit this; and would often tell him, that one day or other he would certainly be reckoned with; and he would often add, in an accent of sorrowful apprehension,—to the uttermost mite. To which Yorick, with his usual carelessness of heart, would as often answer with a pshaw!—and if the subject was started in the fields,—with a hop, skip, and a jump at the end of it; but if close pent up in the social chimney-corner, where the culprit was barricado'd in with a table and a couple of arm-chairs, and could not so readily fly off in a tangent, Eugenius would then go on with his lecture upon discretion, in words to this purpose, though somewhat better put together:—

Trust me, dear Yorick, this unwary

pleasantry of thine will sooner or later bring thee into scrapes and difficulties, which no after-wit can extricate thee out of.——In these sallies, too oft, I see it happens, that a person laughed at considers himself in the light of a person injured, with all the rights of such a situation belonging to him; and when thou viewest him in that light too, and reckonest up his friends, his family, his kindred, and allies,——and musterest up with them the many recruits which will list under him from a sense of common danger,——'tis no extravagant arithmetic to say, that for every ten jokes,—thou hast got an hundred enemies; and till thou hast gone on, and raised a swarm of wasps about thine ears, and art half stung to death by them, thou wilt never be convinced it is so.

I cannot suspect it in the man whom I esteem, that there is the least spur from spleen or malevolence of intent in these sallies;—I believe and know them to be truly honest and sportive:—but consider, my dear lad, that fools cannot distinguish this,—and that knaves will not: and that thou knowest not what it is either to provoke the one, or to make merry with the other:——whenever they associate for mutual defence, depend upon it, they will carry on the war in such a manner against thee, my dear friend, as to make thee heartily sick of it, and of thy life too.

Revenge from some baneful corner shall level a tale of dishonor at thee, which no innocence of heart or integrity of conduct shall set right.——The fortunes of thy house shall totter;—thy character, which led the way to them, shall bleed on every side of it;—thy faith questioned,—thy works belied,—thy wit forgotten,—thy learning trampled on. To wind up the last scene of thy tragedy, *Cruelty* and *Cowardice*, twin ruffians, hired and set on by *Malice* in the dark, shall strike together at all thy infirmities and mistakes;——the best of us, my dear lad, lie open there,——and trust me,——trust me, Yorick, *when to gratify a private appetite, it is once resolved upon, that an innocent and an helpless creature shall be sacrificed, 'tis an easy matter to pick up sticks enough from any thicket where it has strayed, to make a fire to offer it up with.*

Yorick scarce ever heard this sad vaticination of his destiny read over to him, but with a tear stealing from his eye, and a promissory look attending it that he was resolved, for the time to come, to ride his tit with more sobriety.—But, alas, too late!—a grand confederacy, with ***** and ***** at the head of it, was formed before the first prediction of it.—The whole plan of attack, just as Eugenius had foreboded, was put in execution all at once,—with so little mercy on the side of the allies,—and so little suspicion in Yorick, of what was carrying on against him,—that when he thought, good easy man! full surely preferment was o' ripening,—they had smote his root, and then he fell, as many a worthy man had fallen before him.

Yorick, however, fought it out with all imaginable gallantry for some time; till, overpowered by numbers, and worn out at length by the calamities of the war,—but more so by the ungenerous manner in which it was carried on,—he threw down the sword; and, though he kept up his spirits in appearance to the last, he died, nevertheless, as was generally thought, quite broken-hearted.

What inclined Eugenius to the same opinion, was as follows:—

A few hours before Yorick breathed his last, Eugenius stept in, with an intent to take his last sight and last farewell of him. Upon his drawing Yorick's curtain, and asking how he felt himself, Yorick, looking up in his face, took hold of his hand,—and, after thanking him for the many tokens of his friendship to him, for which, he said, if it was their fate to meet hereafter, he would thank him again and again,—he told him, he was within a few hours of giving his enemies the slip for ever.—I hope not, answered Eugenius, with tears trickling down his cheeks, and with the tenderest tone that ever man spoke,—I hope not, Yorick, said he.——Yorick replied with a look up, and a gentle squeeze of Eugenius's hand, and that was all—but it cut Eugenius to his heart.

——Come, come, Yorick, quoth Eugenius, wiping his eyes, and summoning up the man within him,—my dear lad, be comforted,—let not all thy spirits and fortitude forsake thee at this crisis when thou most want'st them;——who knows what resources are in store, and what the power of God may yet do for tnee——Yorick laid his hand upon his heart, and gently shook his head.—For my part, continued Eugenius, crying bitterly as he uttered the words,—I declare I know not, Yorick, how to part with thee; and would gladly flatter my hopes, added Eugenius, cheering up his voice, that there is still enough left of thee to make a Bishop, and that I may live to see it.——I beseech thee, Eugenius, quoth Yorick, taking off his night-cap, as well as he could with his left hand—his right being still clasped close in that of Eugenius,—I beseech thee to take a view of my head.——I see nothing that ails it, replied Eugenius. Then alas! my friend, said Yorick, let me tell you, that 'tis so bruised and misshapen with the blows which ***** and ***** and some others have so unhandsomely given me in the dark, that I might say with Sancho Pança, that, should I recover, and "mitres thereupon be suffered "to rain down from Heaven as thick as hail, "not one of them would fit it."——Yorick's last breath was hanging upon his trembling lips, ready to depart as he uttered this;——yet still it was uttered with something of a Cervantic tone;——and as he spoke it, Eugenius could perceive a stream of lambent fire lighted up for a moment in his eyes:——faint picture of those flashes of his spirit, which (as Shakspeare said of his ancestor) were wont to set the table in a roar!

Eugenius was convinced from this, that the heart of his friend was broke: he squeezed his hand,——and then walked softly out of the room, weeping as he walked. Yorick followed Eugenius with his eyes to the door—he then closed them,—and never opened them more.

He lies buried in the corner of his church-yard in the parish of ——, under a plain marble slab, which his friend Eugenius, by leave of his executors, laid upon his grave, with no more than these three words of inscription, serving both for his epitaph and elegy:—

Alas, poor Yorick!

Ten times a day has Yorick's gnost the consolation to hear his monumental inscription read over with such a variety of plaintive tones as denote a general pity and esteem for him:——a footway crossing the church-yard, close by the side of his grave,—not a passenger goes by without stopping to cast a look upon it,—and sighing, as he walks on,

ALAS, POOR YORICK!

CHAP. XIII.

IT is so long since the reader of this rhapsodical work has been parted from the midwife, that it is high time to mention her again to him, merely to put him in mind that there is such a body still in the world, and whom, upon the best judgment I can form upon my own plan at present, I am going to introduce to him for good and all: but as fresh matter may be started, and much unexpected business fall out betwixt the reader and myself, which may require immediate dispatch,——'twas right to take care that the poor woman should not be lost in the mean time; because, when she is wanted, we can no way do without her.

I think, I told you that this good woman was a person of no small note and consequence throughout our whole village and township;—that her fame had spread itself to the very out-edge and circumference of that circle of importance, of which kind every soul living, whether he has a shirt to his back or not——has one surrounding him;—which said circle, by the way, whenever it is said that such a one is of great weight and importance in the *world*,——I desire may be enlarged or contracted in your worship's fancy, in a compound ratio of the station, profession, knowledge, abilities, height and depth (measuring both ways) of the personage brought before you.

In the present case, if I remember, I fixed it about four or five miles; which not only comprehended the whole parish, but extended itself to two or three of the adjacent hamlets in the skirts of the next parish; which made a considerable thing of it. I must add, that she was, moreover, very well looked on at one large grange-house, and some other odd houses and farms within two or three miles, as I said, from the smoke of her own chimney:——but I must here, once for all, inform you, that all this will be more exactly delineated and explain'd in a map, now in the hands of the engraver, which, with many other pieces and developments of this work, will be added to the end of the twentieth volume,—not to swell the work,—I detest the thought of such a thing;—but by way of commentary, scholium, illustration, and key to such passages, incidents or innuendoes as shall be thought to be either of private interpretation, or of dark or doubtful meaning, after my Life and Opinions shall have been read over (now don't forget the meaning of the word) by all the *world*:——which, betwixt you and me, and in spite of all the gentlemen-reviewers in Great Britain, and of all that their worships shall undertake to write or say to the contrary,—I am determined shall be the case.—I need not tell your Worship that all this is spoke in confidence.

CHAP. XIV.

UPON looking into my mother's marriage-settlement, in order to satisfy myself and reader in a point necessary to be cleared up, before we could proceed any farther in this history,—I had the good fortune to pop upon the very thing I wanted before I had read a day and a half straight forwards:—it might have taken me up a month;—which shows plainly, that when a man sits down to write a history,—though it be but the History of Jack Hickathrift or Tom Thumb, he knows no more than his heels what lets and confounded hindrances he is to meet with in his way,—or what a dance he may be led, by one excursion or another, before all is over. Could a historiographer drive on his history, as a muleteer drives on his mule,—straight forward;——for instance, from Rome all the way to Loretto, without ever once turning his head aside, either to the right hand or to the left——he might venture to foretell you to an hour when he should get to his journey's end;——but the thing is, morally speaking, impossible; for if he is a man of the least spirit, he will have fifty deviations from a straight line to make with this or that party as he goes along, which he can noways avoid. He will have views and prospects to himself perpetually soliciting his eye, which he can no more help standing still to look at than he can fly; he will, moreover, have various

Accounts to reconcile,
Anecdotes to pick up,
Inscriptions to make out,
Stories to weave in,
Traditions to shift,
Personages to call upon

Panegyrics to paste up at this door,

Pasquinades at that:——all which both the man and the mule are exempt from. To sum up all, There are archives at every stage to be look'd into, and rolls, records, documents, and endless genealogies, which justice ever and anon calls him back to stay the reading of:——in short, there is no end of it;—for my own part, I declare I have been at it these six weeks, making all the speed I possibly could,—and am not yet born:—I have just been able, and that is all, to tell you *when* it happened, but not *how;* -so that you see the thing is yet far from being accomplished.

These unforeseen stoppages, which I own I had no conception of when I first set out;—but which, I am convinced now, will rather increase than diminish as I advance, —have struck out a hint which I am resolved to follow;——and that is,—not to be in a hurry;—but to go on leisurely, writing and publishing two volumes of my life every year;—which, if I am suffered to go on quietly, and can make a tolerable bargain with my bookseller, I shall continue to do as long as I live.

CHAP. XV.

THE article in my mother's marriage-settlement, which I told the reader I was at the pains to search for, and which, now that I have found it, I think proper to lay before him,—is so much more fully expressed in the deed itself than ever I can pretend to do it, that it would be barbarity to take it out of the lawyer's hand:—it is as follows:—

"**And this Indenture further** "**witnesseth,** That the said Walter Shan- "dy, merchant, in consideration of the said "intended marriage to be had, and, by God's "blessing, to be well and truly solemnized "and consummated between the said Wal- "ter Shandy and Elizabeth Mollineux "aforesaid, and divers other good and valu- "able causes and considerations him there- "unto especially moving,—doth grant, co- "venant, condescend, consent, conclude, "bargain, and fully agree to and with John "Dixon, and James Turner, Esqrs. the "above-named Trustees, &c &c.—**to wit,** "—That in case it should hereafter so fall "out, chance, happen, or otherwise come to "pass,—That the said Walter Shandy, "merchant, shall have left off business be- "fore the time or times that the said Eliza- "beth Mollineux shall according to the "course of nature, or otherwise, have left "off bearing and bringing forth children;— "and that, in consequence of the said Wal- "ter Shandy having so left off business, he "shall, in despight, and against the free "will, consent and good-liking of the said "Elizabeth Mollineux,—make a departure "from the city of London, in order to retire "to and dwell upon his estate at Shandy "Hall, in the county of ———, or, at any "other country-seat, castle, hall, mansion- "house, messuage, or grange-house, now "purchased or hereafter to be purchased, "or upon any part or parcel thereof:— "That then, and as often as the said Eliza- "beth Mollineux shall happen to be en- "ciente with child or children severally and "lawfully begot, or to be begotten upon the "body of the said Elizabeth Mollineux, "during her said coverture,—he, the said "Walter Shandy, shall, at his own proper "costs and charges, and out of his own "proper moneys, upon good and reasonable "notice, which is hereby agreed to be "within six weeks of her the said Elizabeth "Mollineux's full reckoning, or time of "supposed and computed delivery,—pay, "or cause to be paid, the sum of one hun- "dred and twenty pounds good and lawful "money, to John Dixon and James Turner, "Esqrs. or assigns,—upon *trust* and confi- "dence, and for and unto the use and uses, "intent, end, and purpose following:— "**That is to say**—That the said sum of "one hundred and twenty pounds shall be "paid into the hands of the said Elizabeth "Mollineux, or to be otherwise applied by "them the said Trustees, for the well and "truly hiring of one coach, with able and suf- "ficient horses, to carry and convey the body "of the said Elizabeth Mollineux, and the "child or children which she shall be then "and there enciente and pregnant with,— "unto the city of London; and for the fur- "ther paying and defraying of all other in- "cidental costs, charges, and expenses "whatsoever,—in and about, and for, and "relating to, her said intended delivery "and lying-in, in the said city or suburbs "thereof: and that the said Elizabeth Mollineux shall and may, from time to time, "and at all such time and times as are here "covenanted and agreed upon,—peaceably "and quietly hire the said coach and horses, "and have free ingress, egress, and regress "throughout her journey, in and from the "said coach, according to the tenor, true "intent, and meaning of these presents, "without any let, suit, trouble, disturb- "ance, molestation, discharge, hindrance, "forfeiture, eviction, vexation, interrup- "tion, or encumbrance, whatsoever:—and "that it shall moreover be lawful to and for "the said Elizabeth Mollineux, from time "to time, and as oft or often as she shall "well and truly be advanced in her said "pregnancy, to the time heretofore stipula- "ted and agreed upon,—to live and reside "in such place or places, and in such fam- "ily or families, and with such relations, "friends, and other persons within the said "city of London, as she at her own will "and pleasure, notwithstanding her present "coverture, and as if she was a *femme sole* "and unmarried,—shall think fit.—**And** "**this indenture further witness-** "**eth**, That for the more effectually carrying "of the said covenant into execution, the said "Walter Shandy, merchant, doth hereby "grant bargain, sell, release, and confirm "unto the said John Dixon and James Turn- "er, Esqrs. their heirs, executors, and as- "signs, in their actual possession now being, "by virtue of an indenture of bargain and sale "for a year to them the said John Dixon and "James Turner, Esqrs. by him the said Wal- "ter Shandy, merchant, thereof made; which "said bargain and sale for a year, bears date "the day next before the date of these pres- "ents, and by force and virtue of the statute "for transferring of uses into possession,— "**All** the manor and lordship of Shandy in "the county of ——, with all the rights, "members, and appurtenances thereof; and "all and every the messuages, houses, "buildings, barns, stables, orchards, gar- "dens, backsides, tofts, crofts, garths, cot- "tages, lands, meadows, feedings, pastures, "marshes, commons, woods, underwoods, "drains, fisheries, waters, and water- "courses;—together with all rents, re- "versions, services. annuities, fee-farms, "knight's fees, views of frank-pledge, es- "cheats, reliefs, mines, quarries, goods and "chattels of felons and fugitives, felons of "themselves, and put in exigent, deodands, "freewarrens, and all other royalties and "seigniories, rights and jurisdictions, priv- "ileges and hereditaments whatsoever.—— "**And also** the advowson, donation, pre- "sentation, and free disposition of the rec- "tory or parsonage of Shandy aforesaid, and "all and every the tenths, tythes, glebe- "lands."——

In three words,—My mother was to lie in (if she chose it) in London.

But in order to put a stop to the practice of any unfair play on the part of my mother, which a marriage-article of this nature too manifestly opened a door to, and which indeed had never been thought of at all, but for my uncle Toby Shandy,—a clause was added in security of my father, which was this:—"That in case my mother hereafter "should, at any time, put my father to the "trouble and expense of a London journey, "upon false cries and tokens,——that, for "every such instance, she should forfeit all "the right and title which the covenant "gave her to the next turn:—but no more, "—and so on, *toties quoties*, in as effectual "a manner as if such a covenant betwixt "them had not been made."—This, by the way, was no more than what was reasonable;—and yet, as reasonable as it was, I have ever thought it hard that the whole weight of the article should have fallen entirely, as it did, upon myself.

But I was begot and born to misfortunes;—for my poor mother, whether it was wind or water,—or a compound of both,—or neither;—or whether it was simply the mere swell of imagination and fancy in her:—or how far a strong wish and desire to have it so, might mislead her judgment:—in short, whether she was deceived or deceiving in this matter, it no way becomes me to decide. The fact was this, That in the latter end of September, 1717, which was the year before I was born, my mother having carried my father up to town much against the grain, he peremptorily insisted upon the clause;—so that I was doomed, by marriage-articles, to have my nose squeez'd as flat to my face, as if the destinies had actually spun me without one.

How this event came about,—and what a train of vexatious disappointments, in one stage or other of my life, have pursued me from the mere loss, or rather compression, of this one single member,—shall be laid before the reader all in due time.

CHAP. XVI.

My father, as any body may naturally imagine, came down with my mother into the country, in but a pettish kind of a humor. The first twenty or five-and-twenty miles, he did nothing in the world but fret and tease himself, and indeed my mother too, about the cursed expense, which he said might every shilling of it have been saved.—Then, what vexed him more than every thing else was, the provoking time of the year,—which, as I told you, was towards the end of September, when his wall-fruit, and green gages especially, in which he was very curious, were just ready for pulling.——"Had he been whistled up 'to London, upon a Tom Fool's errand, in 'any other month of the whole year, he "should not have said three words about it."

For the next two whole stages, no subject would go down, but the heavy blow he had sustained from the loss of a son, whom it seems he had fully reckoned upon in his mind, and registered down in his pocket-book, as a second staff for his old age, in case Bobby should fail him. "The disap-"pointment of this (he said) was ten times "more to a wise man than all the money "which the journey, &c. had cost him, put "together:—rot the hundred and twenty "pounds,—he did not mind it a rush."

From Stilton, all the way to Grantham, nothing in the whole affair provoked him so much as the condolences of his friends, and the foolish figure they should both make at church the first Sunday;——of which, in the satirical vehemence of his wit, now sharpened a little by vexation, he would give so many humorous and provoking descriptions,—and place his rib and self in so many tormenting lights and attitudes in the face of the whole congregation, that my mother declared, these two stages were so truly tragi-comical, that she did nothing but laugh and cry in a breath, from one end to the other of them, all the way.

From Grantham, till they had crossed the Trent, my father was out of all kind of patience at the vile trick and imposition which he fancied my mother had put upon him in this affair.—"Certainly," he would say to himself, over and over again, "the woman "could not be deceived herself——if she "could,——what weakness!"—tormenting word! which led his imagination a thorny dance, and before all was over, played the deuce and all with him;——for sure as ever the word *weakness* was uttered, and struck full upon his brain,—so sure it set him upon running divisions upon how many kinds of weaknesses there were;——that there was such a thing as weakness of the body,—as well as weakness of the mind,—and then he would do nothing but syllogize within himself, for a stage or two together, how far the cause of all these vexations might, or might not, have arisen out of himself.

In short, he had so many little subjects of disquietude springing out of this one affair, all fretting successively in his mind as they rose up in it, that my mother, whatever was her journey up, had but an uneasy journey of it down.——In a word, as she complained to my uncle Toby, he would have tired out the patience of any flesh alive.

CHAP. XVII.

Though my father travelled homewards, as I told you, in none of the best of moods,—pshawing and pishing all the way down,—yet he had the complaisance to keep the worst part of the story still to himself;—which was the resolution he had taken of doing himself the justice which my uncle Toby's clause in the marriage-settlement empowered him; nor was it till the very night in which I was begot, which was thirteen months after, that she had the least intimation of his design: when my father, happening, as you remember, to be a little chagrined and out of temper,—took occasion, as they lay chatting gravely in bed afterwards, talking over what was to come,—to let her know that she must accommodate herself as well as she could to the bargain made between them in their marriage-deeds; which was to lie-in of her next child in the country, to balance the last year's journey.

My father was a gentleman of many virtues,—but he had a strong spice of that in his temper, which might, or might not, add to the number.—'Tis known by the name of Perseverance in a good cause,—and of Obstinacy in a bad one: of this my mother had so much knowledge, that she knew 'twas to no purpose to make any remonstrance;—so she e'en resolved to sit down quietly, and make the most of it.

CHAP. XVIII.

As the point was that night agreed, or rather determined, that my mother should lie-in of me in the country, she took her measures accordingly; for which purpose, when she was three days, or thereabouts, gone with child, she began to cast her eyes upon the midwife, whom you have so often heard me mention; and before the week was well got round, as the famous Dr. Manningham was not to be had, she had come to a final determination in her mind,——notwithstanding there was a scientific operator within so near a call as eight miles of us, and who, moreover, had expressly wrote a five-shilling book upon the subject of midwifery, in which he had exposed, not only the blunders of the sisterhood itself,—but had likewise superadded many curious improvements for the quicker extraction of the fœtus in cross-births, and some other cases of danger, which belay us in getting into the world; notwithstanding all this, my mother, I say, was absolutely determined to trust her life, and mine with it, into no soul's hand but this old woman's only.—Now this I like:—When we cannot get at the very thing we wish,——never to take up with the next best in degree to it. No; that's pitiful beyond description.—It is more than a week from this very day, in which I am now writing this book for the edification of the world,—which is March 9, 1759,—that my dear, dear Jenny, observing I looked a little grave, as she stood cheapening a silk of five-and-twenty shillings a yard,—told the mercer, she was sorry she had given him so much trouble;—and immediately went and bought herself a yard-wide stuff of ten-pence a yard.—'Tis the duplication of one and the same greatness of soul; only, what lessened the honor of it somewhat in my mother's case, was, that she could not heroine it into so violent and hazardous an extreme as one in her situation might have wished, because the old midwife had really some little claim to be depended upon,—as much, at least, as success could give her; having, in the course of her practice of near twenty years in the parish, brought every mother's son of them into the world without any one slip or accident which could fairly be laid to her account.

These facts, though they had their weight, yet did not altogether satisfy some few scruples and uneasinesses which hung upon my father's spirits in relation to this choice.—To say nothing of the natural workings of humanity and justice—or of the yearnings of parental and connubial love, all which prompted him to leave as little to hazard as possible in a case of this kind;——he felt himself concerned in a particular manner, that all should go right in the present case;—from the accumulated sorrow he lay open to, should any evil betide his wife and child in lying-in at Shandy-Hall.——He knew the world judged by events, and would add to his afflictions in such a misfortune, by loading him with the whole blame of it.——"Alas o'day!—had "Mrs. Shandy (poor gentlewoman!) had "but her wish in going up to town just to "lie-in and come down again;—which, they "say, she begged and prayed for upon her "bare knees,——and which in my opinion, "considering the fortune which Mr. Shandy "got with her,—was no such mighty matter "to have complied with, the lady and her "babe might both of them have been alive "at this hour."

This exclamation, my father knew, was unanswerable;—and yet, it was not merely to shelter himself,—nor was it altogether for the care of his offspring and wife that he seemed so extremely anxious about this point;—my father had extensive views of things,——and stood moreover, as he thought, deeply concerned in it for the public good, from the dread he entertained of the bad uses an ill-fated instance might be put to.

He was very sensible that all political writers upon the subject had unanimously agreed and lamented, from the beginning of queen Elizabeth's reign down to his own time, that the current of men and money towards the metropolis, upon one frivolous errand or another,—set in so strong,—as to become dangerous to our civil rights,—though, by the bye,——a *current* was not the image he took most delight in;—a *distemper* was here his favorite metaphor, and he would run it down into a perfect allegory, by maintaining it was identically the same in the body national as in the body natural, where the blood and spirits were driven up into the head faster than they could find their ways down;——a stoppage of circulation must ensue, which was death in both cases.

There was little danger, he would say, of losing our liberties by French politics or French invasions;——nor was he so much in pain of a consumption from the mass of corrupted matter and ulcerated humors in our constitution, which he hoped was not so bad as it was imagined:—but he verily feared, that in some violent push we should go off, all at once, in a state-apoplexy;—and then he would say, *The Lord have mercy upon us all.*

My father was never able to give the history of this distemper,—without the remedy along with it.

"Was I an absolute prince," he would say, pulling up his breeches with both his hands, as he rose from his arm-chair, "I "would appoint able judges, at every avenue "of my metropolis, who should take cog-"nizance of every fool's business who came "there;—and if, upon a fair and candid "hearing, it appeared not of weight suffi-"cient to leave his own home, and come "up, bag and baggage, with his wife and "children, farmer's sons, *&c. &c.* at his "backside, they should be all sent back, "from constable to constable, like vagrants "as they were, to the place of their legal "settlements. By this means I should take "care, that my metropolis totter'd not "through its own weight;—that the head "be no longer too big for the body;—that "the extremes, now wasted and pinn'd in, "be restored to their due share of nourish-"ment, and regain with it their natural "strength and beauty:—I would effectually "provide, That the meadows and corn-fields "of my dominions should laugh and sing; "—that good cheer and hospitality flourish "once more;—and that such weight and "influence be put thereby into the hands of "the Squiralty of my kingdom, as should "counterpoise what I perceive my Nobility "are now taking from them.

"Why are there so few palaces and gen-"tlemen's seats," he would ask with some emotion, as he walked across the room, "throughout so many delicious provinces "in France? Whence is it that the few re-"maining *chateaus* amongst them are so "dismantled,—so unfurnished, and in so "ruinous and desolate a condition?——Be-"cause, Sir," (he would say) "in that king-"dom no man has any country-interest to "support:—the little interest of any kind "which any man has anywhere in it, is con-"centrated in the court, and the looks of "the Grand Monarch: by the sunshine of "whose countenance, or the clouds which "pass across it, every Frenchman lives or "dies."

Another political reason which prompted my father so strongly to guard against the least evil accident in my mother's lying-in in the country,——was, That any such instance would infallibly throw a balance of power, too great already, into the weaker vessels of the gentry, in his own, or higher stations;——which, with the many other usurped rights which that part of the constitution was hourly establishing,—would, in the end, prove fatal to the monarchical system of domestic government established in the first creation of things by God.

In this point he was entirely of Sir Robert Filmer's opinion, That the plans and institutions of the greatest monarchies in the eastern parts of the world, were, originally, all stolen from that admirable pattern and prototype of this household and paternal power;—which, for a century, he said, and more, had gradually been degenerating away into a mixed government:——the form of which, however desirable in great combinations of the species,——was very troublesome in small ones,—and seldom produced any thing, that he saw, but sorrow and confusion.

For all these reasons, private and public, put together,—my father was for having the man-midwife by all means;—my mother, by no means. My father begged and entreated she would for once recede from her prerogative in this matter, and suffer him to choose for her:—my mother, on the contrary, insisted upon her privilege in this matter, to choose for herself,—and have no mortal's help but the old woman's.—What could my father do? He was almost at his wit's end;——talked it over with her in all moods;—placed his arguments in all lights;—argued the matter with her like a christian,—like a heathen,—like a husband,—like a father,—like a patriot,—like a man:—My mother answered every thing only like a woman; which was a little hard upon her;—for as she could not assume and fight it out behind such a variety of characters,—'twas no fair match;—'twas seven to one.—What could my mother do? She had the advantage (otherwise she had been certainly overpowered) of a small reinforcement of chagrin personal at the bottom, which bore her up, and enabled her to dispute the affair with my father with so equal an advantage,——that both sides sung *Te Deum.* In a word, my mother was to have the old woman,—and the operator was to have license to drink a bottle of wine with my father and my uncle Toby Shandy in the back parlor,—for which he was to be paid five guineas.

I must beg leave, before I finish this chapter, to enter a caveat in the breast of my fair reader;—and it is this;——not to take it absolutely for granted, from an unguarded word or two which I have dropped in it,——"That I am a married man."—I own, the tender appellation of my dear, dear Jenny,—with some other strokes of conjugal knowledge, interspersed here and there, might naturally enough have misled the most candid judge in the world into such a determination against me.—All I plead for in this case, Madam, is strict justice, and that you do so much of it to me as well as to yourself,—as not to prejudge, or receive such an impression of me, till you have better evidence than, I am positive, at present can be produced against me.—Not that I can be so vain or unreasonable, Madam, as to desire you should therefore think that my dear, dear Jenny is my kept mistress;—no,—that would be flattering my character in the other extreme, and giving it an air of freedom, which, perhaps, it has no kind of right to. All I contend for, is the utter impossibility, for some volumes, that you, or the most penetrating spirit upon earth, should know how this matter really stands.—It is not impossible but that my dear, dear Jenny! tender as the appellation is, may be my child.——Consider,——I was born in the year eighteen.—Nor is there any thing unnatural or extravagant in the supposition, that my dear, dear Jenny may be my friend!——Friend!—My friend.—Surely, Madam, a friendship between the two sexes may subsist, and be supported without——Fy! Mr. Shandy.—Without any thing, Madam, but that tender and delicious sentiment which ever mixes in friendship, where there is a difference of sex. Let me entreat you to study the pure and sentimental parts of the best French romances;—it will really, Madam, astonish you to see with what a variety of chaste expressions this delicious sentiment which I have the honor to speak of, is dress'd out.

CHAP. XIX.

I WOULD sooner undertake to explain the hardest problem in Geometry, than pretend to account for it, that a gentleman of my father's great good sense,—knowing, as the reader must have observed him, and curious too in philosophy,—wise also in political reasoning,—and in polemical (as he will find) no way ignorant,—could be capable of entertaining a notion in his head, so out of the common track,—that I fear the reader, when I come to mention it to him, if he is the least of a choleric temper, will immediately throw the book by; if mercurial, he will laugh most heartily at it;—and if he is of a grave and saturnine cast, he will at first sight absolutely condemn as fanciful and extravagant; and that was in respect to the choice and imposition of christian names, on which he thought a great deal more depended than what superficial minds were capable of conceiving.

His opinion in this matter was, That there was a strange kind of magic bias, which good or bad names, as he called them, irresistibly impressed upon our characters and conduct.

The hero of Cervantes argued not the point with more seriousness,—nor had he more faith,—or more to say on the powers of necromancy in dishonoring his deeds,—or on Dulcinea's name, in shedding lustre upon them, than my father had on those of Trismegistus or Archimedes on the one hand,—or of Nyky and Simkin on the other. How many Cæsars and Pompeys, he would say, by mere inspiration of the names, have been rendered worthy of them! And, how many, he would add, are there, who might have done exceeding well in the world, had not their characters and spirits been totally depressed and Nicodemus'd into nothing!

I see plainly, Sir, by your looks (or as the case happened) my father would say—that you do not heartily subscribe to this opinion of mine,—which, to those, he would add, who have not carefully sifted it to the bottom,—I own has an air more of fancy than of solid reasoning in it;——and yet, my dear Sir, if I may presume to know your character, I am morally assured, I should hazard little in stating a case to you, not as a party in the dispute,—but as a judge, and trusting my appeal upon it to your own good sense and candid disquisition in this matter;——you are a person free from as many narrow prejudices of education as most men:—and, if I may presume to penetrate farther into you,—of a liberality of genius above bearing down an opinion, merely because it wants friends. Your son,—your dear son,—from whose sweet and open temper you have so much to expect;—your Billy, Sir!—would you, for the world, have called him JUDAS?—Would you, my dear Sir, he would say, laying his hand upon your breast, with the genteeiest address,—and in that soft and irresistible *piano* of voice which the nature of the *argumentum ad hominem* absolutely requires,—Would you, Sir if a *Jew* of a godfather had proposed the name for your child, and offered you his purse along with it, would you have consented to such a desecration of him?——O my God! he would say, looking up, if I know your temper right, Sir,—you are incapable of it;—you would have trampled upon the offer;—you would have thrown the temptation at the tempter's head with abhorrence.

Your greatness of mind in this action, which I admire, with that generous contempt of money, which you show me in the whole transaction, is really noble;—and what renders it more so, is the principle of it:—the workings of a parent's love upon the truth and conviction of this very hypothesis, namely, That was your son called Judas,—the sordid and treacherous idea, so inseparable from the name, would have accompanied him through life like his shadow, and, in the end, made a miser and a rascal of him, in spite, Sir, of your example.

I never knew a man able to answer this argument.——But, indeed, to speak of my father as he was;—he was certainly irresistible;—both in his orations and disputations;—he was born an orator;—θεοδίδακτος.—Persuasion hung upon his lips, and the elements of Logic and Rhetoric were so blended up in him,—and, withal, he had so shrewd a guess at the weakness and passions of his respondent,—that NATURE might have stood up and said,—"This man "is eloquent."—In short, whether he was on the weak or the strong side of the question, 'twas hazardous in either case to attack him:—and yet, 'tis strange, he had never read Cicero, nor Quintilian de Oratore, nor Isocrates, nor Aristotle, nor Longinus, amongst the antients;—nor Vossius, nor Skioppius, nor Ramus, nor Farnaby, amongst the moderns; and, what is more astonishing, he had never in his whole life the least light or spark of subtilty struck into his mind, by one single lecture upon Crackenthorp or Burgersdicus or any Dutch logician or commentator;—he knew not so much as in what the difference of an argument *ad ignorantiam*, and an argument *ad hominem*, consisted; so that I well remember, when he went up along with me to enter my name in Jesus' College in ****, —it was a matter of just wonder with my worthy tutor, and two or three fellows of that learned society,—that a man who knew not so much as the names of his tools, should be able to work after that fashion with them.

To work with them in the best manner he could, was what my father was, however, perpetually forced upon;——for he had a thousand little sceptical notions of the comic kind to defend,—most of which notions, I verily believe, at first entered upon the footing of mere whims, and of a *vive la Bagatelle;* and as such he would make merry with them for half an hour or so; and having sharpened his wit upon them, dismiss them till another day.

I mention this, not only as matter of hypothesis or conjecture upon the progress and establishment of my father's many odd opinions,—but as a warning to the learned reader against the indiscreet reception of such guests, who, after a free and undisturbed entrance, for some years, into our brains,—at length claim a kind of settlement there,——working sometimes like yeast;—but more generally after the manner of the gentle passion, beginning in jest, —but ending in downright earnest.

Whether this was the case of the singularity of my father's notions,—or that his judgment, at length, became the dupe of his wit;—or how far, in many of his notions, he might, though odd, be absolutely right;——the reader, as he comes at them, shall decide. All that I maintain here, is, that in this one, of the influence of christian names, however it gained footing, he was serious;—he was all uniformity;—he was systematical, and, like all systematic reasoners, he would move both heaven and earth, and twist and torture every thing in nature, to support his hypothesis. In a word, I repeat it over again,—he was serious; and in consequence of it, he would lose all kind of patience whenever he saw people, especially of condition, who should have known better,—as careless and as indifferent about the name they imposed upon their child,—or more so, than in the choice of Ponto or Cupid for their puppy-dog.

This, he would say, look'd ill;—and had, moreover, this particular aggravation in it, viz. That when once a vile name was wrongfully or injudiciously given, 'twas not like the case of a man's character, which, when wrong'd, might hereafter be cleared;—— and, possibly, some time or other, if not in the man's life, at least after his death—be, somehow or other, set to rights with the world: but the injury of this, he would say, could never be undone,, nay, he doubted even whether an act of parliament could reach it:——He knew as well as you, that the legislature assumed a power over surnames: but for very strong reasons, which he could give, it had never yet adventured, he would say, to go a step farther.

It was observable, that though my father, in consequence of this opinion, had, as I have told you, the strongest likings and dislikings towards certain names,—that there were still numbers of names which hung so equally in the balance before him, that they were absolutely indifferent to him. Jack, Dick, and Tom, were of this class: these my father called neutral names; —affirming of them, without a satire, That there had been as many knaves and fools, at least, as wise and good men, since the world began, who had indifferently borne them;—so that, like equal forces acting against each other in contrary directions, he thought they mutually destroyed each other's effects; for which reason, he would often declare, He would not give a cherry-stone to choose amongst them. Bob, which was my brother's name, was another of these neutral kinds of christian names, which operated very little either way; and as my father happened to be at Epsom when it was given him,—he would ofttimes thank Heaven it was no worse. Andrew was something like a negative quantity in algebra with him;—'twas worse, he said, than nothing,—William stood pretty high:——Numps again was low with him: and Nick, he said, was the *Devil.*

But of all the names in the universe, he had the most unconquerable aversion for *Tristram;*—he had the lowest and most contemptible opinion of it of any thing in the world, thinking it could possibly produce nothing in *rerum naturâ,* but what was extremely mean and pitiful: so that in the midst of a dispute on the subject, in which, by the bye, he was frequently involved,——he would sometimes break off in a sudden and spirited *Epiphonema,* or rather *Erotesis,* raised a third, and sometimes a full fifth above the key of the dis course,——and demand it categorically of his antagonist, Whether he would take upon him to say, he had ever remembered, ——whether he had ever read,—or even whether he had ever heard tell of a man, called Tristram, performing any thing great or worth recording?—No,—he would say, —*Tristram!*—The thing is impossible.

What could be wanting in my father but to have wrote a book to publish this notion of his to the world? Little boots it to the subtle speculatist to stand single in his opinions,—unless he gives them proper vent:—It was the identical thing which my father did:—for in the year sixteen, which was two years before I was born, he was at the pains of writing an express *Dissertation* simply upon the word Tristram,—showing the world, with great candor and modesty, the grounds of his great abhorrence to the name.

When this story is compared with the title-page,—will not the gentle reader pity my father from his soul?—to see an orderly and well-disposed gentleman, who though singular, yet inoffensive in his notions,—so played upon in them by cross-purposes——to look down upon the stage, and see him baffled and overthrown in all his little systems and wishes! to behold a train of events perpetually falling out against him, and in so critical and cruel a way, as if they had purposely been plann'd and pointed against him, merely to insult his speculations!——In a word, to behold such a one, in his old age, ill-fitted for troubles, ten times in a day suffering sorrow!—ten times in a day calling the child of his prayers *Tristram!*—Melancholy dissyllable of sound! which, to his ears, was unison to Nincompoop, and every name vituperative under Heaven.——By his ashes! I swear it,—if ever malignant spirit took pleasure, or busied itself in traversing the purposes of mortal man,—it must have been here;—and if it was not necessary I should be born before I was christened, I would this moment give the reader an account of it.

CHAP. XX.

——How could you, Madam, be so inattentive in reading the last chapter? I told you in it, *That my mother was not a Papist.* ——Papist! you told me no such thing, Sir. —Madam, I beg leave to repeat it over again, that I told you as plain, at least, as words, by direct inference, could tell you such a thing.—Then, Sir, I must have missed a page.—No, Madam,—you have not missed a word.——Then I was asleep, Sir.—My pride, Madam, cannot allow you that refuge. ——Then, I declare, I know nothing at all about the matter.—That, Madam, is the very fault I lay to your charge; and, as a punishment for it, I do insist upon it, that you immediately turn back, that is, as soon as you get to the next full stop, and read the whole chapter over again. I have imposed this penance upon the lady, neither out of wantonness nor cruelty, but from the best of motives; and therefore shall make her no apology for it when she returns back. —'Tis to rebuke a vicious taste, which has crept into thousands besides herself,—of reading straight forwards, more in quest of the adventures than of the deep erudition and knowledge which a book of this cast, if read over as it should be, would infallibly impart with them.——The mind should be accustomed to make wise reflections, and draw curious conclusions, as it goes along; the habitude of which made Pliny the Younger affirm, "That he never read a "book so bad, but he drew some profit from "it." The stories of Greece and Rome, run over without this turn and application,—do less service, I affirm it, than the history of Parismus and Parismenus, or of the Seven Champions of England, read with it.

——But here comes my fair lady. Have you read over again the chapter, Madam, as I desired you?—You have: and did you not observe the passage, upon the second reading, which admits the inference?——Not a word like it! Then, Madam, be pleased to ponder well the last line but one of the chapter, where I take upon me to say, "It "was *necessary* I should be born before I was "christened." Had my mother, Madam, been a Papist, that consequence did not follow.*

* The Romish Rituals direct the baptizing of the child in cases of danger, *before* it is born;—but upon this proviso, That some part or other of the child's body be seen by the baptizer——but the Doctors of the Sorbonne, by a deliberation held amongst them, April 10, 1733,—have enlarged the powers of the midwives.

It is a terrible misfortune for this same book of mine, but more so to the Republic of Letters;—so that my own is quite swallowed up in the consideration of it,—that this self-same vile pruriency for fresh adventures in all things, has got so strongly into our habit and humor,—and so wholly intent are we upon satisfying the impa-

by determining, That though no part of the child's body should appear,——that baptism shall, nevertheless, be administered to it by injection,—*par le moyen d'une petite canulle*,—Anglice,—*a squirt*——'tis very strange that St. Thomas Aquinas, who had so good a mechanical head, both for tying and untying the knots of school divinity, should, after so much pains bestowed upon this—give up the point at last, as a second *La chose impossible*—"Infantes in maternis uteris existentes (quoth St. Thomas!) baptizari possunt *nullo modo*."—O Thomas! Thomas!

If the reader has the curiosity to see the question upon baptism *by injection*, as presented to the Doctors of the Sorbonne, with their consultation thereupon, it is as follows:

MEMOIRE PRESENTE A MESSIEURS LES DOCTEURS DE SORBONNE.*

"Un Chirurgien Accoucheur, represente à Messieurs les Docteurs de Sorbonne, qu'il y a des cas, quoique très rares, où une mere ne sçauroit accoucheur, et même où l'enfant est tellement renfermé dans le sein de sa mere, qu'il ne fait paroître aucune partie de son corps, ce qui seroit un cas, suivant les Rituels, de lui conférer, du moins sous condition, le baptême. Le Chirurgien, qui consulte, prétend, par le moyen d'une petite canulle, de pouvoir baptizer immediatement l'enfant, sans faire aucun tort à la mere——Il demand si ce moyen, qu'il vient de proposer, est permis et légitime, et s'il peut s'en servir dans les cas qu'il vient d'exposer."

REPONSE.

"Le conseil estime, qui la question proposée souffre de grandes difficultés. Les Théologiens posent d'un coté pour principe, que le baptême, qui est une naissance spirituelle, suppose une premiere naissance; il faut être né dans le monde, pour renaitre en Jesus Christ, comme ils l'enseignent. S. Thomas, 3 part quæst. 88. artic. 11. suit cette doctrine comme une verité constante; l'on ne peut, dit ce S. Docteur, baptiser les enfans qui sont renfermé dans le sein de leurs meres, et S. Thomas est fondé sur ce, que les enfans ne sont point nés et ne peuvent être comptés parmi les autres hommes; d'où il conclud, qu'ils ne peuvent être l'objet d'une action extérieure pour reçevoir par leur ministére les sacremens nécessaires au salut: "Pueri in maternis uteris existentes nondum prodierunt in lucem ut cum aliis hominibus vitam ducant: unde non possunt subjici actioni humanæ, ut per eorum ministerium sacramenta recipiant ad salutum." Les rituels ordonnent dans la pratique ce que les théologiens ont établi sur les mémes matiéres, et ils deffendent tous d'une maniére uniforme, de baptiser les enfans qui sont renfermés dans le sein de leurs meres, s'ils ne font paroitre quelque partie de leurs corps. Le concours des théologiens, et des rituels, qui sont les régles des diocéses, paroit former une autorité qui termine la question presente; cependant le conseil de conscience considerant d'un côte, que le raisonnement des théologiens est uniquement fondé sur une raison de convenance, et que la deffense des rituels suppose que l'on ne peut baptiser immediatement les enfans ainsi renfermés dans le sein de leurs meres, ce qui est contre la supposition presente; et d'un autre côté, considerant que les mêmes théologiens enseignent, que l'on peut risquer les sacremens que Jesus Christ à établis comme des moyens faciles, mais nécessaires, pour sanctifier les hommes; et d'ailleurs estimant, que les enfans renfermés dans le sein de leurs meres, pourroient être capables de salut, parcequ'ils sont capables de damnation;—pour ces considerations, et en egard à l'exposé, suivant lequel on assure avoir trouvé un moyen certain de baptiser ces enfans ainsi renfermés, sans faire aucun tort à la mere, le Conseil estime que l'on pourroit se servir du moyen proposé, dans la confiance qu'il a, que Dieu n'a point laissé ces sortes d'enfans sans aucuns secours, et supposant, comme il est exposé, que le moyen dont il s'agit est propre à leur procurer le baptême; cependant comme il s'agiroit, en autorisant la pratique proposée, de changer une règle universellement établie, le Conseil croit que celui qui consulte doit s'addresser à son evêque, et à qu'il il appartient de juger de l'utilité, et du danger du moyen proposé et comme, sous le bon plaisir de l'evêque, le Conseil estime qu'il faudroit recourir au Pape, que a le droit d'expliquer les règles de l'eglise, et d'y déroger dans le cas, ou la loi ne sçauroit obliger, quelque sage et quelque utile que paroisse la manière de baptiser dont il s'agit, le Conseil ne pourroit l'approuver sans le concours de ces deux autorités. On conseile au moins à celui qui consulte, de s'addresser à son evêque, et de lui faire part de la presente décision, afin que, si le prelat entre dans les raisons sur lesquelles les docteurs soussignés s'appuyent, il puisse être autorisé, dans le cas de nécessité, ou il risqueroit trop d'attendre que la permission fût demandée et accordée d'employer le moyen qu'il propose si avantageux au salut de l'enfant. Au reste, le Conseil, en estimant que l'on pourroit s'en servir, croit cependant, que si les enfans dont il s'agit, venoient au monde, contre l'esperance de ceux qui se seroient servis du même moyen, il seroit necessaire de les baptiser sous condition; et en cela le Conseil se conforme à tous les rituels, qui en autorisant le baptême d'un enfant qui fait paroitre quelque partie de son corps, enjoignent néantmoins, et ordonnent de le baptiser sous condition, s'il vient heureusement au monde.

Déliberé en Sorbonne, le 10 Avril, 1733.

A. LE MOYNE.
L. DE ROMIGNY.
DE MARCILLY.

Mr. Tristram Shandy's compliments to Messrs. Le Moyne, De Romigny, and De Marcilly; hopes they all rested well the night after so tiresome a consultation.—He begs to know, whether, after the ceremony of marriage, and before that of consummation, the baptizing all the *Homunculi* at once, slapdash, by *injection*, would not be a shorter and safer cut still; on condition, as above, That if the *Homunculi* do well, and come safe into the world after this, that each and every of them shall be baptized again (*sous condition*)—And provided, in the second place, That the thing can be done, which Mr. Shandy apprehends it may *par le moyen d'une* petite canulle, and *sans faire aucun tort au pere?*

* Vide Deventer, Paris edit. 4to 1734. p. 366.

tience of our concupiscence that way,—that nothing but the gross and more carnal parts of a composition will go down:—the subtle hints and sly communications of science fly off, like spirits, upwards,——the heavy moral escapes downwards; and both the one and the other are as much lost to the world, as if they were still left in the bottom of the ink-horn.

I wish the male-reader has not passed by many a one, as quaint and curious as this one, in which the female-reader has been detected. I wish it may have its effects;—and that all good people, both male and female, from example, may be taught to think as well as read.

CHAP. XXI.

——I wonder what's all that noise, and running backwards and forwards for, above stairs? quoth my father, addressing himself, after an hour and a half's silence, to my uncle Toby,——who, you must know, was sitting on the opposite side of the fire, smoking his social pipe all the time, in mute contemplation of a new pair of black plush-breeches which he had got on:—What can they be doing, brother?—quoth my father,—we can scarce hear ourselves talk.

I think, replied my uncle Toby, taking his pipe from his mouth, and striking the head of it two or three times upon the nail of his left thumb as he began his sentence,——I think, says he,——but to enter rightly into my uncle Toby's sentiments upon this matter, you must be made to enter first a little into his character, the outlines of which I shall just give you, and then the dialogue between him and my father will go on as well again.

Pray, what was that man's name,—for I write in such a hurry, I have no time to recollect or look for it,——who first made the observation, "That there was great inconstancy in our air and climate?" Whoever he was, 'twas a just and good observation in him.—But the corollary drawn from it, namely, "That it is this which has furnished us with such a variety of odd and whimsical characters;"—that was not his;—it was found out by another man, at least a century and a half after him. Then again, —That this copious store-house of original materials, is the true and natural cause that our comedies are so much better than those of France, or any others that either have, or can be wrote upon the Continent:——that discovery was not fully made till about the middle of King William's reign,—when the great Dryden, in writing one of his long prefaces (if I mistake not) most fortunately hit upon it. Indeed, toward the latter end of Queen Anne, the great Addison began to patronize the notion, and more fully explained it to the world in one or two of his Spectators;—but the discovery was not his. —Then, fourthly and lastly, That this strange irregularity in our climate, producing so strange an irregularity in our characters,——doth thereby, in some sort, make us amends, by giving us somewhat to make us merry with when the weather will not suffer us to go out of doors;—that observation is my own;—and was struck out by me this very rainy day, March 26, 1759, and betwixt the hours of nine and ten in the morning.

Thus—thus, my fellow-laborers and associates in this great harvest of our learning, now ripening before our eyes; thus it is, by slow steps of casual increase, that our knowledge, physical, metaphysical, physiological, polemical, nautical, mathematical, enigmatical, technical, biographical, romantical, chemical, and obstetrical, with fifty other branches of it (most of 'em ending, as these do, in *ical*,) have, for these two last centuries and more, gradually been creeping upwards towards that 'Ακμή of their perfections, from which, if we may form a conjecture from the advances of these last seven years, we cannot possibly be far off.

When that happens, it is to be hoped, it will put an end to all kind of writings whatsoever;—the want of all kind of writing will put an end to all kind of reading;—and *that* in time, *as war begets poverty; poverty peace*,—must, in course, put an end to all kind of knowledge,—and then——we shall have all to begin over again; or, in other words, be exactly where we started.

——Happy! thrice happy times! I only wish that the era of my begetting, as well as the mode and manner of it, had been a little alter'd,——or that it could have been put off, with any convenience to my father or mother, for some twenty or five-and-twenty years longer, when a man in the literary world might have stood some chance.——

But I forget my uncle Toby, whom all this while we have left knocking the ashes out of his tobacco-pipe.

His humor was of that particular species which does honor to our atmosphere; and I should have made no scruple of ranking him amongst one of the first-rate productions of it, had not there appeared too many strong lines in it of a family likeness, which showed that he derived the singularity of his temper more from blood, than either wind or water, or any modifications or combinations of them whatever; and I have, therefore, oftentimes wondered, that my father, though I believe he had his reasons for it, upon his observing some tokens of eccentricity in my course when I was a boy,—should never once endeavor to account for them in this way; for all the Shandy Family were of an original character throughout:——I mean the males,—the females had no character at all,—except, indeed, my great-aunt Dinah, who, about sixty years ago, was married and got with child by the coachman; for which my father, according to his hypothesis of christian names, would often say, She might thank her godfathers and godmothers.

It will seem very strange,——and I would as soon think of dropping a riddle in the reader's way, which is not my interest to do, as set him upon guessing how it could come to pass, that an event of this kind, so many years after it had happened, should be reserved for the interruption of the peace and unity, which otherwise so cordially subsisted, between my father and my uncle Toby. One would have thought that the whole force of the misfortune should have spent and wasted itself in the family at first,—as is generally the case.—But nothing ever wrought with our family after the ordinary way. Possibly at the very time this happened, it might have something else to afflict it; and as afflictions are sent down for our good, and that as this had never done the Shandy Family any good at all, it might lie waiting till apt times and circumstances should give it an opportunity to discharge its office.——Observe, I determine nothing upon this.——My way is ever to point out to the curious, different tracts of investigation, to come at the first springs of the events I tell;—not with a pedantic Fescue,—or in the decisive manner of Tacitus, who outwits himself and his reader;—but with the officious humility of a heart devoted to the assistance merely of the inquisitive:—to them I write,——and by them I shall be read,——if any such reading as this could be supposed to hold out so long,—to the very end of the world.

Why this cause of sorrow, therefore, was thus reserved for my father and uncle, is undetermined by me. But how and in what direction it exerted itself so as to become the cause of dissatisfaction between them, after it began to operate, is what I am able to explain with great exactness, and is as follows:

My uncle, Toby Shandy, Madam, was a gentleman, who, with the virtues which usually constitute the character of a man of honor and rectitude,——possessed one in a very eminent degree, which is seldom or never put into the catalogue; and that was a most extreme and unparallel'd modesty of nature;——though I correct the word nature, for this reason, that I may not prejudge a point which must shortly come to a hearing, and that is, Whether this modesty of his was natural or acquired?——Whichever way my uncle Toby came by it, 'twas nevertheless modesty in the truest sense of it; and that is, Madam, not in regard to words, for he was so unhappy as to have very little choice in them,—but to things;——and this kind of modesty so possessed him, and it arose to such a height in him, as almost to equal, if such a thing could be, even the modesty of a woman: that female nicety, Madam, and inward cleanliness of mind and fancy, in your sex, which makes you so much the awe of ours.

You will imagine, Madam, that my uncle Toby had contracted all this from this very source;—that he had spent a great part of his time in converse with your sex; and that, from a thorough knowledge of you, and the force of imitation which such fair examples render irresistible, he had acquired this amiable turn of mind.

I wish I could say so;—for unless it was with his sister-in-law, my father's wife and my mother,——my uncle Toby scarce exchanged three words with the sex in as many years.—No; he got it, Madam, by a blow.——A blow!——Yes, Madam, it was owing to a blow from a stone, broke off by a ball from the parapet of a horn-work at the siege of Namur, which struck full upon my uncle Toby's groin.—Which way could that effect it?—The story of that, Madam, is long and interesting;—but it would be running my history all upon heaps to give it you here.——'Tis for an episode hereafter; and every circumstance relating to it, in its proper place, shall be faithfully laid before you.—Till then, it is not in my power to give farther light into this matter, or say more than what I have said already,——That my uncle Toby was a gentleman of unparallel'd modesty, which happening to be somewhat subtilized and rarefied by the constant heat of a little family pride,——they both so wrought together within him that he could never bear to hear the affair of my aunt Dinah touch'd upon, but with the greatest emotion.——The least hint of it was enough to make the blood fly into his face;—but when my father enlarged upon the story in mixed companies, which the illustration of his hypothesis frequently obliged him to do,—the unfortunate blight of one of the fairest branches of the family, would set my uncle Toby's honor and modesty o'bleeding; and he would often take my father aside, in the greatest concern imaginable, to expostulate and tell him, he would give him any thing in the world, only to let the story rest.

My father, I believe, had the truest love and tenderness for my uncle Toby, that ever one brother bore towards another; and would have done any thing in nature, which one brother in reason could have desir'd of another, to have made my uncle Toby's heart easy in this, or any other point. But this lay out of his power.

——My father, as I told you, was a philosopher in grain,—speculative,—systematical;—and my aunt Dinah's affair was a matter of as much consequence to him, as the retrogradation of the planets to Copernicus:—the backslidings of Venus in her orbit fortified the Copernican system, called so after his name; and the backslidings of my aunt Dinah in her orbit, did the same service in establishing my father's system which, I trust, will for ever hereafter be called the SHANDEAN SYSTEM after his.

In any other family-dishonor, my father, I believe, had as nice a sense of shame as any man whatever;——and neither he, nor I dare say, Copernicus, would have divulged the affair in either case, or have taken the least notice of it to the world, but for the obligation they owed, as they thought, to truth.—*Amicus Plato*,—my father would say, construing the words to my uncle Toby as he went along;—*Amicus Plato*,—that is, Dinah was my aunt;—*sed magis amica veritas*,——but Truth is my sister.

This contrariety of humors betwixt my father and my uncle, was the source of many a fraternal squabble. The one could not bear to hear the tale of family disgrace recorded;——and the other would scarce ever let a day pass to an end without some hint at it.

For God's sake, my uncle Toby would cry,——and for my sake, and for all our sakes, my dear brother Shandy,—do let this story of our aunt's and her ashes sleep in peace.—How can you,—how can you have so little feeling and compassion for the character of our family?——What is the character of a family to an hypothesis? my father would reply.——Nay, if you come to that,—what is the life of a family?——The life of a family—my uncle Toby would say, throwing himself back in his arm-chair, and lifting up his hands, his eyes, and one leg. ——Yes, the life,——my father would say, maintaining his point. How many thousands of 'em are there, every year that comes, cast away, (in all civilized countries at least)——and considered as nothing but common air in competition of an hypothesis! In my plain sense of things, my uncle Toby would answer,——every such instance is downright Murder, let who will commit it.——There lies your mistake, my father would reply;——for, in *Foro Scientiæ* there is no such thing as Murder;——'tis only Death, brother.

My uncle Toby would never offer to answer this by any other kind of argument than that of whistling half a dozen bars of Lillebullero.——You must know it was the usual channel through which his passions got vent, when any thing shocked or surprised him:——but especially when any thing, which he deem'd very absurd, was offered.

As not one of our logical writers, nor any of the commentators upon them, that I remember, have thought proper to give a name to this particular species of argument,—I here take the liberty to do it myself, for two reasons: first, That, in order to prevent all confusion in disputes, it may stand as much distinguished for ever, from every other species of argument——as the *Argumentum ad Vericundiam, ex Absurdo, ex Fortiori*, or any other argument whatsoever;—and, secondly, That it may be said by my children's children, when my head is laid to rest,——that their learn'd grandfather's head had been busied to as much purpose once, as other people's.—That he had invented a name,—and generously thrown it into the Treasury of the *Ars Logica*, for one of the most unanswerable arguments in the whole science; and, if the end of disputation is more to silence than convince,—they may add, if they please,—to one of the best arguments too.

I do therefore, by these presents, strictly order and command, That it be known and distinguished by the name and title of the *Argumentum Fistulatorium*, and no other;—and that it rank hereafter with the *Argumentum Baculinum* and the *Argumentum ad Crumenam*, and for ever hereafter be treated of in the same chapter.

As for the *Argumentum Tripodium*, which is never used but by the woman against the man;—and the *Argumentum ad Rem*, which, contrariwise, is made use of by the man only against the woman:—as these two are enough in conscience for one lecture;——and moreover, as the one is the best answer to the other,—let them likewise be kept apart, and be treated of in a place by themselves.

CHAP. XXII.

The learned Bishop Hall, I mean the famous Dr. Joseph Hall, who was Bishop of Exeter in King James the First's reign, tells us in one of his Decades, at the end of his Divine Art of Meditation, imprinted in London, in the year 1610, by John Beal dwelling in Aldersgate-street, "That it is "an abominable thing for a man to commend himself:"——and I really think it is so.

And yet on the other hand, when a thing is executed in a masterly kind of a fashion, which thing is not likely to be found out;—I think it is full as abominable, that a man should lose the honor of it, and go out of the world with the conceit of it rotting in his head.

This is precisely my situation.

For in this long digression which I was accidentally led into, as in all my digressions (one only excepted) there is a master-stroke of digressive skill, the merit of which has all along, I fear, been overlooked by my reader,—not for want of penetration in him,—but because 'tis an excellence seldom looked for, or expected indeed, in a digression:—and it is this: That, though my digressions are all fair, as you observe,—and that I fly off from what I am about, as far, and as often too, as any writer in Great Britain,—yet I constantly take care to order affairs so, that my main business does not stand still in my absence.

I was just going, for example, to have given you the great outlines of my uncle Toby's most whimsical character:—when my aunt Dinah and the coachman came across us, and led us a vagary some millions of miles into the very heart of the planetary system: notwithstanding all this, you perceive that the drawing of my uncle Toby's character went on gently all the time;—not the great contours of it,—that was impossible,—but some familiar strokes and faint designations of it, were here and there touch'd on, as we went along, so that you are much better acquainted with my uncle Toby now than you was before.

By this contrivance, the machinery of my work is of a species by itself; two contrary motions are introduced into it, and reconciled, which were thought to be at variance with each other. In a word, my work is digressive, and it is progressive too,—and at the same time.

This, Sir, is a very different story from that of the earth's moving round her axis in her diurnal rotation, with her progress in ner elliptic orbit, which brings about the year, and constitutes that variety and vicissitude of seasons we enjoy;—though I own it suggested the thought,—as I believe the greatest of our boasted improvements and discoveries have come from such trifling hints.

Digressions, incontestably, are the sunshine;—they are the life, the soul of reading!—take them out of this book, for instance, you might as well take the book along with them;—one cold eternal winter would reign in every page of it; restore them to the writer;—he steps forth like a bridegroom,—bids All-hail; brings in variety, and forbids the appetite to fail.

All the dexterity is in the good cookery and management of them, so as to be not only for the advantage of the reader, but also of the author, whose distress in this matter is truly pitiable: for if he begins a digression, —from that moment, I observe, his whole work stands stock still;—and if he goes on with his main work, then there is an end of his digression.

——This is vile work.—For which reason, from the beginning of this, you see, I have constructed the main work, and the adventitious parts of it, with such intersections, and have so complicated and involved the digressive and progressive movements, one wheel within another, that the whole machine, in general, has been kept a-going;—and, what's more, it shall be kept a-going these forty years, if it pleases the fountain of health to bless me so long with life and good spirits.

CHAP. XXIII.

I HAVE a strong propensity in me to begin this chapter very nonsensically; and I will not balk my fancy;—accordingly I set off thus:

If the fixture of Momus's glass in the human breast, according to the proposed emendation of that arch-critic, had taken place,——first, This foolish consequence would certainly have followed:—That the very wisest and very gravest of us all, in one coin or other. must have paid window-money every day of our lives.

And, secondly, That had the said glass been there set up, nothing more would have been wanting, in order to have taken a man's character, but to have taken a chair and gone softly, as you would to a dioptrical bee-hive, and look'd in,—viewed the soul stark naked;—observed all her motions,—her machinations;—traced all her maggots from their first engendering to their crawling forth;—watched her loose in her frisks, her gambols, her caprices; and after some notice of her more solemn deportment, consequent upon such frisks, &c.——then taken your pen and ink, and set down nothing but what you had seen, and could have sworn to.—But this is an advantage not to be had by the biographer in this planet;—in the planet Mercury (belike) it may be so; if not, better still for him;——for there, the intense heat of the country, which is proved by computators, from its vicinity to the sun, to be more than equal to that of red-hot iron, —must, I think, long ago have vitrified the bodies of the inhabitants (as the efficient cause) to suit them for the climate (which is the final cause); so that betwixt them both, all the tenements of their souls, from top to bottom, may be nothing else, for aught the soundest philosophy can show to the contrary, but one fine transparent body of clear glass (bating the umbilical knot)—so that, till the inhabitants grow old and tolerably wrinkled, whereby the rays of light, in passing through them, become so monstrously refracted,——or return reflected from their surfaces in such transverse lines to the eye, that a man cannot be seen through,—his soul might as well, unless for mere ceremony, or the trifling advantage which the umbilical point gave her,—might, upon all other accounts, I say, as well play the fool out o'doors as in her own house.

But this, as I said above, is not the case of the inhabitants of this earth:—our minds shine not through the body,—but are wrapt up here in a dark covering of uncrystallized flesh and blood; so that, if we would come to the specific characters of them, we must go some other way to work.

Many, in good truth, are the ways which human wit has been forced to take, to do this thing with exactness.

Some, for instance, draw all their characters with wind-instruments.—Virgil takes notice of that way in the affair of Dido and Æneas :—but it is as fallacious as the breath of fame ;—and, moreover, bespeaks a narrow genius. I am not ignorant that the Italians pretend to a mathematical exactness in their designations of one particular sort of character among them, from the *forte* or *piano* of a certain wind-instrument they use,—which they say is infallible.—I dare not mention the name of the instrument in this place; 'tis sufficient we have it amongst us,—but never think of making a drawing by it :—this is enigmatical, and intended to be so, at least *ad populum* :—and therefore, I beg, Madam, when you come here, that you read on as fast as you can, and never stop to make any inquiry about it.

There are others again, who will draw a man's character from no other helps in the world, but merely from his evacuations ;—but this often gives a very incorrect outline, —unless, indeed, you take a sketch of his repletions too; and by correcting one drawing from the other, compound one good figure out of them both.

I should have no objection to this method, but that I think it must smell too strong of the lamp,—and be render'd still more operose, by forcing you to have an eye to the rest of his non-naturals.——Why the most natural actions of a man's life should be called his non-naturals,—is another question.

There are others, fourthly, who disdain every one of these expedients ;—not from any fertility of their own, but from the various ways of doing it, which they have borrowed from the honorable devices which the Pentagraphic Brethren* of the brush have shown in taking copies.—These, you must know, are your great historians.

One of these you will see drawing a full-length character *against the light* :—that's illiberal,—dishonest,—and hard upon the character of the man who sits.

Others, to mend the matter, will make a drawing of you in the *Camera* ;—that is most unfair of all, because *there* you are sure to be represented in some of your most ridiculous attitudes.

To avoid all and every one of these errors in giving you my uncle Toby's character, I am determined to draw it by no mechanical help whatever ;——nor shall my pencil be guided by any one wind-instrument which ever was blown upon, either on this, or on the other side of the Alps ;—nor will I consider either his repletions or his discharges,—or touch upon his non-naturals; but in a word, I will draw my uncle Toby's character from his Hobby-Horse.

CHAP. XXIV.

If I was not morally sure that the reader must be out of all patience for my uncle Toby's character,—I would here previously have convinced him that there is no instrument so fit to draw such a thing with, as that which I have pitch'd upon.

A man and his Hobby-Horse, though I cannot say that they act and re-act exactly after the same manner in which the soul and body do upon each other; yet, doubtless, there is a communication between them of some kind; and my opinion rather is, that there is something in it more of the manner of electrified bodies ;—and that, by means of the heated parts of the rider, which come immediately into contact with the back of the Hobby-Horse—by long journeys and much friction, it so happens that the body of the rider is at length fill'd as full of Hobby-Horsical matter as it can hold ;——so that if you are able to give but a clear description of the nature of the one, you may form a pretty exact notion of the genius and character of the other.

Now the Hobby-Horse, which my uncle Toby always rode upon, was, in my opinion, a Hobby-Horse well worth giving a description of, if it was only upon the score of his great singularity ;—for you might have travelled from York to Dover,—from Dover to Penzance in Cornwall, and from Penzance to York back again, and not have seen such another upon the road; or if you had seen such a one, whatever haste you had been in, you must infallibly have stopp'd to have taken a view of him. Indeed, the gait and figure of him was so strange, and so utterly unlike was he, from his head to his tail, to any one of the whole species

* Pentagraph, an instrument to copy Prints and Pictures mechanically, and in any proportion.

that it was now and then made a matter of dispute,—whether it was really a HOBBY-HORSE or no: but as the philosopher would use no other argument to the sceptic, who disputed with him against the reality of motion, save that of rising up upon his legs, and walking across the room;—so would my uncle Toby use no other argument to prove his HOBBY-HORSE was a HOBBY-HORSE indeed, but by getting upon his back and riding him about;—leaving the world after that to determine the point as it thought fit.

In good truth, my uncle Toby mounted him with so much pleasure, and he carried my uncle Toby so well,—that he troubled his head very little with what the world either said or thought about it.

It is now high time, however, that I give you a description of him:—but to go on regularly, I only beg you will give me leave to acquaint you first, how my uncle Toby came by him.

CHAP. XXV.

THE wound in my uncle Toby's groin, which he received at the siege of Namur, rendering him unfit for the service, it was thought expedient he should return to England, in order, if possible, to be set to rights.

He was four years totally confined,—part of it to his bed, and all of it to his room; and in the course of his cure, which was all that time in hand, suffer'd unspeakable miseries,—owing to a succession of exfoliations from the *os pubis*, and the outward edge of that part of the *coxendix*, called the *os illium*;——both which bones were dismally crush'd, as much by the irregularity of the stone, which I told you was broke off the parapet,—as by its size,—(though it was pretty large) which inclined the surgeon all along to think, that the great injury which it had done my uncle Toby's groin, was more owing to the gravity of the stone itself, than to the projectile force of it;—which he would often tell him was a great happiness.

My father at that time was just beginning business in London, and had taken a house;—and as the truest friendship and cordiality subsisted between the two brothers,—and that my father thought my uncle Toby could nowhere be so well nursed and taken care of as in his own house,—he assign'd him the best apartment in it;—and, what was a much more sincere mark of his affection still, he would never suffer a friend or an acquaintance to step into the house on any occasion, but he would take him by the hand, and lead him up stairs to see his brother Toby, and chat an hour by his bed-side.

The history of a soldier's wound beguiles the pain of it;—my uncle's visitors at least thought so; and in their daily calls upon him, from the courtesy arising out of that belief, they would frequently turn the discourse to that subject—and from that subject the discourse would generally roll on to the siege itself.

These conversations were infinitely kind; and my uncle Toby received great relief from them, and would have received much more, but that they brought him into some unforeseen perplexities, which, for three months together, retarded his cure greatly; and if he had not hit upon an expedient to extricate himself out of them, I verily believe they would have laid him in his grave.

What these perplexities of my uncle Toby were,——'tis impossible for you to guess:—if you could,—I should blush; not as a relation,—not as a man,—nor even as a woman,—but I should blush as an author; inasmuch as I set no small store by myself upon this very account, that my reader has never yet been able to guess at any thing: and in this, Sir, I am of so nice and singular a humor, that if I thought you was able to form the least judgment, or probable conjecture to yourself, of what was to come in the next page,—I would tear it out of my book.

THE

LIFE AND OPINIONS

OF

Tristram Shandy,

GENTLEMAN.

CHAP. I.

I HAVE begun a new book, on purpose that I might have room enough to explain the nature of the perplexities in which my uncle Toby was involved, from the many discourses and interrogations about the siege of Namur, where he received his wound.

I must remind the reader, in case he has read the history of King William's wars;—but if he has not,—I then inform him, that one of the most memorable attacks in that siege, was that which was made by the English and Dutch upon the point of the advanced counter-scarp, between the gate of St. Nicholas, which inclosed the great sluice or water-stop, where the English were terribly exposed to the shot of the counter-guard and demi-bastion of St, Roch: the issue of which hot dispute, in three words, was this: That the Dutch lodged themselves upon the counter-guard,—and that the English made themselves masters of the covered way before St. Nicholas-gate, notwithstanding the gallantry of the French officers, who exposed themselves upon the glacis sword in hand.

As this was the principal attack of which my uncle Toby was an eye-witness at Namur,——the army of the besiegers being cut off, by the confluence of the Maes and Sambres, from seeing much of each other's operations,——my uncle Toby was generally more eloquent and particular in his account of it; and the many perplexities ne was in, arose out of the almost insurmountable difficulties he found in telling his story intelligibly, and giving such clear ideas of the differences and distinctions between the scarp and counter-scarp,—the glacis and covered way,—the half-moon and ravelin,—as to make his company fully comprehend where and what he was about.

Writers themselves are too apt to confound these terms; so that you will the less wonder, if in his endeavors to explain them, and in opposition to many misconceptions, that my uncle Toby did oft-times puzzle his visitors, and sometimes himself too.

To speak the truth, unless the company my father led up-stairs were tolerably clear-headed, or my uncle Toby was in one of his explanatory moods, 'twas a difficult thing, do what he could, to keep the discourse free from obscurity.

What rendered the account of this affair the more intricate to my uncle Toby was this,—that in the attack of the counterscarp, before the gate of St. Nicholas, extending itself from the bank of the Maes quite up the great water-stop,—the ground was cut and cross-cut with such a multitude of dykes, drains, rivulets, and sluices, on all sides,—and he would get so sadly bewildered, and set fast amongst them, that frequently he could neither get backwards nor forwards to save his life; and was oft-times obliged to give up the attack upon that verv account only.

These perplexing rebuffs gave my uncle Toby Shandy more perturbations than you would imagine; and as my father's kindness to him was continually dragging up fresh friends and fresh inquirers,——he had but a very uneasy task of it.

No doubt, my uncle Toby had great command of himself,—and could guard appearances, I believe, as well as most men,—yet, any one may imagine, that when he could not retreat out of the ravelin without getting into the half-moon, or get out of the covered way without falling down the counter-scarp, nor cross the dyke without danger of slipping into the ditch, but that he must have fretted and fumed inwardly:—He did so;—and the little and hourly vexations, which may seem trifling and of no account to the man who has not read Hippocrates; yet, whoever has read Hippocrates, or Dr. James Mackenzie, and has considered well the effects which the passions and affections of the mind have upon the digestion—(Why not of a wound as well as of a dinner?)—may easily conceive what sharp paroxysms and exacerbations of his wound my uncle Toby must have undergone upon that score only.

—My uncle Toby could not philosophize upon it;—'twas enough he felt it was so:—and having sustained the pain and sorrows of it for three months together, he was resolved, some way or other, to extricate nimself.

He was one morning lying upon his back in his bed, the anguish and nature of the wound upon his groin suffering him to lie in no other position, when a thought came into his head, that if he could purchase such a thing, and have it pasted down upon a board, as a large map of the fortification of the town and citadel of Namur, with its environs, it might be a means of giving him ease.—I take notice of his desire to have the environs along with the town and citadel, for this reason,—because my uncle Toby's wound was got in one of the traverses, about thirty toises from the returning angle of the trench, opposite to the salient angle of the demi-bastion of St. Roch;——so that he was pretty confident he could stick a pin upon the identical spot of ground where he was standing when the stone struck him.

All this succeeded to his wishes; and not only freed him from a world of sad explanations, but, in the end, it proved the happy means, as you will read, of procuring my uncle Toby his Hobby-Horse.

CHAP. II.

There is nothing so foolish, when you are at the expense of making an entertainment of this kind, as to order things so badly, as to let your critics and gentry of refined taste run it down: nor is there any thing so likely to make them do it, as that of leaving them out of the party, or, what is full as offensive, of bestowing your attention upon the rest of your guests in so particular a way, as if there was no such thing as a critic (by occupation) at table.

——I guard against both; for, in the first place, I have left half a dozen places purposely open for them;—and in the next place, I pay them all court.—Gentlemen, I kiss your hands. I protest, no company could give me half the pleasure;—by my soul, I am glad to see you.——I beg only you will make no strangers of yourselves, but sit down, without ceremony, and fall on heartily.

I said I had left six places, and I was on the point of carrying my complaisance so far as to have left a seventh open for them,—and in this very spot I stand on; but being told by a critic (though not by occupation—but by nature) that I had acquitted myself well enough, I shall fill it up directly, hoping, in the mean time, that I shall be able to make a great deal of more room next year.

———How, in the name of wonder! could your uncle Toby, who, it seems, was a military man, and whom you have represented as no fool,——be at the same time such a confused, pudding-headed, muddle-headed fellow, as—Go look.

So, Sir Critic, I could have replied; but I scorn it.—'Tis language unurbane,—and only befitting the man who cannot give clear and satisfactory accounts of things, or dive deep enough into the first causes of human ignorance and confusion. It is moreover the reply valiant,—and therefore I reject it; for though it might have suited my uncle Toby's character as a soldier excellently well,—and had he accustomed himself, in such attacks, to whistle the Lillibullero,* as he wanted no courage, 'tis the

---

* MY UNCLE TOBY'S WHISTLE,
LILLIBULLERO.

The Ballad * to this tune was written in the year 1686, on account of King James II. nominating to the Lieutenancy of Ireland *General Talbot*, newly created Earl of Tyrconnel, a furious Papist, who had recommended himself to his bigoted master by his arbitrary

* See Percy's Reliques of Ancient English Poetry, vol. ii, page 35

very answer he would have given; yet it would by no means have done for me. You see as plain as can be, that I write as a man of erudition;—that even my similies, my allusions, my illustrations, my metaphors, are erudite,—and that I must sustain my character properly, and contrast it properly too,—else what would become of me?——Why, Sir, I should be undone;—at this very moment that I am going here to fill up one place against a critic,—I should have made an opening for a couple.

——Therefore I answer thus;—

Pray, Sir, in all the reading which you have ever read, did you ever read such a book as Locke's Essay upon the Human Understanding?——Don't answer me rashly,—because many, I know, quote the book, who have not read it,—and many have read it who understand it not.—If either of these is your case, as I write to instruct, I will tell you in three words what the book is.—It is a history.—A history! of who? what? where? when? Don't hurry yourself,——It is a history-book, Sir, (which may possibly recommend it to the world) of what passes in a man's own mind; and if you will say so much of the book, and no more, believe me, you will cut no contemptible figure in a metaphysic circle.

But this by the way.

Now if you will venture to go along with me, and look down into the bottom of this matter, it will be found that the cause of obscurity and confusion in the mind of a man, is threefold.

Dull organs, dear Sir, in the first place. Secondly, Slight and transient impressions made by the objects, when the said organs are not dull: and, Thirdly, A memory like unto a sieve; not able to retain what it has received.—Call down Dolly your chamber-maid, and I will give you my cap and bell along with it, if I make not this matter so plain that Dolly herself should understand it as well as Malbranch.——When Dolly has indited her epistle to Robin, and has thrust her arm into the bottom of her pocket hanging by her right side,—take that opportunity to recollect, that the organs and faculties of perception can, by nothing in this world, be so aptly typified and explained as by that one thing which Dolly's hand is in search of.—Your organs are not so dull that I should inform you,—'tis an inch, Sir, of red seal-wax.

When this is melted and dropped upon the letter, if Dolly fumbles too long for her thimble, till the wax is over-hardened, it will not receive the mark of her thimble from the usual impulse which was wont to imprint it. Very well. If Dolly's wax, for want of better, is bees-wax, or of a temper too soft,—tho' it may receive,—it will not hold the impression, how hard soever Dolly thrusts against it: and, last, of all, Supposing the wax good, and eke the thimble, but applied thereto in careless haste, as her mistress rings the bell;—in any one of these three cases, the print left by the thimble will be as unlike the prototype as a brass-jack.

Now you must understand, that not one of these was the true cause of confusion in my uncle Toby's discourse; and it is for that very reason I enlarge upon them so long, after the manner of great physiologists,—to show the world what it did *not* arise from.

What it *did* arise from, I have hinted above; and a fertile source of obscurity it is,—and ever will be,—and that is, the unsteady uses of words, which have perplexed the clearest and most exalted understandings.

It is ten to one (at Arthur's) whether you have ever read the literary history of past ages;—if you have, what terrible battles, yclept logomachies, have they occasioned, and perpetuated with so much gall and ink-shed,—that a good-natured man cannot read the accounts of them without tears in his eyes.

---

treatment of the Protestants in the preceding year, when only Lieutenant-General and whose subsequent conduct fully justified his expectations and their fears.

This foolish Ballad, treating the Papists and chiefly the Irish, in a very ridiculous manner, had a burden, said to be Irish words, "Lero, lero, lillibullero;" and made an impression on the (King's) army, more powerful than either the philippics of Demosthenes or Cicero. The whole army, and at last the people both in city and country, were singing it perpetually. Perhaps never had so slight a thing so great an effect; for it contributed not a little towards the Revolution in 1688.*

LILLIBULLERO and BULLEN-A-LAH, are said to have been the watch-words used among the Irish Papists, in their massacre of the Protestants in 1641.

* See Bishop Burnet's History of his own Times; and King's State of the Protestants in Ireland, 1691, 4to.

Gentle critic! when thou hast weighed all this, and considered within thyself how much of thy own knowledge, discourse, and conversation has been pestered and disordered, at one time or other, by this, and this only;—what a pudder and racket in Councils about ȣσἶα and ὑπόςασις; and in the Schools of the learned about power and about spirit;—about essences, and about quintessences;—about substances and about space;——what confusion in greater Theatres from words of little meaning, and as indeterminate a sense! when thou considerest this, thou wilt not wonder at my uncle Toby's perplexities,—thou wilt drop a tear of pity upon his scarp and his counter-scarp;—his glacis and his covered way;—his ravelin and his half-moon: 'twas not by ideas,—by Heaven; his life was put in jeopardy by words.

CHAP. III.

When my uncle Toby got his map of Namur to his mind, he began immediately to apply himself, and with the utmost diligence, to the study of it; for nothing being of more importance to him than his recovery, and his recovery depending, as you have read, upon the passions and affections of his mind, it behoved him to take the nicest care to make himself so far master of his subject, as to be able to talk upon it without emotion.

In a fortnight's close and painful application, which, by the bye, did my uncle Toby's wound, upon his groin, no good—he was enabled by the help of some marginal documents at the feet of the elephant, together with Gobesius's military architecture and pyroballogy, translated from the Flemish, to form his discourse with passable perspicuity; and before he was two full months gone, —he was right eloquent upon it, and could make not only the attack of the advanced counterscarp with great order;——but having by that time gone much deeper into the art than what his first motive made necessary, my uncle Toby was able to cross the Maes and Sambre; make diversions as far as Vauban's line, the abbey of Salsines, &c. and gave his visitors as distinct a history of each of their attacks as that of the gate of St. Nicholas, where he had the honor to receive his wound.

But desire of knowledge, like the thirst of riches, increases ever with the acquisition of it. The more my uncle Toby pored over his map, the more he took a liking to it!—by the same process and electrical assimilation, as I told you, through which I ween the souls of connoisseurs themselves, by long friction and incumbition, have the happiness, at length, to get all be-virtu'd,—be-pictured,—be-butterflied, and be-fiddled.

The more my uncle Toby drank of this sweet fountain of science, the greater was the heat and impatience of his thirst; so that before the first year of his confinement had well gone round, there was scarce a fortified town in Italy or Flanders, of which, by one means or other, he had not procured a plan, reading over as he got them, and carefully collating therewith the histories of their sieges, their demolitions, their improvements, and new works, all which he would read with that intense application and delight, that he would forget himself, his wound, his confinement, his dinner.

In the second year, my uncle Toby purchased Ramelli and Cataneo, translated from the Italian;—likewise Stevinus, Moralis, the Chevalier de Ville, Lorini, Coehorn, Sheeter, the Count de Pagan, the Marshal Vauban, Mons. Blondel, with almost as many more books of military architecture as Don Quixote was found to have of chivalry, when the curate and barber invaded his library.

Towards the beginning of the third year, which was in August, ninety-nine, my uncle Toby found it necessary to understand a little of projectiles:—and having judged it best to draw his knowledge from the fountain-head, he began with N. Tartaglia, who it seems was the first man who detected the imposition of a cannon-ball's doing all that mischief under the notion of a right line.—This, N. Tartaglia proved, to my uncle Toby, to be an impossible thing.

——Endless is the search of Truth.

No sooner was my uncle Toby satisfied which road the cannon-ball *did not* go, but he was insensibly led on, and resolved in his mind to inquire and find out which road the ball *did* go: for which purpose he was obliged to set off afresh with old Malthus, and studied him devoutly.—He proceeded next to Galileo and Torricellius, wherein, by certain geometrical rules, infallibly laid down, he found the precise path to be a Parabola,—or else a Hyperbola,—and that the parameter, or *latus rectum*, of the conic section of the said path, was to the quantity and amplitude in a direct *ratio*, as the whole line to the sine of double the angle of incidence, formed by the breach upon a horizontal plane;—and that the semiparameter, ——stop! my dear uncle Toby,——stop! —go not one foot farther into this thorny and bewildered track:—intricate are the steps! intricate are the mazes of this labyrinth! intricate are the troubles which the pursuit of this bewitching phantom Knowledge will bring upon thee.—O my uncle, —fly—fly—fly from it as from a serpent! ——Is it fit——good-natured man! thou should'st sit up, with the wound upon thy groin, whole nights baking thy blood with hectic watchings?——Alas! 'twill exasperate thy symptoms,—check thy perspirations,—evaporate thy spirits—waste thy animal strength,—dry up thy radical moisture,—bring thee into a costive habit of body,—impair thy health,—and hasten all the infirmities of thy old age.——O my uncle! my uncle Toby!

CHAP. IV.

I WOULD not give a groat for that man's knowledge in pen-craft, who does not understand this:——That the best plain narrative in the world, tacked very close to the last spirited apostrophe to my uncle Toby——would have felt both cold and vapid upon the reader's palate;—therefore I forthwith put an end to the chapter, though I was in the middle of my story.

———Writers of my stamp have one principle in common with painters. Where an exact copying makes our pictures less striking, we choose the less evil; deeming it even more pardonable to trespass against truth than beauty. This is to be understood *cum grano salis;* but be it as it will,—as the parallel is made more for the sake of letting the apostrophe cool, than any thing else—'tis not very material whether upon any other score the reader approves of it or not.

In the latter end of the third year, my uncle Toby perceiving that the parameter and semi-parameter of the conic section angered his wound, he left off the study of projectiles in a kind of a huff, and betook himself to the practical part of fortification only; the pleasure of which, like a spring held back, returned upon him with redoubled force.

It was in this year that my uncle began to break in upon the daily regularity of a clean shirt,—to dismiss his barber unshaven, and to allow his surgeon scarce time sufficient to dress his wound, concerning himself so little about it, as not to ask him once in seven times' dressing, how it went on: when, lo!—all of a sudden, for the change was as quick as lightning, he began to sigh heavily for his recovery,—complained to my father, grew impatient with the surgeon:—and one morning, as he heard his foot coming up stairs, he shut up his books, and thrust aside his instruments, in order to expostulate with him upon the protraction of the cure, which, he told him, might surely have been accomplished at least by that time.—He dwelt long upon the miseries he had undergone, and the sorrows of his four years' melancholy imprisonment;—adding, that had it not been for the kind looks and fraternal cheerings of the best of brothers,—he had long since sunk under his misfortunes.—My father was by.—My uncle Toby, by nature, was not eloquent,—it had the greater effect.——The surgeon was confounded;—not that there wanted grounds for such, or greater marks of impatience,—but 'twas unexpected too. In the four years he had attended him, he had never seen any thing like it in my uncle Toby's carriage; he had never once dropped one fretful or discontented word;—he had been all patience,—all submission.

—We lose the right of complaining sometimes, by forbearing it;—but we often treble the force;—the surgeon was astonished; but much more so, when he heard my uncle Toby go on, and peremptorily insist upon his healing up the wound directly,—or sending for Monsieur Ronjat, the king's serjeant-surgeon, to do it for him.

The desire of life and health is implanted in man's nature;—the love of liberty and enlargement is a sister-passion to it. These my uncle Toby had in common with his species;—and either of them had been sufficient to account for his earnest desire to get well, and out of doors;—but I have told you before, that nothing wrought with our family after the common way;—and from the time and manner in which this eager desire showed itself in the present case, the penetrating reader will suspect, there was some other cause or crotchet for it in my uncle Toby's head;——There was so, and 'tis the subject of the next chapter to set forth what that cause and crotchet was. I own, when that's done, 'twill be time to return back to the parlor fire-side, where we left my uncle Toby in the middle of his sentence.

CHAP V.

When a man gives himself up to the government of a ruling passion,—or, in other words, when his Hobby-Horse grows headstrong,——farewell cool reason and fair discretion.

My uncle Toby's wound was near well; and as soon as the surgeon recovered his surprise, and could get leave to say as much —he told him, 'twas just beginning to incarnate; and that if no fresh exfoliation happened, which there was no sign of,—it would be dried up in five or six weeks. The sound of as many Olympiads, twelve hours before, would have conveyed an idea of shorter duration to my uncle Toby's mind. ——The succession of his ideas was now rapid,—he broiled with impatience to put his design in execution;—and so, without consulting farther with any soul living,—which, by the bye, I think is right, when you are predetermined to take no one soul's advice,——he privately ordered Trim, his man, to pack up a bundle of lint and dressings, and hire a chariot-and-four, to be at the door exactly by twelve o'clock that day, when he knew my father would be upon 'Change.——So leaving a bank-note upon the table for the surgeon's care of him, and a letter of tender thanks for his brother's—he packed up his maps, his books of fortification, his instruments, *&c.* and by the help of a crutch on one side, and Trim on the other,—my uncle Toby embarked for Shandy-Hall.

The reason, or rather the rise, of this sudden demigration, was as follows:

The table in my uncle Toby's room, and at which, the night before this change happened, he was sitting with his maps, *&c.* about him—being somewhat of the smallest, for that infinity of great and small instruments of knowledge which usually lay crowded upon it—he had the accident, in reaching over for his tobacco-box, to throw down his compasses; and in stooping to take the compasses up, with his sleeve he threw down his case of instruments and snuffers;—and as the dice took a run against him, in his endeavoring to catch the snuffers in falling,—he thrust Monsieur Blondel off the table, and Count de Pagan o'top of him.

'Twas to no purpose for a man, lame as my uncle Toby was, to think of redressing these evils by himself,—he rung his bell for his man Trim.——Trim, quoth my uncle Toby, prithee see what confusion I have here been making—I must have some better contrivance, Trim.——Canst not thou take my rule, and measure the length and breadth of this table, and then go and bespeak me one as big again?——Yes, an please your Honor, replied Trim, making a bow; but I hope your Honor will be soon well enough to get down to your country-seat, where,—as your Honor takes so much pleasure in fortification, we could manage this matter to a T.

I must here inform you, that this servant of my uncle Toby's, who went by the name of Trim, had been a corporal in my uncle's own company,—his real name was James Butler;—but having got the nickname of Trim, in the regiment, my uncle Toby, unless when he happened to be very angry with him, would never call him by any other name.

The poor fellow had been disabled for the service, by a wound on his left knee, by a musket bullet, at the battle of Landen, which was two years before the affair of Namur;—and as the fellow was well-beloved in the regiment, and a handy fellow into the bargain, my uncle Toby took him tor his servant: and of an excellent use was he, attending my uncle Toby in the camp and in his quarters, as a valet, groom, barber, cook, sempster, and nurse; and indeed, from first to last, waited upon him, and served him with great fidelity and affection.

My uncle Toby loved the man in return: and what attached him more to him still, was the similitude of their knowledge;——for Corporal Trim (for so, for the future, I shall call him) by four years' occasional attention to his Master's discourse upon fortified towns, and the advantage of prying and peeping continually into his Master's plans, *&c.* exclusive and besides what he gained Hobby-Horsically, as a body-servant, *Non Hobby-Horsical per se*;—had become no mean proficient in the science; and was thought, by the cook and chambermaid, to know as much of the nature of strong-holds as my uncle Toby himself.

I have but one more stroke to give to finish Corporal Trim's character,—and it is the only dark line in it.—The fellow loved to advise, or rather to hear himself talk: his carriage, however, was so perfectly respectful, 'twas easy to keep him silent when you had him so; but set his tongue a-going, —you had no hold of him—he was voluble; —the eternal interlardings of *your Honor*, with the respectfulness of Corporal Trim's manner, interceding so strong in behalf of his elocution,—that though you might have been incommoded,—you could not well be angry. My uncle Toby was seldom either the one or the other with him.—or, at least, this fault in Trim broke no squares with them. My uncle Toby, as I said, loved the man;—and besides, as he ever looked upon a faithful servant as an humble friend,—he could not bear to stop his mouth.—Such was Corporal Trim.

If I durst presume, continued Trim, to give your Honor my advice, and speak my opinion in this matter——Thou art welcome, Trim, quoth my uncle Toby——speak,—speak what thou thinkest upon the subject, man, without fear.—Why then, replied Trim (not hanging his ears and scratching his head like a country lout, but) stroking his hair back from his forehead, and standing erect as before his division,—I think, quoth Corporal Trim, with humble submission to your Honor's better judgment,—that these ravelins, bastions, curtains, and horn-works, make but a poor, contemptible, fiddle-faddle piece of work of it here upon paper, compared to what your Honor and I could make of it were we in the country by ourselves, and had but a rood, or a rood and a half of ground, to do what we pleased with: as summer is coming on, continued Trim, your Honor might sit out of doors, and give me the nography—(Call it ichnography, quoth my uncle)—of the town or citadel your Honor was pleased to sit down before, and I'll be shot by your Honor upon the glacis of it, if I did not fortify it to your Honor's mind.——I dare say thou would'st, Trim, quoth my uncle.—For if your Honor, continued the corporal, could but mark me the polygon, with its exact lines and angles —(That I could do very well, quoth my uncle)—I would begin with the fossé; and if your Honor could tell me the proper depth and breadth—(I can, to a hair's breadth, Trim, replied my uncle)—I would throw out the earth upon this hand towards the town for the scarp,—and on that hand towards the campaign for the counter-scarp —(Very right, Trim, quoth my uncle Toby) —and when I had sloped them to your mind,—an' please your Honor, I would face the glacis, as the finest fortifications are done in Flanders, with sods,—(and as your Honor knows they should be)—and I would make the walls and parapets of sods too. ——The best engineers call them Gazons, Trim, said my uncle Toby.——Whether they are gazons or sods, is not much matter, replied Trim; your Honor knows they are ten times beyond a facing either of brick or stone.——I know they are, Trim, in some respects,—quoth my uncle Toby, nodding his head:—for a cannon-ball enters into the gazon right onwards, without bringing any rubbish down with it, which might fill the fossé (as was the case at St. Nicholas's gate) and facilitate the passage over it.

Your Honor understands these matters, replied Corporal Trim, better than any officer in his Majesty's service;——but would your Honor please to let the bespeaking of the table alone, and let us but go into the country, I would work under your Honor's directions like a horse, and make fortifications for you something like a tansy, with a their batteries, saps, ditches, and palisadoes, that it should be worth all the world's riding twenty miles to go and see it.

My uncle Toby blushed as red as scarlet as Trim went on;—but it was not a blush of guilt,—of modesty,—or of anger,—it was a blush of joy;—he was fired with Corporal Trim's project and description.——Trim! said my uncle Toby, thou hast said enough. —We might begin the campaign, continued Trim, on the very day that his Majesty and the Allies take the field, and demolish them, town by town, as fast as—Trim, quoth my uncle Toby, say no more. Your Honor, continued Trim, might sit in your arm-chair (pointing to it) this fine weather, giving me your orders, and I would——Say no more, Trim, quoth my uncle Toby—— Besides, your Honor would get not only pleasure and good pastime,—but good air, and good exercise, and good health;—and your Honor's wound would be well in a month. — Thou hast said enough, Trim, quoth my uncle Toby (putting his hand into his breeches' pocket)—I like thy project mightily.—And if your Honor pleases, I'll this moment go and buy a pioneer's spade to take down with us; and I'll bespeak a shovel and a pick-ax, and a couple of——Say no more, Trim, quoth my uncle Toby, leaping up upon one leg, quite overcome with rapture,—and thrusting a guinea into Trim's hand,—Trim, said my uncle Toby, say no more;—but go down, Trim, this moment, my lad, and bring up my supper this instant.

Trim ran down and brought up his master's supper,——to no purpose:—Trim's plan of operation ran so in my uncle Toby's head, he could not taste it.—Trim, quoth my uncle Toby, get me to bed.—'Twas all one.—Corporal Trim's description had fired his imagination;—my uncle Toby could not shut his eyes.—The more he considered it, the more bewitching the scene appeared to him;—so that, two full hours before daylight, he had come to a final determination, and had concerted the whole plan of his and Corporal Trim's decampment.

My uncle Toby had a little neat country-house of his own, in the village where my father's estate lay at Shandy, which had been left him by an old uncle, with a small estate of about one hundred pounds a-year. Behind this house, and contiguous to it, was a kitchen-garden of about half an acre; and at the bottom of the garden, and cut off from it by a tall yew-hedge, was a bowling-green, containing just about as much ground as Corporal Trim wished for;—so that as Trim uttered the words, "A rood "and a half of ground to do what they would "with," this identical bowling-green instantly presented itself, and became curiously painted, all at once, upon the retina of my uncle Toby's fancy;—which was the physical cause of making him change color, or at least of heightening his blush to that immoderate degree I spoke of.

Never did lover post down to a beloved mistress with more heat and expectation than my uncle Toby did, to enjoy the self-same thing in private;—I say in private;—for it was sheltered from the house, as I told you, by a tall yew-hedge, and was covered on the other three sides, from mortal sight, by rough holly and thick-set flowering shrubs:—so that the idea of not being seen, did not a little contribute to the idea of pleasure preconceived in my uncle Toby's mind.—Vain thought! however thick it was planted about,—or private soever it might seem,—to think, dear uncle Toby, of enjoying a thing which took up a whole rood and a half of ground,—and not have it known!

How my uncle Toby and Corporal Trim managed this matter,—with the history of their campaigns, which were no way barren of events,—may make no uninteresting underplot in the epitasis and working up of this drama.——At present the scene must drop, and change for the parlor fire-side.

CHAP. VI.

——What can they be doing, brother? said my father.——I think, replied my uncle Toby,—taking, as I told you, the pipe from his mouth, and striking the ashes out of it as he began his sentence;——I think, replied he,—it would not be amiss, brother, if we rang the bell.

Pray, what's all that racket over our heads, Obadiah?—quoth my father;—my brother and I can scarce hear ourselves speak.

Sir, answered Obadiah, making a bow towards his left shoulder,—my Mistress is taken very badly.—And where's Susannah running, down the garden there, as if they were going to ravish her?——Sir, she is running the shortest cut into the town, replied Obadiah, to fetch the old midwife.—Then saddle a horse, quoth my father, and do you go directly for Dr. Slop, the man-midwife, with all our services,—and let him know your mistress is fallen into labor—and that I desire he will return with you with all speed.

It is very strange, says my father, addressing himself to my uncle Toby, as Obadiah shut the door,—as there is so expert an operator as Dr. Slop so near,—that my wife should persist to the very last in this obstinate humor of hers, in trusting the life of my child, who has had one misfortune already, to the ignorance of an old woman!—and not only the life of my child, brother,—but her own life, and with it the lives of all the children I might, peradventure, have begot out of her hereafter.

Mayhap, brother, replied my uncle Toby, my sister does it to save the expense.—A pudding's end,—replied my father;—the Doctor must be paid the same for inaction as action,—if not better,—to keep him in temper.

——Then it can be out of nothing in the whole world, quoth my uncle Toby, in the simplicity of his heart,—but Modesty.—My sister, I dare say, added he, does not care to let a man come so near her——. I will not say whether my uncle Toby had completed the sentence or not;—'tis for his advantage to suppose he had,—as, I think, he could have added no ONE WORD which would have improved it.

If, on the contrary, my uncle Toby had not fully arrived at the period's end,—then the world stands indebted to the sudden snapping of my father's tobacco-pipe for one of the neatest examples of that ornamental figure in oratory, which rhetoricians style the *Aposiopesis.*——Just Heaven! how does the *Poco piu* and *Poco meno* of the Italian artists;—the insensible MORE or LESS, determine the precise line of beauty in the sentence, as well as in the statue! How do the slight touches of the chisel, the pencil, the pen, the fiddle-stick, *et cætera*,—give the true swell, which gives the true pleasure!—O my countrymen,—be nice:—be cautious of your language,—and never, O! never let it be forgotten upon what small particles your eloquence and your fame depend.

——"My sister, mayhap," quoth my uncle Toby, "does not choose to let a man "come so near her——." Make this dash, ——,—'tis an Aposiopesis;—take the dash away, and write BACKSIDE,——'tis bawdy;—scratch Backside out, and put COVER'D WAY in, 'tis a metaphor;—and, I dare say, as fortification ran so much in my uncle Toby's head, that if it had been left to have added one word to the sentence,—that word was it.

But whether that was the case, or not the case;—or whether the snapping of my father's tobacco-pipe, so critically, happened through accident or anger, will be seen in due time.

CHAP. VII.

THOUGH my father was a good natural philosopher,—yet he was something of a moral philosopher too; for which reason, when his tobacco-pipe snapp'd short in the middle,—he had nothing to do, as such, but to have taken hold of the two pieces, and thrown them gently upon the back of the fire.——He did no such thing; he threw them with all the violence in the world;—and, to give the action still more emphasis,—he started upon both legs to do it.

This looked something like heat;—and the manner of his reply to what my uncle Toby was saying, proved it was so.

—"Not choose," quoth my father (repeating my uncle Toby's words) "to let a "man come so near her!"——By Heaven, brother Toby! you would try the patience of Job; and I think I have the plagues of one already without it.——Why?——Where?—Wherein?——Wherefore?——Upon what account? replied my uncle Toby, in the utmost astonishment.——To think, said my father, of a man living to your age, brother, and knowing so little about women!——I know nothing at all about them,—replied my uncle Toby: and I think, continued he.

that the shock I received the year after the demolition of Dunkirk, in my affair with Widow Wadman:—which shock, you know, I should not have received, but from my total ignorance of the sex,—has given me just cause to say, that I neither know, nor do pretend to know, any thing about 'em, or their concerns either. —— Methinks, brother, replied my father, you might, at least, know so much as the right end of a woman from the wrong.

It is said in Aristotle's Master-Piece, "That when a man doth think of any thing "which is past,—he looketh down upon the "ground;—but that when he thinketh of "something that is to come, he looketh up "towards the heavens."

My uncle Toby, I suppose, thought of neither, for he looked horizontally.—Right end! quoth my uncle Toby, muttering the two words low to himself, and fixing his two eyes insensibly as he muttered them, upon a small crevice, formed by a bad joint in the chimney-piece——Right end of a woman!—I declare, quoth my uncle, I know no more which it is than the man in the moon;—and if I was to think, continued my uncle Toby (keeping his eyes still fixed upon the bad joint) this month together, I am sure I should not be able to find it out.

Then, brother Toby, replied my father, I will tell you.

Every thing in the world, continued my father (filling a fresh pipe)—every thing in the world, my dear brother Toby, has two handles:——Not always, quoth my uncle Toby.——At least, replied my father, every one has two hands,—which comes to the same thing.——Now, if a man was to sit down coolly, and consider within himself the make, the shape, the construction, come-atability and convenience of all the parts which constitute the whole of that animal, called Woman, and compare them analogically,——I never understood rightly the meaning of that word,—quoth my uncle Toby—

Analogy, replied my father, is the certain relation and agreement which different ——Here a devil of a rap at the door snapped my father's definition (like his tobacco-pipe) in two,—and, at the same time, crushing the head of as notable and curious a dissertation as ever was engendered in the womb of speculation:—it was some months before my father could get an opportunity to be safely delivered of it:—and, at this hour, it is a thing full as problematical as the subject of the dissertation itself,—(considering the confusion and distress of our domestic misadventures, which are now coming thick, one upon the back of another) whether I shall be able to find a place for it in the third volume or not.

CHAP. VIII.

It is about an hour and a half's tolerable good reading since my uncle Toby rung the bell, when Obadiah was ordered to saddle a horse, and go for Dr. Slop, the man-midwife;—so that no one can say, with reason, that I have not allowed Obadiah time enough, poetically speaking, and considering the emergency too, both to go and come;—though, morally and truly speaking, the man perhaps has scarce had time to get on his boots.

If the hypercritic will go upon this; and is resolved after all to take a pendulum, and measure the true distance betwixt the ringing of the bell and the rap at the door; and, after finding it to be no more than two minutes, thirteen seconds, and three-fifths,—should take upon him to insult over me for such a breach in the unity, or rather probability of time,—I would remind him, that the idea of duration, and of its simple modes, is got merely from the train and succession of our ideas—and is the true scholastic pendulum,—and by which, as a scholar, I will be tried in this matter,—abjuring and detesting the jurisdiction of all other pendulums whatever.

I would therefore desire him to consider, that it is but poor eight miles from Shandy hall to Dr. Slop the man-midwife's house:—and that whilst Obadiah has been going those said miles and back, I have brought my uncle Toby from Namur, quite across all Flanders, into England;—that I have had him ill upon my hands near four years,—and have since travelled him and Corporal Trim, in a chariot-and-four, a journey of near two hundred miles down into York shire;—all which put together, must have prepared the reader's imagination for the entrance of Dr. Slop upon the stage,—as much, at least (I hope) as a dance, a song, or a concerto between the acts.

If my hypercritic is untractable, alleging that two minutes and thirteen seconds are no more than two minutes and thirteen seconds,—when I have said all I can about them; and that this plea, though it might save me dramatically, will damn me biographically, rendering my book, from this very moment, a professed Romance, which, before, was a book apocryphal:—If I am thus pressed,—I then put an end to the whole objection and controversy about it all at once,—by acquainting him, that Obadiah had not got above threescore yards from the stable-yard, before he met with Dr. Slop:—and indeed he gave a dirty proof that he had met with him, and was within an ace of giving a tragical one too.

Imagine to yourself——But this had better begin a new chapter.

CHAP. IX.

Imagine to yourself a little squat, uncourtly figure of a Doctor Slop, of about four feet and a half perpendicular height, with a breadth of back, and a sesquipedality of belly, which might have done honor to a serjeant in the horse-guards.

Such were the outlines of Dr. Slop's figure; which—if you have read Hogarth's Analysis of Beauty,—and if you have not, I wish you would,——you must know, may as certainly be caricatured and conveyed to the mind by three strokes as three hundred.

Imagine such a one;—for such, I say, were the outlines of Dr. Slop's figure, coming slowly along, foot by foot, waddling through the dirt upon the *vertebræ* of a little diminutive pony, of a pretty color—but of strength,—alack! scarce able to have made an amble of it, under such a fardel, had the roads been in an ambling condition.——They were not.——Imagine to yourself, Obadiah mounted upon a strong monster of a coach-horse, pricked into a full gallop, and making all practicable speed the adverse way.

Pray, Sir, let me interest you a moment in this description.

Had Dr. Slop beheld Obadiah a mile off, posting in a narrow lane directly towards him, at that monstrous rate, splashing and plunging like a devil through thick and thin, as he approached; would not such a phenomenon, with such a vortex of mud and water moving along with it, round its axis,—have been a subject of juster apprehension to Dr. Slop in his situation, than the worst of Whiston's comets?—To say nothing of the Nucleus; that is, of Obadiah and the coach-horse.—In my idea, the vortex alone of 'em was enough to have involved and carried, if not the doctor, at least the doctor's pony, quite away with it. What then do you think must the terror and hydrophobia of Dr. Slop have been, when you read (which you are just going to do) that he was advancing thus warily along towards Shandy-hall, and had approached to within sixty yards of it, and within five yards of a sudden turn, made by an acute-angle of the garden-wall,—and in the dirtiest part of a dirty lane,—when Obadiah and his coach-horse turned the corner, rapid, furious,—pop,—full upon him!—Nothing, I think, in nature, can be supposed more terrible than such a rencounter,—so imprompt! so ill prepared to stand the shock of it as Dr. Slop was.

What could Dr. Slop do?—he crossed himself+ —Pugh!—but the doctor, Sir, was a Papist.—No matter; he had better have kept hold of the pummel.—He had so—nay, as it happened, he had better have done nothing at all; for in crossing himself he let go his whip; and in attempting to save his whip betwixt his knee and his saddle's skirt, as it slipped, he lost his stirrup,—in losing which he lost his seat; and in the multitude of all these losses (which, by the bye, shows what little advantage is in crossing) the unfortunate doctor lost his presence of mind. So that without waiting for Obadiah's onset, he left his pony to its destiny, tumbling off it diagonally, something in the style and manner of a pack of wool, and without any other consequence from the fall save that of being left (as it would have been) with the broadest part of him sunk about twelve inches deep in the mire.

Obadiah pull'd off his cap twice to Dr. Slop;—once as he was falling,—and then again when he saw him seated.——Ill-timed complaisance!—had not the fellow better have stopped his horse, and got off and help'd him?—Sir, he did all that his situation would allow:—but the *momentum* of the coach-horse was so great, that Obadiah could not do it all at once; he rode in a circle three times round Dr. Slop, before he could fully accomplish it any how;—and at the last, when he did stop his beast, 'twas done with such an explosion of mud, that Obadiah had better have been a league off. In short, never was a Dr. Slop so beluted, and so transubstantiated, since that affair came into fashion.

CHAP. X.

When Dr. Slop entered the back parlor, where my father and my uncle Toby were discoursing upon the nature of women,—it was hard to determine whether Dr. Slop's figure, or Dr. Slop's presence, occasioned more surprise to them; for as the accident happened so near the house, as not to make it worth while for Obadiah to remount him, ———Obadiah had led him in as he was; *unwiped, unappointed, unannealed*, with all his stains and blotches on him.—He stood like Hamlet's ghost, motionless and speechless, for a full minute and a half at the parlor-door (Obadiah still holding his hand) with all the majesty of mud;—his hinder parts, upon which he had received his fall, totally besmeared;—and in every other part of him, blotched over in such a manner with Obadiah's explosion, that you would have sworn (without mental reservation) that every grain of it had taken effect.

Here was a fair opportunity for my uncle Toby to have triumphed over my father in his turn;—for no mortal, who had beheld Dr. Slop in that pickle, could have dissented from so much, at least, of my uncle Toby's opinion, "That mayhap his sister "might not care to let such a Dr. Slop "come so near her——." But it was the *argumentum ad hominem;* and if my uncle Toby was not very expert at it, you may think, he might not care to use it.——No; the reason was,—'twas not his nature to insult.

Dr. Slop's presence at that time was no less problematical than the mode of it; tho' it is certain, one moment's reflection in my father might have solved it; for he had apprized Dr. Slop but the week before, that my mother was at her full reckoning; and as the doctor had heard nothing since, 'twas natural and very political too, in him, to have taken a ride to Shandy-hall, as he did, merely to see how matters went on.

But my father's mind took unfortunately a wrong turn in the investigation; running, like the hypercritic's, altogether upon the ringing of the bell and the rap upon the door,—measuring their distance, and keeping his mind so intent upon the operation as to have power to think of nothing else, ——commonplace infirmity of the greatest mathematicians! working with might and main at the demonstration, and so wasting all their strength upon it, that they have none left in them to draw the corollary to do good with.

The ringing of the bell, and the rap upon the door, struck likewise strong upon the *sensorium* of my uncle Toby;—but it excited a very different train of thoughts;—the two irreconcilable pulsations instantly brought Stevinus, the great engineer, along with them, into my uncle Toby's mind. What business Stevinus had in this affair, —is the greatest problem of all:——It shall be solved;—but not in the next chapter.

CHAP. XI.

Writing, when properly managed (as you may be sure I think mine is) is but a different name for conversation. As no one who knows what he is about in good company, would venture to talk all;—so no author who understands the just boundaries of decorum and good-breeding, would presume to think all: the truest respect which you can pay to the reader's understanding, is to halve this matter amicably, and leave him something to imagine, in his turn, as well as yourself.

For my own part, I am eternally paying him compliments of this kind, and do all that lies in my power to keep his imagination as busy as my own.

'Tis his turn now!—I have given an ample description of Dr. Slop's sad overthrow, and of his sad appearance in the back parlor;—his imagination must now go on with it for a while.

Let the reader imagine then, that Dr. Slop has told his tale,—and in what words, and with what aggravations, his fancy chooses;—let him suppose, that Obadiah has told his tale also, and with such rueful looks of affected concern, as he thinks best will contrast the two figures as they stand by each other.——Let him imagine, that my father has stepped up stairs to see my mother;—and, to conclude this work of imagination,—let him imagine the doctor washed,—rubbed down and condoled.—felicitated,—got into a pair of Obadiah's pumps, stepping forwards towards the door, upon the very point of entering upon action.

Truce!—truce, good Dr. Slop!—stay thy obstetric hand;—return it safe unto thy bosom to keep it warm;—little dost thou know what obstacles,——little dost thou think what hidden causes, retard its operation;——Hast thou, Dr. Slop,—hast thou been intrusted with the secret articles of the solemn treaty which has brought thee into this place?—Art thou aware that at this instant a daughter of Lucina is put obstetrically over thy head? Alas!—'tis too true. —Besides, great son of Pilumnus! what canst thou do? Thou hast come forth unarm'd; -thou hast left thy *tire-tête*,—thy new-invented *forceps*,—thy *crotchet*,—thy *squirt*, and all thy instruments of salvation and deliverance behind thee:—by Heaven! at this moment they are hanging up in a green baize bag, betwixt thy two pistols, at the bed's head!—Ring;—call;—send Obadiah back upon the coach-horse to bring them with all speed.

——Make great haste, Obadiah, quoth my father, and I'll give thee a crown!—and, quoth my uncle Toby, I'll give him another!

CHAP. XII.

Your sudden and unexpected arrival, quoth my uncle Toby, addressing himself to Dr. Slop (all three of them sitting down to the fire together, as my uncle Toby began to speak)—instantly brought the great Stevinus into my head, who, you must know, is a favorite author with me. Then, added my father, making use of the argument *ad crumenam*,—I will lay twenty guineas to a single crown piece (which will serve to give away to Obadiah when he gets back) that this same Stevinus was some engineer or other,—or has wrote something or other, either directly or indirectly, upon the science of fortification.

He has so,—replied my uncle Toby.—I knew it, said my father, though, for the soul of me, I cannot see what kind of connexion there can be betwixt Dr. Slop's sudden coming, and a discourse upon fortification;—yet I fear'd it.—Talk of what we will, brother,—or let the occasion be ever so foreign or unfit for the subject,—you are sure to bring it in. I would not, brother Toby, continued my father,——I declare I would not have my head so full of curtains and horn-works.—That I dare say you would not, quoth Dr. Slop, interrupting him, and laughing most immoderately at his pun.

Dennis the critic could not detest and abhor a pun, or the insinuation of a pun, more cordially than my father;—he would grow testy upon it at any time:—but to be broke in upon by one, in a serious discourse, was as bad, he would say, as a fillip upon the nose:—he saw no difference.

Sir, quoth my uncle Toby, addressing himself to Dr. Slop,—the curtains my brother Shandy mentions here, have nothing to do with bedsteads;—though, I know Du Cange says, "That bed-curtains, in all "probability, have taken their name from "them;"—nor have the horn-works he speaks of, any thing in the world to do with the horn-works of cuckoldom: but the *curtain*, Sir, is the word we use in fortification, for that part of the wall or rampart which lies between the two bastions, and joins them.—Besiegers seldom offer to carry on their attacks directly against the curtain, for this reason, because they are so well *flanked* ('Tis the case of other curtains, quoth Dr

Slop, laughing.) However, continued my uncle Toby, to make them sure, he generally chose to place ravelins before them, taking care not only to extend them beyond the *fossé*, or ditch.——The common men, who know very little of fortification, confound the ravelin and the half-moon together,—tho' they are very different things;—not in their figure or construction, for we make them exactly alike, in all points; for they always consist of two faces, making a salient angle, with the gorges not straight, but in form of a crescent.——Where then lies the difference? (quoth my father, a little testily.)—In their situations, answered my uncle Toby:—for when a ravelin, brother, stands before the curtain, it is a ravelin; and when a ravelin stands before a bastion, then the ravelin is not a ravelin;—it is a half-moon; a half-moon likewise is a half-moon, and no more, so long as it stands before its bastion;—but was it to change place, and get before the curtain,—'twould be no longer a half-moon; a half-moon, in that case, is not a half-moon;—'tis no more than a ravelin.——I think, quoth my father, that the noble science of defence has its weak sides—as well as others.

—As for the horn-work (heigh! ho! sigh'd my father) which, continued my uncle Toby, my brother was speaking of, they are a very considerable part of an outwork;—they are called by the French engineers *Ouvrage à corne;* and we generally make them to cover such places as we suspect to be weaker than the rest;—'tis formed by two epaulments or demi-bastions,—they are very pretty,—and if you will take a walk, I'll engage to show you one well worth your trouble. I own, continued my uncle Toby, when we crown them,—they are much stronger; but then they are very expensive, and take up a great deal of ground; so that, in my opinion, they are most of use to cover or defend the head of a camp; otherwise the double *tenaille.*—By the mother who bore us!—brother Toby, quoth my father, not able to hold out any longer,—you would provoke a saint;—here have you got us, I know not how, not only souse into the middle of the old subject again,—but so full is your head of these confounded works, that though my wife is this momen: in the pains of labor, and you hear her cry out, yet nothing will serve you but to carry off the man-midwife——*Accoucheur*,—if you please, quoth Dr. Slop. ——With all my heart, replied my father, I don't care what they call you;—but I wish the whole science of fortification, with all its inventors, at the Devil;—it has been the death of thousands,—and it will be mine in the end.—I would not, I would not, brother Toby, have my brains so full of saps, mines, blinds, gabions, palisadoes, ravelins, half-moons, and such trumpery, to be proprietor of Namur, and of all the towns in Flanders with it.

My uncle Toby was a man patient of injuries;—not from want of courage;—I have told you in a former chapter, "that "he was a man of courage:" and will add here, that where just occasions presented, or called it forth,—I know no man under whose arm I would have sooner taken shelter;—nor did this arise from any insensibility or obtuseness of his intellectual parts;—for he felt this insult of my father as feelingly as a man could do;—but he was of a peaceful, placid nature,—no jarring element in it,—all was mixed up so kindly within him; my uncle Toby had scarce a heart to retaliate upon a fly.

—Go,—says he, one day at dinner, to an overgrown one which had buzzed about his nose, and tormented him cruelly all dinner-time,—and which, after infinite attempts, he had caught at last, as it flew by him;—I'll not hurt thee, says my uncle Toby, rising from his chair, and going across the room, with the fly in his hand,——I'll not hurt a hair of thy head:—Go, says he, lifting up the sash, and opening his hand as he spoke, to let it escape;—go, poor devil, get thee gone, why should I hurt thee?——This world surely is wide enough to hold both thee and me.

I was but ten years old when this happened: but whether it was, that the action itself was more in unison to my nerves in that age of pity, which instantly set my whole frame into one vibration of most pleasurable sensation:—or how far the manner and expression of it might go towards it;—or in what degree, or by what secret magic,—a tone of voice and harmony of movement, attuned by mercy, might find a passage to my heart, I know not;—this

THE FLY.

"This world is surely wide enough to hold both thee and me."—p. 52.

I know, that the lesson of universal good-will then taught and imprinted by my uncle Toby, has never since been worn out of mind: and though I would not depreciate what the study of the *literæ humaniores*, at the university, have done for me in that respect, or discredit the other helps of an expensive education bestowed upon me, both at home and abroad since;—yet I often think that I owe one half of my philanthropy to that one accidental impression.

This is to serve for parents and governors, instead of a whole volume upon the subject.

I could not give the reader this stroke in my uncle Toby's picture, by the instrument with which I drew the other parts of it,—that taking in no more than the mere Hobby-Horsical likeness;——this is a part of his moral character. My father, in this patient endurance of wrongs which I mention, was very different, as the reader must long ago have noted; he had a much more acute and quick sensibility of nature, attended with a little soreness of temper. Though this never transported him to any thing which looked like malignancy;—yet in the little rubs and vexations of life, 'twas apt to show itself in a drollish and witty kind of peevishness: —He was, however, frank and generous in his nature;—at all times open to conviction: and in the little ebullitions of this subacid humor towards others, but particularly towards my uncle Toby, whom he truly loved, ——he would feel more pain, ten times told (except in the affair of my aunt Dinah, or where an hypothesis was concerned) than what he ever gave.

The characters of the two brothers, in this view of them, reflected light upon each other, and appeared with great advantage in this affair which arose about Stevinus.

I need not tell the reader, if he keeps a Hobby-Horse,——that a man's Hobby-Horse is as tender a part as he has about him; and that these unprovoked strokes at my uncle Toby's could not be unfelt by him.——No:——as I said above, my uncle Toby did feel them, and very sensibly too.

Pray, Sir, what said he?—How did he behave?—O, Sir!—it was great; for as soon as my father had done insulting his Hobby-Horse,——he turned his head, without the least emotion, from Dr. Slop, to whom he was addressing his discourse, and looking up into my father's face, with a countenance spread over with so much good-nature;—so placid;—so fraternal;—so inexpressibly tender towards him:—it penetrated my father to his heart; he rose up hastily from his chair, and seizing hold of both my uncle Toby's hands as he spoke:—brother Toby, said he,—I beg thy pardon; —forgive, I pray thee, this rash humor which my mother gave me.——My dear, dear brother, answered my uncle Toby, rising up by my father's help, say no more about it;—you are heartily welcome, had it been ten times as much, brother. But 'tis ungenerous, replied my father, to hurt any man;—a brother worse;—but to hurt a brother of such gentle manners,—so unprovoking,—and so unresenting;—'tis base: —by Heaven, 'tis cowardly.—You are heartily welcome, brother, quoth my uncle Toby, —had it been fifty times as much.——Besides, what have I to do, my dear Toby, cried my father, either with your amusements or your pleasures, unless it was in my power (which it is not) to increase their measure?

——Brother Shandy, answered my uncle Toby, looking wistfully in his face,—you are much mistaken in this point;—for you do increase my pleasure very much, in begetting children for the Shandy family at your time of life.——But, by that, Sir, quoth Dr. Slop, Mr. Shandy increases his own. ——Not a jot, quoth my father.

CHAP. XIII.

My brother does it, quoth my uncle Toby, out of *principle*.——In a family way, I suppose, quoth Dr. Slop.——Pshaw! said my father,—'tis not worth talking of.

CHAP. XIV.

At the end of the last chapter, my father and my uncle Toby were left both standing, like Brutus and Cassius, at the close of the scene, making up their accounts.

As my father spoke the three last words. —he sat down;—my uncle Toby exactly followed his example, only, that before he took his chair, he rung the bell, to order Corporal Trim, who was in waiting, to step home for Stevinus:—my uncle Toby's house being no farther off than the opposite side of the way.

Some men would have dropped the subject of Stevinus;—but my uncle Toby had no resentment in his heart; and he went on with the subject, to show my father he had none.

Your sudden appearance, Dr. Slop, quoth my uncle, resuming the discourse, instantly brought Stevinus into my head. (My father, you may be sure, did not offer to lay any more wagers upon Stevinus's head.) ——Because, continued my uncle Toby, the celebrated sailing chariot, which belonged to Prince Maurice, and was of such wonderful contrivance, and velocity, as to carry half a dozen people thirty German miles, in I don't know how few minutes,—was invented by Stevinus, that great mathematician and engineer.

You might have spared your servant the trouble, quoth Dr. Slop (as the fellow is lame) of going for Stevinus's account of it, because, in my return from Leyden through the Hague, I walked as far as Schevling, which is two long miles, on purpose to take a view of it.

That's nothing, replied my uncle Toby, to what the learned Peireskius did, who walked a matter of five hundred miles, reckoning from Paris to Schevling, and from Schevling to Paris back again, in order to see it,—and nothing else.

Some men cannot bear to be outgone.

The more fool Peireskius, replied Dr. Slop. But, mark, 'twas out of no contempt of Peireskius at all;—but that Peireskius's indefatigable labor in trudging so far on foot, out of love for the sciences, reduced the exploit of Dr. Slop, in that affair, to nothing;—the more fool Peireskius, said he again.—Why so?—replied my father, taking his brother's part, not only to make reparation as fast as he could for the insult he had given him, which sat still upon my father's mind;—but partly, that my father began really to interest himself in the discourse —Why so?—said he. Why is Peireskius, or any man else, to be abused for an appetite for that, or any other morsel of sound knowledge: for notwithstanding I know nothing of the chariot in question, continued he, the inventor of it must have had a very mechanical head; and though I cannot guess upon what principles of philosophy he has achieved it;—yet certainly his machine has been constructed upon solid ones, be they what they will, or it could not have answered at the rate my brother mentions.

It answered, replied my uncle Toby, as well, if not better; for, as Peireskius elegantly expresses it, speaking of the velocity of its motion, *Tam citus erat, quam erat ventus:* which, unless I have forgot my Latin, is, *that it was as swift as the wind itself.*

But pray, Dr. Slop, quoth my father, interrupting my uncle (though not without begging pardon for it at the same time) upon what principles was this self-same chariot set a-going?—Upon very pretty principles to be sure, replied Dr. Slop:—and I have often wondered, continued he, evading the question, why none of our gentry, who live upon large plains like this of ours,—(especially they whose wives are not past child-bearing) attempt nothing of this kind; for it would not only be infinitely expeditious upon sudden calls, to which the sex is subject,—if the wind only served,—but would be excellent good husbandry to make use of the winds, which cost nothing, and which eat nothing, rather than horses, which (the Devil take 'em) both cost and eat a great deal.

For that very reason, replied my father, "Because they cost nothing, and because "they eat nothing,"—the scheme is bad;—it is the consumption of our products, as well as the manufactures of them, which gives bread to the hungry, circulates trade, brings in money, and supports the value of our lands:—and though, I own, if I was a prince, I would generously recompense the scientific head which brought forth such contrivances;—yet I would as peremptorily suppress the use of them.

My father here had got into his element, and was going on as prosperously with his dissertation upon trade, as my uncle Toby had before, upon his of fortification; but to the loss of much sound knowledge, the destinies in the morning had decreed that no dissertation of any kind should be spun by my father that day,—for as he opened his mouth to begin the next sentence,

CHAP. XV.

In popped Corporal Trim with Stevinus: —But 'twas too late;—all the discourse had been exhausted without him, and was running into a new channel.

—You may take the book home again, Trim, said my uncle Toby, nodding to him.

But, prithee, Corporal, quoth my father, drolling,—look first into it, and see if thou canst spy aught of a sailing chariot in it.

Corporal Trim, by being in the service, had learned to obey,—and not to remonstrate;—so taking the book to a side-table, and running over the leaves: an' please your Honour, said Trim, I can see no such thing; however, continued the Corporal, drolling a little in his turn, I'll make sure work of it, an' please your Honor. So taking hold of the two covers of the book, one in each hand, and letting the leaves fall down as he bent the covers back, he gave the book a good sound shake.

There is something fallen out, however, said Trim, an' please your Honor;—but it is not a chariot, or any thing like one. Prithee, Corporal, said my father, smiling, what is it then?—I think, answered Trim, stooping to take it up,—'tis more like a sermon,—for it begins with a text of scripture, and the chapter and verse;—and then goes on, not as a chariot, but like a sermon directly.

The company smiled.

I cannot conceive how it is possible, quoth my uncle Toby, for such a thing as a sermon to have got into my Stevinus.

I think 'tis a sermon, replied Trim;—but if it please your Honors, as it is a fair hand, I will read you a page:—for Trim, you must know, loved to hear himself read almost as well as talk.

I have ever a strong propensity, said my father, to look into things which cross my way, by such strange fatalities as these;—and as we have nothing better to do, at least till Obadiah gets back, I shall be obliged to you, brother, if Dr. Slop has no objection to it, to order the Corporal to give us a page or two of it,—if he is as able to do it as he seems willing. An' please your Honor, quoth Trim, I officiated two whole campaigns in Flanders, as clerk to the chaplain of the regiment.——He can read it, quoth my uncle Toby, as well as I can.——Trim, I assure you, was the best scholar in my company; and should have had the next halberd, but for the poor fellow's misfortune. Corporal Trim laid his hand upon his heart, and made an humble bow to his master;—then laying down his hat upon the floor, and taking up the sermon in his left hand, in order to have his right at liberty,—he advanced, nothing doubting, into the middle of the room, where he could best see, and be best seen by his audience.

CHAP. XVI.

—If you will have any objection,—said my father, addressing himself to Dr. Slop. —Not in the least, replied Dr. Slop:—for it does not appear on which side of the question it is wrote—it may be a composition of a Divine of our church, as well as yours; so that we run equal risks.——'Tis wrote upon neither side, quoth Trim, for 'tis only upon Conscience, an' please your Honors.

Trim's reason put his audience into good-humor,—all but Dr. Slop, who, turning his head about towards Trim, looked a little angry.

Begin, Trim,—and read distinctly, quoth my father.—I will, an' please your Honor, replied the Corporal; making a bow, and bespeaking attention with a slight movement of his right hand.

CHAP. XVII.

———But before the Corporal begins, I must first give you a description of his attitude;—otherwise he will naturally stand represented, by your imagination, in an uneasy posture,—stiff,—perpendicular—dividing the weight of his body equally upon both legs;—his eye fixed, as if on duty;—his look determined, clenching the sermon in his left hand, like his firelock.——In a word, you would be apt to paint Trim as if he was standing in his platoon ready for action.—His attitude was as unlike all this as you can conceive.

He stood before them with his body swayed and bent forwards, just so far as to make an angle of 85 degrees and a half upon the plain of the horizon;—which sound orators, to whom I address this, know very well to be the true persuasive angle of incidence;—in any other angle you may talk and preach;—'tis certain;—and it is done every day;—but with what effect,—I leave the world to judge!

The necessity of this precise angle of 85 degrees and a half to a mathematical exactness,—does it not show us, by the way, how the arts and sciences mutually befriend each other?

How the deuce Corporal Trim, who knew not so much as an acute angle from an obtuse one, came to hit it so exactly;—or whether it was chance or nature, or good sense, or imitation, *&c.* shall be commented upon in that part of the Cyclopædia of Arts and Sciences, where the instrumental parts of the eloquence of the senate, the pulpit, and the bar, the coffee-house, the bed-chamber, and fireside, fall under consideration.

He stood,—for I repeat it, to take the picture of him in at one view, with his body swayed, and somewhat bent forwards;—his right leg from under him, sustaining seven-eighths of his whole weight,——the foot of his left leg, the defect of which was no disadvantage to his attitude, advanced a little,—not laterally, nor forwards, but in a line betwixt them;—his knee bent, but that not violently,—but so as to fall within the limits of the line of beauty;—and I add, of the line of science too; for consider, it had one eighth part of his body to bear up;—so that in this case the position of the leg is determined,—because the foot could be no farther advanced, or the knee more bent, than what would allow him mechanically to receive an eighth part of his whole weight under it, and to carry it too.

☞ This I recommend to painters;—need I add, to orators!—I think not: for unless they practise it,———they must fall upon their noses.

So much for Corporal Trim's body and legs——He held the sermon loosely, not carelessly, in his left hand, raised something above his stomach, and detached a little from his breast;—his right arm falling negligently by his side, as nature and the laws of gravity ordered it,——but with the palm of it open and turned towards his audience, ready to aid the sentiment, in case it stood in need.

Corporal Trim's eyes and the muscles of his face were in full harmony with the other parts of him;—he looked frank,—unconstrained,—something assured,—but not bordering upon assurance.

Let not the critic ask how Corporal Trim could come by all this—I've told him it should be explained;—but so he stood before my father, my uncle Toby, and Dr. Slop;—so swayed his body, so contrasted his limbs, and with such an oratorical sweep throughout the whole figure,—a statuary might have modelled from it;—nay, I doubt whether the oldest Fellow of a College,—or the Hebrew Professor himself, could have much mended it.

Trim made a bow, and read as follows:—

THE SERMON.

HEBREWS, xiii. 18.

———*For we* trust *we have a good Conscience.*

"TRUST!—Trust we have a good con-"science!"

[Certainly, Trim, quoth my father, interrupting him, you give that sentence a very improper accent; for you curl up your nose, man, and read it with such a sneering tone, as if the Parson was going to abuse the Apostle.

He is, an' please your Honor, replied Trim. Pugh! said my father, smiling.

Sir, quoth Dr. Slop, Trim is certainly in the right; for the writer (who I perceive is a Protestant) by the snappish manner in which he takes up the apostle, is certainly going to abuse him;—if this treatment of him has not done it already. But from whence, replied my father, have you concluded so soon, Dr. Slop, that the writer is of our church—for aught I can see yet,—he may be of any church.——Because, answered Dr. Slop, if he was of ours, he durst no more take such a license, than a bear by his beard. If, in our communion, Sir, a man was to insult an apostle,—a saint,—or

THE SERMON.

"Trim made a bow, and read as follows."—p. 56.

even the paring of a saint's nail,—he would have his eyes scratched out.—What, by the saint? quoth my uncle Toby. No, replied Dr. Slop, he would have an old house over his head. Pray is the Inquisition an ancient building, answered my uncle Toby, or is it a modern one?—I know nothing of architecture, replied Dr. Slop.—An' please your Honor, quoth Trim, the Inquisition is the vilest—Prithee spare thy description, Trim, I hate the very name of it, said my father. —No matter for that, answered Dr. Slop,—it has its uses: for though I'm no great advocate for it, yet in such a case as this, he would soon be taught better manners; and I can tell him, if he went on at that rate, would be flung into the Inquisition for his pains. God help him then, quoth my uncle Toby. Amen, added Trim; for Heaven above knows, I have a poor brother who has been fourteen years a captive in it. I never heard one word of it before, said my uncle Toby, hastily:—how came he there, Trim? —O, Sir, the story will make your heart bleed,—as it has made mine a thousand times;—but it is too long to be told now;—your Honor shall hear it from first to last some day when I am working beside you in our fortifications;——but the short of the story is this—that my brother Tom went over a servant to Lisbon,—and then married a Jew's widow who kept a small shop, and sold sausages, which, somehow or other, was the cause of his being taken in the middle of the night out of his bed, where he was lying with his wife and two small children, and carried directly to the Inquisition, where, God help him, continued Trim, fetching a sigh from the bottom of his heart,—the poor honest lad lies confined at this hour. He was as honest a soul, added Trim, (pulling out his handkerchief) as ever blood warmed.—

—The tears trickled down Trim's cheeks faster than he could well wipe them away. —A dead silence in the room ensued for some minutes.—Certain proof of pity!

Come, Trim, quoth my father, after he saw the poor fellow's grief had got a little vent,—read on,—and put this melancholy story out of thy head;—I grieve that I interrupted thee; but prithee begin the sermon again;—for if the first sentence in it is matter of abuse, as thou sayest, I have a great desire to know what kind of provocation the apostle has given.

Corporal Trim wiped his face, and returned his handkerchief into his pocket, and making a bow as he did it,—he began again.

THE SERMON.

Hebrews, xiii. 18.

——*For we* trust *we have a good Conscience.*

"Trust!—Trust we have a good con-"science! Surely, if there is any thing in "this life which a man may depend upon, "and to the knowledge of which he is ca-"pable of arriving upon the most indisputa-"ble evidence, it must be this very thing,—"whether he has a good conscience or no."

[I am positive I am right, quoth Dr. Slop.]

"If a man thinks at all, he cannot well "be a stranger to the true state of this "account:—he must be privy to his own "thoughts and desires;—he must remem-"ber his past pursuits, and know certainly "the true springs and motives, which, in "general, have governed the actions of his "life."

[I defy him, without an assistant, quoth Dr. Slop.]

"In other matters we may be deceived "by false appearances; and, as the wise "man complains, *hardly do we guess aright* "*at the things that are upon the earth*, "*and with labor do we find the things that* "*are before us.* But here the mind has all "the evidence and facts within herself;—"is conscious of the web she has wove;—"knows its texture and fineness, and the "exact share which every passion has had "in working upon the several designs "which virtue or vice has planned before "her."

[The language is good; and I declare Trim reads very well, quoth my father.]

"Now,—as conscience is nothing else "but the knowledge which the mind has "within herself of this; and the judgment, "either of approbation or censure, which it "unavoidably makes upon the successive "actions of our lives; 'tis plain, you will "say, from the very terms of the proposi-"tion,—whenever this inward testimony "goes against a man, and he stands self "accused, that he must necessarily be "guilty man.—And on the contrary, when "the report is favorable on his side, and his "heart condemns him not,—that it is not a "matter of *trust,* as the apostle intimates, "but a matter of *certainty* and fact, that "the conscience is good, and that the man "must be good also."

[Then the apostle is altogether in the wrong, I suppose, quoth Dr. Slop; and the Protestant divine is in the right. Sir, have patience, replied my father, for I think it will presently appear that St. Paul and the Protestant divine are both of an opinion.—As nearly so, quoth Dr. Slop, as east is to west;—But this, continued he, lifting both hands, comes from the liberty of the press.

It is no more, at the worst, replied my uncle Toby, than the liberty of the pulpit; for it does not appear that the sermon is printed, or ever likely to be.

Go on, Trim, quoth my father.]

"At first sight this may seem to be a true "state of the case: and I make no doubt "but the knowledge of right and wrong is "so truly impressed upon the mind of man, "—that did no such thing ever happen, as "that the conscience of a man, by long "habits of sin, might (as the scripture as-"sures it may) insensibly become hard;—"and, like some tender parts of his body, "by much stress and continued hard usage, "lose by degrees that nice sense and per-"ception with which God and nature en-"dowed it:—did this never happen;—or "was it certain that self-love could never "hang the least bias upon the judgment:—"or that the little interests below could rise "up and perplex the faculties of our upper "regions, and encompass them about with "clouds and thick darkness:—Could no "such thing as favor and affection enter this "sacred court:—Did Wit disdain to take a "bribe in it;—or was ashamed to show its "face as an advocate for an unwarrantable "enjoyment: or lastly, were we assured "that Interest stood always unconcerned "whilst the cause was hearing—and that Passion never got into the judgment-seat, "and pronounced sentence in the stead of "Reason, which is supposed always to pre-"side and determine upon the case:—was "this truly so, as the objection must sup-"pose;—no doubt then the religious and "moral state of a man would be exactly "what he himself esteemed it:—and the "guilt or innocence of every man's life "could be known, in general, by no better "measure, than the degrees of his own "approbation and censure."

"I own, in one case, whenever a man's "conscience does accuse him (as it seldom "errs on that side) that he is guilty; and "unless in melancholy and hypochondriac "cases, we may safely pronounce upon it, "that there is always sufficient grounds for "the accusation.

"But the converse of the proposition will "not hold true;—namely, that whenever "there is guilt, the conscience must accuse; "and if it does not, that a man is therefore "innocent.——This is not fact.——So that "the common consolation which some good "christian or other is hourly administering "to himself,—that he thanks God his mind "does not misgive him; and that, conse-"quently, he has a good conscience, because "he hath a quiet one,—is fallacious;—and "as current as the inference is, and as "infallible as the rule appears at first sight, "yet when you look nearer to it, and try "the truth of this rule upon plain facts "—you see it liable to so much error from "a false application; the principle upon "which it goes so often perverted;—the "whole force of it lost, and sometimes so "vilely cast away, that it is painful to pro-"duce the common examples of human life, "which confirm the account.

"A man shall be vicious and utterly de-"bauched in his principles;—exceptionable "in his conduct to the world; shall live "shameless, in the open commission of a "sin which no reason or pretence can jus-"tify,—a sin by which, contrary to all the "workings of humanity, he shall ruin for "ever the deluded partner of his guilt;—"rob her of her best dowry; and not only "cover her own head with dishonor;—but "involve a whole virtuous family in shame "and dishonor for her sake. Surely, you "will think Conscience must lead such a "man a troublesome life; he can have no "rest night or day from its reproaches.

"Alas! Conscience had something else "to do all this time, than break in upon "him: as Elijah reproached the god Baal, "——this domestic god *was either talking,* "*or pursuing, or was on a journey, or* "*peradventure he slept, and could not be* "*awoke.*

"Perhaps he was gone out in company "with Honor, to fight a duel; to pay off "some debt at play;—or dirty annuity, the "bargain of his lust. Perhaps Conscience "all this time was engaged at home, talking "aloud against petty larceny, and exe- "cuting vengeance upon some such puny "crimes, as his fortune and rank of life se- "cured him against all temptation of com- "mitting; so that he lives as merrily"—— [If he was of our church, though, quoth Dr. Slop, he could not.]—"sleeps as soundly in "his bed;—and at last meets death as un- "concernedly!—perhaps much more so than "a much better man."

[All this is impossible with us, quoth Dr. Slop, turning to my father;—the case could not happen in our church.—It happens in ours, however, replied my father, but too often.——I own, quoth Dr. Slop, (struck a little with my father's frank acknowledgment)—that a man in the Romish church may live as badly;—but then he cannot easily die so.——'Tis little matter, replied my father, with an air of indifference, how a rascal dies.—I mean, answered Dr. Slop, he would be denied the benefits of the last sacraments.—Pray, how many have you in all, said my uncle Toby,—for I always forget?——Seven, answered Dr. Slop.—— Humph!—said my uncle Toby;—though not accented as a note of acquiescence, but as an interjection of that particular species of surprise, when a man, in looking into a drawer, finds more of a thing than he expected,——Humph! replied my uncle Toby. Dr. Slop, who had an ear, understood my uncle Toby as well as if he had wrote a whole volume against the seven sacraments. ——Humph! replied Dr. Slop (stating my uncle Toby's argument over again to him) —Why, Sir, are there not seven cardinal virtues?—seven mortal sins?—seven golden candlesticks?—seven heavens?——'Tis more than I know, replied my uncle Toby. ——Are there not seven wonders of the world?—seven days of the creation?—seven planets?—seven plagues?——That there are, quoth my father, with a most affected gravity. But prithee, continued he, go on with the rest of thy characters, Trim.]

"Another is sordid, unmerciful," (here Trim waved his right hand) "a strait- "hearted selfish wretch, incapable either of "private friendship or public spirit. Take "notice how he passes by the widow and "orphan in their distress, and sees all the "miseries incident to human life without "a sigh or a prayer." [An' please your Honors, cried Trim, I think this a viler man than the other.]

"Shall not conscience rise up and sting "him on such occasions?—No; thank God, "there is no occasion, *I pay every man his* "*own;—I have no fornication to answer* "*to my conscience;—no faithless vows or* "*promises to make up;—I have debauched* "*no man's wife or child. Thank God, I* "*am not as other men, adulterers, unjust,* "*or even as this libertine, who stands before* "*me.*

"A third is crafty and designing in his "nature. View his whole life;—'tis nothing "but a cunning contexture of dark arts and "unequitable subterfuges, basely to defeat "the true intent of all laws,—plain dealing, "and the safe enjoyment of our several prop- "erties.——You will see such a one work- "ing out a frame of little designs upon the "ignorance and perplexities of the poor and "needy man;—shall raise a fortune upon "the inexperience of a youth, or the unsus- "pecting temper of his friend, who would "have trusted him with his life.

"When old age comes on, and repent- "ance calls him to look back upon this black "account, and state it over again with his "conscience,—Conscience looks into the "STATUTES at LARGE;—finds no express "law broken by what he has done;—per- "ceives no penalty or forfeiture of goods "and chattels incurred;—sees no scourge "waving over his head, or prison opening "its gates upon him:—What is there to "affright his conscience?—Conscience has "got safely entrenched behind the Letter "of the Law; sits there invulnerable, for- "tified with **Cases** and **Reports**, so "strongly on all sides,—that it is not preach- "ing can dispossess it of its hold."

[Here Corporal Trim and my uncle Toby exchanged looks with each other.—Ay, ay, Trim! quoth my uncle Toby, shaking his head,——these are but sorry fortifications, Trim.——O! very poor work, answered Trim, to what your Honor and I make of it.——The character of this last man, said Dr. Slop, interrupting Trim, is more detestable than all the rest; and seems to have been taken from some pettifogging Lawyer amongst you. Amongst us, a man's conscience could not possibly continue so long *blinded;* three times in a year, at least, he must go to confession.——Will that restore it to sight? quoth my uncle Toby. ——Go on, Trim, quoth my father, or Obadiah will have got back before thou hast got to the end of thy sermon.——'Tis a very short one, replied Trim.——I wish it was longer, quoth my uncle Toby, for I like it hugely.—Trim went on.]

"A fourth man shall want even this "refuge;—shall break through all the cere- "mony of slow chicane;—scorns the doubt- "ful workings of secret plots and cautious "trains to bring about his purpose:—see "the barefaced villain, how he cheats, lies, "perjures, robs, murders!—Horrid!—But "indeed much better was not to be expect- "ed in the present case,—the poor man "was in the dark!—his priest had got the "keeping of his conscience;——and all he "would let him know of it, was, That he "must believe in the Pope,—go to mass,— "cross himself,—tell his beads,—be a good "Catholic; and that this, in all conscience, "was enough to carry him to heaven. "What!—if he perjures?—Why,—he had "a mental reservation in it.—But if he is "so wicked and abandoned a wretch as you "represent him;—if he robs,—if he stabs, "will not conscience, on every such act, "receive a wound itself?—Ay,—but the "man has carried it to confession;—the "wound digests there, and will do well "enough, and in a short time be quite healed "up by absolution. O Popery! what hast "thou to answer for!—when, not content "with the too many natural and fatal ways, "thro' which the heart of man is every day "thus treacherous to itself above all things, "—thou hast wilfully set open the wide "gate of deceit before the face of this un- "wary traveller,—too apt, God knows, to "go astray of himself, and confidently speak "peace to himself, when there is no peace.

"Of this the common instances which I "have drawn out of life, are too notorious to require much evidence. If any man doubts the reality of them, or thinks it "impossible for a man to be such a bubble "to himself,—I must refer him a moment to "his own reflections, and will then venture "to trust my appeal with his own heart.

"Let him consider in how different a de- "gree of detestation, numbers of wicked "actions stand *there,* though equally bad "and vicious in their own natures;—he "will soon find, that such of them as strong "inclination and custom have prompted him "to commit, are generally dressed out and "painted with all the false beauties which "a soft and a flattering hand can give "them;—and that the others, to which he "feels no propensity, appear at once naked "and deformed, surrounded with all the "true circumstances of folly and dishonor.

"When David surprised Saul sleeping "in the cave, and cut off the skirt of his "robe,—we read that his heart smote him "for what he had done:—but in the matter "of Uriah, where a faithful and gallant "servant, whom he ought to have loved and "honored, fell to make way for his lust,—— "where conscience had so much greater "reason to take the alarm, his heart smote "him not. A whole year had almost passed "from the first commission of that crime, "to the time Nathan was sent to reprove "him; and we read not once of the least "sorrow or compunction of heart which he "testified, during all that time, for what he "had done.

"Thus Conscience, this once able moni- "tor,—placed on high as a judge within us, "and intended by our Maker as a just and "equitable one too,—by an unhappy train "of causes and impediments, takes often "such imperfect cognizance of what passes, "—does its office so negligently,—some- "times so corruptly,—that it is not to be "trusted alone; and therefore we find there "is a necessity, an absolute necessity, of "joining another principle with it, to aid, "if not govern, its determinations.

"So that, if you would form a just judg- "ment of what is of infinite importance to "you not to be misled in,—namely, in what "degree of real merit you stand, either as "an honest man, an useful citizen, a faith- "ful subject to your king, or a good servant "to your God, call in religion and morality, "Look: what is written in the law of God? "—How readest thou?—Consult calm rea "son and the unchangeable obligations of "justice and truth; what say they?

"Let CONSCIENCE determine the matter "upon these reports;—and then if thy heart "condemns thee not, which is the case the "apostle supposes,—the rule will be infal- "lible;—[Here Dr. Slop fell asleep]— "*thou wilt have confidence towards God;* "—that is, have just grounds to believe the "judgment thou hast past upon thyself, is "the judgment of God; and nothing else "but an anticipation of that righteous sen- "tence which will be pronounced upon thee "hereafter, by that Being to whom thou art "finally to give an account of thy actions.

"*Blessed is the man*, indeed, then, as the "author of the book of Ecclesiasticus ex- "presses it, *who is not pricked with the* "*multitude of his sins: blessed is the man* "*whose heart hath not condemned him;* '*whether he be rich, or whether he be poor,* "*if he have a good heart* (a heart thus "guided and informed) *he shall at all times* "*rejoice in a cheerful countenance; his* "*mind shall tell him more than seven* "*watchmen that sit above upon a tower on* "*high.*—[A tower has no strength, quoth my uncle Toby, unless 'tis flanked.]—"In "the darkest doubts it shall conduct him "safer than a thousand casuists, and give "the state he lives in a better security for "his behavior than all the causes and "restrictions put together, which law-ma- "kers are forced to multiply:—*forced*, I "say, as things stand; human laws not "being a matter of original choice, but of 'pure necessity, brought in to fence against "the mischievous effects of those con- "sciences which are no law unto them- selves; well intending, by the many pro- 'visions made,—that in all such corrupt "and misguided cases, where principles and "the checks of conscience will not make "us upright,—to supply their force, and, "by the terrors of gaols and halters, oblige "us to it."

[I see plainly, said my father, that this sermon has been composed to be preached at the Temple,—or at some Assize.—I like the reasoning,—and am sorry that Dr. Slop has fallen asleep before the time of his conviction;—for it is now clear, that the Parson, as I thought at first, never insulted St. Paul in the least;—nor has there been, brother, the least difference between them. ——A great matter, if they had differed, replied my uncle Toby!—the best friends in the world may differ sometimes.—— True,—brother Toby, quoth my father, shaking hands with him,—we'll fill our pipes, brother, and then Trim shall go on.

Well,—what dost thou think of it? said my father, speaking to Corporal Trim, as he reached his tobacco-box.

I think, answered the Corporal, that the seven watchmen upon the tower,—who, I suppose, are all sentinels there,—are more, an' please your Honor, than were necessary;—and, to go on at that rate, would harass a regiment all to pieces, which a commanding-officer, who loves his men, will never do, if he can help it; because two sentinels, added the Corporal, are as good as twenty.—I have been a commanding-officer myself in the *Corps de Garde*, a hundred times, continued Trim, rising an inch higher in his figure, as he spoke;—and all the time I had the honor to serve his Majesty King William, in relieving the most considerable posts, I never left more than two in my life.——Very right, Trim, quoth my uncle Toby;—but you do not consider, Trim, that the towers, in Solomon's days, were not such things as our bastions, flanked and defended by other works.— This, Trim, was an invention since Solomon's death; nor had they horn-works, or ravelins before the curtain, in his time;—or such a fossé as we make with a cuvette in the middle of it, and with covered ways and counterscarps pallisadoed along it, to guard against a *coup de main*:—so that the seven men upon the tower were a party, I dare say, from the *Corps de Garde*, set there, not only to look out, but to defend it. ——They could be no more, an' please your Honor, than a corporal's guard.—— My father smiled inwardly, but not outwardly;—the subject being rather too serious, considering what had happened, to make a jest of:—so putting his pipe into his mouth, which he had just lighted,—he contented himself with ordering Trim to read on. He read on as follows:—]

"To have the fear of God before our "eyes, and, in our mutual dealings with "each other, to govern our actions by the "eternal measures of right and wrong:-

"the first of these will comprehend the du-"ties of religion;—the second, those of "morality, which are so inseparably con-"nected together, that you cannot divide "these two *tables*, even in imagination "(though the attempt is often made in "practice) without breaking and mutually "destroying them both.

"I said the attempt is often made; and so "it is;—there being nothing more common "than to see a man who has no sense at "all of religion, and indeed has so much "honesty as to pretend to none, who would "take it as the bitterest affront, should you "but hint at a suspicion of his moral char-"acter,—or imagine he was not conscien-"tiously just and scrupulous to the utter-"most mite.

"When there is some appearance that it "is so,—though one is unwilling even to "suspect the appearance of so amiable a "virtue as moral honesty, yet were we to "look into the grounds of it, in the present "case, I am persuaded we should find little "reason to envy such a one the honor of "his motive.

"Let him declaim as pompously as he "chooses upon the subject, it will be found "to rest upon no better foundation than "either his interest, his pride, his ease, or "some such little and changeable passion "as will give us but small dependence upon "his actions in matters of great distress.

"I will illustrate this by an example.

"I know the banker I deal with, or the "physician I usually call in,"—[There is no need, cried Dr. Slop, *waking*, to call in any physician in this case]—"to be neither "of them men of much religion: I hear "them make a jest of it every day, and "treat all its sanctions with so much scorn, "as to put the matter past doubt. Well; "—notwithstanding this, I put my fortune "into the hands of the one:—and what is "dearer still to me, I trust my life to the "honest skill of the other.

"Now, let me examine what is my rea-"son for this great confidence. Why, in "the first place, I believe there is no proba-"bility that either of them will employ the "power I put into their hands to my disad-"vantage;—I consider that honesty serves "the purposes of this life.—I know their "success in the world depends upon the "fairness of their characters.—In a word, "I'm persuaded that they cannot hurt me "without hurting themselves more.

"But put it otherwise; namely, that in-"terest lay, for once, on the other side; "that a case should happen, wherein the "one, without stain to his reputation, could "secrete my fortune, and leave me naked "in the world;—or that the other could "send me out of it, and enjoy an estate by "my death, without dishonor to himself or "his art;—in this case, what hold have I "of either of them?—Religion, the strong-"est of all motives, is out of the question, "—interest, the next most powerful motive "in the world, is strongly against me:—— "What have I left to cast into the opposite "scale, to balance this temptation?—— "Alas! I have nothing—nothing but what "is lighter than a bubble.——I must lie at "the mercy of Honor, or some such capri-"cious principle,—strait security for two of "the most valuable blessings!—my property "and my life.

"As therefore we can have no depend-"ence upon morality without religion;— "so, on the other hand,—there is nothing "better to be expected from religion with-"out morality; nevertheless, 'tis no prodigy "to see a man whose real moral character "stands very low, who yet entertains the "highest notion of himself in the light of a "religious man.

"He shall not only be covetous, revenge-"ful, implacable,—but even wanting in "points of common honesty; yet inasmuch "as he talks aloud against the infidelity of "the age,—is zealous for some points of "religion,—goes twice a day to church,— "attends the sacraments,—and amuses him-"self with a few instrumental parts of reli-"gion,—shall cheat his conscience into a "judgment, that, for this, he is a religious "man, and has discharged truly his duty to "God: and you will find that such a man, "through force of this delusion, generally "looks down with spiritual pride upon every "other man who has less affectation of "piety,—though, perhaps, ten times more "real honesty, than himself.

"*This likewise is a sore evil under the "sun;* and, I believe, there is no one mis-"taken principle, which, for its time, has "wrought more serious mischiefs.——For "a general proof of this,—examine the "history of the Romish church;"—[Well, what can you make of that? cried Dr. Slop] "see what scenes of cruelty, murder, rap-"ine, bloodshed,"—[They may thank their own obstinacy, cried Dr. Slop]—"have all "been sanctified by a religion not strictly "governed by morality!

"In how many kingdoms of the world"—[Here Trim kept waving his right hand from the sermon to the extent of his arm, returning it backwards and forwards to the conclusion of the paragraph.]

"In how many kingdoms of the world "has the crusading sword of this misguided "saint-errant spared neither age, or merit, "or sex, or condition?—and, as he fought "under the banners of a religion which set "him loose from justice and humanity, he "showed none; mercilessly trampled upon "both,—heard neither the cries of the un-"fortunate, nor pitied their distresses!"

[I have been in many a battle, an' please your Honor, quoth Trim, sighing, but never in so melancholy a one as this:—I would not have drawn a trigger in it against these poor souls,—to have been made a general officer.——Why? what do you understand of the affair? said Dr. Slop, looking towards Trim, with something more of contempt than the Corporal's honest heart deserved. ——What do you know, friend, about this battle you talk of?——I know, replied Trim, that I never refused quarter in my life to any man who cried out for it:—but to a woman or a child, continued Trim, before I would level my musket at them, I would lose my life a thousand times.—— Here's a crown for thee, Trim, to drink with Obadiah to-night, quoth my uncle Toby; and I'll give Obadiah another too. ——God bless your Honor, replied Trim,—I had rather these poor women and children had it.——Thou art an honest fellow, quoth my uncle Toby.——My father nodded his head, as much as to say,—And so he is.——

But prithee, Trim, said my father, make an end,—for I see thou hast but a leaf or two left.

Corporal Trim read on.]

"If the testimony of past centuries in "this matter is not sufficient,—consider at "this instant, how the votaries of that re-"ligion are every day thinking to do ser-"vice and honor to God, by actions which "are a dishonor and scandal to themselves!

"To be convinced of this, go with me for "a moment into the prisons of the Inquisi-"tion."—[God help my poor brother Tom.] —"Behold Religion, with mercy and Jus-"tice chained down under her feet,—there "sitting ghastly upon a black tribunal, "propped up with racks and instruments of "torment.—Hark!—hark!—what a piteous "groan!"—[Here Trim's face turned as pale as ashes.]——"See the melancholy "wretch who uttered it"—[Here the tears began to trickle down]——"just brought "forth to undergo the anguish of a mock "trial, and endure the utmost pains that a "studied system of cruelty has been able "to invent."——[D—n them all, quoth Trim, his color returning into his face as red as blood.]—"Behold this helpless victim "delivered up to his tormentors,—his body "so wasted with sorrow and confinement!" —[Oh! 'tis my brother, cried poor Trim. in a most passionate exclamation, dropping the sermon upon the ground, and clapping his hands together—I fear 'tis poor Tom. ——My father's and my uncle Toby's heart yearned with sympathy for the poor fellow's distress; even Slop himself acknowledged pity for him.——Why, Trim, said my father, this is not a history,—'tis a sermon thou art reading; prithee begin the sentence again.]——"Behold this helpless vic-"tim delivered up to his tormentors,—his "body so wasted with sorrow and confine-"ment, you will see every nerve and mus-"cle as it suffers.

"Observe the last movement of that "horrid engine!"—[I would rather face a cannon, quoth Trim, stamping.]—"See "what convulsions it has thrown him into! "—Consider the nature of the posture in "which he now lies stretched!—what ex-"quisite tortures he endures by it!"—[I hope 'tis not in Portugal.]—"'Tis all nature "can bear! Good God! see how he keeps "his weary soul hanging upon his trembling "lips!"—[I would not read another line of it, quoth Trim, for all this world!—I fear, an' please your Honors, all this is in Portugal, where my poor brother Tom is.——I tell thee, Trim, again, quoth my father, 'tis not an historical account,—'tis a description. —'Tis only a description, honest man quoth

Slop; there's not a word of truth in it.——That's another story, replied my father. ——However, as Trim reads it with so much concern,—'tis cruelty to force him to go on with it.—Give me hold of the sermon, Trim,—I'll finish it for thee, and thou may'st go.——I must stay and hear it too, replied Trim, if your Honor will allow me; —though I would not read it myself for a Colonel's pay.———Poor Trim, quoth my uncle Toby.——My father went on.]

"——Consider the nature of the posture "in which he now lies stretched!—what "exquisite torture he endures by it!—'Tis "all nature can bear! Good God! See how "it keeps his weary soul hanging upon his "trembling lips,—willing to take its leave, "—but not suffered to depart;—Behold the "unhappy wretch led back to his cell!" ——[Then, thank God, however, quoth Trim, they have not killed him.] "See him "dragged out of it again to meet the flames, "and the insults in his last agonies, which "this principle,—this principle, that there "can be religion without mercy, has pre-"pared for him!"——[Then, thank God, he is dead, quoth Trim,—he is out of his pain, and they have done their worst at him. —O Sirs!——Hold your peace, Trim, said my father, going on with the sermon, lest Trim should incense Dr. Slop,—we shall never have done at this rate.]

"The surest way to try the merit of any "disputed notion is, to trace down the con-"sequences such a notion has produced, and "compare them with the spirit of christian-"ity;—'tis the short and decisive rule which "our Savior hath left us for those and such "like cases, and it is worth a thousand ar-"guments—*By their fruits ye shall know* "*them.*

"I will add no farther to the length of "this sermon, than by two or three short "and independent rules deducible from it.

"*First,* Whenever a man talks loudly "against religion, always suspect that it is "not his reason, but his passions, which "have got the better of his CREED. A bad "life and a good belief are disagreeable and "troublesome neighbors: and where they "separate, depend upon it, 'tis for no other "cause but quietness' sake.

"*Secondly,* When a man, thus repre-"sented, tells you in any particular in-"stance,—that such a thing goes against "his conscience—always believe he means "exactly the same thing as when he tells "you such a thing goes against his stomach; "—a present want of appetite being gene-"rally the true cause of both.

"In a word,—trust that man in nothing, "who has not a CONSCIENCE in every thing.

"And in your own case, remember this "plain distinction, a mistake in which has "ruined thousands,—that your conscience "is not a law:—no, God and reason made "the law, and have placed conscience "within you to determine;—not, like an "Asiatic Cadi, according to the ebbs and "flows of his own passions,—but like a "British judge in this land of liberty and "good sense, who makes no new law, but "faithfully declares that law which he "knows already written."

FINIS.

Thou hast read the sermon extremely well, Trim, quoth my father.——If he had spared his comments, replied Dr. Slop,—he would have read it much better.——I should have read it ten times better, Sir, answered Trim, but that my heart was so full. ——That was the very reason, Trim, replied my father, which has made thee read the sermon as well as thou hast done; and if the clergy of our church, continued my father, addressing himself to Dr. Slop, would take part in what they deliver as deeply as this poor fellow has done,—as their compositions are fine;—[I deny it, quoth Dr. Slop.]—I maintain it,—that the eloquence of our pulpits, with such subjects to inflame it, would be a model for the whole world:—But alas! continued my father, and I own it, Sir, with sorrow, that, like French politicians in this respect, what they gain in the cabinet they lose in the field.——'Twere a pity, quoth my uncle, that this should be lost.——I like the sermon well, replied my father,—'tis dramatic; —and there is something in that way of writing, when skilfully managed, which catches the attention.——We preach much in that way with us, said Dr. Slop.—I know that very well, said my father,—but in a tone and manner which disgusted Dr. Slop, full as much as his assent, simply, could have pleased him.——But in this, added Dr. Slop, a little piqued,—our sermons have greatly the advantage, that we never introduce any character into them below a patriarch or a patriarch's wife, or a martyr, or a saint.—There are some very bad characters in this, however, said my father; and I do not think the sermon a jot the worse for 'em.——But pray, quoth my uncle Toby,—whose can this be?—How could it get into my Stevinus?——A man must be as great a conjurer as Stevinus, said my father, to resolve the second question. The first, I think, is not so difficult;—for unless my judgment greatly deceives me,—I know the author; for it was wrote, certainly, by the parson of the parish.

The similitude of the style and manner of it, with those my father constantly had heard preached in his parish-church, was the ground of his conjecture, proving it as strongly as an argument *à priori* could prove such a thing to a philosophic mind, That it was Yorick's and no one's else.—It was proved to be so, *à posteriori*, the day after, when Yorick sent a servant to my uncle Toby's house to inquire after it.

It seems that Yorick, who was inquisitive after all kinds of knowledge, had borrowed Stevinus of my uncle Toby, and had carelessly popped his sermon, as soon as he had made it, into the middle of Stevinus; and by an act of forgetfulness, to which he was ever subject, he had sent Stevinus home, and his sermon to keep him company.

Ill-fated sermon! Thou wast lost, after this recovery of thee, a second time, dropped thro' an unsuspected fissure in thy master's pocket, down into a treacherous and tattered lining,—trod deep into the dirt, by the left hind-foot of his Rosinante inhumanly stepping upon thee as thou falledst;—buried ten days in the mire,—raised up out of it by a beggar,—sold for a half-penny to a parish-clerk, transferred to his parson,—lost for ever to thy own, the remainder of his days,—nor restored to his restless manes till this very moment that I tell the world the story.

Can the reader believe that this sermon of Yorick's was preached at an assize, in the cathedral of York, before a thousand witnesses, ready to give oath of it, by a certain prebendary of that church, and actually printed by him when he had done?—and within so short a space as two years and three months after Yorick's death?—Yorick, indeed, was never better served in his life;—but it was a little hard to maltreat him after, and plunder him after he was laid in his grave.

However, as the gentleman who did it was in perfect charity with Yorick,—and, in conscious justice, printed but a few copies to give away;—and that I am told, he could moreover have made as good a one himself, had he thought fit,—I declare I would not have published this anecdote to the world:—nor do I publish it with an intent to hurt his character and advancement in the church I leave that to others;—but I find myself impelled by two reasons, which I cannot withstand.

The first is, That in doing justice I may give rest to Yorick's ghost:—which,—as the country people, and some others, believe,—*still walks.*

The second reason is, That, by laying open this story to the world, I gain an opportunity of informing it,—That in case the character of Parson Yorick, and the sample of his sermons, is liked,—there are now in the possession of the Shandy family, as many as will make a handsome volume, at the world's service:—and much good may they do it.

CHAP. XVIII.

Obadiah gained the two crowns without dispute; for he came in jingling with all the instruments in the green baize bag we spoke of, slung across his body, just as Corporal Trim went out of the room.

It is now proper, I think, quoth Dr. Slop (clearing up his looks) as we are in a condition to be of some service to Mrs. Shandy, to send up stairs to know how she goes on.

I have ordered, answered my father, the old midwife to come down to us upon the least difficulty;—for you must know, Dr. Slop, continued my father, with a perplexed kind of a smile upon his countenance, that by express treaty, solemnly ratified between me and my wife, you are no more than an auxiliary in this affair,—and not so much as that,—unless the lean old mother of a midwife above stairs cannot do without you. —Women have their particular fancies; and in points of this nature, continued my father, where they bear the whole burden, and suffer so much acute pain for the advantage of our families and the good of the species,—they claim a right of deciding, *en Souveraines*, in whose hands, and in what fashion, they choose to undergo it.

They are in the right of it,—quoth my uncle Toby.——But, Sir, replied Dr. Slop, not taking notice of my uncle Toby's opinion, but turning to my father,——they had better govern in other points;—and a father of a family, who wishes its perpetuity, in my opinion, had better exchange this prerogative with them, and give up some other rights in lieu of it.——I know not, quoth my father, answering a little too testily, to be quite dispassionate in what he said;—I know not, quoth he, what we have left to give up in lieu of who shall bring our children into the world, unless that,—of who shall beget them.——One would almost give up any thing, replied Dr. Slop.——I beg your pardon,—answered my uncle Toby. ——Sir, replied Dr. Slop, it would astonish you to know what improvements we have made of late years in all branches of obstetrical knowledge, but particularly in that one single point of the safe and expeditious extraction of the *fœtus*,—which has received such lights, that, for my part (holding up his hands) I declare, I wonder how the world has——I wish, quoth my uncle Toby, you had seen what prodigious armies we had in Flanders.

CHAP. XIX.

I HAVE dropped the curtain over this scene for a minute,—to remind you of one thing,—and to inform you of another.

What I have to inform you, comes, I own, a little out of its due course;—for it should have been told a hundred and fifty pages ago, but that I foresaw then 'twould come in pat hereafter, and be of more advantage here than elsewhere.—Writers had need look before them, to keep up the spirit and connexion of what they have in hand.

When these two things are done,—the curtain shall be drawn up again, and my uncle Toby, my father and Dr. Slop, shall go on with their discourse, without any more interruption.

First, then, the matter which I have to remind you of, is this:—That from the specimens of singularity in my father's notions in the point of christian names, and that other previous point thereto,—you was led, I think, into an opinion,—(and I am sure I said as much) that my father was a gentleman altogether as odd and whimsical in fifty other opinions. In truth, there was not a stage in the life of man, from the very first act of his begetting,—down to the lean and slippered pantaloon in his second childishness, but he had some favorite notion to himself springing out of it, as sceptical, and as far out of the highway of thinking, as these two which have been explained.

—Mr. Shandy, my father, Sir, would see nothing in the light in which others placed it;—he placed things in his own light;—he would weigh nothing in common scales:—no, he was too refined a researcher to lie open to so gross an imposition.—To come at the exact weight of things in the scientific steel-yard, the *fulcrum*, he would say, should be almost invisible, to avoid all friction from the popular tenets;—without this, the *minutiæ* of philosophy, which would always turn the balance, will have no weight at all. Knowledge, like matter, he would affirm, was divisible *in infinitum*;—that the grains and scruples were as much a part of it, as the gravitation of the whole world.—In a word, he would say, error was error,—no matter where it fell—whether in a fraction,—or a pound,—'twas alike fatal to Truth; and she was kept down at the bottom of her well, as inevitably by a mistake in the dust of a butterfly's wing,—as in the disk of the sun, the moon, and all the stars of Heaven put together.

He would often lament that it was for want of considering this properly, and of applying it skilfully to civil matters, as well as to speculative truths, that so many things in this world were out of joint;—that the political arch was giving way;—and that the very foundations of our excellent constitution in church and state, were so sapped as estimators had reported.

You cry out, he would say, we are a

ruined, undone people. Why? he would ask, making use of the sorites or syllogism of Zeno and Chrysippus, without knowing it belonged to them.—Why? why are we a ruined people?—Because we are corrupted.—Whence is it, dear Sir, that we are corrupted?—Because we are needy;—our poverty, and not our wills, consent:—and wherefore, he would add, are we needy?—From the neglect, he would answer, of our pence and our half-pence:—our bank notes, Sir, our guineas;—nay, our shillings take care of themselves.

'Tis the same, he would say, throughout the whole circle of the sciences;—the great, the established points of them, are not to be broke in upon.—The laws of nature will defend themselves;—but error—(he would add, looking earnestly at my mother)—error, Sir, creeps in through the minute holes and small crevices which human nature leaves unguarded.

This turn of thinking in my father, is what I had to remind you of:—the point you are to be informed of, and which I have reserved for this place, is as follows:—

Amongst the many and excellent reasons with which my father had urged my mother to accept of Dr. Slop's assistance preferably to that of the old woman,—there was one of a very singular nature; which, when he had done arguing the matter with her as a christian, and came to argue it over again with her as a philosopher, he had put his whole strength to, depending indeed upon it as his sheet-anchor.——It failed him, though from no defect in the argument itself: but that, do what he could, he was not able for his soul to make her comprehend the drift of it.——Cursed luck!—said he to himself, one afternoon, as he walked out of the rooom, after he had been stating it for an hour and a half to her, to no manner of purpose;—cursed luck! said he, biting his lip as he shut the door,—for a man to be master of one of the finest chains of reasoning in nature,—and have a wife at the same time with such a head-piece, that he cannot hang up a single inference within side of it, to save his soul from destruction!

This argument, though it was entirely lost upon my mother,—had more weight with him than all his other arguments joined together:—I will therefore endeavor to do it justice,—and set it forth with all the perspicuity I am master of.

My father set out upon the strength of these two following axioms;

First, That an ounce of a man's own wit was worth a ton of other people's; and,

Secondly, (which by the bye was the groundwork of the first axiom,—though it comes last) That every man's wit must come from every man's own soul,—and no other body's.

Now, as it was plain to my father, that all souls were by nature equal,—and that the great difference between the most acute and the most obtuse understanding,—was from no original sharpness or bluntness of one thinking substance above or below another,—but arose merely from the lucky or unlucky organization of the body, in that part where the soul principally took up her residence,—he had made it the object of his inquiry to find out the identical place.

Now, from the best accounts he had been able to get of this matter, he was satisfied it could not be where Des Cartes had fixed it, upon the top of the *pineal* gland of the brain; which, as he philosophized, formed a cushion for her about the size of a marrow-pea; though to speak the truth, as so many nerves did terminate all in that one place,—'twas no bad conjecture:—and my father had certainly fallen with that great philosopher plump into the centre of the mistake, had it not been for my uncle Toby, who rescued him out of it by a story he told him of a Walloon officer at the battle of Landen, who had one part of his brains shot away by a musket ball,—and another part of it taken out after by a French surgeon; and, after all, recovered, and did his duty very well without it.

If death, said my father, reasoning with himself, is nothing but the separation of the soul from the body;—and if it is true that people can walk about and do their business without brains,—then certes the soul does not inhabit there.—Q. E. D.

As for that certain, very thin, subtle, and very fragrant juice which Coglionissimo Borri, the great Milanese physician, affirms, in a letter to Bartholine, to have discovered in the *cellulæ* of the *occipital* parts of the *cerebellum*, and which he likewise affirms to be the principal seat of the reasonable soul (for, you must know, in these latter and more enlightened ages, there are two souls in every man living,—the one, according to the great Metheglingius, being called the *Animus;* the other the *Anima;*)—as for the opinion, I say, of Borri,—my father could never subscribe to it by any means; the very idea of so noble, so refined, so immaterial, and so exalted a being as the *Anima,* or even the *Animus,* taking up her residence and sitting dabbling like a tadpole all day long, both summer and winter, in a puddle,—or in a liquid of any kind, how thick or thin soever, he would say, shocked his imagination; he would scarce give the doctrine a hearing.

What therefore seemed the least liable to objections of any was, that the chief *sensorium,* or head-quarters of the soul, and to which place all intelligences were referred, and from whence all her mandates were issued,—was in, or near, the *cerebellum,*—or rather somewhere about the *medulla oblongata,* wherein it was generally agreed by Dutch anatomists, that all the minute nerves from all the organs of the seven senses concentrated, like streets and winding alleys, into a square.

So far there was nothing singular in my father's opinion,—he had the best of philosophers, of all ages and climates, to go along with him.——But here he took a road of his own, setting up another Shandean hypothesis upon these corner-stones they had laid for him—and which said hypothesis equally stood its ground; whether the subtilty and fineness of the soul depended upon the temperature and clearness of the said liquor, or of the finer net-work and texture in the *cerebellum* itself; which opinion he favored.

He maintained, that next to the due care to be taken in the act of propagation of each individual, which required all the thought in the world, as it laid the foundation of this incomprehensible contexture, in which wit, memory, fancy, eloquence, and what is usually meant by the name of good natural parts, do consist;—that the next to this and his christian name, which were the two original and most efficacious causes of all:—that the third cause, or rather what logicians call the *Causa sine quâ non,* and without which all that was done was of no manner of significance,—was the preservation of this delicate and fine-spun web, from the havoc which was generally made in it by the violent compression and crush which the head was made to undergo, by the nonsensical method of bringing us into the world by that foremost.

——This requires explanation.

My father, who dipped into all kinds of books, upon looking into *Lithopædus Senonesis de Portu difficili**, published by Adrianus Smelvgot, had found out, that the lax and pliable state of a child's head in parturition, the bones of the *cranium* having no sutures at that time, was such,—that by force of the woman's efforts, which, in strong labor-pains, was equal, upon an average, to the weight of 470 pounds avoirdupois acting perpendicularly upon it;—it so happened, that in forty-nine instances out of fifty, the said head was compressed and moulded into the shape of an oblong conical piece of dough, such as a pastry-cook generally rolls up, in order to make a pye of.—Good God! cried my father, what havoc and destruction must this make in the infinitely fine and tender texture of the *cerebellum!*—Or if there is such a juice as Borri pretends,—is it not enough to make the clearest liquid in the world both feculent and mothery?

But how great was his apprehension, when he farther understood, that this force acting upon the very vertex of the head, not only injured the brain itself, or *cerebrum,* —but that it necessarily squeezed and propelled the *cerebrum* towards the *cerebellum,* which was the immediate seat of the understanding!——Angels and ministers of grace defend us! cried my father,—can any soul withstand this shock?—No wonder the intellectual web is so rent and tattered as we see it; and that so many of our best

* The author is here twice mistaken; for *Lithopædus* should be wrote thus: *Lithopædii Senonensis Icon.* The second mistake is, that this *Lithopædus* is not an author, but a drawing of a petrified child. The account of this, published by Athosius, 1580, may be seen at the end of Cordæus's works in Spachius. Mr. Tristram Shandy has been led into this error either from seeing *Lithopædus's* name of late in a catalogue of learned writers in Dr. ——, or by mistaking *Lithopædus* for *Trinecavellius,*—from the too great similitude of the names.

heads are no better than a puzzled skein of silk,—all perplexity,—all confusion within-side.

But when my father read on, and was let into the secret, that when a child was turned topsy-turvy, which was easy for an operator to do, and was extracted by the feet;—that instead of the *cerebrum* being propelled towards the *cerebellum*,—the *cerebellum*, on the contrary, was propelled simply towards the *cerebrum*, where it could do no manner of hurt:—By Heavens! cried he, the world is in conspiracy to drive out what little wit God has given us,—and the professors of the obstetric art are listed into the same conspiracy.—What is it to me which end of my son comes foremost into the world, provided all goes right after, and his *cerebellum* escapes uncrushed?

It is the nature of an hypothesis, when once a man has conceived it, that it assimilates every thing to itself, as proper nourishment; and from the first moment of your begetting it, it generally grows the stronger by every thing you see, hear, read, or understand. This is of great use.

When my father was gone with this about a month, there was scarce a phenomenon of stupidity or of genius, which he could not readily solve by it:—it accounted for the eldest son being the greatest blockhead in the family.——Poor devil, he would say, he made way for the capacity of his younger brothers.——It unriddled the observations of drivellers and monstrous heads,—showing, *à priori*, it could not be otherwise,—unless **** I don't know what. It wonderfully explained and accounted for the *acumen* of the Asiatic genius, and that sprightlier turn, and a more penetrating intuition of minds, in warmer climates; not from the loose and commonplace solution of a clear sky, and a more perpetual sunshine, &c.—which, for aught he knew, might as well rarefy and dilute the faculties of the soul into nothing, by one extreme,—as they are condensed in colder climates by the other;—but he traced the affair up to its spring-head;—showed that, in warmer climates, nature had laid a lighter tax upon the fairest parts of the creation;—their pleasures more;—the necessity of their pains less, insomuch that the pressure and resistance upon the vertex was so slight, that the whole organization of the *cerebellum* was preserved;—nay, he did not believe, in natural births, that so much as a single thread of the net-work was broke or displaced,—so that the soul might just act as she liked.

When my father had got so far,——what a blaze of light did the accounts of the Cæsarian section, and of the towering geniuses who had come safe into the world by it, cast upon this hypothesis! Here you see, he would say, there was no injury done to the *sensorium*:—no pressure of the head against the *pelvis*;—no propulsion of the *cerebrum* towards the *cerebellum*, either by the *os pubis* on this side, or the *os coxygis* on that;——and pray, what were the happy consequences?—Why, Sir, your Julius Cæsar, who gave the operation a name;—and your Hermes Trismegistus, who was born so before ever the operation hrd a name;—your Scipio Africanus; your Manlius Torquatus; our Edward the Sixth,—who, had he lived, would have done the same honor to the hypothesis——These, and many more who figured high in the annals of fame,—all came *side-way*, Sir into the world.

The incision of the *abdomen* and *uterus* ran for six weeks together in my father's head;—he had read, and was satisfied, that wounds in the *epigastrium*, and those in the *matrix*, were not mortal;—so that the belly of the mother might be opened extremely well to give a passage to the child.—He mentioned the thing one afternoon to my mother,—merely as a matter of fact; but seeing her turn as pale as ashes at the very mention of it, as much as the operation flattered his hopes,—he thought it as well to say no more of it,—contenting himself with admiring—what he thought was to no purpose to propose.

This was, my father, Mr. Shandy's hypothesis; concerning which I have only to add, that my brother Bobby did as great honor to it (whatever he did to the family) as any one of the great heroes we spoke of: for happening not only to be christened, as I told you, but to be born too, when my father was at Epsom,—being moreover my mother's first child,—coming into the world with his head *foremost*—and turning out afterwards a lad of wonderful slow parts,—

my father spelt all these together into his opinion; and as he had failed at one end,—he was determined to try the other.

This was not to be expected from one of the sisterhood, who are not easily to be put out of their way;—and was therefore one of my father's great reasons in favor of a man of science,——whom he could better deal with.

Of all men in the world, Dr. Slop was the fittest for my father's purpose:—for though his new-invented forceps was the armor he had proved, and what he maintained to be the safest instrument of deliverance, yet, it seems, he had scattered a word or two in his book, in favor of the very thing which ran in my father's fancy;—though not with a view to the soul's good in extricating by the feet, as was my father's system,—but for reasons merely obstetrical.

This will account for the coalition betwixt my father and Dr. Slop, in the ensuing discourse, which went a little hard against my uncle Toby.——In what manner a plain man, with nothing but common sense, could bear up against two such allies in science,—is hard to conceive.—You may conjecture upon it, if you please;—and whilst your imagination is in motion, you may encourage it to go on, and discover by what causes and effects in nature it could come to pass, that my uncle Toby got his modesty by the wound he received upon his groin.—You may raise a system to account for the loss of my nose by marriage-articles,—and show the world how it could happen, that I should have the misfortune to be called TRISTRAM, in opposition to my father's hypothesis, and the wish of the whole family, godfathers and godmothers not excepted.——These, with fifty other points left unravelled, you may endeavor to solve, if you have time;—but I tell you beforehand it will be in vain, for not the sage Alquise, the magician in Don Belianis of Greece, nor the no less famous Urganda the sorceress, his wife, (were they alive) could pretend to come within a league of the truth.

The reader will be content to wait for a full explanation of these matters till the next year,—when a series of things will be laid open which he little expects.

THE

LIFE AND OPINIONS

OF

Tristram Shandy,

GENTLEMAN.

CHAP. I.

——"I WISH, Dr. Slop," quoth my uncle Toby (repeating his wish for Dr. Slop a second time, and with a degree of more zeal and earnestness in his manner of wishing than he had wished at first*)——"I wish, Dr. Slop," quoth my uncle Toby, "you had seen what prodigious armies we had in Flanders."

My uncle Toby's wish did Dr. Slop a disservice which his heart never intended any man;—Sir, it confounded him,—and thereby putting his ideas first into confusion, and then to flight, he could not rally them again for the soul of him.

In all disputes,—male or female,—whether for honor, for profit, or for love,—it makes no difference in the case;—nothing is more dangerous, Madam, than a wish coming sideways in this unexpected manner upon a man. The safest way in general to take off the force of his wish, is for the party wish'd at, instantly to get upon his legs,—and wish the *wisher* something in return, of pretty near the same value;—so balancing the account upon the spot, you stand as you were:—nay, sometimes gain the advantage of the attack by it.

This will be fully illustrated to the world in my chapter of wishes.—

Dr. Slop did not understand the nature of this defence—he was puzzled with it:—and it put an entire stop to the dispute for four minutes and a half;—five had been fatal to it;—my father saw the danger:—the dispute was one of the most interesting disputes in the world, "whether the child "of his prayers and endeavors should be "born without a head, or with one."—He waited to the last moment, to allow Dr Slop, in whose behalf the wish was made, his right of returning it; but perceiving, I say, that he was confounded, and continued looking with that perplexed vacuity of eye which puzzled souls generally stare with,—first in my uncle Toby's face,—then in his,—then up—then down,—then east,—east and by east, and so on,—coasting it along by the plinth of the wainscot till he had got to the opposite point of the compass,—and that he had actually begun to count the brass nails upon the arm of his chair, my father thought there was no time to be lost with my uncle Toby; so took up the discourse as follows:—

* Vide page 66.

CHAP. II.

—"What prodigious armies you had in Flanders!"——

Brother Toby, replied my father, taking his wig from off his head with his right hand, and with his *left* pulling out a striped India handkerchief from his right coat-pocket, in order to rub his head, as he urged the point with my uncle Toby.——

——Now, in this I think my father was much to blame: and I will give you my reasons for it.

Matters of no more seeming consequence in themselves than "whether my father "should have taken off his wig with his "right hand or with his left,"—have divided the greatest kingdoms, and made the crowns of the monarchs who governed them, to totter upon their heads.——But need I tell you, Sir, that the circumstances with which every thing in this world is begirt, give every thing in this world its size and shape —and by tightening it, or relaxing it, this way or that, make the thing to be, what it is,—great,—little,—good,—bad,—indifferent or not indifferent, just as the case happens?

As my father's India handkerchief was in his right coat-pocket, he should by no means have suffered his right hand to have got engaged: on the contrary, instead of taking off his wig with it, as he did, he ought to have committed that entirely to the left: and then, when the natural exigency my father was under of rubbing his head, called out for his handkerchief, he would have had nothing in the world to have done, but to have put his right hand into his right coat-pocket and taken it out; —which he might have done without any violence, or the least ungraceful twist in any one tendon or muscle of his whole body.

In this case (unless, indeed, my father had been resolved to make a fool of himself by holding the wig stiff in his left hand,—or by making some nonsensical angle or other at his elbow-joint, or arm-pit)—his whole attitude had been easy,—natural,—unforced. Reynolds himself, as great and graceful as he paints, might have painted him as he sat.

Now, as my father managed this matter, —consider what a devil of a figure my father made of himself.

In the latter end of Queen Anne's reign, and in the beginning of the reign of King George the First,—"Coat-pockets were cut "very low down in the skirt."—I need say no more;—the father of mischief, had he been hammering at it a month, could not have contrived a worse fashion for one in my father's situation.

CHAP. III.

It was not an easy matter, in any king's reign (unless you were as lean a subject as myself), to have forced your hand diagonally, quite across your whole body, so as to gain the bottom of your opposite coat-pocket.——In the year one thousand seven hundred and eighteen, when this happened, it was extremely difficult; so that when my uncle Toby discovered the transverse zig-zaggery of my father's approaches towards it, it instantly brought into his mind those he had done duty in, before the gate of St. Nicholas;—the idea of which drew off his attention so entirely from the subject in debate, that he had got his right hand to the bell to ring up Trim to go and fetch his map of Namur, and his compasses and sector along with it, to measure the returning angles of the traverses of that attack,—but particularly of that one where he received his wound upon his groin.

My father knit his brows, and as he knit them, all the blood in his body seemed to rush up into his face—my uncle Toby dismounted immediately.

—I did not apprehend your uncle Toby was on horseback.——

CHAP IV.

A MAN'S body and his mind, with the utmost reverence to both I speak it, are exactly like a jerkin, and a jerkin's lining;—rumple the one,—you rumple the other. There is one certain exception however in this case, and that is, when you are so fortunate a fellow as to have had your jerkin made of gum-taffeta, and the body-lining to it of a sarcenet, or thin Persian.

Zeno, Cleanthes, Diogenes, Babylonius, Dionysius, Heracleotes, Antipater, Panætius, and Possidonius, amongst the Greeks; —Cato, and Varro, and Seneca, amongst the Romans;—Pantenus, and Clemens Alexandrinus, and Montaigne, amongst the Christians; and a score and a half of good, honest, unthinking, Shandean people as ever lived, whose names I cannot recollect, —all pretended that their jerkins were made after this fashion;—you might have rumpled and crumpled, and doubled and creased, and fretted, and fridged the outside of them all to pieces;—in short, you might have play'd the very devil with them, and at the same time, not one of the insides of them would have been one button the worse, for all you had done to them.

I believe in my conscience that mine is made up somewhat after this sort:—for never poor jerkin has been tickled off at such a rate as it has been these last nine months together,—and yet I declare the lining to it,—as far as I am a judge of the matter,—is not a three-penny piece the worse;—pell-mell, helter-skelter, ding-dong, cut and thrust, back stroke and fore stroke, side way and long way, have they been trimming it for me:—had there been the least gumminess in my lining, by Heaven! it had all of it, long ago, been frayed and fretted to a thread.

———You Messrs. the Monthly Reviewers!——how could you cut and slash my jerkin as you did?—how did you know but you would cut my lining too?

Heartily and from my soul, to the protection of that Being who will injure none of us, do I recommend you and your affairs,—so God bless you;—only next month, if any one of you should gnash his teeth, and storm and rage at me, as some of you did last May (in which I remember the weather was very hot)—don't be exasperated if I pass it by again with good temper,—being determined as long as I live or write (which in my case means the same thing,) never to give the honest gentleman a worse word or a worse wish than my uncle Toby gave the fly which buzz'd about his nose all dinner-time:——"Go,—go, poor devil," quoth he;—"get thee gone:—why should I hurt "thee?—This world is surely wide enough "to hold both thee and me."

CHAP. V.

Any man, Madam, reasoning upwards, and observing the prodigious effusion of blood in my father's countenance;—by means of which (as all the blood in his body seemed to rush into his face, as I told you,) he must have reddened, pictorically and scientifically speaking, six whole tints and a half, if not a full octave above his natural color;—any man, Madam, but my uncle Toby, who had observed this,—together with the violent knitting of my father's brows, and the extravagant contortion of his body during the whole affair,—would have concluded my father in a rage; and taking that for granted,—had he been a lover of such kind of concord as arises from two such instruments being put into exact tune,—he would instantly have screw'd up his to the same pitch;—and then the devil and all had broke loose—the whole piece, Madam, must have been played off like the sixth of Avison Scarlatti—*con furia*,—like mad.—Grant me patience!—What has *con furia*,—*con strepito*,—or any other hurly-burly whatever, to do with harmony?

Any man, I say, Madam, but my uncle Toby, the benignity of whose heart interpreted every motion of the body in the kindest sense the motion would admit of, would have concluded my father angry, and blamed him too. My uncle Toby blamed nothing but the tailor who cut the pocket-hole;—so sitting still till my father had got his handkerchief out of it, and looking all the time up in his face with inexpressible good-will,—my father at length went on as follows—

CHAP. VI.

——"What prodigious armies you had in Flanders!"

——Brother Toby, quoth my father, I do believe thee to be as honest a man, and with as good and as upright a heart as ever God created;—nor is it thy fault, if all the children which have been, may, can, shall, will, or ought to be begotten, come with their heads foremost into the world:—but believe me, dear Toby, the accidents which unavoidably waylay them, not only in the article of our begetting 'em,—though these, in my opinion, are well worth considering,—but the dangers and difficulties our children are beset with, after they are got forth into the world, are enow;—little need is there to expose them to unnecessary ones in their passage to it.——Are these dangers, quoth my uncle Toby, laying his hand upon my father's knee, and looking up seriously in his face for an answer,—are these dangers greater now-a-days, brother, than in times past?——Brother Toby, answered my father, if a child was but fairly begot, and born alive, and healthy, and the mother did well after it,—our forefathers never looked farther.—My uncle Toby instantly withdrew his hand from my father's knee, reclined his body gently back in his chair, raised his head till he could just see the cornice of the room, and then directing the buccinatory muscles along his cheeks, and the obicular muscles around his lips to do their duty,—he whistled *Lillibullero.*

CHAP. VII.

Whilst my uncle Toby was whistling *Lillibullero* to my father,—Dr. Slop was stamping, and cursing and damning at Obadiah at a most dreadful rate.——It would have done your heart good, and cured you, Sir, for ever, of the vile sin of swearing, to have heard him. I am determined, therefore, to relate the whole affair to you.

When Dr. Slop's maid delivered the green baize bag with her master's instruments in it, to Obadiah, she very sensibly exhorted him to put his head and one arm through the strings, and ride with it slung across his body. So undoing the bow-knot, to lengthen the strings for him, without any more ado, she helped him on with it. However, as this, in some measure, unguarded the mouth of the bag; lest any thing should bolt out in galloping back, at the speed Obadiah threatened, they concluded to take it off again: and in the great care and caution of their hearts, they had taken the two strings and tied them close (pursing up the mouth of the bag first) with half a dozen hard knots, each of which Obadiah, to make all safe, had twitched and drawn together with all the strength of his body.

This answered all that Obadiah and the maid intended; but was no remedy against some evils which neither he or she foresaw. The instruments, it seems, as tight as the bag was tied above, had so much room to play in it, towards the bottom (the shape of the bag being conical) that Obadiah could not make a trot of it, but with such a terrible jingle, what with the *tire-tête, forceps,* and *squirt,* as would have been enough, had Hymen been taking a jaunt that way, to have frightened him out of the country; but when Obadiah accelerated his motion, and from a plain trot essayed to prick his coach-horse into a full gallop,—by Heaven! Sir, the jingle was incredible.

As Obadiah had a wife and three children,—the turpitude of fornication, and the many other political ill consequences of this jingling, never once entered his brain;—he had however his objection, which came home to himself, and weighed with him, as it has oftentimes done with the greatest patriots.——"The poor fellow, Sir, was not "able to hear himself whistle."

CHAP. VIII.

As Obadiah loved wind-music preferably to all the instrumental music he carried with him,—he very considerately set his imagination to work, to contrive and to invent by what means he should put himself in a condition of enjoying it.

In all distresses (except musical) where small cords are wanted, nothing is so apt to enter a man's head as his hat-band:——the philosophy of this is so near the surface,—I scorn to enter into it.

As Obadiah's was a mixed case:——mark, Sirs,—I say, a mixed case; for it was obstetrical,—*scrip*-tical, squirtical, papistical—and as far as the coach-horse was concerned in it,—cabalistical,—and only partly musical:—Obadiah made no scruple of availing himself of the first expedient which offered; so taking hold of the bag and instruments, and griping them hard together with one hand, and with the finger and thumb of the other, putting the end of the hat-band betwixt his teeth, and then slipping his hand down to the middle of it,—he tied and cross-tied them all fast together from one end to the other (as you would cord a trunk) with such a multiplicity of round-abouts and intricate cross-turns, with a hard knot at every intersection or point where the strings met,—that Dr. Slop must have had three-fifths of Job's patience at least to have unloosed them.—I think, in my conscience, that had Nature been in one of her nimble moods, and in humor for such a contest,—and she and Dr. Slop both fairly started together,—there is no man living who had seen the bag with all that Obadiah had done to it,—and known likewise the great speed the Goddess can make when she thinks proper, who would have had the east doubt remaining in his mind—which of the two would have carried off the prize. My mother, Madam, had been delivered sooner than the green bag infallibly—at least by twenty knots.——Sport of small accidents, Tristram Shandy! that thou art, and ever will be! had that trial been made for thee, and it was fifty to one but it had, —thy affairs had not been so depress'd (at least by the depression of thy nose) as they have been; nor had the fortunes of thy house and the occasions of making them, which have so often presented themselves in the course of thy life, to thee, been so often, so vexatiously, so tamely, so irrevocably abandoned—as thou hast been forced to leave them;—but 'tis over,—all but the account of 'em, which cannot be given to the curious till I am got out into the world.

CHAP. IX.

Great wits jump:—for the moment Dr. Slop cast his eyes upon his bag (which he had not done till the dispute with my uncle Toby about midwifery put him in mind of it) the very same thought occurred.—'Tis God's mercy, quoth he (to himself) that Mrs. Shandy has had so bad a time of it, else she might have been brought to bed seven times told, before one half of these knots could have been got untied.—But here you must distinguish:—the thought floated only in Dr. Slop's mind, without sail or ballast to it, as a simple proposition; millions of which, as your Worship knows, are every day swimming quietly in the middle of the thin juice of a man's understanding, without being carried backwards or forwards, till some little gusts of passion or interest drive them to one side.

A sudden trampling in the room above, near my mother's bed, did the proposition the very service I am speaking of. By all that's unfortunate, quoth Dr. Slop, unless I make haste, the thing will actually befall me as it is.

CHAP. X.

In the case of knots; by which, in the first place, I would not be understood to mean slip-knots,—because in the course of my life and opinions,—my opinions concerning them will come in more properly when I mention the catastrophe of my great-uncle Mr. Hammond Shandy,—a little man,—but of high fancy;—he rushed into the Duke of Monmouth's affair:—nor, secondly, in this place, do I mean that particular species of knots called bow-knots;—there is so little address, or skill, or patience required in the unloosing them, that they are below my giving any opinion at all about them. —But by the knots I am speaking of, may it please your Reverences to believe, that I mean good, honest, devilish tight, hard knots, made *bona fide*, as Obadiah made his: —in which there is no quibbling provision made by the duplication and return of the two ends of the strings through the annulus or noose made by the second implication of them,—to get them slipp'd and undone by. —I hope you apprehend me.

In the case of these knots then, and of the several obstructions, which, may it please your Reverences, such knots cast in our way in getting through life,—every hasty man can whip out his pen-knife and cut through them.—'Tis wrong. Believe me, Sirs, the most virtuous way, and which both reason and conscience dictate,—is to take our teeth or our fingers to them.—Dr. Slop had lost his teeth—his favorite instrument, by extracting in a wrong direction, or by some misapplication of it, unfortunately slipping, he had formerly, in a hard labor, knock'd out three of the best of them with the handle of it:——he tried his fingers;—alas, the nails of his fingers and thumbs were cut close.——The deuce take it! I can make nothing of it either way, cried Dr. Slop.——The trampling over-head near my mother's bed-side increased.—Pox take the fellow! I shall never get the knots untied as long as I live.—My mother gave a groan.——Lend me your pen-knife—I must e'en cut the knots at last.—Pugh!—psha!—Lord! I have cut my thumb quite across to the very bone.—Curse the fellow—if there was not another man-midwife within fifty miles—I am undone for this bout—I wish the scoundrel hang'd —I wish he was shot—I wish all the devils in hell had him for a blockhead!———

My father had a great respect for Oba

diah, and could not bear to hear him disposed of in such a manner:—he had moreover some little respect for himself,—and could as ill bear with the indignity offered to himself in it.

Had Dr. Slop cut any part about him but his thumb,—my father had pass'd it by—his prudence had triumphed:—as it was, he was determined to have his revenge.

Small curses, Dr. Slop, upon great occasions, quoth my father (condoling with him first upon the accident) are but so much waste of our strength and soul's health to no manner of purpose.——I own it, replied Dr. Slop.——They are like sparrow-shot, quoth my uncle Toby (suspending his whistling) fired against a bastion.——They serve, continued my father, to stir the humors—but carry off none of their acrimony;—for my own part, I seldom swear or curse at all—I hold it bad;—but if I fall into it by surprise, I generally retain so much presence of mind (right, quoth my uncle Toby,) as to make it answer my purpose;—that is, I swear on till I find myself easy. A wise and a just man however would always endeavor to proportion the vent given to these humors, not only to the degree of them stirring within himself,—but to the size and ill intent of the offence upon which they are to fall.—"Injuries come only from the heart,"—quoth my uncle Toby.——For this reason, continued my father, with the most Cervantic gravity, I have the greatest veneration in the world for that gentleman, who, in distrust of his own discretion in this point, sat down and composed (that is, at his leisure) fit forms of swearing suitable to all cases, from the lowest to the highest provocations which could possibly happen to him;—which forms being well considered by him, and such moreover as he could stand to, he kept them ever by him on the chimney-piece, within his reach, ready for use.——I never apprehended, replied Dr. Slop, that such a thing was ever thought of,—much less executed.—I beg your pardon, answered my father; I was reading, though not using, one of them to my brother Toby, this morning, whilst he pour'd out the tea:—'tis here upon the shelf over my head: but if I remember right, 'tis too violent for a cut of the thumb.——Not at all, quoth Dr. Slop—the devil take the fellow.——Then, answered my father, 'tis much at your service, Dr. Slop,—on condition you will read it aloud.—So rising up and reaching down a form of excommunication of the church of Rome, a copy of which my father (who was curious in his collections) had procured out of the leger-book of the church of Rochester, writ by Ernulphus the bishop,—with a most affected seriousness of look and voice, which might have cajoled Ernulphus himself,—he put it into Dr. Slop's hands. ——Dr. Slop wrapt his thumb up in the corner of his handkerchief, and with a wry face, though without any suspicion, read aloud, as follows,—my uncle Toby whistling Lillibullero as loud as he could all the time.

TEXTUS DE ECCLESIA ROFFENSI, PER ERNULFUM EPISCOPUM.

CAP. XI.

EXCOMMUNICATIO.*

Ex auctoritate Dei Omnipotentis, Patris, et Filii, et Spiritus Sancti, et sanctorum canonuin, sanctæque et intemeratæ Virginis Dei genetricis Mariæ,—

CHAP. XI.

"By the authority of God Almighty, the "Father, Son, and Holy Ghost, and of the "holy canons, and of the undefiled Virgin "Mary, mother and patroness of our Sa-

---

* As the genuineness of the consultation of the *Sorbonne* upon the question of Baptism, was doubted by some and denied by others,—'twas thought proper to print the original of this excommunication: for the copy of which Mr. Shandy returns thanks to the chapter-clerk of the dean and chapter of Rochester.

vior."—I think there is no necessity, quoth Dr. Slop, dropping the paper down to his knee, and addressing himself to my father, —as you have read it over, Sir, so lately, to read now aloud;—and as Captain Shandy seems to have no great inclination to hear it,—I may as well read it to myself.——That's contrary to treaty, replied my father —Besides, there is something so whimsical, especially in the latter part of it, I should grieve to lose the pleasure of a second reading.—Dr. Slop did not altogether like it; but my uncle Toby offering at that instant to give over whistling, and read it himself to them,—Dr. Slop thought he might as well read it, under the cover of my uncle Toby's whistling—as suffer my uncle Toby to read it alone:—so raising up the paper to his face, and holding it quite parallel to it, in order to hide his chagrin,—he read it aloud, as follows—my uncle Toby whistling *Lillibullero*, though not quite so loud as before.

——Atque omnium cœlestium virtutum, angelorum, archangelorum, thronorum, dominationum, protestatuum, cherubin ac seraphin, & sanctorum patriarcharum, prophetarum, & omnium apostolorum & evangelistarum, and sanctorum innocentum, qui in conspectu Agni Sancti digni inventi sunt canticum cantare novum, et sanctorum martyrum & sanctorum confessorum, et sanctarum virginum, atque omnium simul sanctorum et electorum Dei,—Excommuni-
vel os s
camus, et anathematizamus hunc furem,
vel os s
vel hunc malefactorem, N.N. et à liminibus sanctæ Dei ecclesiæ sequestramus, et æternis
vel i n
suppliciis excruciandus, mancipetur, cum Dathan et Abiram, et cum his qui dixerunt Domino Deo, Recede à nobis, scientiam viarum tuarum nolumus: et sicut aquâ ignis
vel eorum
extinguitur, sic extinguatur, lucerna ejus in
n
secula seculorum nisi respuerit, et ad satis-
n
factionem venerit. Amen.
os
Maledicant illum Deus Pater qui hominem
os
creavit. Maledicat illum Dei Filius qui pro

"By the authority of God Almighty, the "Father, Son, and Holy Ghost, and of the "undefiled Virgin Mary, mother and pa-"troness of our Savior, and of all the ce-"lestial virtues, angels, archangels, thrones, "dominions, powers, cherubims and sera-"phims, and of all the holy patriarchs, pro-"phets, and of all the apostles and evan-"gelists, and of the holy innocents, who in "the sight of the Holy Lamb, are found "worthy to sing the new song of the holy "martyrs and holy confessors, and of the "holy virgins, and of all the saints, to-"gether with the holy and elect of God,— "May he" (Obadiah) "be damn'd" (for tying these knots)—"We excommunicate "and anathematize him; and from the "thresholds of the holy church of God Al-"mighty we sequester him, that he may be "tormented, disposed, and delivered over "with Dathan and Abiram, and with those "who say unto the Lord God, Depart from "us, we desire none of thy ways. And as "fire is quenched with water, so let the "light of him be put out for evermore, un-"less it shall repent him" (Obadiah, of the knots which he has tied) "and make satis-"faction!" (for them) "Amen."

"May the Father who created man, curse "him.—May the Son who suffered for us, "curse him!——May the Holy Ghost, who

os
homine passus est. Maledicat illum Spiritus Sanctus qui in baptismo effusus est. Male-
os
dicat illum sancta crux, quam Christus pro nostrâ salute hostem triumphans ascendit.
os
Maledicat illum sancta Dei genetrix et
os
perpetua Virgo Maria. Maledicat illum sanctus Michael, animarum susceptor sa-
os
crarum. Maledicant illum omnes angeli et archangeli, principatus et potestates, omnesque militia cœlestes.

os
Maledicat illum patriarcharum et prophe-
os
tarum laudabilis numerus. Maledicant illum sanctus Johannes Præcursor et Baptista Christi, et sanctus Petrus, et sanctus Paulus, atque sanctus Andreas, omnesque Christi apostoli, simul et cæteri discipuli quatuor quoque evangelistæ, qui sua prædicatione mundum universum converterunt. Maledi-
os
cat illum cuneus martyrum et confessorum mirificus, qui Deo bonis operibus placitus inventus est.

os
Maledicant illum sacrarum virginum chori, quæ mundi vana causa honoris Christi
os
respuenda contempserunt. Maledicant illum omnes sancti qui ab initio mundi usque in finem seculi Deo dilecti inveniuntur.

os
Maledicant illum cœli et terra, et omnia sancta in eis manentia.

i n n
Maledictus sit ubicunque, fuerit, sive in domo, sive in agro, sive in viâ, sive in semitâ, sive in silvâ, sive in aquâ, sive in ecclesiâ.

i n
Maledictus sit vivendo, moriendo,—

——— ——— ———
——— ——— ———
——— ——— ———
——— ——— ———
——— ——— ———

manducando, bibendo, esuriendo, sitiendo, jejunando, dormitando, dormiendo, vigilando, ambulando, stando, sedendo, jacendo, oper-

"was given to us in baptism, curse him! (Obadiah)——"May the holy cross which "Christ, for our salvation, triumphing over "his enemies, ascended, curse him!

"May the holy and eternal Virgin Mary, "mother of God, curse him!—May St. "Michael, the advocate of holy souls, curse "him!——May all the angels and arch- "angels, principalities and powers, and all "the heavenly armies, curse him!" [Our armies swore terribly in Flanders, cried my uncle Toby,—but nothing to this.——For my own part, I could not have a heart to curse my dog so.]

"May the praiseworthy multitude of "patriarchs and prophets curse him!

"May St. John, the Præcursor, and St. "John the Baptist, and St. Peter, and St. "Paul, and St. Andrew, and all other "Christ's apostles, together curse him! "And may the rest of his disciples and "four evangelists, who, by their preaching "converted the universal world, and may the "holy and wonderful company of martyrs "and confessors, who by their holy works "are found pleasing to God Almighty, curse "him!" (Obadiah.)

"May the holy choir of the holy virgins, "who for the honor of Christ have despised "the things of the world, damn him!—May "all the saints who, from the beginning of "the world to everlasting ages, are found "to be beloved of God, damn him!—May "the heavens and earth, and all the holy "things remaining therein, damn him," (Obadiah) "or her!" (or whoever else had a hand in tying these knots.)

"May he" (Obadiah) "be damn'd wherever "he be,—whether in the house or the "stables, the garden, or the field, or the "highway, or in the path, or in the wood, "or in the water, or in the church!——May "he be cursed, in living, in dying!" [Here my uncle Toby, taking the advantage of a *minim* in the second bar of his tune, kept whistling one continued note to the end of the sentence,—Dr. Slop, with his division of curses, moving under him, like a running bass, all the way.] "May he be cursed in "eating and drinking, in being hungry, in

ando, quiescendo, mingendo, cacando, flebotomando.

ı n

Maledictus sit in totis viribus corporis.

i n

Maledictus sit intus ex exterius.

i n i n

Maledictus sit in capillis; maledictus sit

i n

in cerebro. Maledictus sit in vertice, in temporibus, in fronte, in auriculis, in superciliis, in oculis, in genis, in maxillis, in naribus, in dentibus, mordacibus, in labris sive molibus, in labiis, in guttere, in humeris, in carpis, in brachiis, in manubus, in digitis, in pectore, in corde, et in omnibus interioribus stomacho tenus, in renibus, in inguine, in femore, in genitalibus, in coxis, in genubus, in cruribus, in pedidus, et in unguibus.

i n

Maledictus sit in totis compagibus membrorum, a vertice capitis, usque ad plantam pedis.—Non sit in eo sanitas.

os

Maledicat illum Christus Filius Dei vivi toto suæ majestatis imperio——

"being thirsty, in fasting, in sleeping, in "slumbering, in waking, in walking, in "standing, in sitting, in lying, in working, "in resting, in pissing, in shitting, and in "blood-letting!

"May he" (Obadiah) "be cursed in all "the faculties of his body!

"May he be cursed inwardly and out- "wardly!——May he be cursed in the hair "of his head!——May he be cursed in his "brains, and in his vertex," [That is a sad curse, quoth my father] "in his temples in "his forehead, in his ears, in his eyebrows. "in his cheeks, in his jaw-bones, in his "nostrils, in his fore-teeth and grinders, in "his lips, in his throat, in his shoulders, in "his wrists, in his arms, in his hands, in "his fingers!

"May he be damn'd in his mouth, in his "breast, in his heart and purtenance, down "to the very stomach!

"May he be cursed in his reins, and in "his groin," [God in Heaven forbid! quoth "my uncle Toby] "in his thighs, in his "genitals" [My father shook his head] "and "in his hips, and in his knees, his legs, and "feet, and toe-nails!

"May he be cursed in all the joints and "articulations of his members, from the top "of his head to the sole of his foot! May "there be no soundness in him!"

"May the Son of the living God, with "all the glory of his Majesty,——" [Here my uncle Toby throwing back his head, gave a monstrous, long, loud Whew--w——w——; something betwixt the interjectional whistle of *Heyday!* and the word itself.——

——By the golden beard of Jupiter,—and of Juno (if her majesty wore one), and by the beards of the rest of your heathen Worships, which, by the bye, was no small number, since, what with the beards of your celestial gods, and gods aerial and aquatic,—to say nothing of the beards of town-gods and country-gods, or of the celestial goddesses your wives, or of the infernal goddesses your whores and concubines (that is in case they wore them)——all which beards, as Varro tells me, upon his word and honor, when mustered up together, made no less than thirty thousand effective beards upon the Pagan establishment·-

every beard of which claimed the rights and privileges of being stroken and sworn by:—by all these beards together then,—I vow and protest that of the two bad cassocks I am worth in the world, I would have given the better of them, as freely as ever Cid Hamet offered his,—to have stood by and heard my uncle Toby's accompaniment.]

——et insurgat adversus illum cœlum cum omnibus virtutibus quæ in eo moventur ad *damnandum* eum nisi pœnituerit et ad satisfactionem venerit. Amen. Fiat, fiat. Amen.

——"curse him!"—continued Dr. Slop,—"and may Heaven, with all the powers "which move therein, rise up against him, "curse and damn him," (Obadiah) "unless "he repent and make satisfaction! Amen. "So be it,—so be it.—Amen."

I declare, quoth my uncle Toby, my heart would not let me curse the devil himself with so much bitterness.——He is the father of curses, replied Dr. Slop.——So am not I, replied my uncle.——But he is cursed and damn'd already to all eternity, replied Dr. Slop.

I am sorry for it, quoth my uncle Toby.

Dr. Slop drew up his mouth, and was just beginning to return my uncle Toby the compliment of his Whu—u—u, or interjectional whistle,—when the door hastily opening in the next chapter but one,—put an end to the affair.

CHAP. XII.

Now don't let us give ourselves a parcel of airs, and pretend that the oaths we make free with in this land of liberty of ours are our own; and because we have the spirit to swear them,—imagine that we have had the wit to invent them too.

I'll undertake this moment to prove it to any man in the world, except to a connoisseur;——though I declare I object only to a connoisseur in swearing,—as I would do to a connoisseur in painting, &c. &c. the whole set of 'em are so hung round and *befetish'd* with the bobs and trinkets of criticism,—or, to drop my metaphor, which by the bye is a pity,—for I have fetch'd it as far as from the coast of Guinea,—their heads, Sir, are stuck so full of rules and compasses, and have that eternal propensity to apply them upon all occasions, that a work of genius had better go to the devil at once, than stand to be prick'd and tortur'd to death by 'em.

—And how did Garrick speak the soliloquy last night?—Oh, against all rule, my Lord,—most ungrammatically! betwixt the substantive and the adjective, which should agree together in *number*, *case*, and *gender*, he made a breach thus,—stopping, as if the point wanted settling;—and betwixt the nominative case, which your Lordship knows should govern the verb, he suspended his voice in the epilogue a dozen times three seconds and three fifths by a stop-watch, my Lord, each time.——Admirable grammarian!—But in suspending his voice,—was the sense suspended likewise? Did no expression of attitude or countenance fill up the chasm?—Was the eye silent?—Did you narrowly look?——I look'd only at the stop-watch, my Lord.——Excellent observer!

And what of this new book the whole world makes such a rout about?—Oh! 'tis out of all plumb, my Lord,—quite an irregular thing!—not one of the angles at the four corners was a right angle.——I had my rule and compasses. &c. my Lord, in my pocket.——Excellent critic!

——And for the epic poem your Lordship bid me look at,—upon taking the length, breadth, height, and depth of it, and trying them at home upon an exact scale of Bossu's,——'tis out, my Lord, in every one of its dimensions.——Admirable connoisseur!

——And did you step in, to take a look at the grand picture in your way back?——'Tis a melancholy daub, my Lord, not one principle of the pyramid in any one group!—and what a price!—for there is nothing of the coloring of Titian—the expression of Rubens—the grace of Raphael—the purity of Dominichino—the *corregiescity* of Corregio—the learning of Poussin—the airs of Guido—the taste of the Carrachis—or the grand contour of Angelo.——Grant me patience, just Heaven!—Of all the cants which are canted in this canting world,—though the cant of hypocrites may be the worst,—the cant of criticism is the most tormenting!

I would go fifty miles on foot, for I have not a horse worth riding on, to kiss the hand of that man whose generous heart will give up the reins of his imagination into his author's hands,—be pleased he knows not why, and cares not wherefore.

Great Apollo!—if thou art in a giving humor,—give me,—I ask no more, but one stroke of native humor, with a single spark of thy own fire along with it,—and send Mercury, with the *rules* and *compasses*, if he can be spared, with my compliments to,—no matter.

Now to any one else I will undertake to prove, that all the oaths and imprecations which we have been puffing off upon the world for these two hundred and fifty years last past as originals,—except *St. Paul's thumb*,—*God's flesh*, and *God's fish*, which were oaths monarchical, and, considering who made them, not much amiss; and as king's oaths, 'tis not much matter whether they were fish or flesh;—else, I say, there is not an oath, or at least a curse amongst them, which has not been copied over and over again out of Ernulphus a thousand times; but, like all other copies, how infinitely short of the force and spirit of the original!—It is thought to be no bad oath, —and by itself passes very well,—"G—d damn you."——Set it beside Ernulphus's —"God Almighty the Father damn you, "—God the Son damn you,—God the Holy "Ghost damn you,"—you see 'tis nothing. ——There is an orientality in his we cannot rise up to: besides, he is more copious in his invention,—possess'd more of the excellencies of a swearer,—had such a thorough knowledge of the human frame, its membranes, nerves, ligaments, knittings of the joints, and articulations,—that when Ernulphus cursed,—no part escaped him. ——'Tis true, there is something of a *hardness* in his manner,—and, as in Michael Angelo, a want of *grace*;—but then there is such a greatness of *gusto*!

My father, who generally look'd upon every thing in a light very different from all mankind, would, after all, never allow this to be an original.—He considered rather Ernulphus's anathema as an institute of swearing, in which, as he suspected, upon the decline of swearing in some milder pontificate, Ernulphus, by order of the succeeding pope, had with great learning and diligence collected together all the laws of it;—for the same reason that Justinian, in the decline of the empire, had ordered his chancellor Tribonias to collect the Roman or civil laws together into one code or digest—lest, through the rust of time, and the fatality of all things committed to oral tradition,—they should be lost to the world for ever.

For this reason my father would often times affirm, there was not an oath from the great and tremendous oath of William the conqueror ("By the splendor of God") down to the lowest oath of a scavenger ("Damn your eyes") which was not to be found in Ernulphus.——In short, he would add—I defy a man to swear out of it.

The hypothesis is, like most of my father's, singular and ingenious too;—nor have I any objection to it, but that it overturns my own.

CHAP. XIII.

——Bless my soul!—my poor mistress is ready to faint—and her pains are gone—and the drops are done—and the bottle of julap is broke—and the nurse has cut her arm—(and I my thumb, cried Dr. Slop;) and the child is where it was, continued Susannah,—and the midwife has fallen backwards upon the edge of the fender, and bruised her hip as black as your hat.——I'll look at it, quoth Dr. Slop.——There is no need of that, replied Susannah,—you had better look at my mistress—but the midwife would gladly first give you an account how things are; so desires you would go up stairs and speak to her this moment.

Human nature is the same in all professions.

The midwife had just before been put over Dr. Slop's head,——he had not digested it.—No, replied Dr. Slop, 'twould be full as proper, if the midwife came down to me,——I like subordination, quoth my uncle Toby,—and but for it, after the reduction of Lisle, I know not what might have become of the garrison of Ghent, in the mutiny for bread, in the year Ten.——Nor, replied Dr. Slop, (parodying my uncle Toby's hobby-horsical reflection; though fully as hobby-horsical himself)—do I know, Captain Shandy, what might have become of the garrison above stairs, in the mutiny and confusion I find all things are in at present, but for the subordination of fingers and thumbs to ******.—the application of which, Sir, under this accident of mine, comes in so *à propos*, that, without it, the cut upon my thumb might have been felt by the Shandy family as long as the Shandy family had a name.

CHAP. XIV.

Let us go back to the ******—in the last chapter.

It is a singular stroke of eloquence (at least it was so when eloquence flourished at Athens and Rome; and would be so now, did orators wear mantles) not to mention the name of a thing, when you had the thing about you *in petto*, ready to produce, pop, in the place you want it. A scar, an ax, a sword, a pink'd doublet, a rusty helmet, a pound and a half of pot-ashes in an urn, or a three-halfpenny pickle-pot;—but above all, a tender infant royally accoutred.—Though if it was too young, and the oration as long as Tully's second Philippic,—it must certainly have beshit the orator's mantle.—And then again, if too old,—it must have been unwieldy and incommodious to his action,—so as to make him lose by his child almost as much as he could gain by it.—Otherwise, when a state-orator has hit the precise age to a minute,—hid his BAMBINO in his mantle so cunningly that no mortal could smell it,—and produced it so critically, that no soul could say it came in by head and shoulders—Oh, Sirs, it has done wonders!—it has open'd the sluices, and turn'd the brains, and shook the principles, and unhinged the politics of half a nation!

These feats however are not to be done, except in those states and times, I say, where orators wore mantles,—and pretty large ones too, my brethren, with some twenty or five-and-twenty yards of good purple, superfine, marketable cloth in them,—with large flowing folds and doubles, and in a great style of design.—All which plainly shows, may it please your Worships, that the decay of eloquence, and the little good service it does at present, both within and without doors, is owing to nothing else in the world but short coats and the disuse of trunk-hose.——We can conceal nothing under ours, Madam, worth showing.

CHAP. XV.

Dr. Slop was within an ace of being an exception to all this argumentation: for happening to have his green baize bag upon his knees when he began to parody my uncle Toby,—'twas as good as the best mantle in the world to him: for which purpose, when he foresaw the sentence would end in his new-invented forceps, he thrust his hand into the bag, in order to have them ready to clap in, when your Reverences took so much notice of the ******, which, had he managed,—my uncle Toby had certainly been overthrown: the sentence and the argument in that case jumping closely in one point, so like the two lines which form the salient angle of a ravelin,—Dr. Slop would never have given them up;—and my uncle Toby would as soon have thought of flying, as taking them by force: but Dr. Slop fumbled so vilely in pulling them out, it took off the whole effect, and, what was a ten times worse evil (for they seldom come alone in this life) in pulling out his forceps, his forceps unfortunately drew out the squirt along with it.

When a proposition can be taken in two senses—'tis a law in disputation, that the respondent may reply to which of the two he pleases, or finds most convenient for him.—This threw the advantage of the argument quite on my uncle Toby's side.——"Good God!" cried my uncle Toby, "*are* "*children brought into the world with a* "*squirt?*"

CHAP. XVI.

—Upon my honor, Sir, you have torn every bit of skin quite off the back of both my hands with your forceps, cried my uncle Toby;—and you have crush'd all my knuckles into the bargain with them to a jelly.——'Tis your own fault, said Dr. Slop;—you should have clinch'd your two fists together into the form of a child's head, as I told you, and sat firm.——I did so, answered my uncle Toby.——Then the points of my forceps have not been sufficiently arm'd, or the rivet wants closing,—or else the cut on my thumb has made me a little awkward,—or possibly——'Tis well, quoth my father, interrupting the detail of possibilities,—that the experiment was not first made upon my child's head-piece.——It would not have been a cherry-stone the worse, answered Dr. Slop.——I maintain it, said my uncle Toby, it would have broke the cerebellum (unless indeed the skull had been as hard as a granado) and turn'd it all into a perfect posset.——Pshaw! replied Dr. Slop, a child's head is naturally as soft as the pap of an apple;—the sutures give way;—and besides, I could have extracted by the feet after.——Not you, said she.——I rather wish you would begin that way, quoth my father.

Pray do, added my uncle Toby

CHAP. XVII.

——And pray, good woman, after all, will you take upon you to say, it may not be the child's hip, as well as the child's head?—('Tis most certainly the head, replied the midwife.) Because, continued Dr. Slop (turning to my father), as positive as these old ladies generally are,—'tis a point very difficult to know,—and yet of the greatest consequence to be known,——because, Sir, if the hip is mistaken for the head,—there is a possibility (if it is a boy) that the forceps * * * * * * * * * * * * * *

——What the possibility was, Dr. Slop whispered very low to my father, and then to my uncle Toby.——There is no such danger, continued he, with the head.——No, in truth, quoth my father;—but when your possibility has taken place at the hip,—you may as well take off the head too.

——It is morally impossible that the reader should understand this,—'tis enough Dr. Slop understood it;—so taking the green baize bag in his hand, with the help of Obadiah's pumps, he tripp'd pretty nimbly, for a man of his size, across the room to the door;—and from the door was shown the way, by the good old midwife, to my mother's apartments.

CHAP. XVIII.

It is two hours and ten minutes,—and no more,—cried my father, looking at his watch, since Dr. Slop and Obadiah arrived;—and I know not how it happens, brother Toby,—but, to my imagination, it seems almost an age.

——Here—pray, Sir, take hold of my cap:—nay, take the bell along with it, and my pantofles too.

Now, Sir, they are all at your service; and I freely make you a present of 'em, on condition you give me all your attention to this chapter.

Though my father said, "*he knew not* "*how it happen'd*,"—yet he knew very well how it happen'd:—and at the instant he spoke it, was predetermined in his mind to give my uncle Toby a clear account of the matter, by a metaphysical dissertation upon the subject of *duration and its simple modes*, in order to show my uncle Toby by what mechanism and mensurations in the brain it came to pass, that the rapid succession of their ideas, and the eternal scampering of the discourse from one thing to another, since Dr. Slop had come into the room, had lengthened out so short a period to so inconceivable an extent.——"I know "not how it happens,"—cried my father—"but it seems an age."

——'Tis owing entirely, quoth my uncle Toby, to the succession of our ideas.

My father, who had an itch, in common with all philosophers, of reasoning upon every thing which happened, and accounting for it too,—proposed infinite pleasure to himself in this, of the succession of ideas; and had not the least apprehension of having it snatch'd out of his hands by my uncle Toby, who (honest man!) generally took every thing as it happened;—and who of all things in the world troubled his brain the least with abstruse thinking;—the ideas of time and space,—or how we came by those ideas,—or of what stuff they were made,—or whether they were born with us,—or we picked them up afterwards as we went along,—or whether we did it in frocks,—or not till we had got into breeches;—with a thousand other inquiries and disputes about INFINITY, PRESCIENCE, LIBERTY, NECESSITY, and so forth, upon whose desperate and unconquerable theories so many fine heads have been turned and cracked,—never did my uncle Toby's the least injury at all; my father knew it,—and was no less surprised than he was disappointed with my uncle's fortuitous solution.

Do you understand the theory of that affair? replied my father.

Not I, quoth my uncle.

—But you have some ideas, said my father, of what you talk about?

No more than my horse, replied my uncle Toby.

Gracious Heaven! cried my father, looking upwards, and clasping his two hands together,—there is a worth in thy honest ignorance, brother Toby;—'twere almost a pity to exchange it for a knowledge.—But I'll tell thee.——

To understand what Time is aright, without which we never can comprehend Infinity, insomuch as one is a portion of the other,—we ought seriously to sit down and consider what idea it is we have of *duration*, so as to give a satisfactory account how we came by it.——What is that to any body? quoth my uncle Toby. * "For if you will "turn your eyes inwards upon your mind," continued my father, "and observe atten-"tively, you will perceive, brother, that "whilst you and I are talking together, and "thinking, and smoking our pipes, or whilst "we receive successively ideas in our minds, "we know that we do exist; and so we es-"timate the existence, or the continuation "of the existence of ourselves, or any thing "else, commensurate to the succession of "any ideas in our minds, the duration of "ourselves, or any such other thing co-ex-"isting with our thinking:—and so, accord-"ing to that preconceived"——You puzzle me to death, cried my uncle Toby.

——'Tis owing to this, replied my father, that in our computations of time we are so used to minutes, hours, weeks, and months—and of clocks (I wish there was not a clock in the kingdom) to measure out their several portions to us, and to those who belong to us,—that 'twill be well if, in time to come, the *succession of our ideas* be of any use or service to us at all.

Now, whether we observe it or no, continued my father, in every sound man's head there is a regular succession of ideas, of one sort or other, which follow each other in a train just like——a train of artillery? said my uncle Toby——A train of a fiddle-stick!—quoth my father—which follow and succeed one another in our minds at certain distances, just like the images in the inside of a lantern turned round by the heat of a candle.—I declare, quoth my uncle Toby, mine are more like a smoke-jack.——Then, brother Toby, I have nothing more to say to you upon the subject, said my father.

CHAP. XIX.

——WHAT a conjecture was here lost! ——My father, in one of his best explanatory moods,—in eager pursuit of a meta-

* Vide Locke

physical point, into the very regions where clouds and thick darkness would soon have encompassed it about;—my uncle Toby, in one of the finest dispositions for it in the world;—his head like a smoke-jack;—the funnel unswept, and the ideas whirling round and round about in it, all obfuscated and darkened over with fuliginous matter! ——By the tomb-stone of Lucian,—if it is in being;—if not, why then by his ashes! by the ashes of my dear Rabelais, and dearer Cervantes!——my father and my uncle Toby's discourse upon TIME and ETERNITY,—was a discourse devoutly to be wished for! and the petulancy of my father's humor, in putting a stop to it as he did, was a robbery of the *Ontologic Treasury* of such a jewel, as no coalition of great occasions and great men are ever likely to restore to it again.

CHAP. XX.

THOUGH my father persisted in not going on with the discourse—yet he could not get my uncle Toby's smoke-jack out of his head,—piqued as he was at first with it;—there was something in the comparison at bottom which hit his fancy; for which purpose, resting his elbow upon the table, and reclining the right side of his head upon the palm of his hand,—but looking first stedfastly in the fire,—he began to commune with himself, and philosophize about it: but his spirits being worn out by the fatigues of investigating new tracts, and the constant exertion of his faculties upon that variety of subjects which had taken their turn in the discourse—the idea of the smoke-jack soon turned all his ideas upside down,—so that he fell asleep almost before he knew what he was about.

As for my uncle Toby, his smoke-jack had not made a dozen revolutions before he fell asleep also.——Peace be with them both!——Dr. Slop is engaged with the midwife and my mother, above stairs.——Trim is busy in turning an old pair of jackboots into a couple of mortars, to be employed in the siege of Messina next summer;—and is this instant boring a touchhole with the point of a hot poker.——All my heroes are off my hands;—'tis the first time I have had a moment to spare,—and I'll make use of it, and write my preface.

THE AUTHOR'S PREFACE.

No, I'll not say a word about it;——here it is.—In publishing it,—I have appealed to the world,—and to the world I leave it;—it must speak for itself.

All I know of the matter is, when I sat down, my intent was to write a good book; and as far as the tenuity of my understanding would hold out,—a wise, ay, and a discreet; taking care only, as I went along, to put into it all the wit and the judgment (be it more or less) which the great Author and Bestower of them had thought fit originally to give me;—so that, as your Worships see,—'tis just as God pleases.

Now, Agalastes (speaking dispraisingly) saith, That there may be some wit in it, for aught he knows,—but no judgment at all: and Triptolemus and Phutatorius agreeing thereto, ask, How is it possible there should? for that wit and judgment in this world never go together; inasmuch as they are two operations differing from each other as wide as east from west.—So says Locke:—so are farting and hickuping, say I. But in answer to this, Didius the great church-lawyer, in his code *de fartendi et illustrandi fallaciis*, doth maintain and make fully appear, That an illustration is no argument:—nor do I maintain the wiping of a looking-glass clean to be a syllogism;—but you all, may it please your Worships, see the better for it;—so that the main good these things do, is only to clarify the understanding previous to the application of the argument itself, in order to free it from any little motes, or specks of *opacular* matter, which, if left swimming therein, might hinder a conception, and spoil all.

Now, my dear anti-Shandeans, and thrice able critics and fellow-laborers (for to you I write this preface)—and to you, most subtle statesmen and discreet doctors (do,—pull off your beards) renowned for gravity and wisdom;—Monopolus, my politician;—Didius, my counsel;—Kysarcius, my friend;—Phutatorius, my guide;—Gastripheres the preserver of my life;—Somnolentius, the balm and repose of it,—not forgetting all others, as well sleeping as waking, ecclesiastical as civil, whom for brevity, but out of no resentment to you, I lump all together.——Believe me, Right Worthy.

My most zealous wish and fervent prayer in your behalf, and in my own too, in case the thing is not done already for us,—is, That the great gifts and endowments both of wit and judgment, with every thing which usually goes along with them,—such as memory, fancy, genius, eloquence, quick parts, and what not,—may this precious moment, without stint or measure, let or hindrance, be poured down warm as each of us could bear it,—scum and sediment and all (for I would not have a drop lost) into the several receptacles, cells, cellules, domiciles, dormitories, refectories, and spare-places of our brains,——in such sort, that they might continue to be injected and turn'd into, according to the true intent and meaning of my wish, until every vessel of them, both great and small, be so replenish'd, saturated, and filled up therewith, that no more, would it save a man's life, could possibly be got either in or out.

Bless us!—what noble work we should make:—how should I tickle it off!—and what spirits should I find myself in, to be writing away for such readers!—and you,—just Heaven!—with what raptures would you sit and read!—but oh!—'tis too much!—I am sick,—I faint away deliciously at the thoughts of it!—'tis more than nature can bear!—lay hold of me,—I am giddy,—I am stone blind,—I am dying,—I am gone. ——Help! Help! Help!—But hold,—I grow something better again, for I am beginning to foresee, when this is over, that as we shall all of us continue to be great wits,—we should never agree amongst ourselves one day to an end;—there would be so much satire and sarcasm,—scoffing and flouting, with rallying and reparteeing of it,—thrusting and parrying in one corner or another,—there would be nothing but mischief among us.——Chaste stars! what biting and scratching, and what a racket and a clatter we should make, what with breaking of heads, rapping of knuckles, and hitting of sore places,—there would be no such thing as living for us.

But then again, as we should all of us be men of great judgment, we should make up matters as fast as ever they went wrong; and though we should abominate each other ten times worse than so many devils or devilesses, we should nevertheless, my dear creatures, be all courtesy and kindness, milk and honey,—'twould be a second land of promise,—a paradise upon earth, if there was such a thing to be had;—so that, upon the whole, we should have done well enough.

All I fret and fume at, and what most distresses my invention at present, is how to bring the point itself to bear; for as your Worships well know, that of these heavenly emanations of *wit* and *judgment*, which I have so bountifully wished both for your Worships and myself,—there is but a certain *quantum* stored up for us all, for the use and behoof of the whole race of mankind; and such small *modicums* of 'em are only sent forth into this wide world, circulating here and there in one bye-corner or another,—and in such narrow streams, and at such prodigious intervals from each other, that one would wonder how it holds out, or could be sufficient for the wants and emergencies of so many great states and populous empires.

Indeed, there is one thing to be considered: That in Nova Zembla, North Lapland, and in all those cold and dreary tracks of the globe which lie more directly under the arctic and antarctic circles, where the whole province of a man's concernments lies for near nine months together within the narrow compass of his cave,—where the spirits are compressed almost to nothing,—and where the passions of a man, with every thing which belongs to them, are as frigid as the zone itself,—there the least quantity of *judgment* imaginable does the business;—and of *wit*,—there is a total and an absolute saving,—for as not one spark is wanted,—so not one spark is given. Angels and ministers of grace defend us! what a dismal thing would it have been to have governed a kingdom, to have fought a battle, or made a treaty, or run a match, or wrote a book, or got a child, or held a provincial chapter there, with so *plentiful a lack* of wit and judgment about us!—For mercy's sake, let us think no more about it, but travel on as fast as we can southwards into Norway,—crossing over Swedeland, if you please, through the small triangular province of Angermania, to the lake of Bothnia, coasting along it through East and West Bothnia, down to Carelia, and so on, through all those states and provinces which border upon the far side of the Gulf of Finland, and the north-east of the Baltic, up to Petersburgh, and just stepping into Ingria;—then stretching over directly from thence through the north parts of the Russian empire, leaving Siberia a little upon the left hand, till we got into the very heart of Russia and Asiatic Tartary.

Now through this long tour which I have led you, you observe the good people are better off by far, than in the polar countries which we have just left:——for if you hold your hand over your eyes, and look very attentively, you may perceive some small glimmerings (as it were) of wit, with a comfortable provision of good plain household judgment, which, taking the quality and quantity of it together, they make a very good shift with;—and had they either more of one or the other, it would destroy the proper balance betwixt them; and I am satisfied, moreover, they would want occasions to put them to use.

Now, Sir, if I conduct you home again into this warmer and more luxuriant island, where you perceive the spring-tide of our blood and humors runs high;—where we have more ambition, and pride, and envy, and lechery, and other whoreson passions upon our hands to govern and subject to reason,—the *height* of our wit, and the *depth* of our judgment, you see, are exactly proportioned to the *length* and *breadth* of our necessities;—and accordingly we have them sent down amongst us in such a flowing kind of decent and creditable plenty, that no one thinks he has any cause to complain.

It must however be confessed on this head, that, as our air blows hot and cold,—wet and dry, ten times in a day, we have them in no regular and settled way;—so that sometimes for near half a century together, there shall be very little wit or judgment either to be seen or heard of amongst us:—the small channels of them shall seem quite dried up;—then all of a sudden the sluices shall break out, and take a fit of running again like fury,—you would think they would never stop:——and then it is that, in writing, and fighting, and twenty other gallant things, we drive all the world before us.

It is by these observations, and a wary reasoning by analogy in that kind of argumentative process, which Suidas calls *dialectic induction*,—that I draw and set up this position as most true and veritable:

That of these two luminaries, so much of their irradiations are suffered from time to time to shine down upon us, as He, whose infinite wisdom which dispenses every thing in exact weight and measure, knows will just serve to light us on our way in this night of our obscurity; so that your Reverences and Worships now find out, nor is it a moment longer in my power to conceal it from you, That the fervent wish in your behalf with which I set out, was no more than the first insinuating *How d'ye* of a caressing prefacer, stifling his reader, as a lover sometimes does a coy mistress, into silence. For alas! could this effusion of light have been as easily procured, as the exordium wished it,—I tremble to think how many thousands for it, of benighted travellers (in the learned sciences at least) must have groped and blundered on in the dark, all the nights of their lives,—running their heads against posts, and knocking out their brains, without ever getting to their journey's end;—some falling with their noses perpendicularly into sinks;—others horizontally with their tails into kennels:—Here one half of a learned profession tilting *full but* against the other half of it; and then tumbling and rolling one over the other in the dirt like hogs:—Here the brethren of another profession, who should have run in opposition to each other, flying on the contrary, like a flock of wild geese, all in a row the same way.—What confusion!—what mistakes!—fiddlers and painters judging by their eyes and ears—admirable!—trusting to the passions excited,—in an air sung, or a story painted to the heart,—instead of measuring them by a quadrant!

In the fore-ground of this picture, a *statesman* turning the political wheel, like a brute, the wrong way round—*against* the stream of corruption,—by Heaven!—instead of *with* it!

In this corner, a son of the divine Esculapius, writing a book against predestination; perhaps worse,—feeling his patient's pulse instead of his apothecary's:—a brother of the Faculty in the back-ground upon his knees in tears,—drawing the curtains of a mangled victim, to beg his forgiveness:—offering a fee, instead of taking one.

In that spacious HALL, a coalition of the gown, from all the bars of it, driving a damn'd, dirty, vexatious cause before them, with all their might and main, the wrong way!—kicking it *out* of the great doors instead of *in!*—and with such fury in their looks, and such a degree of inveteracy in their manner of kicking it, as if the laws had been originally made for the peace and preservation of mankind;——perhaps a more enormous mistake committed by them still,—a litigated point fairly hung up;—for instance, Whether *John o'Nokes* his nose could stand in *Tom o'Stiles* his face, without a trespass, or not?—rashly determined by them in five-and-twenty minutes, which, with the cautious pro's and con's required in so intricate a proceeding, might have taken up as many months;—and if carried on upon a military plan, as your Honors know an ACTION should be, with all the stratagems practicable therein,—such as feints,—forced marches,—surprises—ambuscades,—mask-batteries, and a thousand other strokes of generalship, which consist in catching at all advantages on both sides,—might reasonably have lasted them as many years, finding food and raiment all that term for a centumvirate of the profession.

As for the Clergy,—No;—if I say a word against them, I'll be shot.——I have no desire; and besides, if I had,—I durst not for my soul touch upon the subject. With such weak nerves and spirits, and in the condition I am in at present, 'twould be as much as my life was worth, to deject and contrist myself with so bad and melancholy an account;—and therefore 'tis safer to draw a curtain across, and hasten from it, as fast as I can, to the main and principal point I have undertaken to clear up;—and that is, How it comes to pass, that your men of least *wit* are reported to be men of most *judgment?*—But mark—I say, *reported to be;*—for it is no more, my dear Sirs, than a report, and which, like twenty others taken up every day upon trust, I maintain to be a vile and a malicious report into the bargain.

This, by the help of the observation already premised, and I hope already weighed and perpended by your Reverences and Worships, I shall forthwith make appear.

I hate set dissertations; and, above all things in the world, 'tis one of the silliest things in one of them, to darken your hypothesis by placing a number of tall, opake words, one before another, in a right line, betwixt your own and your reader's conception,—when, in all likelihood, if you had looked about, you might have seen something standing, or hanging up, which would have cleared the point at once;—"for what hindrance, "hurt, or harm doth the laudable desire of "knowledge bring to any man, if even "from a sot, a pot, a fool, a stool, a winter-"mitten, a truckle for a pulley, the lid of a "goldsmith's crucible, an oil-bottle, an old "slipper, or a cane-chair?"—I am this moment sitting upon one. Will you give me leave to illustrate this affair of wit and judgment, by the two knobs on the top of the back of it?—they are fastened on, you see, with two pegs stuck slightly into two gimblet-holes, and will place what I have to say in so clear a light, as to let you see through the drift and meaning of my whole preface, as plainly as if every point and particle of it was made up of sun-beams.

I enter now directly upon the point.

—Here stands *wit*,—and there stands *judgment*, close beside it, just like the two knobs I'm speaking of, upon the back of this self-same chair on which I am sitting.

You see, they are the highest and most ornamental parts of its *frame*,—as wit and judgment are of *ours*,—and, like them too, indubitably both made and fitted to go together, in order, as we may say in all such cases of duplicated embellishment, *to answer one another.*

Now, for the sake of an experiment, and for the clearer illustrating this matter,—let us for a moment take off one of these two curious ornaments (I care not which) from the point or pinnacle of the chair it now stands on;—nay, don't laugh at it,—but did you ever see, in the whole course of your lives, such a ridiculous business as this has made of it?—Why, 'tis as miserable a sight as a sow with one ear; and there is just as much sense and symmetry in the one as in the other.——Do,—pray, get off your seats, only to take a view of it.—Now, would any man who valued his character a straw, have turned a piece of work out of his hand in such a condition?—Nay, lay your hands upon your hearts, and answer this plain question, Whether this one single knob, which now stands here like a blockhead by itself, can serve any purpose upon earth, but to put one in mind of the want of the other?—and let me farther ask, in case the chair was your own, if you would not in your consciences think, rather than be as it is, that it would be ten times better without any knobs at all?

Now these two knobs, or top-ornaments of the mind of man, which crown the whole entablature,—being, as I said, wit and judgment, which, of all others, as I have proved it, are the most needful,—the most priz'd, —the most calamitous to be without, and consequently the hardest to come at;—for all these reasons put together, there is not a mortal among us so destitute of a love of good fame or feeding,—or so ignorant of what will do him good therein,—who does not wish and stedfastly resolve in his own mind, to be, or to be thought at least, master of the one or the other, and indeed of both of them, if the thing seems any way feasible, or likely to be brought to pass.

Now, your graver gentry having little or no kind of chance in aiming at the one,—unless they laid hold of the other,—pray what do you think would become of them? ——Why, Sirs, in spite of all their *gravities*, they must e'en have been contented to have gone with their insides naked:—this was not to be borne but by an effort of philosophy not to be supposed in the case we are upon;—so that no one could well have been angry with them, had they been satisfied with what little they could have snatched up and secreted under their cloaks and great periwigs, had they not raised a *hue* and *cry* at the same time against the lawful owners.

I need not tell your Worships, that this was done with so much cunning and artifice,—that the great Locke, who was seldom outwitted by false sounds,—was nevertheless bubbled here.——The cry, it seems, was so deep and solemn a one, and what with the help of great wigs, grave faces, and other implements of deceit, was rendered so general a one against the *poor wits* in this matter, that the philosopher himself was deceived by it:—it was his glory to free the world from the lumber of a thousand vulgar errors;—but this was not of the number; so that, instead of sitting down coolly, as such a philosopher should have done, to have examined the matter of fact before he philosophized upon it,—on the contrary he took the fact for granted, and so join'd in with the cry, and halloo'd it as boisterously as the rest.

This has been made the Magna Charta of stupidity ever since:—but your Reverences plainly see, it has been obtained in such a manner, that the title to it is not worth a groat:——which, by the bye, is one of the many and vile impositions which gravity and grave folks have to answer for hereafter.

As for great wigs, upon which I may be thought to have spoken my mind too freely, —I beg leave to qualify whatever has been unguardedly said to their dispraise or prejudice, by one general declaration,—That I have no abhorrence whatever, nor do I detest and abjure either great wigs or long beards, any farther than when I see they are bespoke and let grow on purpose to carry on this self-same imposture,—for any purpose.—Peace be with them!—☞ Mark only,—I write not for them.

CHAP. XXI.

Every day for at least ten years together, did my father resolve to have it mended:—'tis not mended yet.—No family but ours would have borne with it an hour;—and, what is most astonishing, there was not a subject in the world upon which my father was so eloquent, as upon that of door-hinges:——and yet at the same time, he was certainly one of the greatest bubbles to them, I think, that history can produce: his rhetoric and conduct were at perpetual handy-cuffs.—Never did the parlor-door open,—but his philosophy or his principles fell a victim to it.—Three drops of oil with a feather, and a smart stroke of a hammer, had saved his honor for ever.

——Inconsistent soul that man is!—languishing under wounds, which he has the power to heal!—his whole life a contradiction to his knowledge!—his reason, that precious gift of God to him,—(instead of pouring in oil) serving but to sharpen his sensibilities,—to multiply his pains, and render him more melancholy and uneasy under them!—Poor unhappy creature, that he should do so!—Are not the necessary causes of misery in this life enough, but he must add voluntary ones to his stock of sorrow!—struggle against evils which cannot be avoided!—and submit to others, which a tenth part of the trouble they create him would remove from his heart for ever!

By all that is good and virtuous, if there are three drops of oil to be got, and a hammer to be found within ten miles of Shandy-hall,—the parlor door-hinge shall be mended this reign.

CHAP. XXII.

When Corporal Trim had brought his two mortars to bear, he was delighted with his handywork above measure; and knowing what a pleasure it would be to his master to see them, he was not able to resist the desire he had of carrying them directly into his parlor.

Now, next to the moral lesson I had in view in mentioning the affair of *hinges*, I had a speculative consideration arising out of it, and it is this:—

Had the parlor-door opened and turn'd upon its hinges, as a door should do,—

Or, for example, as cleverly as our government has been turning upon its hinges,—(that is, in case things have all along gone well with your Worship,—otherwise I give up my simile)—in this case, I say, there had been no danger, either to master or man, in Corporal Trim's peeping in: the moment he had beheld my father and my uncle Toby fast asleep,—the respectfulness of his carriage was such, he would have retired as silent as death, and left them both in their arm-chairs, dreaming as happy as he had found them: but the thing was, morally speaking, so very impracticable, that for the many years in which this hinge was suffered to be out of order, and amongst the hourly grievances my father submitted to upon its account,—this was one; that he never folded his arms to take his nap after dinner, but the thoughts of being unavoidably awakened by the first person who should open the door, was always uppermost in his imagination, and so incessantly stepp'd in betwixt him and the first balmy presage of his repose, as to rob him, as he often declared, of the whole sweets of it.

"When things move upon bad hinges, "an' please your Worships, how can it be "otherwise?"

Pray what's the matter? who is there? cried my father, waking, the moment the door began to creak.——I wish the smith would give a peep at that confounded hinge.——'Tis nothing, an' please your Honor, said Trim, but two mortars I am bringing in.——They shan't make a clatter with them here, cried my father hastily.——If Dr. Slop has any drugs to pound, let him do it in the kitchen.——May it please your Honor, cried Trim, they are two mortar-pieces for a siege next summer, which I have been making out of a pair of jack-boots, which Obadiah told me your Honor had left off wearing.——By Heaven! cried my father, springing out of his chair, as he swore,—I have not one appointment belonging to me which I set so much store by, as I do by these jack-boots:—they were our great-grandfather's, brother Toby:—they were *hereditary*.——Then I fear, quoth my uncle Toby, Trim has cut off the entail.——I have only cut off the tops, an' please your Honor, cried Trim.——I hate *perpetuities* as much as any man alive, cried my father,—but these jack-boots, continued he (smiling, though very angry at the same time), have been in the family, brother, ever since the civil wars;—Sir Roger Shandy wore them at the battle of Marston-Moor.—I declare I would not have taken ten pounds for them.——I'll pay you the money, brother Shandy, quoth my uncle Toby, looking at the two mortars with infinite pleasure, and putting his hand into his breeches'-pocket, as he viewed them,—I'll pay you the ten pounds this moment, with all my heart and soul.——

Brother Toby, replied my father, altering his tone, you care not what money you dissipate and throw away, provided, continued he, 'tis but upon a SIEGE.——Have I not one hundred and twenty pounds a year, besides my half-pay? cried my uncle Toby. ——What is that,—replied my father hastily,—to ten pounds for a pair of jack-boots? —twelve guineas for your *pontoons*?—half as much for your Dutch draw-bridge?—to say nothing of the train of little brass artillery you bespoke last week, with twenty other preparations for the siege of Messina! Believe me, dear brother Toby, continued my father, taking him kindly by the hand, —these military operations of yours are above your strength:—you mean well, brother,—but they carry you into greater expenses than you were at first aware of;—and take my word, dear Toby, they will in the end quite ruin your fortune, and make a beggar of you.——What signifies it if they do, brother, replied my uncle Toby, so long as we know 'tis for the good of the nation?——

My father could not help smiling for his soul:—his anger at the worst was never more than a spark; and the zeal and simplicity of Trim,—and the generous (though hobby-horsical) gallantry of my uncle Toby, brought him into perfect good humor with them in an instant.

Generous souls!—God prosper you both, and your mortar-pieces too! quoth my father to himself.

CHAP. XXIII.

ALL is quiet and hush, cried my father, at least above stairs:—I hear not one foot stirring.—Prithee, Trim, who's in the kitchen?——There is no one soul in the kitchen, answered Trim, making a low bow as he spoke, except Dr. Slop.——Confusion! cried my father (getting up upon his legs a second time)—not one single thing has gone right this day! Had I faith in astrology, brother, (which, by the bye, my father had) I would have sworn some retrograde planet was hanging over this unfortunate house of mine, and turning every individual thing in it out of its place.—Why, I thought Dr. Slop had been above stairs with my wife; and so said you.—What can the fellow be puzzling about in the kitchen!——He is busy, an' please your Honor, replied Trim, in making a bridge.——'Tis very obliging in him, quoth my uncle Toby:——pray give my humble service to Dr. Slop, Trim, and tell him I thank him heartily.

You must know, my uncle Toby mistook the bridge,—as widely as my father mistook the mortars:—but to understand how my uncle Toby could mistake the bridge,—I fear I must give you an exact account of the road which led to it;—or, to drop my metaphor (for there is nothing more dishonest in an historian than the use of one) —in order to conceive the probability of this error in my uncle Toby aright, I must give you some account of an adventure of Trim's, though much against my will; I say much against my will, only because the story, in one sense, is certainly out of its place here; for by right, it should come in, either amongst the anecdotes of my uncle Toby's amours with Widow Wadman, in which Corporal Trim was no mean actor, —or else in the middle of his and my uncle Toby's campaigns on the bowling-green, for it will do very well in either place;—but then if I reserve it for either of those parts of my story,—I ruin the story I'm upon;—and if I tell it here,—I anticipate matters, and ruin it there.

—What would your Worships have me to do in this case?

—Tell it, Mr. Shandy, by all means.——You are a fool, Tristram, if you do.

O ye powers! (for powers ye are, and great ones too)—which enable mortal man to tell a story worth the hearing,—that kindly show him where he is to begin it,—and where he is to end it,—what he is to put into it,—and what he is to leave out,—how much of it he is to cast into a shade,—and whereabouts he is to throw his light!—Ye who preside over this vast empire of biographical freebooters, and see how many scrapes and plunges your subjects hourly fall into,—will you do one thing?

I beg and beseech you (in case you will do nothing better for us), that wherever in any part of your dominions it so falls out, that three several roads meet in one point, as they have done just here,—that at least you set up a guide-post in the centre of them, in mere charity, to direct an uncertain devil which of the three he is to take.

CHAP. XXIV.

THOUGH the shock my uncle Toby received the year after the demolition of Dunkirk, in his affair with Widow Wadman, had fixed him in a resolution never more to think of the sex,—or of aught which belonged to it;—yet Corporal Trim had made no such bargain with himself.—Indeed, in my uncle Toby's case there was a strange and unaccountable concurrence of circumstances, which insensibly drew him in, to lay siege to that fair and strong citadel.—In Trim's case there was a concurrence of nothing in the world, but of him and Bridget in the kitchen;—though in truth, the love and veneration he bore his master was such, and so fond was he of imitating him in all he did, that had my uncle Toby employed his time and genius in tagging of points,—I am persuaded the honest Corporal would have laid down his arms, and followed his example with pleasure. When therefore my uncle Toby sat down before the mistress,—Corporal Trim incontinently took ground before the maid.

Now, my dear friend Garrick, whom I have so much cause to esteem and honor—(why or wherefore, 'tis no matter)—can it escape your penetration,—I defy it,—that so many playwrights, and opificers of chit-chat, have ever since been working upon Trim's and my uncle Toby's pattern?—I care not what Aristotle, or Pacuvius, or Bossu, or Ricaboni, say—(though I never read one of them)—there is not a greater difference between a single-horse chair and Madam Pompadour's *vis à vis*, than betwixt a single amour and an amour thus nobly doubled, and going upon all-four, prancing throughout a grand drama.—Sir, a simple, single, silly affair of that kind,—is quite lost in five acts;—but that is neither here nor there.

After a series of attacks and repulses in a course of nine months on my uncle Toby's quarter, a most minute account of every particular of which shall be given in its proper place, my uncle Toby, honest man! found it necessary to draw off his forces and raise the siege somewhat indignantly.

Corporal Trim, as I said, had made no such bargain either with himself,—or with any one else;—the fidelity however of his heart not suffering him to go into a house which his master had forsaken with disgust,—he contented himself with turning his part of the siege into a blockade;—that is, he kept others off;—for though he never afterwards went to the house, yet he never met Bridget in the village but he would either nod, or wink, or smile, or look kindly at her,—or (as circumstances directed) he would shake her by the hand,—or ask her lovingly how she did,—or would give her a ribbon,—and now and then, though never but when it could be done with decorum, would give Bridget a ——.

Precisely in this situation did these things stand for five years; that is, from the demolition of Dunkirk in the year thirteen, to the latter end of my uncle Toby's campaign in the year eighteen, which was about six or seven weeks before the time I'm speaking of,——when Trim, as his custom was, after he had put my uncle Toby to bed, going down one moon-shiny night to see that every thing was right at his fortifications,—in the lane separated from the bowling-green with flowering shrubs and holly,—he espied his Bridget.

As the Corporal thought there was nothing in the world so well worth showing as the glorious works which he and my uncle Toby had made, Trim courteously and gallantly took her by the hand, and led her in. This was not done so privately, but that the foul-mouth'd trumpet of Fame carried it from ear to ear, till at length it reach'd my father's, with this untoward circumstance along with it, that my uncle Toby's curious draw-bridge, constructed and painted after the Dutch fashion, and which went quite across the ditch,—was broke down, and somehow or other crushed all to pieces, that very night.

My father, as you have observed, had no great esteem for my uncle Toby's HOBBY-HORSE; he thought it the most ridiculous horse that ever gentleman mounted; and indeed, unless my uncle Toby vexed him about it, could never think of it once, without smiling at it;—so that it could never get lame, or happen any mischance, but it tickled my father's imagination beyond measure; but this being an accident much more to his humor than any one which had yet befallen it, it proved an inexhaustible fund of entertainment to him.—Well,—but dear Toby! my father would say, do tell me seriously how this affair of the bridge happened.——How can you tease me so much about it? my uncle Toby would reply;—I have told it you twenty times, word for word, as Trim told it me.——Prithee, now was it then, Corporal? my father would cry, turning to Trim.——It was a mere misfortune, an' please your Honor;—I was showing Mrs. Bridget our fortifications; and in going too near the edge of the *fossé*, I unfortunately slipp'd in——Very well, Trim! my father would cry—(smiling mysteriously, and giving a nod,—but without interrupting him)——and being link'd fast, an' please your Honor, arm in arm with Mrs. Bridget, I dragg'd her after me; by means of which she fell backwards soss against the bridge;—and Trim's foot (my uncle Toby would cry, taking the story out of his mouth) getting into the cuvette, he tumbled full against the bridge too.——It was a thousand to one, my uncle Toby would add, that the poor fellow did not break his leg.——Ay, truly, my father would say,—a limb is soon broke, brother Toby, in such encounters.——And so, an' please your Honor, the bridge, which your Honor knows was a very slight one, was broke down betwixt us, and splintered all to pieces.

At other times, but especially when my uncle Toby was so unfortunate as to say a syllable about cannons, bombs, or petards,—my father would exhaust all the stores of his eloquence (which indeed were very great) in a panegyric upon the battering-rams of the ancients—the vinea which Alexander made use of at the siege of Troy.—He would tell my uncle Toby of the *catapultæ* of the Syrians, which threw such monstrous stones so many hundred feet, and shook the strongest bulwarks from their very foundations;—he would go on and describe the wonderful mechanism of the *balista*, which Marcellinus makes so much rout about!—the terrible effects of the *pyraboli*, which cast fire;—the danger of the *terebra* and *scorpio*, which cast javelins.—But what are these, would he say, to the destructive machinery of Corporal Trim!—Believe me, brother Toby, no bridge or bastion, or sally-port, that ever was constructed in this world, can hold out against such artillery.

My uncle Toby would never attempt any defence against the force of this ridicule, but that of redoubling the vehemence of smoking his pipe; in doing which, he raised so dense a vapor one night after supper, that it set my father, who was a little phthisical, into a suffocating fit of violent coughing; my uncle Toby leap'd up, without feeling the pain upon his groin,—and, with infinite pity, stood beside his brother's chair, tapping his back with one hand, and holding his head with the other, and from time to time wiping his eyes with a clean cambric handkerchief, which he pull'd out of his pocket. The affectionate and endearing manner in which my uncle Toby did these little offices,—cut my father through his reins, for the pain he had just been giving him.——May my brains be knock'd out with a battering-ram or a catapulta, I care not which, quoth my father to himself—if ever I insult this worthy soul more!

CHAP. XXV.

The draw-bridge being held irreparable, Trim was ordered directly to set about another,——but not upon the same model; for Cardinal Alberoni's intrigues at that time being discovered, and my uncle Toby rightly foreseeing that a flame would inevitably break out betwixt Spain and the Empire, and that the operations of the ensuing campaign must in all likelihood be either in Naples or Sicily,—he determined upon an Italian bridge—(my uncle Toby, by the bye, was not far out of his conjectures);—but my father, who was infinitely the better politician, and took the lead as far of my uncle Toby in the cabinet, as my uncle Toby took it of him in the field,—convinced him that if the King of Spain and the Emperor went together by the ears,—England France, and Holland, must, by force of their pre-engagements, all enter the lists too;—

and if so, he would say, the combatants, brother Toby, as sure as we are alive, will fall to it again, pell-mell, upon the old prize-fighting stage of Flanders,—then what will you do with your Italian bridge?

We will go on with it then upon the old model, cried my uncle Toby.

When Corporal Trim had about half finished it in that style,—my uncle Toby found out a capital defect in it, which he had never thoroughly considered before. It turned, it seems, upon hinges at both ends of it, opening in the middle, one half of which turning to one side of the fossé, and the other to the other; the advantage of which was this, that by dividing the weight of the bridge into two equal portions, it empowered my uncle Toby to raise it up or let it down with the end of his crutch, and with one hand, which, as his garrison was weak, was as much as he could well spare;—but the disadvantages of such a construction were insurmountable;—for by this means, he would say, I leave one half of my bridge in my enemy's possession;—and pray, of what use is the other?

The natural remedy for this was, no doubt, to have his bridge fast only at one end with hinges, so that the whole might be lifted up together, and stand bolt upright;—but that was rejected, for the reason given above.

For a whole week after, he was determined in his mind to have one of that particular construction which is made to draw back horizontally, to hinder a passage; and to thrust forwards again, to gain a passage,—of which sorts your Worships might have seen three famous ones at Spires before its destruction—and one now at Brisac, if I mistake not;—but my father advising my uncle Toby, with great earnestness, to have nothing more to do with thrusting bridges;—and my uncle foreseeing moreover that it would but perpetuate the memory of the Corporal's misfortune,—he changed his mind for that of the Marquis d'Hôpital's invention, which the younger Bernouilli has so well and learnedly described, as your Worships may see——— *Act. Erud. Lips.* an. 1695:—to these a lead weight is an eternal balance, and keeps watch as well as a couple of sentinels, inasmuch as the construction of them was a curve line approximating to a cycloid——if not a cycloid itself.

My uncle Toby understood the nature of a parabola as well as any man in England:—but was not quite such a master of the cycloid:—he talked however about it every day——the bridge went not forwards.——We'll ask somebody about it, cried my uncle Toby to Trim.

CHAP. XXVI.

When Trim came in and told my father, that Dr. Slop was in the kitchen, and busy in making a bridge,—my uncle Toby,——the affair of the jack-boots having just then raised a train of military ideas in his brain,——took it instantly for granted that Dr. Slop was making a model of the Marquis d'Hôpital's bridge.——'Tis very obliging in him, quoth my uncle Toby;—pray give my humble service to Dr. Slop, Trim, and tell him I thank him heartily.

Had my uncle Toby's head been a Savoyard's box, and my father peeping in all the time at one end of it,—it could not have given him a more distinct conception of the operations of my uncle Toby's imagination than what he had; so, notwithstanding the catapulta and battering-ram, and his bitter imprecation about them, he was just beginning to triumph,—

When Trim's answer in an instant tore the laurel from his brows, and twisted it to pieces.

CHAP. XXVII.

——This unfortunate draw-bridge of yours, quoth my father,——God bless your Honor, cried Trim, 'tis a bridge for master's nose.——In bringing him into the world with his vile instruments, he has crush'd his nose, Susannah says, as flat as a pan-cake to his face, and he is making a false bridge with a piece of cotton, and a thin piece of whalebone out of Susannah's stays, to raise it up.

——Lead me, brother Toby, cried my father, to my room this instant.

CHAP. XXVIII.

From the first moment I sat down to write my life for the amusement of the world, and my opinions for its instruction, has a cloud insensibly been gathering over my father.—A tide of little evils and distresses has been setting in against him.—Not one thing, as he observed himself, has gone right: and now is the storm thicken'd and going to break, and pour down full upon his head.

I enter upon this part of my story in the most pensive and melancholy frame of mind that ever sympathetic breast was touched with.—My nerves relax as I tell it.—Every line I write, I feel an abatement of the quickness of my pulse, and of that careless alacrity with it, which every day of my life prompts me to say and write a thousand things I should not:—and this moment, that I last dipp'd my pen into my ink, I could not help taking notice what a cautious air of sad composure and solemnity there appear'd in my manner of doing it.—Lord! how different from the rash jerks and hare-brain'd squirts thou art wont, Tristram, to transact it with in other humors—dropping thy pen,—spurting thy ink about thy table and thy books,—as if thy pen and thy ink, thy books and thy furniture, cost thee nothing!

CHAP. XXIX.

——I won't go about to argue the point with you:—'tis so;—and I am persuaded of it, Madam, as much as can be, "That "both man and woman bear pain or sorrow "(and, for aught I know, pleasure too) best "in a horizontal position."

The moment my father got up into his chamber, he threw himself prostrate across his bed in the wildest disorder imaginable, but at the same time in the most lamentable attitude of a man borne down with sorrows, that ever the eye of pity dropp'd a tear for.—The palm of his right hand, as he fell upon the bed, receiving his forehead, and covering the greatest part of both his eyes, gently sunk down with his head (his elbow giving way backwards) till his nose touch'd the quilt; his left arm hung insensibly over the side of the bed, his knuckles reclining upon the handle of the chamber-pot, which peep'd out beyond the valance;—his right leg (his left being drawn up towards his body) hung half over the side of the bed, the edge of it pressing upon his shin-bone,—He felt it not. A fix'd, inflexible sorrow took possession of every line of his face.—He sigh'd once,—heav'd his breast often,—but uttered not a word.

An old set-stitch'd chair, valanced and fringed around with party-colored worsted bobs, stood at the bed's head, opposite to the side where my father's head reclin'd.—My uncle Toby sat him down in it.

Before an affliction is digested,—consolation ever comes too soon;—and after it is digested,—it comes too late; so that you see, Madam, there is but a mark between these two, as fine almost as a hair, for a comforter to take aim at.—My uncle Toby was always either on this side or on that of it, and would often say, he believed in his heart he could as soon hit the longitude; for this reason, when he sat down in the chair, he drew the curtain a little forwards, and having a tear at every one's service,—he pull'd out a cambric handkerchief,—gave a low sigh,—but held his peace.

CHAP. XXX.

——"All is not gain that is got into the "purse."——So that, notwithstanding my father had the happiness of reading the oddest books in the universe, and had, moreover, in himself, the oddest way of thinking that ever man in it was bless'd with, yet it had this drawback upon him after all,——That it laid him open to some of the oddest and most whimsical distresses; of which this particular one, which he sunk under at present, is as strong an example as can be given.

No doubt, the breaking down of the bridge of a child's nose, by the edge of a pair of forceps,—however scientifically applied.—would vex any man in the world who was at so much pains in begetting a child as my father was;—yet it will not account for the extravagance of his affliction, nor will it justify the unchristian manner he abandoned and surrendered himself up to.

To explain this, I must leave him upon the bed for half an hour,—and my uncle Toby, in his old fringed chair, sitting beside him.

CHAP. XXXI.

——I THINK it a very unreasonable demand, cried my great-grandfather, twisting up the paper, and throwing it upon the table. ——By this account, Madam, you have but two thousand pounds fortune, and not a shilling more;—and you insist upon having three hundred pounds a year jointure for it.——

—"Because," replied my great-grandmother, "you have little or no nose, Sir."——

Now, before I venture to make use of the word *Nose* a second time,—to avoid all confusion in what will be said upon it, in this interesting part of my story, it may not be amiss to explain my own meaning, and define, with all possible exactness and precision, what I would willingly be understood to mean by the term: being of opinion, that 'tis owing to the negligence and perverseness of writers in despising this precaution, and to nothing else,—that all the polemical writings in divinity are not as clear and demonstrative as those upon *a Will o' the Wisp*, or any other sound part of philosophy and natural pursuit; in order to which, what have you to do, before you set out, unless you intend to go puzzling on to the day of judgment,—but to give the world a good definition, and stand to it, of the main word you have most occasion for, —changing it, Sir, as you would a guinea, into small coin,—which done, let the father of confusion puzzle you, if he can; or put a different idea either into your head, or your reader's head, if he knows how.

In books of strict morality and close reasoning, such as this I am engaged in,—the neglect is unexcusable; and heaven is witness how the world has revenged itself upon me for leaving so many openings to equivocal strictures.—and for depending so much as I have done, all along, upon the cleanliness of my readers' imaginations.—

——Here are two senses, cried Eugenius as we walk'd along, pointing with the fore-finger of his right hand to the word *crevice*, in the forty-eighth page of this book of books: ——here are two senses,—quoth he.—And here are two roads, replied I, turning short upon him,—a dirty and a clean one,—which shall we take?——The clean, by all means, replied Eugenius.——Eugenius, said I, stepping before him, and laying my hand upon his breast,—to define is to distrust.— Thus I triumphed over Eugenius; but I triumphed over him, as I always do, like a fool.—'Tis my comfort, however, I am not an obstinate one: therefore,

I define a nose as follows,—entreating only beforehand, and beseeching my readers, both male and female, of what age, complexion, and condition soever, for the love of God and their own souls, to guard against the temptations and suggestions of the Devil, and suffer him by no art or wile to put any other ideas into their minds than what I put into my definition:—for by the word *Nose*, throughout all this long chapter of noses, and in every other part of my work where the word *Nose* occurs,—I declare by that word I mean a nose, and nothing more or less.

CHAP. XXXII.

——"BECAUSE," quoth my great-grand mother, repeating the words again,—"you "have little or no nose, Sir."——

S'death! cried my great-grandfather, clapping his hand upon his nose,—'tis not so small as that comes to;—'tis a full inch longer than my father's.——Now, my great-grandfather's nose was for all the world like unto the noses of all the men, women, and children whom Pantagruel found dwelling upon the island of Ennasin.—By the way, if you would know the strange way of getting a-kin amongst so flat-nosed a people, you must read the book;—find it out yourself you never can.——

—'Twas shaped, Sir, like an ace of clubs.

——'Tis a full inch, continued my great-grandfather, pressing up the ridge of his nose with his finger and thumb; and repeating his assertion,—'tis a full inch longer

Madam, than my father's.——You must mean your uncle's, replied my great-grandmother.

——My great-grandfather was convinced.—He untwisted the paper, and signed the article.

CHAP. XXXIII.

——What an unconscionable jointure, my dear do we pay out of this small estate of ours! quoth my grandmother to my grandfather.——

My father, replied my grandfather, had no more nose, my dear, saving the mark, than there is upon the back of my hand.——

Now, you must know, that my great-grandmother outlived my grandfather twelve years; so that my father had the jointure to pay, a hundred and fifty pounds half-yearly—(on Michaelmas and Lady-day)—during all that time.

No man discharged pecuniary obligations with a better grace than my father;—and as far as a hundred pounds went, he would fling it upon the table, guinea by guinea, with that spirited jerk of an honest welcome, with which generous souls, and generous souls only, are able to fling down money: but as soon as ever he enter'd upon the odd fifty,—he generally gave a loud *hem!* rubb'd the side of his nose leisurely with the flat part of his fore-finger,—inserted his hand cautiously betwixt his head and the cawl of his wig,—look'd at both sides of every guinea as he parted with it,—and seldom could get to the end of the fifty pounds, without pulling out his handkerchief, and wiping his temples.

Defend me, gracious Heaven! from those persecuting spirits who make no allowance for these workings within us.—Never,—O never may I lay down in their tents, who cannot relax the engine, and feel pity for the force of education, and the prevalence of opinions long derived from ancestors.

For three generations at least, this *tenet* in favor of long noses had gradually been taking root in our family.—Tradition was all along on its side, and Interest was every half-year stepping in to strengthen it; so that the whimsicality of my father's brain was so far from having the whole honor of this, as it had of almost all his other strange notions;—for in a great measure, he might have said to have suck'd this in with his mother's milk. He did his part, however.—If education planted the mistake (in case it was one) my father watered it, and ripened it to perfection.

He would often declare, in speaking his thoughts upon the subject, that he did not conceive how the greatest family in England could stand it out against an uninterrupted succession of six or seven short noses.—And, for the contrary reason, he would generally add, That it must be one of the greatest problems in civil life, where the same number of long and jolly noses, following one another in a direct line, did not raise and hoist it up into the best vacancies in the kingdom.—He would often boast that the Shandy Family rank'd very high in king Harry the VIIIth's time; but owed its rise to no state engine,—he would say,—but to that only;—but that, like other families, he would add,—it had left the turn of the wheel, and had never recovered the blow of my great-grandfather's nose.—It was an ace of clubs indeed, he would cry, shaking his head:—and as vile a one for an unfortunate family as ever turn'd up trumps.

——Fair and softly, gentle reader!—where is thy fancy carrying thee!—If there is truth in man, by my great-grandfather's nose, I mean the external organ of smelling, or that part of man which stands prominent in his face,—and which, painters say, in good jolly noses and well-proportioned faces, should comprehend a full third!—that is, measured downwards from the setting on of the hair.——

——What a life of it has an author, at this pass!

CHAP. XXXIV.

It is a singular blessing, that nature has form'd the mind of man with the same happy backwardness and renitency against conviction, which is observed in old dogs,—"of not learning new tricks."

What a shuttlecock of a fellow would the greatest philosopher that ever existed be whisk'd into at once, did he read such books, and observe such facts, and think such thoughts, as would eternally be making him change sides!

Now, my father, as I told you last year, detested all this:—He pick'd up an opinion, Sir, as a man in a state of nature picks up an apple:—it becomes his own:—and if he is a man of spirit, he would lose his life rather than give it up.

I am aware that Didius, the great civilian, will contest this point, and cry out against me, Whence comes this man's right to this apple? *ex confesso*, he will say,—things were in a state of nature;—the apple is as much Frank's apple as John's.—Pray, Mr. Shandy, what patent has he to show for it? and how did it begin to be his? was it when he set his heart upon it? or when he gathered it? or when he chew'd it? or when he roasted it? or when he peel'd, or when he brought it home? or when he digested? —or when he——?—For 'tis plain, Sir, if the first picking up of the apple, made it not his,—that no subsequent act could.

Brother Didius, Tribonius will answer—(now Tribonius the civilian and church-lawyer's beard being three inches and a half, and three-eighths longer than Didius his beard,—I'm glad he takes up the cudgels for me; so I give myself no farther trouble about the answer.)—Brother Didius, Tribonius will say, it is a decreed case, as you may find it in the fragments of Gregorius and Hermogines's codes, and in all the codes from Justinian's down to the codes of Louis and Des Eaux,—that the sweat of a man's brows, and the exudations of a man's brains, are as much a man's own property as the breeches upon his backside;—which said exudations, &c. being dropp'd upon the said apple by the labor of finding it, and picking it up; and being moreover indissolubly wasted, and as indissolubly annex'd, by the picker up, to the thing pick'd up, carried home, roasted, peel'd, eaten, digested, and so on,—'tis evident that the gatherer of the apple, in so doing, has mix'd up something which was his own, with the apple which was not his own; by which means he has acquired a property;—or, in other words, the apple is John's apple.

By the same learned chain of reasoning, my father stood up for all his opinions; he had spared no pains in picking them up; and the more they lay out of the common way, the better still was his title.—No mortal claimed them; they had cost him, moreover, as much labor in cooking and digesting as in the case above; so that they might well and truly be said to be of his own goods and chattels.—Accordingly he held fast by 'em, both by teeth and claws,—would fly to whatever he could lay his hands on,—and, in a word, would intrench and fortify them round with as many circumvallations and breast-works as my uncle Toby would a citadel.

There was one plaguy rub in the way of this:—the scarcity of materials to make any thing of a defence with, in case of a smart attack; inasmuch as few men of great genius had exercised their parts in writing books upon the subject of great noses. By the trotting of my lean horse, the thing is incredible! and I am quite lost in my understanding, when I am considering what a treasure of precious time and talents together has been wasted upon worse objects,—and how many millions of books, in all languages, and in all possible types and bindings, have been fabricated on points not half so much tending to the unity and peace-making of the world! What was to be had, however, he set the greater store by; and though my father would oft-times sport with my uncle Toby's library,—which, by the bye, was ridiculous enough,—yet at the very same time he did it, he collected every book and treatise which had been systematically wrote upon noses, with as much care as my honest uncle Toby had done those upon military architecture.—'Tis true, a much less table would have held them;—but that was not thy transgression, my dear uncle.—

Here,——but why here,—rather than in any other part of my story?——I am not able to tell——but here it is———my heart stops me to pay to thee, my dear uncle Toby, once for all, the tribute I owe thy goodness.—Here let me thrust my chair aside, and kneel down upon the ground whilst I am pouring forth the warmest sentiment of love for thee, and veneration for the excellency of thy character, that ever virtue and nature kindled in a nephew's bosom.—Peace and comfort rest for evermore upon thy head!—Thou enviedst no man's comforts, insultedst no man's opinions;—thou blackenedst no man's character,—devouredst no man's bread! Gentle, with faithful Trim behind thee, didst thou amble round the little circle of pleasure, justling no creature in the way: for each one's sorrows thou hadst a tear;—for each man's need thou hadst a shilling.

Whilst I am worth one to pay a weeder, —thy path from the door to thy bowling-green shall never be grown up.—Whilst there is a rood and a half of land in the Shandy family, thy fortifications, my dear uncle Toby, shall never be demolish'd.

CHAP. XXXV.

My father's collection was not great; but, to make amends, it was curious; and consequently he was some time in making it; he had the great good fortune, however, to set off well, in getting Bruscambille's prologue upon long noses, almost for nothing; —for he gave no more for Bruscambille than three half-crowns, owing indeed to the strong fancy which the stall-man saw my father had for the book, the moment he laid his hands upon it.—There are not three Bruscambilles in Christendom, said the stall-man, except what are chain'd up in the libraries of the curious. My father flung down the money as quick as lightning,—took Bruscambille into his bosom, —hied home from Piccadilly to Coleman-street with it, as he would have hied home with a treasure, without taking his hand once off from Bruscambille all the way.

To those who do not yet know of which gender Bruscambille is,—inasmuch as a prologue upon long noses might easily be done by either,—'twill be no objection against the simile—to say, That when my father got home, he solaced himself with Bruscambille after the manner in which, 'tis ten to one, your Worship solaced yourself with your first mistress!—that is, from morning even unto night: which, by the bye, how delightful soever it may prove to the enamorato,—is of little or no entertainment at all to by-standers.—Take notice, I go no farther with the simile;—my father's eye was greater than his appetite,—his zeal greater than his knowledge,—he cool'd,—his affections became divided;——he got hold of Prignitz, purchased Scroderus, Andrea Paræus, Bouchet's Evening Conferences, and, above all, the great and learned Hafen Slawkenbergius; of which, as I shall have much to say by and by,—I will say nothing now.

CHAP. XXXVI.

Of all the tracts my father was at the pains to procure and study, in support of his hypothesis, there was not any one wherein he felt a more cruel disappointment at first, than the celebrated Dialogue between Pamphagus and Cocles, written by the chaste pen of the great and venerable Erasmus, upon the various uses and seasonable applications of long noses.——Now don't let Satan, my dear girl, in this chapter, take advantage of any one spot of rising ground to get astride of your imagination, if you can any ways help it; or, if he is so nimble as to slip on,—let me beg of you, like an unback'd filly, to *frisk it, to squirt it, to jump it, to rear it, to bound it —and to kick it, with long kicks, and short kicks*, till, like Tickletoby's mare, you break a strap or a crupper, and throw his Worship into the dirt.—You need not kill him.—

—And pray, who was Tickletoby's mare? —'Tis just as discreditable and unscholar-like a question, Sir, as to have asked what year (*ab urb. con.*) the second Punic war broke out.—Who was Tickletoby's mare? ——Read, read, read, read, my unlearned reader!—read,—or, by the knowledge of the great Saint Paraleipomenon,—I tell you beforehand, you had better throw down the book at once; for without *much reading*, by which your Reverence knows I mean *much knowledge*, you will no more be able to penetrate the moral of the next marbled page (motley emblem of my work!) than the world with all its sagacity has been able to unravel the many opinions, transactions, and truths, which still lie mystically hid under the dark veil of the black one

LIFE AND OPINIONS

CHAP. XXXVII.

"*NIHIL me pœnitet hujus nasi,*" quoth Pamphagus;—that is,—"My nose has been the making of me."——"*Nec est cur pœniteat,*" replies Cocles; that is, "How the deuce should such a nose fail?"

The doctrine, you see, was laid down by Erasmus, as my father wished it, with the utmost plainness; but my father's disappointment was, in finding nothing more from so able a pen, but the bare fact itself; without any of that speculative subtilty or ambidexterity of argumentation upon it, which Heaven had bestow'd upon man, on purpose to investigate Truth, and fight for her on all sides.—My father pish'd and pugh'd at first most terribly.——'Tis worth something to have a good name. As the dialogue was of Erasmus, my father soon came to himself, and read it over and over again with great application, studying every word and every syllable of it, through and through, in its most strict and literal interpretation.—He could still make nothing of it, that way. Mayhap, there is more meant than is said in it, quoth my father.—Learned men, brother Toby, don't write dialogues upon long noses for nothing.—I'll study the mystic and the allegoric sense.—Here is some room to turn a man's self in, brother.

My father read on,——

Now I find it needful to inform your Reverences and Worships, that besides the many nautical uses of long noses enumerated by Erasmus, the dialogist affirmeth, That a long nose is not without its domestic conveniences also; for that, in case of distress,—and for want of a pair of bellows, it will do excellently well, *ad excitandum focum* (to stir up the fire).

Nature had been prodigal in her gifts to my father beyond measure, and had sown the seeds of verbal criticism as deep within him, as she had done the seeds of all other knowledge;—so that he had got out his penknife, and was trying experiments upon the sentence, to see if he could not scratch some better sense into it.—I've got within a single letter, brother Toby, cried my father, of Erasmus his mystic meaning.——You are near enough, brother, replied my uncle, in all conscience.——Pshaw! cried my father, scratching on,—I might as well be seven miles off—I've done it,—said my father, snapping his fingers. See, my dear brother Toby, how I have mended the sense.—But you have marr'd a word, replied my uncle Toby.——My father put on his spectacles,—bit his lip,—and tore out the leaf in a passion.

CHAP. XXXVIII.

O SLAWKENBERGIUS! thou faithful analyzer of my Disgrazias,—thou sad foreteller of so many of the whips and short turns which in one stage or other of my life have come slap upon me from the shortness of my nose, and no other cause that I am conscious of,—tell me, Slawkenbergius! what secret impulse was it? what intonation of voice? whence came it?—how did it sound in thy ears?—art thou sure thou heard'st it?—which first cried out to thee,—Go,—go,—Slawkenbergius! dedicate the labors of thy life,—neglect thy pastimes,—call forth all the powers and faculties of thy nature,—macerate thyself in the service of mankind! and write a grand FOLIO for them, upon the subject of their noses.

How the communication was conveyed into Slawkenbergius's sensorium,—so that Slawkenbergius should know whose finger touch'd the key—and whose hand it was that blew the bellows,—as Hafen Slawkenbergius has been dead and laid in his grave above fourscore and ten years,—we can only raise conjectures.

Slawkenbergius was play'd upon, for aught I know, like one of Whitfield's disciples;—that is, with such a distinct intelligence, Sir, of which of the two masters it was that had been practising upon his *instrument,*—as to make all reasoning upon it needless.

——For in the account which Hafen Slawkenbergius gives the world of his motives and occasions for writing, and spending so many years of his life upon this one work,—towards the end of his prolegomena;—which, by the bye, should have come first,—but the bookbinder has most injudiciously placed it betwixt the analytical contents of the book and the book itself,—he informs his reader, That ever since he had arrived at the age of discernment, and was able to sit down coolly, and consider within himself the true state and condition of man, and distinguish the main end and design of his being;—or,—to shorten my translation, for Slawkenbergius's book is in Latin, and not a little prolix in this passage;—ever since I understood, quoth Slawkenbergius, any thing,—or rather *what was what*,—and could perceive that the point of long noses had been too loosely handled by all who had gone before,—have I, Slawkenbergius, felt a strong impulse, with a mighty and unresistible call within me, to gird up myself to this undertaking.

And to do justice to Slawkenbergius, he has entered the list with a stronger lance, and taken a much larger career in it, than any one man who had ever entered it before him:—and indeed, in many respects, deserves to be *en-nich'd* as a prototype for all writers, of voluminous works at least, to model their books by;—for he has taken in, Sir, the whole subject,—examined every part of it *dialectically*,—then brought it into full day; dilucidating it with all the light which either the collision of his own natural parts could strike,—or the profoundest knowledge of the sciences had empowered him to cast upon it;—collating, collecting, and compiling;—begging, borrowing, and stealing, as he went along, all that had been wrote or wrangled thereupon in the schools and porticoes of the learned; so that Slawkenbergius his book may properly be considered, not only as a model,—but as a thorough-stitched DIGEST and regular institute of noses, comprehending in it all that is or can be needful to be known about them

For this cause it is that I forbear to speak of so many (otherwise) valuable books and treatises of my father's collecting, wrote either plump upon noses,—or collaterally touching them;—such for instance as Prignitz, now lying upon the table before me, who with infinite learning, and from the most candid and scholar-like examination of above four thousand different skulls, in upwards of twenty charnel-houses in Silesia, which he had rummaged,—has informed us, that the mensuration and configuration of the osseous or bony parts of human noses, in any given tract of country, except Crim Tartary, where they are all crush'd down by the thumb, so that no judgment can be formed upon them,—are much nearer alike than the world imagines;—the difference amongst them being, he says, a mere trifle, not worth taking notice of;—but that the size and jollity of every individual nose, and by which one nose ranks above another, and bears a higher price, is owing to the cartilaginous and muscular parts of it, into whose ducts and sinuses the blood and animal spirits being impell'd and driven by the warmth and force of the imagination, which is but a step from it (bating the case of idiots, whom Prignitz, who had lived many years in Turkey, supposes under the more immediate tutelage of Heaven)—it so happens, and ever must, says Prignitz, that the excellency of the nose is in a direct arithmetical proportion to the excellency of the wearer's fancy.

It is for the same reason; that is, because 'tis all comprehended in Slawkenbergius, that I say nothing likewise of Scroderus (Andrea) who, all the world knows, set himself to oppugn Prignitz with great violence;—proving it in his own way, first logically, and then by a series of stubborn facts, "That so far was Prignitz from the truth, in affirming that the fancy begat the nose, that, on the contrary,—the nose begat the fancy."

—The learned suspected Scroderus of an indecent sophism in this;—and Prignitz cried out aloud in the dispute, that Scroderus had shifted the idea upon him;—but Scroderus went on maintaining his thesis.

My father was just balancing within himself, which of the two sides he should take in this affair; when Ambrose Paræus decided it in a moment, and, by overthrowing the systems both of Prignitz and Scroderus, drove my father out of both sides of the controversy at once.

Be witness,——

I don't acquaint the learned reader—in saying it,—I mention it only to show the learned, I know the fact myself,——

That this Ambrose Paræus was chief surgeon and nose-mender to Francis the Ninth of France; and in high credit with him and the two preceding, or succeeding kings (I know not which)—and that, except in the slip he made in his story of Taliacotius's noses, and in his manner of setting them on,—he was esteemed by the whole college of physicians at that time, as more knowing in matters of noses, than any one who had ever taken them in hand.

Now, Ambrose Paræus convinced my father, that the true and efficient cause of what had engaged so much the attention of the world, and upon which Prignitz and Scroderus had wasted so much learning and fine parts,—was neither this nor that;—but that the length and goodness of the nose was owing simply to the softness and flaccidity in the nurse's breast,—as the flatness and shortness of *puisne* noses was to the firmness and elastic repulsion of the same organ of nutrition in the hale and lively;—which, though happy for the woman, was the undoing of the child, inasmuch as his nose was so snubb'd, so rebuff'd, so rebated, and so refrigerated thereby, as never to arrive *ad mensuram suam legitimam;*—but that in case of the flaccidity and softness of the nurse or mother's breast—by sinking into it, quoth Paræus, as into so much butter, the nose was comforted, nourish'd, plump'd up, refresh'd, refocillated, and set a growing for ever.

I have but two things to observe of Paræus; first, That he proves and explains all this with the utmost chastity and decorum of expression:—for which, may his soul for ever rest in peace!

And, secondly, That besides the systems of Prignitz and Scroderus, which Ambrose Paræus his hypothesis effectually overthrew,—it overthrew at the same time the system of peace and harmony of our family; and for three days together, not only embroiled matters between my father and my mother, but turn'd likewise the whole house and every thing in it, except my uncle Toby, quite upside down.

Such a ridiculous tale of a dispute between a man and his wife, never surely in any age or country, got vent through the key-hole of a street-door.

My mother, you must know,——but I have fifty things more necessary to let you know first;—I have a hundred difficulties which I have promised to clear up, and a thousand distresses and domestic misadventures crowding in upon me thick and three-fold, one upon the neck of another. A cow broke in (to-morrow morning) to my uncle Toby's fortifications, and eat up two rations and a half of dried grass, tearing up the sods with it, which faced his horn-work and covered way.——Trim insists upon being tried by a court-martial,—the cow to be shot,—Slop to be *crucifix'd*,—myself to be *Tristram'd*, and at my very baptism made a martyr of;—poor unhappy Devils that we all are!—I want swaddling:—but there is no time to be lost in exclamations,—I have left my father lying across his bed, my uncle Toby in his old fringed chair, sitting beside him, and promised I would go back to them in half an hour; and five-and-thirty minutes are laps'd already.—Of all the perplexities a mortal author was ever seen in,—this certainly is the greatest; for I have Hafen Slawkenbergius's folio, Sir, to finish;—a dialogue between my father and my uncle Toby, upon the solution of Prignitz, Scroderus, Ambrose Paræus, Panocrates, and Grangousier to relate;—a tale out of Slawkenbergius to translate; and all this in five minutes less than no time at all.—Such a head!—would to Heaven my enemies only saw the inside of it.

CHAP. XXXIX.

There was not any one scene more entertaining in our family;—and to do it justice in this point,—I here put off my cap and lay it upon the table, close beside my ink-horn, on purpose to make my declaration to the world concerning this one article the more solemn,—That I believe, in my soul (unless my love and partiality to my understanding blinds me) the hand of the Supreme Maker and First Designer of all things, never made or put a family together (in that period at least of it which I have sat down to write the story of)—where the characters of it were cast or contrasted with so dramatic a felicity as ours was, for this end: or in which the capacities of affording such exquisite scenes, and the powers of shifting them perpetually from morning to night, were lodged and intrusted with so unlimited a confidence, as in the Shandy Family.

Not any one of these was more diverting

I say, in this whimsical theatre of ours,—than what frequently arose out of this self-same chapter of · long noses,—especially when my father's imagination was heated with the inquiry, and nothing would serve him but to heat my uncle Toby's too.

My uncle Toby would give my father all possible fair play in this attempt; and with infinite patience would sit smoking his pipe for whole hours together, whilst my father was practising upon his head, and trying every accessible avenue to drive Prignitz and Scroderus's solutions into it.

Whether they were above my uncle Toby's reason,—or contrary to it,—or that his brain was like *damp* tinder, and no spark could possibly take hold; or that it was so full of saps, mines, blinds, curtains, and such military disqualifications to his seeing clearly into Prignitz and Scroderus's doctrines,—I say not;—let schoolmen,—scullions,—anatomists, and engineers, fight for it among themselves.——

'Twas some misfortune, I make no doubt, in this affair, that my father had every word of it to translate for the benefit of my uncle Toby, and render out of Slawkenbergius's Latin, of which, as he was no great master, his translation was not always of the purest, —and generally least so where 'twas most wanted. This naturally open'd a door to a second misfortune;—that in the warmer paroxysms of his zeal to open my uncle Toby's eyes,—my father's ideas ran on as much faster than the translation, as the translation outmoved my uncle Toby's——neither the one or the other added much to the perspicuity of my father's lecture.

CHAP. XL.

THE gift of ratiocination and making syllogisms,—I mean in man,—for in superior classes of beings, such as angels and spirits, —'tis all done, may it please your Worships, as they tell me, by INTUITION;—and beings inferior, as your Worships all know, —syllogize by their noses; though there is an island swimming in the sea (though not altogether at its ease) whose inhabitants, if my intelligence deceives me not, are so wonderfully gifted, as to syllogize after the same fashion, and oft-times to make very well out too:——but that's neither here nor there:—

The gift of doing it as it should be, amongst us, or, the great and principal act of ratiocination in man, as logicians tell us, is the finding out the agreement or disagreement of two ideas one with another, by the intervention of a third (called the *medius terminus!*) just as a man, as Locke well observes, by a yard, finds two men's nine-pin-alleys to be of the same length, which could not be brought together, to measure their equality, by *juxta-position.*

Had the same great reasoner looked on, as my father illustrated his systems of noses, and observed my uncle Toby's deportment,—what great attention he gave to every word; —and as oft as he took his pipe from his mouth, with what wonderful seriousness he contemplated the length of it!—surveying it transversely as he held it betwixt his finger and his thumb;—then fore-right,—then this way, and then that, in all its possible directions and fore-shortenings,—he would have concluded my uncle Toby had got hold of the *medius terminus*, and was syllogizing and measuring with it the truth of each hypothesis of long noses, in order, as my father laid them before him. This, by the bye, was more than my father wanted:—his aim in all the pains he was at in these philosophic lectures,—was to enable my uncle Toby not to *discuss*,—but *comprehend;*—to hold the grains and scruples of learning,—not to *weigh* them.——My uncle Toby, as you will read in the next chapter, did neither the one or the other.

CHAP. XLI.

'TIS a pity, cried my father, one winter's night after a three hours' painful translation of Slawkenbergius,—'tis a pity, cried my father, putting my mother's thread-paper into the book for a mark as he spoke,—that Truth, brother Toby, should shut herself up in such impregnable fastnesses, and be so obstinate as not to surrender herself up sometimes upon the closest siege.—

Now it happened then, as indeed it had often done before, that my uncle Toby's fancy, during the time of my father's explanation of Prignitz to him,—having nothing to stay it there, had taken a short flight to the bowling-green:--his body might as well have taken a turn there too:—so that with all the semblance of a deep school-man intent upon the *medius terminus*,—my uncle Toby was in fact as ignorant of the whole lecture, and all its pro's and con's, as if my father had been translating Hafen Slawkenbergius from the Latin tongue into the Cherokee. But the word *siege*, like a talismanic power, in my father's metaphor, wafting back my uncle Toby's fancy, quick as a note could follow the touch,—he open'd his ears;—and my father observing that he took his pipe out of his mouth, and shuffled his chair nearer the table, as with a desire to profit,—my father with great pleasure began his sentence again, changing only the plan, and dropping the metaphor of the siege in it, to keep clear of some dangers my father apprehended from it.

'Tis a pity, said my father, that truth can only be on one side, brother Toby,—considering what ingenuity these learned men have all shown in their solutions of noses. ——Can noses be dissolved? replied my uncle Toby.

—My father thrust back his chair, rose up,—put on his hat,—took four long strides to the door,—jerked it open,—thrust his head half-way out,—shut the door again,—took no notice of the bad hinge,—returned to the table,—pluck'd my mother's thread-paper out of Slawkenbergius's book,—went hastily to his bureau,—walked slowly back,—twisted my mother's thread-paper about his thumb,—unbutton'd his waistcoat,—threw my mother's thread-paper into the fire,—bit her satin pin-cushion in two,—fill'd his mouth with bran,—confounded it:—but mark!—the oath of confusion was levell'd at my uncle Toby's brain,—which was e'en confused enough already;—the curse came charged only with the bran—the bran, may it please your Honors, was no more than powder to the ball.

'Twas well my father's passions lasted not long; for so long as they did last, they led him a busy life on't; and it is one of the most unaccountable problems that ever I met with in my observations of human nature, that nothing should prove my father's mettle so much, or make his passions go off so like gun-powder, as the unexpected strokes his science met with from the quaint simplicity of my uncle Toby's questions. ——Had ten dozen of hornets stung him behind in so many different places all at one time,—he could not have exerted more mechanical functions in fewer seconds,—or started half so much, as with one single *quære* of three words unseasonably popping in full upon him in his hobby-horsical career.

'Twas all one to my uncle Toby;—he smoked his pipe on with unvaried composure; his heart never intended offence to his brother;—and as his head could seldom find out where the sting of it lay,—he always gave my father the credit of cooling by himself.——He was five minutes and thirty-five seconds about it in the present case.

By all that's good! said my father, swearing, as he came to himself, and taking the oath out of Ernulphus's digest of curses—(though, to do my father justice, it was a fault, as he told Dr. Slop in the affair of Ernulphus, which he as seldom committed as any man upon earth,)——By all that's good and great! brother Toby, said my father, if it was not for the aids of philosophy, which befriend one so much as they do,—you would put a man beside all temper. —Why, by the *solutions* of noses, of which I was telling you, I meant, as you might have known, had you favored me with one grain of attention, the various accounts, which learned men of different kinds of knowledge have given the world of the causes of short and long noses.——There is no cause but one, replied my uncle Toby, —why one man's nose is longer than another's, but because that God pleases to have it so.——That is Grangousier's solution, said my father.——'Tis he, continued my uncle Toby looking up, and not regarding my father's interruption, who makes us all, and frames and puts us together in such forms and proportions, and for such ends, as is agreeable to his infinite wisdom. —'Tis a pious account, cried my father, but not philosophical;—there is more religion in it than sound science. 'Twas no inconsistent part of my uncle Toby's character—that he feared God, and reverenced religion.—So the moment my father finished his remark,—my uncle Toby fell a whistling *Lillibullero* with more zeal (though more out of tune) than usual.—

What is become of my wife's thread-paper?

CHAP. XLII.

No matter;—as an appendage to seamstressy, the thread-paper might be of some consequence to my mother;—of none to my father as a mark in Slawkenbergius.—Slawkenbergius, in every page of him, was a rich treasure of inexhaustible knowledge to my father;—he could not open him amiss; and he would often say in closing the book, That if all the arts and sciences in the world, with the books which treated of them, were lost,—should the wisdom and policies of governments, he would say, through disuse, ever happen to be forgot; and all that statesmen had wrote or caused to be written, upon the strong or the weak sides of courts and kingdoms, should they be forgot also, —and Slawkenbergius only left,—there would be enough in him in all conscience, he would say, to set the world a-going again. A treasure, therefore, was he indeed! an institute of all that was necessary to be known of noses, and every thing else:—at matin, noon, and vespers, was Hafen Slawkenbergius his recreation and delight: 'twas for ever in his hands:—you would have sworn, Sir, it had been a canon's prayer book:—so worn, so glazed, so contrited and attrited was it with fingers and with thumbs in all its parts, from one end even unto the other.

I am not such a bigot to Slawkenbergius as my father:——there is a fund in him, no doubt! but in my opinion, the best, I don't say the most profitable, but the most amusing part of Hafen Slawkenbergius is his Tales;—and considering he was a German, many of them told not without fancy.——

These take up his second book, containing nearly one half of his folio, and are comprehended in ten decades; each decade containing ten tales.—Philosophy is not built upon tales: and therefore 'twas certainly wrong in Slawkenbergius to send them into the world by that name!—there are a few of them in his eighth, ninth, and tenth decades, which, I own, seem rather playful and sportive than speculative;—but, in general, they are to be looked upon by the learned as a detail of so many independent facts, all of them turning round, somehow or other, upon the main hinges of his subject, and collected by him with great fidelity and added to his work as so many illustrations upon the doctrines of noses.

As we have leisure enough upon our hands,—if you give me leave, Madam, I'll tell you the ninth tale of his tenth decade

THE

LIFE AND OPINIONS

OF

Tristram Shandy,

GENTLEMAN.

SLAWKENBERGII FABELLA.*

Vespera quâdam frigidulâ, posteriori in parte mensis Augusti, peregrinus, mulo fusco colore incidens, manticâ a tergo, paucis indusiis, binis calceis, braccisque sericis coccineis repleta, Argentoratum ingressus est.

Militi eum percontanti, quum portus intraret dixit, se apud Nasorum Promontorium fuisse, Francofurtum proficisci, et Argentoratum, transitu ad fines Sarmatiæ mensis intervallo, reversurum.

Miles peregrini in faciem suspexit:——Di boni, nova forma nasi!

At multum mihi profuit, inquit peregrinus, carpum amento extrahens, è quo pependit acinaces: Loculo manum inseruit; et magnâ cum urbanitate, pilei parte anteriore tactâ manu sinistrâ, ut extendit dextram, militi florinum dedit et processit.

Dolet mihi, ait miles, tympanistam manum et valgum alloquens, virum adeo urbanum vaginam perdidisse: itineravi haud poterit nudâ acinaci: neque vaginam toto Argentorato, habilem inveniet.——Nullam unquam habui, respondit peregrinus respiciens ——seque comiter inclinans—hoc more gesto, nudam acinacem elevans, mulo lentè progrediente, ut nasum tueri possim.

SLAWKENBERGIUS'S TALE.

It was one cool, refreshing evening, at the close of a very sultry day, in the latter end of the month of August, when a stranger, mounted upon a dark mule, with a small cloak-bag behind him, containing a few shirts, a pair of shoes, and a crimson-satin pair of breeches, entered the town of Strasburg.

He told the sentinel, who questioned him as he entered the gates, that he had been at the Promontory of Noses,—was going on to Frankfort,—and should be back again at Strasburg that day month, in his way to the borders of Crim Tartary.

The sentinel looked up into the stranger's face:——he never saw such a Nose in his life!

—I have made a very good venture of it, quoth the stranger;—so slipping his wrist out of the loop of a black ribbon, to which a short scimitar was hung, he put his hand into his pocket, and with great courtesy touching the fore-part of his cap with his left hand, as he extended his right,—he put a florin into the sentinel's hand, and passed on.

It grieves me, said the sentinel, speaking to a little dwarfish bandy-legg'd drummer, that so courteous a soul should have lost his scabbard;—he cannot travel without one to his scimitar; and will not be able to get a scabbard to fit it in all Strasburg.——I never had one, replied the stranger, looking back to the sentinel, and putting his hand up to his cap as he spoke.—I carry it, continued he, thus:—holding up his naked

---

* As Hafen Slawkenbergius de Nasis is extremely scarce, it may not be unacceptable to the learned reader to see the specimen of a few pages of his original, I will make no reflection upon it, but that his story-telling Latin is much more concise than his philosophic,—and, I think, has more of Latinity in

Non immerito, benigne peregrine, respondit miles.

Nihili æstimo, ait ille tympanista, è pergamenâ factitius est.

Prout christianus sum, inquit miles, nasus ille, ni sexties major sit, meo esset conformis.

Crepitare audivi, ait tympanista.

Mehercule! sanguinam emisit, respondit miles.

Miseret me, inquit tympanista, qui non ambo tetigimus!

Eodem temporis puncto, quo hæc res argumentata fuit inter militem et tympanistam, disceptabatur ibidem tubicine et uxore suâ, qui tunc accesserunt, et peregrino prætereunte, restiterunt.

Quantus nasus! æque longus est, ait tubicina, ac tuba.

Et ex eodem metallo, ait tubicen, velut sternutamento audias.

Tantum abest, respondit illa, quod fistulam dulcedine vincit.

Æneus est, ait tubicen.

Nequaquam, respondit uxor.

Rursum affirmo, ait tubicen, quod æneus est.

Rem penitus explorabo; prius, enim digito tangam, ait uxor, quam dormivero.

Mulus peregrini gradu lento progressus est, ut unumquodque verbum controversiæ, non tantum inter militem et tympanistam, verum etiam inter tubicinem et uxorem ejus, audiret.

Nequaquam, ait ille, in muli collum fræna demittens, et manibus ambabus in pectus positis (mulo lentè progrediente) nequaquam, ait ille respiciens, non necesse est ut res isthæc dilucidata foret. Minime gentium! meus nasus nunquam tangetur, dum spiritus hos reget artus—Ad quid agendum? ait uxor burgomagistri.

Peregrinus illi non respondit. Votum faciebat tunc temporis sancto Nicolao: quo facto, in sinum dextrum inserens, e quâ

scimitar, his mule moving on slowly all the time,—on purpose to defend my nose.

It is well worth it, gentle stranger, replied the sentinel.

——'Tis not worth a single stiver, said the bandy-legg'd drummer:——'tis a nose of parchment.

As I am a true Catholic,—except that it is six times as big,—'tis a nose, said the sentinel, like my own.

—I heard it crackle, said the drummer.

By dunder, said the sentinel, I saw it bleed.

What a pity, cried the bandy-legg'd drummer, we did not both touch it!

At the very time that this dispute was maintaining by the sentinel and the drummer—was the same point debating betwixt a trumpeter and a trumpeter's wife, who were just then coming up, and had stopp'd to see the stranger pass by.

Benedicity!——What a nose!—'tis as long, said the trumpeter's wife, as a trumpet.

And of the same metal, said the trumpeter, as you hear by its sneezing.

'Tis as soft as a flute, said she.

—'Tis brass, said the trumpeter.

—'Tis a pudding's end, said his wife.

I tell thee again, said the trumpeter, 'tis a brazen nose.

I'll know the bottom of it, said the trumpeter's wife, for I will touch it with my finger before I sleep.

The stranger's mule moved on at so slow a rate, that he heard every word of the dispute, not only betwixt the sentinel and the drummer, but betwixt the trumpeter and the trumpeter's wife.

No! said he, dropping his reins upon his mule's neck, and laying both his hands upon his breast, the one over the other in a saint-like position (his mule going on easily all the time) No! said he, looking up,—I am not such a debtor to the world,—slandered and disappointed as I have been,—as to give it that conviction:——no! said he, my nose shall never be touched whilst Heaven gives me strength——To do what? said a burgomaster's wife.

The stranger took no notice of the burgomaster's wife;—he was making a vow to Saint Nicholas; which done, having un

negligenter pependit acinaces, lento gradu processit per plateam Argentorati latam quæ ad diversorium templo ex adversum ducit.

crossed his arms with the same solemnity with which he crossed them, he took up the reins of his bridle with his left hand, and putting his right hand into his bosom, with his scimitar hanging loosely to the wrist of it, he rode on, as slowly as one foot of the mule could follow another, through the principal streets of Strasburg, till chance brought him to the great inn in the market-place, over-against the church.

Peregrinus mulo descendens stabulo includi, et manticam inferri jussit; quâ apertâ et coccineis sericis femorabilis extractis cum argento laciniato Περιζομαυτὲ, his sese induit, statimque, acinaci in manu, ad forum deambulavit.

The moment the stranger alighted, he ordered his mule to be led into the stable, and his cloak-bag to be brought in; then opening, and taking out of it his crimson-satin breeches, with a silver-fringed—(appendage to them, which I dare not translate)—he put his breeches, with his fringed cod-piece on, and forthwith, with his short scimitar in his hand, walked out to the grand parade.

Quod ubi peregrinus esset ingressus, uxorem tubicinis obviam euntem aspicit; illico cursum flectit, metuens ne nasus suus exploraretur, atque ad diversorium, regressus est—exuit se vestibus; braccas coccineas sericas manticæ imposuit mulumque educi jussit.

The stranger had just taken three turns upon the parade, when he perceived the trumpeter's wife at the opposite side of it; —so turning short, in pain lest his nose should be attempted, he instantly went back to his inn,—undressed himself, packed up his crimson-satin breeches, &c. in his cloak-bag, and called for his mule.

Francofurtum proficiscor, ait ille, et Argentoratem quatuor abhinc hebdomadis revertar.

I am going forwards, said the stranger, for Frankfort—and shall be back at Strasburg this day month.

Bene curasti hoc jumentum? (ait) muli faciem manu demulcens—me, manticamque meam, plus sexcentis mille passibus portavit.

I hope, continued the stranger, stroking down the face of his mule with his left hand as he was going to mount it, that you have been kind to this faithful slave of mine:—it has carried me and my cloak-bag, continued he, tapping the mule's back, above six hundred leagues.

Longa via est! respondit hospes, nisi plurimum esset negotii.—Enimvero, ait peregrinus, a Nasorum Promontorio redivi, et nasum speciosissimum, egregiosissimumque quem unquam quisquam sortitus est, acquisivi.

——'Tis a long journey, Sir, replied the master of the inn,—unless a man has great business.——Tut! tut! said the stranger, I have been at the Promontory of Noses; and have got me one of the goodliest and jolliest, thank Heaven, that ever fell to a single man's lot.

Dum peregrinus hanc miram rationem de seipso reddit, hospes et uxor ejus, oculis intentis, peregrini nasum contemplantur ——Per sanctos sanctasque omnes, ait hospitis uxor, nasis duodecim maximis in toto Argentorato major est!—estne, ait illa mariti in aurem insusurrans, nonne est nasus prægrandis?

Whilst the stranger was giving this odd account of himself, the master of the inn and his wife kept both their eyes fixed full upon the stranger's nose.——By Saint Radagunda, said the inn-keeper's wife to herself, there is more of it than in any dozen of the largest noses put together in all Strasburg! Is it not, said she, whispering

Dolus inest, anime mî, ait hospes—nasus est falsus.

Verus est, respondit uxor.

Ex abiete factus est, ait ille, terebinthinum olet.—

Carbunculus inest, ait uxor.

Mortuus est nasus, respondit hospes.

Vivus est, ait illa,—et si ipsa vivam, tangam.

Votum feci sancto Nicolao, ait peregrinus, nasum meum intactum fore usque ad —Quodnam tempus? illico respondit illa.

Minimè tangetur, inquit ille (manibus in pectus compositis) usque ad illam horam ——Quam horam? ait illa——Nullam, respondit peregrinus, donec pervenio ad—Quem locum,—obsecro? ait illa——Peregrinus nil respondens mulo conscenso discessit.

her husband in his ear, is it not a noble nose?

'Tis an imposture, my dear, said the master of the inn;—'tis a false nose.

'Tis a true nose, said his wife.

'Tis made of fir-tree, said he; I smell the turpentine.——

There's a pimple on it, said she.

'Tis a dead nose, replied the inn-keeper.

'Tis a live nose; and if I am alive myself, said the inn-keeper's wife, I will touch it.

I have made a vow to St. Nicholas this day, said the stranger, that my nose shall not be touched till——. Here the stranger, suspending his voice, looked up.——Till when? said she hastily.

It never shall be touched, said he, clasping his hands and bringing them close to his breast, till that hour——What hour? cried the inn-keeper's wife——Never!—never! said the stranger, never till I am got——For Heaven's sake, into what place? said she.——The stranger rode away without saying a word.

The stranger had not got half a league on his way towards Frankfort, before all the city of Strasburg was in an uproar about his nose. The Compline bells were just ringing, to call the Strasburgers to their devotions, and shut up the duties of the day in prayer;—no soul in all Strasburg heard 'em,—the city was like a swarm of bees,—men, women, and children, (the Compline bells tinkling all the time) flying here and there,—in at one door and out at another,—this way and that way,—long ways and cross ways,—up one street, down another street,—in at this alley, out at that; did you see it? did you see it? did you see it? O! did you see it?——who saw it? who did see it? for mercy's sake, who saw it?

Alack-a-day! I was at vespers!—I was washing, I was starching, I was scouring, I was quilting.——God help me! I never saw it—I never touch'd it!—would I had been a sentinel, a bandy-legg'd drummer, a trumpeter, a trumpeter's wife, was the general cry and lamentation in every street and corner of Strasburg.

Whilst all this confusion and disorder triumphed throughout the great city of Strasburg, was the courteous stranger going on as gently upon his mule, in his way to Frankfort, as if he had no concern at all in the affair,——talking all the way he rode in broken sentences, sometimes to his mule, —sometimes to himself,—sometimes to his Julia.

O Julia, my lovely Julia;—nay, I cannot stop to let thee bite that thistle:—that ever the suspected tongue of a rival should have robbed me of enjoyment when I was upon the point of tasting it!——

——Pugh!—'tis nothing but a thistle—never mind it;—thou shalt have a better supper at night.

——Banish'd from my country,—my friends,—from thee.——

Poor devil, thou'rt sadly tired with thy journey!——Come, get on a little faster, —there's nothing in my cloak-bag but two shirts,—a crimson-satin pair of breeches,—and a fringed——Dear Julia!

——But why to Frankfort?—is it that there is a hand unfelt, which secretly is conducting me through these meanders and unsuspected tracts?

——Stumbling! by Saint Nicholas, every step!—Why, at this rate, we shall be all night in getting in———

——To happiness;—or am I to be the sport of fortune and slander?—destined to be driven forth unconvicted,——unheard, ——untouch'd;—if so, why did I not stay at Strasburg, where justice—but I had sworn! Come, thou shalt drink—to St. Nicholas—O Julia!——What dost thou prick up thy ears at?—'tis nothing but a man, &c.

The stranger rode on communing in this manner with his mule and Julia,—till he arrived at his inn, where, as soon as he arrived, he alighted;—saw his mule, as he had promised it, taken good care of,—took off his cloak-bag, with his crimson-satin breeches, &c. in it,—called for an omelet for his supper, went to his bed about twelve o'clock. and in five minutes fell fast asleep.

It was about the same hour when the tumult in Strasburg being abated for that night,—the Strasburgers had all got quietly into their beds,—but not like the stranger, for the rest either of their minds or bodies; Queen Mab, like an elf as she was, had taken the stranger's nose, and, without reduction of its bulk, had that night been at the pains of slitting and dividing it into as many noses of different cuts and fashions, as there were heads in Strasburg to hold them. The abbess of Quedlingberg, who, with the four great dignitaries of her chapter, the prioress, the deaness, the sub-chantress, and senior-canoness, had that week come to Strasburg, to consult the university upon a case of conscience relating to their placket-holes,—was ill all the night.

The courteous stranger's nose had got perched upon the top of the pineal gland of her brain, and made such rousing work in the fancies of the four great dignitaries of her chapter, they could not get a wink of sleep the whole night through for it;—there was no keeping a limb still amongst them:—in short, they got up like so many ghosts.

The penitentiaries of the third order of Saint Francis,—the nuns of Mount Calvary, —the Præmonstratenses,—the Clunienses*, —the Carthusians,—and all the severer orders of nuns who lay that night in blankets or hair-cloth, were still in a worse condition than the abbess of Quedlingberg;—by tumbling and tossing, and tossing and tumbling from one side of their beds to the other, the whole night long;—the several sisterhoods had scratch'd and maul'd themselves all to death;—they got out of their beds almost flay'd alive;—every body thought Saint Anthony had visited them for probation with his fire;—they had never once, in short, shut their eyes the whole night long from vespers to matins.

The nuns of Saint Ursula acted the wisest;—they never attempted to go to bed at all.

The dean of Strasburg, the prebendaries, the capitulars and domiciliars (capitularly assembled in the morning to consider the case of butter'd buns) all wished they had followed the nuns of Saint Ursula's example.

In the hurry and confusion every thing had been in the night before, the bakers had all forgot to lay their leaven,—there were no butter'd buns to be had for breakfast in all Strasburg:—the whole close of the cathedral was in one eternal commotion:—

* Hafen Slawkenbergius means the Benedictine nuns of Cluny, founded in the year 940, by Odo, abbe de Cluny.

such a cause of restlessness and disquietude, and such a zealous inquiry into the cause of that restlessness, had never happened in Strasburg, since Martin Luther, with his doctrines, had turned the city upside down.

If the stranger's nose took this liberty of thrusting himself thus into the dishes* of religious orders, &c. what a carnival did his nose make of it in those of the laity!—'tis more than my pen, worn to the stump as it is, has power to describe; though, I acknowledge, (*cries* Slawkenbergius, *with more gaiety of thought than I could have expected from him*) that there is many a good simile now subsisting in the world which might give my countrymen some idea of it; but at the close of such a folio as this, wrote for their sakes, and in which I have spent the greatest part of my life,—though I own to them the simile is in being, yet would it not be unreasonable in them to expect I should have either time or inclination to search for it? Let it suffice to say, that the riot and disorder it occasioned in the Strasburgers' fantasies was so general,—such an overpowering mastership had it got of all the faculties of the Strasburgers' minds,—so many strange things, with equal confidence on all sides, and with equal eloquence in all places, were spoken and sworn to concerning it, that turned the whole stream of all discourse and wonder towards it; every soul, good and bad,—rich and poor,—learned and unlearned,—doctor and student,—mistress and maid,—gentle and simple,—nun's flesh and woman's flesh, in Strasburg, spent their time in hearing tidings about it;—every eye in Strasburg languished to see it;—every finger,—every thumb in Strasburg,—burned to touch it.

Now what might add, if any thing may be thought necessary to add, to so vehement a desire, was this,—that the sentinel, the bandy-legg'd drummer, the trumpeter, the trumpeter's wife, the burgomaster's widow, the master of the inn, and the master of the inn's wife, how widely soever they all differed every one from another in their testimonies and descriptions of the stranger's nose,—they all agreed together in two points,—namely, that he was gone to Frankfort, and would not return to Strasburg till that day month; and secondly, whether his nose was true or false, that the stranger himself was one of the most perfect paragons of beauty,—the finest made man,—the most genteel!—the most generous of his purse,—the most courteous in his carriage, that had ever entered the gates of Strasburg;—that as he rode, with his scimitar slung loosely to his wrist, through the streets,—and walked with his crimson-satin breeches across the parade,—'twas with so sweet an air of careless modesty, and so manly withal,—as would have put the heart in jeopardy (had his nose not stood in his way) of every virgin who had cast her eyes upon him.

I call not upon that heart which is a stranger to the throbs and yearnings of curiosity, so excited, to justify the abbess of Quedlingberg, the prioress, the deaness, and sub-chantress, for sending at noon-day for the trumpeter's wife: she went through the streets of Strasburg with her husband's trumpet in her hand,—the best apparatus the straitness of the time would allow her, for the illustration of her theory,—she staid no longer than three days.

The sentinel and the bandy-legg'd drummer!—nothing on this side of old Athens could equal them! they read their lectures under the city-gates to comers and goers, with all the pomp of a Chrysippus and a Crantor in their porticoes.

The master of the inn, with his ostler on his left hand, read his also in the same style,—under the portico or gateway of his stable-yard;—his wife, hers more privately in a back room. All flocked to their lectures; not promiscuously,—but to this or that, as is ever the way, as faith and credulity marshall'd them. In a word, each Strasburger came crowding for intelligence;—and every Strasburger had the intelligence he wanted.

'Tis worth remarking, for the benefit of all demonstrators in natural philosophy, &c. that as soon as the trumpeter's wife had finished the abbess of Quedlingberg's private lecture, and had begun to read in public, which she did upon a stool in the middle

* Mr. Shandy's compliments to orators,—is very sensible that Slawkenbergius has here changed his metaphor,—which he is very guilty of;—that, as a translator, Mr. Shandy has all along done what he could to make him stick to it,—bu that here 'twas impossible

of the great parade,—she incommoded the other demonstrators mainly, by gaining incontinently the most fashionable part of the city of Strasburg for her auditory.——But when a demonstrator in philosophy (cries Slawkenbergius) has a trumpet for an apparatus, pray what rival in science can pretend to be heard besides him?

Whilst the unlearned, through these conduits of intelligence, were all busied in getting down to the bottom of the well, where TRUTH keeps her little court,——were the learned in their way as busy in pumping her up through the conduits of dialect induction;—they concerned themselves not with facts,—they reasoned.——

Not one profession had thrown more light upon this subject than the Faculty,—had not all their disputes about it run into the affair of *wens* and œdematous swellings, they could not keep clear of them for their bloods and souls.—The stranger's nose had nothing to do either with wens or œdematous swellings.

It was demonstrated, however, very satisfactorily, that such a ponderous mass of heterogeneous matter could not be congested and conglomerated to the nose, whilst the infant was *in utero*, without destroying the statical balance of the fœtus, and throwing it plump upon its head nine months before the time.—

——The opponents granted the theory;—they denied the consequences.

And if a suitable provision of veins, arteries, &c. said they, was not laid in, for the due nourishment of such a nose, in the very first *stamina* and rudiments of its formation, before it came into the world (bating the case of wens), it could not regularly grow and be sustained afterwards.

This was all answered by a dissertation upon nutriment, and the effect which nutriment had in extending the vessels; and in the increase and prolongation of the muscular parts of the greatest growth and expansion imaginable.—In the triumph of which theory, they went so far as to affirm, That there was no cause in nature why a nose should not grow to the size of the man himself.

The respondents satisfied the world this event could never happen to them so long as a man had but one stomach and one pair of lungs:—for the stomach, said they, being the only organ destined for the reception of food, and turning it into chyle, and the lungs the only engine of sanguification,—it could possibly work off no more than what the appetite brought it: or, admitting the possibility of a man's overloading his stomach, nature had set bounds however to his lungs,—the engine was of a determined size and strength, and could elaborate but a certain quantity in a given time;—that is, it could produce just as much blood as was sufficient for one single man, and no more; so that, if there was as much nose as man,—they proved a mortification must necessarily ensue; and forasmuch as there could not be a support for both, that the nose must either fall off from the man, or the man inevitably fall off from his nose.

Nature accommodates herself to these emergencies, cried the opponents,—else what do you say to the case of a whole stomach,—a whole pair of lungs, and but *half* a man, when both his legs have been unfortunately shot off?

He dies of a plethora, said they,—or must spit blood, and in a fortnight or three weeks go off in a consumption.——

——It happens otherwise, replied the opponents.——

It ought not, said they.

The more curious and intimate inquirers after Nature and her doings, though they went hand in hand a good way together, yet they all divided about the nose at last, almost as much as the Faculty itself.

They amicably laid it down, that there was a just and geometrical arrangement and proportion of the several parts of the human frame to its several destinations, offices, and functions, which could not be transgressed but within certain limits;—that Nature, though she sported,—she sported within a certain circle,—and they could not agree about the diameter of it.

The logicians stuck much closer to the point before them than any of the classes of the *literati*;—they began and ended with the word *Nose*; and had it not been for a *petitio principii*, which one of the ablest of them ran his head against in the beginning of the combat, the whole controversy had been settled at once.

A nose, argued the logician, cannot bleed

without blood,—and not only blood,—but blood circulating in it to supply the phenomenon with a succession of drops—(a stream being but a quicker succession of drops, that is included, said he.)——Now death, continued the logician, being nothing but the stagnation of the blood,——

I deny the definition:—death is the separation of the soul from the body, said his antagonist.——Then we don't agree about our weapons, said the logician.——Then there is an end of the dispute, replied the antagonist.——

The civilians were still more concise: what they offered being more in the nature of a decree—than a dispute.——

Such a monstrous nose, said they, had it been a true nose, could not possibly have been suffered in civil society;—and if false, to impose upon society with such false signs and tokens, was a still greater violation of its rights, and must have had still less mercy shown it.

The only objection to this was, that if it proved any thing, it proved the stranger's nose was neither true nor false.

This left room for the controversy to go on. It was maintained by the advocates of the ecclesiastical court, that there was nothing to inhibit a decree, since the stranger *ex mero motu* had confessed he had been at the Promontory of Noses, and had got one of the goodliest, &c. &c.——To this it was answered, It was impossible there should be such a place as the Promontory of Noses, and the learned be ignorant where it lay. The commissary of the Bishop of Strasburg undertook the advocates' part, explained this matter in a treatise upon proverbial phrases, showing them, that the Promontory of Noses was a mere allegoric expression, importing no more than that nature had given him a long nose: in proof of which, with great learning, he cited the underwritten authories,* which had decided the point incontestably, had it not appeared that a dispute about some franchises of dean and chapter-lands, had been determined by it nineteen years before.

It happened,—I must not say unluckily for Truth, because they were giving her a lift another way in so doing, that the two universities of Strasburg,—the Lutheran founded in the year 1538, by Jacobus Sturmius, counsellor of the senate,—and the Popish, founded by Leopold, archduke of Austria, were, during all this time, employing the whole depth of their knowledge (except just what the affair of the abbess of Quedlingberg's placket-holes required) —in determining the point of Martin Luther's damnation.

The Popish doctors had undertaken to demonstrate, *à priori*, that from the necessary influence of the planets on the twenty-second day of October, 1483,—when the moon was in the twelfth house, Jupiter, Mars, and Venus in the third; the Sun, Saturn, and Mercury, all got together in the fourth;—that he must in course, and unavoidably, be a damn'd man; and that his doctrines, by a direct corollary, must be damn'd doctrines too.

By inspection into his horoscope, where five planets were in coition all at once with Scorpio* (in reading this, my father would always shake his head) in the ninth house, which the Arabians allotted to religion,—it appeared that Martin Luther did not care one stiver about the matter:—and that, from the horoscope directed to the conjunction of Mars—they made it plain likewise he must die cursing and blaspheming;—with the blast of which his soul (being

* Nonnulli ex nostratibus eadem loquendi formula utun. Quinimo & Logistæ & Canonistæ.——Vid. Parce Barne Jas in d. L. Provincial. Constitut. de conjec. vid. Vol. Lib. 4. Titul. 1. n. 7. qua etiam in re conspir. Om. de Promontorio Nas. Tichmak. ff. d. tit. 3. fol. 189. passim. Vid. Glos. de contrahend. empt. &c. necnon. J. Scrudr. in cap. § refut per totum. Cum his cons. Rever. J. Tubal, Sentent. & Pro cap. 9. ff. 11, 12. obiter. V. & Librum, cui Tit. de Terris & Phras. Belg. ad finem, cum comment. N. Bardy Belg. Vid. Scrip. Argentoratens. de Antiq. Ecc. in Episc. Archiv fid. coll. per Von Jacobum Koinshoven Folio Argent. 1583. præcip. ad finem. Quibus add. Rebuff in L. obvenire de Signif. Nom. ff. fol. & de jure Gent. & Civil. de protib. alinea feud. per fedcra, test. Joha. Luxius in prolegom. quem velim videas, de Analy. Cap. 1, 2, 3. Vid. Idea.

* Hæc miro, satisque horrenda. Planetarum coitio sub Scorpio Asterismo in nona cœli statione, quam Arabes religioni deputabant efficit *Martinum Lutherum* sacrilegium hereticum, Christianæ religionis hostem acerrimum atque prophanum, ex horoscopi directione ad Martis coitum, religiosissimus obiit, ejus Anima scelestissima ad infernos navigat,—ab Alecto, Tisiphone & Megara flagellis igneis cruciata periuntur.

——Lucas Gaurieus in Tractatu astrologico de præteritis multorum hominum accidentibus per genituras examinatis.

steep'd in guilt) sailed before the wind in the lake of hell-fire.

The little objection of the Lutheran doctors to this, was, that it must certainly be the soul of another man, born October 22, '83, which was forced to sail down before the wind in that manner,—inasmuch as it appeared from the register of Islaben, in the county of Mansfelt; that Luther was not born in the year 1483, but in 84; and not on the 22d day of October, but on the 10th of November, the eve of Martinmas-day, from whence he had the name of Martin.

[——I must break off my translation for a moment; for, if I did not, I know I should no more be able to shut my eyes in bed, than the abbess of Quedlingberg.—It is to tell the reader, that my father never read this passage of Slawkenbergius to my uncle Toby, but with triumph,—not over my uncle Toby, for he never opposed him in it,—but over the whole world.

Now you see, brother Toby, he would say, looking up, "that Christian names are "not such indifferent things;"—had Luther here been called by any other name but Martin, he would have been damn'd to all eternity;—not that I look upon Martin, he would add, as a good name,—far from it,—'tis something better than a neutral, and but a little;—yet, little as it is, you see it was of some service to him.

My father knew the weakness of this prop to his hypothesis, as well as the best logician could show him,—yet so strange is the weakness of man at the same time, as it fell in his way, he could not for his life but make use of it; and it was certainly for this reason that though there are many stories in Hafen Slawkenbergius's Decades full as entertaining as this I am translating, yet there is not one amongst them which my father read over with half the delight;—it flattered two of his strangest hypotheses together,—his *Names* and his *Noses*.—I will be bold to say, he might have read all the books in the Alexandrian Library, had not fate taken other care of them, and not have met with a book or passage in one, which hit two such nails as these upon the head at one stroke.]

The two universities of Strasburg were hard tugging at this affair of Luther's navigation The Protestant doctors had demonstrated, that he had not sailed right before the wind, as the Popish doctors had pretended; and as every one knew there was no sailing full in the teeth of it,—they were going to settle, in case he had sailed, how many points he was off; whether Martin had doubled the Cape, or had fallen upon a lee-shore; and no doubt, as it was an inquiry of much edification, at least to those who understood this sort of *navigation*, they had gone on with it in spite of the size of the stranger's nose, had not the size of the stranger's nose drawn off the attention of the world from what they were about:—it was their business to follow.

The abbess of Quedlingberg and her four dignitaries were no stop; for the enormity of the stranger's nose running full as much in their fancies as their case of conscience,—the affair of their placket-holes kept cold—in a word, the printers were ordered to distribute their types:—all controversies dropp'd.

'Twas a square cap with a silver tassel upon the crown of it—to a nut-shell,—to have guessed on which side of the nose the two universities would split.

'Tis above reason, cried the doctors on one side.

'Tis below reason, cried the others.

'Tis faith, cried one.

'Tis a fiddle-stick, said the other.

'Tis possible, cried the one.

'Tis impossible, said the other.

God's power is infinite, cried the Nosarians; he can do any thing.

He can do nothing, replied the Antinosarians, which implies contradictions.

He can make matter think, said the Nosarians.

As certainly as you can make a velvet cap out of a sow's ear, replied the Antinosarians.

He cannot make two and two five, replied the Popish doctors.——'Tis false, said the other opponents.

Infinite power is infinite power, said the doctors who maintained the reality of the nose.—It extends only to all possible things, replied the Lutherans.

By God in Heaven, cried the Popish doctors, he can make a nose, if he thinks fit, as big as the steeple of Strasburg.

Now the steeple of Strasburg being the

biggest and the tallest church-steeple to be seen in the whole world, the Antinosarians denied that a nose of 575 geometrical feet in length, could be worn, at least by a middle-siz'd man.—The Popish doctors swore it could:—the Lutheran doctors said No;—it could not.

This at once started a new dispute, which they pursued a great way, upon the extent and limitation of the moral and natural attributes of God.—That controversy led them naturally into Thomas Aquinas; and Thomas Aquinas to the Devil.

The stranger's nose was no more heard of in the dispute;—it just served as a frigate, to launch them into the gulf of school divinity,—and then they all sailed before the wind.

Heat is in proportion to the want of true knowledge.

The controversy about the attributes, &c. instead of cooling, on the contrary had inflamed the Strasburgers' imaginations to a most inordinate degree.—The less they understood of the matter, the greater was their wonder about it;—they were left in all the distresses of desire unsatisfied,—saw their doctors, the ***Parchmentarians***, the ***Brassarians***, the ***Turpentarians***, on one side,—the Popish doctors on the other, like Pantagruel and his companions in quest of the oracle of the bottle, all embarked out of sight.

——The poor Strasburgers left upon the beach!

——What was to be done!—No delay;—the uproar increased,—every one in disorder,—the city-gates set open.

Unfortunate Strasburgers! was there in the store-house of nature,—was there in the lumber-rooms of learning,—was there in the great arsenal of chance, one single engine left undrawn forth to torture your curiosities, and stretch your desires, which was not pointed by the hand of Fate to play upon your hearts?—I dip not my pen into my ink to excuse the surrender of yourselves,—'tis to write your panegyric. Show me a city so macerated with expectation,—who neither eat, or drank, or slept, or prayed, or hearkened to the calls either of religion or nature, for seven-and-twenty days together, who could have held out one day longer!

On the twenty-eighth the courteous stranger had promised to return to Strasburg.

Seven thousand coaches (Slawkenbergius must certainly have made some mistake in his numerical characters) 7000 coaches,—15,000 single-horse chairs,—20,000 waggons, crowded as full as they could all hold with senators, counsellors, syndics,—beguines, widows, wives, virgins, canons, concubines, all in their coaches:—The abbess of Quedlingberg, with the prioress, the deaness, and subchantress, leading the procession in one coach, and the dean of Strasburg, with the four great dignitaries of his chapter, on her left hand,—the rest following higglety-pigglety as they could; some on horseback,—some on foot,—some led, some driven, some down the Rhine,—some this way,—some that,—all set out at sunrise to meet the courteous stranger on the road.

Haste we now towards the catastrophe of my tale,—I say catastrophe (cries Slawkenbergius) inasmuch as a tale, with parts rightly disposed, not only rejoiceth (*gaudet*) in the *Catastrophe* and *Peripeitia* of a DRAMA, but rejoiceth moreover in all the essential and integrant parts of it;—it has its ***Protasis***, ***Epitasis***, ***Catastasis***, its ***Catastrophe***, or ***Peripeitia***, growing one out of the other in it, in the order Aristotle first planted them,—without which a tale had better never be told at all, says Slawkenbergius, but be kept to a man's self.

In all my ten tales, in all my ten decades, have I, Slawkenbergius, tied down every tale of them as tightly to this rule, as I have done this of the stranger and his nose.

—From his first parley with the sentinel, to his leaving the city of Strasburg, after pulling off his crimson-satin pair of breeches, is the ***Protasis*** or first entrance,—where the characters of the ***Personæ Dramatis*** are just touched in, and the subject slightly begun.

The *Epitasis*, wherein the action is more fully entered upon and heightened, till it arrives at its state or height, called the *Catastasis*, and which usually takes up the 2nd and 3d act, is included within that busy period of my tale, betwixt the first night's uproar about the nose, to the conclusion of the trumpeter's wife's lectures upon it in the middle of the grand parade; and from the first embarking of the learned in the dispute,—to the doctors' finally sailing away, and leaving the Strasburgers upon the beach in distress, is the *Catastasis*, or the ripening of the incidents and passions for their bursting forth in the fifth act.

This commences with the setting out of the Strasburgers on the Frankfort road, and terminates in unwinding the labyrinth and bringing the hero out of a state of agitation (as Aristotle calls it) to a state of rest and quietness.

This, says Hafen Slawkenbergius, constitutes the *Catastrophe* or *Peripeitia* of my tale;—and that is the part of it I am going to relate.

We left the stranger behind the curtain asleep:—he enters now upon the stage.

—What dost thou prick up thy ears at? —'tis nothing but a man upon a horse; was the last word the stranger uttered to his mule. It was not proper then to tell the reader that the mule took his master's word for it; and without any more *ifs* or *ands*, let the traveller and his horse pass by.

The traveller was hastening with all diligence to get to Strasburg that night. What a fool am I, said the traveller to himself, when he had rode about a league farther, to think of getting into Strasburg this night!—Strasburg!—the great Strasburg! —Strasburg, the capital of all Alsatia! Strasburg, an imperial city! Strasburg, a sovereign state! Strasburg, garrisoned with five thousand of the best troops in all the world! —Alas! if I was at the gates of Strasburg this moment, I could not gain admittance into it for a ducat,—nay, a ducat and a half; —'tis too much,—better go back to the last inn I have passed,—than lie I know not where,—or give I know not what. The traveller, as he made these reflections in his mind, turned his horse's head about, and three minutes after the stranger had been conducted into his chamber, he arrived at the same inn.

——We have bacon in the house, said the host, and bread;—and till eleven o'clock this night had three eggs in it;—but a stranger, who arrived an hour ago, has had them dressed into an omelet, and we have nothing.—

Alas! said the traveller, harassed as I am, I want nothing but a bed.——I have one as soft as is in Alsatia, said the host.

—The stranger, continued he, should have slept in it, for 'tis my best bed, but upon the score of his nose.——He has got a defluxion, said the traveller.——Not that I know cried the host.—But 'tis a camp-bed, and Jacinta, said he, looking towards the maid, imagined there was not room in it to turn his nose in.——Why so, cried the traveller, starting back.——It is so long a nose, replied the host.——The traveller fixed his eyes upon Jacinta, then upon the ground, —kneeled upon his right knee, had just got his hand laid upon his breast——Trifle not with my anxiety, said he, rising up again. ——'Tis no trifle, said Jacinta, 'tis the most glorious nose!——The traveller fell upon his knee again,—laid his hand upon his breast,—then, said he, looking up to heaven, thou hast conducted me to the end of my pilgrimage,—'Tis Diego.

The traveller was the brother of Julia, so often invoked that night by the stranger as he rode from Strasburg upon his mule; and was come, on her part, in quest of him. He had accompanied his sister from Valladolid across the Pyrennean mountains through France, and had many an entangled skein to wind off in pursuit of him, through the many meanders and abrupt turnings of a lover's thorny tracks.

——Julia had sunk under it,—and had not been able to get a step farther than to Lyons, where, with the many disquietudes of a tender heart, which all talk of,—but few feel,—she sicken'd, but had just strength to write a letter to Diego; and having conjured her brother never to see her face till he had found him out, and put the letter into his hands, Julia took to her bed.

Fernandez (for that was her brother's name)—though the camp-bed was as soft as any one in Alsace, yet he could not shut his eyes in it.—As soon as it was day, he rose; and hearing Diego was risen too, he entered his chamber and discharged his sister's commission.

The letter was as follows:

"Seig. Diego,

"Whether my suspicions of your nose "were justly excited or not,—'tis not now "to inquire;—it is enough I have not had "firmness to put them to farther trial.

"How could I know so little of myself, "when I sent my duenna to forbid your "coming more under my lattice? or how "could I know so little of you, Diego, as to "imagine you would have staid one day in "Valladolid to have given ease to my doubts? "—Was I to be abandoned, Diego, because "I was deceived? or was it kind to take "me at my word, whether my suspicions "were just or no, and leave me, as you did, "a prey to much uncertainty and sorrow?

"In what manner Julia has resented this, "—my brother, when he puts this letter "into your hands, will tell you; he will "tell you in how few moments she repented "of the rash message she had sent you,— "in what frantic haste she flew to her lat- "tice, and how many days and nights to- "gether she leaned immovably upon her "elbow, looking through it towards the "way which Diego was wont to come.

"He will tell you, when she heard of "your departure,—how her spirits deserted "her, how her heart sicken'd,—how pite- "ously she mourned,—how low she hung "her head. O Diego! how many weary "steps has my brother's pity led me by the "hand languishing to trace out yours! how "far has desire carried me beyond strength! "—and how oft have I fainted by the way, "and sunk into his arms, with only power "to cry out,—O my Diego!

"If the gentleness of your carriage has "not belied your heart, you will fly to me "almost as fast as you fled from me:—haste "as you will,—you will arrive but to see "me expire.—'Tis a bitter draught, Diego; "but oh! 'tis embittered still more by dying "*un———!*"

She could proceed no farther.

Slawkenbergius supposes the word intended was *unconvinced;* but her strength would not enable her to finish her letter.

The heart of the courteous Diego overflowed as he read the letter:—he ordered his mule forthwith and Fernandez's horse to be saddled; and as no vent in prose is equal to that of poetry in such conflicts,——chance, which as often directs us to remedies as to *diseases*, having thrown a piece of charcoal into the window,—Diego availed himself of it; and, whilst the ostler was getting ready his mule, he eased his mind against the wall as follows:

ODE.

Harsh and untuneful are the notes of love
 Unless my Julia strikes the key,
Her hand alone can touch the part.
 Whose dulcet move-
 ment charms the heart,
And governs all the man with sympathetic sway.

2d.

O Julia!

The lines were very natural,—for they were nothing at all to the purpose, says Slawkenbergius, and 'tis a pity there were no more of them; but whether it was that Seig. Diego was slow in composing verses,—or the ostler quick in saddling mules,—is not averred; certain it was, that Diego's mule and Fernandez's horse were ready at the door of the inn before Diego was ready for his second stanza; so, without staying to finish his ode, they both mounted, sallied forth, passed the Rhine, traversed Alsace, shaped their course towards Lyons, and, before the Strasburgers and the abbess of Quedlingberg had set out on their cavalcade, had Fernandez, Diego, and his Julia, crossed the Pyrennean mountains, and got safe to Valladolid.

'Tis needless to inform the geographical reader, that, when Diego was in Spain, it was not possible to meet the courteous stranger in the Frankfort road; it is enough to say, that of all restless desires, curiosity being the strongest,—the Strasburgers felt the full force of it; and that for three days and nights they were tossed to and fro in the Frankfort road, with the tempestuous fury of this passion, before they could submit to return home;—when, alas! an event was prepared for them, of all others, the most grievous that could befall a free people.

As this revolution of the Strasburgers' affairs is often spoken of, and little understood, I will, in ten words, says Slawkenbergius, give the world an explanation of it, and with it put an end to my tale.

Every body knows of the grand system of Universal Monarchy, wrote by order of Mon. Colbert, and put in manuscript into the hands of Louis the Fourteenth, in the year 1664.

'Tis as well known, that one branch out of many of that system was the getting possession of Strasburg, to favor an entrance at all times into Suabia, in order to disturb the quiet of Germany;—and that, in consequence of this plan, Strasburg unhappily fell at length into their hands.

It is the lot of a few to trace out the true springs of this and such like revolutions; —the vulgar look too high for them,—statesmen look too low;—Truth (for once) lies in the middle.

What a fatal thing is the popular pride of a free city! cries one historian.—The Strasburgers deemed it a diminution of their freedom to receive an imperial garrison,—so fell a prey to a French one.

The fate, says another of the Strasburgers, may be a warning to all free people to save their money.—They anticipated their revenues,—brought themselves under taxes, exhausted their strength, and, in the end, became so weak a people, they had not strength to keep their gates shut; and, so the French pushed them open!

Alas! alas! cries Slawkenbergius, 'twas not the French,—'twas *curiosity* pushed them open.—The French, indeed, who are ever upon the catch, when they saw the Strasburgers, men, women, and children, all marched out to follow the stranger's nose,—each man followed his own, and marched in.

Trade and manufactures have decayed and gradually grown down ever since,—but not from any cause which commercial heads have assigned; for it is owing to this only, that Noses have ever so run in their heads, that the Strasburgers could not follow their business.

Alas! alas! cries Slawkenbergius, making an exclamation,—it is not the first,—and I fear will not be the last fortress that has been either won—or lost by *Noses.*

THE END OF SLAWKENBERGIUS'S TALE.

CHAP. I.

WITH all this learning upon Noses running perpetually in my father's fancy,—with so many family prejudices,—and ten decades of such tales running on for ever along with them,—how was it possible with such exquisite,—was it a true nose?—that a man with such exquisite feelings as my father had, could bear the shock at all below stairs,—or indeed above stairs, in any other posture but the very posture I have described?

——Throw yourself down upon the bed a dozen times,—taking care only to place a looking-glass first in a chair on one side of it before you do it.—But was the stranger's nose a true nose, or was it a false one?

To tell that beforehand, Madam, would be to do injury to one of the best tales in the Christian world; and that is the tenth of the tenth decade, which immediately follows this.

This tale, cried Slawkenbergius, somewhat exultingly, has been reserved by me for the concluding tale of my whole work; knowing right well, that when I shall have told it, and my reader shall have read it through, —'twould be even high time for both of us to shut up the book; inasmuch, continues Slawkenbergius, as I know of no tale which could possibly ever go down after it.

—'Tis a tale indeed!

This sets out with the first interview in the inn at Lyons, when Fernandez left the courteous stranger and his sister Julia alone in her chamber, and is overwritten

THE INTRICACIES

OF

DIEGO AND JULIA.

Heavens! thou art a strange creature, Slawkenbergius! what a whimsical view of the involutions of the heart of woman hast thou opened! how this can ever be translated, and yet if this specimen of Slawkenbergius's tales, and the exquisiteness of his moral, should please the world,—translated shall a couple of volumes be.—Else, how this can ever be translated into good English, I have no sort of conception.—There seems, in some passages, to want a sixth sense to do it rightly.—What can he mean by the lambent pupilability of slow, low, dry chat, five notes below the natural tone,—which you know, Madam, is little more than a whisper? The moment I pronounced the words, I could perceive an attempt towards a vibration in the strings about the region of the heart.—The brain made no acknowledgment.—There's often no good understanding betwixt 'em:—I felt as if I understood it.—I had no ideas.—The movement could not be without cause.—I'm lost.—I can make nothing of it,—unless, may it please your Worships, the voice, in that case being little more than a whisper, unavoidably forces the eyes to approach not only within six inches of each other,—but to look into the pupils.—Is not that dangerous?—But it can't be avoided;—for to look up to the ceiling, in that case the two chins unavoidably meet;—and, to look down into each other's lap, the foreheads come into immediate contact, which at once puts an end to the conference,—I mean to the sentimental part of it.—What is left, Madam, is not worth stooping for.

CHAP. II.

My father lay stretched across the bed as still as if the hand of death had pushed him down, for a full hour and a half before he began to play upon the floor with the toe of that foot which hung over the bedside. My uncle Toby's heart was a pound lighter for it.—In a few moments, his left hand, the knuckles of which had all the time reclined upon the handle of the chamber-pot, came to its feeling;—he thrust it a little more within the valance,—drew up his hand, when he had done, into his bosom,—gave a hem! My good uncle Toby, with infinite pleasure, answered it; and full gladly would have ingrafted a sentence of consolation upon the opening it afforded: but having no talents, as I said, that way, and fearing, moreover, that he might set out with something which might make a bad matter worse, he contented himself with resting his chin placidly upon the cross of his crutch.

Now, whether the compression shortened my uncle Toby's face into a more pleasurable oval,—or that the philanthropy of his heart, in seeing his brother beginning to emerge out of the sea of his afflictions, had braced up his muscles,—so that the compression upon his chin only doubled the benignity which was there before, is not hard to decide.—My father, in turning his eyes, was struck with such a gleam of sun-shine in his face, as melted down the sullenness of his grief in a moment.

He broke silence as follows:—

CHAP. III.

Did ever man, brother Toby, cried my father, raising himself upon his elbow, and turning himself round to the opposite side of the bed, where my uncle Toby was sitting in his old fringed chair, with his chin resting upon his crutch,—did ever a poor unfortunate man, brother Toby, cried my father, receive so many lashes?——The most I ever saw given, quoth my uncle Toby (ringing the bell at the bed's head for Trim) was to a grenadier, I think, in Mackay's regiment.

——Had my uncle Toby shot a bullet through my father's heart, he could not have fallen down with his nose upon the quilt more suddenly.

Bless me! said my uncle Toby.

CHAP. IV.

Was it Mackay's regiment, quoth my uncle Toby, where the poor grenadier was so unmercifully whipp'd at Bruges, about the ducats?——O Christ! he was innocent! cried Trim, with a deep sigh.—And he was whipp'd, may it please your Honor, almost to Death's door.—They had better have shot him outright, as he begg'd, and he had gone directly to Heaven; for he was as innocent as your Honor.——I thank thee, Trim, quoth my uncle Toby.——I never think of his, continued Trim, and my poor brother Tom's misfortunes, for we were all three school-fellows, but I cry like a coward.——Tears are no proof of cowardice, Trim.—I drop them oft-times myself, cried my uncle Toby.——I know your Honor does, replied Trim, and so am not ashamed of it myself.—But to think, may it please your Honor, continued Trim, a tear stealing into the corner of his eye as he spoke,—to think of two virtuous lads with hearts as warm in their bodies, and as honest as God could make them,—the children of honest people, going forth with gallant spirits to seek their fortunes in the world,—and fall into such evils!—poor Tom! to be tortured upon a rack for nothing—but marrying a Jew's widow who sold sausages!—honest Dick Johnson's soul to be scourged out of his body, for the ducats another man put into his knapsack!—O!—these are misfortunes, cried Trim,—pulling out his handkerchief,—these are misfortunes, may it please your Honor, worth lying down and crying over.

—My father could not help blushing.

'Twould be a pity, Trim, quoth my uncle Toby, thou shouldst ever feel sorrow of thy own;—thou feelest it so tenderly for others. —Alack-a-day, replied the corporal brightening up his face,—your Honor knows I have neither wife or child;—I can have no sorrows in this world.——My father could not help smiling.——As few as any man, Trim, replied my uncle Toby; nor can I see how a fellow of thy light heart can suffer, but from the distress of poverty in thy old age, when thou art passed all services, Trim,—and hast outlived thy friends.—— An' please your Honor, never fear, replied Trim, cheerly.——But I would have thee never fear, Trim, replied my uncle Toby; and therefore, continued my uncle Toby, throwing down his crutch, and getting up upon his legs as he uttered the word *therefore*,—in recompense, Trim, of thy long fidelity to me, and that goodness of thy heart I have had such proofs of,—whilst thy master is worth a shilling,—thou shalt never ask elsewhere, Trim, for a penny. ——Trim attempted to thank my uncle Toby,—but had not power;—tears trickled down his cheeks faster than he could wipe them off.—he laid his hands upon his breast, —made a bow to the ground, and shut the door.

——I have left Trim my bowling-green, cried my uncle Toby.—My father smiled. —I have left him, moreover, a pension, continued my uncle Toby.——My father looked grave.

CHAP. V.

Is this a fit time, said my father to himself, to talk of *pensions* and *grenadiers?*

CHAP. VI.

When my uncle Toby first mentioned the grenadier, my father, I said, fell down with his nose flat to the quilt, and as suddenly as if my uncle Toby had shot him but it was not added that every other limb and member of my father instantly relapsed, with his nose, into the same precise attitude in which he lay first described; so that when Corporal Trim left the room, and my father found himself disposed to rise off the bed,—he had all the little preparatory movements to run over again before he could do it.—Attitudes are nothing, Madam, —'tis the transition from one attitude to another,—like the preparation and resolution of the discord into harmony, which is all in all.

For which reason, my father played the same jig over again with his toe upon the floor,—pushed the chamber-pot still a little farther within the valance,—gave a hem, —raised himself up upon his elbow,—and was just beginning to address himself to my uncle Toby,—when, recollecting the unsuccessfulness of his first effort in that attitude,—he got upon his legs, and in making the third turn across the room, he stopped short before my uncle Toby; and laying the three first fingers of his right hand in the palm of his left, and stooping a little, he addressed himself to my uncle Toby as follows:—

CHAP. VII.

When I reflect, brother Toby, upon MAN; and take a view of that dark side of him which represents his life as open to so many causes of trouble;—when I consider, brother Toby, how oft we eat the bread of affliction, and that we are born to it, as to the portion of our inheritance,——I was born to nothing, quoth my uncle Toby, interrupting my father,—but my commission. ——Zooks! said my father, did not my uncle leave you a hundred and twenty pounds a year.——What could I have done without it? replied my uncle Toby.—— That's another concern, said my father testily;—but I say, Toby, when one runs over the catalogue of all the cross-reckonings and sorrowful *items* with which the heart of man is overcharged, 'tis wonderful by what hidden resources the mind is enabled to stand it out, and bear itself up, as it does, against the impositions laid upon our nature.——'Tis by the assistance of Almighty God, cried my uncle Toby, looking up, and pressing the palms of his hands close together,—'tis not from our own strength, brother Shandy;—a sentinel in a wooden sentry-box might as well pretend to stand it out against a detachment of fifty men.—We are upheld by the grace and the assistance of the best of Beings.

——That is cutting the knot, said my father, instead of untying it.—But give me leave to lead you, brother Toby, a little deeper into the mystery.

With all my heart, replied my uncle Toby.

My father instantly exchanged the attitude he was in, for that in which Socrates is so finely painted by Raphael, in his school of Athens; which your connoisseurship knows is so exquisitely imagined, that even the particular manner of the reasoning of Socrates is expressed by it,—for he holds the fore-finger of his left-hand between the fore-finger and the thumb of his right; and seems as if he was saying to the libertine he is reclaiming,—"*You grant me* this,— "and this: and this, and this, I don't ask "of you;—they follow of themselves in "course."

So stood my father, holding fast his fore-finger betwixt his finger and his thumb, and reasoning with my uncle Toby as he sat in his old fringed chair, valanced around with party-colored worsted bobs.——O Garrick! —what a rich scene of this would thy exquisite powers make! and how gladly would I write such another to avail myself of thy immortality, and secure my own behind it!

CHAP. VIII.

Though man is of all others the most curious vehicle, said my father; yet, at the same time, 'tis of so slight a frame, and so totteringly put together, that the sudden jerks and hard jostlings it unavoidably meets with in this rugged journey, would overset and tear it to pieces a dozen times a day,—was it not, brother Toby, that there is a secret spring within us.——Which spring, said my uncle Toby, I take to be Religion.——Will that set my child's nose on? cried my father, letting go his finger, and striking one hand against the other. ——It makes every thing straight for us, answered my uncle Toby.——Figuratively speaking, dear Toby, it may, for aught I know, said my father; but the spring I am speaking of, is that great and elastic power within us of counterbalancing evil; which, like a secret spring in a well-ordered machine, though it can't prevent the shock,—at least, it imposes upon our sense of it.

Now, my dear brother, said my father, replacing his fore-finger as he was coming closer to the point,—had my child arrived safe into the world, unmartyr'd in that precious part of him, fanciful and extravagant as I may appear to the world in my opinion of christian names, and of that magic bias which good or bad names irresistibly impress upon our characters and conducts,—Heaven is witness, that in the warmest transports of my wishes for the prosperity of my child, I never once wished to crown his head with more glory and honor than what George or Edward would have spread around it.

But alas! continued my father, as the greatest evil has befallen him,—I must counteract and undo it with the greatest good.

He shall be christened Trismegistus, brother.

I wish it may answer,—replied my uncle Toby, rising up.

CHAP. IX.

What a chapter of chances! said my father, turning himself about on the first landing, as he and my uncle Toby were going down stairs:—what a long chapter of chances do the events of this world lay open to us! Take pen and ink in hand brother Toby, and calculate it fairly.——I know no more of calculation than this baluster, said my uncle Toby (striking short of it with his crutch, and hitting my father a desperate blow souse upon his shin-bone.) —'Twas a hundred to one,—cried my uncle Toby——I thought, quoth my father (rubbing his shin) you had known nothing of calculations, brother Toby.——'Twas a mere chance, said my uncle Toby.——Then it adds one to the chapter,—replied my father.

The double success of my father's repartees tickled off the pain of his shin at once:—it was well it so fell out—(chance! again)—or the world to this day had never known the subject of my father's calculation;—to guess it there was no chance.—What a lucky chapter of chances has this turned out! for it has saved me the trouble of writing one express; and in truth I have enough already upon my hands without it. Have I not promised the world a chapter of knots? two chapters upon the right and the wrong end of a woman? a chapter upon whiskers? a chapter upon wishes? a chapter of noses?—No: I have done that;—a chapter upon my uncle Toby's modesty?—to say nothing of a chapter upon chapters, which I will finish before I sleep.—By my great-grandfather's whiskers, I shall never get half of 'em through this year.

Take pen and ink in hand, and calculate it fairly, brother Toby, said my father; and it will turn out a million to one, that of all the parts of the body, the edge of the forceps should have the ill-luck just to fall upon and break down that one part, which should break down the fortunes of our house with it.

It might have been worse, replied my uncle Toby.——I don't comprehend, said my father.——Suppose the hip had presented, replied my uncle Toby, as Dr. Slop foreboded?

My father reflected half a minute;—looked down,—touched the middle of his forehead slightly with his finger——

—True, said he.

CHAP. X.

Is it not a shame to make two chapters of what passed in going down one pair of stairs? for we are got no farther yet than to the first landing, and there are fifteen more steps down to the bottom; and, for aught I know, as my father and my uncle Toby are in a talking humor, there may be as many chapters as steps. Let that be as it will, Sir, I can no more help it than my destiny.—A sudden impulse comes across me;——drop the curtain, Shandy:—I drop it.—Strike a line here across the paper, Tristram:—I strike it,—and hey for a new chapter.

The deuce of any other rule have I to govern myself by in this affair;—and if I had one,—as I do all things out of all rule,—I would twist it and tear it to pieces, and throw it into the fire when I had done.—Am I warm? I am, and the cause demands it:—a pretty story! is a man to follow rules, or rules to follow him?

Now this, you must know, being my chapter upon chapters, which I promised to write before I went to sleep, I thought it meet to ease my conscience entirely before I laid down, by telling the world all I knew about the matter at once. Is not this ten times better than to set out dogmatically with a sententious parade of wisdom, and telling the world a story of a roasted horse?—that chapters relieve the mind,—that they assist,—or impose upon the imagination,—and that in a work of this dramatic cast they are as necessary as the shifting of scenes,—with fifty other cold conceits, enough to extinguish the fire which roasted him! O! but to understand this, which is a puff at the fire of Diana's temple,—you must read Longinus:—read away:—if you are not a jot the wiser by reading him the first time over,—never fear,—read him again.—Avicenna and Licetus read Aristotle's Metaphysics forty times through a-piece, and never understood a single word!—But mark the consequence.—Avicenna turned out a desperate writer at all kinds of writing;—for he wrote books *de omni scribili;* and for Licetus (Fortunio)—though all the world knows he was born a *fœtus*,* of no more than five

* Ce fœtus n'etoit pas plus grand que la paume de la main; mais son pere l'ayant éxaminé en qualité de Médecin, & ayant trouvé que c'etoit quelque chose de plus qu'un Embryon, le fit transporter tout vivant à Rapallo, ou il le fit voir à Jerôme Bardi & a d'autres Médecins du lieu. On trouva qu'il ne lui manquoi

inches and a half in length, yet he grew to that astonishing height in literature, as to write a book with a title as long as himself. The learned know I mean his *Gonopsychanthropologia* upon the origin of the Human Soul.

So much for my chapter upon chapters, which I hold to be the best chapter in my whole work; and, take my word, whoever reads it, is full as well employed as in picking straws.

CHAP. XI.

We shall bring all things to rights, said my father, setting his foot upon the first step from the landing.—This Trismegistus, continued my father, drawing his leg back, and turning to my uncle Toby,—was the greatest (Toby) of all earthly beings;—he was the greatest king,—the greatest lawgiver,—the greatest philosopher,—and the greatest priest;——and engineer,—said my uncle Toby.

——In course, said my father.

CHAP. XII.

—And how does your mistress? cried my father, taking the same step over again from the landing, and calling to Susannah, whom he saw passing by the foot of the stairs with a huge pin-cushion in her hand, —how does your mistress?——As well, said Susannah, tripping by, but without looking up, as can be expected.——What a fool am I! said my father, drawing his leg back again,—let things be as they will, brother Toby, 'tis ever the precise answer.—And how is the child, pray?——No answer.—And where is Dr. Slop?—added my father, raising his voice aloud, and looking over the balusters.—Susannah was out of hearing.

Of all the riddles of a married life, said my father, crossing the landing, in order to set his back against the wall whilst he propounded it to my uncle Toby,—of all the puzzling riddles, said he, in the marriage state,—of which, you may trust me, brother Toby, there are more asses' loads than all Job's stock of asses could have carried,—there is not one that has more intricacies in it than this:—that from the very moment the mistress of the house is brought to bed, every female in it, from my lady's gentlewoman down to the cinder-wench, becomes an inch taller for it; and gives herself more airs upon that single inch, than all her other inches put together.

I think rather, replied my uncle Toby, that 'tis we who sink an inch lower.—If I meet but a woman with child,—I do it. —'Tis a heavy tax upon that half of our fellow-creatures, brother Shandy, said my uncle Toby.—'Tis a piteous burden upon 'em, continued he, shaking his head.——Yes, yes, 'tis a painful thing,—said my father, shaking his head too:—but certainly since shaking of heads came into fashion, never did two heads shake together, in concert, from two such different springs.

God bless }
Deuce take } 'em all,—said my uncle Toby and my father; each to himself.

CHAP. XIII.

Holla!—you chairman!—here's sixpence:—do step into that bookseller's shop, and call me a *day-tall* critic. I am very willing to give any one of 'em a crown to help me with his tackling to get my fathe

rien d'essentiel à la vie; & son pere pour faire voir un essai de son experience, entreprit d'achever l'ouvrage de la Nature, & de travailler à la formation de l'Enfant avec le même artifice que celui dont on se sert pour faire ècclore les Poulets en Egypte. Il instruisit une Nourisse de tout ce qu'elle avoit à faire, & ayant fait mettre son fils dans un pour proprement accommodé, il recussit à l'élever & à lui faire prendre ses accroissemens necessaires, par l'uniformité d'une chaleur étrangere mesurée exactement sur les dégrés d'un Thermomètre, ou d'un autre instrument equivalent. (Vide Mich. Giustinian, ne gli Scritt Liguri à Cart. 223. 488.

On auroit toujours été très satisfait de l'industrie d un pere si experimenté dans l'Art de la Generation, quand il n'auroit pü prolonger la vie à son fils que pour quelques mois, ou pour peu d'années.

Mois quand on se represente que l'Enfant a veçu prés pe quatre-vingts ans, & qu'il a composé quatre-vingts Ouvrages differents tous fruits d'une longue lecture—il faut convenir que tout ce qui est incroyable n'est pas toujours faux, & que la "Vraisemblance n'est pas toujours du côté de la Verité."

Il n'avoit que dix-neuf ans lorsqu'il composa Gonopsychanthropologia de Origine Animæ humanæ.

(Les Enfans celebres, revùs & corrigés par M. de la Monnoye de l'Academie Françoise.)

and my uncle Toby off the stairs, and to put them to bed.

—'Tis even high time; for, except a short nap which they both got whilst Trim was boring the jack-boots,—and which, by the bye, did my father no sort of good, upon the score of the bad hinge,—they have not else shut their eyes since nine hours before the time that Doctor Slop was led into the back-parlor in that dirty pickle by Obadiah.

Was every day of my life to be as busy a day as this,—and to take up——Truce;

I will not finish that sentence till I have made an observation upon the strange state of affairs between the reader and myself, just as things stand at present:—an observation never applicable before to any one biographical writer since the creation of the world, but to myself;—and, I believe, will never hold good to any other, until its final destruction;—and, therefore, for the very novelty of it alone, it must be worth your Worships' attending to.

I am this month one whole year older than I was this time twelve-month; and having got, as you perceive, almost into the middle of my third volume,*—and no farther than to my first day's life,—'tis demonstrative that I have 364 days more life to write just now, than when I first set out, so that, instead of advancing, as a common writer, in my work with what I have been doing at it;—on the contrary, I am just thrown so many volumes back.—Was every day of my life to be as busy a day as this,—And why not?—and the transactions and opinions of it to take up as much description,—And for what reason should they be cut short? as at this rate I should just live 364 times faster than I should write,—it must follow, an' please your Worships, that the more I write, the more I shall have to write,—and, consequently, the more your Worships read, the more your Worships will have to read.

Will this be good for your Worships' eyes?

It will do well for mine; and was it not that my *Opinions* will be the death of me, I perceive I shall lead a fine life of it out of this self-same *Life* of mine; or, in other words, shall lead a couple of fine lives together.

As for the proposal of twelve volumes a year, or a volume a month, it no way alters my prospects:—write as I will, and rush as I may into the middle of things, as Horace advises,—I shall never overtake myself, whipp'd and driven to the last pinch. At the worst I shall have one day the start of my pen,—and one day is enough for two volumes!—and two volumes will be enough for one year.—

Heaven prosper the manufacturers of paper under this propitious reign, which is now opened to us! as I trust its providence will prosper every thing else in it that is taken in hand.

As for the propagation of geese, I give myself no concern,—Nature is all-bountiful;—I shall never want tools to work with.

—So then, friend, you have got my father and my uncle Toby off the stairs, and seen them to bed?—And how did you manage it?—You dropp'd a curtain at the stair-foot. I thought you had no other way for it.—Here's a crown for your trouble.

CHAP. XIV.

—THEN reach my breeches off the chair, said my father to Susannah,——There is not a moment's time to dress you, Sir, cried Susannah,—the child is as black in the face as my —— As your what? said my father; for, like all orators, he was a dear searcher into comparisons.——Bless me, Sir, said Susannah, the child's in a fit.——And where's Mr. Yorick?——Never where he should be, said Susannah; but his curate's in the dressing-room, with the child upon his arm, waiting for the name;—and my mistress bid me run as fast as I could to know, as Captain Shandy is the godfather, whether it should not be called after him?

Were one sure, said my father to himself, scratching his eye-brow, that the child was expiring, one might as well compliment my brother Toby as not,—and it would be a pity, in such a case, to throw away so great

* According to the original editions.

a name as Trismegistus upon him:—but he may recover.

No, no—said my father to Susannah, I'll get up,——There is no time, cried Susannah, the child's as black as my shoe.——Trismegistus, said my father.—But stay,—thou art a leaky vessel, Susannah, added my father; canst thou carry Trismegistus in thy head the length of the gallery without scattering?——Can I? cried Susannah, shutting the door in a huff.——If she can, I'll be shot, said my father, bouncing out of bed in the dark, and groping for his breeches.

Susannah ran with all speed along the gallery.

My father made all possible speed to find his breeches.

Susannah got the start, and kept it.—'Tis Tris—something, cried Susannah.——There is no christian name in the world, said the curate, beginning with Tris—, but Tristram.——Then 'tis Tristram-gistus, quoth Susannah.

——There is no gistus to it, noodle!—'tis my own name, replied the curate, dipping his hand, as he spoke, into the bason; Tristram! said he, &c. &c. &c. &c.:—so Tristram was I called, and Tristram shall I be to the day of my death.

My father followed Susannah, with his night-gown across his arm, with nothing more than his breeches on; fastened, through haste, with but a single button; and that button, through haste, thrust only half into the button-hole.

——She has not forgot the name? cried my father, half-opening the door.——No, no, said the curate, with a tone of intelligence.——And the child is better, cried Susannah.——And how does your mistress?——As well, said Susannah, as can be expected.——Pish! said my father, the button of his breeches slipping out of the button-hole;—so that whether the interjection was levelled at Susannah or the button-hole;—whether Pish was an interjection of contempt, or an interjection of modesty, is a doubt; and must be a doubt till I shall have time to write the three following favorite chapters; that is, my chapter of chamber-maids, my chapter of pishes, and my chapter of button-holes.

All the light I am able to give the reader at present is this, That the moment my father cried Pish! he whisk'd himself about,—and with his breeches held up by one hand, and his night-gown thrown across the arm of the other, he returned along the gallery to bed, something slower than he came.

CHAP. XV.

I wish I could write a chapter upon sleep.

A fitter occasion could never have presented itself, than what this moment offers, when all the curtains of the family are drawn,—the candles put out,—and no creature's eyes are open but a single one—for the other has been shut these twenty years, of my mother's nurse.

It is a fine subject.

And yet, as fine as it is, I would undertake to write a dozen chapters upon button-holes, both quicker and with more fame, than a single chapter upon this.

Button holes! there is something lively in the very idea of 'em;—and trust me, when I get amongst 'em,—you gentry with great beards, look as grave as you will,—I'll make merry work with my button-holes,—I shall have 'em all to myself,—'tis a maiden subject,—I shall run foul of no man's wisdom or fine saying in it.

But for sleep,—I know I shall make nothing of it before I begin;—I am no dab at your fine sayings, in the first place;—and in the next, I cannot for my soul set a grave face upon a bad matter, and tell the world,—'tis the refuge of the unfortunate,—the enfranchisement of the prisoner,—the downy lap of the hopeless, the weary, and the broken-hearted; nor could I set out with a lie in my mouth, by affirming that of all the soft and delicious functions of our nature, by which the great Author of it, in his bounty, has been pleased to recompense the sufferings wherewith his justice and his good pleasure has wearied us,—that this is the chiefest (I know pleasures worth ten of :—or what a happiness it is to man, the anxieties and passions of the day are over, and he lies down upon his back, that his soul shall be so seated within him, that whichever way she turns her eyes, the heavens shall look calm and sweet above her,—no desire,—or fear,—or doubt, that troubles the air; nor any difficulty, past, present, or to come, that the imagination may not pass over without offence, in that sweet secession.

"God's blessing," said Sancho Pança, "be upon the man who first invented this "self-same thing called Sleep:—it covers "a man all over like a cloak."——Now there is more to me in this, and it speaks warmer to my heart and affections, than all the dissertations squeez'd out of the heads of the learned together upon the subject.

—Not that I altogether disapprove of what Montaigne advances upon it;—'tis admirable in its way:—(I quote by memory.)

The world enjoys other pleasures, says he, as they do that of sleep, without tasting or feeling it as it slips and passes by.—We should study and ruminate upon it, in order to render proper thanks to him who grants it to us.——For this end, I cause myself to be disturbed in my sleep, that I may the better and more sensibly relish it:——and yet I see few, says he again, who live with less sleep, when need requires: my body is capable of a firm, but not of a violent and sudden agitation,—I evade of late all violent exercises,—I am never weary with walking:—but from my youth, I never liked to ride upon pavements. I love to lie hard and alone, and even without my wife.——This last word may stagger the faith of the world;—but remember, "La Vraisemblance," (as Bayle says in the affair of Liceti) "n'est pas toujours du Côté "de la Verité."——And so much for sleep.

CHAP. XVI.

If my wife will but venture him,—brother Toby, Trismegistus shall be dress'd and brought down to us, whilst you and I are getting our breakfast together.

Go, tell Susannah, Obadiah, to step here.

She is run up-stairs, answered Obadiah, this very instant, sobbing and crying, and wringing her hands as if her heart would break.——

We shall have a rare month of it, said my father, turning his head from Obadiah, and looking wistfully in my uncle Toby's face for some time,—we shall have a devilish month of it, brother Toby, said my father, setting his arms a-kimbo, and shaking his head: fire, water, women, wind,—brother Toby!——'Tis some misfortune, quoth my uncle Toby.——That it is, cried my father,—to have so many jarring elements breaking loose, and riding triumph in every corner of a gentleman's house.—Little boots it to the peace of a family, brother Toby, that you and I possess ourselves, and sit here silent and unmov'd,—whilst such a storm is whistling over our heads.—

And what's the matter, Susannah?——They have called the child Tristram;—and my mistress is just got out of an hysteric fit about it.——No!—'tis not my fault, said Susannah,—I told him it was Tristram gistus.

——Make tea for yourself, brother Toby said my father, taking down his hat;—but how different from the sallies and agitations of voice and members which a common reader would imagine!

For he spake in the sweetest modulation, and took down his hat with the genteelest movement of limbs, that ever affliction harmonized and attuned together.

Go to the bowling-green for Corporal Trim, said my uncle Toby, speaking to Obadiah, as soon as my father left the room.

CHAP. XVII.

When the misfortune of my Nose fell so heavily upon my father's head,—the reader remembers that he walked instantly up stairs, and cast himself down upon his bed; and from hence, unless he has a great insight into human nature, he will be apt to expect a rotation of the same ascending and descending movements from him, upon this misfortune of my Name.—No.

The different weight, dear Sir,—nay

even the different package of two vexations of the same weight,—makes a very wide difference in our manners of bearing and getting through with them.—It is not half an hour ago, when (in the great hurry and precipitation of a poor Devil's writing for daily bread) I threw a fair sheet, which I had just finished, and carefully wrote out, slap into the fire, instead of the foul one.

Instantly I snatched off my wig, and threw it perpendicularly, with all imaginable violence, up to the top of the room:—indeed I caught it as it fell:—but there was an end of the matter; nor do I think any thing else in Nature would have given such immediate ease. She, dear goddess, by an instantaneous impulse, in all *provoking cases*, determines us to a sally of this or that member,—or else she thrusts us into this or that place, or posture of the body, we know not why;—but mark, Madam, we live amongst riddles and mysteries:—the most obvious things which come in our way have dark sides, which the quickest sight cannot penetrate into: and even the clearest and most exalted understandings amongst us find ourselves puzzled and at a loss in almost every cranny of Nature's works: so that this, like a thousand other things, falls out for us in a way, which though we cannot reason upon it, yet we find the good of it, may it please your Reverences and your Worships,—and that's enough for us.

Now, my father could not lie down with this affliction for his life,—nor could he carry it up stairs like the other;—he walked composedly out with it to the fish-pond.

Had my father leaned his head upon his hand, and reasoned an hour which way to have gone,—Reason, with all her force, could not have directed him to any thing like it: there is something, Sir, in fish-ponds:—but what it is, I leave to system-builders and fish-pond-diggers betwixt 'em to find out;—but there is something, under the first disorderly transport of the humors, so unaccountably becalming in an orderly and a short walk towards one of them, that I have often wondered that neither Pythagoras, nor Plato, nor Solon, nor Lycurgus, nor Mahomet, nor any one of your noted lawgivers, ever gave order about them.

CHAP. XVIII.

Your Honor, said Trim, shutting the parlor-door before he began to speak, has heard, I imagine, of this unlucky accident. ——O yes, Trim, said my uncle Toby, and it gives me great concern.——I am heartily concerned too; but I hope your Honor, replied Trim, will do me the justice to believe, that it was not in the least owing to me.——To thee,—Trim?—cried my uncle Toby, looking kindly in his face,—'twas Susannah's and the curate's folly betwixt them,——What business could they have together, an' please your Honor, in the garden?——In the gallery thou meanest, replied my uncle Toby.

Trim found he was upon a wrong scent, and stopped short with a low bow.——Two misfortunes, quoth the Corporal to himself, are twice as many at least as are needful to be talked over at one time;—the mischief the cow has done in breaking into the fortifications, may be told his Honor hereafter.——Trim's casuistry and address, under the cover of his low bow, prevented all suspicion in my uncle Toby; so he went on with what he had to say to Trim as follows:

——For my own part, Trim, though I can see little or no difference betwixt my nephew's being called Tristram or Trismegistus;—yet as the thing sits so near my brother's heart, Trim,—I would freely have given a hundred pounds rather than it should have happened.——A hundred pounds, an' please your Honor! replied Trim,—I would not give a cherry-stone to boot.——Nor would I, Trim, upon my own account, quoth my uncle Toby;—but my brother, whom there is no arguing with in this case, —maintains that a great deal more depends, Trim, upon christian names than what ignorant people imagine!—for he says there never was a great or heroic action performed, since the world began, by one called Tristram.—Nay, he will have it, Trim, that a man can neither be learned, or wise, or brave.——'Tis all fancy, an' please your Honor:—I fought just as well, replied the Corporal, when the regiment called me Trim, as when they called me James Butler.——And for my own part, said my uncle Toby, though I should blush to boast of myself, Trim:—yet, had my name been Alexander, I could have done no more at Namur than my duty.——Bless your Honor! cried Trim, advancing three steps as he spoke, does a man think of his christian name when he goes upon the attack?——Or when he stands in the trench, Trim? cried my uncle Toby, looking firm.——Or when he enters a breach? said Trim, pushing in between two chairs.——Or forces the lines? cried my uncle, rising up, and pushing his crutch like a pike,——Or facing a platoon? cried Trim, presenting his stick like a firelock.——Or when he marches up the glacis? cried my uncle Toby, looking warm and setting his foot upon his stool.——

CHAP. XIX.

My father was returned from his walk to he fish-pond,—and opened the parlor-door in the very height of the attack, just as my uncle Toby was marching up the glacis.—Trim recovered his arms.—Never was my uncle Toby caught in riding at such a desperate rate in his life! Alas! my uncle Toby! had not a weightier matter called forth all the ready eloquence of my father,—how hadst thou then, and thy poor *hobby-horse* too, been insulted!

My father hung up his hat with the same air he took it down; and, after giving a slight look at the disorder of the room, he took hold of one of the chairs which had formed the corporal's breach, and placing it over-against my uncle Toby, he sat down in it, and, as soon as the tea-things were taken away, and the door shut, he broke out into a lamentation as follows:

MY FATHER'S LAMENTATION.

It is in vain longer, said my father, addressing himself as much to Ernulphus's curse, which was laid upon the corner of the chimney-piece,—as to my uncle Toby, who sat under it;—it is in vain longer, said my father, in the most querulous monotony imaginable, to struggle as I have done against this most uncomfortable of human persuasions.—I see it plainly, that either for my own sins, brother Toby, or the sins and follies of the Shandy family, Heaven has thought fit to draw forth the heaviest of its artillery against me; and that the prosperity of my child is the point upon which the whole force of it is directed to play.—Such a thing would batter the whole universe about our ears, brother Shandy, said my uncle Toby, if it was so.——Unhappy Tristram! child of wrath! child of decrepitude! interruption! mistake! and discontent! What one misfortune or disaster in the book of embryotic evils, that could unmechanize thy frame, or entangle thy filaments, which has not fallen upon thy head, or even thou camest into the world; what evils in thy passage into it!—what evils since! produced into being, in the decline of thy father's days,—when the powers of his imagination and of his body were waxing feeble,—when radical heat and radical moisture, the elements which should have temper'd thine, were drying up; and nothing left to found thy stamina in, but negations!—'Tis pitiful,—brother Toby, at the best, and called out for all the little helps that care and attention on both sides could give it.—But how were we defeated! You know the event, brother Toby!—'tis too melancholy a one to be repeated now—when the few animal spirits I was worth in the world, and with which memory, fancy, and quick parts should have been convey'd,—were all dispersed, confused, confounded, scattered, and sent to the devil!—

Here then was the time to have put a stop to this persecution against him,—and tried an experiment at least, whether calmness and serenity of mind in your sister, with a due attention, brother Toby, to her evacuations and repletions,—and the rest of her non-naturals, might not, in the course of nine months' gestation, have set all things to rights.—My child was bereft of these!—What a teasing life did she lead herself, and, consequently, her fœtus too, with that nonsensical anxiety of hers about lying-in in town!——I thought my sister submitted with the greatest patience, replied my uncle Toby;—I never heard her utter one fretful word about it.——She fumed inwardly, cried my father; and that, let me tell you, brother, was ten times worse for the child,—and then, what battles did she fight with me! and what perpetual storms about the midwife!——There she gave vent, said my uncle Toby.——Vent! cried my father, looking up.

But what was all this, my dear Toby, to the injuries done us by my child's coming head-foremost into the world, when all I wished in this general wreck of his frame, was to have saved this little casket unbroke, unrifled!—

With all my precautions, how was my system turned topsy-turvy in the womb with my child! his head exposed to the hand of violence, and a pressure of 470 pounds avoirdupois weight acting perpendicularly upon its apex,—that at this hour, 'tis ninety *per cent.* insurance, that the fine net-work of the intellectual web be not rent and torn to a thousand tatters.

——Still we could have done!—Fool, Coxcomb, Puppy,—give him but a *Nose*;—Cripple, Dwarf, Driveller, Goosecap,—(shape him as you will) the door of fortune stands open,—O Licetus! Licetus! had I been bless'd with a fœtus five inches long and a half, like thee,—Fate might have done her worst.

Still, brother Toby, there was one cast of the die left for our child, after all:—O Tristram! Tristram! Tristram!

We will send for Mr. Yorick, said my uncle Toby.

You may send for whom you will, replied my father.

CHAP. XX.

What a rate have I gone on at, curveting and frisking it away, two up and two down, for three volumes* together, without looking once behind, or even on one side of me, to see whom I trod upon!—I'll tread upon no one,—quoth I to myself, when I mounted·—I'll take a good rattling gallop: but I'll not hurt the poorest jackass upon the road.—So off I set,—up one lane,—down another,—through this turnpike,—over that, as if the arch-jockey of jockeys had got behind me.

Now, ride at this rate with what good intention and resolution you may,—'tis a million to one you'll do some one a mischief, if not yourself.—He's flung,—he's off,—he's lost his seat,—he's down,—he'll break his neck;—see! if he has not galloped full among the scaffolding of the undertaking critics!—he'll knock his brains out against some of their posts!—he's bounced out!—look,—he's now riding like a madcap, full tilt through a whole crowd of painters, fiddlers, poets, biographers, physicians, lawyers, logicians, players, schoolmen, churchmen, statesmen, soldiers, casuists, connoisseurs, prelates, popes, and engineers.—Don't fear, said I,—I'll not hurt the poorest jackass upon the King's highway.——But your horse throws dirt; see, you've splash'd a bishop!—I hope in God, 'twas only Ernulphus, said I.—But you have squirted full in the faces of Mess. Le Moyne, De Romigny, and De Marcilly, doctors of the Sorbonne.—That was last year, replied I.—But you have trod this moment upon a king.—Kings have bad times on't, said I, to be trod upon by such people as me.

You have done it, replied my accuser.

I deny it, quoth I, and so have got off; and here am I standing with my bridle in one hand, and with my cap in the other, to tell my story.——And what is it? You shall hear in the next chapter.

* According to the original editions.

CHAP. XXI.

As Francis the First, of France, was one winterly night warming himself over the embers of a wood-fire, and talking with his first minister of sundry things for the good of the state,*—it would not be amiss, said the king, stirring up the embers with his cane, if this good understanding betwixt ourselves and Switzerland was a little strengthened.——There is no end, Sire, replied the minister, in giving money to these people,—they would swallow up the treasury of France——Poo! poo! answered the king,—there are more ways, Mons. le Premier, of bribing states, besides that of giving money;—I'll pay Switzerland the

* Vide Menagiana, Vol. I.

honor of standing godfather for my next child.——Your majesty, said the minister, in so doing, would have all the grammarians in Europe upon your back;—Switzerland, as a republic, being a female, can in no construction be godfather.——She may be godmother, replied Francis, hastily;—so, announce my intentions by a courier tomorrow morning.

I am astonished, said Francis the First (that day fortnight), speaking to his minister as he entered the closet, that we have had no answer from Switzerland.——Sire, I wait upon you this moment, said Mons. le Premier, to lay before you my dispatches upon that business.——They take it kindly, said the king.——They do, Sire, replied the minister, and have the highest sense of the honor your majesty has done them,—but the republic, as godmother, claims her right, in this case, of naming the child.

In all reason quoth the king;—she will christen him Francis, or Henry, or Lewis, or some other name that she knows will be agreeable to us.——Your majesty is deceived, replied the minister.—I have this hour received a dispatch from our resident, with the determination of the republic on that point also.—And what name has the republic fixed upon for the Dauphin? Shadrach, Meshech, Abed-nego, replied the minister.——By Saint Peter's girdle, I will have nothing to do with the Swiss, cried Francis the First, pulling up his breeches, and walking hastily across the floor.

Your majesty, replied the minister calmly, cannot bring yourself off.

We'll pay them in money,—said the king.

Sire, there are not sixty thousand crowns in the treasury, answered the minister.——I'll pawn the best jewel in my crown, quoth Francis the First.

Your honor stands pawned already in this matter, answered Monsieur le Premier.

Then, Mons. le Premier, said the king, by —— we'll go to war with 'em.

CHAP. XXII.

Albeit, gentle reader, I have lusted earnestly, and endeavored carefully (according to the measure of such a slender skill as God has vouchsafed me, and as convenient leisure from other occasions of needful profit and healthful pastime have permitted) that these little books which I here put into thy hands, might stand instead of many bigger books,—yet have I carried myself towards thee in such fanciful guise of careless disport, that right sore am I ashamed now to entreat thy lenity seriously,—in beseeching thee to believe it of me, that, in the story of my father and his christian names,—I have no thoughts of treading upon Francis the First,—nor, in the affair of the nose,—upon Francis the Ninth,—nor, in the character of my uncle Toby, of characterizing the militating spirits of my country;—the wound upon his groin is a wound to every comparison of that kind:—nor by Trim,—that I meant the Duke of Ormond,—or that my book is wrote against predestination, or free will, or taxes;—if 'tis wrote against any thing,—'tis wrote, an't please your Worships, against the Spleen! in order, by a more frequent and a more convulsive elevation and depression of the diaphragm, and the succussations of the intercostal and abdominal muscles in laughter, to drive the *gall* and other *bitter juices* from the gall-bladder, liver, and sweet-bread of his majesty's subjects, with all the inimicitious passions which belong to them, down into their duodenums.

CHAP. XXIII.

But can the thing be undone, Yorick? said my father:—for in my opinion, continued he, it cannot. I am a vile canonist, replied Yorick;——but of all evils, holding suspense to be the most tormenting, we shall at least know the worst of this matter. —I hate these great dinners, said my father. ——The size of the dinner is not the point, answered Yorick,—we want, Mr. Shandy, to dive into the bottom of this doubt, whether the name can be changed or not;—and as the beards of so many commissaries, officials, advocates, proctors, registers, and of the most eminent of our school-divines, and others, are all to meet in the middle of one table, and Didius has so pressingly invited you,—who, in your distress would miss such an occasion? All that is requisite, continued Yorick, is to apprize Didius, and let him manage a conversation after dinner so as to introduce the subject.—Then my brother Toby, cried my father, clapping his two hands together, shall go with us.

——Let my old tie-wig, quoth my uncle Toby, and my laced regimentals, be hung to the fire all night, Trim.

CHAP. XXV.

——No doubt, Sir,—there is a whole chapter wanting here,—and a chasm of ten pages made in the book by it;—but the bookbinder is neither a fool, nor a knave, nor a puppy,—nor is the book a jot more imperfect (at least upon that score);—but, on the contrary the book is more perfect and complete by wanting the chapter, than having it, as I shall demonstrate to your Reverences in this manner.—I question first, by the bye, whether the same experiment might not be made as successfully upon sundry other chapters,—but there is no end, an' please your Reverences, in trying experiments upon chapters,—we have had enough of it;——so there's an end of that matter.

But before I begin my demonstration, let me only tell you, that the chapter which I have torn out, and which otherwise you would all have been reading just now instead of this,—was the description of my father's, my uncle Toby's, Trim's, and Obadiah's setting out and journeying to the visitation at ****.

We'll go in the coach, said my father.—Prithee, have the arms been altered, Obadiah?—It would have made my story much better to have begun with telling you that at the time my mother's arms were added to the Shandy's, when the coach was repainted upon my father's marriage, it had so fallen out, that the coach-painter, whether by performing all his works with the left hand, like Turphilius the Roman, or Hans Holbein of Basil,—or whether 'twas more from the blunder of his head than hand,—or whether, lastly, it was from the sinister turn which every thing relating to our family was apt to take,—it so fell out, however, to our reproach, that instead of the *bend-dexter*, which, since Harry the Eighth's reign, was honestly our due,—a *bend-sinister*, by some of these fatalities, had been drawn quite across the field of the Shandy arms. 'Tis scarce credible that the mind of so wise a man as my father was, could be so much incommoded with so small a matter. The word coach,—let it be whose it would,—or coach-man, or coach-horse, or coach-hire, could never be named in the family, but he constantly complained of carrying this vile mark of illegitimacy upon the door of his own: he never once was able to step into the coach, or out of it, without turning round to take a view of the arms, and making a vow at the same time, that it was the last time he would ever set his foot in it again, till the *bend-sinister* was taken out;—but, like the affair of the hinge, it was one of the many things which the Destinies had set down in their books ever to be grumbled at (and in wiser families than ours)—but never to be mended.

——Has the *bend-sinister* been brush'd out, I say? said my father.——There has been nothing brush'd out, Sir, answered Obadiah, but the lining.——We'll go o' horseback, said my father, turning to Yorick.——Of all things in the world, except politics, the clergy know the least of heraldry, said Yorick.——No matter for that, cried my father; I should be sorry to appear with a blot in my escutcheon before them.——Never mind the *bend-sinister*, said my uncle Toby, putting on his tie-wig. ——No, indeed, said my father: you may go with my aunt Dinah to a visitation with a *bend-sinister*, if you think fit.——My poor uncle Toby blushed. My father was vexed at himself.——No,—my dear brother Toby, said my father, changing his tone; but the damp of the coach-lining about my loins, may give me the sciatica again, as it did December, January, and February, last winter: so, if you please, you shall ride my wife's pad;—and, as you are to preach,

Yorick, you had better make the best of your way before, and leave me to take care of my brother Toby, and to follow at our own rates.

Now, the chapter I was obliged to tear out, was the description of this cavalcade, in which corporal Trim and Obadiah, upon two coach-horses abreast, led the way as slow as a patrol,—whilst my uncle Toby, in his laced regimentals and tie-wig, kept his rank with my father, in deep roads and dissertations alternately, upon the advantage of learning and arms, as each could get the start.

——But the painting of this journey, upon reviewing it, appears to be so much above the style and manner of any thing else I have been able to paint in this book, that it could not have remained in it, without depreciating every other scene, and destroying, at the same time, that necessary equipoise and balance (whether of good or bad) betwixt chapter and chapter, from whence the just proportions and harmony of the whole work result. For my own part, I am but just set up in the business, so know little about it;—but, in my opinion, to write a book, is for all the world like humming a song;—be but in tune with yourself, Madam, 'tis no matter how high or how low you take it.

—This is the reason, may it please your Reverences, that some of the lowest and flattest compositions pass off very well—(as Yorick told my uncle Toby one night) by siege.——My uncle Toby looked brisk at the sound of the word *siege;* but could make neither head nor tail of it.

I'm to preach at court next Sunday, said Homenas:—run over my notes:——so I humm'd over Doctor Homenas's notes;—the modulation's very well;—'twill do, Homenas, if it holds on at this rate;—so on I humm'd,—and a tolerable tune I thought it was; and to this hour, may it please your Reverences, had never found out how low, how flat, how spiritless and jejune it was, but that, all of a sudden, up started an air in the middle of it, so fine, so rich, so heavenly,—it carried my soul up with it into the other world: now had I (as Montaigne complained in a parallel accident)—had I found the declivity easy, or the ascent accessible, -certes I had been outwitted.—Your notes, Homenas, I should have said, are good notes;—but it was so perpendicular a precipice,—so wholly cut off from the rest of the work, that, by the first note I humm'd, I found myself flying into the other world, and from thence discovered the vale from whence I came, so deep, so low, and dismal, that I shall never have the heart to descend into it again.

☞ A dwarf who brings a standard along with him to measure his own size,—take my word, is a dwarf in more articles than one.—And so much for tearing out of chapters.

CHAP. XXVI.

—See, if he is not cutting it all into slips!——and giving them about him to light their pipes! 'Tis abominable, answered Didius.——It should not go unnoticed, said Doctor Kysarcius:——☞ he was of the Kysarcii of the Low Countries.

Methinks, said Didius, half rising from his chair, in order to remove a bottle and a tall decanter, which stood in a direct line betwixt him and Yorick,—you might have spared this sarcastic stroke, and have hit upon a more proper place, Mr. Yorick;—or at least upon a more proper occasion to have shown your contempt of what we have been about. If the sermon is of no better worth than to light pipes with,—'twas certainly, Sir, not good enough to be preached before so learned a body; and, if 'twas good enough to be preached before so learned a body,—'twas certainly, Sir, too good to light their pipes with afterwards.

——I have got him fast hung up, quoth Didius to himself, upon one of the two horns of my dilemma;—let him get off as he can.

I have undergone such unspeakable torments, in bringing forth this sermon, quoth Yorick, upon this occasion,—that I declare, Didius, I would suffer martyrdom,—and, if it was possible, my horse with me, a thousand times over, before I would sit down and make such another: I was delivered of it at the wrong end of me;—it came from my head instead of my heart;—and it is for the pain it gave me, both in the writing and preaching of it, that I revenge myself of it in this manner.——To preach, to show the extent of our reading, or the subtleties of our wit,—to parade it in the eyes of the vulgar with the beggarly accounts of a little learning, tinsell'd over with a few words, which glitter, but convey little light and less warmth,—is a dishonest use of the poor single half hour in a week which is put into our hands:—'tis not preaching the gospel,—but ourselves.—For my own part, continued Yorick, I had rather direct five words point-blank to the heart.

As Yorick pronounced the word *point-blank*, my uncle Toby rose up to say something upon projectiles,—when a single word, and no more, uttered from the opposite side of the table, drew every one's ears towards it:—a word of all others in the dictionary the last in that place to be expected:—a word I am ashamed to write,—yet must be written, must be read;—illegal, uncanonical,—guess ten thousand guesses, multiplied into themselves,—rack,—torture your invention for ever, you're where you was.—In short, I'll tell it in the next chapter.

CHAP. XXVII.

ZOUNDS! ——————————————

——————————————

——————Z——ds! cried Phutatorius, partly to himself,—and yet high enough to be heard;—and, what seemed odd, 'twas uttered in a construction of look, and in a tone of voice, somewhat between that of a man in amazement, and one in bodily pain.

One or two who had very nice ears, and could distinguish the expression and mixture of the two tones as plainly as a *third* or a *fifth*, or any other chord in music,—were the most puzzled and perplexed with it.—The concord was good itself;—but then 'twas quite out of the key, and no way applicable to the subject started:—so that, with all their knowledge, they could not tell what in the world to make of it.

Others, who knew nothing of musical expression, and merely lent their ears to the plain import of the word, imagined that Phutatorius, who was somewhat of a choleric spirit, was just going to snatch the cudgels out of Didius's hands, in order to bemaul Yorick to some purpose;—and that the desperate monosyllable Z——ds, was the exordium to an oration, which, as they judged from the sample, presaged but a rough kind of handling of him; so that my uncle Toby's good-nature felt a pang for what Yorick was about to undergo. But seeing Phutatorius stop short, without any attempt or desire to go on,—a third party began to suppose, that it was no more than an involuntary respiration, casually forming itself into the shape of a twelve-penny oath,—without the sin or substance of one.

Others, and especially one or two who sat next him, looked upon it, on the contrary, as a real and substantial oath, propensely formed against Yorick, to whom he was known to bear no good liking;—which said oath, as my father philosophized upon it, actually lay fretting and fuming at that very time in the upper regions of Phutatorius's purtenance; and so was naturally, and according to the due course of things, first squeezed out by the sudden influx of blood which was driven into the right ventricle of Phutatorius's heart, by the stroke of surprise which so strange a theory of preaching had excited.

How finely we argue upon mistaken facts!

There was not a soul busied in all these various reasonings upon the monosyllable which Phutatorius uttered,—who did not take this for granted, proceeding upon it as from an axiom, namely, that Phutatorius's mind was intent upon the subject of debate which was arising between Didius and Yorick; and indeed, as he looked first towards the one, and then towards the other, with the air of a man listening to what was going forwards,—who would not have thought the same? But the truth was, that Phutatorius knew not one word or one syllable of what was passing;—but his whole thoughts and attention were taken up with a transaction which was going forwards at that very instant within the precincts of his own Galligaskins, and in a part of them, where of all others he stood most interested to watch accidents: so that, notwithstanding he looked with all the attention in the world, and had gradually screwed up every nerve and muscle in his face to the utmost pitch the instrument would bear, in order, as it was thought, to give a sharp reply to Yorick, who sat over-against him,—yet, I say, was Yorick never once in any one domicil of Phutatorius's brain;—but the true cause of his exclamation lay at least a yard below.

This I will endeavor to explain to you with all imaginable decency.

You must be informed then, that Gastripheres, who had taken a turn into the kitchen a little before dinner, to see how things went on,—observing a wicker-basket of fine chestnuts standing upon the dresser, had ordered that a hundred or two of them might be roasted and sent in as soon as dinner was over;—Gastripheres enforcing his orders about them, that Didius, but Phutatorius especially, were particularly fond of 'em.

About two minutes before the time that my uncle Toby interrupted Yorick's harangue, — Gastripheres's chestnuts were brought in:—and as Phutatorius's fondness for 'em was uppermost in the waiter's head, he laid them directly before Phutatorius, wrapt up hot in a clean damask napkin.

Now, whether it was physically impossible, with half a dozen hands all thrust into the napkin at a time,—but that some one chestnut, of more life and rotundity than the rest, must be put in motion,—it so fell out, however, that one was actually sent rolling off the table; and as Phutatorius sat straddling under,—it fell perpendicularly into that particular aperture of Phutatorius's breeches, for which, to the shame and indelicacy of our language be it spoke, there is no chaste word throughout all Johnson's Dictionary:—let it suffice to say,—it was that particular aperture which, in all good societies, the laws of decorum do strictly require, like the temple of Janus (in peace at least) to be universally shut up.

The neglect of this punctilio in Phutatorius (which by the bye should be a warning to all mankind) had opened a door to this accident.—

Accident I call it, in compliance to a received mode of speaking;—but in no opposition to the opinion either of Acrites or Mythogeras in this matter; I know they were both prepossessed and fully persuaded of it,—and are so to this hour, That there was nothing of accident in the whole event,—but that the chestnut's taking that particular course, and in a manner of its own accord,—and then falling with all its heat directly into that one particular place, and no other,—was a real judgment upon Phutatorius for that filthy and obscene treatise *de Concubinis retinendis*, which Phutatorius had published about twenty years ago,—and was that identical week going to give the world a second edition of.

It is not my business to dip my pen in this controversy: much, undoubtedly, may be wrote on both sides of the question:—all that concerns me, as an historian, is to represent the matter of fact, and render it credible to the reader, that the hiatus in Phutatorius's breeches was sufficiently wide to receive the chestnut;—and that the chestnut, somehow or other, did fall perpendicularly, and piping hot, into it, without Phutatorius's perceiving it, or any one else at that time.

The genial warmth which the chestnut imparted, was not undelectable for the first twenty or five-and-twenty seconds;—and did no more than gently solicit Phutatorius's attention towards the part:—but the heat gradually increasing, and, in a few seconds more, getting beyond the point of all sober pleasure, and then advancing with all speed into the regions of pain, the soul of Phutatorius, together with all his ideas, his thoughts, his attention, his imagination, judgment, resolution, deliberation, ratiocination, memory, fancy, with ten battalions of animal spirits, all tumultuously crowded down, through different defiles and circuits, to the place in danger, leaving all his upper regions, as you may imagine, as empty as my purse.

With the best intelligence which all these messengers could bring him back, Phutatorius was not able to dive into the secret of what was going forward below; nor could he make any kind of conjecture what the devil was the matter with it. However, as he knew not what the true cause might turn out, he deemed it most prudent, in the situation he was in at present,—to bear it, if possible, like a Stoic; which, with the help of some wry faces and compursions of the mouth, he had certainly accomplished, had his imagination continued neuter:—but the sallies of the imagination are ungovernable in all things of this kind:—a thought instantly darted into his mind, that though the anguish had the sensation of glowing heat,—it might, notwithstanding that, be a bite as well as a burn; and if so, that possibly a newt or an asker, or some such detested reptile, had crept up, and was fastening his teeth;—the horrid idea of which, with a fresh glow of pain arising that instant from the chestnut, seized Phutatorius with a sudden panic,—and in the first terrifying disorder of the passion, it threw him, as it has done the best generals upon earth, quite off his guard:—the effect of which was this, that he leap'd incontinently up, uttering as he rose that interjection of surprise so much descanted upon, with the aposiopestic break after it, marked thus, Z——ds!—which, though not strictly canonical, was still as little as any man could have said upon the occasion;—and which, by the bye, whether canonical or not, Phutatorius could no more help than he could the cause of it.

Though this has taken up some time in the narrative, it took up little more time in the transaction than just to allow time for Phutatorius to draw forth the chestnut, and throw it down with violence upon the floor,—and for Yorick to rise from his chair, and pick the chestnut up.

It is curious to observe the triumph of slight incidents over the mind.—What incredible weight they have in forming and governing our opinions, both of men and things!—that trifles, light as air, shall waft a belief into the soul, and plant it so immovably within it,—that Euclid's demonstrations, could they be brought to batter it in breach, should not all have power to overthrow it!

Yorick, I said, picked up the chestnut which Phutatorius's wrath had flung down:—the action was trifling;—I am ashamed to account for it:—he did it,—for no reason, but that he thought the chestnut not a jot worse for the adventure;—and that he thought a good chestnut worth stooping for.—But this incident, trifling as it was, wrought differently in Phutatorius's head. He considered this act of Yorick's, in getting off his chair and picking up the chestnut, as a plain acknowledgment in him, that the chestnut was originally his;—and, in course, that it must have been the owner of the chestnut, and no one else, who could have played him such a prank with it. What greatly confirmed him in this opinion, was this, That the table being parallelogramical, and very narrow, it afforded a fair opportunity for Yorick, who sat directly over-against Phutatorius, of slipping the chestnut in:—and consequently that he did it. The look of something more than suspicion, which Phutatorius cast full upon Yorick as these thoughts arose, too evidently spoke his opinion;—and as Phutatorius was naturally supposed to know more of the matter than any person besides, his opinion at once became the general one; and for a reason very different from any which have been yet given, in a little time it was put out of all manner of dispute.

When great or unexpected events fall out upon the stage of this sublunary world,—the mind of man, which is an inquisitive kind of a substance, naturally takes a flight behind the scenes, to see what is the cause and first spring of them.—The search was not long in this instance.

It was well known that Yorick had never a good opinion of the Treatise which Phutatorius had wrote, *de Concubinis retinendis*, as a thing which he feared had done hurt in the world:—and 'twas easily found out, that there was a mystical meaning in Yorick's prank,—and that his chucking the chestnut hot into Phutatorius's ***—*****, was a sarcastical fling at his book;—the doctrines of which, they said, had inflamed many an honest man in the same place.

This conceit awaken'd Somnolentius;—made Agelastes smile;—and, if you can recollect the precise look and air of a man's face intent in finding out a riddle,—it threw Gastripheres's into that form;—and, in short, was thought by many to be a master-stroke of arch wit.

This, as the reader has seen from one end to the other, was as groundless as the dreams of philosophy. Yorick, no doubt, as Shakspeare said of his ancestor,—"was a "man of jest," but it was temper'd with something which withheld him from that and many other ungracious pranks, of which he as undeservedly bore the blame;—but it was his misfortune, all his life long, to bear the imputation of saying and doing a thousand things, of which (unless my esteem blinds me) his nature was incapable. All I blame him for,—or rather, all I blame and alternately like him for, was that singularity of his temper, which would never suffer him to take pains to set a story right with the world, however in his power. In every ill-usage of that sort, he acted precisely as in the affair of his lean horse.—He could have explained it to his honor, but his spirit was above it; and besides, he ever looked upon the inventor, the propagator, and believer, of an illiberal report, alike so injurious to him,—he could not stoop to tell his story to them;—and so trusted to time and truth to do it for him.

This heroic cast produced him inconveniences in many respects;—in the present, it was followed by the fixed resentment of Phutatorius, who, as Yorick had just made an end of his chestnut, rose up from his chair a second time, to let him know it;—which indeed he did with a smile;—saying only,—that he would endeavor not to forget the obligation.

But you must mark and carefully separate and distinguish these two things in your mind:—

—The smile was for the company;

—The threat was for Yorick.

CHAP. XXVIII.

—Can you tell me, quoth Phutatorius, speaking to Gastripheres, who sat next to him,—for one would not apply to a surgeon in so foolish an affair,—can you tell me, Gastripheres, what is best to take out the fire?——Ask Eugenius, said Gastripheres. ——That greatly depends, said Eugenius, pretending ignorance of the adventure, upon the nature of the part.—If it is a tender part, and a part which can conveniently be wrapt up,——It is both the one and the other, replied Phutatorius, laying his hand as he spoke, with an emphatical nod of his head, upon the part in question, and lifting up his right leg at the same time, to ease and ventilate it.——If that is the case, said Eugenius, I would advise you, Phutatorius, not to tamper with it by any means; but if you will send to the next printer, and trust your cure to such a simple thing as a soft sheet of paper just come off the press,—you need do nothing more than twist it round.——The damp paper, quoth Yorick (who sat next to his friend Eugenius) though I know it has a refreshing coolness in it,—yet, I presume, is no more than the vehicle;—and that the oil and lamp-black, with which the paper is so strongly impregnated, does the business. ——Right, said Eugenius; and is, of any outward application I would venture to recommend, the most anodyne and safe.

Was it my case, said Gastripheres, as the main thing is the oil and lamp-black, I should spread them thick upon a rag, and clap it on directly.——That would make a very devil of it, replied Yorick.——And besides, added Eugenius, it would not answer the intention, which is the extreme neatness and elegance of the prescription; which the faculty hold to be half in half:—for consider, if the type is a very small one (which it should be) the sanative particles, which come into contact in this form, have the advantage of being spread so infinitely thin, and with such a mathematical equality (fresh paragraphs and large capitals excepted) as no art or management of the spatula can come up to.——It falls out very luckily, replied Phutatorius, that the second edition of my Treatise, *De Concubinis retinendis* is at this instant in the press. ——You may take any leaf of it, said Eugenius;—no matter which.——Provided, quoth Yorick, there is no bawdy in it.——

They are just now, replied Phutatorius, printing off the ninth chapter;—which is the last chapter but one in the book.——Pray, what is the title of that chapter? said Yorick; making a respectful bow to Phutatorius, as he spoke.——I think, answered Phutatorius, 'tis that *de Re Concubinariâ*.

For Heaven's sake, keep out of that chapter, quoth Yorick.

——By all means,—added Eugenius.

CHAP. XXIX.

—Now, quoth Didius, rising up, and laying his right hand, with his fingers spread, upon his breast,—had such a blunder about a christian name happened before the Reformation,——[It happened the day before yesterday, quoth my uncle Toby to himself] —and when baptism was administer'd in Latin,—['Twas all in English, said my uncle]—many things might have coincided with it; and upon the authority of sundry decreed cases, to have pronounced the baptism null,—with a power of giving the child a new name.—Had a priest, for instance, which was no uncommon thing, through ignorance of the Latin tongue, baptized a child of Tom-o'Stiles, *in nomine patriæ & filia & spiritum sanctos*,—the baptism was held null.——I beg your pardon, replied Kysarcius;—in that case, as the mistake was only the terminations, the baptism was valid;—and to have rendered it null, the blunder of the priest should have fallen upon the first syllable of each noun;—and not, as in your case, upon the last.

My father delighted in subtleties of this kind, and listen'd with infinite attention.

Gastripheres, for example, continued Kysarcius, baptizes a child of John Stradling's *in gomine Gatris, &c. &c.* instead of *in nomine Patris, &c.*—Is this a baptism?—No,—say the ablest canonists; inasmuch as the radix of each word is hereby torn up, and the sense and meaning of them removed and changed quite to another object;—for *gomine* does not signify a name, nor *gatris* a father.——What do they signify? said my uncle Toby. Nothing at all, —quoth Yorick.——Ergo, such a baptism is null, said Kysarcius.——

In course, answered Yorick,——in a tone two parts jest and one part earnest.——

But in the case cited, continued Kysarcius, where *patriæ* is put for *patris*, *filia* for *filii*, and so on;—as it is a fault only in the declension, and the roots of the words continue untouch'd, the inflections of their branches, either this way or that, does not in any sort hinder the baptism, inasmuch as the same sense continues in the words as before.——But then, said Didius, the intention of the priest's pronouncing them grammatically must have been proved to have gone along with it.——Right, answered Kysarcius; and of this, brother Didius, we have an instance in a decree of the decretals of Pope Leo the Third.—— But my brother's child, cried my uncle Toby, has nothing to do with the Pope;— 'tis the plain child of a Protestant gentleman, christen'd Tristram against the wills and wishes both of his father and mother, and all who are akin to it.——

If the wills and wishes, said Kysarcius, interrupting my uncle Toby, of those only who stand related to Mr. Shandy's child, were to have weight in this matter, Mrs. Shandy, of all people, has the least to do in it.——My uncle Toby laid down his pipe, and my father drew his chair still closer to the table, to hear the conclusion of so strange an introduction.

——It has not only been a question, Captain Shandy, amongst the* best lawyers and civilians in this land, continued Kysarcius, "Whether the mother be of kin to "her child;"—but, after much dispassionate inquiry and jactitation of the arguments on all sides,—it has been adjudged for the negative;—namely, "That the mother is "not of kin to her child."† My father instantly clapp'd his hand upon my uncle Toby's mouth, under color of whispering in his ear;—the truth was, he was alarmed for *Lillibullero*,—and having a great desire to hear more of so curious an argument,— he begg'd my uncle Toby, for Heaven's sake, not to disappoint him in it.——My uncle Toby gave a nod,—resumed his pipe, and contenting himself with whistling *Lillibullero* inwardly,—Kysarcius, Didius, and Triptolemus went on with the discourse as follows:—

This determination, continued Kysarcius, how contrary soever it may seem to run to the stream of vulgar ideas, yet had reason strongly on its side, and has been put out of all manner of dispute from the famous case, known commonly by the name of the Duke of Suffolk's Case.——It is cited in Brooke, said Triptolemus.——And taken notice of by Lord Coke, added Didius.—— And you may find it in Swinburn on Testaments, said Kysarcius.

* Vide Swinburn on Testaments, Part 7. § 8.

† Vide Brooke's Abridg. Tit. Administr. N. 47.

The case, Mr. Shandy, was this—

In the reign of Edward the Sixth, Charles Duke of Suffolk having issue a son by one venter, and a daughter by another venter, made his last will, wherein he devised goods to his son, and died: after whose death the son died also;—but without will, without wife, and without child;—his mother and his sister by the father's side (for she was born of the former venter) then living. The mother took the administration of her son's goods, according to the statute of the 21st of Harry the eighth; whereby it is enacted, That in case any person die intestate, the administration of his goods shall be committed to the next of kin.

The administration being thus (surreptitiously) granted to the mother,—the sister, by the father's side, commenced a suit before the Ecclesiastical Judge, alleging, 1st, That she herself was next of kin; and, 2dly, That the mother was not of kin at all to the party deceased; and, therefore, prayed the court, that the administration granted to the mother might be revoked, and be committed unto her, as next of kin to the deceased, by force of the said statute.

Hereupon, as it was a great cause, and much depending upon its issue,—and many causes of great property likely to be decided in times to come, by the precedent to be then made,—the most learned, as well in the laws of this realm as in the civil law, were consulted together, Whether the mother was of kin to her son, or no?—Whereunto not only the temporal lawyers,—but the church-lawyers,—the juris-consulti,—the jurisprudentes,—the civilians,—the advocates,—the commissaries,—the judges of the consistory and prerogative courts of Canterbury and York, with the master of the faculties, were all unanimously of opinion, That the mother was not of* kin to her child.——

And what said the Duchess of Suffolk to it? said my uncle Toby.

The unexpectedness of my uncle Toby's question, confounded Kysarcius more than the ablest advocate.—He stopp'd a full minute, looking in my uncle Toby's face without replying;—and in that single minute Triptolemus put by him, and took the lead as follows:

'Tis a ground and principle in the law, said Triptolemus, that things do not ascend, but descend in it; and I make no doubt 'tis for this cause, that however true it is that the child may be of the blood and seed of its parents,—that the parents, nevertheless, are not of the blood and seed of it; inasmuch as the parents are not begot by the child, but the child by the parents;—for so they write, *Liberi sunt de sanguine patris & matris, sed pater & mater non sunt de sanguine liberorum.*

——But this, Triptolemus, cried Didius, proves too much;—for, from this authority cited, it would follow, not only what indeed is granted on all sides, that the mother is not of kin to her child,—but the father likewise.——It is held, said Triptolemus, the better opinion; because the father, the mother, and the child, though they be three persons, yet are they but (*una caro**) one flesh; and consequently no degree of kindred,—or any method of acquiring one *in nature.*——There you push the argument again too far, cried Didius,—for there is no prohibition *in nature,* though there is in the Levitical law,—but that a man may beget a child upon his grandmother;—in which case, supposing the issue a daughter, she would stand in relation both of——But who ever thought, cried Kysarcius, of lying with his grandmother?——The young gentleman, replied Yorick, whom Selden speaks of,—who not only thought of it, but justified his intention to his father by the argument drawn from the law of retaliation:—"You lay, Sir, with my mother," said the lad; "why may not I lie with yours?"——'Tis the *argumentum commune,* added Yorick.——'Tis as good, replied Eugenius, taking down his hat, as they deserve.

The company broke up.

CHAP. XXX.

—And pray, said my uncle Toby, leaning upon Yorick, as he and my father were helping him leisurely down the stairs,—

* Mater non numeratur inter consanguineos, Bald. in ult. C. de Verb. signific.

* Vide Brooke's Abridg. tit. Administr. N 47.

don't be terrified, Madam; this stair-case conversation is not so long as the last.—And pray, Yorick, said my uncle Toby, which way is this said affair of Tristram at length settled by these learned men?——Very satisfactorily, replied Yorick; no mortal, Sir, has any concern with it;—for Mrs. Shandy, the mother, is nothing at all akin to him;—and as the mother's is the surest side,—Mr. Shandy, in course, is still less than nothing.—In short he is not as much akin to him, Sir, as I am.—

——That may well be, said my father, shaking his head.

——Let the learned say what they will, there must certainly, quoth my uncle Toby, have been some sort of consanguinity betwixt the Duchess of Suffolk and her son.

The vulgar are of the same opinion, quoth Yorick, to this hour.

CHAP. XXXI.

Though my father was hugely tickled with the subtleties of these learned discourses,—'twas still but like the anointing of a broken bone.—The moment he got home, the weight of his afflictions returned upon him but so much the heavier, as is ever the case when the staff we lean on slips from under us.—He became pensive,—walked frequently forth to the fish-pond,—let down one loop of his hat,—sigh'd often,—forbore to snap;—and, as the hasty sparks of temper, which occasion snapping, so much assist perspiration and digestion, as Hippocrates tell us,—he had certainly fallen ill with the extinction of them, had not his thoughts been critically drawn off, and his health rescued by a fresh train of disquietudes left him, with a legacy of a thousand pounds, by my aunt Dinah.

My father had scarce read the letter, when, taking the thing by the right end, he instantly began to plague and puzzle his head how to lay it out mostly to the honor of his family.—A hundred and fifty odd projects took possession of his brains by turns;—he would do this, and that, and t'other.—He would go to Rome;—he would go to law;—he would buy stock;—he would buy John Hobson's farm,—he would new forefront his house, and add a new wing to make it even.—There was a fine water-mill on this side; and he would build a wind-mill on the other side of the river, in full view, to answer it.—But above all things in the world, he would inclose the great Ox-moor, and send out my brother Bobby immediately upon his travels.

But as the sum was *finite*, and consequently could not do every thing;—and in truth very few of these to any purpose,—of all the projects which offered themselves upon this occasion, the two last seemed to make the deepest impression; and he would infallibly have determined upon both at once, but for the small inconvenience hinted at above, which absolutely put him under a necessity of deciding in favor either of the one or the other.

This was not altogether so easy to be done; for though 'tis certain my father had long before set his heart upon this necessary part of my brother's education, and, like a prudent man, had actually determined to carry it into execution, with the first money that returned from the second creation of actions in the Mississippi-scheme, in which he was an adventurer;—yet the Ox-moor, which was a fine, large, whinny, undrained, unimproved common, belonging to the Shandy-estate, had almost as old a claim upon him: he had long and affectionately set his heart upon turning it likewise to some account.

But having never hitherto been pressed with such a conjuncture of things as made it necessary to settle either the priority or justice of their claims,—like a wise man, he had refrained entering into any nice or critical examination about them: so that, upon the dismission of every other project at this crisis,—the two old projects, the Ox-moor, and my brother, divided him again; and so equal a match were they for each other, as to become the occasion of no small contest in the old gentleman's mind,—which of the two should be set a-going first.

——People may laugh as they will;—but the case was this:—

It had ever been the custom of the family, and by length of time was almost become a matter of common right, that the eldest son of it should have free ingress, egress, and regress into foreign parts before marriage,—not only for the sake of bettering his own private parts, by the benefit of exercise and change of so much air,—but simply for the mere delectation of his fancy, by the feather put into his cap of having been abroad.—*Tantum valet*, my father would say, *quantum sonat.*

Now as this was a reasonable, and in course a most Christian indulgence,—to deprive him of it, without why or wherefore, —and thereby make an example of him, as the first Shandy unwhirl'd about Europe in a post-chaise, and only because he was a heavy lad,—would be using him ten times worse than a Turk.

On the other hand, the case of the Oxmoor was full as hard.

Exclusive of the original purchase-money, which was eight hundred pounds,—it had cost the family eight hundred pounds more in a law-suit about fifteen years before,—besides the Lord knows what trouble and vexation.

It had been moreover in possession of the Shandy family ever since the middle of the last century; and though it lay full in view before the house, bounded on one extremity by the water-mill; and on the other by the projected wind-mill spoken of above;—and for all these reasons seemed to have the fairest title of any part of the estate to the care and protection of the family,—yet, by an unaccountable fatality, common to men, as well as the ground they tread on,—it had all along most shamefully been overlook'd; and, to speak the truth of it, had suffered so much by it, that it would have made any man's heart have bled (Obadiah said) who understood the value of land, to have rode over it, and only seen the condition it was in.

However, as neither the purchasing this tract of ground,—nor indeed the placing of it where it lay, were either of them, properly speaking, of my father's doing,—he had never thought himself any way concerned in the affair—till the fifteen years before, when the breaking out of that cursed law-suit mentioned above (and which had arose about its boundaries)—which being altogether my father's own act and deed, it naturally awakened every other argument in its favor; and upon summing them all up together, he saw, not merely in interest, but in honor, he was bound to do something for it;—and that now or never was the time.

I think there must certainly have been a mixture of ill-luck in it, that the reasons on both sides should happen to be so equally balanced by each other; for though my father weigh'd them in all humors and conditions, spent many an anxious hour in the most profound and abstracted meditation upon what was best to be done;—reading books of farming one day,—books of travels another,—laying aside all passion whatever, —viewing the arguments on both sides in all their lights and circumstances,—communing every day with my uncle Toby,—arguing with Yorick, and talking over the whole affair of the Ox-moor with Obadiah, —yet nothing in all that time appeared so strongly in behalf of the one, which was not either strictly applicable to the other, or at least so far counterbalanced by some consideration of equal weight, as to keep the scales even.

For to be sure, with proper helps, and in the hands of some people, though the Oxmoor would undoubtedly have made a different appearance in the world from what it did, or ever could do, in the condition it lay,—yet every tittle of this was true with regard to my brother Bobby,—let Obadiah say what he would.——

In point of interest, the contest, I own, at first sight, did not appear so undecisive betwixt them; for whenever my father took pen and ink in hand, and set about calculating the simple expense of paring and burning, and fencing in the Oxmoor, &c. &c.—with the certain profit it would bring him in return,—the latter turned out so prodigiously in his way of working the account, that you would have sworn the Ox-moor would have carried all before it; for it was plain he should reap a hundred lasts of rape, at twenty pounds a last, the very first year,—besides an excellent crop of wheat the year following;—and the year after that, to speak within bounds, a hundred,—but, in all likelihood, a hundred and fifty,—if not two hundred quarters of pease and beans, besides potatoes without end.—But then, to think he was all this while breeding up my brother like a hog to eat them,—knocked all on the head again, and generally left the old gentleman in such a state of suspense,—that, as he often declared to my uncle Toby,—he knew no more than his heels what to do.

Nobody but he who has felt it, can conceive what a plaguing thing it is to have a man's mind torn asunder by two projects of equal strength, both obstinately pulling in a contrary direction at the same time; for, to say nothing of the havoc, which by a certain consequence is unavoidably made by it all over the finer system of the nerves, which you know convey the animal spirits and more subtle juices from the heart to the head, and so on,—it is not to be told in what a degree such a wayward kind of friction works upon the more gross and solid parts, wasting the fat and impairing the strength of a man, every time, as it goes backwards and forwards.

My father had certainly sunk under this evil, as certainly as he had done under that of my Christian Name, had he not been rescued out of it, as he was out of that, by a fresh evil:—the misfortune of my brother Bobby's death.

What is the life of man? Is it not to shift from side to side?—from sorrow to sorrow?—to button up one cause of vexation,—and unbutton another?

CHAP. XXXII.

From this moment I am to be considered as heir-apparent to the Shandy family;—and it is from this point, properly, that the story of my Life and Opinions sets out. With all my hurry and precipitation, I have been but clearing the ground to raise the building;—and such a building do I foresee it will turn out, as never was planned, and as never was executed, since Adam. In less than five minutes I shall have thrown my pen into the fire, and the little drop of thick ink which is left remaining at the bottom of my ink-horn, after it:—I have but half a score of things to do in the time;—I have a thing to name,—a thing to lament,—a thing to hope,—a thing to promise,—and a thing to threaten.—I have a thing to suppose,—a thing to declare,—a thing to conceal,—a thing to choose,—and a thing to pray for.—This chapter, therefore, I *name* the chapter of Things,—and my next chapter to it, that is, the first chapter of my next volume, if I live, shall be my chapter upon Whiskers, in order to keep up some sort of connexion in my works.

The thing I lament is, that things have crowded in so thick upon me, that I have not been able to get into that part of my work, towards which I have all the way looked forwards with so much earnest desire; and that is the campaigns, but especially the amours, of my uncle Toby, the events of which are of so singular a nature, and so Cervantic a cast, that if I can so manage it, as to convey but the same impressions to every other brain which the occurrences themselves excite in my own,—I will answer for it, the book shall make its way in the world much better than its master has done before it.—Oh Tristram! Tristram! can this but be once brought about,—the credit which will attend thee as an author, shall counterbalance the many evils which have befallen thee as a man;—thou wilt feast upon the one,—when thou hast lost all sense and remembrance of the other!——

No wonder I itch so much as I do to get at these amours:—they are the choicest morsel of my whole story! and when I do get at 'em,—assure yourselves, good folks,—(nor do I value whose squeamish stomach takes offence at it) I shall not be at all nice in the choice of my words!—and that's the thing I have to *declare*.—I shall never get all through in five minutes, that I *fear*:—and the thing I *hope* is, that your Worships and Reverences are not offended:—if you are, depend upon't I'll give you something, my good gentry, next year, to be offended at;—that's my dear Jenny's way;—but who my Jenny is,—and which is the right and which the wrong end of a woman,—is the thing to be *concealed*:—it shall be told you in the next chapter but one to my chapter of Button-holes;—and not one chapter before.

And now that you have just got to the end of these four volumes,*—the thing I have to *ask* is, how you feel your heads?

* According to the original edition.

my own aches dismally! — As for your healths, I know they are much better.— True Shandeism, think what you will against it, opens the heart and lungs; and, like all those affections which partake of its nature, it forces the blood and other vital fluids of the body to run freely through their channels, and makes the wheel of life run long and cheerfully round.

Was I left, like Sancho Pança, to choose my kingdom, it should not be maritime,— or a kingdom of blacks, to make a penny of;—no, it should be a kingdom of hearty laughing subjects: and as the bilious and more saturnine passions, by creating disorders in the blood and humors, have as bad an influence, I see, upon the body politic as body natural;—and as nothing but a habit of virtue can fully govern those passions, and subject them to reason, — I should add to my prayer,—that God would give my subjects grace to be WISE as they were MERRY; and then I should be the happiest monarch, and they the happiest people, under Heaven.

And so with this moral for the present, may it please your Worships and your Reverences, I take my leave of you till this time twelve-month, when (unless this vile cough kills me in the mean time) I'll have another pluck at your beards, and lay open a story to the world you little dream of

THE

LIFE AND OPINIONS

OF

Tristram Shandy,

GENTLEMAN.

CHAP. I.

IF it had not been for those two mettlesome tits, and that madcap of a postilion who drove them from Stilton to Stamford, the thought had never entered my head. He flew like lightning:—there was a slope of three miles and a half;—we scarce touched the ground,—the motion was most rapid,—most impetuous;—'twas communicated to my brain,—my heart partook of it.—"By "the great God of day," said I, looking towards the sun, and thrusting my arm out of the fore-window of the chaise, as I made my vow, "I will lock up my study-door "the moment I get home, and throw the "key of it ninety feet below the surface, in "the draw-well at the back of my house."

The London wagon confirmed me in my resolution; it hung tottering upon the hill, scarce progressive, dragg'd,—dragg'd up by eight *heavy beasts*,—"by main "strength!"—quoth I, nodding; "but your "betters draw the same way, and something "of every body's!——O rare!"

Tell me, ye learned, shall we for ever be adding so much to the *bulk*,—so little to the *stock?*

Shall we for ever make new books, as apothecaries make new mixtures, by pouring only out of one vessel into another?

Are we for ever to be twisting, and untwisting, the same rope? for ever in the same track,—for ever at the same pace?

Shall we be destined to the days of eternity, on holydays as well as working-days, to be showing the *relics of learning*, as monks do the relics of their saints,—without working one,—one single miracle with them?

Who made Man, with powers which dart him from earth to heaven in a moment;—that great, that most excellent, and most noble creature of the world—the *miracle* of nature, as Zoroaster, in his book ωερι φυσεως, called him;—the *Shekinah* of the Divine Presence, as Chrysostom:—the *image* of God, as Moses;—the *ray* of Divinity, as Plato;—the *marvel* of *marvels*, as Aristotle,—to go sneaking on at this pitiful,—pimping,—pettifogging rate?

I scorn to be as abusive as Horace upon the occasion;—but if there is no catachresis in the wish, and no sin in it, I wish from my soul, that every imitator in Great Britain, France, and Ireland, had the farcy for his pains; and that there was a good farcical house, large enough to hold,—ay,—and sublimate them, *tag-rag* and *bob-tail*, male and female, all together: and this leads me to the affair of *whiskers*;—but by what chain of ideas,—I leave as a legacy in *mortmain* to Prudes and Tartufs, to enjoy and make the most of.

UPON WHISKERS.

I'm sorry I made it;—'twas as inconsiderate a promise as ever entered a man's head.—A chapter upon whiskers! alas! the world will not bear it!—'tis a delicate world;—but I knew not of what mettle it was made,—nor had I ever seen the under-written fragment; otherwise, as surely as noses are noses, and whiskers are whiskers still (let the world say what it will to the contrary), so surely would I have steered clear of this dangerous chapter.

THE FRAGMENT.

* * * * * * * *
* * * * * * * *

——You are half asleep, my good lady, said the old gentleman, taking hold of the old lady's hand, and giving it a gentle squeeze as he pronounced the word *whiskers.*—Shall we change the subject?——By no means, replied the old lady;—I like your account of those matters: so throwing a thin gauze handkerchief over her head, and leaning it back upon the chair, with her face turned towards him, and advancing her two feet as she reclined herself,—I desire, continued she, you will go on.

The old gentleman went on as follows:—Whiskers! cried the Queen of Navarre, dropping her knotting-ball as La Fosseuse uttered the word.——Whiskers, Madam! said La Fosseuse, pinning the ball to the queen's apron, and making a courtesy as she repeated it.

La Fosseuse's voice was naturally soft and low, yet 'twas an articulate voice; and every letter of the word *whiskers* fell distinctly upon the Queen of Navarre's ear. ——Whiskers! cried the queen, laying a greater stress upon the word, and as if she had still distrusted her ears.——Whiskers! replied La Fosseuse, repeating the word a third time.—There is not a cavalier, Madam, of his age in Navarre, continued the maid of honor, pressing the page's interest upon the queen, that has so gallant a pair——Of what? cried Margaret, smiling. ——Of whiskers, said La Fosseuse, with infinite modesty.

The word *whiskers* still stood its ground, and continued to be made use of in most of the best companies throughout the little kingdom of Navarre, notwithstanding the indiscreet use which La Fosseuse had made of it: the truth was, La Fosseuse had pronounced the word not only before the queen, but upon sundry other occasions at court, with an accent which always implied something of a mystery.—And as the court of Margaret, as all the world knows, was at that time a mixture of gallantry and devotion,—and whiskers being as applicable to the one as the other, the word naturally stood its ground;—it gained full as much as it lost; that is, the clergy were for it,—the laity were against it,—and, for the women, *they* were divided.

The excellency of the figure and mien of the young Sieur De Croix, was at that time beginning to draw the attention of the maids of honor towards the terrace before the palace-gate, where the guard was mounted. The lady De Baussiere fell deeply in love with him,—La Battarelle did the same; it was the finest weather for it that ever was remembered in Navarre.—La Guyol, La Maronette, La Sabatiere, fell in love with the Sieur de Croix also; La Rebours and La Fosseuse knew better:—De Croix had failed in an attempt to recommend himself to La Rebours; and La Rebours and La Fosseuse were inseparable.

The Queen of Navarre was sitting with her ladies in the painted bow-window, facing the gate of the second court, as De Croix passed through it.—He is handsome, said the Lady Baussiere.——He has a good mien, said La Battarelle.——He is finely shaped, said La Guyol,——I never saw an officer of the horse-guards in my life, said La Maronette, with two such legs;——Or who stood so well upon them, said La Sabatiere. ——But he has no whiskers, cried La Fosseuse.——Not a pile, said La Rebours.

The queen went directly to her oratory, musing all the way as she walked through the gallery, upon the subject; turning t this way and that way in her fancy.—Ave Maria †—what can La Fosseuse mean? said she, kneeling down upon the cushion.

La Guyol, La Battarelle, La Maronette, La Sabatiere, retired instantly to their chambers. Whiskers! said all four of them to themselves, as they bolted the doors on the inside.

The Lady Carnavallette was counting her beads with both hands, unsuspected under her farthingale.—From St. Anthony down to St. Ursula, inclusive, not a saint passed through her finger without whiskers: St. Francis, St. Dominick, St. Bennet, St. Basil, St. Bridget, had all whiskers.

The Lady Baussiere had got into a wilderness of conceits, with moralizing too intricately upon La Fosseuse's text:—she mounted her palfrey, her page followed her. —the host passed by,—the Lady Baussiere rode on.

One denier, cried the Order of Mercy,—one single denier, in behalf of a thousand patient captives, whose eyes look towards Heaven and you for their redemption.

——The Lady Baussiere rode on.

Pity the unhappy, said a devout, venerable, hoary-headed man, meekly holding up a box begirt with iron in his withered hands. —I beg for the unfortunate:—good my lady, 'tis for a prison,—for an hospital,—'tis for an old man,—a poor man undone by shipwreck, by suretiship, by fire;—I call God and all his angels to witness,—'tis to clothe the naked, to feed the hungry;—'tis to comfort the sick and the broken-hearted.

——The Lady Baussiere rode on.

A decayed kinsman bowed himself to the ground.

——The Lady Baussiere rode on.

He ran begging bare-headed on one side of her palfrey, conjuring her by the former bonds of friendship, alliance, consanguinity, &c.—Cousin, aunt, sister, mother,—for virtue's sake, for your own, for mine, for Christ's sake, remember me!—pity me!

——The Lady Baussiere rode on.

Take hold of *my whiskers*, said the Lady Baussiere.——The page took hold of *her palfrey*. She dismounted at the end of the terrace.

There are some trains of certain ideas which leave prints of themselves about our eyes and eye-brows: and there is a consciousness of it, somewhere about the heart, which serves but to make these etchings the stronger.—We see, spell, and put them together, without a dictionary.

Ha, ha! he, hee! cried La Guyol and La Sabatiere, looking close at each other's prints.—Ho, ho! cried La Battarelle and Maronette, doing the same.—Whist! cried one;—st, st, said a second;—hush, quoth a third;—poo, poo, replied a fourth;—gramercy! cried the Lady Carnavallette;—'twas she who bewhisker'd St. Bridget.

La Fosseuse drew her bodkin from the knot of her hair, and having traced the outline of a small whisker, with the blunt end of it, upon one side of her upper lip, put it into La Rebours' hand.—La Rebours shook her head.

The Lady Baussiere coughed thrice into the inside of her muff.—La Guyol smiled.

—Fy! said the Lady Baussiere. The Queen of Navarre touched her eye with the tip of her fore-finger,—as much as to say, I understand you all.

'Twas plain to the whole court the word was ruined: La Fosseuse had given it a wound, and it was not the better for passing through all these defiles.—It made a faint stand, however, for a few months; by the expiration of which, the Sieur de Croix, finding it high time to leave Navarre for want of whiskers,—the word in course became indecent, and (after a few efforts) absolutely unfit for use.

The best word in the best language of the best world, must have suffered under such combinations.——The Curate d'Estella wrote a book against them, setting forth the dangers of accessory ideas, and warning the Navarrois against them.

Does not all the world know, said the Curate d'Estella, at the conclusion of his work, that Noses ran the same fate, some centuries ago, in most parts of Europe, which whiskers have now done in the kingdom of Navarre?—The evil, indeed, spread no farther then; but have not beds and bolsters, and night-caps and chamber-pots, stood upon the brink of destruction ever since? Are not trouse, and placket-holes, and pump-handles,—and spigots, and faucets, in danger still from the same association?—Chastity, by nature the gentlest of all affections, —give it but its head,—'tis like a ramping and a roaring lion.

The drift of the Curate d'Estella's argument was not understood.—They ran the scent the wrong way.—The world bridled his ass at the tail.—And when the *extremes* of *Delicacy*, and the *beginnings* of *Concupiscence*, hold their next provincial chapter together, they may decree *that* bawdy also.

CHAP. II.

When my father received the letter which brought him the melancholy account of my brother Bobby's death, he was busy calculating the expense of his riding post from Calais to Paris, and so on to Lyons.

'Twas a most inauspicious journey; my father having had every foot of it to travel over again, and his calculation to begin afresh when he had almost got to the end of it, by Obadiah's opening the door to acquaint him the family was out of yeast,—and to ask whether he might not take the great coach-horse early in the morning, and ride in search of some.——With all my heart, Obadiah, said my father (pursuing his journey);—take the coach-horse, and welcome.——But he wants a shoe, poor creature! said Obadiah.——Poor creature! said my uncle Toby, vibrating the note back again, like a string in unison.——Then ride the Scotch horse, quoth my father hastily.——He cannot bear a saddle upon his back, quoth Obadiah, for the whole world.——The Devil's in that horse; then take Patriot, cried my father, and shut the door.——Patriot is sold, said Obadiah.——Here's for you! cried my father, making a pause, and looking in my uncle Toby's face as if the thing had not been a matter of fact.——Your Worship ordered me to sell him last April, said Obadiah.——Then go on foot for your pains, cried my father.——I had much rather walk than ride, said Obadiah, shutting the door.

What plagues! cried my father, going on with his calculation.——But the waters are out, said Obadiah,—opening the door again.

Till that moment, my father, who had a map of Sanson's, and a book of the post-roads before him, had kept his hand upon the head of his compasses, with one foot of them fixed upon Nevers, the last stage he had paid for,—purposing to go on from that point with his journey and calculation, as soon as Obadiah quitted the room: but this second attack of Obadiah's, in opening the door and laying the whole country under water, was too much.—He let go his compasses,—or rather, with a mixed motion between accident and anger, he threw them upon the table: and then there was nothing for him to do, but to return back to Calais (like many others) as wise as he set out.

When the letter was brought into the parlor, which contained the news of my brother's death, my father had got forwards again upon his journey to within a stride of the compasses of the very same stage of Nevers.——By your leave, Mons. Sanson, cried my father, striking the point of his compasses through Nevers into the table,—and nodding to my uncle Toby, to see what was in the letter,—twice in one night is too much for an English gentleman and his son, Mons. Sanson, to be turned back from so lousy a town as Nevers. What think'st thou, Toby? added my father in a sprightly tone.——Unless it be a garrison town, said my uncle Toby, for then——I shall be a fool, said my father, smiling to himself, as long as I live.—So giving a second nod, and keeping his compasses still upon Nevers with one hand, and holding his book of the post-roads in the other,—half calculating and half listening, he leaned forwards upon the table with both elbows, as my uncle Toby hummed over the letter.

—— —— —— —— ——
—— —— —— —— ——
—— —— —— —— ——
—— —— —— —— — he's gone! said my uncle Toby.——Where?—Who? cried my father,——My nephew, said my uncle Toby.——What, without leave,—without money,—without governor? cried my father in amazement.——No:—he is dead, my dear brother, quoth my uncle Toby.——Without being ill? cried my father again.——I dare say not, said my uncle Toby, in a low voice, and fetching a deep sigh from the bottom of his heart; he has been ill enough, poor lad! I'll answer for him,—for he is dead.

When Agrippina was told of her son's death, Tacitus informs us, that not being able to moderate the violence of her passions, she abruptly broke off her work.——My father stuck his compasses into Nevers but so much the faster.—What contrarieties! his, indeed, was matter of calculation! Agrippina's must have been quite a different affair; who else could pretend to reason from history?

How my father went on, in my opinion, deserves a chapter to itself.

CHAP. III.

————And a chapter it shall have, and a devil of a one too; so look to yourselves.

'Tis either Plato, or Plutarch, or Seneca, or Xenophon, or Epictetus, or Theophrastus, or Lucian,—or some one, perhaps, of later date,—either Cardan, or Budæus, or Petrarch, or Stella,—or, possibly, it may be some divine or father of the church;—St. Austin, or St. Cyprian, or Barnard, who affirms, that it is an irresistible and natural passion to weep for the loss of our friends or children:—and Seneca (I'm positive) tells us somewhere, that such griefs evacuate themselves best by that particular channel: and, accordingly, we find, that David wept for his son Absalom, Adrian for his Antinous, Niobe for her children, and that Apollodorus and Crito both shed tears for Socrates before his death.

My father managed his affliction otherwise; and, indeed, differently from most men, either ancient or modern; for he neither wept it away, as the Hebrews and the Romans,—nor slept it off, as the Laplanders,—nor hanged it, as the English,—nor drowned it, as the Germans; nor did he curse it, or damn it, or excommunicate it, or rhyme it, or *lillebullero* it.—

—He got rid of it, however.

Will your Worships give me leave to squeeze in a story between these two pages?

When Tully was bereft of his dear daughter Tullia, at first he laid it to his heart,—he listened to the voice of nature, and modulated his own unto it.—O my Tullia! my daughter! my child!—still, still, still,—'twas O my Tullia!—my Tullia! Methinks I see my Tullia, I hear my Tullia, I talk with my Tullia.—But, as soon as he began to look into the stores of philosophy, and consider how many excellent things might be said upon the occasion,—nobody upon earth can conceive, says the great orator, how happy, how joyful it made me.

My father was as proud of his eloquence as Marcus Tullius Cicero could be for his life, and, for aught I am convinced of to the contrary at present, with as much reason: it was, indeed, his strength and his weakness too.—His strength, for he was by nature eloquent; and his weakness, for he was hourly a dupe to it; and, provided an occasion in life would but permit him to show his talents, or say either a wise thing, a witty, or a shrewd one—(bating the case of a systematic misfortune)—he had all he wanted.—A blessing which tied up my father's tongue, and a misfortune which set it loose with a good grace, were pretty equal: sometimes, indeed, the misfortune was the better of the two; for instance, where the pleasure of the harangue was as *ten*, and the pain of the misfortune but as *five*,—my father gained half in half; and, consequently, was as well again off, as if it had never befallen him.

This clue will unravel what otherwise would seem very inconsistent in my father's domestic character; and it is this that, in the provocations arising from the neglects and blunders of servants, or other mishaps, unavoidable in a family, his anger, or rather the duration of it, eternally ran counter to all conjecture.

My father had a favorite little mare, which he had consigned over to a most beautiful Arabian horse, in order to have a pad out of her for his own riding. He was sanguine in all his projects; so talked about his pad every day with as absolute a security, as if he had been reared, broke,—and bridled and saddled at his door ready for mounting. By some neglect or other in Obadiah, it so fell out, that my father's expectations were answered with nothing better than a mule, and as ugly a beast of the kind as ever was produced.

My mother and my uncle Toby expected my father would be the death of Obadiah.—and that there would never be an end of the disaster.——See here! you rascal, cried my father, pointing to the mule, what you have done!——It was not me, said Obadiah.——How do I know that? replied my father.——

Triumph swam in my father's eyes at the repartee,—the Attic salt brought water into them;—and so Obadiah heard no more about it.

Now let us go back to my brother's death.

Philosophy has a fine saying for every thing.—For Death, it has an entire set: the misery was, they all at once rushed so into my father's head, that 'twas difficult to string them together, so as to make any thing of a consistent show out of them.—He took them as they came.—

"'Tis an inevitable chance,—the first "statute in Magna Charta;—it is an ever-"lasting act of parliament, my dear bro-"ther,—*All must die.*

"If my son could not have died, it had been "matter of wonder;—not that he is dead

"Monarchs and princes dance in the same "ring with us.

"*To die*, is the great debt and tribute "due unto nature: tombs and monuments, "which should perpetuate our memories, "pay it themselves; and the proudest pyr- "amid of them all, which Wealth and Sci- "ence have erected, has lost its apex, and "stands obtruncated in the traveller's hori- "zon."——(My father found he got great ease, and went on)—"Kingdoms and prov- "inces, and towns and cities, have they not "their periods? and when those principles "and powers, which at first cemented and "put them together, have performed their "several evolutions, they fall back."—— Brother Shandy, said my uncle Toby, laying down his pipe at the word *evolutions*,—— Revolutions, I meant, quoth my father;— by Heaven! I meant revolutions, brother Toby;—evolutions is nonsense.——'Tis not nonsense, said my uncle Toby.——But is it not nonsense to break the thread of such a discourse upon such an occasion? cried my father;—do not, dear Toby, continued he, taking him by the hand, do not—do not, I beseech thee, interrupt me at this crisis. ——My uncle Toby put his pipe into his mouth.

"Where is Troy and Mycenæ, and Thebes "and Delos, and Persepolis and Agrigen- "tum?" continued my father, taking up his book of post-roads, which he had laid down.— "What is become, brother Toby, of Nineveh "and Babylon, of Cyzicum and Mitylenæ? "The fairest towns that ever the sun rose "upon, are now no more; the names only "are left; and those (for many of them are "wrong spelt) are falling themselves by "piecemeal to decay, and in length of time "will be forgotten, and involved with every "thing in a perpetual night. The world "itself, brother Toby, must,—must come "to an end.

"Returning out of Asia, when I sailed "from Ægina towards Megara," (when can this have been? thought my uncle Toby) "I began to view the country round about. "—Ægina was behind me, Megara was be- "fore, Pyræus on the right hand, Corinth "on the left.—What flourishing towns now "prostrate upon the earth! Alas! alas! "said I to myself, that man should disturb "his soul for the loss of a child, when so "much as this lies awfully buried in his "presence!—Remember, said I to myself "again,—remember thou art a man."

Now, my uncle Toby knew not that this last paragraph was an extract of Servius Sulpicius's consolatory letter to Tully:— he had as little skill, honest man, in the fragments, as he had in the whole pieces of antiquity:—and as my father, whilst he was concerned in the Turkey trade, had been three or four different times in the Levant, in one of which he had staid a whole year and an half at Zante, my uncle Toby naturally concluded, that, in some one of these periods, he had taken a trip across the Archipelago into Asia; and that all this sailing affair, with Ægina behind, and Megara before, and Pyræus on the right hand, &c. &c. was nothing more than the true course of my father's voyage and reflections.— 'Twas certainly in his *manner;* and many an undertaking critic would have built two stories higher upon worse foundations.—— And pray, brother, quoth my uncle Toby, laying the end of his pipe upon my father's hand in a kindly way of interruption,—but waiting till he finished the account,—What year of our Lord was this?——'Twas no year of our Lord, replied my father.—— That's impossible, cried my uncle Toby. ——Simpleton! said my father,—'twas forty years before Christ was born.

My uncle Toby had but two things for it; either to suppose his brother to be the Wandering Jew, or that his misfortunes had disordered his brain.——"May the Lord "God of heaven and earth protect him and "restore him!" said my uncle Toby, praying silently for my father, and with tears in his eyes.——

My father placed the tears to a proper account, and went on with his harangue with great spirit.—

"There is not such great odds, brother "Toby, betwixt good and evil, as the world "imagines."—(This way of setting off, by the bye, was not likely to cure my uncle Toby's suspicions.)——"Labor, sorrow, "grief, sickness, want, and woe, are the "sauces of life."——Much good may it do them,—said my uncle Toby to himself.——

"My son is dead!—so much the better, "—'tis a shame, in such a tempest, to have "but one anchor.

"But he is gone for ever from us!—be it so.—He is got from under the hands of "his barber before he was bald;—he is but "risen from a feast before he was surfeit- "ed;—from a banquet before he had got "drunken.

"The Thracians wept when a child was "born,"—(and we were very near it, quoth my uncle Toby)—"and feasted and made "merry when a man went out of the world; "and with reason.—Death opens the gate "of Fame, and shuts the gate of Envy after "it:—it unlooses the chain of the captive, "—and puts the bondsman's task into an- "other man's hands.

"Show me the man, who knows what "life is, who dreads it,—and I'll show thee "a prisoner who dreads his liberty."——

Is it not better, my dear brother Toby (for mark,—our appetites are but diseases)—is it not better not to hunger at all, than to eat?—not to thirst, than to take physic to cure it?

Is it not better to be freed from cares and agues,—from love and melancholy,—and the other hot and cold fits of life, than, like a galled traveller, who comes weary to his inn, to be bound to begin his journey afresh?

There is no terror, brother Toby, in its looks, but what it borrows from groans and convulsions, and the blowing of noses and the wiping away of tears with the bottoms of curtains, in a dying man's room.—Strip it of these,—What is it?——'Tis better in battle than in bed, said my uncle Toby.—Take away its hearses, its mutes, and its mourning,—its plumes, escutcheons, and other mechanic aids,—What is it?——*Better in battle!* continued my father, smiling, for he had absolutely forgot my brother Bobby;—'tis terrible no way,—for consider, brother Toby,—when we *are*, death is *not;* —and when death *is*,—we are *not.*——My uncle Toby laid down his pipe, to consider the proposition; my father's eloquence was too rapid to stay for any man;—away it went,—and hurried my uncle Toby's ideas along with it.——

For this reason, continued my father, 'tis worthy to recollect, how little alteration, in great men, the approaches of death have made.—Vespasian died in a jest upon his close-stool;—Galba with a sentence;—Septimus Severus in a dispatch;—Tiberius in dissimulation;—and Cæsar Augustus in a compliment.——I hope 'twas a sincere one, —quoth my uncle Toby.——

'Twas to his wife,—said my father.

CHAP. IV.

——And lastly,—for of all the choice anecdotes which history can produce of this matter, continued my father,—this, like the gilded dome which covers in the fabric, —crowns all.——

'Tis of Cornelius Gallus, the prætor,—which, I dare say, brother Toby, you have read.——I dare say I have not, replied my uncle.——He died, said my father, as * * * * * * * * * * * * * * * * *——And if it was with his wife, said my uncle Toby,—there could be no hurt in it.——That's more than I know,—replied my father.

CHAP. V.

My mother was going very gingerly in the dark along the passage which led to the parlor, as my uncle Toby pronounced the word *wife.*—'Tis a shrill penetrating sound of itself, and Obadiah had helped it by leaving the door a little ajar, so that my mother heard enough of it to imagine herself the subject of the conversation; so laying the edge of her finger across her two lips,—holding in her breath, and bending her head a little downwards, with a twist of her neck —(not towards the door, but from it, by which means her ear was brought to the chink)—she listened with all her powers: —the listening slave, with the Goddess of Silence at his back, could not have given a finer thought for an intaglio.

In this attitude I am determined to let her stand for five minutes,—till I bring up the affairs of the kitchen (as Rapin does those of the church) to the same period.

CHAP. VI.

Though, in one sense, our family was certainly a simple machine, as it consisted of a few wheels; yet there was thus much to be said for it, that these wheels were set in motion by so many different springs, and acted one upon the other from such a variety of strange principles and impulses, —that though it was a simple machine, it had all the honor and advantages of a complex one,—and a number of as odd movements within it, as ever were beheld in the inside of a Dutch silk-mill.

Amongst these there was one, I am going to speak of, in which, perhaps, it was not altogether so singular as in many others: and it was this, that whatever motion, debate, harangue, dialogue, project, or dissertation, was going forward in the parlor, there was generally another at the same time, and upon the same subject, running parallel along with it in the kitchen.

Now to bring this about, whenever an extraordinary message, or letter, was delivered in the parlor,—or a discourse suspended till a servant went out,—or the lines of discontent were observed to hang upon the brows of my father or mother;—or, in short, when any thing was supposed to be upon the tapis worth knowing or listening to, 'twas the rule to leave the door, not absolutely shut, but somewhat ajar,—as it stands just now;—which, under covert of the bad hinge (and that possibly might be one of the many reasons why it was never mended) it was not difficult to manage; by which means, in all these cases, a passage was generally left, not indeed so wide as the Dardanelles, but wide enough, for all that, to carry on as much of this windward trade as was sufficient to save my father the trouble of governing his house;—my mother at this moment stands profiting by it.—Obadiah did the same thing, as soon as he had left the letter upon the table which brought the news of my brother's death; so that before my father had well got over his surprise, and entered upon his harangue,—had Trim got upon his legs, to speak his sentiments upon the subject.

A curious observer of nature, had he been worth the inventory of all Job's stock, —though, by the bye, *your curious observers are seldom worth a groat*,—would have given the half of it to have heard Corporal Trim and my father, two orators so contrasted by nature and education, haranguing over the same bier.

My father,—a man of deep reading,—prompt memory,—with Cato, and Seneca, and Epictetus, at his fingers' ends:—

The Corporal,—with nothing—to remember;—of no deeper reading than his muster-roll,—or greater names at his fingers' ends, than the contents of it.

The one proceeding from period to period, by metaphor and allusion, and striking the fancy as he went along (as men of wit and fancy do) with the entertainment and pleasantry of his pictures and images.

The other, without wit or antithesis, or point, or turn, this way or that; but leaving the images on one side, and the pictures on the other, going straight-forwards, as nature could lead him, to the heart.—O Trim! would to Heaven thou hadst a better historian!—Would thy historian had a better pair of breeches!—O ye critics! will nothing melt you?

CHAP. VII.

My young master in London is dead! said Obadiah.

——A green satin night-gown of my mother's, which had been twice scoured, was the first idea which Obadiah's exclamation brought into Susannah's head.——Well might Locke write a chapter upon the imperfections of words.——Then, quoth Susannah, we must all go into mourning. ——But note a second time: the word *mourning*, notwithstanding Susannah made use of it herself,—failed also of doing its office; it excited not one single idea, tinged either with grey or black:—all was green. —The green satin night-gown hung there still.

—O! 'twill be the death of my poor mistress, cried Susannah.—My mother's whole wardrobe followed.—What a possession! her red damask,—her orange-tawny,—her white and yellow lutestrings,—her brown taffeta,—her bone-laced caps, her bed-gowns, and comfortable under-petticoats.—Not a rag was left behind.—"*No;—she* "*will never look up again!*" said Susannah.

We had a fat, foolish scullion;—my

father, I think, kept her for her simplicity;—she had been all autumn struggling with a dropsy.——He is dead, said Obadiah;—he is certainly dead!——So am not I, said the foolish scullion.

——Here is sad news, Trim, cried Susannah, wiping her eyes as Trim stepp'd into the kitchen;—Master Bobby is dead and *buried!*—the funeral was an interpolation of Susannah's; we shall have all to go into mourning, said Susannah.

I hope not, said Trim.——You hope not! cried Susannah earnestly.—The mourning ran not in Trim's head, whatever it did in Susannah's.—I hope,—said Trim, explaining himself, I hope in God the news is not true.——I heard the letter read with my own ears, answered Obadiah; and we shall have a terrible piece of work of it in stubbing the Ox-moor.——Oh! he's dead, said Susannah,——As sure, said the scullion, as I'm alive.

I lament for him from my heart and my soul, said Trim, fetching a sigh.—Poor creature!—poor boy!—poor gentleman!

——He was alive last Whitsuntide! said the coachman.——Whitsuntide! alas! cried Trim, extending his right arm, and falling instantly into the same attitude in which he read the sermon,—what is Whitsuntide, Jonathan, (for that was the coachman's name) or Shrovetide, or any tide or time past to this? Are we not here now, continued the Corporal (striking the end of his stick perpendicularly upon the floor, so as to give an idea of health and stability;)—and are we not—(dropping his hat upon the ground) gone! in a moment!—'Twas infinitely striking! Susannah burst into a flood of tears.—We are not stocks and stones.——Jonathan, Obadiah, the cook-maid, all melted.—The foolish fat scullion herself, who was scouring a fish-kettle upon her knees, was rous'd with it.—The whole kitchen crowded about the Corporal.

Now, as I perceive plainly, that the preservation of our constitution in church and state,—and possibly the preservation of the whole world,—or, what is the same thing, the distribution and balance of its property and power, may, in time to come, depend greatly upon the right understanding of this stroke of the Corporal's eloquence,—I do demand your attention:—your Worships and Reverences, for any ten pages together, take them where you will in any other part of the work, shall sleep for it at your ease.

I said, "We are not stocks and stones:"—'tis very well. I should have added, nor are we angels,—I wish we were;—but men clothed with bodies, and governed by our imaginations:—and what a junketing piece of work of it there is betwixt these and our seven senses, especially some of them; for my own part, I own it, I am ashamed to confess. Let it suffice to affirm that of all the senses, the eye (for I absolutely deny the touch, though most of your *Barbati*, I know, are for it) has the quickest commerce with the soul,—gives a smarter stroke, and leaves something more inexpressible upon the fancy than words can either convey,—or sometimes get rid of.

I've gone a little about;—no matter, 'tis for health,—let us only carry it back in our mind, to the mortality of Trim's hat.—"Are we not here now,—and gone in a "moment?"—There was nothing in the sentence;—'twas one of your self-evident truths we have the advantage of hearing every day; and if Trim had not trusted more to his hat than his head,—he had made nothing at all of it.

——"Are we not here now?" continued the Corporal; "and are we not——" (dropping his hat plump upon the ground,—and pausing, before he pronounced the word)—"gone in a moment?" The descent of the hat was as if a heavy lump of clay had been kneaded into the crown of it.—Nothing could have expressed the sentiment of mortality, of which it was the type and forerunner, like it;—his hand seemed to vanish from under it;—it fell dead;—the Corporal's eye fixed upon it as upon a corpse;—and Susannah burst into a flood of tears.

Now,—ten thousand, and ten thousand times ten thousand (for matter and motion are infinite) are the ways by which a hat may be dropped upon the ground without any effect.—Had he flung it, or thrown it, or cast it, or skimmed it, or squirted it, or let it slip or fall in any possible direction under Heaven,—or in the best direction, that could be given to it!—had he dropped it like a goose—like a puppy,—like an ass;—or in doing it, or even after he had done it, had he looked like a fool,—like a ninny,—like a nincompoop,—it had fail'd, and the effect upon the heart had been lost.

Ye who govern this mighty world and its mighty concerns with the engines of eloquence;—who heat it, and cool it, and melt it, and mollify it,—and then harden it again to your purpose:——

Ye who wind and turn the passions with this great windlass; and, having done it, lead the owners of them whither ye think meet:——

Ye, lastly, who drive——; and why not? Ye also who are driven like turkeys to market, with a stick and a red clout,—meditate,—meditate, I beseech you, upon Trim's hat.

CHAP. VIII.

Stay,—I have a small account to settle with the reader before Trim can go on with his harangue.—It shall be done in two minutes.

Amongst many other book-debts, all of which I shall discharge in due time,—I own myself a debtor to the world for two items, a chapter upon chamber-maids and button-holes: which, in the former part of my work, I promised and fully intended to pay off this year: but some of your Worships and Reverences telling me that the two subjects, especially so connected together, might endanger the morals of the world,—I pray the chapter upon chamber-maids and button-holes may be forgiven me,—and that they will accept of the last chapter in lieu of it; which is nothing, an't please your Reverences, but a chapter of chamber-maids, green gowns, and old hats.

Trim took his hat off the ground,—put it upon his head,—and then went on with his oration upon death, in manner and form following:—

CHAP. IX.

——To us, Jonathan, who know not what want or care is,—who live here in the service of two of the best of masters—(bating, in my own case, his majesty King William the Third, whom I had the honor to serve both in Ireland and Flanders)—I own it; that from Whitsuntide to within three weeks of Christmas,—'tis not long,—'tis like nothing;—but to those, Jonathan, who know what death is, and what havoc and destruction he can make, before a man can well wheel about,—'tis like a whole age,—O Jonathan!—'twould make a good-natured man's heart bleed, to consider, continued the Corporal, (standing perpendicularly) how low many a brave and upright fellow has been laid since that time!—And trust me, Susy, added the Corporal, turning to Susannah, whose eyes were swimming in water,—before that time comes round again,—many a bright eye will be dim.——Susannah placed it to the right side of the page;—she wept,—but she court'sied too.—Are we not, continued Trim, looking still at Susannah,—are we not like a flower of the field?——A tear of pride stole in betwixt every two tears of humiliation—else no tongue could have described Susannah's affliction.—Is not all flesh grass?—'Tis clay,—'tis—dirt.——They all looked directly at the scullion;—the scullion had just been scouring a fish-kettle.—It was not fair.—

—What is the finest face that ever man looked at!——I could hear Trim talk so for ever, cried Susannah,—what is it!—(Susannah laid her hand upon Trim's shoulder)—but corruption!——Susannah took it off.

Now I love you for this;—and 'tis this delicious mixture within you which makes you dear creatures what you are;—and he who hates you for it——all I can say of the matter is,—That he has either a pumpkin for his head,—or a pippin for his heart;—and whenever he is dissected 'twill be found so.

CHAP. X.

Whether Susannah by taking her hand too suddenly from off the Corporal's shoulder, (by the whisking about of her passions)—broke a little the chain of his reflections,—

Or whether the Corporal began to be

suspicious he had got into the Doctor's quarters, and was talking more like the Chaplain than himself,

Or whether, - - - - - - - - - -

Or whether,—for in all such cases a man of invention and parts may, with pleasure, fill a couple of pages with suppositions,—which of all these was the cause, let the curious physiologist, or the curious any body, determine,—'tis certain, at least, the Corporal went on thus with his harangue.—

For my own part, I declare it, that out of doors, I value not death at all: — not this . . added the Corporal, snapping his fingers; — but with an air which no one but the Corporal could have given to the sentiment. — In battle I value death not this . . . and let him not take me cowardly, like poor Joe Gibbons, in scouring his gun.—What is he?—A pull of a trigger;—a push of a bayonet an inch this way or that,—makes the difference. Look along the line—to the right,—see! Jack's down! Well, — 'tis worth a regiment of horse to him. — No; —'tis Dick. — Then Jack's no worse.—Never mind which;—we pass on,—in hot pursuit; the wound itself which brings him is not felt,—the best way is to stand up to him;—the man who flies, is in ten times more danger than the man who marches up into his jaws. —I've looked him, added the Corporal, an hundred times in the face,—and know what he is. He's nothing, Obadiah, at all in the field.——But he's very frightful in a house, quoth Obadiah.——I never mind it myself, said Jonathan, upon a coach-box. ——It must, in my opinion, be most natural in bed, replied Susannah,——And could I escape him by creeping into the worst calf's skin that ever was made into a knapsack, I would do it there,—said Trim;—but that is nature.

——Nature is nature, said Jonathan. ——And that is the reason, cried Susannah, I so much pity my mistress. — She will never get the better of it.——Now I pity the Captain the most of any one in the family, answered Trim.—Madam will get ease of heart in weeping,—and the Squire in talking about it,—but my poor master will keep it all in silence to himself.—I shall hear him sigh in his bed for a whole month together, as he did for Lieutenant Le Fevre. An' please your Honor, do not sigh so piteously, I would say to him as I lay beside him.—I cannot help it, Trim, my master would say;—tis so melancholy an accident,—I cannot get it off my heart.——Your Honor fears not death yourself.——I hope, Trim, I fear nothing, he would say, but the doing a wrong thing.—Well, he would add, whatever betides, I will take care of Le Fevre's boy.—And with that, like a quieting draught, his Honor would fall asleep.

I like to hear Trim's stories about the Captain, said Susannah.——He is a kindly-hearted gentleman, said Obadiah, as ever lived.——Ay, and as brave a one too, said the Corporal, as ever stept before a platoon.—There never was a better officer in the King's army,—or a better man in God's world; for he would march up to the mouth of a cannon, though he saw the lighted match at the very touch-hole: and yet, for all that, he has a heart as soft as a child for other people:—he would not hurt a chicken.——I would sooner, quoth Jonathan, drive such a gentleman for seven pounds a year,—than some for eight.——Thank thee, Jonathan! for thy twenty shillings,—as much, Jonathan, said the Corporal, shaking him by the hand, as if thou hadst put the money into my own pocket.—I would serve him to the day of my death out of love. He is a friend and a brother to me;—and could I be sure my poor brother Tom was dead,—continued the Corporal, taking out his handkerchief, —was I worth ten thousand pounds, I would leave every shilling of it to the Captain.—Trim could not refrain from tears at this testamentary proof he gave of his affection to his master. The whole kitchen was affected.——Do tell us the story of the poor Lieutenant, said Susannah.—With all my heart, answered the Corporal.

Susannah, the cook, Jonathan, Obadiah, and Corporal Trim, formed a circle about the fire; and as soon as the scullion had shut the kitchen-door,—the Corporal began,——

CHAP. XI.

I AM a Turk if I had not as much forgot my mother, as if Nature had plastered me up, and set me down naked upon the banks of the river Nile, without one.—Your most obedient servant, Madam,—I've cost you a great deal of trouble.—I wish it may answer;—but you have left a crack in my back;—and here's a great piece fallen off here before:—and what must I do with this foot?—I shall never reach England with it.

For my own part, I never wonder at any thing;—and so often has my judgment deceived me in my life, that I always suspect it, right or wrong;—at least, I am seldom hot upon cold subjects. For all this, I reverence truth as much as any body; and when it has slipped us, if a man will but take me by the hand, and go quietly and search for it, as for a thing we have both lost, and can neither of us do well without,—I'll go to the world's end with him.—But I hate disputes,—and therefore (bating religious points, or such as touch society) I would almost subscribe to any thing which does not choke me in the first passage, rather than be drawn into one.—But I cannot bear suffocation;—and bad smells worst of all.—For which reasons, I resolved from the beginning, that if ever the army of martyrs was to be augmented,—or a new one raised,—I would have no hand in it, one way or t'other.

CHAP. XII.

—BUT to return to my mother.

My uncle Toby's opinion, Madam, "That "there could be no harm in Cornelius Gal- "lus, the Roman prætor's lying with his "wife;"—or rather the last word of that opinion,—(for it was all my mother heard of it) caught hold of her by the weak part of the whole sex; —you shall not mistake me,—I mean her curiosity;—she instantly concluded herself the subject of the conversation, and with that prepossession upon her fancy, you will readily conceive, every word my father said was accommodated either to herself or her family-concerns.

—Pray, Madam, in what street does the lady live who would not have done the same?

From the strange mode of Cornelius's death, my father had made a transition to that of Socrates, and was giving my uncle Toby an abstract of his pleading before his judges;—'twas irresistible:——not the oration of Socrates,—but my father's temptation to it.—He had wrote the * Life of Socrates himself the year before he left off trade; which, I fear, was the means of hastening him out of it;—so that no one was able to set out with so full a sail, and in so swelling a tide of heroic loftiness upon the occasion, as my father was. Not a period in Socrates's oration which closed with a shorter word than transmigration, or annihilation,—or a worse thought in the middle of it than *to be—or not to be*,—the entering upon a new and untried state of things,—or upon a long, a profound and peaceful sleep, without dreams, without disturbance!—*That we and our children were born to die,—but neither of us born to be slaves.*—No, there I mistake; that was part of Eleazer's oration, as recorded by Josephus (de Bell. Judaic.) —Eleazer owns he had it from the philosophers of India. In all likelihood, Alexander the Great, in his irruption into India, after he had overrun Persia, amongst the many things he stole,—stole that sentiment also; by which means it was carried, if not all the way by himself (for we all know he died at Babylon) at least by some of his marauders, into Greece,—from Greece it got to Rome, from Rome to France,—and from France to England.—So things come round:—

By land-carriage; I can conceive no other way.—

By water, the sentiment might easily have come down the Ganges, into the Sinus Gangeticus, or Bay of Bengal, and so into the Indian Sea; and following the course of trade (the way from India by the Cape of Good Hope being then unknown) might be carried, with other drugs and spices, up the Red Sea to Joddah, the port of Mecca, or else to Tor or Suez, towns at

* This book my father would never consent to publish; 'tis in manuscript, with some other tracts of his, in the family; all, or most of which, will be printed in due time.

the bottom of the Gulf; and from thence by caravans to Coptos, but three days' journey distant, so down the Nile directly to Alexandria, where the *sentiment* would be landed at the very foot of the great staircase of the Alexandrian library;—and from that storehouse it would be fetched.—Bless me! what a trade was driven by the learned in those days!

CHAP. XIII.

—Now my father had a way, a little like that of Job's (in case there ever was such a man)—if not, there's an end of the matter.—

Though, by the bye, because your learned men find some difficulty in fixing the precise era in which so great a man lived;—whether, for instance, before or after the patriarchs, &c.—to vote, therefore, that he never lived at all, is a little cruel;—'tis not doing as they would be done by.—Happen that as it may,—my father, I say, had a way, when things went extremely wrong with him, especially upon the first sally of his impatience—of wondering why he was begot;—wishing himself dead;—sometimes worse:—and when the provocation ran high, and grief touched his lips with more than ordinary powers,—Sir, you scarce could have distinguished him from Socrates himself.—Every word would breathe sentiments of a soul disdaining life, and careless about all its issues; for which reason, though my mother was a woman of no deep reading, yet the abstract of Socrates's oration, which my father was giving my uncle Toby, was not altogether new to her.—She listened to it with composed intelligence, and would have done so to the end of the chapter, had not my father plunged (which he had no occasion to have done) into that part of the pleading where the great philosopher reckons up his connexions, his alliances, and children; but renounces a security to be so won, by working upon the passions of his judges.—"I have friends,—I have "relations,—I have three desolate chil- "dren,"—says Socrates.—

——Then, cried my mother, opening the door,—you have one more, Mr. Shandy, than I know of.

——By Heaven! I have one less,—said my father, getting up and walking out of the room.

CHAP. XIV.

——They are Socrates's children, said my uncle Toby.——He has been dead a hundred years ago, replied my mother.

My uncle Toby was no chronologer;—so not caring to advance one step but upon safe ground, he laid down his pipe deliberately upon the table, and rising up, and taking my mother most kindly by the hand, without saying another word, either good or bad, to her, he led her out after my father, that he might finish the eclaircissement himself.

CHAP. XV.

Had this volume been a farce, which, unless every one's Life and Opinions are to be looked upon as a farce as well as mine, I see no reason to suppose,—the last chapter, Sir, had finished the first act of it; and then this chapter must have set off thus:—

Ptr..r..r..ing,—twing,—twang,—prut,—trut;—'tis a cursed bad fiddle.—Do you know whether my fiddle's in tune or no?—trut..prut..—They should be fifths.—'Tis wickedly strung,—tr...a.e.i.o.u.-twang.—The bridge is a mile too high, and the sound-post absolutely down,—else,—trut.. prut.—Hark! 'tis not so bad a tone.—Diddle diddle, diddle diddle, diddle diddle, dum. There is nothing in playing before good judges;—but there's a man there,—no,—not him with the bundle under his arm,—the grave man in black.—'Sdeath! not the gentleman with the sword on.—Sir, I had rather play a Caprichio to Calliope herself, than draw my bow across my fiddle before that very man; and yet I'll stake my Cremona to a Jew's trump, which is the greatest musical odds that ever were laid, that I will this moment stop three hundred and fifty leagues out of tune upon my fiddle, without punishing one single nerve that belongs to him.—Twaddle diddle,—tweddle diddle,— twiddle diddle,—twoddle diddle,—twuddle diddle;—prut-trut,—krish,—krash,—krush.—I've undone you, Sir,—but you see he's no worse;—and was Apollo to take his fiddle after me, he can make him no better.

Diddle diddle, diddle diddle, diddle diddle,—hum,—dum,—drum.

Your Worships and your Reverences love music,—and God has made you all with good ears,—and some of you play delightfully yourselves;—trut-prut,—prut-trut.

O! there is—whom I could sit and hear whole days,—whose talents lie in making what he fiddles to be felt;—who inspires me with his joys and hopes, and puts the most hidden springs of my heart into motion.—If you would borrow five guineas of me, Sir,—which is generally ten guineas more than I have to spare,—or you, Messrs. Apothecary and Taylor, want your bills paid,—that's your time.

CHAP. XVI.

The first thing which entered my father's head, after affairs were a little settled in the family, and Susannah had got possession of my mother's green satin night-gown.—was to sit down coolly, after the example of Xenophon, and write a *Tristrapædia*, or system of education for me; collecting first for that purpose his own scattered thoughts, counsels, and notions; and binding them together, so as to form an INSTITUTE for the government of my childhood and adolescence.—I was my father's last stake,—he had lost my brother Bobby entirely,—he had lost, by his own computation, full three-fourths of me,—that is, he had been unfortunate in his three first great casts for me:—my geniture, nose, and name!—there was but this one left; and accordingly my father gave himself up to it with as much devotion as ever my uncle Toby had done to his doctrine of projectiles.—The difference between them was, that my uncle Toby drew his whole knowledge of projectiles from Nicholas Tartaglia.—My father spun his, every thread of it, out of his own brain,—or had so reeled and cross-twisted what all other spinners and spinsters had spun before him, that 'twas pretty near the same torture to him.

In about three years, or something more, my father had got advanced almost into the middle of his work.—Like all other writers, he met with disappointments.—He imagined he should be able to bring whatever he had to say, into so small a compass, that when it was finished and bound, it might be rolled up in my mother's housewife.—Matter grows under our hands.—Let no man say,—"Come,—I'll write a *duodecimo*."

My father gave himself up to it, however, with the most painful diligence, proceeding step by step in every line, with the same kind of caution and circumspection (though I cannot say upon quite so religious a principle) as was used by John de la Casse, the Lord Archbishop of Benevento, in composing his Galatea; in which his Grace of Benevento spent near forty years of his life; and, when the thing came out, it was not of above half the size or thickness of a Rider's Almanac.—How the holy man managed the affair, unless he spent the greatest part of his time in combing his whiskers, or playing at *primero* with his chaplain,—would pose any mortal not let into the true secret;—and therefore 'tis worth explaining to the world, was it only for the encouragement of those few in it, who write not so much to be fed,—as to be famous.

I own, had John de la Casse, the Archbishop of Benevento, for whose memory (notwithstanding his Galatea) I retain the highest veneration,—had he been, Sir, a slender clerk,—of dull wit, slow parts,—costive head, and so forth,—he and his Galatea might have jogged on together to the age of Methuselah for me;—the phenomenon had not been worth a parenthesis.—

But the reverse of this was the truth. John de la Casse was a genius of fine parts and fertile fancy; and yet with all these great advantages of nature, which should have pricked him forwards with his Galatea, he lay under an impuissance at the same time of advancing above a line and a half in the compass of a whole summer's day. This disability in his Grace arose from an opinion he was afflicted with;—which opinion was this,—viz. That whenever a Christian was writing a book (not for his private amusement, but) where his intent and purpose was, *bonâ fide*, to print and publish it to the world,—his first thoughts were always the temptations of the evil one.—This was the state of ordinary writers: but when a personage in venerable character and high station, either in church or state, once turned author,—he maintained, that from the very moment he took pen in hand,—all the Devils in hell broke out of their holes to cajole him.—'Twas Term-time with them;—every thought, first and last, was captious;—how specious and good soever,—'twas all one;—in whatever form or color it presented itself to the imagination,—'twas still a stroke of one or other of 'em levell'd at him, and was to be fenced off.—So that the life of a writer, whatever he might fancy to the contrary, was not so much a state of *composition*, as a state of *warfare;* and his probation in it, precisely that of any other man militant upon earth, —both depending alike, not half so much upon the degrees of his wit,—as his *resistance.*

My father was hugely pleased with this theory of John de la Casse, Archbishop of Benevento; and (had it not cramped him a little in his creed) I believe would have given ten of the best acres in the Shandy estate to have been the broacher of it.—How far my father actually believed in the Devil, will be seen, when I come to speak of my father's religious notions, in the progress of this work: 'tis enough to say here, as he could not have the honor of it, in the literal sense of the doctrine,—he took up with the allegory of it; and would often say, especially when his pen was a little retrograde, there was as much good meaning, truth, and knowledge, couched under the veil of John de la Casse's parabolical representation,—as was to be found in any one poetic fiction or mystic record of antiquity.—Prejudice of education, he would say, *is the Devil,*—and the multitudes of them which we suck in with our mother's milk, *are the Devil and all.*—We are haunted with them, brother Toby, in all our lucubrations and researches; and was a man fool enough to submit tamely to what they obtruded upon him,—what would his book be? Nothing;—he would add, throwing his pen away with a vengeance;—nothing but a farrago of the clack of nurses, and of the nonsense of the old women (of both sexes) throughout the kingdom.

This is the best account I am determined to give of the slow progress my father made in his *Tristrapædia;* at which (as I said) he was three years, and something more, indefatigably at work, and, at last, had scarce completed, by his own reckoning, one half of his undertaking; the misfortune was, that I was all that time totally neglected and abandoned to my mother; and, what was almost as bad, by the very delay, the first part of the work, upon which my father had spent the most of his pains, was rendered entirely useless;—every day a page or two became of no consequence.—

——Certainly it was ordained as a scourge upon the pride of human wisdom, That the wisest of us all should thus outwit ourselves, and eternally forego our purposes in the intemperate act of pursuing them.

In short, my father was so long in all his acts of resistance,—or, in other words,—he advanced so very slow with his work, and I began to live and get forwards at such a rate, that if an event had not happened,—which, when we get to it, if it can be told with decency, shall not be concealed a moment from the reader,—I verily believe, I had put by my father, and left him drawing a sun-dial, for no better purpose than to be buried under ground.

CHAP. XVII.

——'Twas nothing:—I did not lose two drops of blood by it:—'twas not worth calling in a surgeon had he lived next door to us.—Thousands suffer by choice, what I did by accident.—Doctor Slop made ten times more of it than there was occasion.—Some men rise by the art of hanging great weights upon small wires:—and I am this day (August the 10th, 1761) paying part of the price of this man's reputation.—O, 'twould provoke a stone to see how things are carried on in this world!—The chambermaid had left no ****** *** under the bed. ——Cannot you contrive, master, quoth Susannah, lifting up the sash with one hand, as she spoke, and helping me up into the window-seat with the other,—cannot you manage, my dear, for a single time, to **** *** ** *** ******?——

I was five years old.—Susannah did not consider that nothing was well hung in our family;—so, slap came the sash down like lightning upon us.——Nothing is left,—cried Susannah,—nothing is left,—for me, but to run my country.——

My uncle Toby's house was a much kinder sanctuary; and so Susannah fled to it.

CHAP. XVIII.

When Susannah told the Corporal the misadventure of the sash, with all the circumstances which attended the *murder* of me,—(as she called it)—the blood forsook his cheeks;—all accessaries in murder being principals,—Trim's conscience told him he was as much to blame as Susannah;—and if the doctrine had been true, my uncle Toby had as much of the bloodshed to answer for to Heaven as either of 'em;—so that neither reason nor instinct, separate nor together, could possibly have guided Susannah's steps to so proper an asylum.—It is in vain to leave this to the reader's imagination:—to form any kind of hypothesis that will render these propositions feasible, he must cudgel his brains sore; and to do it without,—he must have such brains as no reader ever had before him.—Why should I put them either to trial or to torture?—'Tis my own affair: I'll explain it myself.

CHAP. XIX.

'Tis a pity, Trim, said my uncle Toby, resting with his hand upon the Corporal's shoulder, as they both stood surveying their works,—that we have not a couple of field-pieces to mount in the gorge of that new redoubt;—'twould secure the lines all along there, and make the attack on that side quite complete.—Get me a couple cast, Trim.——

Your Honor shall have them, replied Trim, before to-morrow morning.——

It was the joy of Trim's heart; nor was his fertile head ever at a loss for expedients in doing it, to supply my uncle Toby, in his campaigns, with whatever his fancy called for: had it been his last crown, he would have sat down and hammered it into a paderero, to have prevented a single wish in his master.—The Corporal had already,—what with cutting off the ends of my uncle Toby's spouts,—hacking and chisseling up the sides of his leaden gutters,—melting down his pewter shaving-bason;—and going at last, like Lewis the Fourteenth, on to the top of the church for spare ends, &c.—he had that very campaign brought no less than eight new battering cannons, besides three demi-culverins, into the field. My uncle Toby's demand for two more pieces for the redoubt, had set the Corporal at work again; and no better resource offering, he had taken the two leaden weights from the nursery-window; and as the sash-pulleys, when the lead was gone, were of no kind of use, he had taken them away also, to make a couple of wheels for one of their carriages.

He had dismantled every sash-window in my uncle Toby's house long before, in the very same way,—though not always in the same order; for sometimes the pulleys had been wanted, and not the lead,—so then he began with the pulleys; and the pulleys being picked out, then the lead became useless;—and so the lead went to pot too.

——A great MORAL might be picked handsomely out of this, but I have not time;—'tis enough to say, Wherever the demolition began, 'twas equally fatal to the sash-window.

CHAP. XX.

The Corporal had not taken his measures so badly in this stroke of artilleryship, but that he might have kept the matter entirely to himself, and left Susannah to have sustained the whole weight of the attack as she could:—true courage is not content with coming off so.—The Corporal, whether as general or comptroller of the train,—'twas no matter,—had done that, without which, as he imagined, the misfortune cou never have happened,—*at least in Susannah's hands.*—How would your Honors have behaved?—He determined at once, not to take shelter behind Susannah,—but to give it, and, with this resolution upon his mind, he marched upright into the parlor, to lay the whole *manœuvre* before my uncle Toby.

My uncle Toby had just then been giving Yorick an account of the battle of Steinkirk, and of the strange conduct of Count Solmes, in ordering the foot to halt, and the horse to march where it could not act; which was directly contrary to the king's command, and proved the loss of the day.

There are incidents in some families so pat to the purpose of what is going to follow,—they are scarce exceeded by the invention of a dramatic writer,—I mean of ancient days.—

Trim, by the help of his fore-finger laid flat upon the table, and the edge of his hand striking across it at right angles, made a shift to tell his story so that priests and virgins might have listened to it;—and the story being told, the dialogue went on as follows:—

CHAP. XXI.

——I WOULD be picqueted to death, cried the Corporal, as he concluded Susannah's story, before I would suffer the woman to come to any harm:—'twas my fault, an' please your Honor,—not her's.

Corporal Trim, replied my uncle Toby, putting on his hat, which lay upon the table, if any thing can be said to be a fault, when the service absolutely requires it should be done, 'tis I certainly who deserve the blame; you obeyed your orders.

Had Count Solmes, Trim, done the same at the battle of Steinkirk, said Yorick, drolling a little upon the Corporal, who had been run over by a dragoon in the retreat, --he had saved thee——Saved! cried Trim, interrupting Yorick, and finishing the sentence for him after his own fashion,—he had saved five battalions, and please your Reverence, every soul of them.—There was Cutts's continued the Corporal, clapping the fore-finger of his right hand upon the thumb of his left, and counting round his hand,—there was Cutts's,—Mackay's,—Angus's,—Graham's,—and Leven's, all cut to pieces;—and so had the English life-guards, too, had it not been for some regiments upon the right, who marched up boldly to their relief, and received the enemy's fire in their faces, before any one of their own platoons discharged a musket.—They'll go to Heaven for it, added Trim. ——Trim is right, said my uncle Toby, nodding to Yorick;—he's perfectly right. ——What signified his marching the horse, continued the Corporal, where the ground was so strait, and the French had such a nation of hedges, and copses, and ditches, and fell'd trees laid this way and that, to cover them (as they always have.)—Count Solmes should have sent us;—we would have fired muzzle to muzzle with them for their lives.—There was nothing to be done for the horse:—he had his foot shot off, however, for his pains, continued the Corporal, the very next campaign at Landen. ——Poor Trim got his wound there, quoth my uncle Toby.——'Twas owing, an please your Honor, entirely to Count Solmes; had he drubbed them soundly at Steinkirk, they would not have fought us at Landen.——Possibly not, Trim, said my uncle Toby; though, if they have the advantage of a wood, or you give them a moment's time to intrench themselves, they are a nation which will pop and pop for ever at you. There is no way but to march coolly up to them,—receive their fire, and fall in upon them, pell-mell;——Ding-dong, added Trim;——Horse and foot, said my uncle Toby;——Helter-skelter, said Trim; ——Right and left, cried my uncle Toby. ——Blood an' ounds! shouted the Corporal:—the battle raged; Yorick drew his chair a little to one side for safety; and, after a moment's pause, my uncle Toby, sinking his voice a note, resumed the discourse as follows:—

CHAP. XXII.

KING William, said my uncle Toby, addressing himself to Yorick, was so terribly provoked at Count Solmes for disobeying his orders, that he would not suffer him to come into his presence for many months after.——I fear, answered Yorick, the Squire will be as much provoked at the Corporal, as the King at the Count.—But 'twould be singularly hard in this case, continued he, if Corporal Trim, who has behaved so diametrically opposite to Count Solmes, should have the fate to be rewarded with the same disgrace:—too often, in this world, do things take that train.——I would spring a mine, cried my uncle Toby, rising up, and blow up my fortifications, and my house with them, and we would perish under their ruins, ere I would stand by and see it.——Trim directed a slight, but a grateful bow towards his master,—and so the chapter ends.

CHAP. XXIII.

—Then, Yorick, replied my uncle Toby, you and I will lead the way abreast:—— and do you, Corporal, follow a few paces behind us.——And Susannah, an' please your Honor, said Trim, shall be put in the rear. 'Twas an excellent disposition, and in this order, without either drums beating, or colors flying, they marched slowly from my uncle Toby's house to Shandy-hall.

——I wish, said Trim, as they entered the door, instead of the sash-weights, I had cut off the church-spout, as I once thought to have done.——You have cut off spouts enow, replied Yorick.

CHAP. XXIV.

As many pictures as have been given of my father, how like him soever in different airs and attitudes,—not one, or all of them, can ever help the reader to any kind of preconception of how my father would think, speak, or act, upon any untried occasion or occurrence of life.—There was that infinitude of oddities in him, and of chances along with it, by which handle he would take a thing,—it baffled, Sir, all calculations.—The truth was, his road lay so very far on one side, from that wherein most men travelled, that every object before him presented a face and section of itself to his eye, altogether different from the plan and elevation of it seen by the rest of mankind.—In other words, 'twas a different object, and, in course, was differently considered.

This is the true reason that my dear Jenny and I, as well as all the world besides us, have such eternal squabbles about nothing.—She looks at her outside;—I, at her in.—How is it possible we should agree about her value?

CHAP. XXV.

'Tis a point settled,—and I mention it for the comfort of Confucius*, who is apt to get entangled in telling a plain story,— that provided he keeps along the line of his story, he may go backwards and forwards as he will, 'tis still held to be no digression.

This being premised, I take the benefit of the *act of going backwards* myself.

CHAP. XXVI.

Fifty thousand pannier loads of Devils —(not of the Archbishop of Benevento's,— I mean of Rabelais's Devils) with their tails chopped off by their rumps, could not have made so diabolical a scream of it as I did— when the accident befell me: it summoned up my mother instantly into the nursery;— so that Susannah had but just time to make her escape down the back stairs, as my mother came up the fore.

Now, though I was old enough to have told the story myself,—and young enough, I hope, to have done it without malignity, —yet Susannah, in passing by the kitchen, for fear of accidents, had left it in short hand with the cook,—the cook had told it, with a commentary, to Jonathan; and Jonathan to Obadiah; so that, by the time my father had rung the bell half a dozen times,

* Mr. Shandy is supposed to mean ***** ****** Esq. member for *****,—and not the Chinese Legislator.

to know what was the matter above,—was Obadiah enabled to give him a particular account of it, just as it had happened.——I thought as much, said my father, tucking up his night-gown,—and so walked up stairs.

One would imagine from this—(though for my own part I somewhat question it)—that my father, before that time, had actually wrote that remarkable chapter in the *Tristra-pædia*, which to me is the most original and entertaining one in the whole book,—and that is the *chapter upon sash-windows*, with a bitter *Philippic* at the end of it, upon the forgetfulness of chamber-maids. I have but two reasons for thinking otherwise.

First, had the matter been taken into consideration before the event happened, my father certainly would have nailed up the sash-window for good an' all; which, considering with what difficulty he composed books, he might have done with ten times less trouble than he could have wrote the chapter. This argument, I foresee, holds good against his writing a chapter, even after the event; but 'tis obviated under the second reason, which I have the honor to offer to the world in support of my opinion, that my father did not write the chapter upon sash-windows and chamber-pots at the time supposed,—and it is this:—

—That, in order to render the *Tristra-pædia* complete, I wrote the chapter myself.

CHAP. XXVII.

My father put on his spectacles,—looked,—took them off,—put them into the case,—all in less than a statutable minute; and, without opening his lips, turned about and walked precipitately down stairs. My mother imagined he had stepped down for lint and basilicon: but seeing him return with a couple of folios under his arm, and Obadiah following him with a large reading-desk, she took it for granted it was an Herbal, and so drew him a chair to the bed-side, that he might consult upon the case at his ease.

——If it be but right done, said my father, turning to the section,—*de sede vel subjecti circumcisionis*,—for he had brought up *Spenser de Legibus Hebræorum Ritualibus*,—and *Maimonides*, in order to confront and examine us altogether;——

——If it be but right done, quoth he,—Only tell us, cried my mother, interrupting him, what herbs?——For that, replied my father, you must send for Dr. Slop.

My mother went down, and my father went on, reading the section as follows:

* * * * * * * *
* * * * * * * *
* * ——Very well,—said my father,
* * * * * * * *
* * * * * * * *
* * *—nay, if it has that convenience,—and so without stopping a moment to settle it first in his mind, whether the Jews had it from the Egyptians, or the Egyptians from the Jews,—he rose up, and rubbing his forehead two or three times across with the palm of his hand, in the manner we rub out the footsteps of care, when evil has trod lighter upon us than we foreboded,—he shut the book, and walked down stairs.——Nay, said he, mentioning the name of a different great nation upon every step as he set his foot upon it,—if the Egyptians,—the Syrians,—the Phœnicians,—the Arabians,—the Cappadocians,—if the Colchi and Troglodytes did it,—if Solon and Pythagoras submitted,—what is Tristram?—Who am I, that I should fret or fume one moment about the matter?

CHAP. XXVIII.

Dear Yorick, said my father, smiling (for Yorick had broke his rank with my uncle Toby, in coming through the narrow entry, and so had stept first into the parlor) this Tristram of ours, I find, comes very hardly by all his religious rites. Never was the son of Jew, Christian, Turk, or Infidel, initiated into them in so oblique and slovenly a manner.——But he is no worse, I trust, said Yorick.——There has been certainly, continued my father, the deuce and all to do in some part or other of the ecliptic, when this offspring of mine was formed.——*That* you are a better judge of than I, replied Yorick.——Astrologers, quoth my father, know better than us both:—the trine and sextile aspects have jumped awry,—or the opposite of their ascendants have not hit it, as they should,—or the lords of the genitures (as they call them) have been at *bo-peep*,—or something has been wrong above or below with us.

'Tis possible, answered Yorick.——But is the child, cried my uncle Toby, the worse?——The Troglodytes say not, replied my father.—And your theologists, Yorick, tell us —— Theologically? said Yorick;—or speaking after the manner of apothecaries? *—statesmen? †—or washer-women? ‡

———I'm not sure, replied my father;—but they tell us, brother Toby, he's the better for it.——Provided, said Yorick, you travel him into Egypt.——Of that, answered my father, he will have the advantage, when he sees the Pyramids.

——Now, every word of this, quoth my uncle Toby, is Arabic to me.——I wish, said Yorick, 'twas so to half the world.

—— § Ilus, continued my father, circumcised his whole army one morning.——Not without a court-martial? cried my uncle Toby.——Though the learned, continued he, taking no notice of my uncle Toby's remark, but turning to Yorick,—are greatly divided still, who Ilus was;—some say Saturn:—some, the Supreme Being;—others, no more than a brigadier-general under Pharaoh-Neco.——Let him be who he will, said my uncle Toby, I know not by what article of war he could justify it.

The controvertists, answered my father, assign two-and-twenty different reasons for it:—others, indeed, who have drawn their pens on the opposite side of the question, have shown the world the futility of the greatest part of them.—But then again our best polemic divines,——I wish there was not a polemic divine, said Yorick, in the kingdom;—one ounce of practical divinity—is worth a painted ship-load of all their Reverences have imported these fifty years.——Pray, Mr. Yorick, quoth my uncle Toby,—do tel me what a polemic divine is?——The best description, Captain Shandy, I have ever read, is of a couple of 'em, replied Yorick, in the account of the battle fought, single hands, betwixt Gymnast and Captain Tripet; which I have in my pocket.——I beg I may hear it, quoth my uncle Toby, earnestly——You shall, said Yorick,——And as the Corporal is waiting for me at the door,——and I know the description of a battle will do the poor fellow more good than his supper,—I beg, brother, you'll give him leave to come in.—With all my soul, said my father.——Trim came in, erect and happy as an emperor; and having shut the door, Yorick took a book from his right-hand coat-pocket, and read, or pretended tc read, as follows:—

CHAP. XXIX.

——"Which words being heard by all "the soldiers which were there, divers of "them, being inwardly terrified, did shrink "back and make room for the assailant.—"All this did Gymnast very well remark "and consider; and, therefore, making as "if he would have alighted from off his "horse, as he was poising himself on the "mounting side, he most nimbly (with his "short sword by his thigh) shifting his feet "in the stirrup, and performing the stirrup-"leather feat, whereby after the inclining "of his body downwards, he forthwith "launched himself aloft into the air, and "placed both his feet together upon the "saddle, standing upright, with his back "turned towards his horse's head.—Now "(said he) my case goes forward. Then, "suddenly, in the same posture wherein he "was, he fetched a gambol upon one foot, "and turning to the left hand, failed not to "carry his body perfectly round, just into "his former position, without missing one "jot.——Ha! said Tripet, I will not do "that at this time; and not without cause "——Well, said Gymnast, I have failed,—"I will undo this leap; then with a mar"vellous strength and agility, turning to"wards the right hand, he fetched another

* Χαλεπῆς νόσυ, καὶ δυσιάτυ ἀπαλλαγὴ, ἣν α"νθρακα καλοῦσιν.—PHILO

† Τὰ τεμνόμενα τῶν ἐθῶν πολυγονωτατα, καὶ πολυανθρωπότατα εἶναι.

‡ Καθαριδηῖος εινεκεν.—BOCHART.

§ Ὁ Ἶλος, τὰ αἰδοια περιτέμνεται. ταυτο ποῖησαι καὶ τως ἅμ' αυ'τῶ συμμάχυς καταναγκασάς.—SANCHUNIATHO.

"frisking gambol as before; which done, "he set his right-hand thumb upon the bow "of the saddle, raised himself up, and "sprung into the air, poising and upholding "his whole weight upon the muscle and "nerve of the said thumb, and so turned "and whirled himself about three times, "at the fourth, reversing his body, and over-"turning it upside down, and foreside back, "without *touching any thing*, he brought "himself betwixt the horse's two ears, and "then giving himself a jerking swing, he "seated himself upon the crupper."—

[This can't be fighting, said my uncle Toby.——The Corporal shook his head at it.——Have patience, said Yorick.]

"Then (Tripet) pass'd his right leg over "his saddle, and placed himself *en croup*. "—But, said he, 'twere better for me to get "into the saddle; then putting the thumbs "of both hands upon the crupper before "him, and thereupon leaning himself, as "upon the only supporters of his body, he "incontinently turned heels over head into "the air, and straight found himself be-"twixt the bow of the saddle, in a tolerable "seat; then springing into the air with a "summerset, he turned him about like a "wind-mill, and made above an hundred "frisks, turns, and demipommadas."—Good God! cried Trim, losing all patience——one home thrust of a bayonet is worth it all. ——I think so, too, replied Yorick.—

I am of a contrary opinion, quoth my father.

CHAP. XXX.

—No;—I thing I have advanced nothing, replied my father, making answer to a question which Yorick had taken the liberty to put to him,—I have advanced nothing in the *Tristra-pædia*, but what is as clear as any one proposition in Euclid. ——Reach me, Trim, that book from off the scrutoire.—It has oft-times been in my mind, continued my father, to have read it over, both to you, Yorick, and to my brother Toby; and I think it a little unfriendly in myself, in not having done it long ago. —Shall we have a short chapter or two now,——and a chapter or two hereafter, as occasions serve, and so on, till we get through the whole? My uncle Toby and Yorick made the obeisance which was proper; and the Corporal, though he was not included in the compliment, laid his hand upon his breast, and made his bow at the same time.—The company smiled.—Trim, quoth my father, has paid the full price for staying out the entertainment.—He did not seem to relish the play, replied Yorick. ——'Twas a Tom-fool battle, an' please your Reverences, of Captain Tripet's and that other officer, making so many summersets as they advanced:——the French come on capering now and then in that way,—but not quite so much.

My uncle Toby never felt the consciousness of his existence with more complacency, than what the Corporal's, and his own reflections, made him do at that moment;—he lighted his pipe,—Yorick drew his chair closer to the table,—Trim snuff'd the candle,—my father stirr'd up the fire, —took up the book,——cough'd twice, and began.

CHAP. XXXI.

The first thirty pages, said my father, turning over the leaves,——are a little dry; and as they are not closely connected with the subject,—for the present we'll pass them by: 'tis a prefatory introduction, continued my father, or an introductory preface (for I am not determined which name to give it) upon political or civil government, the foundation of which being laid in the first conjunction betwixt male and female, for procreation of the species,—I was insensibly led into it.—'Twas natural, said Yorick.

The original of society, continued my father, I'm satisfied, is, what Politian tells us, i. e. merely conjugal, and nothing more than the getting together of one man and one woman;—to which, (according to Hesiod) the philosopher adds a servant:—but supposing, in the first beginning, there were no men-servants born,—he lays the foundation of it, in a man, —a woman,—and a bull.——I believe 'tis an ox, quoth Yorick, quoting the passage (*υἶκον μὲν πρωτιστατα, γυναῖκα τε, βȣν τ' αροτηρα*)—A bull must have given more trouble than his head was worth.—but there is a better reason still, said my father, (dipping his pen into his ink;) for the ox, being the most patient of animals, and the most useful withal in tilling the ground for their nourishment,—was the properest instrument, and emblem too, for the new-joined couple, that the creation could have associated with them. —And there is a stronger reason, added my uncle Toby, than them all for the ox.——My father had not power to take his pen out of his inkhorn, till he had heard my uncle Toby's reason.——For, when the ground was tilled, said my uncle Toby, and made worth inclosing, then they began to secure it by walls and ditches, which was the origin of fortification.——True, true, dear Toby, cried my father, striking out the bull, and putting the ox in his place.

My father gave Trim a nod, to snuff the candle, and resumed his discourse.

——I enter upon this speculation, said my father, carelessly, and half shutting the book, as he went on, merely to show the foundation of the natural relation between a father and his child; the right and jurisdiction over whom he acquires these several ways:—

1st, by marriage.

2d, by adoption.

3d, by legitimation.

And, 4th, by procreation; all which I consider in their order.

I lay a slight stress upon one of them, replied Yorick,—the act, especially where it ends there, in my opinion, lays as little obligation upon the child, as it conveys power to the father.——You are wrong,—said my father, argutely; and for this plain reason * * * * * * *
* * * * * * * *
* * * * * * * *

——I own, added my father, that the offspring, upon this account, is not so under the power and jurisdiction of the mother.—But the reason, replied Yorick, equally holds good for her.—She is under authority herself, said my father:—and besides, continued my father, nodding his head, and laying his finger upon the side of his nose, as he assigned his reason,—"she is not the principal agent," Yorick.—In what? quoth my uncle Toby, stopping his pipe.—Though, by all means, added my father, (not attending to my uncle Toby) "The son ought to "pay her respect," as you may read, Yorick, at large, in the first book of the Institutes of Justinian, at the eleventh title, and the tenth section.——I can read it as well, replied Yorick, in the Catechism.

CHAP. IX.

Trim can repeat every word of it by heart, quoth my uncle Toby.—Pugh! said my father, not caring to be interrupted with Trim's saying his Catechism.—He can, upon my honor, replied my uncle Toby. —Ask him, Mr. Yorick, any question you please.——

—The Fifth Commandment, Trim—said Yorick, speaking mildly, and with a gentle nod, as to a modest catechumen.—The Corporal stood silent.——You don't ask him right, said my uncle Toby, raising his voice, and giving it rapidly like the word of command;—the fifth?—cried my uncle Toby. ——I must begin with the first, an' please your Honor, said the Corporal.—

—Yorick could not forbear smiling.—Your Reverence does not consider, said the Corporal, shouldering his stick like a musket, and marching into the middle of the room, to illustrate his position,—that 'tis exactly the same thing as doing one's exercise in the field.——

"Join your right hand to your firelock,' cried the Corporal, giving the word of command, and performing the motion.——

"Poise your firelock," cried the Corporal, doing the duty still of both adjutant and private man.—

"Rest your firelock,"—one motion, an' please your Reverence, you see leads into another.—If his Honor will begin but with the first—

The first?—cried my uncle Toby, setting his hand upon his side.—* * * *
* * * * * *

The second?—cried my uncle Toby, waving his tobacco-pipe, as he would have done his sword at the head of a regiment.—The Corporal went through his manual with exactness; and having honored his father and mother, made a low bow, and fell back to the side of the room.

Every thing in the world, said my father,

is big with jest,—and has wit in it, and instruction too,—if we can but find it out.

—Here is the scaffold-work of INSTRUCTION, its true point of folly, without the BUILDING behind it.——

—Here is the glass for pedagogues, preceptors, tutors, governors, gerund-grinders, and bear-leaders, to view themselves in, in their true dimensions.——

Oh! there is a husk and shell, Yorick, which grows up with learning, which their unskilfulness knows not how to fling away! SCIENCES MAY BE LEARNED BY ROTE, BUT WISDOM NOT.

Yorick thought my father inspired.——I will enter into obligations this moment, said my father, to lay out all my aunt Dinah's legacy in charitable uses, (of which, by the bye, my father had no high opinion) if the Corporal has any one determinate idea annexed to any one word he has repeated.—Prithee, Trim, quoth my father turning round to him,—what dost thou mean by "honoring thy father and mother?"

Allowing them, an' please your Honor, three half-pence a day out of my pay, when they grow old.——And didst thou do that, Trim? said Yorick.—He did, indeed, replied my uncle Toby.—Then, Trim, said Yorick, springing out of his chair, and taking the Corporal by the hand, thou art the best commentator on that part of the Decalogue; and I honor thee more for it, Corporal Trim, than if thou hadst had a hand in the Talmud itself.

CHAP. XXXIII.

O BLESSED health! cried my father, making an exclamation as he turned over the leaves to the next chapter,—thou art above all gold and treasure; 'tis thou who enlargest the soul,—and openest all its power to receive instruction and to relish virtue.——He that has thee, has little more to wish for;——and he that is so wretched as to want thee,—wants every thing with thee.

I have concentrated all that can be said upon this important head, said my father, into very little room; therefore we'll read the chapter quite through.

My father read as follows:

"The whole secret of health depending "upon the due contention for mastery be-"twixt the radical heat and the radical "moisture,"——You have proved that matter of fact, I suppose, above, said Yorick. Sufficiently, replied my father.

In saying this, my father shut the book, ——not as if he resolved to read no more of it, for he kept his fore-finger in the chapter: ——not pettishly,—for he shut the book slowly; his thumb resting, when he had done it, upon the upper side of the cover, as his three fingers supported the lower side of it, without the least compressive violence.—

I have demonstrated the truth of that point, quoth my father, nodding to Yorick, most sufficiently, in the preceding chapter.

Now, could the man in the moon be told, that a man in the earth had wrote a chapter, sufficiently demonstrating, That the secret of all health depended upon the due contention for mastery betwixt the radical heat and the radical moisture,—and that he had managed the point so well, that there was not one single word wet or dry upon radical heat or radical moisture, throughout the whole chapter,—or a single syllable in it, pro or con, directly or indirectly, upon the contention betwixt these two powers in any part of the animal economy,——

"O thou eternal Maker of all beings!" —he would cry, striking his breast with his right hand, (in case he had one)——"Thou whose power and goodness can "enlarge the faculties of thy creatures to "this infinite degree of excellence and "perfection,—What have we MOONITES "done?"

CHAP. XXXIV.

WITH two strokes, the one at Hippocrates, the other at Lord Verulam, did my father achieve it.

The stroke at the prince of physicians, with which he began, was no more than a short insult upon his sorrowful complaint of the *ars longa*,—and *vita brevis*.—Life short, cried my father,—and the art of healing tedious! and who are we to thank for both the one and the other, but the ignorance of quacks themselves,—and the stage-loads of chemical nostrums, and peripatetic lumber, with which in all ages they have first flatter'd the world, and at last deceived it!

——O my Lord Verulam! cried my father, turning from Hippocrates, and making his second stroke at him, as the principal of nostrum-mongers, and the fittest to be made an example of to the rest,—What shall I say to thee, my great lord Verulam? What shall I say to thy internal spirit,—thy opium, thy saltpetre,—thy greasy unction,—thy daily purges, thy nightly glisters, and succedaneums?

——My father was never at a loss what to say to any man, upon any subject; and had the least occasion for the exordium of any man breathing: how he dealt with his lordship's opinion,—you shall see;—but when——I know not:—we must first see what his lordship's opinion was.

CHAP. XXXV.

"The two great causes which conspire "with each other to shorten life, says Lord "Verulam, are, first,—

"The internal spirit, which, like a gentle "flame, wastes the body down to death:— "and, secondly, the external air, that "parches the body up to ashes:—which two "enemies attacking us on both sides of our "bodies together, at length destroy our or-"gans, and render them unfit to carry on "the functions of life."

This being the state of the case, the road to longevity was plain; nothing more being required, says his lordship, but to repair the waste committed by the internal spirit, by making the substance of it more thick and dense, by a regular course of opiates on one side, and by refrigerating the heat of it on the other, by three grains and a half of saltpetre every morning before you get up.—

Still this frame of ours was left exposed to the inimical assaults of the air without;—but this was fenced off again by a course of greasy unctions, which so fully saturated the pores of the skin, that no spicula could enter;—nor could any one get out.——This put a stop to all perspiration, sensible and insensible, which being the cause of so many scurvy distempers,—a course of glisters was requisite to carry off redundant humors,—and render the system complete.

What my father had to say to my lord of Verulam's opiates, his saltpetre, and greasy unctions and glisters, you shall read,—but not to-day—or to-morrow:—time presses upon me,—my reader is impatient,——I must get forwards.——You shall read the chapter at your leisure, (if you choose it) as soon as ever the *Tristram-pædia* is published.——

Sufficeth it at present to say, my father levelled the hypothesis with the ground, and in doing that, the learned know, he built up and established his own.—

CHAP. XXXVI.

The whole secret of health, said my father, beginning the sentence again, depending evidently upon the due contention betwixt the radical heat and radical moisture within us;—the least imiginable skill had been sufficient to have maintained it, had not the schoolmen confounded the task, merely, (as Van Hemont the famous chymist has proved) by all along mistaking the radical moisture for the tallow and fat of animal bodies.

Now the radical moisture is not the tallow or fat of animals, but an oily and balsamous substance; for the fat or tallow, as also the phlegm or watery parts, are cold: whereas the oily and balsamous parts are of a lively heat and spirit, which accounts for the observation of Aristotle, "*Quod omne animal post coitum est triste.*"

Now it is certain, that the radical heat lives in the radical moisture; but whether *vice versa*, is a doubt; however, when the one decays, the other decays also; and then is produced, either an unnatural heat, which causes an unnatural dryness,—or an unnatural moisture, which causes dropsies:——so that if a child, as he grows up, can but be taught to avoid running into fire or water, as either of them threaten his destruction,—'twill be all that is needful to be done upon that head.——

CHAP. XXXVII.

The description of the siege of Jericho itself, could not have engaged the attention of my uncle Toby more powerfully than the last chapter;—his eyes were fixed upon my father, throughout it;—he never mentioned radical heat and radical moisture, but my uncle Toby took his pipe out of his mouth and shook his head; and as soon as the chapter was finished, he beckoned to the Corporal to come close to his chair, to ask him the following question,—*aside:*— * * * * * * * * * * * * * * * *

It was at the siege of Limerick, an' please your honor, replied the Corporal, making a bow.

The poor fellow and I, quoth my uncle Toby, addressing himself to my father, were scarce able to crawl out of our tents, at the time the siege of Limerick was raised, upon the very account you mention.—Now what can have got into that precious noddle of thine, my dear brother Toby? cried my father mentally.——By heaven! continued he, communing still with himself, it would puzzle an Œdipus to bring it in point.——

I believe, an' please your Honor, quoth the Corporal, that if it had not been for the quantity of brandy we set fire to every night, and the claret and cinnamon with which I plied your Honor off,—And the Geneva, Trim, added my uncle Toby, which did us more good than all,—I verily believe, continued the Corporal, we had both, an' please your Honor, left our lives in the trenches, and been buried in them too.—The noblest grave, Corporal, cried my uncle Toby, his eyes sparkling as he spoke, that a soldier could wish to lie down in!——But a pitiful death for him! an' please your Honor, replied the Corporal.

All this was as much Arabic to my father, as the rites of the Colchi and Troglodytes had been before to my uncle Toby; my father could not determine whether he was to frown or to smile.

My uncle Toby, turning to Yorick, resumed the case at Limerick, more intelligibly than he had begun it,—and so settled the point for my father at once.——

CHAP. XXXVIII.

It was undoubtedly, said my uncle Toby a great happiness for myself and the Corporal, that we had all along a burning fever, attended with a most raging thirst, during the whole five-and-twenty days the flux was upon us in the camp; otherwise, what my brother calls the radical moisture, must, as I conceive it, inevitably have got the better.——My father drew in his lungs topfull of air, and looking up, blew it forth again, as slowly as he possibly could.

It was Heaven's mercy to us, continued my uncle Toby, which put it into the Corporal's head to maintain that due contention betwixt the radical heat and the radical moisture, by reinforcing the fever, as he did all along, with hot wine and spices; whereby the Corporal kept up (as it were) a continual firing; so that the radical heat stood its ground from the beginning to the end, and was a fair match for the moisture, terrible as it was.—Upon my honor, added my uncle Toby, you might have heard the contention within our bodies, brother Shandy, twenty toises.——If there was no firing, said Yorick.——

Well, said my father, with a full aspiration, and pausing a while after the word,—was I a judge, and the laws of the country which made me one permitted it, I would condemn some of the worst malefactors, provided they had their clergy,——

——Yorick, foreseeing the sentence was likely to end with no sort of mercy, laid his hand upon my father's breast, and begged he would respite it for a few minutes, till he asked the Corporal a question. Prithee, Trim, said Yorick, without staying for my father's leave,—tell us honestly,—what is thy opinion concerning this self-same radical heat and radical moisture?—

With humble submission to his Honor's better judgment, quoth the Corporal, making a bow to my uncle Toby,——Speak thy opinion freely, Corporal, said my uncle Toby.——The poor fellow is my servant, not my slave, added my uncle Toby, turning to my father.——

The Corporal put his hat under his left arm, and with his stick hanging upon the wrist of it, by a black thong split into a tassel about the knot, he marched up to the ground where he had performed his catechism; then touching his under jaw with the thumb and finger of his right hand before he opened his mouth,—he delivered his notion thus:—

CHAP. XXXIX.

Just as the Corporal was hemming to begin,—in waddled Dr. Slop.——'Tis not two-pence matter,—the Corporal shall go on in the next chapter, let who will come in.——

Well, my good Doctor, cried my father, sportively, for the transitions of his passions were unaccountably sudden;—and what has this whelp of mine to say to the matter?—

Had my father been asking after the amputation of the tail of a puppy-dog,—he could not have done it in a more careless air: the system which Dr. Slop had laid down, to treat the accident by, no way allowed of such a mode of inquiry.—He sat down.—

Pray, Sir, quoth my uncle Toby, in a manner which could not go unanswered,—in what condition is the boy?——'Twill end in a *phimosis*, replied Dr. Slop.——

I am no wiser than I was, quoth my uncle Toby, returning his pipe into his mouth.——Then let the Corporal go on, said my father, with his medical lecture.——The Corporal made a bow to his old friend, Dr. Slop, and then delivered his opinion concerning radical heat and radical moisture, in the following words:—

CHAP. XL.

The city of Limerick, the siege of which was begun under his majesty King William himself, the year after I went into the army,—lies, an' please your Honors, in the middle of a devilish wet swampy country.—'Tis quite surrounded, said my uncle Toby, with the Shannon: and is, by its situation, one of the strongest fortified places in Ireland.—

I think this is a new fashion, quoth Dr. Slop, of beginning a medical lecture.——'Tis all true, answered Trim.——Then I wish the faculty would follow the cut of it, said Yorick.——'Tis all cut through, an please your Reverence, said the Corporal, with drains and bogs: and besides, there was such a quantity of rain fell during the siege, the whole country was like a puddle;—'twas that, and nothing else, which brought on the flux, and which had like to have killed both his Honor and myself. Now there was no such thing, after the first ten days, continued the Corporal, for a soldier to lie dry in his tent, without cutting a ditch round it, to draw off the water;—nor was that enough for those who could afford it, as his Honor could, without setting fire every night to a pewter dish full of brandy, which took off the damp of the air, and made the inside of the tent as warm as a stove.——

And what conclusion dost thou draw, Corporal Trim, cried my father, from all these premises?—

I infer, an' please your Worship, replied Trim, that the radical moisture is nothing in the world but ditch-water;—and that the radical heat of those who can go to the expense of it, is burnt brandy:—the radical heat and moisture of a private man, an please your Honor, is nothing but ditch-water—and a dram of Geneva;—and give us but enough of it, with a pipe of tobacco, to give us spirits and drive away the vapors,—we know not what it is to fear death.

I am at a loss, Captain Shandy, quoth Doctor Slop, to determine in which branch of learning your servant shines most; whether in physiology or divinity.——Slop had not forgot Trim's comment upon the sermon.——

It is but an hour ago, replied Yorick, since the Corporal was examined in the latter, and passed muster with great honor.——

The radical heat and moisture, quoth Doctor Slop, turning to my father, you must know, is the basis and foundation of our being,—as the root of a tree is the source and principle of its vegetation.—It is inherent in the seeds of all animals, and may be preserved sundry ways; but principally, in my opinion, by *consubstantials, impriments* and *occludents.*—Now this poor fellow, continued Dr. Slop, pointing to the Corporal, has had the misfortune to have heard some superficial empiric discourse upon this nice point.——That he has,—said my father.——Very likely,—said my uncle. ——I'm sure of it,—quoth Yorick.

CHAP. XLI.

Doctor Slop being called out to look at a cataplasm he had ordered, it gave my father an opportunity of going on with another chapter in the *Tristra-pædia.*—— Come! cheer up, my lads; I'll show you land;—for when we have tugged through that chapter, the book shall not be opened again this twelve-month. Huzza!—

CHAP. XLII.

——Five years with a bib under his chin;

Four years in travelling from Christ-cross-row to Malachi;

A year and a half in learning to write his own name;

Seven long years and more τυπτωing it, at Greek and Latin;

Four years at his *probations* and his *negations*;—the fine statue still lying in the middle of the marble block, and nothing done, but his tools sharpened to hew it out! —'Tis a piteous delay!—Was not the great Julius Scaliger within an ace of never getting his tools sharpened at all?—Forty-four years old was he before he could manage his Greek;—and Peter Damianus, Lord Bishop of Ostia, as all the world knows, could not so much as read when he was of man's estate;—and Baldus himself, as eminent as he turned out after, entered upon the law so late in life, that every body imagined he intended to be an advocate in the other world. No wonder, when Eudamidas, the son of Archidamas, heard Xenocrates at seventy-five disputing about *wisdom*, that he asked gravely,—"If the old man be yet "disputing and inquiring concerning wis- "dom,—what time will he have to make "use of it?"

Yorick listened to my father with great attention; there was a seasoning of wisdom unaccountably mixed up with his strangest whims; and he had sometimes such illuminations in the darkest of his eclipses, as almost atoned for them.—Be wary, Sir, when you imitate him.

I am convinced, Yorick, continued my father, half reading and half discoursing, that there is a north-west passage to the intellectual world; and that the soul of man has shorter ways of going to work, in furnishing itself with knowledge and instruction, than we generally take with it.—But, alack! all fields have not a river or a spring running beside them;—every child, Yorick, has not a parent to point it out.

—The whole entirely depends, added my father, in a low voice, upon the *auxiliary verbs*, Mr. Yorick.

Had Yorick trod upon Virgil's snake, he could not have looked more surprised.—I am surprised too, cried my father, observing it;—and I reckon it as one of the greatest calamities which ever befell the republic of letters, That those who have been intrusted with the education of our children, and whose business it was to open their minds, and stock them early with ideas, in order to set the imagination loose upon them, have made so little use of the auxiliary verbs in doing it, as they have done;—so that, except Raymond Lullius, and the elder Pelegrini, the last of whom arrived to such perfection in the use of 'em, with his topics, that, in a few lessons, he could teach a young gentleman to discourse with plausibility upon any subject, *pro* and *con*, and to say and write all that could be spoken or written concerning it, without blotting a word, to the admiration of all who beheld him.——I should be glad, said Yorick, interrupting my father, to be made to comprehend this matter.——You shall, said my father.

The highest stretch of improvement a single word is capable of, is a high metaphor;—for which, in my opinion, the idea is generally the worse, and not the better:—but, be that as it may,—when the mind has done that with it,—there is an end;—the mind and the idea are at rest,—until a second idea enters:—and so on.

Now the use of the *Auxiliaries* is, at once to set the soul a-going by herself upon the materials as they are brought her; and by the versability of this great engine, round which they are twisted, to open new tracts of inquiry, and make every idea engender millions.

You excite my curiosity greatly, said Yorick.

For my own part, quoth my uncle Toby, I have given it up.——The Danes, an' please your Honor, quoth the Corporal, who were on the left at the siege of Limerick, were all auxiliaries.——And very good ones, said my uncle Toby.——And your Honor roul'd with them,—captains with captains,—very well, said the Corporal.——But the auxiliaries, Trim, my brother is talking about, answered my uncle Toby,—I conceive to be different things.

——You do? said my father, rising up.

CHAP. XLIII.

My father took a single turn across the room, then sat down and finished the chapter.

The verbs auxiliary we are concerned in here, continued my father, are, *am, was, have, had, do, did, make, made, suffer, shall, should, will, would, can, could, owe, ought, used*, or *is wont;*—and these varied with tenses, *present, past, future*, and conjugated with the verb *see*,—or with these questions added to them:—*Is it? Was it? Will it be? Would it be? May it be? Might it be?*—and these again put negatively,—*Is it not? Was it not? Ought it not?*—or affirmatively, *It is, It was, It ought to be:*—or chronologically,—*Has it been always? Lately? How long ago?* or hypothetically,—*If it was? If it was not?*—what would follow?—If the French should beat the English? If the Sun go out of the Zodiac?

Now by the right use and application of these, continued my father, in which a child's memory should be exercised, there is no one idea can enter his brain, how barren soever, but a magazine of corruptions and conclusions may be drawn forth from it.——Didst thou ever see a white bear? cried my father, turning his head round to Trim, who stood at the back of the chair.—No, an please your Honor, replied the Corporal.——But thou couldst discourse about one, Trim, said my father, in case of need?——How is it possible, brother, quoth my uncle Toby, if the Corporal never saw one?—'Tis the fact I want, replied my father;—and the possibility of it is as follows:—

A WHITE BEAR! Very well. Have I ever seen one? Might I ever have seen one? Am I ever to see one? Ought I ever to have seen one? Or can I ever see one?

Would I had seen a white bear! (for how can I imagine it?)

If I should see a white bear, what should I say? If I should never see a white bear, what then?

If I never have, can, must, or shall see a white bear alive,—have I ever seen the skin of one? Did I ever see one painted?—described? Have I never dreamed of one?

Did my father, mother, uncle, aunt, brothers, or sisters, ever see a white bear. What would they give? How would they behave? How would the white bear have behaved? Is he wild? Tame? Terrible? Rough? Smooth?

—Is the white bear worth seeing?

—Is there no sin in it?

Is it better than a *black one?*

THE

LIFE AND OPINIONS

OF

Tristram Shandy,

GENTLEMAN.

CHAP. I.

WE'LL not stop two moments, my dear Sir,—only as we have got through these seven volumes,* (do, Sir, sit down upon a seat —they are better than nothing) let us just look back upon the country we have passed through.—

What a wilderness has it been! and what a mercy that we have not both of us been lost, or devoured by wild beasts in it!

Did you think the world itself, Sir, had contained such a number of Jack-Asses?—How they view'd and review'd us, as we passed over the rivulet at the bottom of that little valley!—and when we climbed over that hill, and were just getting out of sight,—good God! what a braying did they all set up together!

—Prithee, Shepherd, who keeps all these Jack-Asses? * * *

—Heaven be their comforter—What! are they never curried?—are they never taken in in winter?—Bray,—bray,—bray, bray on,—the world is deeply your debtor; —louder still—that's nothing;—in good sooth, you are ill used.—Was I a Jack-Ass, I solemnly declare, I would bray in G-sol-re-ut from morning, even unto night.

CHAP. II.

WHEN my father had danced his white bear backwards and forwards through half a dozen pages, he closed the book for good and all,—and, in a kind of triumph, re-delivered it into Trim's hand, with a nod to lay it upon the scrutoire where he found it.

* According to the original editions.

Tristram, said he, shall be made to conjugate every word in the dictionary backwards and forwards the same way:—every word, Yorick, by this means, you see, is converted into a thesis or an hypothesis;—every thesis and hypothesis have an offspring of propositions;—and each proposition has its own consequences and conclusions;—every one of which leads the mind on again, into fresh tracts of inquiries and doubtings.—The force of this engine, added my father, is incredible, in opening a child's head.——'Tis enough, brother Shandy, cried my uncle Toby, to burst it into a thousand splinters.——

I presume, said Yorick, smiling,—it must be owing to this,—(for, let logicians say what they will, it is not to be accounted for sufficiently from the bare use of the ten predicaments),—that the famous Vincent Quirino, amongst the many other astonishing feats of his childhood, of which the Cardinal Bembo has given the world so exact a story—should be able to paste up in the public schools at Rome, so early as in the eighth year of his age, no less than four thousand five hundred and sixty different theses, upon the most abstruse points of the most abstruse theology;—and to defend and maintain them in such sort, as to cramp and dumbfound his opponents.—What is that, cried my father, to what is told us of Alphonsus Tostatus, who, almost in his nurse's arms, learned all the sciences and liberal arts, without being taught any one of them?—What shall we say of the great Peireskius?—That's the very man, cried my uncle Toby, I once told you of, brother Shandy, who walked a matter of five hundred miles, reckoning from Paris to Scheveling, and from Scheveling back again, merely to see Stevinus's flying chariot.—He was a very great man! added my uncle Toby, (meaning Stevinus).—He was so, brother Toby, said my father, (meaning Peireskius)—and had multiplied his ideas so fast, and increased his knowledge to such a prodigious stock, that, if we may give credit to an anecdote concerning him, which we cannot withhold here, without shaking the authority of all anecdotes whatever,—at seven years of age, his father committed entirely to his care the education of his younger brother, a boy of five years old,—with the sole management of all his concerns.—Was the father as wise as the son? quoth my uncle Toby.—I should think not, said Yorick. — But what are these, continued my father—(breaking out in a kind of enthusiasm) — what are these to those prodigies of childhood in Grotius, Scioppius, Heinsius, Politian, Pascal, Joseph Scaliger, Ferdinand de Cordouè, and others, — some of whom left off their substantial forms at nine years old, or sooner, and went on reasoning without them?—Others went through their classes at seven;—wrote tragedies at eight.—Ferdinand de Cordouè was so wise at nine, 'twas thought the devil was in him; —and at Venice gave such proofs of his knowledge and goodness, that the monks imagined he was Antichrist, or nothing.—Others were masters of fourteen languages at ten;—finished the course of their rhetoric, poetry, logic, and ethics, at eleven; — put forth their commentaries upon Servius and Martianus Capella at twelve;—and at thirteen received their degrees in philosophy, laws, and divinity.—But you forget the great Lipsius, quoth Yorick, who composed a work* the day he was born.—They should have wiped it up, said my uncle Toby, and said no more about it.

* Nous aurions quelque interêt, says Baillet, de montrer qu'il n'a rien de ridicule s'il etoit veritable, au moins dans le sens enigmatique que Nicius Erythræus a tâché de lui donner. Cet auteur dit que pour comprendre comme Lipse, il a pu composer un ouvrage le premier jour de sa vie il faut s'imaginer, que ce premier jour n'est pas celui de la naissance charnelle, mais celui au quel il a commencé d'user de la raison: il veut que ç'ait-été à l'age de neuf ans; et il nous veut persuader que ce fût en cet age, que Lipse fit un poeme ——Le tour est ingenieux, &c. &c.

CHAP. III.

When the cataplasm was ready, a scruple of decorum had unseasonably rose up in Susannah's conscience about holding the candle, whilst Slop tied it on; Slop had not treated Susannah's distemper with anodynes,—and so a quarrel had ensued betwixt them.

Oh! oh!—said Slop, casting a glance of undue freedom in Susannah's face, as she declined the office;—then, I think, I know you, Madam.—You know me, Sir, cried Susannah, fastidiously, and with a toss of her head, levelled evidently, not at his profession, but at the doctor himself,—you know me! cried Susannah again.—Dr. Slop clapped his finger and his thumb instantly upon his nostrils;—Susannah's spleen was ready to burst at it;—'Tis false, said Susannah.—Come, come, Mrs. Modesty, said Slop, not a little elated with the success of his last thrust,—if you won't hold the candle and look—you may hold it and shut your eyes.—That's one of your popish shifts, cried Susannah.—'Tis better, said Slop, with a nod, than no shift at all, young woman.—I defy you, Sir, cried Susannah, pulling her shift-sleeve below her elbow.

It was almost impossible for two persons to assist each other, in a surgical case, with a more splenetic cordiality.

Slop snatched up the cataplasm:—Susannah snatched up the candle.—A little this way, said Slop.—Susannah looking one way, and rowing another, instantly set fire to Slop's wig, which being somewhat bushy and unctuous withal, was burnt out before it was well kindled.—You impudent whore! cried Slop,—(for what is passion but a wild beast)—you impudent whore! cried Slop, getting upright, with the cataplasm in his hand.—I never was the destruction of any body's nose, said Susannah—which is more than you can say.——Is it?—cried Slop, throwing the cataplasm in her face.—Yes, it is, cried Susannah, returning the compliment with what was left in the pan

CHAP. IV.

Doctor Slop and Susannah filed cross bills against each other in the parlor; which done, as the cataplasm had failed, they retired into the kitchen, to prepare a fomentation for me;—and whilst that was doing, my father determined the point, as you will read.

CHAP. V.

You see 'tis high time, said my father, addressing himself equally to my uncle Toby and Yorick, to take this young creature out of these women's hands, and put him into those of a private governor. Marcus Antoninus provided fourteen governors all at once to superintend his son Commodus's education;—and in six weeks cashiered five of them.—I know very well, continued my father, that Commodus's mother was in love with a gladiator at the time of her conception; which accounts for a great many of Commodus's cruelties when he became emperor;—but still I am of opinion, that those five whom Antoninus dismissed, did Commodus's temper, in that short time, more hurt than the other nine were able to rectify all their lives long.

Now, as I consider the person who is to be about my son, as the mirror in which he is to view himself from morning to night, and by which he is to adjust his looks, his carriage, and, perhaps, the inmost sentiments of his heart,—I would have one, Yorick, if possible, polished at all points, fit for my child to look into.—This is very good sense, quoth my uncle Toby to himself.

—There is, continued my father, a certain mien and motion of the body and all its parts, both in acting and speaking, which argues a man well within;—and I am not at all surprised, that Gregory of Nazianzum, upon observing the hasty and untoward gestures of Julian, should foretell he would one day become an apostate;—or that St. Ambrose should turn his amanuensis out of doors, because of an indecent motion of his head, which went backwards and forwards like a flail;—or that Democritus should conceive Protagoras to be a scholar from seeing him bind up a fagot, and thrusting, as he did it, the small twigs inwards.—There are a thousand unnoticed openings, continued my father, which let a penetrating eye at once into a man's soul; and I maintain it, added he, that a man of sense does not lay down his hat in coming into a room,—or take it up in going out of it, but something escapes which discovers him.

It is for these reasons, continued my father, that the governor I make choice of, shall neither lisp,* nor squint, nor wink, nor talk loud, nor look fierce, nor foolish;—nor bite his lips, nor grind his teeth, nor speak through his nose, nor pick it, nor blow it with his fingers.

He shall neither walk fast, nor slow, nor fold his arms,—for that is laziness; nor hang them down,—for that is folly; nor hide them in his pocket,—for that is nonsense.

He shall neither strike, nor pinch, nor tickle,—nor bite, nor cut his nails, nor hawk, nor spit, nor snift, nor drum with his feet or fingers in company;—nor (according to Erasmus) shall he speak to any one, in making water,—nor shall he point to carrion or excrement.—Now this is all nonsense again, quoth my uncle Toby to himself.

I will have him, continued my father, cheerful, faceté, jovial; at the same time prudent, attentive to business, vigilant, acute, argute, inventive, quick in resolving doubts and speculative questions;—he shall be wise, and judicious, and learned.—And why not humble, and moderate, and gentle-tempered, and good? said Yorick.—And why not, cried my uncle Toby, free, and generous, and bountiful, and brave?—He shall, my dear Toby, replied my father, getting up and shaking him by his hand.—Then, brother Shandy, answered my uncle Toby, raising himself off the chair, and laying down his pipe to take hold of my father's other hand,—I humbly beg I may recommend poor Le Fevre's son to you—(a tear of joy of the first water sparkled in my uncle Toby's eye,—and another, the fellow to it, in the Corporal's, as the proposition was made)—you will see why, when you read Le Fevre's story. Fool that I was! nor can I recollect, (nor perhaps you) without turning back to the place, what it was that hindered me from letting the Cor-

* Vide Pellegrina.

poral tell it in his own words;—but the occasion is lost,—I must tell it now in my own.

CHAP. VI.

THE STORY OF LE FEVRE.

It was some time in the summer of that year in which Dendermond was taken by the allies,—which was about seven years before my father came into the country,—and about as many after the time that my uncle Toby and Trim had privately decamped from my father's house in town, in order to lay some of the finest sieges to some of the finest fortified cities in Europe; —when my uncle Toby was one evening getting his supper, with Trim sitting behind him at a small sideboard,—I say, sitting,—for in consideration of the Corporal's lame knee (which sometimes gave him exquisite pain)—when my uncle Toby dined or supped alone, he would never suffer the Corporal to stand; and the poor fellow's veneration for his master was such, that, with a proper artillery, my uncle Toby could have taken Dendermond itself with less trouble than he was able to gain his point over him; for many a time, when my uncle Toby supposed the Corporal's leg was at rest, he would look back, and detect him standing behind him with the most dutiful respect. —This bred more little squabbles betwixt them, than all other causes, for five and twenty years together.—But this is neither here nor there—why do I mention it?—Ask my pen;—it governs me,—I govern not it.

He was one evening sitting thus at his supper, when the landlord of a little inn in the village, came into the parlor with an empty phial in his hand, to beg a glass or two of sack.—'Tis for a poor gentleman, I think, of the army, said the landlord, who has been taken ill at my house four days ago, and has never held up his head since, or had a desire to taste any thing, till just now, that he has a fancy for a glass of sack, and a thin toast.—I think, says he, taking his hand from his head, it would comfort me.

If I could neither beg borrow, or buy such a thing, added the landlord, I would almost steal it for the poor gentleman, he is so ill. I hope in God he will still mend, continued he; we are all of us concerned for him.

—Thou art a good-natured soul, I will answer for thee, cried my uncle Toby; and thou shalt drink the poor gentleman's health in a glass of sack thyself,—and take a couple of bottles, with my service, and tell him he is heartily welcome to them, and to a dozen more, if they will do him good.

Though I am persuaded, said my uncle Toby, as the landlord shut the door, he is a very compassionate fellow, Trim, yet I cannot help entertaining a high opinion of his guest too. There must be something more than common in him, that, in so short a time, should win so much upon the affections of his host:—And of his whole family, added the Corporal, for they are all concerned for him.—Step after him, said my uncle Toby, do, Trim; and ask if he knows his name.

—I have quite forgot it truly, said the landlord, coming back into the parlor with the Corporal;—but I can ask his son again. —Has he a son with him, then? said my uncle Toby.—A boy, replied the landlord, of about eleven or twelve years of age;—but the poor creature has tasted almost as little as his father: he does nothing but mourn and lament for him night and day. He has not stirred from the bed-side these two days.

My uncle Toby laid down his knife and fork, and thrust his plate from before him, as the landlord gave him the account; and Trim, without being ordered, took it away without saying one word, and, in a few minutes after, brought him his pipe and tobacco.

—Stay in the room a little, said my uncle Toby.

Trim! said my uncle Toby, after he lighted his pipe, and smoked about a dozen whiffs.—Trim came in front of his master, and made his bow;—my uncle Toby smoked on, and said no more.—Corporal! said my uncle Toby,—the Corporal made his bow.—My uncle Toby proceeded no farther, but finished his pipe.

Trim! said my uncle Toby, I have a project in my head, as it is a bad night, of wrapping myself up warm in my roquelaure, and paying a visit to this poor gentleman. —Your Honor's roquelaure, replied the Corporal, has not once been had on, since the night before your Honor received your wound, when we mounted guard in the trenches before the gate of St. Nicholas; and, besides, it is so cold and rainy a night, that what with the roquelaure, and what with the weather, 'twill be enough to give your Honor your death, and bring on your Honor's torment in your groin.—I fear so, replied my uncle Toby; but I am not at rest in my mind, Trim, since the account the landlord has given me.—I wish I had not known so much of this affair, added my uncle Toby, or that I had known more of it.—How shall we manage it? Leave it, an' please your Honor, to me, quoth the Corporal. I'll take my hat and stick, and go to the house and reconnoitre, and act accordingly; and I will bring your Honor a full account in an hour.—Thou shalt go, Trim, said my uncle Toby, and here's a shilling for thee to drink with his servant.—I shall get it all out of him, said the Corporal, shutting the door.

My uncle Toby filled his second pipe; and had it not been that he now and then wandered from the point, with considering whether it was not full as well to have the curtain of the ténaille a straight line, as a crooked one,—he might be said to have thought of nothing else but poor Le Fevre and his boy the whole time he smoked it.

CHAP. VII.

THE STORY OF LE FEVRE CONTINUED.

—It was not till my uncle Toby had knocked the ashes out of his third pipe, that Corporal Trim returned from the inn, and gave him the following account:—

—I despaired at first, said the Corporal, of being able to bring back your Honor any kind of intelligence concerning the poor sick lieutenant.—Is he in the army then? said my uncle Toby.—He is, said the Corporal.—And in what regiment? said my uncle Toby.—I'll tell your Honor, replied the Corporal, every thing straight-forwards, as I learnt it.—Then, Trim, I'll fill another pipe, said my uncle Toby, and not interrupt thee, till thou hast done; so sit down at thy ease, Trim, in the window-seat, and begin thy story again.—The Corporal made his old bow, which generally spoke as plain as a bow could speak it—Your Honor is good:—And having done that, he sat down, as he was ordered, and began the story to my uncle Toby over again, in pretty near the same words.

I despaired at first, said the Corporal, of being able to bring back any intelligence to your Honor, about the lieutenant and his son:—for, when I asked where his servant was, from whom I made myself sure of knowing every thing which was proper to be asked,—(That's a right distinction, Trim, said my uncle Toby)—I was answered, an' please your Honor, that he had no servant with him;—that he had come to the inn with hired horses, which, upon finding himself unable to proceed, (to join, I suppose, the regiment) he had dismissed the morning after he came.—If I get better, my dear, said he, as he gave his purse to his son to pay the man,—we can hire horses from hence.—But alas! the poor gentleman will never go from hence, said the landlady to me,—for I heard the death-watch all night long;—and, when he dies, the youth, his son, will certainly die with him; for he is broken-hearted already.

I was hearing this account, continued the Corporal, when the youth came into the kitchen, to order the thin toast the landlord spoke of:—but I will do it for my father, myself, said the youth.—Pray let me save you the trouble, young gentleman, said I, taking up a fork for the purpose, and offering him my chair to sit down upon by the fire, whilst I did it.—I believe, Sir, said he, very modestly, I can please him best myself.—I am sure, said I, his Honor will not like the toast the worse for being toasted by an old soldier.—The youth took hold of my hand, and instantly burst into tears.—Poor youth! said my uncle Toby; —he has been bred up from an infant in the army; and the name of a soldier, Trim, sounded in his ears like the name of a friend!—I wish I had him here.

—I never, in the longest march, said the Corporal, had so great a mind for my dinner, as I had to cry with him for company: —What could be the matter with me, an please your Honor?—Nothing in the world, Trim, said my uncle Toby, blowing his nose,—but that thou art a good-natured fellow.

--When I gave him the toast, continued the Corporal, I thought it was proper to tell him, I was Captain Shandy's servant, and that your Honor (though a stranger) was extremely concerned for his father;—and that if there was any thing in your house or cellar—(And thou might'st have added my purse too, said my uncle Toby)—he was heartily welcome to it.——He made a very low bow (which was meant to your Honor) but no answer;—for his heart was full:—so he went up stairs with the toast. —I warrant you, my dear, said I, as I opened the kitchen-door, your father will be well again.——Mr. Yorick's curate was smoking a pipe by the kitchen-fire,—but said not a word, good or bad, to comfort the youth.—I thought it wrong, added the Corporal.——I think so too, said my uncle Toby.

When the lieutenant had taken his glass of sack and toast, he felt himself a little revived, and sent down into the kitchen, to let me know, that in about ten minutes, he should be glad if I would step up stairs. ——I believe, said the landlord, he is going to say his prayers,—for there was a book laid upon the chair by his bed-side, and as I shut the door, I saw his son take up a cushion.

—I thought, said the curate, that you gentlemen of the army, Mr. Trim, never said your prayers at all.—I heard the poor gentleman say his prayers last night, said the landlady, very devoutly, and with my own ears, or I could not have believed it. ——Are you sure of it? replied the curate. —A soldier, an' please your Reverence, said I, prays as often (of his own accord) as a parson; and when he is fighting for his king, and for his own life, and for his honor too, he has the most reason to pray to God of any one in the whole world.—'Twas well said of thee, Trim, said my uncle Toby.——But when a soldier, said I, an' please your Reverence, has been standing for twelve hours together in the trenches, up to his knees in cold water,—or engaged, said I, for months together, in long and dangerous marches;—harassed, perhaps, in his rear to-day;—harassing others to morrow;—detached here;—countermanded there;—resting this night out upon his arms;—beat up in his shirt the next;—benumbed in his joints; perhaps without straw in his tent to kneel on;—must say his prayers how and when he can.——I believe, said I, for I was piqued, quoth the Corporal, for the reputation of the army,—I believe, an' please your Reverence, said I, that when a soldier gets time to pray,—he prays as heartily as a parson—though not with all his fuss and hypocrisy.—Thou shouldst not have said that, Trim, said my uncle Toby,—for God only knows who is a hypocrite, and who is not:—At the great and general review of us all, Corporal, at the day of judgment, (and not till then)—it will be seen who have done their duties in this world,—and who have not; and we shall be advanced, Trim, accordingly.—I hope we shall, said Trim.——It is in the scripture, said my uncle Toby; and I will show it thee to-morrow.—In the mean time we may depend upon it, Trim, for our comfort, said my uncle Toby, that God Almighty is so good and just a governor of the world, that if we have but done our duties in it,—it will never be inquired into, whether we have done them in a red coat or a black one.—I hope not, said the Corporal.—But go on, Trim, said my uncle Toby, with thy story.—

When I went up, continued the Corporal, into the lieutenant's room, which I did not do till the expiration of the ten minutes,—he was lying in his bed, with his head raised upon his hand, with his elbow upon the pillow, and a clean white cambric handkerchief beside it.—The youth was just stooping down to take up the cushion, upon which, I supposed, he had been kneeling;—the book was laid upon the bed;—and as he rose, in taking up the cushion with one hand, he reached out his other to take it away at the same time.—Let it remain there, my dear, said the lieutenant.—

He did not offer to speak to me, till I had walked up close to to his bed-side.—If you are Captain Shandy's servant, said he, you must present my thanks to your master, with my little boy's thanks along with them, for his courtesy to me.—If he was of Levens's,—said the lieutenant.—I told him your Honor was.—Then, said he, I served three campaigns with him in Flanders, and remember him,—but 'tis most likely, as I had not the honor of any acquaintance with him, that he knows nothing of me.—You will tell him, however, that the person his good-nature has laid under obligations to him, is one Le Fevre, a lieutenant in Angus's;—but he knows me not,—said he, a second time, musing;—possibly he may my story, added he.—Pray tell the captain, I was the ensign at Breda, whose wife was most unfortunately killed with a musket-shot, as she lay in my arms in my tent.——I remember the story, an' please your Honor, said I, very well.—Do you so?—said he, wiping his eyes with his handkerchief,—then well may I.——In saying this, he drew a little ring out of his bosom, which seemed tied with a black ribbon about his neck, and kissed it twice.——Here, Billy, said he;—the boy flew across the room to the bed-side,—and falling down upon his knee, took the ring in his hand, and kissed it too,—then kissed his father, and sat down upon the bed and wept.

I wish, said my uncle Toby, with a deep sigh,—I wish, Trim, I was asleep.—

Your Honor, replied the Corporal, is too much concerned.—Shall I pour out your Honor a glass of sack, to your pipe?—Do, Trim, said my uncle Toby.

I remember, said my uncle Toby, sighing again, the story of the ensign and his wife, with a circumstance his modesty omitted;—and particularly well that he, as well as she, upon some account or other, (I forget what) was universally pitied by the whole regiment;—but finish the story thou art upon.—'Tis finished already, said the Corporal,—for I could stay no longer;—so wished his Honor a good night. Young Le Fevre rose from off the bed, and saw me to the bottom of the stairs; and as we went down together, told me, they had come from Ireland, and were on their route to join the regiment in Flanders.——But alas! said the Corporal,—the lieutenant's last day's march is over!——Then what is to become of his poor boy? cried my uncle Toby.

CHAP. VIII.

THE STORY OF LE FEVRE CONTINUED.

It was to my uncle Toby's eternal honor—though I tell it only for the sake of those who, when coop'd in betwixt a natural and a positive law, know not, for their souls, which way in the world to turn themselves,—That notwithstanding my uncle Toby was warmly engaged at that time in carrying on the siege of Dendermond, parallel with the allies, who pressed theirs so vigorously, that they scarce allowed him time to get his dinner:—that nevertheless he gave up Dendermond, though he had already made a lodgment upon the counterscarp;—and bent his whole thoughts towards the private distresses at the inn; and, except that he ordered the garden-gate to be bolted up, by which he might be said to have turned the siege of Dendermond into a blockade,—he left Dendermond to itself,—to be relieved or not by the French king, as the French king thought good; and only considered how he himself should relieve the poor lieutenant and his son.

—That kind Being, who is a friend to the friendless, shall recompense thee for this.—

Thou hast left this matter short, said my uncle Toby to the Corporal, as he was putting him to bed, and I will tell thee in what, Trim.—In the first place, when thou mad'st an offer of my services to Le Fevre,—as sickness and travelling are both expensive, and thou knew'st he was but a poor lieutenant, with a son to subsist as well as himself, out of his pay,—that thou didst not make an offer to him of my purse; because, had he stood in need, thou knowest, Trim, he had been as welcome to it as myself.—Your Honor knows, said the Corporal, I had no orders.—True, quoth my uncle Toby,—thou didst very right, Trim, as a soldier,—but certainly very wrong as a man.

In the second place, for which, indeed, thou hast the same excuse, continued my uncle Toby,—when thou offeredst him whatever was in my house, thou shouldst have offered him my house too.—A sick brother officer should have the best quarters, Trim,

THE STORY OF LEFEVRE.

"And the Corporal shall be your nurse;—and I'll be your servant, Lefevre."—p. 179

and if we had him with us,—we could tend and look to him.——Thou art an excellent nurse thyself, Trim, and what with thy care of him, and the old woman's, and his boy's, and mine together, we might recruit him again at once, and set him upon his legs.——

—In a fortnight or three weeks, added my uncle Toby, smiling,—he might march. —He will never march, an' please your Honor, in this world, said the Corporal. He will march, said my uncle Toby, rising up from the side of the bed with one shoe off. —An' please your Honor, said the Corporal, he will never march, but to his grave. ——He shall march, cried my uncle Toby, marching the foot which had a shoe on, though without advancing an inch,—he shall march to his regiment.—He cannot stand it, said the Corporal.—He shall be supported, said my uncle Toby.—He'll drop at last, said the Corporal, and what will become of his boy?—He shall not drop, said my uncle Toby, firmly.—A-well-a-day! do what we can for him, said Trim, maintaining his point,—the poor soul will die.—He shall not die, by G—, cried my uncle Toby.

——The accusing spirit which flew up to Heaven's chancery with the oath, blush'd as he gave it in; and the recording angel, as he wrote it down, dropp'd a tear upon the word, and blotted it out for ever.

CHAP. IX.

—My uncle Toby went to his bureau,—put his purse into his breeches-pocket, and having ordered the Corporal to go early in the morning for a physician,—he went to bed, and fell asleep.

CHAP. X.

THE STORY OF LE FEVRE CONCLUDED.

The sun looked bright the morning after, to every eye in the village but Le Fevre's and his afflicted son's; the hand of death press'd heavy upon his eye-lids;—and hardly could the wheel at the cistern turn round its circle,—when my uncle Toby, who had rose up an hour before his wonted time, entered the lieutenant's room, and without preface or apology, sat himself down upon the chair by the bed-side, and, independently of all modes and customs, opened the curtain in the manner an old friend and brother-officer would have done it, and asked him how he did,—how he had rested in the night,—what was his complaint,—where was his pain,—and what he could do to help him;—and without giving him time to answer any one of the inquiries, went on and told him of the little plan which he had been concerting with the Corporal the night before for him.

—You shall go home directly, Le Fevre, said my uncle Toby, to my house, and we'll send for a doctor to see what's the matter, —and we'll have an apothecary,—and the Corporal shall be your nurse;—and I'll be your servant, Le Fevre.—

There was a frankness in my uncle Toby, —not the effect of familiarity,—but the cause of it,—which let you at once into his soul, and showed you the goodness of his nature. To this, there was something in his looks, and voice, and manner, superadded, which eternally beckoned to the unfortunate to come and take shelter under him; so that before my uncle Toby had half finished the kind offers he was making to the father, had the son insensibly pressed up close to his knees, and had taken hold of the breast of his coat, and was pulling it towards him. ——The blood and spirits of Le Fevre, which were waxing cold and slow within him, and were retreating to their last citadel, the heart—rallied back,—the film forsook his eyes for a moment;—he looked up wishfully in my uncle Toby's face;—then cast a look upon his boy;—and that ligament, fine as it was, was never broken.—

Nature instantly ebb'd again;—the film returned to its place;—the pulse fluttered, —stopp'd,—went on,—throbb'd,—stopp'd again,—mov'd,—stopp'd,—shall I go on? ——No.

CHAP. XI.

I am so impatient to return to my own story, that what remains of young Le

Fevre's, that is, from this turn of his fortune, to the time my uncle Toby recommended him for my preceptor, shall be told in a very few words, in the next chapter. —All that is necessary to be added to this chapter is as follows:—

That my uncle Toby, with young Le Fevre in his hand, attended the poor lieutenant, as chief mourners, to his grave.

That the governor of Dendermond paid his obsequies all military honors; and that Yorick, not to be behind-hand,—paid him all ecclesiastic,—for he buried him in his chancel.—And it appears likewise, he preached a funeral sermon over him,—I say, it appears,—for it was Yorick's custom which I suppose a general one with those of his profession, on the first leaf of every sermon which he composed, to chronicle down the time, the place, and the occasion of its being preached: to this, he was ever wont to add some short comment or stricture upon the sermon itself,—seldom, indeed, much to its credit.—For instance, "This sermon upon the Jewish dispensation —I don't like it at all; though I own there is a world of WATER-LANDISH knowledge in it;—but 'tis all tritical, and most tritically put together.—This is but a flimsy kind of composition. What was in my head when I made it?

"—N. B. The excellency of this text is, that it will suit any sermon;—and of this sermon, that it will suit any text.

"—For this sermon I shall be hanged,—for I have stolen the greatest part of it. Doctor Paidagunes found me out.

"☞ Set a thief to catch a thief."

On the back of half a dozen I find written, "So so," and no more:—and upon a couple "Moderato;" by which, as far as one may gather from Altieri's Italian Dictionary,—but mostly from the authority of a piece of green whip-cord, which seemed to have been the unravelling of Yorick's whip-lash, with which he has left us the two sermons marked Moderato, and the half dozen of So so's, tied fast together in one bundle by themselves, one may safely suppose he meant pretty nearly the same thing.

There is but one difficulty in the way of this conjecture, which is this, that the Moderato's are five times better than the So so's;—show ten times more knowledge of the human heart;—have seventy times more wit and spirit in them;—(and to rise properly in my climax)—discover a thousand times more genius; and, to crown all, are infinitely more entertaining, than those tied up with them:—for which reason, whenever Yorick's dramatic sermons are offered to the world, though I shall admit but one out of the whole number of the So so's, I shall, nevertheless, adventure to print the two moderato's without any sort of scruple.

What Yorick could mean by the words *lentamente*,—*tenute*,—*grave*,—and sometimes *adagio*,—as applied to theological compositions, and with which he has characterized some of these sermons, I dare not venture to guess.—I am more puzzled still upon finding a *l'octavo alta!* upon one:—*Constrepito* upon the back of another;—*Scicilliana* upon a third;—*Alla capella* upon a fourth;—*Con l'arco* upon this;—*Senza l'arco* upon that.—All I know is, that they are musical terms, and have a meaning;—and as he was a musical man, I will make no doubt, but that by some quaint application of such metaphors to the compositions in hand, they impressed very distinct ideas of their several characters upon his fancy, whatever they may do upon that of others.

Amongst these, there is that particular sermon which has unaccountably led me into this digression,—The funeral sermon upon poor Le Fevre, wrote out very fairly, as if from a hasty copy.—I take notice of it the more, because it seems to have been his favorite composition.—It is upon mortality; and is tied length-ways and cross-ways with a yarn thrum, and then rolled up and twisted round with a half sheet of dirty blue paper, which seems to have been once the cast-cover of a general review, which to this day smells horribly of horse drugs.—Whether these marks of humiliation were designed,—I something doubt;—because at the end of the sermon, (and not at the beginning of it)—very different from his way of treating the rest, he had wrote—

BRAVO!

—though not very offensively,—for it is at two inches, at least, and a half's distance from, and below the concluding line of the sermon, at the very extremity of the page, and in that right-hand corner of it, which, you know, is generally covered with your thumb; and, to do it justice, it is wrote besides with a crow's quill so faintly in a small Italian hand, as scarce to solicit the eye towards the place, whether your thumb is there or not;—so that, from the manner of it, it stands half excused; and being wrote, moreover, with very pale ink, diluted almost to nothing,—'tis more like the ritratto of the shadow of vanity, than of VANITY herself—of the two; resembling rather a faint thought of transient applause, secretly stirring up in the heart of the composer, than a gross mark of it, coarsely obtruded upon the world.

With all these extenuations, I am aware, that in publishing this, I do no service to Yorick's character as a modest man;—but all men have their failings; and what lessens this still farther, and almost wipes it away, is this, that the word was struck through some time afterwards (as appears from a different tint of the ink) with a line quite across it in this manner, ~~BRAVO~~—as if he had retracted, or was ashamed of the opinion he had once entertained of it.

These short characters of his sermons were always written, excepting in this one instance, upon the first leaf of his sermon, which served as a cover to it; and usually upon the inside of it, which was turned toward the text;—but at the end of his discourse, where, perhaps, he had five or six pages, and sometimes, perhaps, a whole score to turn himself in,—he took a larger circuit, and indeed a much more mettlesome one;—as if he had snatched the occasion of unlacing himself with a few more frolicsome strokes at vice, than the straitness of the pulpit allowed.—These, though hussar-like they skirmish lightly, and out of all order, are still auxiliaries on the side of virtue;—tell me, then, Mynheer Vander Blonederdondergewdenstronke, why they should not be printed together?

CHAP. XII.

WHEN my uncle Toby had turned every thing into money, and settled all accounts betwixt the agent of the regiment and Le Fevre, and betwixt Le Fevre and all mankind, there remained nothing more in my uncle Toby's hands than an old regimental coat, and a sword; so that my uncle Toby found little or no opposition from the world in taking administration. The coat my uncle Toby gave the Corporal.—Wear it, Trim said my uncle Toby, as long as it will hold together, for the sake of the poor lieutenant.—And this,—said my uncle Toby, taking up the sword in his hand, and drawing it out of the scabbard as he spoke,—and this, Le Fevre, I'll save for thee:—'tis all the fortune, continued my uncle Toby, hanging it upon a crook, and pointing to it,—'tis all the fortune, my dear Le Fevre, which God has left thee; but if he has given thee a heart to fight thy way with it in the world,—and thou doest it like a man of honor,—'tis enough for us.

As soon as my uncle Toby had laid a foundation and taught him to inscribe a regular polygon in a circle, he sent him to a public school, where, excepting Whitsuntide and Christmas, at which times the Corporal was punctually dispatched for him,—he remained to the spring of the year seventeen; when the stories of the Emperor's sending his army into Hungary, against the Turks, kindling a spark of fire in his bosom, he left his Greek and Latin without leave, and throwing himself upon his knees before my uncle Toby, begged his father's sword, and my uncle Toby's leave along with it, to go and try his fortune under Eugene.—Twice did my uncle Toby forget his wound, and cry out, Le Fevre! I will go with thee, and thou shalt fight beside me,—and twice he laid his hand upon his groin, and hung down his head in sorrow and disconsolation.—

My uncle Toby took down the sword from the crook, where it had hung untouched ever since the lieutenant's death, and delivered it to the Corporal to brighten up;—and having detained Le Fevre a single fortnight to equip him, and contract for his passage to Leghorn,—he put the sword into his hands.—If thou art brave, Le Fevre, said my uncle Toby, this will not fail thee,—but Fortune, said he, (musing a little)—Fortune may:—And if she does—added my uncle Toby, embracing him,—come back again to me, Le Fevre, and we will shape thee another course.

The greatest injury could not have oppressed the heart of Le Fevre more than my uncle Toby's paternal kindness;—he parted from my uncle Toby, as the best of sons from the best of fathers—both dropped tears—and as my uncle Toby gave him his last kiss, he slipped sixty guineas, tied up in an old purse of his father's, in which was his mother's ring, into his hand,—and bid God bless him.

CHAP. XIII.

Le Fevre got up to the Imperial army just time enough to try what metal his sword was made of, at the defeat of the Turks before Belgrade; but a series of unmerited mischances had pursued him from that moment, and trod close upon his heels for four years together after. He had withstood these buffetings to the last, till sickness overtook him at Marseilles, from whence he wrote my uncle Toby word, he had lost his time, his services, his health, and, in short, every thing but his sword;—and was waiting for the first ship to return back to him.

As this letter came to hand about six weeks before Susannah's accident, Le Fevre was hourly expected, and was uppermost in my uncle Toby's mind all the time my father was giving him and Yorick a description of what kind of a person he would choose for a preceptor to me: but as my uncle Toby thought my father at first somewhat fanciful in the accomplishments he required, he forbore mentioning Le Fevre's name—till the character, by Yorick's interposition, ending, unexpectedly, in one who should be gentle-tempered, and generous, and good, it impressed the image of Le Fevre, and his interest, upon my uncle Toby so forcibly, that he rose instantly off his chair; and laying down his pipe, in order to take hold of both my father's hands—I beg, brother Shandy, said my uncle Toby, I may recommend poor Le Fevre's son to you.—I beseech you do, added Yorick.—He has a good heart, said my uncle Toby.—And a brave one too, an' please your Honor, said the Corporal.

—The best hearts, Trim, are ever the bravest, replied my uncle Toby.—And the greatest cowards, an' please your Honor, in our regiment, were the greatest rascals in it:—there was Serjeant Kumber, and Ensign——

We'll talk of them, said my father, an other time.

CHAP. XIV.

What a jovial and a merry world would this be, may it please your Worships, but for that inextricable labyrinth of debts, cares, woes, want, grief, discontent, melancholy, large jointures, impositions, and lies!

Dr. Slop, like a son of a w——, as my father called him for it,—to exalt himself—debased me to death, and made ten thousand times more of Susannah's accident than there was any grounds for; so that in a week's time, or less, it was in every body's mouth, that poor Master Shandy * * * * * * * entirely—and Fame, who loves to double every thing,—in three days more, had sworn positively she saw it; and all the world, as usual, gave credit to her evidence—"That the nursery window "had not only * * * * * * * * * "* * *; but that * * * * * * * "* * * * * * *'s also."

Could the world have been sued like a body-corporate,—my father had brought an action upon the case, and trounced it sufficiently; but, to fall foul of individuals about it—as every soul who had mentioned the affair, did it with the greatest pity imaginable—'twas like flying in the very face of his best friends:—and yet, to acquiesce under the report, in silence—was to acknowledge it openly,—at least in the opinion of one half of the world; and to make a bustle again, in contradicting it—was to confirm it as strongly in the opinion of the other half.—

—Was ever poor devil of a country-gentleman so hampered? said my father.

I would show him publicly, said my uncle Toby, at the market-cross.

—'Twill have no effect, said my father

CHAP. XV.

——I'll put him, however, into breeches, said my father, let the world say what it will.

CHAP. XVI.

There are a thousand resolutions, Sir, both in church and state, as well as in matters, Madam, of a more private concern,—which, though they have carried all the appearance in the world of being taken and entered upon in a hasty, harebrained, and unadvised manner, were, notwithstanding this, (and could you or I have got into the cabinet, or stood behind the curtain, we should have found it was so) weighed, poised, and perpended—argued upon—canvassed through—entered into, and examined on all sides with so much coolness, that the goddess of coolness herself (I do not take upon me to prove her existence) could neither have wished it, or done it better.

Of the number of these was my father's resolution of putting me into breeches; which though determined at once—in a kind of huff, and a defiance of all mankind, had, nevertheless, been pro'd and con'd, and judicially talked over betwixt him and my mother about a month before, in two several beds of justice, which my father had held for that purpose. I shall explain the nature of these beds of justice in my next chapter; and, in the chapter following that, you shall step with me, Madam, behind the curtain, only to hear in what kind of manner my father and my mother debated between themselves this affair of the breeches, from which you may form an idea how they debated all lesser matters.

CHAP. XVII.

The ancient Goths of Germany, who (the learned Cluverius is positive) were first seated in the country between the Vistula and the Oder, and who afterwards incorporated the Herculi, the Bugians, and some other Vandalic clans to 'em, had all of them a wise custom of debating every thing of importance to their state, twice; that is, once drunk, and once sober; drunk—that their councils might not want vigor;—and sober—that they might not want discretion

Now my father, being entirely a water-drinker,—was a long time gravelled almost to death, in turning this as much to his advantage, as he did every other thing, which the ancients did or said: and it was not till the seventh year of his marriage, after a thousand fruitless experiments and devices, that he hit upon an expedient which answered the purpose:—and that was, when any difficult and momentous point was to be settled in the family, which required great sobriety, and great spirit too, in its determination,—he fixed and set apart the first Sunday night in the month, and the Saturday night which immediately preceded it, to argue it over in bed with my mother: by which contrivance, if you consider, Sir, with yourself, * * * * * * * * * * * * * *.

These my father, humorously enough, called his beds of justice;—for, from the two different counsels taken in these two different humors, a middle one was generally found out, which touched the point of wisdom as well as if he had got drunk and sober an hundred times.

It must not be made a secret of to the world, that this answers full as well in literary discussions, as either in military or conjugal; but it is not every author that can try the experiment as the Goths and Vandals did it—or, if he can, may it be always for his body's health? and to do it, as my father did it,—am I sure it would be always for his soul's?

My way is this:——

In all nice and ticklish discussions,—(of which, Heaven knows, there are but too many in my book)—where I find I cannot take a step without the danger of having either their Worships or their Reverences upon my back,—I write one half full,—and t'other fasting;—or write it all full and correct it fasting; or write it fasting and correct it full—for they all come to the same thing.—So that, with a less variation from my father's plan, than my father's from the Gothic—I feel myself upon a par with him in his first bed of justice,—and no way inferior to him in his second.—These different and almost irreconcilable effects, flow uniformly from the wise and wonderful mechanism of nature—of which—be hers the honor.—All that we can do, is, to turn and work the machine to the improvement and better manufactory of the arts and sciences.—

Now, when I write full,—I write as if I was never to write fasting again as long as I live;—that is, I write free from the cares, as well as the terrors of the world—I count not the number of my scars, nor does my fancy go forth into dark entries and by-corners to antedate my stabs.—In a word, my pen takes its course; and I write on, as much from the fullness of my heart as my stomach.—

But when, an' please your Honors, I indite fasting, 'tis a different story.—I pay the world all possible attention and respect,—and have as great a share (whilst it lasts) of that understrapping virtue of discretion as the best of you.—So that betwixt both, I write a careless kind of a civil, nonsensical, good-humored, Shandean book, which will do all your hearts good.

——And all your heads too,—provided you understand it.

CHAP. XVIII.

We should begin, said my father, (turning himself half round in bed, and shifting his pillow a little towards my mother's, as he opened the debate)—we should begin to think, Mrs. Shandy, of putting this boy into breeches.—

We should so,—said my mother.—We defer it, my dear, quoth my father, shamefully.——

I think we do, Mr. Shandy,—said my mother.

—Not but the child looks extremely well, said my father, in his vests and tunics.—

—He does look very well in them,—replied my mother.

—And for that reason it would be almost a sin, added my father, to take him out of em.

It would so,—said my mother.—But, indeed, he is growing a very tall lad, —rejoined my father.

—He is very tall for his age, indeed—said my mother.—

—I can not (making two syllables of it) imagine, quoth my father, who the deuce he takes after.—

I cannot conceive, for my life,—said my mother.—

Humph!—said my father.

(The dialogue ceased for a moment.)

—I am very short myself,—continued my father, gravely.

You are very short, Mr. Shandy,—said my mother.

Humph! quoth my father to himself, a second time; in muttering which, he plucked his pillow a little farther from my mother's—and turning about again, there was an end of the debate for three minutes and an half.

—When he gets these breeches made, cried my father, in a higher tone, he'll look like a beast in 'em.

He will be very awkward in them at first, replied my mother.

—And 'twill be lucky, if that's the worst on't, added my father.

It will be very lucky, answered my mother.

I suppose, replied my father,—making some pause first—he'll be exactly like other people's children.—

Exactly, said my mother.—

—Though I should be sorry for that, added my father: and so the debate stopp'd again.

—They should be of leather, said my father, turning him about again.—

They will last him, said my mother, the longest.

But he can have no linings to 'em, replied my father.

He cannot, said my mother.

'Twere better to have them of fustian, quoth my father.

Nothing can be better, quoth my mother.—

—Except dimity, replied my father.—

'Tis best of all,—replied my mother.—

—One must not give him his death, however,—interrupted my father.

By no means, said my mother.—And so the dialogue stood still again.

I am resolved, however, quoth my father, breaking silence the fourth time, he shall have no pockets in them.

—There is no occasion for any,—said my mother.

I mean, in his coat and waistcoat,—cried my father.

—I mean so too,—replied my mother.

Though if he gets a gig or a top—poor souls! it is a crown and a sceptre to them, —they should have where to secure it.

Order it as you please, Mr. Shandy, replied my mother.

But don't you think it right? added my father, pressing the point home to her.

Perfectly, said my mother, if it pleases you, Mr. Shandy.——

—There's for you! cried my father, losing temper.—Pleases me!—You never will distinguish, Mrs. Shandy, nor shall I ever teach you to do it, betwixt a point of pleasure and a point of convenience.—This was on the Sunday-night;—and farther this chapter sayeth not.)

CHAP. XIX.

After my father had debated the affair of the breeches with my mother,—he consulted Albertus Rubenius upon it; and Albertus Rubenius used my father ten times worse in the consultation (if possible) than even my father had used my mother; for as Rubenius had wrote a quarto express, *De re Vestiaria Veterum*,—it was Rubenius' business to have given my father some lights.—On the contrary, my father might as well have thought of extracting the seven cardinal virtues out of a long beard, as of extracting a single word out of Rubenius upon the subject.

Upon every other article of ancient dress, Rubenius was very communicative to my father; he gave him a full and satisfactory account of

The Toga, or loose gown.
The Chlamys.
The Ephod.
The Tunica, or Jacket.
The Synthesis.
The Pænula.
The Lacerna, with its Cucullus.
The Paludamentum.
The Prætexta.
The Sagum, or soldier's jerkin.
The Trabea; of which, according to Suetonius, there were three kinds——

—But what are all these to the breeches? said my father.

Rubenius threw him down upon the counter all kinds of shoes which had been in fashion with the Romans.—There was,

The open shoe.
The close shoe.
The slip shoe.
The wooden shoe.
The sock.
The buskin.
And The military shoe with hob nails in it, which Juvenal takes notice of.

There were, The clogs.
The pattens.
The pantoufles.
The brogues.
The sandals, with latches to them.

There was, The felt shoe.
The linen shoe.
The braided shoe.
The laced shoe.
The calceus insisus.
And The calceus rostratus.

Rubenius showed my father how well they all fitted,—in what manner they laced on, —with what points, straps, thongs, latchets, ribbons, jaggs, and ends.

—But I want to be informed about the breeches, said my father.—

Albertus Rubenius informed my father that the Romans manufactured stuffs of various fabrics:—some plain,—some striped, ——others diapered throughout the whole contexture of the wool, with silk and gold: —That linen did not begin to be in common use till towards the declension of the empire, when the Egyptians, coming to settle amongst them, brought it into vogue.

—That persons of quality and fortune distinguished themselves by the fineness and whiteness of their clothes: which color (next to purple, which was appropriated to the great officers) they most affected and wore on their birth-days and public rejoicings:—That it appeared from the best historians of those times, that they frequently sent their clothes to the fuller, to be clean'd and whitened:—but that the inferior people, to avoid that expense, generally wore brown clothes, and of a something coarser texture—till towards the beginning of Augustus's reign, when the slave dressed like his master, and almost every distinction of habiliment was lost, but the *Latus Clavus*.

And what was the *Latus Clavus?* said my father.

Rubenius told him, that the point was still litigating amongst the learned;—that Egnatius, Sigonius, Bossius, Ticinensis, Baysius, Budæus, Salmasius, Lipsius, Lizius, Isaac Causabon, and Joseph Scaliger, all differed from each other,—and he from them:—That some took it to be the button;—some the coat itself;—others only the color of it:—That the great Baysius, in his Wardrobe of the Ancients, chap. 12,—honestly said, he knew not what it was,—whether a tribula,—a stud,—a button,—a loop,—a buckle,—or clasps and keepers.—

My father lost the horse, but not the saddle.—They are *hooks* and *eyes*, said my father—and with hooks and eyes he ordered my breeches to be made.

CHAP. XX.

We are now going to enter upon a new scene of events.

Leave we then the breeches in the taylor's hands, with my father standing over him with his cane, reading him as he sat at work a lecture upon the *latus clavus*, and pointing to the precise part of the waistband where he was determined to have it sewed on.

Leave we my mother—(truest of all the *Pococurantes* of her sex!)—careless about it, as about every thing else in the world which concerned her;—that is,—indifferent whether it was done this way or that,—providing it was but done at all.

Leave we Slop likewise to the full profits of all my dishonors.

Leave we poor Le Fevre to recover, and get home from Marseilles as he can:—and last of all,—because the hardest of all,—

Let us leave, if possible, *myself*:—but tis impossible,—I must go along with you to the end of the work.

CHAP. XXI.

If the reader has not a clear conception of the rood and a half of ground which lay at the bottom of my uncle Toby's kitchen-garden, and which was the scene of so many of his delicious hours,—the fault is not in me, but in his imagination; for I am sure I gave him so minute a description, I was almost ashamed of it.

When *Fate* was looking forwards one afternoon, into the great transactions of future times,—and recollected for what purposes this little plot, by a decree fast bound down in iron, had been destined,—she gave a nod to *Nature*:—'twas enough—Nature threw half a spadefull of her kindliest compost upon it, with just so *much* clay in it, as to retain the forms of angles and indentings,—and so *little* of it too, as not to cling to the spade, and render works of so much glory, nasty in foul weather.

My uncle Toby came down, as the reader has been informed, with plans along with him, of almost every fortified town in Italy and Flanders; so, let the Duke of Marlborough, or the allies, have set down before what town they pleased, my uncle Toby was prepared for them.

His way, which was the simplest one in the world, was this:—As soon as ever a town was invested, (but sooner when the design was known) to take the plan of it (let it be what town it would) and enlarge it upon a scale to the exact size of his bowling-green; upon the surface of which, by means of a large roll of pack-thread, and a number of small piquets driven into the ground, at the several angles, and redans, he transferred the lines from his paper; then taking the profile of the place, with its works, to determine the depths and slopes of the ditches,—the talus of the glacis, and the precise height of the several *banquettes*, parapets, &c.—he set the Corporal to work; and sweetly went it on.—The nature of the soil,—the nature of the work itself,—and, above all, the good-nature of my uncle Toby, sitting by from morning to night, and chatting kindly with the Corporal upon past-done deeds—left *labor* little else but the ceremony of the name.

When the place was finished in this manner, and put into a proper posture of defence,—it was invested;—and my uncle

Toby and the Corporal began to run their first parallel.—I beg I may not be interrupted in my story, by being told, *That the first parallel should be at least three hundred toises distant from the main body of the place,—and that I have not left a single inch for it;*—for my uncle Toby took the liberty of encroaching upon his kitchen-garden, for the sake of enlarging his works on the bowling-green; and for that reason generally ran his first and second parallels betwixt two rows of his cabbages and his cauliflowers: the conveniencies and inconveniencies of which will be considered at large in the history of my uncle Toby's and the Corporal's campaigns, of which this I'm now writing is but a sketch, and will be finished, if I conjecture right, in three pages (but there is no guessing).—The campaigns themselves will take up as many books; and therefore I apprehend it would be hanging too great a weight of one kind of matter in so flimsy a performance as this, to rhapsodize them, as I once intended, into the body of the work;—surely they had better be printed apart.—We'll consider the affair;—so take the following sketch of them in the mean time:—

CHAP. XXII.

WHEN the town, with its works, was finished, my uncle Toby and the Corporal began to run their first parallel, not at random, or any how,—but from the same points and distances the allies had begun to run theirs; and regulating their approaches and attacks by the accounts my uncle Toby received from the daily papers,—they went on during the whole siege, step by step, with the allies.

When the Duke of Marlborough made a lodgment,—my uncle Toby made a lodgment too:—and when the face of a bastion was battered down, or a defence ruined,—the Corporal took his mattock and did as much,—and so on;—gaining ground and making themselves masters of the works, one after another, till the town fell into their hands.

To one who took pleasure in the happy state of others, there could not have been a greater sight in the world than on a post morning, in which a practicable breach had been made by the Duke of Marlborough in the main body of the place,—to have stood behind the horn-beam hedge, and observed the spirit with which my uncle Toby, with Trim behind him, sallied forth;—the one with the Gazette in his hand,—the other with a spade on his shoulder to execute the contents.—What an honest triumph in my uncle Toby's looks, as he marched up to the ramparts! what intense pleasure swimming in his eye, as he stood over the Corporal, reading the paragraph ten times over to him, as he was at work, lest, peradventure, he should make the breach an inch too wide,—or leave it an inch too narrow!—But when the *chamade* was beat, and the Corporal helped my uncle up it, and followed with the colors in his hand, to fix them upon the ramparts, Heaven! Earth! Sea!—but what avail apostrophes?—with all your elements, wet or dry, you never compounded so intoxicating a draught.

In this track of happiness for many years, without one interruption to it, except now and then when the wind continued to blow due west for a week or ten days together, which detained the Flanders mail, and kept them so long in torture, but still 'twas the torture of the happy:—in this track, I say, did my uncle Toby and Trim move for many years, every year of which, and sometimes every month, from the invention of either the one or the other of them, adding some new conceit or quirk of improvement to their operations, which always opened fresh springs of delight in carrying them on.

The first year's campaign was carried on, from beginning to end, in the plain and simple method I've related.

In the second year, in which my uncle Toby took Liege and Ruremond, he thought he might afford the expense of four handsome draw-bridges; of two of which I have given an exact description in the former part of my work.

At the latter end of the same year, he added a couple of gates with portcullises:—these last were converted afterwards into orgues, as the better thing; and during the winter of the same year, my uncle Toby, instead of a new suit of clothes, which he always had at Christmas treated himself with a handsome sentry-box, to stand at the corner of the bowling-green, betwixt which point and the foot of the glacis, there was left a little kind of an esplanade, for him and the Corporal to confer and hold councils of war upon.

The sentry-box was in case of rain.

All these were painted white three times over the ensuing spring, which enabled my uncle Toby to take the field with great splendor.

My father would often say to Yorick, that if any mortal in the whole universe had done such a thing except his brother Toby, it would have been looked upon by the world as one of the most refined satires upon the parade and prancing manner in which Louis XIV. from the beginning of the war, but particularly that very year, had taken the field.—But 'tis not in my brother Toby's nature, kind soul! my father would add, to insult any one.

—But let us go on.

CHAP. XXIII.

I MUST observe, that although in the first year's campaign, the word town is often mentioned,—yet there was no town at that time within the polygon; that addition was not made till the summer following, the spring in which the bridges and sentry-box were painted, which was the third year of my uncle Toby's campaigns,—when, upon his taking Amberg, Bonn, and Rhinberg, and Huy and Limbourg, one after another, a thought came into the Corporal's head, that to talk of taking so many towns, *without one town to show for it,*—was a very nonsensical way of going to work; and so proposed to my uncle Toby, that they should have a little model of a town built for them, —to be run up together, of slit deals, and then painted, and clapped within the interior polygon to serve for all.

My uncle Toby felt the good of the project instantly, and instantly agreed to it; but with the addition of two singular improvements, of which he was almost as proud, as if he had been the original inventor of the project itself.

The one was, to have the town built exactly in the style of those of which it was most likely to be the representative; —with grated windows, and the gable-ends of the houses facing the streets, &c. &c.— as those in Ghent and Bruges, and the rest of the towns in Brabant and Flanders.

The other was, not to have the houses run up together, as the Corporal proposed, but to have every house independent, to hook on, or off, so as to form into the plan of whatever town they pleased.—This was put directly into hand; and many and many a look of mutual congratulation was exchanged between my uncle Toby and the Corporal, as the carpenter did the work.

It answered prodigiously the next summer;—the town was a perfect Proteus.—It was Landen, and Trerebach, and Stantvliet, and Drusen, and Hagenau;—and then it was Ostend, and Menin, and Aeth, and Dendermond.

—Surely never did any TOWN act so many parts, since Sodom and Gomorrah, as my uncle Toby's town did.

In the fourth year, my uncle Toby, thinking a town looked foolishly without a church, added a very fine one with a steeple.—Trim was for having bells in it.——My uncle Toby said, the metal had better be cast into cannon.

This led the way, the next campaign, for half a dozen brass field-pieces,—to be planted three and three, on each side of my uncle Toby's sentry-box; and, in a short time, these led the way for a train somewhat larger,—and so on—(as must always be the case in hobby-horsical affairs) from pieces of half an inch bore, till it came at last to my father's jack-boots.

The next year, which was that in which Lisle was besieged, and at the close of which both Ghent and Bruges fell into our hands, —my uncle Toby was sadly put to it for *proper* ammunition: I say proper ammunition,—because his great artillery would not bear powder;—and 'twas well for the Shandy family they would not.—For so full were the papers, from the beginning to the end of the siege, of the incessant firings kept up by the besiegers;—and so heated was my uncle Toby's imagination with the accounts of them, that he had infallibly shot away all his estate.

Something therefore was wanting, as a *succedaneum*, especially in one or two of the more violent paroxysms of the siege, to keep up something like a continual firing in the imagination,—and this *something* the Corporal, whose principal strength lay in invention, supplied by an entire new system of battering of his own,—without which, this had been objected to by military critics, to the end of the world, as one of the great *desiderata* of my uncle Toby's apparatus.

This will not be explained the worse, for setting off, as I generally do, at a little distance from the subject.

CHAP. XXIV.

WITH two or three other trinkets, small in themselves, but of great regard, which poor Tom, the Corporal's unfortunate brother, had sent him over, with the account of his marriage with the Jew's widow,—there was

A Montero-cap and two Turkish tobacco-pipes.

The Montero-cap I shall describe by and by.—The Turkish tobacco-pipes had nothing particular in them; they were fitted up and ornamented as usual, with flexible tubes of Morocco leather and gold wire, and mounted at their ends, the one of them with ivory,—the other with black ebony, tipp'd with silver.

My father, who saw all things in lights different from the rest of the world, would say to the Corporal, that he ought to look upon these two presents more as tokens of his brother's nicety than his affection.—Tom did not care, Trim, he would say, to put on the cap, or to smoke in the tobacco-pipe of a Jew.——God bless your Honor, the Corporal would say, (giving a strong reason to the contrary)—how can that be?

The Montero-cap was scarlet, of a superfine Spanish cloth, dyed in grain, and mounted all round with fur, except about four inches in the front, which was faced with a light blue, slightly embroidered; and seemed to have been the property of a Portuguese quarter-master, not of foot, but of horse, as the word denotes.

The Corporal was not a little proud of it, as well for its own sake, as for the sake of the giver,—so seldom or never put it on but upon GALA days; and yet never was a Montero-cap put to so many uses; for in all controverted points, whether military or culinary, provided the Corporal was sure he was in the right,—it was either his *oath*,—his *wager*,—or his *gift*.

——'Twas his gift in the present case.

I'll be bound, said the Corporal, speaking to himself, to give away my Montero-cap to the first beggar who comes to the door, if I do not manage this matter to his Honor's satisfaction.

The completion was no farther off, than the very next morning; which was that of the storm of the counterscarp betwixt the Lower Deule, to the right, and the gate of St. Andrew;—and on the left, between St. Magdalen's and the river.

As this was the most memorable attack in the whole war,—the most gallant and obstinate on both sides,—and, I must add, the most bloody too, (for it cost the allies themselves that morning above eleven hundred men),—my uncle Toby prepared himself for it with a more than ordinary solemnity.

The eve which preceded, as my uncle Toby went to bed, he ordered his Ramillie wig, which had lain, inside out, for many years, in the corner of an old campaigning trunk, which stood by his bed-side, to be taken out and laid upon the lid of it, ready for the morning;—and the very first thing he did, in his shirt, when he had stepped out of bed, my uncle Toby, after he had turned the rough side outwards,—put it on.—This done, he proceeded next to his breeches; and having buttoned the waistband, he forthwith buckled on his sword-belt, and had got his sword half-way in,—when he considered he should want shaving, and that it would be but very inconvenient doing it with his sword on,—so took it off.—In essaying to put on his regimental coat and waistcoat, my uncle Toby found the same objection in his wig,—so that went off too:—so that, what with one thing and what with another, as it always falls out when a man is in the most haste,—'twas ten o'clock, which was half an hour later than his usual time, before my uncle Toby sallied out.

CHAP. XXV.

My uncle Toby had scarce turned the corner of his yew-hedge, which separated his kitchen-garden from his bowling-green, when he perceived the Corporal had begun the attack without him.—

Let me stop and give you a picture of the Corporal's apparatus, and of the Corporal himself in the height of this attack, just as it struck my uncle Toby, as he turned towards the sentry-box, where the Corporal was at work,—for in Nature there is not such another;—nor can any combination of all that is grotesque and whimsical in her works produce its equal.

The corporal——

Tread lightly on his ashes, ye men of genius,—for he was your kinsman:

Weed his grave clean, ye men of goodness,—for he was your brother.—Oh, Corporal! had I thee, but now,—now, that I am able to give thee a dinner and protection,—how would I cherish thee! thou should'st wear thy Montero-cap every hour of the day, and every day of the week;—and when it was worn out, I would purchase thee a couple like it.—But alas! alas! alas! now that I can do this, in spite of their Reverences,—the occasion is lost,—for thou art gone:—thy genius fled up to the stars, from whence it came;—and that warm heart of thine, with all its generous and open vessels, compressed into a *clod of the valley!*

But what,—what is this, to that future and dreaded page, where I look towards the velvet pall, decorated with the military ensigns of thy Master,—the first,—the foremost of created beings; where,—I shall see thee, faithful servant! laying his sword and scabbard, with a trembling hand, across his coffin, and then returning pale as ashes to the door, to take his mourning-horse by the bridle to follow his hearse, as he directed thee:—where all my father's systems shall be baffled by his sorrows; and, in spite of his philosophy, I shall behold him, as he inspects the lacquered plate, twice taking his spectacles from off his nose, to wipe away the dew which Nature has shed upon them.—When I see him cast in the rosemary with an air of disconsolation, which cries through my ears,—O Toby! in what corner of the world shall I seek thy fellow?

—Gracious powers! which erst have opened the lips of the dumb in his distress, and made the tongue of the stammerer speak plain,—when I shall arrive at this dreaded page, deal not with me, then, with a stinted hand.

CHAP. XXVI.

The Corporal, who the night before had resolved in his mind to supply the grand *desideratum*, of keeping up something like an incessant firing upon the enemy during the heat of the attack,—had no farther idea in his fancy at that time, than a contrivance of smoking tobacco against the town, out of one of my uncle Toby's six field-pieces, which were planted on each side of his sentry-box; the means of effecting which occurring to his fancy at the same time, though he had pledged his cap, he thought it in no danger from the miscarriage of his projects.

Upon turning it this way and that a little in his mind, he soon began to find out, that, by means of his two Turkish tobacco-pipes, with the supplement of three smaller tubes of wash-leather at each of their lower ends, to be tagg'd by the same number of tin-pipes fitted to the touch-holes, and sealed with clay next the cannon, and then tied hermetically with waxed silk at their several insertions into the morocco tube,—he should be able to fire the six field-pieces all together, and with the same ease as to fire one.

—Let no man say from what tags and jaggs hints may not be cut out for the advancement of human knowledge. Let no man, who has read my father's first and second *beds of justice*, ever rise up and say again, from collision of what kinds of bodies light may or may not be struck out, to carry the Arts and Sciences up to perfection.—Heaven! thou knowest how I love them;—thou knowest the secrets of my heart, and that I would this moment give my shirt——Thou art a fool, Shandy, says Eugenius,—for thou hast but a dozen in the world, and 'twill break thy set.—

No matter for that, Eugenius; I would give the shirt off my back to be burnt into tinder, were it only to satisfy one feverish inquirer. How many sparks, at one good stroke, a good flint and steel could strike into the tail of it.—Think ye not, that in striking these *in*,—he might, peradventure, strike something *out?*—as sure as a gun.

—But this project by the bye.

The Corporal sat up the best part of the night, in bringing *his* to perfection; and having made a sufficient proof of his cannon, with charging them to the top with tobacco,—he went with contentment to bed.

CHAP. XXVII.

THE Corporal had slipped out about ten minutes before my uncle Toby, in order to fix his apparatus, and just give the enemy a shot or two before my uncle Toby came.

He had drawn the six field-pieces for this end, all close up together in front of my uncle Toby's sentry-box, leaving only an interval of about a yard and a half betwixt the three, on the right and left, for the convenience of charging, &c.—and the sake, possibly, of two batteries, which he might think double the honor of one.

In the rear, and facing this opening, with his back to the door of his sentry-box, for fear of being flanked, had the Corporal wisely taken his post.—He held the ivory pipe appertaining to the battery on the right, betwixt the finger and thumb of his right hand:—and the ebony pipe tipp'd with silver, which appertained to the battery on the left, betwixt the finger and thumb of the other;—and with his right knee fixed firm upon the ground, as if in the front rank of his platoon, was the Corporal, with his Montero-cap upon his head, furiously playing off his two cross-batteries at the same time against the counter-guard, which faced the counterscarp, where the attack was to be made that morning. His first intention, as I said, was no more than giving the enemy a single puff or two;—but the pleasure of the *puffs*, as well as the *puffing*, had insensibly got hold of the Corporal, and drawn him on from puff to puff, into the very height of the attack, by the time my uncle Toby joined him.

'Twas well for my father, that my uncle Toby had not his will to make that day.

CHAP. XXVIII.

MY uncle Toby took the ivory pipe out of the Corporal's hand;—looked at it for half a minute, and returned it.

In less than two minutes, my uncle Toby took the pipe from the Corporal again, and raised it half-way to his mouth,—then hastily gave it back a second time.

The Corporal redoubled the attack;—my uncle Toby smiled,—then looked grave,—then smiled for a moment,—then looked serious for a long time.—Give me hold of the ivory pipe, Trim, said my uncle Toby.—My uncle Toby put it to his lips,—drew it back directly,—gave a peep over the horn-beam hedge.—Never did my uncle Toby's mouth water so much for a pipe in his life.—My uncle Toby retired into the sentry-box with the pipe in his hand.—

—Dear uncle Toby! don't go into the sentry-box with the pipe;—there's no trusting a man's self with such a thing in such a corner.

CHAP. XXIX.

I BEG the reader will assist me here, to wheel off my uncle Toby's ordnance behind the scenes;—to remove his sentry-box, and clear the theatre, if possible, of horn-works and half-moons, and get the rest of his military apparatus out of the way;—that done, my dear friend Garrick, we'll snuff the candles bright, sweep the stage with a new broom,—draw up the curtain, and exhibit my uncle Toby dressed in a new character, throughout which the world can have no idea how he will act: and yet, if pity be akin to love,—and bravery no alien to it, you have seen enough of my uncle Toby in these, to trace these family likenesses betwixt the two passions (in case there is one) to your heart's content.

Vain science! thou assistest us in no case of this kind,—and thou puzzlest us in every one.

There was, Madam, in my uncle Toby, a singleness of heart, which misled him so far out of the little serpentine tracks in which things of this nature usually go on, you can—you can have no conception of it: with this, there was a plainness and simplicity of thinking, with such an unmistrusting ignorance of the plies and foldings of the heart of woman;—and so naked and defenceless did he stand before you (when a siege was out of his head) that you might have stood behind any one of your serpentine walks, and shot my uncle Toby, ten times in a day, through his liver; if nine times in a day, Madam, had not served your purpose.

With all this, Madam,—and what confounded every thing as much on the other hand, my uncle Toby had that unparalleled modesty of nature I once told you of, and which, by the bye, stood eternal sentry upon his feelings, that you might as soon ——But where am I going? These reflections crowd in upon me ten pages at least too soon, and take up that time which I ought to bestow upon facts.

CHAP. XXX.

Of the few legitimate sons of Adam, whose breasts never felt what the sting of love was—(maintaining first all misogynists to be bastards)—the greatest heroes of ancient and modern story have carried off amongst them nine parts in ten of the honor; and I wish, for their sakes, I had the key of my study, out of the draw-well, only for five minutes, to tell you their names;—recollect them I cannot,—so be content to accept of these, for the present, in their stead.

There was the great king Aldrovandus, and Bosphorus, and Cappadocius, and Dardanus, and Pontus, and Asius,—to say nothing of the iron-hearted Charles the XIIth, whom the Countess of K***** herself could make nothing of.—There was Babylonicus, and Mediterraneus, and Polixenes, and Persicus, and Prusicus; not one of whom (except Cappadocius and Pontus, who were both a little suspected) ever once bowed down his breast to the goddess.—The truth is, they had all of them something else to do;—and so had my uncle Toby,—till Fate,—till Fate, I say, envying his name the glory of being handed down to posterity with Aldrovandus's and the rest,—she basely patched up the peace of Utrecht.

—Believe me, Sirs, 'twas the worst deed she did that year.

CHAP. XXXI.

Amongst the many ill consequences of the treaty of Utrecht, it was within a point of giving my uncle Toby a surfeit of sieges; and though he recovered his appetite afterwards, yet Calais itself left not a deeper scar in Mary's heart, than Utrecht upon my uncle Toby's. To the end of his life he never could hear Utrecht mentioned upon any account whatever,—or so much as read an article of news extracted out of the Utrecht Gazette, without fetching a sigh, as if his heart would break in twain.

My father, who was a great *motive-monger*, and consequently a very dangerous person for a man to sit by, either laughing or crying,—for he generally knew your motive for doing both, much better than you knew it yourself,—would always console my uncle Toby upon these occasions, in a way which showed plainly he imagined my uncle Toby grieved for nothing in the whole affair, so much as the loss of his HOBBY-HORSE.—Never mind, brother Toby, he would say,—by God's blessing, we shall have another war break out again some of these days; and when it does, the belligerent powers, if they would hang themselves, cannot keep us out of play.—I defy 'em, my dear Toby, he would add, to take countries without taking towns,—or towns without sieges.

My uncle Toby never took this backstroke of my father's at his HOBBY-HORSE kindly.—He thought the stroke ungenerous; and the more so, because in striking the horse he hit the rider too, and in the most dishonorable part a blow could fall; so that, upon these occasions, he always laid down his pipe upon the table with more fire to defend himself than common.

I told the reader, this time two years, that my uncle Toby was not eloquent; and in the very same page gave an instance to the contrary.—I repeat the observation, and a fact which contradicts it again.—He was not eloquent,—it was not easy to my uncle Toby to make long harangues,—and he hated florid ones; but there were occasions where the stream overflowed the man, and ran so counter to its usual course, that in some parts, my uncle Toby, for a time, was at least equal to Tertullus;—but in others, in my own opinion, infinitely above him.

My father was so highly pleased with one of these apologetical orations of my uncle Toby, which he had delivered one evening before him and Yorick, that he wrote it down before he went to bed.

I have had the good fortune to meet with it amongst my father's papers, with here and there an insertion of his own, betwixt two crooks, thus, [ ], and is indorsed,

My brother Toby's justification of his own principles and conduct in wishing to continue the war.

I may safely say, I have read over this apologetical oration of my uncle Toby's a hundred times; and think it so fine a model of defence, and shows so sweet a temperament of gallantry and good principles in him, that I give it the world, word for word (interlineations and all) as I find it.

CHAP. XXXII.

MY UNCLE TOBY'S APOLOGETICAL ORATION.

I AM not insensible, brother Shandy, that when a man, whose profession is arms, wishes, as I have done, for war, it has an ill aspect to the world:—and that, how just and right soever his motives and intentions may be,—he stands in an uneasy posture in vindicating himself from private views in doing it.

For this cause, if a soldier is a prudent man, which he may be without being a jot the less brave, he will be sure not to utter his wish in the hearing of an enemy; for say what he will, an enemy will not believe him.—He will be cautious of doing it even to a friend,—lest he may suffer in his esteem; but if his heart is overcharged, and a secret sigh for arms must have its vent, he will reserve it for the ear of a brother, who knows his character to the bottom, and what his true notions, dispositions, and principles of honor are. What, I hope, I have been in all these, brother Shandy, would be unbecoming in me to say:—much worse, I know, have I been than I ought,—and something worse, perhaps, than I think: but such as I am, you, my dear brother Shandy, who have sucked the same breasts with me,—and with whom I have been brought up from my cradle,—and from whose knowledge, from the first hours of our boyish pastimes, down to this, I have concealed no one action of my life, and scarce a thought in it;—such as I am, brother, you must, by this time, know me, with all my vices, and with all my weaknesses too, whether of my age, my temper, my passions, or my understanding.

Tell me then, my dear brother Shandy, upon which of them it is, that when I condemned the peace of Utrecht, and grieved the war was not carried on with vigor a little longer, you should think your brother did it upon unworthy views; or that, in wishing for war, he should be bad enough to wish more of his fellow-creatures slain,—more slaves made,—and more families driven from their peaceful habitations, merely for his own pleasure.—Tell me, brother Shandy, upon what one deed of mine do you ground it,?—[*The devil a deed do I know of, dear Toby, but one for an hundred pounds, which I lent thee to carry on these cursed sieges.*]

If, when I was a school-boy, I could not hear a drum beat, but my heart beat with it,—was it my fault?—Did I plant the propensity there?—Did I sound the alarm within, or Nature.

When Guy, Earl of Warwick, and Parismus and Parismenus, and Valentine and Orson, and the Seven Champions of England, were handed around the school,—were they not all purchased with my own pocket-money?—Was that selfish, brother Shandy?—When we read over the siege of Troy, which lasted ten years and eight months,—though with such a train of artillery as we had at Namur, the town might have been carried in a week—was I not as much concerned for the destruction of the Greeks and Trojans as any boy of the whole school?—Had I not three strokes of a ferula given me, two on my right hand, and one on my left, for calling Helena a bitch for it?—Did any one of you shed more tears for Hector?—And when king Priam came to the camp to beg his body, and returned weeping back to Troy without it,—you know, brother, I could not eat my dinner.

——Did that bespeak me cruel?—Or because, brother Shandy, my blood flew out into the camp, and my heart panted for war,—was it a proof it could not ache for the distresses of war too?

O brother! 'tis one thing for a soldier to gather laurels,—and 'tis another to scatter cypress.—[*Who told thee, my dear Toby, that cypress was used by the ancients on mournful occasions?*]—

'Tis one thing, brother Shandy, for a soldier to hazard his own life,—to leap first down into the trench, where he is sure to be cut in pieces:—'Tis one thing, from public spirit and a thirst of glory, to enter the breach the first man, to stand in the foremost rank, and march bravely on with drums and trumpets, and colors flying about his ears:—'Tis one thing, I say, brother Shandy, to do this;—and 'tis another thing to reflect on the miseries of war;—to view the desolations of whole countries, and consider the intolerable fatigues and hardships which the soldier himself, the instrument who works them, is forced (for sixpence a day, if he can get it) to undergo.

Need I be told, dear Yorick, as I was by you in Le Fevre's funeral sermon, *That so soft and gentle a creature, born to love, to mercy, and kindness, as man is, was not shaped for this?*—But why did you not add, Yorick,—if not by *Nature*—that he is so by *Necessity?*—For what is war? what is it, Yorick, when fought, as ours has been, upon principles of *liberty*, and upon principles of *honor?*—what is it, but the getting together of quiet and harmless people, with their swords in their hands, to keep the ambitious and the turbulent within bounds? —And Heaven is my witness, brother Shandy, that the pleasure I have taken in these things,—and that infinite delight, in particular, which has attended my sieges in my bowling-green, has arose within me, and I hope in the Corporal too, from the consciousness we both had, that, in carrying them on, we were answering the great end of our creation.

CHAP. XXXIII.

I TOLD the christian reader;—I say *christian*,—hoping he is one;—and if he is not, I am sorry for it,—and only beg he will consider the matter with himself, and not lay the blame entirely upon this book;—

I told him, Sir,—for in good truth, when a man is telling a story in the strange way I do mine, he is obliged continually to be going backwards and forwards to keep all tight together in the reader's fancy;—which, for my own part, if I did not take heed to do more than at first, there is so much unfixed and equivocal matter starting up, with so many breaks and gaps in it,—and so little service do the stars afford, which nevertheless I hang up in some of the darkest passages, knowing that the world is apt to lose its way, with all the lights the sun itself at noon-day can give it,—and now you see, I'm lost myself!

But 'tis my father's fault; and whenever my brains come to be dissected, you will perceive, without spectacles, that he has left a large uneven thread, as you sometimes see in an unsaleable piece of cambric, running along the whole length of the web, and so untowardly, you cannot so much as cut out a * *, (here I hang up a couple of lights again)—or a fillet, or a thumb-stall, but it is seen or felt.—

Quanto id diligentius in liberis procreandis cavendum, sayeth Carden.——All which being considered, and that you see 'tis morally impracticable for me to wind this round to where I set out,—I begin the chapter over again.

CHAP. XXXIII.

I TOLD the christian reader, in the beginning of the chapter which preceded my uncle Toby's apologetical oration,—though or a different trope from what I shall make use of now, That the peace of Utrecht was within an ace of creating the same shyness betwixt my uncle Toby and his Hobby-horse, as it did betwixt the Queen and the rest of the confederating powers.

There is an indignant way in which a man sometimes dismounts his horse, which as good as says to him, "I'll go afoot, Sir, "all the days of my life, before I would "ride a single mile upon your back again." Now, my uncle Toby could not be said to dismount his horse in this manner; for, in strictness of language, he could not be said to dismount his horse at all,—his horse rather flung him,—and somewhat *viciously*, which made my uncle Toby take it ten times more unkindly. Let this matter be settled by state jockeys as they like;—it created, I say, a sort of shyness betwixt my uncle Toby and his Hobby-horse:—He had no occasion for him from the month of March to November, which was the summer after the articles were signed, except it was now and then to take a short ride out, just to see that the fortifications and harbor of Dunkirk were demolished, according to stipulation.

The French were so backward all that summer in setting about that affair; and Monsieur Tugghe, the deputy from the magistrates of Dunkirk, presented so many affecting petitions to the Queen, beseeching her Majesty to cause only her thunderbolts to fall upon the martial works which might have incurred her displeasure,—but to spare, —to spare the mole, for the mole's sake; which, in its naked situation, could be no more than an object of pity;—and the Queen (who was but a woman) being of a pitiful disposition,—and her ministers also, they not wishing in their hearts to have the town dismantled, for these private reasons, * * * * * * *
* * * * * * * *
* * * * *——* * *
* * * * * * ; so that the whole went heavily on with my uncle Toby; insomuch, that it was not within three full months, after he and the Corporal had constructed the town, and put it in a condition to be destroyed, that the several commandants, commissaries, deputies, negotiators, and intendants, would permit him to set about it.—Fatal interval of in activity!

The Corporal was for beginning the demolition, by making a breach in the ramparts, or main fortifications of the town.—No;—that will never do, Corporal, said my uncle Toby; for, in going that way to work with the town, the English garrison will not be safe in it an hour; because, if the French are treacherous,—They are as treacherous as Devils, an' please your Honor, said the Corporal.—It gives me concern always when I hear it, Trim, said my uncle Toby,—for they don't want personal bravery; and if a breach is made in the ramparts, they may enter it, and make themselves masters of the place when they please.——Let them enter it, said the Corporal, lifting up the pioneer's spade in both his hands, as if he was going to lay about him with it,—let them enter, an' please your Honor, if they dare.——In cases like this, Corporal, said my uncle Toby, slipping his right hand down to the middle of his cane, and holding it afterwards truncheon-wise, with his fore-finger extended,—'tis no part of the consideration of a commandant, what the enemy dare, or what they dare not do; he must act with prudence. We will begin with the outworks both towards the sea and the land, and particularly with Fort Louis, the most distant of them all, and demolish it first;—and the rest one by one, both on our right and left, as we retreat towards the town;—then we'll demolish the mole,—next fill up the harbor,—then retire into the citadel, and blow it up into the air; and having done that, Corporal, we'll embark for England.——We are there, quoth the Corporal, recollecting himself.—Very true, said my uncle Toby,—looking at the church.

CHAP. XXXIV.

A DELUSIVE, delicious consultation or two of this kind, betwixt my uncle Toby and Trim, upon the demolition of Dunkirk,—for a moment rallied back the ideas of those pleasures, which were slipping from under him. Still,—still all went on heavily; the magic left the mind the weaker, *Stillness*, with

Silence at her back, entered the solitary parlor, and drew their gauzy mantle over my uncle Toby's head;—and *Listlessness*, with her lax fibre and undirected eye, sat quietly down beside him in his arm-chair. —No longer Amberg, and Rhinberg, and Limbourg, and Huy, and Bonn, in one year; —and the prospect of Landen, and Trerebach, and Drusen, and Dendermond, the next,—hurried on the blood:—No longer did saps, and mines, and blinds, and gabions, and palisadoes, keep out this fair enemy of man's repose:—No more could my uncle Toby, after passing the French lines, as he eat his egg at supper, from thence break into the heart of France,—cross over the Oyse, and with all Picardie open behind him, march up to the gates of Paris, and fall asleep with nothing but ideas of glory: —No more was he to dream he had fixed the royal standard upon the tower of the Bastile, and awake with it streaming in his head:

—Softer visions,——gentler vibrations, stole sweetly in upon his slumbers; the trumpet of war fell out of his hands;—he took up the lute, sweet instrument! of all others the most delicate! the most difficult! —how wilt thou touch it, my dear uncle Toby?

CHAP. XXXV.

Now, because I have once or twice said, in my inconsiderate way of talking, that I was confident the following memoirs of my uncle Toby's courtship of Widow Wadman, whenever I got time to write them, would turn out one of the most complete systems, both of the elementary and practical part of love and love-making, that ever was addressed to the world,—are you to imagine from thence, that I shall set out with a description of *what love is?* whether part God and part Devil? as Plotinus will have it;—

—Or, by a more critical equation, and, supposing the whole of love to be as ten? to determine, with Ficinus, "*how many* "*parts of it the one? and how many the other?*"—or whether it is *all of it one great devil*, from head to tail; as Plato has taken upon him to pronounce; concerning which conceit of his, I shall not offer my opinion:—but my opinion of Plato is this: That he appears, from this instance, to have been a man of much the same temper and way of reasoning with Dr. Baynard; who being a great enemy to blisters, as imagining that half a dozen of 'em on at once, would draw a man as surely to his grave, as a hearse and six,—rashly concluded, that the Devil himself was nothing in the world, but one great bouncing *Cantharides*.

I have nothing to say to people who allow themselves this monstrous liberty in arguing, but what Nazianzen cried out (that is, polemically) to Philagrius.

"Ευγε!" *O rare! 'tis fine reasoning, Sir, indeed!*—οτι φιλοσοφεις εν Παθεσι——*and most nobly do you aim at truth, when you philosophize about it in your moods and passions.*

Nor is it to be imagined, for the same reason, I should stop to inquire, whether love is a disease,—or embroil myself with Rhasis and Dioscorides, whether the seat of it is in the brain or liver,—because this would lead me on to an examination of the two very opposite manners in which patients have been treated,—the one, of Aætius, who always began with a cooling clyster of hemp-seed and bruised cucumbers; —and followed on with thin potations of water-lilies and purslane,—to which he added a pinch of snuff; of the herb Hanea; and, where Aætius durst venture it, his topaz ring.

—The other, that of Gordonius, who (in his cap. 15, *de Amore*) directs they should be thrashed "*ad putorem usque*,"—till they stink again.

These are the disquisitions which my father, who had laid in a great stock of knowledge of this kind, will be very busy with in the progress of my uncle Toby's affairs: I must anticipate thus much: That from his theories of love (with which, by the way, he contrived to crucify my uncle Toby's mind almost as much as his amours themselves)—he took a single step into practice; and, by means of a camphorated cerecloth, which he found means to impose upon the taylor for buckram, whilst he was making my uncle Toby a new pair of breeches, he produced Gordonius's effect upon my uncle Toby, without the disgrace.

What changes this produced, will be read in its proper place: all that is needful to be added to the anecdote, is this: That whatever effect it had upon my uncle Toby, it had a vile effect upon the house; and, if my uncle Toby had not smoked it down as he did, it might have had a vile effect upon my father too.

CHAP. XXXVI.

—'Twill come out of itself, by and bye. —All I contend for is, that I am not obliged to set out with a definition of what love is; and so long as I can go on with my story intelligibly, with the help of the word itself, without any other idea to it than what I have in common with the rest of the world, why should I differ from it a moment before the time?—When I can get on no further,—and find myself entangled on all sides in this mystic labyrinth,—my opinion will then come in, in course,—and lead me out.

At present, I hope I shall be sufficiently understood, in telling the reader, my uncle Toby *fell in love:*

—Not that the phrase is at all to my liking: for to say a man is *fallen* in love, —or that he is *deeply* in love;—or up to the ears in love;—and sometimes even *over head and ears in it*, carries an idiomatical kind of implication, that love is a thing *below* a man.—This is recurring again to Plato's opinion, which, with all his divinityship,—I hold to be damnable and heretical;—and so much for that.

Let love therefore be what it will,—my uncle Toby fell into it.

—And possibly, gentle reader, with such a temptation,—so would'st thou:—For never did thy eyes behold, or thy concupiscence covet, any thing in this world more concupiscible than Widow Wadman.

CHAP. XXXVII.

To conceive this right,—call for pen and ink;—here's paper ready to your hand.—Sit down, Sir, paint her to your own mind; —as like your mistress as you can,—as unlike your wife as your conscience will let you,—'tis all one to me,—please bu your own fancy in it.

Was ever any thing in nature so sweet! —so exquisite!

—Then, dear Sir, how could my uncle Toby resist it?

Thrice happy book! thou wilt have one page, at least, within thy covers, which *Malice* will not blacken, and which *Ignorance* cannot misrepresent.

CHAP. XXXIX.

As Susannah was informed, by an express from Mrs. Bridget, of my uncle Toby's falling in love with her mistress, fifteen days before it happened,—the contents of which express Susannah communicated to my mother the next day;—it has just given me an opportunity of entering upon my uncle Toby's amours a fortnight before their existence.

I have an article of news to tell you, Mr. Shandy, quoth my mother, which will surprise you greatly.—

Now my father was then holding one of his second beds of justice, and was musing within himself about the hardships of matrimony, as my mother broke silence.

"—My brother Toby, quoth she, is going to be married to Mrs. Wadman!"

—Then he will never, quoth my father, be able to lie *diagonally* in his bed again, as long as he lives.

It was a consuming vexation to my father, that my mother never asked the meaning of a thing she did not understand.

—That she is not a woman of science, my father would say, is her misfortune;—but she might ask a question.—

My mother never did.—In short, she went out of the world, at last, without knowing whether it *turned round*, or *stood still*.—My father had officiously told her above a thousand times, which way it was;—but she always forgot.

For these reasons, a discourse seldom went on much farther betwixt them than a proposition,—a reply, and a rejoinder; at the end of which, it generally took breath for a few minutes (as in the affair of the breeches) and then went on again.

If he marries, 'twill be the worse for us, quoth my mother.

—Not a cherry-stone, said my father;—he may as well batter away his means upon that, as any thing else.

—To be sure, said my mother. So here ended the proposition,—the reply,—and the rejoinder, I told you of.

—It will be some amusement to him, too, said my father.

—A very great one, answered my mother, if he should have children.

—Lord have mercy upon me! said my father to himself.—— * * * *

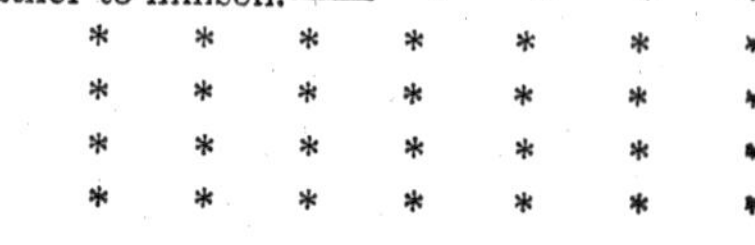

CHAP. XL.

I AM now beginning to get fairly into my work; and by the help of a vegetable diet, with a few of the cold seeds, I make no doubt but I shall be able to go on with my uncle Toby's story and my own, in a tolerable straight line. Now,

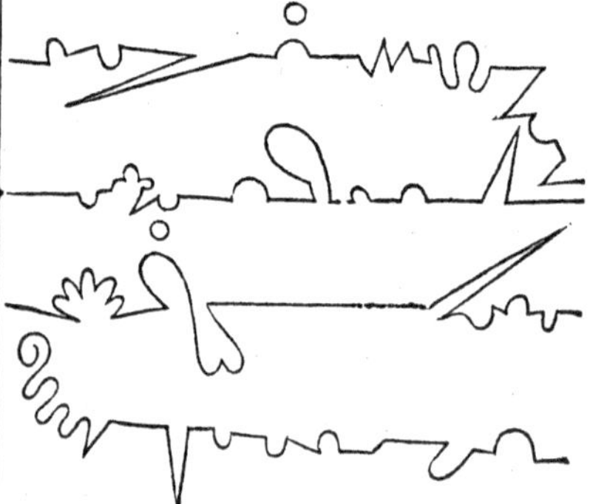

These were the four lines I moved in through my first, second, third, and fourth volumes. *—In the fifth volume I have been very good,—the precise line I have described in it being this:—

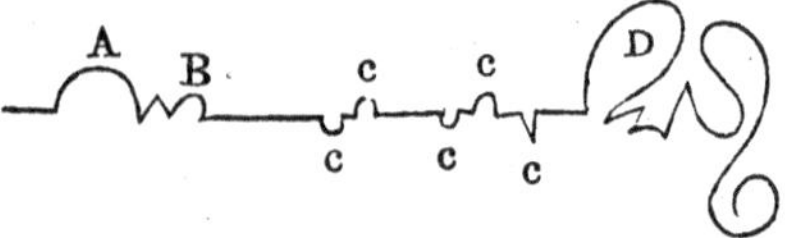

By which it appears, that except at the curve, marked A, where I took a trip to

* Alluding to the first edition

Navarre;—and the indented curve B, which is the short airing when I was there with the lady Baussiere and her page,—I have not taken the least frisk of a digression, till John de la Casse's Devils led me the round you see marked D;—for as for *c c c c c*, they are nothing but parentheses, and the common ins and outs incident to the lives of the greatest ministers of state; and when compared with what men have done,—or with my own transgressions at the letters A B D,—they vanish into nothing.

In this last volume I have done better still,—for from the end of Le Fevre's episode, to the beginning of my uncle Toby's campaigns—I have scarce stepped a yard out of my way.

If I mend at this rate, it is not impossible,—by the good leave of his Grace of Benevento's Devils, but I may arrive hereafter at the excellency of going on even thus:

———————————————————

which is a line drawn as straight as I could draw it by a writing-master's ruler (borrowed for that purpose) turning neither to the right hand nor to the left.

—This *right line*,—the pathway for christians to walk in! say divines,—

—The emblem of moral rectitude! says Cicero,—

—The *best line!* say cabbage-planters,—is the shortest line, says Archimedes, which can be drawn from one given point to another.

I wish your Ladyships would lay this matter to heart, in your next birth-day suits!

—What a journey!

Pray can you tell me,—that is, without anger, before I write my chapter upon straight lines,—by what mistake,—who told them so,—or how it has come to pass, that your men of wit and genius have all along confounded this line with the line of *gravitation?*

THE

LIFE AND OPINIONS

OF

Tristram Shandy,

GENTLEMAN.

CHAP. I.

NO:—I think I said, I would write two volumes every year, provided the vile cough, which then tormented me, and which to this hour I dread worse than the Devil, would but give me leave;—and in another place—(but where, I can't recollect now) speaking of my book as a *machine*, and laying my pen and ruler down cross-wise upon the table, in order to gain the greater credit to it,—I swore it should be kept a-going at that rate these forty years, if it pleased but the Fountain of Life to bless me so long with health and good spirits.

Now, as for my spirits, little have I to say to their charge,—nay, so very little (unless the mounting me upon a long stick, and playing the fool with me nineteen hours out of the twenty-four, be accusations)—that, on the contrary, I have much,—much to thank 'em for. Cheerily have ye made me tread the path of life, with all the burdens of it (except its cares) upon my back: in no one moment of my existence, that I remember, have ye once deserted me, or tinged the objects which came in my way, either with sable, or with a sickly green: in dangers ye gilded my horizon with hope; and when DEATH himself knocked at my door,—ye bade him come again; and in so gay a tone of careless indifference did ye do it, that he doubted of his commission.

"—There must certainly be some mistake "in this matter," quoth he.

Now there is nothing in this world I abominate worse, than to be interrupted in a story;—and I was that moment telling Eugenius a most tawdry one, in my way, of a nun who fancied herself a shell-fish; and of a monk damn'd for eating a muscle; and was showing him the grounds and justice of the procedure.

"—Did ever so grave a personage get "into so vile a scrape?" quoth Death.——Thou hast had a narrow escape, Tristram, said Eugenius, taking hold of my hand as I finished my story.—

But there is no *living*, Eugenius, replied I, at this rate; for as this *son of a whore* has found out my lodgings,—

——You call him rightly, said Eugenius,—for by sin, we are told, he enter'd the world.—I care not which way he enter'd, quoth I, provided he be not in such a hurry to take me out with him,—for I have forty volumes to write, and forty thousand things to say and do, which nobody in the world will say and do for me, except thyself; and as thou seest he has got me by the throat, (for Eugenius could scarce hear me speak across the table) and that I am no match for him in the open field, had I not better whilst these few scatter'd spirits remain, and these two spider legs of mine (holding one of them up to him) are able to support me,—had I not better, Eugenius, fly for my life?—'Tis my advice, my dear Tristram, said Eugenius.—Then, by Heaven! I will lead him a dance he little thinks of;—for I will gallop, quoth I, without looking once behind me, to the banks of the Garrone;—and if I hear him clattering at my heels,—I'll scamper away to Mount Vesuvius;—from thence to Joppa, and from Joppa to the world's end; where, if he follows me, I pray God he may break his neck.—

He runs more risk *there*, said Eugenius, than thou.

Eugenius's wit and affection brought blood into the cheek from whence it had been some months banish'd:—'twas a vile moment to bid adieu in: he led me to my chaise.—*Allons!* said I; the post-boy gave a crack with his whip,—off I went like a cannon, and at half a dozen bounds got into Dover.

CHAP. II.

Now, hang it! quoth I, as I look'd towards the French coast,—a man should know something of his own country too, before he goes abroad;—and I never gave a peep into Rochester church, or took notice of the dock of Chatham, or visited St. Thomas at Canterbury, though they all three lay in my way.

—But mine, indeed, is a particular case.

—So, without arguing the matter further with Thomas o'Becket, or any one else,—I skipp'd into the boat, and in five minutes we got under sail, and scudded away like the wind.

Pray, Captain, quoth I, as I was going down into the cabin, is a man never overtaken by Death in this passage?—

Why, there is not time for a man to be sick in it, replied he.—What a cursed liar! for I am sick as a horse, quoth I, already.—What a brain!—upside down!—hey-day!—the cells are broke loose one into another, and the blood, and the lymph, and the nervous juices, with the fix'd and volatile salts, are all jumbled into one mass!—good G—! every thing turns round in it like a thousand whirlpools.—I'd give a shilling to know if I shan't write the clearer for it.—

Sick! sick! sick! sick!—

When shall we get to land, Captain?—they have hearts like stones.—O I am deadly sick!—Reach me that thing, boy:—'tis the most discomfiting sickness,—I wish I was at the bottom.—Madam, how is it with you?—Undone! undone! un——O! undone, Sir.—What! the first time?—No, 'tis the second, third, sixth, tenth time, Sir.—Hey-day,—what a trampling over-head!—Hollo! cabin-boy! what's the matter?—

The wind chopp'd about!—S'death!—then I shall meet him full in the face.

—What luck!—'tis chopp'd about again, master.—O the Devil chop it.——

Captain, quoth she, for Heaven's sake, let us get ashore.

CHAP. III.

It is a great inconvenience to a man in a haste, that there are three distinct roads between Calais and Paris; in behalf of which, there is so much to be said by the several deputies from the towns which lie along them, that half a day is easily lost in settling which you'll take.

First, The road by Lisle and Arras, which is the most about,—but most interesting and instructing:

The second, That by Amiens; which you may go, if you would see Chantilly:

And that by Beauvais, which you may go if you will.

For this reason, a great many choose to go by Beauvais.

CHAP. IV.

"Now, before I quit Calais," a travel-writer would say, "it would not be amiss to "give some account of it."—

Now, I think it very much amiss,—that a man cannot go quietly through a town and let it alone when it does not meddle with him, but that he must be turning about, and drawing his pen at every kennel he crosses over, merely, o' my conscience, for the sake of drawing it; because, if we may judge from what has been wrote of these things, by all who have *wrote and gallop'd*,—or who have *gallop'd and wrote*, which is a different way still; or who, for more expedition than the rest, *wrote galloping*,—which is the way I do at present,—from the great Addison, who did it with his satchel of school-books hanging at his a—, and galling his beast's crupper at every stroke, there is not a galloper of us all, who might not have gone on ambling quietly on his own ground (in case he had any) and have wrote all he had to write, dry-shod, as well as not.

For my own part, as Heaven is my judge, and to which I shall ever make my last appeal,—I know no more of Calais, (except the little my barber told me of it as he was whetting his razor) than I do this moment of Grand Cairo; for it was dusky in the evening when I landed, and as dark as pitch in the morning when I set out; and yet, by merely knowing what is what, and by drawing this from that in one part of the town, and by spelling and putting this and that together in another,—I would lay any travelling odds, that I this moment write a chapter upon Calais as long as my arm; and with so distinct and satisfactory a detail of every item which is worth a stranger's curiosity in the town,—that you would take me for the town-clerk of Calais itself;—and where, Sir, would be the wonder? was not Democritus, who laughed ten times more than I,—town-clerk of Abdera? and was not (I forget his name) who had more discretion than us both, town-clerk of Ephesus?—It should be penn'd, moreover Sir, with so much knowledge, and good sense, and truth, and precision,——

—Nay,—if you don't believe me, you may read the chapter for your pains.

CHAP. V.

Calais, Calatium, Calusium, Calesium.

This town, if we may trust its archives, the authority of which I see no reason to call in question in this place,—was once no more than a small village, belonging to one of the first Counts de Guignes, and as it boasts at present of no less than fourteen thousand inhabitants, exclusive of four hundred and twenty distinct families in the *basse ville*, or suburbs,—it must have grown up by little and little, I suppose, to its present size.

Though there are four convents, there is but one parochial church in the whole town. I had not an opportunity of taking its exact dimensions, but it is pretty easy to make a tolerable conjecture of 'em:—for as there are fourteen thousand inhabitants in the town, if the church holds them all, it must be considerably large;—and if it will not,—'tis a very great pity they have not another.—It is built in form of a cross, and dedicated to the Virgin Mary; the steeple, which has a spire to it, is placed in the middle of the church, and stands upon four pillars, elegant and light enough, but sufficiently strong at the same time.—It is decorated with eleven altars, most of which are rather fine than beautiful. The great altar is a masterpiece in its kind,—'tis of white marble, and, as I was told, near sixty feet high:—had it been much higher, it had been as high as Mount Calvary itself;—therefore, I suppose it must be high enough in all conscience.

There was nothing struck me more than the great square: though I cannot say 'tis either well paved or well built; but 'tis in the heart of the town, and most of the streets, especially those in that quarter, all terminate in it. Could there have been a fountain in all Calais, which it seems there cannot, as such an object would have been a great ornament, it is not to be doubted but that the inhabitants would have had it in the very centre of this square;—not that it is properly a square,—because 'tis forty feet longer from east to west, than from north to south; so that the French in general have more reason on their side in calling them Places than Squares, which, strictly speaking, to be sure, they are not.

The town-house seems to be but a sorry building, and not to be kept in the best repair; otherwise it had been a second great ornament to this place: it answers, however, its destination, and serves very well for the reception of the magistrates, who assemble in it from time to time; so that 'tis presumable, justice is regularly distributed.

I had heard much of it, but there is nothing at all curious in the Courgain: 'tis a distinct quarter of the town, inhabited solely by sailors and fishermen: it consists of a number of small streets, neatly built, and mostly of brick. 'Tis extremely populous; but as that may be accounted for from the principles of their diet,—there is nothing curious in that neither.—A traveller may see it, to satisfy himself:—he must not omit however taking notice of La Tour de Guet, upon any account; 'tis so called from its particular destination, because in war it serves to discover and give notice of the enemies which approach the place, either by sea or land;—but 'tis monstrous high, and catches the eye so continually, you cannot avoid taking notice of it if you would.

It was a singular disappointment to me, that I could not have permission to take an exact survey of the fortifications, which are the strongest in the world and which, from first to last, that is, from the time they were set about by Philip of France, Count of Boulogne, to the present war, wherein many reparations were made, have cost (as I learnt afterwards from an engineer in Gascony)—above a hundred millions of livres.—It is very remarkable, that at the Tête de Gravelenes, and where the town is naturally the weakest, they have expended the most money; so that the outworks stretch a great way into the campaign, and consequently occupy a large tract of ground.—However, after all that is *said* and *done*, it must be acknowledged that Calais was never upon any account so considerable from itself, as from its situation, and that easy entrance which it gave our ancestors, upon all occasions, into France. It was not without its inconveniences also; being no less troublesome to the English, in those times, than Dunkirk has been to us, in ours; so that it was deservedly looked upon as the key to both kingdoms; which no doubt is the reason that there have arisen so many contentions who should keep it: of these, the siege of Calais, or rather the blockade (for it was shut up both by land and sea) was the most memorable, as it withstood the efforts of Edward the Third a whole year, and was not terminated, at last, but by famine and extreme misery; the gallantry of Eustace de St. Pierre, who first offered himself a victim for his fellow-citizens, has rank'd his name with heroes.—As it will not take up above fifty pages, it would be injustice to the reader, not to give a minute account of that romantic transaction, as well as of the siege itself, in Rapin's own words:—

CHAP. VI.

—But courage! gentle reader!—I scorn it:—'tis enough to have thee in my power;—but to make use of the advantage which the fortune of the pen has now gained over thee, would be too much.—No!—by that all-powerful fire which warms the visionary brain, and lights the spirits through unworldly tracts! ere I would force a helpless creature upon this hard service, and make thee pay, poor soul! for fifty pages, which I have no right to sell thee,—naked as I am, I would browse upon the mountains, and smile that the north wind brought me neither my tent nor my supper.

—So put on, my brave boy! and make the best of thy way to Boulogne.

CHAP. VII.

—Boulogne!—hah!—so we are all got together,—debtors and sinners before Heaven, a jolly set of us;—but I can't stay and quaff it off with you.—I'm pursued myself like a hundred Devils, and shall be overtaken before I can well change horses:—for Heaven's sake, make haste.——'Tis for high treason, quoth a very little man, whispering as low as he could to a very tall man that stood next him.—Or else for murder, quoth the tall man.—Well thrown, Size-Ace! quoth I.—No; quoth a third, the gentleman has been committing——

Ah! ma chere fille! said I, as she tripped by from her matins,—you look as rosy as the morning (for the sun was rising, and it made the compliment the more gracious)—No; it can't be that, quoth a fourth—(she made a court'sy to me,—I kiss'd my hand) 'tis a debt, continued he.—'Tis certainly for debt, quoth a fifth.—I would not pay that gentleman's debts, quoth Ace, for a thousand pound. Nor would I, quoth Size, for six times the sum.—Well thrown, Size-Ace again! quoth I;—but I have no debt but the debt of Nature, and I want but patience of her, and I will pay her every farthing I owe her.—How can you be so hard-hearted, Madam, to arrest a poor traveller going along, without molestation to any one, upon his lawful occasions?—Do stop that death-looking, long-striding scoundrel of a scare sinner, who is posting after me.—He never would have followed me but for you. If it be but for a stage or two, just to give me start of him, I beseech you, Madam.—Do, dear lady.—

Now, in troth, 'tis a great pity, quoth mine Irish host, that all this good courtship should be lost; for the young gentlewoman has been after going out of hearing of it all along.—

Simpleton! quoth I.

So you have nothing *else* in Boulogne worth seeing?—

—By Jasus! there is the finest *seminary* for the *Humanities.*—

There cannot be a finer, quoth I.

CHAP. VIII.

When the precipitancy of a man's wishes hurries on his ideas ninety times faster than the vehicle he rides in,—woe be to truth! and woe be to the vehicle and its tackling (let 'em be made of what stuff you will) upon which he breathes forth the disappointment of his soul!

As I never give general characters either of men or things in choler, "the most haste "the worst speed," was all the reflection I made upon the affair the first time it happen'd;—the second, third, fourth, and fifth time, I confined it respectively to those times, and accordingly blamed only the second, third, fourth, and fifth post-boy for it, without carrying my reflections further; but the event continuing to befall me from the fifth to the sixth, seventh, eighth, ninth, and tenth time, and without one exception, I then could not avoid making a national reflection of it, which I do, in these words:—

That something is always wrong in a French post-chaise upon first setting out.

Or the proposition may stand thus:—

A French postilion has always to alight before he has got three hundred yards out of town.

What's wrong now?—*Diable!*—a rope's broke!—a knot has slipt!—a staple's drawn!—a bolt's to whittle!—a tag, a rag, a jagg, a strap, a buckle, or a buckle's tongue, want altering.

Now, true as all this is, I never think myself empowered to excommunicate thereupon either the post-chaise, or its driver; nor do I take it into my head to swear by the living G—, I would rather go afoot ten thousand times,—or that I will be damn'd if ever I get into another;—but I take the matter coolly before me, and consider, that some tag, or rag, or jagg, or bolt, or buckle, or buckle's tongue, will ever be a-wanting, or want altering, travel where I will;—so I never chaff, but take the good and the bad as they fall in my road, and get on.—Do so, my lad! said I: he had lost five minutes already in alighting, in order to get at a luncheon of black bread, which he had cramm'd into the chaise-pocket, and was remounted, and going leisurely on, to relish it the better.—Get on, my lad, said I, briskly;—but in the most persuasive tone imaginable; for I jingled a four-and-twenty sous piece against the glass, taking care to hold the flat side towards him, as he look'd back. The dog grinn'd intelligence from his right ear to his left; and behind his sooty muzzle discover'd such a pearly row of teeth, that *sovereignty* would have pawn'd her jewels for them.

Just Heaven! { What masticators!—
What bread!—

and so, as he finish'd the last mouthful of it, we enter'd the town of Montreuil.

CHAP. IX.

There is not a town in all France, which, in my opinion, looks better in the map than Montreuil.—I own, it does not look so well in the book of post-roads;—but when you come to see it,—to be sure it looks most pitifully.

There is one thing, however, in it at present very handsome; and that is, the inn-keeper's daughter.—She has been eighteen months at Amiens, and six at Paris, in going through her classes; so knits, and sews, and dances, and does the little coquetries very well.

A slut! in running them over within these five minutes that I have stood looking at her, she has let fall at least a dozen loops in a white thread stocking.—Yes, yes,—I see, you cunning gipsy!—'tis long and taper,—you need not pin it to your knee:—and that 'tis your own,—and fits you exactly.

That Nature should have told this creature a word about a *statue's thumb!*

But as this sample is worth all their thumbs,—besides, I have her thumbs and fingers in at the bargain, if they can be any guide to me,—and as Janatone withal (for that is her name) stands so well for a drawing,—may I never draw more; or rather, may I draw like a draught-horse, by main strength, all the days of my life,—if I do not draw her in all her proportions, and with as determin'd a pencil, as if I had her in the wettest drapery.

—But your Worships choose rather that I give you the length, breadth, and perpendicular height of the great parish-church, or a drawing of the façade of the abbey of St. Austreberte, which has been transported from Artois hither:—every thing is just I suppose as the masons and carpenters left them;—and if the belief in Christ continues so long, will be so these fifty years to come; —so your Worships and Reverences may all measure them at your leisures;—but he who measures thee, Janatone, must do it now;—thou carriest the principles of change within thy frame; and, considering the chances of a transitory life, I would not answer for thee a moment: ere twice twelve months are pass'd and gone, thou mayest grow out like a pumpkin, and lose thy shapes:—or, thou mayest go off like a flower, and lose thy beauty;—nay, thou mayest go off like a hussy—and lose thyself.—I would not answer for my aunt Dinah, was she alive; 'faith, scarce for her picture, were it but painted by Reynolds.—

But if I go on with my drawing, after naming that son of Apollo, I'll be shot.

So you must e'en be content with the original; which, if the evening is fine in passing through Montreuil, you will see at your chaise-door, as you change horses: but unless you have as bad a reason for haste as I have,—you had better stop.—She has a little of the *devote;* but that, Sir, is a terce to a nine in your favor.

L— help me! I could not count a single point: so had been piqued, and re-piqued, and capotted to the Devil.

CHAP. X.

All which being considered, and that Death moreover might be much nearer me than I imagined,—I wish I was at Abbeville, quoth I, were it only to see how they card and spin:—so off we set.

* *de Montreuil a Nampont-poste et demi*
de Nampont a Bernay - poste
de Bernay a Nouvion - poste
de Nouvion a Abbeville - poste.

—but the carders and spinners were all gone to bed.

CHAP. XI.

What a vast advantage is travelling! only it heats one; but there is a remedy for that, which you may pick out of the next chapter.

CHAP. XII.

Was I in a condition to stipulate with Death, as I am this moment with my apothecary, how and where I will take his clyster, —I should certainly declare against submitting to it before my friends; and therefore I never seriously think upon the mode and manner of this great catastrophe, which generally takes up and torments my thoughts as much as the catastrophe itself, —but I constantly draw the curtain across it with this wish,—That the Disposer of all things may so order it, that it happen not to me in my own house,—but rather in some decent inn;—at home I know it;—the concern of my friends, and the last services of wiping my brows and smoothing my pillow, which the quivering hand of pale Affection shall pay me, will so crucify my soul, that I shall die of a distemper which my physician is not aware of: but in an inn, the few cold offices I wanted, would be purchased with a few guineas, and paid me with an undisturbed, but punctual attention;—but mark;—This inn should not be the inn at Abbeville:—if there was not another in the universe, I would strike that inn out of the capitulation: so

Let the horses be in the chaise exactly by four in the morning.—Yes, by four, Sir, —or, by Genevieve! I'll raise a clatter in the house shall wake the dead.

---

* Vide Book of French Post-Roads, page 36, edition of 1762.

CHAP. XIII.

"*Make them like unto a wheel*," is a bitter sarcasm, as all the learned know, against the *grand tour*, and that restless spirit for making it, which David prophetically foresaw would haunt the children of men in the latter days; and, therefore, as thinketh the great Bishop Hall, 'tis one of the severest imprecations which David ever utter'd against the enemies of the Lord,—and, as if he had said, "I wish them no "worse luck than always to be rolling "about."—So much motion, continues he (for he was very corpulent)—is so much unquietness; and so much of rest, by the same analogy, is so much of Heaven.

Now, I (being very thin) think differently; and that so much of motion, is so much of life, and so much of joy;—and that to stand still, or get on but slowly, is death and the devil.

—Hollo! ho!—the whole world's asleep!—bring out the horses,—grease the wheels,—tie on the mail;—and drive a nail into that moulding,—I'll not lose a moment.—

Now, the wheel we are talking of, and *whereinto* (but not *whereonto*, for that would make an Ixion's wheel of it) he curseth his enemies, according to the bishop's habit of body, should certainly be a post-chaise wheel, whether they were set up in Palestine at that time or not;—and my wheel, for the contrary reasons, must as certainly be a cart-wheel, groaning round its revolution once in an age; and of which sort, were I to turn commentator, I should make no scruple to affirm, they had great store in that hilly country.

I love the Pythagoreans (much more than ever I dare tell my dear Jenny) for their "χοριςμον απο τȣ Σωματος, εις το καλως φιλοσοφειν."—[their] "*getting out of the body, in order "to think well.*" No man thinks right whilst he is in it; blinded, as he must be, with his congenial humors, and drawn differently aside, as the bishop and myself have been, with too lax or too tense a fibre;—Reason is, half of it, Sense; and the measure of Heaven itself is but the measure of our present appetites and connexions.—

–But which of the two, in the present case, do you think to be mostly in the wrong?

—You, certainly, quoth she, to disturb a whole family so early.

CHAP. XIV.

—But she did not know I was under a vow not to shave my beard till I got to Paris;—yet I hate to make mysteries of nothing;—'tis the cold cautiousness of one of those little souls from which Lessius (*lib.* 13. *de Moribus Divinis, cap.* 24.) hath made his estimate, wherein he setteth forth, That one Dutch mile, cubically multiplied, will allow room enough, and to spare, for eight hundred thousand millions, which he supposes to be as great a number of souls (counting from the fall of Adam) as can possibly be damn'd to the end of the world.

From what he has made this second estimate,—unless from the parental goodness of God,—I don't know:—I am much more at a loss what could be in Franciscus Ribbera's head, who pretends that no less a space than one of two hundred Italian miles multiplied into itself, will be sufficient to hold the like number;—he certainly must have gone upon some of the old Roman souls, of which he had read, without reflecting how much, by a gradual and most tabid decline, in a course of eighteen hundred years, they must unavoidably have shrunk so as to have come, when he wrote, almost to nothing.

In Lessius's time, who seems the cooler man, they were as little as can be imagined.—

—We find them less *now*;—

—And next winter we shall find them less again; so that, if we go on from little to less, and from less to nothing, I hesitate not one moment to affirm, that in half a century, at this rate, we shall have no souls at all; which being the period, beyond which I doubt likewise of the existence of the Christian faith, 'twill be one advantage, that both of them will be exactly worn out together.

Blessed Jupiter! and blessed every other heathen god and goddess! for now ye will come into play again, and with Priapus at your tails.—What jovial times!—but where am I? and into what a delicious riot of things am I rushing? I—I, who must be cut short in the midst of my days, and taste no more of 'em than what I borrow from my imagination:—Peace to thee, generous fool! and let me go on.

CHAP. XV.

—"So hating, I say, to make mysteries "of *nothing*,"—I intrusted it with the post-boy, as soon as ever I got off the stones: he gave a crack with his whip to balance the compliment; and with the thill-horse trotting, had a sort of an up and a down of the other, we danced it along to Ailly au Clochers, famed in days of yore for the finest chimes in the world; but we danced through it without music,—the chimes being greatly out of order—(as in truth they were through all France.)

And so making all possible speed from Ailly au Clochers, I got to Hixcourt;—from Hixcourt, I got to Perquignay; and from Perquignay, I got to Amiens; concerning which town I have nothing to inform you, but what I have informed you once before,—and that was, that Janatone went there to school.

CHAP. XVI.

In the whole catalogue of those whiffling vexations which come puffing across a man's canvas, there is not one of a more teasing or tormenting nature than this particular one which I am going to describe,—and for which (unless you travel with an *avance-courier*, which numbers do, in order to prevent it) there is no help; and it is this:—

That be you in ever so kindly a propensity to sleep,—though you are passing perhaps through the finest country, upon the best roads, and in the easiest carriage for doing it in the world;—nay, were you sure you could sleep fifty miles straight-forwards, without once opening your eyes;—nay, what is more, was you as demonstratively satisfied as you can be of any truth in Euclid, that you should upon all accounts be full as well asleep as awake,—nay, perhaps, better;—yet the incessant returns of paying for the horses at every stage,—with the necessity thereupon of putting your hand into your pocket, and counting out from thence three livres fifteen sous (sous by sous) puts an end to so much of the project, that you cannot execute above six miles of it (or, supposing it is a post and an half, that is but nine)—were it to save your soul from destruction.

—I'll be even with 'em, quoth I; for I'll put the precise sum into a piece of paper, and hold it ready in my hand all the way: "Now, I shall have nothing to do," said I, (composing myself to rest) "but to drop "this gently into the post-boy's hat, and not "say a word."—Then there wants two sous more to drink,—or there is a twelve sous piece of Louis XIV. which will not pass,—or a livre and some old liards to be brought over from the last stage, which Monsieur had forgot; which altercations (as a man cannot dispute very well asleep) rouse him: still is sweet sleep retrievable; and still might the flesh weigh down the spirit, and recover itself of these blows;—but then, by Heaven! you have paid but a single post,—whereas 'tis a post and a half; and this obliges you to pull out your book of post-roads, the print of which is so very small, it forces you to open your eyes, whether you will or no: then Monsieur le Curé offers you a pinch of snuff,—or a poor soldier shows you his leg,—or a shaveling his box,—or the priestess of the cistern will water your wheels;—(they do not want it;—but she swears by her *priesthood* (throwing it back) that they do)—then you have all these points to argue, or consider over in your mind; in doing of which, the rational powers get so thoroughly awakened,—you may get them to sleep again as you can.

It was entirely owing to one of these misfortunes, or I had pass'd clean by the stables of Chantilly.—But the postilion first affirming, and then persisting in it to my face, that there was no mark upon the two sous piece, I open'd my eyes to be convinced;—and seeing the mark upon it as plain as my nose,—I leap'd out of the chaise in a passion, and so saw every thing at Chantilly in spite.—I tried it but for three posts and a half, but believe 'tis the best principle in the world to travel speedily upon; for as few objects look very inviting in that mood,—you have little or nothing to stop you; by which means it was that I passed through St. Dennis, without turning my head so much as on the side towards the Abbey—

Richness of their treasury!—stuff and nonsense!—Bating their jewels, which are all false, I would not give three sous for any one thing in it, but Jaidas's lantern;—nor for that neither, only, as it grows dark, it might be of use.

CHAP. XVII.

Crack, crack,—crack, crack,—crack, crack;—so this is Paris! quoth I (continuing in the same mood)—and this is Paris!—humph!—Paris! cried I, repeating the name the third time,—

The first, the finest, the most brilliant!

The streets, however, are nasty.

But it looks, I suppose, better than it smells.—Crack, crack,—crack, crack;—what a fuss thou makest!—as if it concerned the good people to be informed, that a man with a pale face and clad in black, had the honor to be driven into Paris at nine o'clock at night, by a postilion in a tawny yellow jerkin, turned up with red calamanco!—Crack,—crack, crack,—crack, crack.—I wish thy whip—

—But 'tis the spirit of thy nation; so crack—crack on.

Ha!—and no one gives the wall! but in the School of Urbanity herself, if the walls are besh-t—how can you do otherwise?

And prithee, when do they light the lamps? What!—never in the summer months!—Ho! 'tis the time of salads.—O rare! salad and soup,—soup and salad,—salad and soup, *encore*—

—'Tis *too much* for sinners.

Now I cannot bear the barbarity of it. How can that unconscionable coachman talk so much bawdy to that lean horse? don't you see, friend, the streets are so villanously narrow, that there is not room in all Paris to turn a wheelbarrow? In the grandest city of the whole world, it would not have been amiss if they had been left a thought wider; nay, were it only so much in every single street, as that a man might know (was it only for satisfaction) on which side of it he was walking.

One,—two,—three,—four,—five,—six,—seven,—eight,—nine,—ten.—Ten cooks' shops! and twice the number of barbers! and all within three minutes' driving! one would think that all the cooks in the world, on some great merry-meeting with the barbers, by joint consent, had said,—Come, let us all go live at Paris: the French love good eating;—they are all *gourmands*;—we shall rank high; if their god is their belly,—their cooks must be gentlemen: and, forasmuch as *the periwig maketh the man*, and the periwig-maker maketh the periwig,—*ergo*, would the barbers say, we shall rank higher still,—we shall be above you all,—we shall be * *Capitouls* at least,—*pardi!* we shall all wear swords:

—And so, one would swear (that is by candle-light,—but there is no depending upon it) they continue to do to this day.

CHAP. XVIII.

The French are certainly misunderstood:—but whether the fault is theirs, in not sufficiently explaining themselves; or speaking with that exact limitation and precision which one would expect on a point of such importance, and which, moreover, is so likely to be contested by us;—or whether the fault may not be altogether on our side, in not understanding their language always so critically as to know "what they "would be at,"—I shall not decide; but 'tis evident to me, when they affirm, "That "*they who have seen Paris, have seen every* "*thing*," they must mean to speak of those who have seen it by day-light.

As for candle-light,—I give it up;—I have said before, there was no depending upon it;—and I repeat it again;—but not because the lights and shades are too sharp,—or the tints confounded,—or that there is

* Chief Magistrate in Toulouse, &c.

neither beauty nor keeping, &c. . . . for that's not truth;—but it is an uncertain light in this respect, that in all the five hundred grand hotels, which they number up to you in Paris;—and the five hundred good things, at a modest computation (for tis only allowing one good thing to a hotel) which by candle-light are best to be *seen*, *felt*, *heard*, and *understood* (which, by the bye, is a quotation from Lilly)—the devil a one of us, out of fifty, can get our heads fairly thrust in amongst them.

This is no part of the French computation; 'tis simply this:—

That by the last survey, taken in the year 1716, since which time there have been considerable augmentations, — Paris doth contain nine hundred streets, (*viz.*)

In the quarter called the City, there are fifty-three streets;

In St. James of the Shambles, fifty-five streets;

In St. Oportune, thirty-four streets;

In the quarter of the Louvre, twenty-five streets;

In the Palace Royal, or St. Honorius, forty-nine streets;

In Mont Martyr, forty-one streets;

In St. Eustace, twenty-nine streets;

In the Halles, twenty-seven streets;

In St. Dennis, fifty-five streets;

In St. Martin, fifty-four streets;

In St. Paul, or the Mortellerie, twenty-seven streets;

The Greve, thirty-eight streets;

In St. Avoy, or the Verrerie, nineteen streets;

In the Marias, or the Temple, fifty-two streets;

In St. Anthony, sixty-eight streets;

In the Place Maubert, eighty-one streets;

In St. Bennet, sixty streets;

In St. Andrew de Arcs, fifty-one streets;

In the quarter of the Luxembourg, sixty-two streets;

And in that of St. Germain, fifty-five streets; into any of which you may walk; and that when you have seen them, with all that belongs to them, fairly by day-light,—their gates, their bridges, their squares, their statues - - - and have crusaded it, moreover, through all their parish-churches, by no means omitting St. Roche and Sulpice; - and to crown all, have taken a walk to the four palaces, which you may see, either with or without the statues and pictures, just as you choose.

—Then you have seen—

—but 'tis what no one needeth to tell you, for you will read of it yourself, upon the portico of the Louvre, in these words:—

* Earth no such Folks!—no Folks e'er such a town
As Paris is!—sing Derry, derry, down.

The French have a *gay* way of treating every thing that is Great; and that is all can be said upon it.

CHAP. XIX.

In mentioning the word *gay* (as in the close of the last chapter) it puts one (*i. e.* an author) in mind of the word *spleen;*—especially if he has any thing to say upon it. Not that by any analysis, — or that from any table of interest or genealogy, there appears much more ground of alliance betwixt them, than betwixt light and darkness, or any two of the most unfriendly opposites in nature;—only 'tis an undercraft of authors to keep up a good understanding amongst words, as politicians do amongst men, — not knowing how near they may be under a necessity of placing them to each other;—which point being now gain'd, and that I may place mine exactly to my mind, I write it down here,

SPLEEN.

This, upon leaving Chantilly, I declared to be the best principle in the world to travel speedily upon; but I gave it only as matter of opinion. I still continue in the same sentiments;—only I had not then experience enough of its working to add this, That though you do get on at a tearing rate, yet you get on but uneasily to yourself at the same time; for which reason, I here quit it entirely, and for ever; and 'tis heartily at any one's service:—it has spoiled me the digestion of a good supper, and brought on a bilious diarrhœa, which has brought me back again to my first principle on which I set out;—and with

* Non orbis gentem, non urbem gens habet ullam
——————————ulla parem.

which I shall now scamper it away to the banks of the Garonne.

—No;—I cannot stop a moment to give you the character of the people,—their genius,—their manners,—their customs,—their laws,—their religion,—their government,—their manufactures,—their commerce,—their finances, with all the resources and hidden springs which sustain them; qualified as I may be, by spending three days and two nights amongst them, and during all that time making these things the entire subject of my inquiries and reflections.—

Still,—still I must away,—the roads are paved,—the posts are short,—the days are long,—'tis no more than noon,—I shall be at Fontainbleau before the King.

—Was he going there? Not that I know.

CHAP. XX.

Now I hate to hear a person, especially if he be a traveller, complain that we do not get on so fast in France as we do in England; whereas we get on much faster, *consideratis considerandis*; thereby always meaning, that if you weigh their vehicles with the mountains of baggage which you lay both before and behind upon them,—and then consider their puny horses, with the very little they give them,—'tis a wonder they get on at all. Their suffering is most unchristian; and 'tis evident thereupon to me, that a French post-horse would not know what in the world to do, was it not for the two words ****** and ******, in which there is as much sustenance as if you gave them a peck of corn. Now as these words cost nothing, I long, from my soul, to tell the reader what they are; but here is the question,—they must be told him plainly, and with the most distinct articulation, or it will answer no end;—and yet to do it in that plain way,—though their Reverences may laugh at it in the bed-chamber,—full well I wot, they will abuse it in the parlor; for which cause, I have been volving and revolving in my fancy some time, but to no purpose, by what clean device, or *facette* contrivance, I might so modulate them, that whilst I satisfy *that ear* which the reader chooses to *lend* me,—I might not dissatisfy the other which he keeps to himself.

—My ink burns my finger to try; and when I have,—'twill have a worse consequence,—it will burn (I fear) my paper.

—No;—I dare not.

But if you wish to know how the Abbess of Andouillets and a novice of her convent got over the difficulty, (only first wishing myself all imaginable success)—I'll tell you without the least scruple.

CHAP. XXI.

The Abbess of Andouillets, which, if you look into the large set of provincial maps now publishing at Paris, you will find situated amongst the hills which divide Burgundy from Savoy, being in danger of an *anchylosis*, or stiff joint, (the *sinovia* of her knee becoming hard by long matins) and having tried every remedy:—First, prayers and thanksgivings;—then invocations to all the saints in Heaven, promiscuously;—then particularly to every saint who had ever had a stiff leg before her;—then touching it with all the relics of the convent, principally with the thigh-bone of the man of Lystra, who had been impotent from his youth; then wrapping it up in her veil when she went to bed;—then cross-wise her rosary;—then bringing in to her aid the secular arm, and anointing it with oils and hot fat of animals;—then treating it with emollient and resolving fomentations;—then with poultices of marsh-mallows, mallows, bonus Henricus, white lilies, and fenugreek;—then taking the woods, I mean the smoke of 'em, holding her scapulary across her lap;—then decoctions of wild chicory, water-cresses, chervil, sweet cecily, and cochlearia; and nothing all this while answering, was prevailed on at last to try the hot baths of Bourbon:—so having first obtained leave of the visitor-general to take care of her existence,—she ordered all to be got ready for her journey. A novice of the convent, of about seventeen, who had been troubled with a whitloe in her middle finger, by sticking it constantly into the Abbess's cast poultices, &c.—had gained such an interest, that overlooking a sciatical old nun, who might have been set up for ever by the hot baths of Bourbon, Margarita, the little novice, was elected as the companion of the journey.

An old calash, belonging to the Abbess, lined with green frieze, was ordered to be drawn out into the sun. The gardener of the convent, being chosen muleteer, led out the two old mules, to clip the hair from the rump-ends of their tails; whilst a couple of lay-sisters were busied, the one in darning the lining, and the other in sewing on the shreds of yellow binding, which the teeth of time had unravelled;—the under-gardener dressed the muleteer's hat in hot wine-lees;—and a taylor sat musically at it, in a shed over-against the convent, in assorting four dozen of bells for the harness, whistling to each bell as he tied it on with a thong.

—The carpenter and the smith of Andouillets held a council of wheels; and by seven, the morning after, all look'd spruce, and was ready at the gate of the convent for the hot baths of Bourbon.—Two rows of the unfortunate stood ready there an hour before.

The Abbess of Andouillets, supported by Margarita the novice, advanced slowly to the calash, both clad in white, with their black rosaries hanging at their breasts.

—There was a simple solemnity in the contrast; they entered the calash; the nuns in the same uniform, sweet emblem of innocence, each occupied a window, and as the Abbess and Margarita look'd up,—each (the sciatical poor nun excepted)—each stream'd out the end of her veil in the air,—then kiss'd the lily hand which let it go. The good Abbess and Margarita laid their hands saint-wise upon their breasts,—look'd up to Heaven,—then to them,—and look'd "God "bless you, dear sisters."

I declare I am interested in this story, and wish I had been there.

The gardener, whom I shall now call the muleteer, was a little, hearty, broad-set, good-natured, chattering, toping kind of a fellow, who troubled his head very little with the *hows* and *whens* of life; so had mortgag'd a month of his conventicle wages in a borrachio, or leathern cask of wine, which he had disposed behind the calash, with a large russet-colored riding-coat over it to guard it from the sun; and as the weather was hot, and he not a niggard of his labors, walking ten times more than he rode,—he found more occasions than those of nature, to fall back to the rear of his carriage; till by frequent coming and going it had so happen'd, that all his wine had leak'd out at the *legal* vent of the borrachio, before one half of the journey was finish'd.

Man is a creature born to habitudes. The day had been sultry,—the evening was delicious,—the wine was generous,—the Burgundian hill on which it grew was steep,—a little tempting bush, over the door of a cool cottage, at the foot of it, hung vibrating in full harmony with the passions,—a gentle air rustled distinctly through the leaves,—"Come,—come,—thirsty muleteer,—come in."

—The muleteer was a son of Adam: I need not say one word more. He gave the mules, each of 'em, a sound lash, and looking in the Abbess's and Margarita's faces (as he did it)—as much as to say, "here I "am,"—he gave a second good crack,—as much as to say to his mules, "get on;"—so slinking behind, he enter'd the little inn at the foot of the hill.

The muleteer, as I told you, was a little joyous, chirping fellow, who thought not of to-morrow, nor of what had gone before, or what was to follow it, provided he got but his scantling of Burgundy, and a little chitchat along with it; so entering into a long conversation, as how he was chief gardener to the convent of Andouillets, &c. &c. and out of friendship for the Abbess and Mademoiselle Margarita, who was only in her noviciate, he had come along with them from the confines of Savoy, &c. &c.—and as how she had got a white swelling by her devotions; and what a nation of herbs he had procured to mollify her humors, &c. &c.—and that if the waters of Bourbon did not mend that leg,—she might as well be lame of both, &c. &c. &c.—He so contrived his story, as absolutely to forget the heroine of it,—and with her the little novice; and what was a more ticklish point to be forgot than both,—the two mules; who being creatures that take advantage of the world, inasmuch as their parents took it of them,—and they not being in a condition to return the obligation *downwards* (as men, and women, and beasts are)—they do it side-ways, and long-ways, and back-ways, — and up hill, and down hill, and which way they can.— Philosophers, with all their ethics, have never considered this rightly:—how should the poor muleteer, then, in his cups, consider it at all? He did not in the least;— 'tis time we do. Let us leave him then in the vortex of his element, the happiest and most thoughtless of mortal men,—and for a moment let us look after the mules, the Abbess, and Margarita.

By virtue of the muleteer's two last strokes, the mules had gone quietly on, following their own consciences up the hill, till they had conquer'd about one half of it; when the elder of them, a shrewd crafty old devil, at the turn of an angle, giving a side-glance and no muleteer behind them,—

By my fig! said she, swearing, I'll go no further. — And if I do, replied the other, they shall make a drum of my hide.

—And so, with one consent, they stopp'd thus:—

CHAP. XXII.

—Get on with you, said the Abbess.

—Wh - - - - - ysh, — ysh, — ysh, — cried Margarita.

—Sh - - - a,—shu - u,—shu - u,—sh - - aw, —shaw'd the Abbess.

—Whu — v — w, — whew — w — w, — whuv'd Margarita, pursing up her sweet lips betwixt a hoot and a whistle.

Thump, — thump, — thump, — obstreperated the Abbess of Andouillets, with the end of her gold-headed cane against the bottom of the calash.

-The old mule let a f—

CHAP. XXIII.

We are ruin'd and undone, my child, said the Abbess to Margarita; — we shall be here all night:—we shall be plunder'd,— we shall be ravish'd!

We shall be ravish'd, said Margarita, as sure as a gun.

—*Sancta Maria!* cried the Abbess (forgetting the *O!*)—why was I govern'd by this wicked stiff joint? why did I leave the convent of Andouillets? and why didst thou not suffer thy servant to go unpolluted to her tomb?—

O my finger! my finger! cried the novice, catching fire at the word *servant*,— why was I not content to put it here, or there? anywhere, rather than be in this strait?

—Strait! said the Abbess.

—Strait! said the novice; for terror had struck their understandings,—the one knew not what she said, — the other what she answer'd.

—O my virginity! virginity! cried the Abbess.

—inity!—inity! said the novice, sobbing.

CHAP. XXIV.

My dear mother, quoth the novice, coming a little to herself,—there are two certain words, which I have been told will force any horse, or ass, or mule, to go up a hill whether he will or not: be he ever so obstinate or ill-will'd, the moment he hears them uttered, he obeys.—They are words magic! cried the Abbess, in the utmost horror. — No, replied Margarita, calmly, but they are words sinful—What are they? quoth the Abbess, interrupting her.—They are sinful in the first degree, answered Margarita;—they are mortal;—and if we are ravish'd and die unabsolv'd of them, we shall both—But you may pronounce them to me, quoth the Abbess of Andouillets.— They cannot, my dear mother, said the novice, be pronounced at all; they will make all the blood in one's body fly up into one's face.—But you may whisper them in my ear, quoth the Abbess.

Heaven! hadst thou no guardian angel to delegate to the inn at the bottom of the hill? Was there no generous and friendly spirit unemployed?—no agent in nature, by some monitory shivering creeping along the artery which led to his heart, to rouse the muleteer from his banquet?—no sweet minstrelsy to bring back the fair idea of the Abbess and Margarita, with their black rosaries?

Rouse! rouse!—but 'tis too late;—the

horrid words are pronounced this moment,—and how to tell them,—Ye, who can speak of every thing existing with unpolluted lips,—instruct me,—guide me!

CHAP. XXV.

All sins whatever, quoth the Abbess, turning casuist in the distress they were under, are held by the confessor of our convent to be either mortal or venial: there is no further division.—Now, a venial sin being the slightest and least of all sins,—being halved,—by taking either only the half of it, and leaving the rest,—or, by taking it all, and amicably halving it betwixt yourself and another person,—in course becomes diluted into no sin at all.

Now I see no sin in saying *bou, bou, bou, bou, bou*, a hundred times together; nor is there any turpitude in pronouncing the syllable *ger, ger, ger, ger, ger*, were it from our matins to our vespers.—Therefore, my dear daughter, continued the Abbess of Andouillets,—I will say *bou*, and thou shalt say *ger;* and then alternately, as there is no more sin in *fou* than in *bou;*—thou shalt say *fou,*—and I will come in (like fa, sol, la, re, mi, ut, at our complines) with *ter:*—and accordingly the Abbess, giving the pitch-note, set off thus:

Abbess, } Bou - - bou - - bou - -
Margarita, } ——ger, - - ger, - - ger.
Margarita, } Fou - - fou - - fou - -
Abbess, } ——ter, - - ter, - - ter.

The two mules acknowledged the notes by a mutual lash of their tails; but it went no further.—'Twill answer by and by, said the novice.—

Abbess, } Bou- bou- bou- bou- bou- bou-
Margarita, } —ger, ger, ger, ger, ger, ger.

Quicker still, cried Margarita.

Fou, fou, fou, fou, fou, fou, fou, fou, fou, fou.

Quicker still, cried Margarita.

Bou, bou, bou, bou, bou, bou, bou, bou, bou.

Quicker still.—God preserve me, said the Abbess.—They do not understand us, cried Margarita.—But the Devil does, said the Abbess of Andouillets.

CHAP. XXVI.

What a tract of country have I run!—how many degrees nearer to the warm sun am I advanced, and how many fair and goodly cities have I seen, during the time you have been reading and reflecting, Madam, upon this story!—There's Fontainbleau, and Sens, and Joigny, and Auxerre, and Dijon the capital of Burgundy, and Challon, and Mâcon the capital of the Maconese, and a score more upon the road to Lyons;—and now I have run them over,—I might as well talk to you of so many market-towns in the moon, as tell you one word about them: it will be this chapter at the least, if not both this and the next entirely lost, do what I will.—

Why, 'tis a strange story! Tristram.

—Alas! Madam, had it been upon some melancholy lecture of the cross,—the peace of meekness, or the contentment of resignation,—I had not been incommoded; or had I thought of writing it upon the purer abstractions of the soul, and that the food of wisdom, and holiness, and contemplation, upon which the spirit of man (when separated from the body) is to subsist for ever,—you would have come with a better appetite from it.

I wish I never had wrote it: but as I never blot any thing out,—let us use some honest means to get it out of our heads directly.

Pray reach me my fool's cap:—I fear you sit upon it, Madam;—'tis under the cushion:—I'll put it on.—

Bless me! you have had it upon your head this half hour.—There then let it stay, with a

Fa-ra diddle di
and a fa-ri diddle d
and a high-dum,—dye-dum
fiddle - - - dum - c.

And now, madam, we may venture, I hope, a little to go on.

CHAP. XXVII.

All you need say of Fontainbleau (in case you are ask'd,) is, that it stands about fortv miles (south *something*) from Paris, in the middle of a large forest:—that there is something great in it:—that the King goes there once every two or three years, with his whole court, for the pleasure of the chase; and that, during that carnival of sporting, an English gentleman of fashion (you need not forget yourself) may be accommodated with a nag or two, to partake of the sport, taking care only not to outgallop the King—

Though there are two reasons why you need not talk loud of this to every one.

First, Because 'twill make the said nags the harder to be got; and,

Secondly, 'Tis not a word of it true.—*Allons!*

As for Sens, you may dispatch it in a word;—" 'Tis an archiepiscopal see."

For Joigny,—the less, I think, one says of it, the better.

But for Auxerre, I could go on for ever: for in my *grand tour* through Europe, in which, after all, my father (not caring to trust me with any one) attended me himself, with my uncle Toby, and Trim, and Obadiah, and indeed most of the family, except my mother, who being taken up with a project of knitting my father a pair of large worsted breeches—(the thing is common sense)—and she not caring to be put out of her way, she staid at home, at Shandy-hall, to keep things right during the expedition; in which, I say, my father stopping us two days at Auxerre, and his researches being ever of such a nature, that they would have found fruit even in a desert,—he has left me enough to say upon Auxerre. In short, wherever my father went;—but 'twas more remarkably so in this journey through France and Italy, than in any other stages of his life;—his road seemed to lie so much on one side of that, wherein all other travellers have gone before him,—he saw Kings, and courts, and silks of all colors, in such strange lights;—and his remarks, and reasonings upon the characters, the manners, and customs of the countries we pass'd over, were so opposite to those of all other mortal men, particularly those of my uncle Toby and Trim—(to say nothing of myself;)—and to crown all,—the occurrences and scrapes which we were perpetually meeting and getting into, in consequence of his systems and opiniatry, — they were of so odd, so mix'd and tragi-comical a contexture,—that the whole put together, it appears of so different a shade and tint from any tour in Europe, which was ever executed,—that I will venture to pronounce,—the fault must be mine, and mine only,—if it be not read by all travellers and travel-readers, till travelling is no more,—or, which comes to the same point,—till the world, finally, takes it into its head to stand still.

But this rich bale is not to be opened now, except a small thread or two of it, merely to unravel the mystery of my father's stay at Auxerre.

As I have mentioned it,—'tis too slight to be kept suspended; and when 'tis wove in, there is an end of it.—

We'll go, brother Toby, said my father, whilst dinner is coddling,—to the abbey of Saint Germain, if it be only to see these bodies, of which Monsieur Sequier has given such a recommendation.—I'll go see any body, quoth my uncle Toby; for he was all compliance through every step of the journey.—Defend me! said my father,—they are all mummies.—Then one need not shave, quoth my uncle Toby.—Shave! no,—cried my father,—'twill be more like relations to go with our beards on.—So out we sallied, the Corporal lending his master his arm, and bringing up the rear, to the abbey of St. Germain.—

Every thing is very fine, and very rich, and very superb, and very magnificent, said my father, addressing himself to the sacristan, who was a younger brother of the order of Benedictines;—but our curiosity has led us to see the bodies, of which Monsieur Sequier has given the world so exact a description.—The sacristan made a bow, and lighting a torch first, which he had always in the vestry ready for the purpose, he led us into the tomb of St. Heribald.—This, said the sacristan, laying his hand upon the tomb, was a renown'd prince of the house of Bavaria, who, under the successive reigns of Charlemagne, Louis le Debonnair, and Charles the Bald, bore a great sway in the government, and had a principal hand in bringing every thing into order and discipline.—

Then he has been as great, said my uncle, in the field as in the cabinet—I dare say he has been a gallant soldier.—He was a monk,—said the sacristan.—

My uncle Toby and Trim sought comfort in each other's faces,—but found it not. —My father clapp'd both his hands upon his cod-piece, which was a way he had when any thing hugely tickled him: for though he hated a monk, and the very smell of a monk, worse than all the Devils in hell,—yet, the shot hitting my uncle Toby and Trim so much harder than him, 'twas a relative triumph, and put him into the gayest humor in the world.—

And pray what do you call this gentleman? quoth my father, rather sportingly.— This tomb, said the young Benedictine, looking downwards, contains the bones of St. Maxima, who came from Ravenna on purpose to touch the body——

Of St. Maximus, said my father, popping in with his saint before him,—they were two of the greatest saints in the whole martyrology, added my father.—Excuse me, said the sacristan,—'twas to touch the bones of St. Germain, the builder of the abbey.—And what did she get by it? said my uncle Toby.—What does any woman get by it? said my father.—*Martyrdom*, replied the young Benedictine, making a bow down to the ground, and uttering the word with so humble but decisive a cadence, it disarmed my father for a moment.—'Tis supposed, continued the Benedictine, that St. Maxima has lain in this tomb four hundred years, and two hundred before her canonization.—'Tis but a slow rise, brother Toby, quoth my father, in this self-same army of martyrs.—A desperate slow one, an' please your Honor, said Trim, unless one could purchase.—I should rather sell out entirely, quoth my uncle Toby.—I am pretty much of your opinion, brother Toby, said my father.—

Poor St. Maxima! said my uncle Toby, low to himself, as we turn'd from the tomb. —She was one of the fairest and most beautiful ladies either of Italy or France, continued the sacristan.—But who the deuce has got lain down here, beside her? quoth my father, pointing with his cane to a large tomb as we walked on.—It is Saint Optat, Sir, answered the sacristan.—And properly is Saint Optat placed! said my father; and what is Saint Optat's story? continued he. —Saint Optat, replied the sacristan, was a bishop.—

—I thought so, by Heaven! cried my father, interrupting him;—Saint Optat!— how should Saint Optat fail?—So snatching out his pocket-book, and the young Benedictine holding him the torch as he wrote, he set it down as a new prop to his system of Christian names: and I will be bold to say, so disinterested was he in the search of truth, that, had he found a treasure in Saint Optat's tomb, it would not have made him half so rich; 'twas as successful a short visit as ever was paid to the dead; and so highly was his fancy pleased with all that had passed in it, that he determined at once to stay another day in Auxerre.

—I'll see the rest of these good gentry to-morrow, said my father, as we crossed over the square.—And while you are paying that visit, brother Shandy, quoth my uncle Toby, the Corporal and I will mount the ramparts.

CHAP. XXVIII

—Now this is the most puzzled skein of all;—for in this last chapter, as far as it has help'd me through Auxerre, I have been getting forwards in two different journeys together, and with the same dash of the pen;—for I have got entirely out of Auxerre in this journey which I am writing now, and I am got half-way out of Auxerre in that which I shall write hereafter.—There is but a certain degree of perfection in every thing; and, by pushing at something beyond that, I have brought myself into such a situation, as no traveller ever stood before me; for I am this moment walking across the market-place of Auxerre, with my father and my uncle Toby, in our way back to dinner;—and I am this moment also entering Lyons, with my post-chaise broke into a thousand pieces:—and I am, moreover, this moment in a handsome pavilion, built by Pringello,* upon the banks of the Garonne, which Mons. Sligniac has

* The famous Don Pringello, the celebrated Spanish architect, of whom my cousin Anthony has made such honorable mention, in a scholium to the Tale inscribed to his name.—Vid. p. 129, small edit.

lent me, and where I now sit rhapsodizing all these affairs.

—Let me collect myself, and pursue my journey.

CHAP. XXIX.

I AM glad of it, said I, settling the account with myself, as I walk'd into Lyons,—my chaise being all laid higgledy-piggledy with my baggage in a cart, which was moving slowly before me.—I am heartily glad, said I, that 'tis all broke to pieces; for now I can go directly by water to Avignon, which will carry me on a hundred and twenty miles of my journey, and not cost me seven livres;—and from thence, continued I, bringing forwards the accounts, I can hire a couple of mules,—or asses, if I like (for nobody knows me) and cross the plains of Languedoc for almost nothing:—I shall gain four hundred livres by the misfortune clear into my purse; and pleasure! worth,—worth double the money, by it. With what velocity, continued I, clapping my two hands together, shall I fly down the rapid Rhone, with the Vivares on my right hand, and Dauphiny on my left, scarce seeing the ancient cities of Vienne, Valence, and Vivieres! What a flame will it rekindle in the lamp, to snatch a blushing grape from the Hermitage and Cotê Roti, as I shoot by the foot of them! and what a fresh spring in the blood! to behold upon the banks, advancing and retiring, the castles of romance, whence courteous knights have whilom rescued the distress'd;—and see, vertiginous, the rocks, the mountains, the cataracts, and all the hurry which Nature is in with all her great works about her!

As I went on thus, methought my chaise, the wreck of which look'd stately enough at the first, insensibly grew less and less in its size; the freshness of the painting was no more,—the gilding lost its lustre,—and the whole affair appeared so poor in my eyes!—so sorry!—so contemptible!—and, in a word, so much worse than the Abbess of Andouillet's itself,—that I was just opening my mouth to give it to the Devil,—when a pert, vamping chaise-undertaker, stepping nimbly across the street, demanded if Monsieur would have his chaise refitted.—No, no, said I, shaking my head sideways.—Would Monsieur choose to sell it? rejoined the undertaker.—With all my soul, said I;—the iron-work is worth forty livres,—and the glasses worth forty more,—and the leather you may take to live on.

—What a mine of wealth, quoth I, as he counted me the money, has this post-chaise brought me in! And this is my usual method of book-keeping, at least with the disasters of life,—making a penny of every one of 'em as they happen to me.

—Do, my dear Jenny, tell the world for me how I behaved under one, the most oppressive of its kind, which could befall me as a man, proud as he ought to be of his manhood.

'Tis enough, saidst thou, coming close up to me, as I stood with my garters in my hand, reflecting upon what had *not* passed,—'Tis enough, Tristram, and I am satisfied, saidst thou, whispering these words in my ear, * * * * * * * * * ;— * * * * —any other man would have sunk down to the centre.

—Every thing is good for something, quoth I.

—I'll go into Wales for six weeks, and drink goat's whey,—and I'll gain seven years longer life for the accident. For which reason I think myself inexcusable for blaming Fortune so often as I have done, for pelting me all my life long, like an ungracious duchess, as I call'd her, with so many small evils. Surely, if I have any cause to be angry with her, 'tis that she has not sent me great ones:—a score of good cursed, bouncing losses, would have been as good as a pension to me.

—One of a hundred a year, or so, is all I wish:—I would not be at the plague of paying land-tax for a larger

CHAP. XXX.

To those who call vexations, *vexations*, as knowing what they are, there could not be a greater, than to be the best part of a day at Lyons, the most opulent and flourishing city in France, enriched with the most fragments of antiquity,—and not be able to see it. To be withheld upon *any* account, must be a vexation; but to be withheld *by* a vexation,—must certainly be what philosophy justly calls

VEXATION
upon
VEXATION.

I had got my two dishes of milk-coffee (which, by the bye, is excellently good for a consumption; but you must boil the milk and coffee together,—otherwise 'tis only coffee and milk)—and as it was no more than eight in the morning, and the boat did not go off till noon, I had time to see enough of Lyons to tire the patience of all the friends I had in the world with it. I will take a walk to the cathedral, said I, looking at my list, and see the wonderful mechanism of this great clock of Lippius of Basil, in the first place.

Now, of all things in the world, I understand the least of mechanism;—I have neither genius, or taste, or fancy,—and have a brain so entirely unapt for every thing of that kind, that I solemnly declare I was never yet able to comprehend the principles of motion of a squirrel-cage, or a common knife-grinder's wheel,—though I have many an hour of my life look'd up with great devotion at the one,—and stood by with as much patience as any christian ever could do at the other.

I'll go see the surprising movements of this great clock, said I, the very first thing I do: and then I will pay a visit to the great library of the Jesuits, and procure, if possible, a sight of the thirty volumes of the general history of China, wrote (not in the Tartarian, but) in the Chinese language, and in the Chinese character too.

Now, I almost know as little of the Chinese language, as I do of the mechanism of Lippius's clock-work: so, why these should have jostled themselves into the two first articles of my list,—I leave to the curious as a problem of Nature. I own, it looks like one of her ladyship's obliquities; and they who court her, are interested in finding out her humor as much as I.

When these curiosities are seen, quoth I, half addressing myself to my valet de place, who stood behind me,—'twill be no hurt if we go to the church of St. Irenæus, and see the pillar to which Christ was tied,—and, after that, the house where Pontius Pilate lived.—'Twas at the next town, said the valet de place, at Vienne.—I am glad of it, said I, rising briskly from my chair, and walking across the room with strides twice as long as my usual pace;—"for so "much the sooner shall I be at the *Tomb* "*of the Two Lovers.*"

What was the cause of this movement, and why I took such long strides in uttering this,—I might leave to the curious too; but, as no principle of clock-work is concerned in it,—'twill be as well for the reader if I explain it myself.

CHAP. XXXI.

O! THERE is a sweet era in the life of man, when (the brain being tender and fibrillous, and more like pap than any thing else)—a story read of two fond lovers, separated from each other by cruel parents, and by still more cruel destiny—

Amandus—He,
Amanda—She,—

each ignorant of the other's course;

He—east,
She—west:

Amandus taken captive by the Turks, and carried to the Emperor of Morocco's court, where the Princess of Morocco, falling in love with him, keeps him twenty years in prison for the love of his Amanda.

She (Amanda) all the time wandering barefoot, and with dishevell'd hair, o'er rocks and mountains, inquiring for Amandus!—Amandus! Amandus!—making every hill and valley to echo back his name—

Amandus! Amandus!

at every town and city, sitting down forlorn at the gate:—Has Amandus!—has my Amandus enter'd!—till,—going round, and round, and round the world,—chance unexpectedly bringing them at the same moment of the night, though by different ways, to the gate of Lyons, their native city, and each in well-known accents calling out aloud,

Is Amandus } still alive?
Is my Amanda }

they fly into each other's arms, and both drop down dead for joy.

There is a soft era in every gentle mortal's life, where such a story affords more *pabulum* to the brain than all the Frusts, and Crusts, and Rusts of antiquity, which travellers can cook up for it.

—'Twas all that stuck on the right side of the cullender in my own, of what Spon and others, in their accounts of Lyons, had *strained* into it; and finding, moreover, in some Itinerary, but in what, God knows,—that, sacred to the fidelity of Amandus and Amanda, a tomb was built without the gates, where, to this hour, lovers called upon them to attest their truths,—I never could get into a scrape of that kind in my life, but this *tomb of the lovers* would, somehow or other, come in at the close; nay, such a kind of empire had it establish'd over me, that I could seldom think or speak of Lyons;—and sometimes, not so much as see even a Lyons-waistcoat, but this remnant of antiquity would present itself to my fancy; and I have often said in my wild way of running on,—though I fear with some irreverence,—"I thought this shrine (neglected as it was) as valuable as that of Mecca, and so little short, except in wealth, of the *Santa Casa* itself, that, some time or other, I would go a pilgrimage (though I had no other business at Lyons) on purpose to pay it a visit."

In my list, therefore, of Videnda at Lyons, this, though *last*,—was not, you see, *least;* so taking a dozen or two of longer strides than usual across my room, just while it passed my brain, I walked down calmly into the *Basse Cour*, in order to sally forth; and, having called for my bill,—as it was uncertain whether I should return to my inn, I had paid it,—and, moreover, given the maid ten sous, and was just receiving the dernier compliments of Monsieur Le Blanc, for a pleasant voyage down the Rhône,—when I was stopp'd at the gate

CHAP. XXXII.

'Twas by a poor ass, who had just turned in with a couple of large panniers upon his back, to collect eleemosynary turnip-tops and cabbage-leaves; and stood dubious, with his two fore-feet on the inside of the threshold, and with his two hinder-feet towards the street, as not knowing very well whether he was to go in or no.

Now, 'tis an animal (be in what hurry I may) I cannot bear to strike:—there is a patient endurance of sufferings, wrote so unaffectedly in his looks and carriage, which pleads so mightily for him, that it always disarms me; and to that degree, that I do not like to speak unkindly to him: on the contrary, meet him where I will, whether in town or country,—in cart, or under panniers,—whether in liberty or bondage,—I have ever something civil to say to him on my part; and as one word begets another (if he has as little to do as I)—I generally fall into conversation with him; and surely never is my imagination so busy as in framing his responses from the etchings of his countenance, and where those carry me not deep enough,—in flying from my own heart into his, and seeing what is natural for an ass to think,—as well as a man, upon the occasion. In truth, it is the only creature of all the classes of beings below me, with whom I can do this;—for parrots, jackdaws, &c. I never exchange a word with them,—nor with apes, &c. for pretty near the same reason; they act by rote, as the others speak by it, and equally make me silent: nay, my dog and my cat, though I value them both—(and, for my dog, he would speak if he could)—yet, somehow or other, they neither of them possess the talents for conversation;—I can make nothing of a discourse with them beyond the *proposition*, the *reply*, and *rejoinder*, which terminated my father's and my mother's conversation in his beds of justice;—and those utter'd,—there's an end of the dialogue.

—But with an ass, I can commune for ever.

—Come, Honesty! said I,- seeing it was impracticable to pass betwixt him and the gate,—art thou for coming in or going out?

—The ass twisted his head round, to look up the street.

—Well, replied I, we'll wait a minute for thy driver.

—He turned his head thoughtful about, and looked wistfully the opposite way

I understand thee perfectly, answered I:—if thou takest a wrong step in this affair, he will cudgel thee to death.—Well, a minute is but a minute, and, if it saves a fellow-creature a drubbing, it shall not be set down as ill spent.

He was eating the stem of an artichoke as this discourse went on, and, in the little peevish contentions of nature betwixt hunger and unsavoriness, had dropt it out of his mouth half a dozen times, and pick'd it up again.—God help thee, Jack! said I, thou hast a bitter breakfast on't,—and many a bitter day's labor,—and many a bitter blow, I fear, for its wages!—'tis all—all bitterness to thee, whatever life is to others!—And now, thy mouth, if one knew the truth of it, is as bitter, I dare say, as soot—(for he had cast aside the stem) and thou hast not a friend, perhaps, in all this world, that will give thee a macaroon.—In saying this, I pull'd out a paper of 'em, which I had just purchased, and gave him one,—and, at this moment that I am telling it, my heart smites me, that there was more of pleasantry in the conceit of seeing *how* an ass would eat a macaroon,—than of benevolence in giving him one, which presided in the act.

When the ass had eaten his macaroon, I press'd him to come in;—the poor beast was heavy loaded,—his legs seemed to tremble under him,—he hung rather backwards; and, as I pull'd at his halter, it broke short in my hand.—He look'd up pensive in my face—"Don't thrash me with it;—but, if you will, you may."—"If I do," said I, "I'll be d——d."

The word was but one half of it pronounced, like the Abbess of Andouillets'—(so there was no sin in it)—when a person coming in, let fall a thundering bastinado upon the poor devil's crupper, which put an end to the ceremony.

Out upon it!

cried I;—but the interjection was equivocal, and, I think, wrong placed too,—for the end of an osier which had started out from the contexture of the ass's pannier, had caught hold of my breeches-pocket as he rush'd by me, and rent it in the most disastrous direction you can imagine;—so that the

Out upon it! in my opinion, should have come in here;—but this I leave to be settled by

THE

REVIEWERS

OF

MY BREECHES,

which I have brought over along with me for that purpose.

CHAP. XXXIII.

When all was set to rights, I came down stairs again into the *Basse Cour* with my *valet de place*, in order to sally out towards the tomb of the two lovers, &c.—and was a second time stopp'd at the gate;—not by the ass,—but by the person who struck him; and who, by that time, had taken possession (as is not uncommon after a defeat) of the very spot of ground where the ass stood.

It was a commissary sent to me from the post-office, with a rescript in his hand, for the payment of some six livres odd sous.

Upon what account? said I.—'Tis upon the part of the King, replied the commissary, heaving up both his shoulders.

—My good friend, quoth I,—as sure as I am I,—and you are you,—

—And who are you? said he,

—Don't puzzle me, said I.

CHAP. XXXVII.

—But it is an indubitable verity, continued I, addressing myself to the commissary, changing only the form of my asseveration,—that I owe the King of France nothing but my good-will; for he is a very honest man, and I wish him all health and pastime in the world.

Pardonnez moi,—replied the commissary; you are indebted to him six livres four sous for the next post from hence to St. Fons, in your route to Avignon;—which being a post royal, you pay double for the horses and postilion—otherwise, 'twould have amounted to no more than three livres two sous.

—But I don't go by land, said I.

—You may, if you please, replied the commissary.

—Your most obedient servant,—said I, making him a low bow.

The commissary, with all the sincerity of grave good breeding,—made me one as low again,—I never was more disconcerted with a bow in my life.

—The Devil take the serious character of these people! quoth I—(aside)—they understand no more of *irony* than this—

The comparison was standing close by with his panniers,—but something sealed up my lips;—I could not pronounce the name.

—Sir, said I, collecting myself.—it is not my intention to take post.

—But you may,—said he, persisting in his first reply;—you may take post, if you choose.

—And I may take salt to my pickled herring, said I, if I choose.

—But I do not choose.

—But you must pay for it, whether you do or no.

—Ay! for the salt, said I (I know).

—And for the post too, added he.—Defend me! cried I.

—I travel by water;—I am going down the Rhone this very afternoon;—my baggage is in the boat,—and I have actually paid nine livres for my passage.

C'est tout egal,—'tis all one, said he.

—*Bon Dieu!* what, pay for the way I go! and for the way I do *not* go!

C'est tout egal, replied the commissary.

—The Devil it is! said I;—but I will go to ten thousand Bastiles first.

O England! England! thou land of liberty, and climate of good sense! thou tenderest of mothers, and gentlest of nurses! cried I, kneeling upon one knee as I was beginning my apostrophe,—

When the director of Madame Le Blanc's conscience coming in at that instant, and seeing a person in black, with a face as pale as ashes, at his devotions,—looking still paler by the contrast and distress of his drapery,—ask'd if I stood in want of the aids of the church?

—I go by *water*, said I;—and here's another will be for making me pay for going by *oil!*

CHAP. XXXV.

As I perceived the commissary of the post-office would have his six livres four sous, I had nothing else for it, but to say some smart thing upon the occasion, worth the money:

And so I set off thus:—

And pray, Mr. Commissary, by what law of courtesy is a defenceless stranger to be used just the reverse from what you use a Frenchman in this matter?

—By no means, said he.

—Excuse me, said I;—for you have begun, Sir, with tearing off my breeches,—and now you want my pocket.

Whereas,—had you first taken my pocket, as you do with your own people,—and then left me bare a—'d after,—I had been a beast to have complain'd.

As it is,—

—'Tis contrary to *the law of nature*.

—'Tis contrary to *reason*,

—'Tis contrary to the *Gospel*.

—But not to this,—said he,—putting a printed paper into my hand:—

PAR LE ROY.

—'Tis a pithy prolegomenon, quoth I;—and so read on — — — —
— — — — — — —
— — — — — — —
— — — — — — —
— — — — — — —

—By all which it appears, quoth I, having read it over a little too rapidly, that if a man sets out in a post-chaise from Paris,—he must go on travelling in one all the days of his life,—or pay for it.—Excuse me, said the commissary, the spirit of the ordinance is this:—That if you set out with an intention of running post from Paris to Avignon, &c. you shall not change that intention, or mode of travelling, without first satisfying the fermiers for two posts further than the place you repent at;—and 'tis founded, continued he, upon this, That the *Revenues* are not to fall short through your *fickleness*.

—O by Heavens! cried I,—if fickleness is taxable in France,—we have nothing to do but to make the best peace with you we can.

And so the peace was made;

—And if it is a bad one,—as Tristram

Shandy laid the corner-stone of it,—nobody but Tristram Shandy ought to be hanged.

CHAP. XXXVI.

Though I was sensible I had said as many clever things to the commissary as came to six livres four sous, yet I was determined to note down the imposition amongst my remarks, before I retired from the place; so putting my hand into my coat pocket for my remarks—(which, by the bye, may be a caution to travellers to take a little more care of *their* remarks for the future)—"my remarks were *stolen.*"—Never did sorry traveller make such a pother and racket about his remarks, as I did about mine, upon the occasion.

Heaven! earth! sea! fire! cried I, calling in every thing to my aid but what I should,—my remarks are stolen!—What shall I do?—Mr. Commissary! pray did I drop any remarks as I stood beside you?—

You dropp'd a good many very singular ones, replied he.—Pugh! said I, those were but a few, not worth above six livres two sous;—but these are a large parcel.—He shook his head.—Monsieur Le Blanc! Madame Le Blanc! did you see any papers of mine?—You, maid of the house, run up stairs!—François, run up after her!

—I must have my remarks;—they were the best remarks, cried I, that ever were made,—the wisest,—the wittiest.—What shall I do?—Which way shall I turn myself?

Sancho Pança, when he lost his ass's *furniture*, did not exclaim more bitterly.

CHAP. XXXVII.

When the first transport was over, and the registers of the brain were beginning to get a little out of the confusion into which this jumble of cross accidents had cast them,—it then presently occurr'd to me, that I left the remarks in the pocket of the chaise;—and that, in selling my chaise, I had sold my remarks along with it, to the chaise-vamper.

I leave this void space, that the reader may swear into it any oath he is most accustomed to.—For my own part, if ever I swore a *whole* oath into a vacancy in my life, I think it was into that—* * * * * * * * *, said I;—and so my remarks through France, which were as full of wit as an egg is full of meat,—and as well worth four hundred guineas as the said egg is worth a penny,—have I been selling here to a chaise-vamper,—for four Louis d'Ors;—and giving him a post-chaise (by Heaven!) worth six into the bargain; had it been to Dodsley, or Becket, or any creditable bookseller, who was either leaving off business, and wanted a post-chaise,—or who was beginning it—and wanted my remarks, and two or three guineas along with them,—I could have borne it; but to a chaise-vamper!—Show me to him this moment, François, said I.—The *valet de place* put on his hat, and led the way;—and I pull'd off mine as I pass'd the commissary, and followed him.

CHAP. XXXVIII.

When we arrived at the chaise-vamper's house, both the house and the shop were shut up: it was the eighth of September, the nativity of the blessed Virgin Mary, mother of God.

—Tantarra-ra-tan-tivi,—the whole world was going out a May-poling,—frisking here,—capering there,—nobody cared a button for me or my remarks; so I sat me down upon a bench by the door, philosophizing upon my condition. By a better fate than usually attends me, I had not waited half an hour, when the mistress came in to take the papilliotes from off her hair, before she went to the May-poles.

The French women, by the bye, love May-poles *à la folie*;—that is, as much as their matins.—Give 'em but a May-pole, whether in May, June, July, or September,—they never count the times,—down it goes,—'tis meat, drink, washing, and lodging to 'em;—and had we but the policy, an' please your Worships (as wood is a little scarce in France) to send them but plenty of May-poles,—

The women would set them up; and when they had done, they would dance round them (and the men for company) till they were all blind.

The wife of the chaise-vamper stepp'd in, I told you, to take the papilliotes from off her hair,—the toilet stands still for no man,—so she jerk'd off her cap, to begin with them, as she open'd the door; in doing which one of them fell upon the ground:—I instantly saw it was my own writing.

O Seigneur! cried I,—you have got all my remarks upon your head, Madam!—*J'en suis bien mortifiée*, said she:—'Tis well, thinks I, they have stuck there,—for could they have gone deeper, they would have made such confusion in a French woman's noddle,—she had better have gone with it unfrizzled to the day of eternity.

Tenez, said she:—so without any idea of the nature of my suffering, she took them from her curls, and put them gravely, one by one, into my hat;—one was twisted this way,—another twisted that.—Ay! by my faith, and when they are published, quoth I,—

They will be worse twisted still.

CHAP. XXXIX.

And now for Lippius's clock! said I, with the air of a man who had got through all his difficulties;—nothing can prevent us seeing that, and the Chinese History, &c.—Except the time, said François;—for 'tis almost eleven.—Then we must speed the faster, said I, striding it away to the cathedral.

I cannot say, in my heart, that it gave me any concern in being told by one of the minor canons, as I was entering the west door,—that Lippius's great clock was all out of joints, and had not gone for some years.—It will give me the more time, thought I, to peruse the Chinese history; and besides, I shall be able to give the world a better account of the clock in its decay, than I could have done in its flourishing condition.

—And so away I posted to the college of the Jesuits.

Now it is with the project of getting a peep at the History of China, in Chinese characters,—as with many others I could mention, which strike the fancy only at a distance; for as I came nearer and nearer to the point,—my blood cool'd,—the freak gradually went off, till at length I would not have given a cherry-stone to have it gratified.—The truth was, my time was short, and my heart was at the Tomb of the Lovers.—I wish to God, said I, as I got the rapper in my hand, that the key of the library may be but lost. It fell out as well,—

For all the Jesuits had got the colic,—and to that degree, as never was known in the memory of the oldest practitioner.

CHAP. XL.

As I knew the geography of the Tomb of the Lovers, as well as if I had lived twenty years in Lyons; namely, that it was upon the turning of my right hand, just without the gate leading to the Fauxbourg de Vaise,—I dispatched François to the boat, that I might pay the homage I so long ow'd it, without a witness of my weakness;—I walk'd with all imaginable joy towards the place.—When I saw the gate which intercepted the tomb, my heart glowed within me.

—Tender and faithful spirits! cried I, addressing myself to Amandus and Amanda,—long,—long have I tarried to drop this tear upon your tomb.—I come,—I come—

When I came,—there was no tomb to drop it upon.

What would I have given for my uncle Toby to have whistled *Lillibullero!*

CHAP. XLI.

No matter how or in what mood,—but I flew from the Tomb of the Lovers,—or rather I did not fly *from* it—for there was no such thing existing, and just got time enough to the boat to save my passage:—and ere I had sailed a hundred yards) the Rhône and the Saôn met together, and carried me down merrily betwixt them.

But I have described this voyage down the Rhône before I made it.

—So now I am at Avignon; and as there is nothing to see but the old house in which the Duke of Ormond resided, and nothing to stop me but a short remark upon the place, in three minutes you will see me crossing the bridge upon a mule, with François upon a horse with my portmanteau behind him, and the owner of both, striding the way before us, with a long gun upon his shoulder, and a sword under his arm, lest peradventure we should run away with his cattle. Had you seen my breeches in entering Avignon,—though you'd have seen them better, I think, as I mounted,—you would not have thought the precaution amiss, or found in your heart to have taken it in dudgeon: for my own part, I took it most kindly; and determined to make him a present of them, when we got to the end of our journey, for the trouble they had put him to, of arming himself at all points against them.

Before I go further, let me get rid of my remark upon Avignon, which is this:—That I think it wrong, merely because a man's hat has been blown off his head, by chance, the first night he comes to Avignon, —that he should therefore say, "Avignon "is more subject to high winds than any "town in all France:" for which reason I laid no stress upon the accident till I had inquired of the master of the inn about it; who telling me seriously it was so;—and hearing, moreover, the windiness of Avignon spoken of in the country about as a proverb,—I set it down merely to ask the learned what can be the cause?—the consequence I saw, for they are all Dukes, Marquisses, and Counts there,—the deuce a baron in all Avignon;—so that there is scarce any talking to them on a windy day.

Prithee, friend, said I, take hold of my mule for a moment;—for I wanted to pull off one of my jack-boots, which hurt my heel:—the man was standing quite idle at the door of the inn: and as I had taken it into my head he was someway concerned about the house or stable, I put the bridle into his hand,—so begun with my boot.—When I had finished the affair, I turned about to take the mule from the man, and thank him,—

But Monsieur le Marquis had walked in.

CHAP. XLII.

I HAD now the whole south of France. from the banks of the Rhône to those of the Garonne, to traverse upon my mule at my own leisure,—*at my own leisure*,—for I had left Death, the Lord knows,—and he only,—how far behind me!—"I have followed many a man through France," quoth he;—"but never at this mettlesome rate." —Still he followed,—and still I fled him,—but I fled him cheerfully;—still he pursued, —but, like one who pursued his prey without hope,—as he lagg'd, every step he lost softened his looks.—Why should I fly him at this rate?

So, notwithstanding all the commissary of the post-office had said, I changed the *mode* of my travelling once more; and, after so precipitate and rattling a course as I had run, I flattered my fancy with thinking of my mule, and that I should traverse the rich plains of Languedoc upon his back, as slowly as foot could fall.

There is nothing more pleasing to a traveller,—or more terrible to travel-writers, than a large rich plain, especially if it is without great rivers or bridges; and presents nothing to the eye but one unvaried picture of plenty: for after they have once told you, that 'tis delicious (or delightful as the case happens;)—that the soil was grateful, and that Nature pours out all her abundance, &c. . . . . they have then a large plain upon their hands, which they know not what to do with,—and which is of little or no use to them, but to carry them to some town; and that town, perhaps of little more, but a new place to start from to the next plain,—and so on.

This is most terrible work;—judge if I don't manage my plains better.

CHAP. XLIII.

I HAD not gone above two leagues and a half, before the man with his gun began to look at his priming.

I had three several times loiter'd *terribly* behind; half a mile at least every time once in deep conference with a drum-maker, who was making drums for the fairs of Bau caria and Tarascone:—I did not understand the principles.—

The second time, I cannot so properly say I stopp'd,—for meeting a couple of Franciscans straitened more for time than myself, and not being able to get to the bottom of what I was about,—I had turned back with them.—

The third was an affair of trade with a gossip, for a hand-basket of Provence figs for four sous: this would have been transacted at once, but for a case of conscience at the close of it; for when the figs were paid for, it turn'd out, that there were two dozen of eggs covered over with vine-leaves at the bottom of the basket:—as I had no intention of buying eggs,—I made no sort of claim of them:—as for the space they had occupied, what signified it? I had figs enow for my money.—

But it was my intention to have the basket;—it was the gossip's intention to keep it, without which she could do nothing with her eggs;—and unless I had the basket, I could do as little with my figs, which were too ripe already, and some of 'em burst at the side: this brought on a short contention, which terminated in sundry proposals what we should both do.—

How we disposed of our eggs and figs, I defy you or the Devil himself, had he not been there (which I am persuaded he was) to form the least probable conjecture.— You will read the whole of it,—not this year, for I am hastening to the story of my uncle Toby's amours;—but you will read it in the collection of those which have arose out of the journey across this plain;—and which, therefore, I call my

PLAIN STORIES.

How far my pen has been fatigued, like those of other travellers, in this journey of it, over so barren a track,—the world must judge; but the traces of it, which are now all set o' vibrating together this moment, tell me 'tis the most fruitful and busy period of my life; for as I had made no convention with my man with the gun, as to time,—by stopping and talking to every soul I met, who was not in a full trot,—joining all parties before me,—waiting for every soul behind,—hailing all those who were coming through cross-roads, arresting all kinds of beggars, pilgrims, fiddlers, friars,—not passing by a woman in a mulberry-tree without commending her legs, and tempting her into conversation with a pinch of snuff:—in short, by seizing every handle, of what size or shape soever, which chance held out to me in this journey,—I turned my *plain* into a *city*.—I was always in company, and with great variety too; and as my mule loved society as much as myself, and had some proposals always on his part to offer to every beast he met,—I am confident we could have passed through Pall-mall or St. James's Street, for a month together, with fewer adventures,—and seen less of human nature.

O! there is that sprightly frankness, which at once unpins every plait of a Languedocian's dress,—that whatever is beneath it, it looks so like the simplicity which poets sung of in better days! I will delude my fancy, and believe it is so.

'Twas in the road betwixt Nismes, and Lunel, where there is the best Muscatto wine in all France, and which, by the bye, belongs to the honest canons of Montpellier:—and foul befall the man who has drunk it at their table, who grudges them a drop of it.

The sun was set;—they had done their work; the nymphs had tied up their hair afresh,—and the swains were preparing for a carousal;—my mule made a dead point. —'Tis the fife and tabourine, said I.—I'm frighten'd to death, quoth he.—They are running at the ring of pleasure, said I, giving him a prick.—By Saint Boogar, and all the saints at the backside of the door of purgatory, said he,—(making the same resolution with the Abbess of Andouillet's) I'll not go a step further.—'Tis very well, Sir, said I.—I never will argue a point with one of your family as long as I live; so leaping off his back, and kicking off one boot into this ditch, and t'other into that,—I'll take a dance, said I;—so stay you here

A sun-burnt daughter of Labor rose up from the group to meet me, as I advanced towards them; her hair, which was a dark chestnut, approaching rather to a black, was tied up in a knot, all but a single tress.—

We want a cavalier, said she, holding out both her hands, as if to offer them.—And a cavalier you shall have, said I, taking hold of both of them.

Hadst thou, Nannette, been array'd like a *Duchesse!*

But that cursed slit in thy petticoat!

Nannette cared not for it.—

We could not have done without you, said she, letting go one hand, with self-taught politeness, and leading me up with the other.—

A lame youth, whom Apollo had recompensed with a pipe, and to which he had added a tabourine of his own accord, ran sweetly over the prelude, as he sat upon the bank.—Tie me up this tress instantly, said Nannette, putting a piece of string into my hand.—It taught me to forget I was a stranger.—The whole knot fell down. —We had been seven years acquainted.

The youth struck the note upon the tabourine, his pipe followed, and off we bounded,—"the deuce take that slit!"

The sister of the youth, who had stolen her voice from Heaven, sung alternately with her brother;—'twas a Gascoigne roundelay.

VIVA LA JOIA!
FIDON LA TRISTESSA!

The nymphs join'd in unison, and their swains an octave below them.—

I would have given a crown to have had it sew'd up.—Nannette would not have given a sous,—*Viva la joia* was in her lips:—*Viva la joia* was in her eyes.—A transient spark of amity shot across the space betwixt us.—She look'd amiable!—Why could I not live, and end my days thus? Just Disposer of our joys and sorrows, cried I, why could not a man sit down in the lap of content here,—and dance and sing, and say his prayers, and go to Heaven with this nut-brown maid? Capriciously did she bend her head on one side, and dance up insidious.—Then 'tis time to dance off, quoth I; so changing only partners and tunes, I danced it away from Lunel to Montpellier;—from thence to Pesçnas, Beziers.—I danced it along through Narbonne, Carcasson, and Castle Naudairy, till at last I danced myself into Pedrillo's pavilion; where, pulling out a paper of black lines, that I might go on straight-forwards, without digression or parenthesis, in my uncle Toby's amours.

I began thus:—

THE

LIFE AND OPINIONS

OF

Tristram Shandy,

GENTLEMAN.

CHAP. I.

—BUT softly,—for in these sportive plains, and under this genial sun, where at this instant all flesh is running out piping, fiddling, and dancing to the vintage, and every step that's taken, the judgment is surprised by the imagination, I defy, notwithstanding all that has been said upon *straight lines*,* in sundry pages of my book, —I defy the best cabbage-planter that ever existed, whether he plants backwards or forwards, it makes little difference in the account (except that he will have more to answer for in the one case than in the other) —I defy him to go on coolly, critically, and canonically, planting his cabbages one by one, in straight lines, and stoical distances, especially if slits in petticoats are unsew'd up,—without ever and anon straddling out, or sliding into some bastardly digression.— In Freeze-land, Fog-land, and some other lands I wot of,—it may be done!—

But in this clear climate of fantasy and perspiration, where every idea, sensible and insensible, gets vent,—in this land, my dear Eugenius,—in this fertile land of chivalry and romance, where I now sit, unscrewing my inkhorn to write my uncle Toby's amours, and with all the meanders of Julia's track in quest of her Diego, in full view of my study-window,—if thou comest not and takest me by the hand,—

What a work it is likely to turn out!

Let us begin it.

* Vide page 199.

CHAP. II.

IT is with Love as with Cuckoldom.— but now I am talking of beginning a book, and have long had a thing upon my mind to be imparted to the reader, which, if not imparted now, can never be imparted to him as long as I live (whereas the *comparison* may be imparted to him any hour in the day)—I'll just mention it, and begin in good earnest.

The thing is this:—

That of all the several ways of beginning a book which are now in practice throughout the known world, I am confident my own way of doing it is the best.—I'm sure it is the most religious,—for I begin with writing the first sentence,—and trusting to Almighty God for the second.

'Twould cure an author for ever of the fuss and folly of opening the street-door, and calling in his neighbors, and friends, and kinsfolk, with the Devil and all his imps, with their hammers, and engines, &c. only to observe how one sentence of mine follows another, and how the plan follows the whole.

I wish you saw me half starting out of my chair, with what confidence, as I grasp the elbow of it, I look up,—catching the idea even sometimes before it half-way reaches me!

—I believe, in my conscience, I intercept many a thought which Heaven intended for another man.

Pope and his portrait are fools to me:— no martyr is ever so full of faith or fire.— I wish I could say of good works too;—but I have no

Zeal or Anger,—or
Anger or Zeal;—
and, till gods and men agree together to call it by the same name,—the arrantest *Tartuffe* in science, in politics, or in religion, shall never kindle a spark within me, or have a worse word, or a more unkind greeting, than what he will read in the next chapter.

CHAP. III.

—*Bon jour!* — good-morrow! — so you have got your cloak on betimes!—but 'tis a cold morning, and you judge the matter rightly;—'tis better to be well mounted than go o' foot;—and obstructions in the glands are dangerous.—And how goes it with thy concubine,—thy wife,—and thy little ones o' both sides? and when did you hear from the old gentleman and lady,—your sister, aunt, uncle, and cousins?—I hope they have got the better of their colds, coughs, claps, tooth-aches, fevers, stranguaries, sciaticas, swellings, and sore eyes.

—What a devil of an apothecary! to take so much blood,—give such a vile purge,—puke,—poultice,—plaster,—night-draught,—clyster,—blister!—And why so many grains of calomel? *Santa Maria!* and such a dose of opium! periclitating, pardi! the whole family of ye, from head to tail!—By my great-aunt Dinah's old black velvet mask! I think there was no occasion for it.

Now this being a little bald about the chin, by frequently putting off and on, *before* she was got with child by the coachman,—not one of our family would wear it after. To cover the *mask* afresh, was more than the mask was worth;—and to wear a mask which was bald, or which could be half seen through, was as bad as having no mask at all.

—This is the reason, may it please your Reverences, that in all our numerous family, for these four generations, we count no more than one Archbishop, a Welsh Judge, some three or four Aldermen, and a single Mountebank.

In the sixteenth century, we boast of no less than a dozen alchymists.

CHAP. IV.

"It is with Love as with Cuckoldom;"—the suffering party is at least the *third*, but, generally, the last in the house who knows any thing about the matter: this comes, as all the world knows, from having half a dozen words for one thing; and so long as what in this vessel of the human frame is *Love*,—may be *Hatred* in that,—*Sentiment* half a yard higher,—and *Nonsense*,—No, Madam,—not there; I mean at the part I am now pointing to with my fore-finger,—how can we help ourselves?

Of all mortal, and immortal men too, if you please, who ever soliloquized upon this mystic subject, my uncle Toby was the worst fitted to have push'd his researches through such a contention of feelings; and he had infallibly let them all run on, as we do worse matters, to see what they would turn out,—had not Bridget's pre-notification of them to Susannah, and Susannah's repeated manifestoes thereupon to all the world, made it necessary for my uncle Toby to look into the affair.

CHAP. V.

Why weavers, gardeners, and gladiators,—or a man with a pined leg (proceeding from some ailment in the *foot*)—should ever have had some tender nymph breaking her heart in secret for them, are points well and duly settled and accounted for, by ancient and modern physiologists.

A water-drinker, provided he is a professed one, and does it without fraud or covin, is precisely in the same predicament: not that, at first sight, there is any consequence, or show of logic in it, "That a rill of cold "water dribbling through my inward parts, "should light up a torch in my Jenny's—"

—The proposition does not strike one; on the contrary, it seems to run opposite to the natural workings of causes and effects:—

But it shows the weakness and imbecility of human reason.

—"And in perfect good health with it!"

—The most perfect, Madam, that Friendship herself could wish me.

—"And drink nothing!—nothing but water?"

—Impetuous fluid! the moment thou pressest against the flood-gates of the brain,—see how they give way!

—In swims *Curiosity*, beckoning to her damsels to follow;—they dive into the centre of the current.

Fancy sits musing upon the bank, and, with her eyes following the stream, turns straws and bulrushes into masts and bowsprits.—And *Desire*, with vest held up to the knee in one hand, snatches at them, as they swim by her, with the other.

O ye water-drinkers! is it then by this delusive fountain, that ye have so often governed and turn'd this world about like a mill-wheel,—grinding the faces of the impotent, bepowdering their ribs,—bepeppering their noses, and changing sometimes even the very frame and face of nature!

—If I was you, quoth Yorick, I would drink more water, Eugenius.—And, if I was you, Yorick, replied Eugenius, so would I.

Which shows they had both read Longinus.

For my own part, I am resolved never to read any book but my own as long as I live.

CHAP. VI.

I wish my uncle Toby had been a water-drinker, for then the thing had been accounted for, That the first moment Widow Wadman saw him, she felt something stirring within her in his favor;—something!—something.

—Something, perhaps, more than friendship,—less than love:—something,—no matter what,—no matter where;—I would not give a single hair of my mule's tail, and be obliged to pluck it off myself (indeed, the villain has not many to spare, and is not a little vicious into the bargain) to be let by your Worships into the secret.

But the truth is, my uncle Toby was not a water-drinker; he drank it neither pure nor mix'd, nor anyhow, nor anywhere, except fortuitously upon some advanced posts, where better liquor was not to be had,—or during the time he was under cure; when, the surgeon telling him it would extend the fibres, and bring them sooner into contact,—my uncle Toby drank it for quietness' sake.

Now, as all the world knows that no effect in nature can be produced without a cause, and as it is as well known that my uncle Toby was neither a weaver, a gardener, nor a gladiator,—unless, as a captain, you will needs have him one,—but then he was only a captain of foot,—and, besides, the whole is an equivocation.—There is nothing left for us to suppose, but that my uncle Toby's leg,—but that will avail us little in the present hypothesis, unless it had proceeded from some ailment *in the foot*,—whereas his leg was not emaciated from any disorder in his foot,—for my uncle Toby's leg was not emaciated at all. It was a little stiff and awkward, from a total disuse of it for the three years he lay confined at my father's house in town; but it was plump and muscular, and, in all other respects, as good and promising a leg as the other.

I declare, I do not recollect any one opinion or passage of my life, where my understanding was more at a loss to make ends meet, and torture the chapter I had been writing, to the service of the chapter following it, than in the present case: one would think I took a pleasure in running into difficulties of this kind, merely to make fresh experiments of getting out of 'em.—Inconsiderate soul that thou art! What! are not the unavoidable distresses with which, as an author and a man, thou art hemm'd in on every side of thee;—are they, Tristram, not sufficient, but thou must entangle thyself still more?

Is it not enough that thou art in debt, and that thou hast ten cart-loads of thy fifth and sixth volumes* still,—still unsold, and art almost at thy wit's ends how to get them off thy hands?

To this hour art thou not tormented with the vile asthma that thou gattest in skating against the wind in Flanders? and it is but two months ago that, in a fit of laughter, on seeing a cardinal make water like a quirister (with both hands) thou brakest a vessel in thy lungs, whereby, in two hours, thou lost as many quarts of blood; and, hadst thou

* Alluding to the first edition.

lost as much more, did not the faculty tell thee,—it would have amounted to a gallon?—

CHAP. VII.

—But, for Heaven's sake, let us not talk of quarts or gallons, let us take the story straight before us; it is so nice and intricate a one, it will scarce bear the transposition of a single tittle; and somehow or other, you have got me thrust almost into the middle of it.

I beg we may take more care.

CHAP. VIII.

My uncle Toby and the Corporal had posted down with so much heat and precipitation, to take possession of the spot of ground we have so often spoke of, in order to open their campaign as early as the rest of the allies; that they had forgot one of the most necessary articles of the whole affair; it was neither a pioneer's spade, a pick-ax, or a shovel;—

It was a bed to lie on: so that as Shandy-hall was at that time unfurnished; and the little inn where poor Le Fevre died, not yet built,—my uncle Toby was constrained to accept of a bed at Mrs. Wadman's, for a night or two, till Corporal Trim (who, to the character of an excellent valet, groom, cook, sempster, surgeon, and engineer, superadded that of an excellent upholsterer too) with the help of a carpenter and a couple of tailors, constructed one in my uncle Toby's house.

A daughter of Eve, for such was Widow Wadman, and it's all the character I intend to give of her,

—"*That she was a perfect woman,*—" had better be fifty leagues off,—or in her warm bed, or playing with a case-knife,—or any thing you please,—than make a man the object of her attention, when the house and all the furniture is her own.

There is nothing in it out of doors and in broad daylight, where a woman has a power, physically speaking, of viewing a man in more lights than one;—but here, for her soul, she can see him in no light without mixing something of her own goods and chattels along with him,—till, by reiterated acts of such combinations, he gets foisted into her inventory,

And then, good night.

But this is not matter of *System;* for I have delivered that above:—nor is it matter of *Breviary;*—for I make no man's creed but my own:—nor matter of *Fact,*—at least that I know of: but 'tis matter copulative and introductory to what follows.

CHAP. IX.

I do not speak it with regard to the coarseness or cleanness of them,—or the strength of their gussets;—but pray, Do not night-shifts differ from day-shifts as much in this particular, as in any thing else in the world, That they so far exceed the others in length, that, when you are laid down in them, they fall almost as much below the feet as the day-shifts fall short of them?

Widow Wadman's night-shifts (as was the mode, I suppose, in King William's and Queen Anne's reigns) were cut, however, after this fashion; and, if the fashion is changed (for in Italy they are come to nothing)—so much the worse for the public; they were two Flemish ells and a half in length; so that, allowing a moderate woman two ells, she had half an ell to spare, to do what she would with.

Now, from one little indulgence gained after another, in the many bleak and Decemberly nights of a seven years' widowhood, things had insensibly come to this pass, and, for the two last years, had got establish'd into one of the ordinances of the bed-chamber,—That as soon as Mrs. Wadman was put to bed, and had got her legs stretched down to the bottom of it, of which she always gave Bridget notice,—Bridget with all suitable decorum, having first open'd the bed-clothes at the feet, took hold of the half-ell of cloth we are speaking of, and having gently, and with both her hands, drawn it downwards to its furthest extension, and then contracted it again sidelong by four or five even plaits, she took a large corking-pin out of her sleeve, and, with the point directed towards her, pinn'd the plaits all fast together, a little above the hem; which done, she tuck'd all in tight at the feet, and wish'd her mistress a good-night.

This was constant, and without any other variation than this; that, on shivering and tempestuous nights, when Bridget untuck'd the feet of the bed, &c. to do this, she consulted no thermometer but that of her own passions; and so performed it standing,—kneeling,—or squatting, according to the different degrees of faith, hope, and charity, she was in, and bore towards her mistress that night. In every other respect, the etiquette was sacred, and might have vied with the most mechanical one of the most inflexible bed-chamber in Christendom.

The first night, as soon as the Corporal had conducted my uncle Toby up stairs, which was about ten,—Mrs. Wadman threw herself into her arm-chair, and crossing her left knee with her right, which formed a resting-place for her elbow, she reclin'd her cheek upon the palm of her hand, and, leaning forwards, ruminated till midnight upon both sides of the question.

The second night she went to her bureau, and, having ordered Bridget to bring her up a couple of fresh candles and leave them upon the table, she took out her marriage-settlement, and read it over with great devotion: and the third night (which was the last of my uncle Toby's stay) when Bridget had pull'd down the night-shift, and was essaying to stick in the corking-pin,—

—With a kick of both heels at once, but at the same time the most natural kick that could be kick'd in her situation;—for supposing * * * * * * * * * * to be the sun in its meridian, it was a north-east kick; she kick'd the pin out of her fingers,—the etiquette which hung upon it, down,—down it fell to the ground, and was shiver'd into a thousand atoms.

From all which, it was plain that Widow Wadman was in love with my uncle Toby.

CHAP. X.

My uncle Toby's head at that time was full of other matters, so that it was not till the demolition of Dunkirk, when all the other civilities of Europe were settled, that he found leisure to return this.

This made an armistice (that is, speaking with regard to my uncle Toby,—but, with respect to Mrs. Wadman, a vacancy)—of almost eleven years. But in all cases of this nature, as it is the second blow, happen at what distance of time it will, which makes the fray,—I choose, for that reason, to call these the amours of my uncle Toby with Mrs. Wadman, rather than the amours of Mrs. Wadman with my uncle Toby.

This is not a distinction without a difference.

It is not like the affair of *an old hat cock'd*,—and *a cock'd old hat*, about which your Reverences have so often been at odds with one another;—but there is a difference here in the nature of things;—

And, let me tell you gentry, a wide one too.

CHAP. XI.

Now, as Widow Wadman did love my uncle Toby,—and my uncle Toby did not love Widow Wadman, there was nothing for Widow Wadman to do, but to go on and love my uncle Toby,—or let it alone.

Widow Wadman would do neither the one nor the other.

—Gracious Heaven!—but I forget I am a little of her temper myself: for whenever it so falls out, which it sometimes does, about the equinoxes, that an earthly goddess is so much this, and that, and t'other, that I cannot eat my breakfast for her,—and that she careth not three half-pence whether I eat my breakfast or not,—

—Curse on her! and so I send her to Tartary, and from Tartary to Terra del Fuego, and so on to the Devil. In short, there is not an infernal niche where I do not take her divinityship and stick it.

But as the heart is tender, and the passions in these tides ebb and flow ten times in a minute, I instantly bring her back again; and, as I do all things in extremes, I place her in the very centre of the milky way,—Brightest of stars! thou wilt shed thy influence upon some one.

—The deuce take her and her influence too:—for, at that word, I lose all patience:—much good may it do him!—By all that is hirsute and gashly! I cry, taking off my furr'd cap, and twisting it round my finger,—I would not give sixpence for a dozen such!

—But 'tis an excellent cap too (putting it upon my head, and pressing it close to my ears)—and warm,—and soft, especially if you stroke it the right way:—but, alas! that will never be my luck:—(so here my philosophy is shipwreck'd again.)

—No; I shall never have a finger in the pye (so here I break my metaphor.)

Crust and crumb,
Inside and out,
Top and bottom;—I detest it, I hate it, I repudiate it;—I am sick at the sight of it:—

'Tis all pepper,
garlic,
staragen,
salt, and
Devil's dung.—By the great arch-cook of cooks, who does nothing, I think, from morning to night, but sit down by the fire-side and invent inflammatory dishes for us, I would not touch it for the world.

—O Tristram! Tristram! cried Jenny.

O Jenny! Jenny! replied I, and so went on with the twelfth chapter

CHAP. XII.

—"Not touch it for the world," did I say?

Lord, how I have heated my imagination with this metaphor!

CHAP. XIII.

Which shows, let your Reverences and Worships say what you will of it (for, as for *thinking*,—all who do think,—think pretty much alike both upon it and other matters)—Love is certainly, at least alphabetically speaking, one of the most

A gitating,
B ewitching,
C onfounded,
D evilish affairs of life;——the most
E xtravagant,
F utilitous,
G aligaskinish,
H andy-dandyish,
I racundulous (there is no K to it) and
L yrical of all human passions: at the same time, the most
M isgiving,
N innyhammering,
O bstipating,
P ragmatical,
S tridulous,
R idiculous,——though, by the bye, the R should have gone first:—but, in short, 'tis of such a nature, as my father once told my uncle Toby, upon the close of a long dissertation upon the subject:—"You can scarce," said he, "combine two ideas together upon "it, brother Toby, without an hypallage;"—What's that? cried my uncle Toby.

The cart before the horse, replied my father.

—And what is he to do there? cried my uncle Toby.

—Nothing, quoth my father, but to get in,—or let it alone.

Now Widow Wadman, as I told you before, would do neither the one nor the other.

She stood, however, ready harnessed and caparisoned at all points, to watch accidents.

CHAP. XIV.

The Fates, who certainly all foreknew of these amours of Widow Wadman and my uncle Toby, had, from the first creation of matter and motion (and with more courtesy than they usually do things of this kind) established such a chain of causes and effects hanging so fast to one another, that it was scarce possible for my uncle Toby to have dwelt in any other house in the world, or to have occupied any other garden in Christendom but the very house and garden which join'd and lay parallel to Mrs. Wadman's: this, with the advantage of a thickset arbor in Mrs. Wadman's garden, but planted in the hedge-row of my uncle Toby's, put all the occasions into her hands which love-militancy wanted: she could observe my uncle Toby's motions, and was mistress likewise of his councils of war; and as his unsuspecting heart had given leave to the Corporal, through the mediation of Bridget, to make her a wicker-gate of communication to enlarge her walks, it enabled her to carry on her approaches to the very door of the sentry-box; and sometimes, out of gratitude, to make an attack, and endeavor to blow my uncle Toby up in the very sentry-box itself.

CHAP. XV.

It is a great pity;—but 'tis certain, from every day's observation of man, that he may be set on fire, like a candle, at either end,—provided there is a sufficient wick standing out; if there is not—there's an end of the affair; and if there is,—by lighting it at the bottom, as the flame in that case has the misfortune generally to put out itself,—there's an end of the affair again.

For my part, could I always have the ordering of it which way I would be burnt myself,—for I cannot bear the thoughts of being burnt like a beast,—I would oblige a housewife constantly to light me at the top; for then I should burn down decently to the socket; that is from my head to my heart, from my heart to my liver, from my liver to my bowels, and so on by the mesenteric veins and arteries, through all the turns and lateral insertions of the intestines and their tunicles to the blind gut.—

I beseech you, Doctor Slop, quoth my uncle Toby, interrupting him as he mentioned the *blind gut*, in a discourse with my father the night my mother was brought to bed of me,—I beseech you, quoth my uncle Toby, to tell me which is the blind gut; for, old as I am, I vow I do not know to this day where it lies.

—The *blind gut*, answered Doctor Slop, lies betwixt the *Ilion* and *Colon.*

—In man? said my father.

—'Tis precisely the same, cried Doctor Slop, in a woman.

—That's more than I know, quoth my father.

CHAP. XVI.

—And so, to make sure of both systems, Mrs. Wadman predetermined to light my uncle Toby neither at this end nor that; but, like a prodigal's candle, to light him, if possible, at both ends at once.

Now, through all the lumber-rooms of military furniture, including both of horse and foot, from the great arsenal of Venice to the Tower of London (exclusive) if Mrs. Wadman had been rummaging for seven years together, and with Bridget to help her, she could not have found any one *blind* or *mantelet* so fit for her purpose as that which the expediency of my uncle Toby's affairs had fix'd up ready to her hands.

I believe I have told you,—but I don't know,—possibly I have;—be it as it will, 'tis one of the number of those many things which a man had better do over again than dispute about it,—That whatever town or fortress the Corporal was at work upon, during the course of their campaign, my uncle Toby always took care, on the inside of his sentry-box, which was towards his left hand, to have a plan of the place, fasten'd up with two or three pins at the top, but loose at the bottom, for the conveniency of holding it up to the eye, &c. . . . as occasions required; so that when an attack was resolved upon, Mrs. Wadman had nothing more to do, when she had got advanced to the door of the sentry-box, but to extend her right hand; and edging in her left foot at the same movement, to take hold of the map or plan, or upright, or whatever it was, and with out-stretched neck meeting it half-way,—to advance it towards her; on which my uncle Toby's passions were sure to catch fire,—for he would instantly take hold of the other corner of the map in his left hand, and with the end of his pipe in the other, begin an explanation.

When the attack was advanced to this point,—the world will naturally enter into the reasons of Mrs. Wadman's next stroke of generalship;—which was, to take my uncle Toby's tobacco-pipe out of his hand as soon as she possibly could; which, under one pretence or other, but generally that of pointing more distinctly at some redoubt or breastwork in the map, she would effect before my uncle Toby (poor soul!) had well march'd above half a dozen toises with it.

—It obliged my uncle Toby to make use of his fore-finger.

The difference it made in the attack was this:—That in going upon it, as in the first case, with the end of her fore-finger against the end of my uncle Toby's tobacco-pipe, she might have travelled with it along the lines, from Dan to Beersheba, had my uncle Toby's lines reached so far, without any effect: for as there was no arterial or vital heat in the end of the tobacco-pipe, it could excite no sentiment,—it could neither give fire by pulsation,—nor receive it by sympathy;—'twas nothing but smoke.

Whereas, in following my uncle Toby's fore-finger with hers, close through all the little turns and indentings of his works,—pressing sometimes against the side of it,—then treading upon its nail,—then tripping it up,—then touching it here,—then there, and so on,—it set something at least in motion.

This, though slight skirmishing, and at a distance from the main body, yet drew on the rest; for here, the map usually falling with the back of it close to the side of the sentry-box, my uncle Toby, in the simplicity of his soul, would lay his hand flat upon it, in order to go on with his explanation; and Mrs. Wadman, by a manœuvre as quick as thought, would as certainly place hers close beside it. This at once opened a communication, large enough for any sentiment to pass or repass, which a person skill'd in the elementary and practical part of love-making has occasion for.—

By bringing up her fore-finger parallel (as before) to my uncle Toby's—it unavoidably brought the thumb into action; and the fore-finger and thumb being once engaged, as naturally brought in the whole hand. Thine, dear uncle Toby! was never now in its right place,—Mrs. Wadman had it ever to take up, or, with the gentlest pushings, protrusions, and equivocal compressions, that a hand to be removed is capable of receiving, to get it press'd a hair-breadth of one side out of her way.

Whilst this was doing, how could she forget to make him sensible that it was her leg (and no one's else) at the bottom of the sentry-box, which slightly press'd against the calf of his!—So that my uncle Toby being thus attack'd, and sore push'd on both his wings,—was it a wonder, if now and then, it put his centre into disorder?

—The deuce take it! said my uncle Toby.

CHAP. XVII.

These attacks of Mrs. Wadman, you will readily conceive to be of different kinds; varying from each other like the attacks which history is full of, and from the same reasons. A general looker-on would scarce allow them to be attacks at all;—or if he did, would confound them all together;—but I write not to them. It will be time enough to be a little more exact in my descriptions of them as I come up to them, which will not be for some chapters; having nothing more to add in this, but that in a bundle of original papers and drawings, which my father took care to roll up by themselves, there is a plan of Bouchain in perfect preservation (and shall be kept so—whilst I have power to preserve any thing;) upon the lower corner of which, on the right hand side, there are still remaining the marks of a snuffy finger and thumb; which, there is all the reason in the world to imagine, were Mrs. Wadman's; for the opposite side of the margin, which I suppose to have been my uncle Toby's, is absolutely clean. This seems an authenticated record of one of these attacks; for there are *vestigia* of the two punctures partly grown up, but still visible on the opposite corner of the map, which are unquestionably the very holes through which it has been pricked up in the sentry-box.—

By all that is priestly! I value this precious relic, with its *stigmata* and *pricks*, more than all the relics of the Romish church;—always excepting when I am writing upon these matters, the pricks which entered the flesh of St. Radagunda in the desert; which, in your road from *Fesse* to *Cluny*, the nuns of that name will show you for love.

CHAP. XVIII.

I THINK, an' please your Honor, quoth Trim, the fortifications are quite destroyed; —and the bason is upon a level with the mole.—I think so too,—replied my uncle Toby, with a sigh half suppress'd; — but step into the parlor, Trim, for the stipulation;—it lies upon the table.

—It has lain there these six weeks, replied the Corporal; till this very morning that the old woman kindled the fire with it.

—Then, said my uncle Toby, there is no further occasion for our services.——The more, an' please your Honor, the pity, said the Corporal; in uttering which, he cast his spade into the wheel-barrow, which was beside him, with an air the most expressive of disconsolation that can be imagined, and was heavily turning about to look for his pick-ax, his pioneer's shovel, his piquets, and other little military stores, in order to carry them off the field,—when an heigh-ho! from the sentry-box, which being made of thin slit deal, reverberated the sound more sorrowfully to his ear, forbade him.

—No, said the Corporal to himself, I'll do it before his Honor rises to-morrow morning; so taking his spade out of the wheel-barrow again, with a little earth in it, as if to level something at the foot of the glacis, —but with a real intent to approach nearer to his master, in order to divert him,—he loosen'd a sod or two,—pared their edges with his spade, and having given them a gentle blow or two with the back of it, he sat himself down close by my uncle Toby's feet, and began as follows:—

CHAP. XIX.

IT was a thousand pities;—though I believe, an' please your Honor, I am going to say but a foolish kind of a thing for a soldier,—

A soldier, cried my uncle Toby, interrupting the Corporal, is no more exempt from saying a foolish thing, Trim, than a man of letters,—But not so often, an' please your Honor, replied the Corporal.——My uncle Toby gave a nod.

—It was a thousand pities, then, said the Corporal, casting his eye upon Dunkirk and the Mole, as Servius Sulpicius, in returning out of Asia (when he sailed from Ægina towards Megara) did upon Corinth and Pyræus,—

"It was a thousand pities, an' please your Honor, to destroy these works,—and a thousand pities to have let them stand."

—Thou art right, Trim, in both cases, said my uncle Toby.—This, continued the Corporal, is the reason, that from the beginning of their demolition to the end,—I have never once whistled, or sung, or laugh'd, or cry'd, or talk'd of past-done deeds, or told your Honor one story, good or bad.

—Thou hast many excellencies, Trim, said my uncle Toby; and I hold it not the least of them, as thou happenest to be a story-teller, that of the number thou hast told me, either to amuse me in my painful hours, or divert me in my grave ones,—thou hast seldom told me a bad one.

—Because, an' please your Honor, except one of a *King of Bohemia and his seven castles*,—they are all true; for they are about myself.

—I do not like the subject the worse, Trim, said my uncle Toby, on that score. But, prithee, what is this story? Thou hast excited my curiosity.

—I'll tell it your Honor, quoth the Corporal, directly.—Provided, said my uncle Toby, looking earnestly towards Dunkirk and the Mole again,—provided it is not a merry one: to such, Trim, a man should ever bring one half of the entertainment along with him; and the disposition I am in at present,—would wrong both thee, Trim, and thy story.—It is not a merry one, by any means, replied the Corporal.—Nor would I have it altogether a grave one, added my uncle Toby.—It is neither the one nor the other, replied the Corporal; but will suit your Honor exactly.—Then I'll thank thee for it with all my heart, cried my uncle Toby; so prithee begin it, Trim.

The Corporal made his reverence; and though it is not so easy a matter as the world imagines, to pull off a lank Montero-cap with grace,—or a whit less difficult, in my conceptions, when a man is sitting squat upon the ground, to make a bow so teeming with respect as the Corporal was wont yet, by suffering the palm of his right hand, which was towards his master, to slip back wards upon the grass, a little beyond his body, in order to allow it the greater sweep, —and by an unforced compression, at the same time, of his cap with the thumb and the two fore-fingers of his left, by which the diameter of the cap became reduced; so that it might be said rather to be insensibly squeez'd,—than pull'd off with a flatus, —the Corporal acquitted himself of both in a better manner than the posture of his affairs promised; and having *hemmed* twice, to find in what key his story would best go, and best suit his master's humor,—he exchanged a single look of kindness with him, and set off thus:—

THE STORY OF THE KING OF BOHEMIA AND HIS SEVEN CASTLES.

There was a certain King of Bo—he—

As the Corporal was entering the confines of Bohemia, my uncle Toby obliged him to halt for a single moment. He had set out bare-headed; having, since he pull'd off his Montero-cap in the latter end of the last chapter, left it lying beside him on the ground.

—The eye of Goodness espieth all things; so that before the Corporal had well got through the first five words of his story, had my uncle Toby twice touch'd his Montero-cap with the end of his cane, interrogatively:—as much as to say, Why don't you put it on, Trim?—Trim took it up with the most respectful slowness, and casting a glance of humiliation, as he did it, upon the embroidery of the fore-part, which being dismally tarnish'd and fray'd, moreover, in some of the principal leaves and boldest parts of the pattern, he laid it down again between his two feet, in order to moralize upon the subject.

—'Tis every word of it but too true, cried my uncle Toby, that thou art about to observe:—

"*Nothing in this world, Trim, is made* "*to last for ever.*"

—But when tokens, dear Tom, of thy love and remembrance wear out, said Trim, what shall we say?

—There is no occasion, Trim, quoth my uncle Toby, to say any thing else; and was a man to puzzle his brains till Doomsday, I believe, Trim, it would be impossible.

The Corporal perceiving my uncle Toby was in the right, and that it would be in vain for the wit of man to think of extracting a purer moral from his cap, without further attempting it, he put it on; and passing his hand across his forehead to rub out a pensive wrinkle, which the text and doctrine between them had engender'd, he return'd, with the same look and tone of voice, to his story of the King of Bohemia and his seven castles.

THE STORY OF THE KING OF BOHEMIA AND HIS SEVEN CASTLES, CONTINUED.

There was a certain King of Bohemia; but in whose reign, except his own, I am not able to inform your Honor.—

I do not desire it of thee, Trim, by any means, cried my uncle Toby.

—It was a little before the time, an' please your Honor, when giants were beginning to leave off breeding:—but in what year of our Lord that was,—

—I would not give a halfpenny to know, said my uncle Toby.

—Only, an' please your Honor, it makes a story look the better in the face.

—'Tis thy own, Trim, so ornament it after thy own fashion; and take any date, continued my uncle Toby, looking pleasantly upon him;—take any date in the whole world thou choosest, and put it to,—thou art heartily welcome.—

The Corporal bowed; for of every century, and of every year of that century, from the first creation of the world down to Noah's flood; and from Noah's flood to the birth of Abraham; through all the pilgrimages of the patriarchs, to the departure of the Israelites out of Egypt;—and throughout all the Dynasties, Olympiads, Urbeconditas, and other memorable epochas of the different nations of the world, down to the coming of Christ, and from thence to the very moment in which the Corporal was telling his story,—had my uncle Toby subjected this vast empire of time, and all its abysses, at his feet; but as *Modesty* scarce touches with a finger what *Liberality* offers her with both hands open,—the Corporal contented himself with the very *worst year* of the whole bunch; which, to prevent your Honors of the Majority and Minority from tearing the very flesh off your bones in contestation, 'Whether that year is not always the last-cast year of the last-cast almanac?'—I tell you plainly, it was; but from a different reason than you wot of.

—It was the year next him;—which being the year of our Lord seventeen hundred and twelve, when the Duke of Ormond was playing the Devil in Flanders,—the Corporal took it, and set out with it afresh on his expedition to Bohemia.

THE STORY OF THE KING OF BOHEMIA AND HIS SEVEN CASTLES, CONTINUED.

In the year of our Lord one thousand seven hundred and twelve, there was, an' please your Honor,—

—To tell thee truly, Trim, quoth my uncle Toby, any other date would have pleased me much better, not only on account of the sad stain upon our history that year, in marching off our troops, and refusing to cover the siege of Quesnoi, though Fagel was carrying on the works with such incredible vigor,—but likewise on the score, Trim, of thy own story; because if there are,—and which, from what thou hast dropt, I partly suspect to be the fact,—if there are giants in it,—

—There is but one, an' please your Honor.

—'Tis as bad as twenty, replied my uncle Toby; thou should'st have carried him back some seven or eight hundred years out of harm's way, both of critics and other people; and therefore, I would advise thee, if ever thou tellest it again,—

—If I live, an' please your Honor, but once to get through it, I will never tell it again, quoth Trim, either to man, woman, or child.—Poo—poo! said my uncle Toby;—but with accents of such sweet encouragement did he utter it, that the Corporal went on with his story with more alacrity than ever.

THE STORY OF THE KING OF BOHEMIA AND HIS SEVEN CASTLES, CONTINUED.

There was, an' please your Honor, said the Corporal, raising his voice and rubbing the palms of his two hands cheerly together as he began, a certain King of Bohemia,—

—Leave out the date entirely, Trim, quoth my uncle Toby, leaning forwards, and laying his hand gently upon the Corporal's shoulder to temper the interruption,—leave it out entirely, Trim; a story passes very well without these niceties, unless one is pretty sure of 'em.—Sure of 'em! said the Corporal, shaking his head.

—Right, answered my uncle Toby; it is not easy, Trim, for one, bred up as thou and I have been to arms, who seldom looks further forward than to the end of his musket, or backwards beyond his knapsack, to know much about this matter.—God bless your Honor! said the Corporal, won by the *manner* of my uncle Toby's reasoning, as much as by the reasoning itself, he has something else to do; if not in action, or on a march, or upon duty in his garrison,—he has his firelock, an' please your Honor, to furbish,—his accoutrements to take care of,—his regimentals to mend,—himself to shave and keep clean, so as to appear always like what he is upon the parade what business, added the Corporal triumphantly, has a soldier, an' please your Honor to know any thing at all of *geography?*

—Thou would'st have said *chronology*, Trim, said my uncle Toby; for as for geography, 'tis of absolute use to him; he must be acquainted intimately with every country and its boundaries where his profession carries him; he should know every town and city, and village and hamlet, with the canals, the roads, and hollow-ways, which lead up to them. There is not a river or a rivulet he passes, Trim, but he should be able, at first sight, to tell thee what is its name,—in what mountains it takes its rise,—what is its course,—how far it is navigable,—where fordable,—where not;—he should know the fertility of every valley, as well as the hind who plows it; and be able to describe, or, if it is required, to give thee an exact map of all the plains and defiles, the forts, the acclivities, the woods and morasses, through and by which his army is to march; he should know their produce, their plants, their minerals, their waters, their animals, their seasons, their climates, their heats and colds, their inhabitants, their customs, their language, their policy, and even their religion.

Is it else to be conceived, Corporal, continued my uncle Toby, rising up in his sentry-box as he began to warm in this part of his discourse,—how Marlborough could have marched his army from the banks of the Maes to Belburg; from Belburg to Kerpenord—(here the Corporal could sit no longer)—from Kerpenord, Trim, to Kalsaken; from Kalsaken to Newdorf; from Newdorf to Landenbourg; from Landenbourg to Mildenheim; from Mildenheim to Elchingen; from Elchingen to Gingen; from Gingen to Balmerchoffen; from Balmerchoffen to Skellenburg, where he broke in upon the enemy's works, forced his passage over the Danube, crossed the Lech,—push'd on his troops into the heart of the empire, marching at the head of them through Fribourg, Hokenwert and Schonevelt, to the plains of Blenheim and Hochstet?—Great as he was, Corporal, he could not have advanced a step, or made one single day's march, without the aids of Geography.—As for Chronology, I own, Trim, continued my uncle Toby, sitting down again coolly in his sentry-box, that, of all others, it seems a science which the soldier might best spare, was it not for the lights which that science must one day give him, in determining the invention of powder; the furious execution of which, renversing every thing, like thunder, before it, has become a new era to us of military improvements, changing so totally the nature of attacks and defences, both by sea and land, and awakening so much art and skill in doing it, that the world cannot be too exact in ascertaining the precise time of its discovery, or too inquisitive in knowing what great man was the discoverer, and what occasions gave birth to it.

I am far from controverting, continued my uncle Toby, what historians agree in, that in the year of our Lord 1380, under the reign of Wencelaus, son of Charles the Fourth,—a certain priest, whose name was Schwartz, show'd the use of powder to the Venetians, in their wars against the Genoese; but 'tis certain he was not the first; because, if we are to believe Don Pedro, the bishop of Leon,—How came priests and bishops, an' please your Honor, to trouble their heads so much about gunpowder?—God knows, said my uncle Toby,—his providence brings good out of every thing—and he avers, in his chronicle of King Alphonsus, who reduced Toledo, that in the year 1343, which was full thirty-seven years before that time, the secret of powder was well known, and employed with success, both by Moors and Christians, not only in their sea-combats, at that period, but in many of their most memorable sieges in Spain and Barbary;—and all the world knows, that Friar Bacon had wrote expressly about it, and had generously given the world a receipt to make it by, above a hundred and fifty years before even Schwartz was born:—and that the Chinese, added my uncle Toby, embarrass us, and all accounts of it, still more, by boasting of the invention some hundreds of years even before him.—

They are a pack of liars, I believe, cried Trim.—

They are somehow or other deceived, said my uncle Toby, in this matter, as is plain to me from the present miserable state of military architecture amongst them; which consists of nothing more than a *fossé* with a brick wall without flanks;—and for what they give us as a bastion at each angle of it, 'tis so barbarously constructed, that it looks for all the world,—like one of my seven castles, an' please your Honor, quoth Trim.—

My uncle Toby, though in the utmost distress for a comparison, most courteously refused Trim's offer,—till Trim, telling him he had half a dozen more in Bohemia, which he knew not how to get off his hands,—my uncle Toby was so touch'd with the pleasantry of heart of the Corporal,—that he discontinued his dissertation upon gunpowder,—and begged the Corporal forthwith to go on with his story of the King of Bohemia and his seven castles.

THE STORY OF THE KING OF BOHEMIA AND HIS SEVEN CASTLES, CONTINUED.

This *unfortunate* King of Bohemia, said Trim,—Was he unfortunate, then? cried my uncle Toby, for he had been so wrapt up in his dissertation upon gunpowder, and other military affairs, that though he had desired the Corporal to go on, yet the many interruptions he had given, dwelt not so strong on his fancy as to account for the epithet.—Was he *unfortunate*, then, Trim? said my uncle Toby, pathetically.—The Corporal, wishing first the *word* and all its synonimas at the Devil, forthwith began to run back in his mind the principal events in the King of Bohemia's story; from every one of which, it appearing that he was the most fortunate man that ever existed in the world,—it put the Corporal to a stand; for not caring to retract his epithet,—and less to explain it,—and least of all to twist his tale (like men of lore) to serve a system,—he looked up in my uncle Toby's face for assistance;—but seeing it was the very thing my uncle Toby sat in expectation of himself, after a *hum* and a *haw*, he went on—

The King of Bohemia, an' please your Honor, replied the Corporal, was *unfortunate*, as thus:—That taking great pleasure and delight in navigation and all sort of sea affairs;—and there *happening* throughout the whole kingdom of Bohemia to be no sea-port town whatever,—

—How the deuce should there, Trim? cried my uncle Toby; for Bohemia being totally inland, it could have happen'd no otherwise.

—It might, said Trim, if it had pleased God.—

My uncle Toby never spoke of the being and natural attributes of God, but with diffidence and hesitation.—

I believe not, replied my uncle Toby, after some pause;—for being inland, as I said, and having Silesia and Moravia to the east; Lusatia and Upper Saxony to the north; Franconia to the west; and Bavaria to the south,—Bohemia could not have been propell'd to the sea without ceasing to be Bohemia;—nor could the sea, on the other hand, have come up to Bohemia, without overflowing a great part of Germany, and destroying millions of unfortunate inhabitants who could make no defence against it.—Scandalous, cried Trim.—Which would bespeak, added my uncle Toby, mildly, such a want of compassion in him who is the father of it,—that, I think, Trim,—the thing could have happen'd no way.—

The Corporal made the bow of unfeign'd conviction, and went on.—

Now the King of Bohemia, with his Queen and courtiers, *happening* one fine summer's evening to walk out,—Ay, there the word *happening* is right, Trim, cried my uncle Toby; for the King of Bohemia and his Queen might have walked out or let it alone:—'twas a matter of contingency which might happen or not, just as chance ordered it.—

King William was of an opinion, an' please your Honor, quoth Trim, that every thing was predestined for us in this world; insomuch, that he would often say to his soldiers, that "every ball had its billet."—He was a great man, said my uncle Toby.—And I believe, continued Trim, to this day that the shot which disabled me at the battle of Landen, was pointed at my knee for no other purpose but to take me out of his service, and place me in your Honor's, where I should be taken so much better care of in my old age.—It shall never, Trim, be construed otherwise, said my uncle Toby.—

The heart, both of the master and the man, were alike subject to sudden overflowings;—a short silence ensued.—

Besides, said the Corporal, resuming the discourse, but in a gayer accent,—if it had not been for that single shot, I had never, an' please your Honor, been in love.—

So thou wast once in love, Trim? said my uncle Toby, smiling.—

Souse! replied the Corporal,—over head and ears! an' please your Honor.—Prithee, when? where? and how came it to pass?—I never heard one word of it before, quoth my uncle Toby.—I dare say, answered Trim, that every drummer and serjeant's son in the regiment knew of it.—'Tis high time I should,—said my uncle Toby.—

Your Honor remembers with concern, said the Corporal, the total rout and confusion of our camp and army at the affair of Landen: every one was left to shift for himself; and if it had not been for the regiments of Wyndham, Lumley, and Galway, which covered the retreat over the bridge of Neerspeeken, the king himself could scarce have gained it;—he was press'd hard, as your Honor knows, on every side of him.—

Gallant mortal! cried my uncle Toby, caught with enthusiasm, this moment, now that all is lost, I see him galloping across me, Corporal, to the left, to bring up the remains of the English horse along with him, to support the right, and tear the laurel from Luxembourg's brows, if yet 'tis possible:—I see him with the knot of his scarf just shot off, infusing fresh spirits into poor Galway's regiment,—riding along the line;—then wheeling about, and charging Conti at the head of it.—Brave! brave, by Heaven! cried my uncle Toby; he deserves a crown——As richly, as a thief a halter, shouted Trim.

My uncle Toby knew the Corporal's loyalty—otherwise the comparison was not at all to his mind:—it did not altogether strike the Corporal's fancy when he had made it; —but it could not be recall'd; so he had nothing to do, but proceed.

As the number of wounded was prodigious, and no one had time to think of any thing but his own safety,—Though Talmash, said my uncle Toby, brought off the foot with great prudence.—But I was left upon the field, said the Corporal.—Thou wast so, poor fellow! replied my uncle Toby.—So that it was noon the next day, continued the Corporal, before I was exchanged, and put into a cart with thirteen or fourteen more, in order to be conveyed to our hospital.

There is no part of the body, an' please your Honor, where a wound occasions more intolerable anguish than upon the knee.—

Except the groin, said my uncle Toby.—An' please your Honor, replied the Corporal, the knee, in my opinion, must certainly be the most acute, there being so many tendons and what-d'ye-call-'ems all about it.—

It is for that reason, quoth my uncle Toby, that the groin is infinitely more sensible;—there being not only as many tendons and what-d'ye-call-'ems (for I know their names as little as thou dost)—about it,—but moreover,* * *—

Mrs. Wadman, who had been all the time in her arbor,—instantly stopp'd her breath, unpinn'd her mob at the chin, and stood up upon one leg.

The dispute was maintained with amicable and equal force betwixt my uncle Toby and Trim for some time; till Trim at length recollecting that he had often cried at his master's sufferings, but never shed a tear at his own,—was for giving up the point; which my uncle Toby would not allow.—'Tis a proof of nothing, Trim, said he, but the generosity of thy temper.

So that whether the pain of a wound in the groin (*cæteris paribus*) is greater than the pain of a wound in the knee,—or

Whether the pain of a wound in the knee is not greater than the pain of a wound in the groin,—are points which to this day remain unsettled.

CHAP. XX.

The anguish of my knee, continued the Corporal, was excessive in itself; and the uneasiness of the cart, with the roughness of the roads, which were terribly cut up,—making bad still worse,—every step was death to me; so that with the loss of blood, and the want of care-taking of me, and a fever I felt coming on besides,—(Poor soul! said my uncle Toby.)—All together, an' please your Honor, was more than I could sustain.

I was telling my sufferings to a young woman at a peasant's house, where our cart, which was the last of the line, had halted; they had help'd me in, and the young woman had taken a cordial out of her pocket and dropp'd it upon some sugar; and seeing it had cheer'd me, she had given it me a second and a third time.—So I was telling her, an' please your Honor, the anguish I was in, and was saying it was so intolerable to me, that I had much rather lie down upon the bed, turning my face towards one which was in the corner of the room,—and die,—than go on,—when, upon the attempting to lead me to it, I fainted away in her arms.—She was a good soul! as your Honor, said the Corporal, wiping his eyes, will hear.—

I thought *love* had been a joyous thing, quoth my uncle Toby.—

'Tis the most serious thing, an' please your Honor (sometimes) that is in the world.—

By the persuasion of the young woman, continued the Corporal, the cart with the wounded men set off without me; she had assured them I should expire immediately if I was put into the cart. So when I came to myself,—I found myself in a still quiet cottage, with no one but the young woman, and the peasant and his wife. I was laid across the bed in the corner of the room, with my wounded leg upon a chair, and the young woman beside me, holding the corner of her handkerchief dipp'd in vinegar to my nose with one hand, and rubbing my temples with the other.

I took her at first for the daughter of the peasant (for it was no inn);—so had offer'd her a little purse with eighteen florins, which my poor brother Tom (here Trim wip'd his eyes) had sent me as a token, by a recruit, just before he set out for Lisbon.

I never told your Honor that piteous story yet,—(Here Trim wip'd his eyes a third time.)

The young woman call'd the old man and his wife into the room to show them the money, in order to gain me credit for a bed and what little necessaries I should want, till I should be in a condition to be got to the hospital.—Come then, said she, tying up the little purse,—I'll be your banker;—but as that office alone will not keep me employ'd, I'll be your nurse too.—

I thought by her manner of speaking this, as well as by her dress, which I then began to consider more attentively,—that the young woman could not be the daughter of the peasant.

She was in black down to her toes, with her hair concealed under a cambric border, laid close to her forehead: she was one of those kind of nuns, an' please your Honor, of which your Honor knows there are a good many in Flanders, which they let go loose.—By thy description, Trim, said my uncle Toby, I dare say she was a young Beguine, of which there are none to be found anywhere but in the Spanish Netherlands,—except at Amsterdam:—they differ from nuns in this, that they can quit their cloister if they choose to marry; they visit and take care of the sick by profession. I had rather, for my own part, they did it out of good-nature.—

She often told me, quoth Trim, she did it for the love of Christ.—I did not like it.—I believe, Trim, we are both wrong, said my uncle Toby:—we'll ask Mr. Yorick about it to-night, at my brother Shandy's; so put me in mind, added my uncle Toby.—

The young Beguine, continued the Corporal, had scarce given herself time to tell me, "she would be my nurse," when she hastily turned about to begin the office of one, and prepare something for me;—and in a short time,—though I thought it a long one,—she came back with flannels, &c. &c. and having fomented my knee soundly for a couple of hours, &c. and made me a bason of thin gruel for my supper,—she wish'd me rest, and promised to be with me early in the morning.—She wish'd me, an' please your Honor, what was not to be had.—My fever ran very high that night;—her figure made sad disturbance within me;—I was every moment cutting the world in two,—to give her half of it;—and every moment was I crying, That I had nothing but a knapsack and eighteen florins to share with her.—The whole night long was the fair Beguine, like an angel, close by my bed-side, holding back my curtain, and offering me cordials;—and I was only awakened from my dream by her coming there at the hour promised, and giving them in reality. —In truth, she was scarce ever from me; and so accustomed was I to receive life from her hands, that my heart sickened, and I lost color, when she left the room; and yet, continued the Corporal (making one of the strangest reflections upon it, in the world)—

"It was not love;"—for during the three weeks she was almost constantly with me, fomenting my knee with her hand night and day,—I can honestly say, an' please your Honor,—that * once.—

That was very odd, Trim, quoth my uncle Toby.—

I think so too,—said Mrs. Wadman.

It never did, said the Corporal.

CHAP. XXI.

—But 'tis no marvel, continued the Corporal,—seeing my uncle Toby musing upon it,—for love, an' please your Honor, is exactly like war, in this; that a soldier, though he has escaped three weeks complete o' Saturday night,—may, nevertheless, be shot through his heart on Sunday morning.—*It happened so here*, an' please your Honor, with this difference only,—that it was on Sunday in the afternoon, when I fell in love all at once with a *sisserara*.—It burst upon me, an' please your Honor, like a bomb,—scarce giving me time to say, "God bless me."—

I thought, Trim, said my uncle Toby, a man never fell in love so very suddenly.—

Yes, an' please your Honor, if he is in the way of it,—replied Trim.

I prithee, quoth my uncle Toby, inform me how this matter happened.—

With all pleasure, said the Corporal, making a bow.

CHAP. XXII.

I HAD escaped, continued the Corporal, all that time from falling in love, and had gone on to the end of the chapter, had it not been predestined otherwise.—There is no resisting our fate.—It was on a Sunday, in the afternoon, as I told your Honor.

The old man and his wife had walked out.—

Every thing was still and hush as midnight about the house.

There was not so much as a duck or a duckling about the yard,—

When the fair Beguine came in to see me.

My wound was then in a fair way of doing well,—the inflammation had been gone off for some time; but it was succeeded with an itching both above and below my knee, so insufferable, that I had not shut my eyes the whole night for it.—

Let me see it, said she, kneeling down upon the ground parallel to my knee, and laying her hand upon the part below it.—It only wants rubbing a little, said the Beguine; so covering it with the bed-clothes, she began with the fore-finger of her right hand to rub under my knee, guiding her fore-finger backwards and forwards by the edge of the flannel which kept on the dressing.

In five or six minutes I felt slightly the end of her second finger, and presently it was laid flat with the other, and she continued rubbing in that way round and round for a good while; it then came into my head, that I should fall in love:—I blush'd when I saw how white a hand she had.—I shall never, an please your Honor, behold another hand so white whilst I live.—

Not in that place, said my uncle Toby.—

Though it was the most serious despair in nature to the Corporal,—he could not forbear smiling.—

The young Beguine, continued the Corporal, perceiving it was of great service to me,—from rubbing for some time with two fingers,—proceeded to rub at length with three, -till by little and little she brought down the fourth, and then rubb'd with her whole hand. I will never say another word, an' please your Honor, upon hands again;—but it was softer than satin.—

—Prithee, Trim, commend it as much as thou wilt, said my uncle Toby; I shall hear thy story with the more delight.—The Corporal thank'd his master most unfeignedly; but having nothing to say upon the Beguine's hand but the same over again,—he proceeded to the effects of it.

The fair Beguine, said the Corporal, continued rubbing with her whole hand under my knee,—till I fear'd her zeal would weary her.—"I would do a thousand times more," said she, "for the love of Christ."—In saying which, she pass'd her hand across the flannel, to the part above my knee, which I had equally complain'd of, and rubb'd it also.

I perceived then, I was beginning to be in love.—

As she continued rub-rub-rubbing, I felt it spread from under her hand, an' please your Honor, to every part of my frame.

The more she rubb'd, and the longer strokes she took, the more the fire kindled in my veins,—till at length, by two or three strokes longer than the rest, my passion rose to the highest pitch.—I seiz'd her hand,—

And then thou clapped'st it to thy lips, Trim, said my uncle Toby, and madest a speech.

Whether the Corporal's amour terminated precisely in the way my uncle Toby described it, is not material; it is enough that it contained in it the essence of all the love-romances which ever have been wrote since the beginning of the world.

CHAP. XXIII.

As soon as the Corporal had finished the story of his amour,—or rather my uncle Toby for him,—Mrs. Wadman silently sallied forth from her arbor, replaced the pin in her mob, pass'd the wicker-gate, and advanced slowly towards my uncle Toby's sentry-box: the disposition which Trim had made in my uncle Toby's mind, was too favorable a crisis to be let slip.

—The attack was determin'd upon: it was facilitated still more by my uncle

Toby's having ordered the Corporal to wheel off the pioneer's shovel, the spade, the pick-ax, the piquets, and other military stores which lay scatter'd upon the ground where Dunkirk stood.—The Corporal had march'd;—the field was clear.

Now, consider, Sir, what nonsense it is, either in fighting, or writing, or any thing else (whether in rhyme to it, or not) which a man has occasion to do,—to act by plan: for if ever Plan, independent of all circumstances, deserved registering in letters of gold (I mean in the archives of Gotham)—it was certainly the Plan of Mrs. Wadman's attack of my uncle Toby in his sentry-box, *by plan.*—Now, the plan hanging up in it at this juncture, being the plan of Dunkirk, —and the tale of Dunkirk a tale of relaxation, it opposed every impression she could make: and, besides, could she have gone upon it, — the manœuvre of fingers and hands in the attack of the sentry-box, was so outdone by that of the fair Beguine's, in Trim's story,—that just then, that particular attack, however successful before,—became the most heartless attack that could be made.

O! let woman alone for this. Mrs. Wadman had scarce open'd the wicker-gate, when her genius sported with the change of circumstances.

She formed a new attack in a moment.

CHAP. XXIV.

—I am half distracted, Captain Shandy, said Mrs. Wadman, holding up her cambric handkerchief to her left eye, as she approach'd the door of my uncle Toby's sentry-box; a mote,—or sand,—or something,—I know not what, has got into this eye of mine;—do look into it:—it is not in the white.—

In saying which, Mrs. Wadman edged herself close in beside my uncle Toby, and squeezing herself down upon the corner of his bench, she gave him an opportunity of doing it without rising up,—Do look into it, said she.

Honest soul! thou didst look into it with as much innocency of heart as ever child look'd into a raree show-box; and 'twere as much a sin to have hurt thee.

If a man will be peeping of his own accord into things of that nature, I've nothing to say to it.

My uncle Toby never did; and I will answer for him, that he would have sat quietly upon a sofa from June to January (which, you know, takes in both the hot and cold months) with an eye as fine as the Thracian * Rhodope's beside him, without being able to tell whether it was a black or a blue one.

The difficulty was, to get my uncle Toby to look at one at all.

'Tis surmounted. And

I see him yonder, with his pipe pendulous in his hand, and the ashes falling out of it, — looking, — and looking, — then rubbing his eyes,—and looking again, with twice the good-nature that ever Galileo look'd for a spot in the sun.

In vain! for, by all the powers which animate the organ,—Widow Wadman's left eye shines this moment as lucid as her right;—there is neither mote, nor sand, nor dust, nor chaff, nor speck, nor particle of opake matter floating in it.—There is nothing, my dear paternal uncle! but one lambent delicious fire, furtively shooting out from every part of it, in all directions, into thine.

If thou lookest, uncle Toby, in search of this mote one moment longer, thou art undone.

CHAP. XXV.

An eye is, for all the world, exactly like a cannon, in this respect, That it is not so much the eye or the cannon, in themselves, as it is the carriage of the eye—and the carriage of the cannon; by which both the one and the other are enabled to do so much execution. I don't think the comparison a bad one: however, as 'tis made and placed at the head of the chapter, as much for use as ornament, all I desire in return, is, that whenever I speak of Mrs. Wadman's eyes (except once in the next period) that you keep it in your fancy.

* Rhodope Thracia tam inevitabili fascino instructo, tam exactè oculis intuens attraxit, ut si in illam quis incidisset, fieri non posset, quin caperetur.—I KNOW NOT WHO.

I protest, Madam, said my uncle Toby, I can see nothing whatever in your eye.

—It is not in the white, said Mrs. Wadman.—My uncle Toby look'd with might and main into the pupil.

Now, of all the eyes which ever were created; from your own, Madam, up to those of Venus herself, which certainly were as venereal a pair of eyes as ever stood in a head, there never was an eye of them all so fitted to rob my uncle Toby of his repose, as the very eye at which he was looking;—it was not, Madam, a rolling eye,—a romping, or a wanton one;—nor was it an eye sparkling, petulant, or imperious,—of high claims and terrifying exactions, which would have curdled at once that milk of human nature, of which my uncle Toby was made up;—but 'twas an eye full of gentle salutations,—and soft responses,—speaking,—not like the trumpet-stop of some ill-made organ, in which many an eye I talk to holds coarse converse, but whispering soft,—like the last low accents of an expiring saint,—"How can you live comfortless, "Captain Shandy, and alone, without a "bosom to lean your head on,—or trust "your cares to?"

It was an eye——

But I shall be in love with it myself, if I say another word about it.

It did my uncle Toby's business.

CHAP. XXVI.

There is nothing shows the characters of my father and my uncle Toby in a more entertaining light, than their different manner of deportment under the same accident;—for I call not love a misfortune; from a persuasion, that a man's heart is ever the better for it.—Great God! what must my uncle Toby's have been, when 'twas all benignity without it!—

My father, as appears from many of his papers, was very subject to this passion before he married;—but, from a little subacid kind of drollish impatience in his nature, whenever it befell him, he would never submit to it like a Christian; but would pish, and huff, and bounce, and kick, and play the Devil, and write the bitterest Philippics against the eye that ever man wrote:—there is one in verse upon somebody's eye or other, that, for two or three nights together, had put him by his rest; which, in his first transport of resentment against it, he begins thus:—

> "A devil 'tis—and mischief such doth work
> "As never yet did Pagan, Jew, or Turk."*

In short, during the whole paroxysm, my father was all abuse and foul language, approaching rather towards malediction;—only he did not do it with as much method as Ernulphus;—he was too impetuous; nor with Ernulphus's policy;—for though my father, with the most intolerant spirit, would curse both this and that, and every thing under Heaven, which was either aiding or abetting to his love,—yet he never concluded his chapter of curses upon it, without cursing himself in at the bargain, as one of the most egregious fools and coxcombs, he would say, that ever was let loose in the world.

My uncle Toby, on the contrary, took it like a lamb,—sat still, and let the poison work in his veins without resistance;—in the sharpest exacerbations of his wound (like that on his groin) he never dropt one fretful or discontented word,—he blamed neither heaven nor earth,—nor thought, nor spoke an injurious thing of any body, or any part of it; he sat solitary and pensive with his pipe,—looking at his lame leg,—then whiffing out a sentimental heigh-ho! which, mixing with the smoke, incommoded no one mortal.

He took it like a lamb, I say.

In truth, he had mistook it at first; for, having taken a ride with my father that very morning, to save, if possible, a beautiful wood, which the dean and chapter were hewing down to give to the poor;† which said wood being in full view of my uncle Toby's house, and of singular service to him in his description of the battle of Wynnendale,—by trotting on too hastily to save it, upon an uneasy saddle, worse horse. &c. &c. . . it had so happened, that the serous part of the blood had got betwixt the two skins, in the nethermost part of my un-

* This will be printed with my father's Life of Socrates, &c.

† Mr. Shandy must mean the poor in spirit! inasmuch as they divided the money amongst themselves

cle Toby,—the first shootings of which (as my uncle Toby had no experience of love) he had taken for a part of the passion, till the blister breaking in the one case, and the other remaining, my uncle Toby was presently convinced that his wound was not a skin-deep wound, but that it had gone to his heart.

CHAP. XXVII.

THE world is ashamed of being virtuous. —My uncle Toby knew little of the world; and therefore, when he felt he was in love with Widow Wadman, he had no conception that the thing was any more to be made a mystery of, than if Mrs. Wadman had given him a cut with a gap'd knife across his finger. Had it been otherwise,—yet, as he ever look'd upon Trim as an humble friend, and saw fresh reasons every day of his life to treat him as such,—it would have made no variation in the manner in which he informed him of the affair.

"I am in love, Corporal!" quoth my uncle Toby.

CHAP. XXVIII.

IN love!—said the Corporal,—your Honor was very well the day before yesterday, when I was telling your Honor the story of the King of Bohemia.—Bohemia! said my uncle Toby - - - - musing a long time - - - - What became of that story, Trim?

—We lost it, an' please your Honor, somehow betwixt us;—but your Honor was as free from love then, as I am.—'Twas just whilst thou went'st off with the wheel-barrow,—with Mrs. Wadman, quoth my uncle Toby.—She has left a ball here, added my uncle Toby, pointing to his breast.

—She can no more, an' please your Honor, stand a siege, than she can fly, cried the Corporal.

But as we are neighbors, Trim, the best way, I think, is to let her know it civilly first, quoth my uncle Toby.

Now, if I might presume, said the Corporal, to differ from your Honor,—

Why else do I talk to thee, Trim? said my uncle Toby, mildly.

—Then I would begin, an' please your Honor, with making a good thundering attack upon her, in return,—and telling her civilly afterwards;—for if she knows any thing of your Honor's being in love, beforehand——L—d help her!—she knows no more at present of it, Trim, said my uncle Toby,—than the child unborn.

Precious souls!—

Mrs. Wadman had told it, with all its circumstances, to Mrs. Bridget, twenty-four hours before; and was, at that very moment, sitting in council with her, touching some slight misgivings with regard to the issue of the affair, which the Devil, who never lies dead in a ditch, had put into her head, —before he would allow her half time to get quietly through her *Te Deum.*

I am terribly afraid, said Widow Wadman, in case I should marry him, Bridget, —that the poor Captain will not enjoy his health, with the monstrous wound upon his groin.

—It may not, Madam, be so very large, replied Bridget, as you think;—and I believe, besides, added she,—that 'tis dried up.

—I could like to know,—merely for his sake, said Mrs. Wadman.

—We'll know the long and the broad of it in ten days, answered Mrs. Bridget; for whilst the Captain is paying his addresses to you,—I'm confident Mr. Trim will be for making love to me;—and I'll let him as much as he will, added Bridget, to get it all out of him.

The measures were taken at once;—and my uncle Toby and the Corporal went on with theirs.

Now, quoth the Corporal, setting his left hand a-kimbo, and giving such a flourish with his right, as just promised success,—and no more,—if your Honor will give me leave to lay down the plan of this attack,—

Thou wilt please me by it, Trim, said my uncle Toby, exceedingly;—and as I foresee thou must act in it as my *aid-de-camp*, here's a crown, Corporal, to begin with, to steep thy commission.

—Then, an' please your Honor, said the Corporal, (making a bow first for his commission)—we will begin with getting your Honor's laced clothes out of the great can paign-trunk, to be well air'd, and have the blue and gold taken up at the sleeves;—and I'll put your white ramillie-wig fresh into pipes;—and send for a taylor to have your Honor's thin scarlet breeches turn'd.—

I had better take the red plush ones, quoth my uncle Toby.—They will be too clumsy, said the Corporal.

CHAP. XXIX.

—Thou wilt get a brush and a little chalk to my sword.—'Twill be only in your Honor's way, replied Trim.

CHAP. XXX.

—But your Honor's two razors shall be new set—and I will get my Montero-cap furbish'd up, and put on poor Lieutenant Le Fevre's regimental coat, which your Honor gave me to wear for his sake;—and as soon as your Honor is clean shaved,—and has got your clean shirt on, with your blue and gold or your fine scarlet,—sometimes one and sometimes t'other,—and every thing is ready for the attack,—we'll march up boldly, as if 'twas to the face of a bastion; and whilst your Honor engages Mrs. Wadman in the parlor, to the right.—I'll attack Mrs. Bridget in the kitchen, to the left; and having seiz'd that pass, I'll answer for it, said the Corporal, snapping his fingers over his head,—that the day is your own.

—I wish I may but manage it right, said my uncle Toby;—but I declare, Corporal, I had rather march up to the very edge of a trench.

—A woman is quite a different thing, said the Corporal.

—I suppose so, quoth my uncle Toby.

CHAP. XXXI.

If any thing in this world which my father said, could have provoked my uncle Toby, during the time he was in love, it was the perverse use my father was always making of an expression of Hilarion, the hermit; who, in speaking of his abstinence. his watchings, flagellations, and other instrumental parts of his religion,—would say —though with more facetiousness than became a hermit, "That they were the means " he used to make his *ass* (meaning his body) " leave off kicking."

It pleased my father well; it was not only a laconic way of expressing,—but of libelling, at the same time, the desires and appetites of the lower part of us; so that for many years of my father's life, 'twas his constant mode of expression;—he never used the word *passions* once,—but *ass* always, instead of them;—so that he might be said truly to have been upon the bones, or the back of his own ass, or else of some other man's, during all that time.

I must here observe to you the difference betwixt

My father's Ass and

My Hobby-Horse,—in order to keep characters as separate as may be, in our fancies as we go along.

For my Hobby-Horse, if you recollect a little, is no way a vicious beast; he has scarce one hair or lineament of the ass about him. —'Tis the sporting little filly-folly which carries you out for the present hour,—a maggot, a butterfly, a picture, a fiddle-stick, —an uncle Toby's siege, or an *any thing* which a man makes a shift to get astride on, to canter it away from the cares and solicitudes of life.—'Tis as useful a beast as is in the whole creation;—nor do I really see how the world could do without it.

—But for my father's ass.—Oh! mount him,—mount him,—mount him,—(that's three times, is it not?)—mount him not:— 'tis a beast concupiscent;—and foul befall the man who does not hinder him from kicking.

CHAP. XXXII.

Well, dear brother Toby, said my father, upon his first seeing him after he fell in love,—and how goes it with your Ass?

Now, my uncle Toby thinking more of the *part* where he had had the blister, than of Hilarion's metaphor,—and our preconceptions having (you know) as great a power over the sounds of words as the shapes of things, he had imagined that my father, who was not very ceremonious in his choice of words, had inquired after the part by its proper name: so, notwithstanding my mother, Dr. Slop, and Mr. Yorick, were sitting in the parlor, he thought it rather civil to conform to the term my father had made use of than not. When a man is hemm'd in by two indecorums, and must commit one of 'em, I always observe,—let him choose which he will, the world will blame him; —so I should not be astonish'd if it blames my uncle Toby.

My a—e, quoth my uncle Toby, is much better, brother Shandy.—My father had formed great expectations from his Ass in this onset: and would have brought him on again; but Doctor Slop setting up an intemperate laugh, and my mother crying out L—— bless us!—it drove my father's Ass off the field:—and the laugh then becoming general,—there was no bringing him back to the charge for some time:—

And so the discourse went on without him.

Every body, said my mother, says you are in love, brother Toby;—and we hope it is true.

I am as much in love, sister, I believe, replied my uncle Toby, as any man usually is.—Humph! said my father.—And when did you know it? quoth my mother.

—When the blister broke, replied my uncle Toby.

My uncle Toby's reply put my father into good temper,—so he charged o' foot.

CHAP. XXXIII.

As the ancients agree, brother Toby, said my father, that there are two different and distinct kinds of *love*, according to the different parts which are affected by it,—the brain or liver,—I think when a man is in love, it behoves him a little to consider which of the two he has fallen into.

—What signifies it, brother Shandy, replied my uncle Toby, which of the two it is, provided it will but make a man marry, and love his wife, and get a few children?

—A few children! cried my father, rising out of his chair, and looking full in my mother's face, as he forced his way betwixt hers and Doctor Slop's,—a few children! cried my father, repeating my uncle Toby's words as he walked to and fro.

Not, my dear brother Toby, cried my father, recovering himself all at once, and coming close up to the back of my uncle Toby's chair,—not that I should be sorry hadst thou a score:—on the contrary, I should rejoice,—and be as kind, Toby, to every one of them as a father.—

My uncle Toby stole his hand, unperceived, behind his chair, to give my father's a squeeze.—

Nay, moreover continued he, keeping hold of my uncle Toby's hand,—so much dost thou possess, my dear Toby, of the milk of human nature, and so little of its asperities,—'tis piteous the world is not peopled by creatures which resemble thee! and was I an Asiatic monarch, added my father, heating himself with his new project,—I would oblige thee, provided it would not impair thy strength,—or dry up thy radical moisture too fast,—or weaken thy memory, or fancy, brother Toby, which these gymnics, inordinately taken, are apt to do,—else, dear Toby, I would procure thee the most beautiful women in my empire, and I would oblige thee, *nolens volens*, to beget for me one subject every *month*.

As my father pronounced the last word of the sentence,—my mother took a pinch of snuff.—

Now I would not, quoth my uncle Toby, get a child, *nolens volens*, that is, whether I would or no, to please the greatest prince upon earth.—

And 'twould be cruel in me, brother Toby, to compel thee, said my father;—but 'tis a case put, to show thee, that it is not thy begetting a child,—in case thou should'st be able,—but the system of Love and Marriage thou goest upon, which I would set thee right in.—

There is, at least, said Yorick, a great deal of reason and plain sense in Captain Shandy's opinion of love; and 'tis amongst the ill-spent hours of my life, which I have to answer for, that I have read so many flourishing poets and rhetoricians in my time from whom I never could extract so much.—

I wish, Yorick, said my father, you had read Plato: for there you would have learnt that there are two *loves*.—I know there were two *religions*, replied Yorick, amongst the ancients;—one for the vulgar, and another for the learned:—but I think *one love* might have served both of them very well.—

It could not, replied my father,—and for the same reasons; for, of these loves, according to Ficinus's comment upon Velasius, the one is rational,—

The other is *natural;*—

the first ancient,—without mother,—where Venus had nothing to do; the second begotten of Jupiter and Dione,—

Pray, brother, quoth my uncle Toby, what has a man who believes in God to do with this?—My father could not stop to answer, for fear of breaking the thread of his discourse.—

This latter, continued he, partakes wholly of the nature of Venus.

The first, which is the golden chain let down from Heaven, excites to love heroic, which comprehends in it, and excites to, the desire of philosophy and truth;—the second excites to *desire* simply.—

I think the procreation of children as beneficial to the world, said Yorick, as the finding out the longitude.

To be sure, said my mother, *love* keeps peace in the world.—

In the *house*,—my dear, I own.—

It replenishes the earth, said my mother.

But it keeps Heaven empty, my dear,—replied my father.

'Tis Virginity, cried Slop, triumphantly, which fills Paradise.—

Well push'd, nun! quoth my father.

CHAP. XXXIV.

My father had such a skirmishing, cutting kind of a slashing way with him in his disputations, thrusting and ripping, and giving every one a stroke to remember him by, in his turn, that if there were twenty people in company,—in less than half an hour he was sure to have every one of 'em against him.

What did not a little contribute to leave him thus without an ally, was, that if there was any one post more untenable than the rest, he would be sure to throw himself into it; and to do him justice, when he was once there, he would defend it so gallantly, that 'twould have been a concern, either to a brave man, or a good-natured one, to have seen him driven out.

Yorick, for this reason, though he would often attack him,—yet could never bear to do it with all his force.

Doctor Slop's *Virginity*, in the close of the last chapter, had got him for once on the right side of the rampart; and he was beginning to blow up all the convents in Christendom about Slop's ears, when Corporal Trim came into the parlor to inform my uncle Toby, that his thin scarlet breeches, in which the attack was to be made upon Mrs. Wadman, would not do; for that the taylor, in ripping them up, in order to turn them, had found that they had been turn'd before.—Then turn them again, brother, said my father, rapidly, for there will be many a turning of 'em yet before all's done in the affair.—They are as rotten as dirt, said the Corporal.—Then by all means, said my father, bespeak a new pair, brother;—for though I know, continued my father, turning himself to the company, that Widow Wadman has been deeply in love with my brother Toby for many years, and has used every art and circumvention of woman to outwit him into the same passion, yet now that she has caught him,—her fever will be past its height.

She has gained her point.

In this case, continued my father, which Plato, I am persuaded, never thought of,—Love, you see, is not so much a *sentiment* as a *situation*, into which a man enters, as my brother Toby would do into a *corps*,—no matter whether he loves the service or no; being once in it,—he acts as if he did, and takes every step to show himself a man of prowess.

The hypothesis, like the rest of my father's, was plausible enough, and my uncle Toby had but a single word to object to it,—in which Trim stood ready to second him;—but my father had not drawn his conclusion.—

For this reason, continued my father, (stating the case over again)—notwithstanding all the world knows that Mrs. Wadman *affects* my brother Toby;—and my brother Toby contrariwise *affects* Mrs. Wadman, and no obstacle in nature to forbid the music striking up this very night, yet will I answer for it, that this self-same tune will not be play'd this twelvemonth.

We have taken our measures badly, quoth my uncle Toby, looking up interrogatively in Trim's face.—

I would lay my Montero-cap, said Trim.—

Now Trim's Montero-cap, as I once told you, was his constant wager; and having furbish'd it up that very night, in order to go upon the attack,—it made the odds look more considerable.—I would lay, an' please your Honor, my Montero-cap to a shilling, —was it proper, continued Trim (making a bow) to offer a wager before your Honors.—

There is nothing improper in it, said my father,—'tis a mode of expression; for in saying thou would'st lay thy Montero-cap to a shilling,—all thou meanest is this,—that thou believest,—

Now, what dost thou believe?

That Widow Wadman, an' please your Worship, cannot hold it out ten days.—

And whence, cried Slop, jeeringly, hast thou all this knowledge of woman, friend?—

By falling in love with a popish clergywoman, said Trim.—

'Twas a Beguine, said my uncle Toby.—

Doctor Slop was too much in wrath to listen to the distinction; and my father taking that very crisis to fall in helter-skelter upon the whole order of Nuns and Beguines, a set of silly, fusty baggages,—Slop could not stand it;—and my uncle Toby having some measures to take about his breeches,—and Yorick about his fourth general division,—in order for their several attacks next day,—the company broke up; and my father being left alone, and having half an hour upon his hands betwixt that and bed-time, he called for pen, ink, and paper, and wrote my uncle Toby the following letter of instructions:

My dear brother Toby,

What I am going to say to thee, is upon the nature of women, and of love-making to them; and perhaps it is as well for thee, —though not so well for me,—that thou hast occasion for a letter of instructions upon that head, and that I am able to write it to thee.

Had it been the good pleasure of Him who disposes of our lots, and thou no sufferer by the knowledge, I had been well content that thou should'st have dipp'd the pen this moment into the ink, instead of myself; but that not being the case,—Mrs. Shandy being now close beside me, preparing for bed, —I have thrown together, without order, and just as they have come into my mind, such hints and documents as I deem may be of use to thee, intending, in this, to give thee a token of my love; not doubting, my dear Toby, of the manner in which it will be accepted.

In the first place, with regard to all which concerns religion in the affair,—though I perceive, from a glow in my cheek, that I blush as I begin to speak to thee upon the subject, as well knowing notwithstanding thy unaffected secrecy, how few of its offices thou neglectest,—yet I would remind thee of one (during the continuance of thy courtship) in a particular manner, which I would not have omitted; and that is, never to go forth upon the enterprise, whether it be in the morning or the afternoon, without first recommending thyself to the protection of Almighty God, that he may defend thee from the evil one.

Shave the whole top of thy crown clean once at least every four or five days, but oftener if convenient; lest, in taking off thy wig before her, through absence of mind, she should be able to discover how much has been cut away by Time:—how much by Trim.

'Twere better to keep ideas of baldness out of her fancy.

Always carry it in thy mind, and act upon it as a sure maxim, Toby,—

"That women are timid;" and 'tis well they are,—else there would be no dealing with them.

Let not thy breeches be too tight, or hang too loose about thy thighs, like the trunk-hose of our ancestors:

A just medium prevents all conclusions.

Whatever thou hast to say, be it more or less, forget not to utter it in a low soft tone of voice;—silence, and whatever approaches it, weaves dreams of midnight secrecy into the brain; for this cause, if thou canst help it, never throw down the tongs and poker.

Avoid all kinds of pleasantry and facetiousness in thy discourse with her, and do whatever lies in thy power, at the same time, to keep from her all books and writings which tend thereto: there are some devotional tracts, which if thou canst entice her to read over,—it will be well; but suffer her not to look into Rabelais, or Scarron, or Don Quixote:

They are all books which excite laughter; and thou knowest, dear Toby, that there is no passion so serious as lust.

Stick a pin in the bosom of thy shirt, before thou enterest her parlor.

And if thou art permitted to sit upon the same sofa with her, and she gives thee occasion to lay thy hand upon hers—beware of taking it;—thou canst not lay thy hand on hers, but she will feel the temper of thine. — Leave that and as many other things as thou canst, quite undetermined; by so doing, thou wilt have her curiosity on thy side; and if she is not conquered by that, and thy *ass* continues still kicking, which there is great reason to suppose,—thou must begin with first losing a few ounces of blood below the ears, according to the practice of the ancient Scythians, who cured the most intemperate fits of the appetite by that means.

Avicenna, after this, is for having the part anointed with the syrup of hellebore, using proper evacuations and purges;—and I believe rightly.—But thou must eat little or no goat's flesh, nor red deer;—nor even foal's flesh by any means;—and carefully abstain, — that is, as much as thou canst, from peacocks, cranes, coots, didappers, and water-hens.

As for thy drink, I need not tell thee, it must be the infusion of *Vervain* and the herb *Hanea*, of which Ælian relates such effects;—but if thy stomach palls with it, —discontinue it from time to time,—taking cucumbers, melons, purslain, water-lilies, woodbine, and lettuce in the stead of them.

There is nothing further for thee which occurs to me at present,

Unless the breaking out of a fresh war —So wishing every thing, dear Toby, for the best,

I rest thy affectionate brother,

WALTER SHANDY.

CHAP. XXXV.

WHILST my father was writing his letter of instructions, my uncle Toby and the Corporal were busy in preparing every thing for the attack. As the turning of the thin scarlet breeches was laid aside (at least for the present) there was nothing which should put it off beyond the next morning; so, accordingly, it was resolved upon for eleven o'clock.

Come, my dear, said my father to my mother, 'twill be but like a brother and sister, if you and I take a walk down to my brother Toby's, — to countenance him in this attack of his.

My uncle Toby and the Corporal had both been accoutred some time, when my father and mother enter'd, and the clock striking eleven, were that moment in motion to sally forth;—but the account of this is worth more than to be wove into the fag-end of the eighth* volume of such a work as this.—My father had no time but to put the letter of instructions into my uncle Toby's coat-pocket, and join with my mother in wishing his attack prosperous.

I could like, said my mother, to look through the key-hole, out of *curiosity.*— Call it by its right name, my dear, quoth my father,—

And look through the key-hole as long as you will.

---

* Alluding to the first edition.

A

DEDICATION

TO

A GREAT MAN.

Having, *a priori*, intended to dedicate The Amours of my uncle Toby to Mr. * * *, —I see more reasons, *a posteriori*, for doing it to Lord * * * * * * *.

I should lament from my soul, if this exposed me to the jealousy of their Reverences: because, *a posteriori*, in Court Latin, signifies the kissing hands for preferment,—or any thing else,—in order to get it.

My opinion of Lord * * * * * * * is neither better nor worse than it was of Mr. * * *. Honors, like impressions upon coin, may give an ideal and local value to a bit of base metal; but gold and silver will pass all the world over, without any other recommendation than their own weight.

The same good-will that made me think of offering up half an hour's amusement to Mr. * * * when out of place, operates more forcibly at present, as half an hour's amusement will be more serviceable and refreshing after labor and sorrow, that after a philosophical repast.

Nothing is so perfectly *amusement* as a total change of ideas; no ideas are so totally different as those of Ministers and innocent Lovers: for which reason, when I come to talk of Statesmen and Patriots, and set such marks upon them as will prevent confusion and mistake concerning them for the future,—I propose to dedicate that volume to some gentle Shepherd,

Whose thoughts proud Science never taught to stray,
Far as the Statesman's walk or Patriot's way;
Yet *simple Nature* to his hopes had given,
Out of a cloud-capp'd hill, an humbler heaven;
Some *untam'd* World in depth of woods embrac'd—
Some happier Island in the wat'ry waste—
And where, admitted to that equal sky,
His *faithful Dog* shall bear him company.

In a word, by thus introducing an entire new set of objects to his imagination, I shall unavoidably give a *Diversion* to his passionate and love-sick contemplations. In the mean time,

I am

The Author.

4

THE

LIFE AND OPINIONS

OF

Tristram Shandy,

GENTLEMAN.

CHAP. I.

I CALL all the powers of time and chance, which severally check us in our careers in this world, to bear me witness, that I could never yet get fairly to my uncle Toby's amours, till this very moment, that my mother's *curiosity*, as she stated the affair,—or a different impulse in her, as my father would have it,—wished her to take a peep at them through the key-hole.

"Call it, my dear, by its right name," quoth my father, "and look through the key-hole as long as you will."

Nothing but the fermentation of that little subacid humor, which I have often spoken of, in my father's habit, could have vented such an insinuation;—he was, however, frank and generous in his nature, and at all times open to conviction; so that he had scarce got to the last word of this ungracious retort, when his conscience smote him.

My mother was then conjugally swinging with her left arm twisted under his right, in such wise, that the inside of her hand rested upon the back of his;—she raised her fingers, and let them fall,—it could scarce be called a tap; or, if it was a tap,—'twould have puzzled a casuist to say, whether 'twas a tap of remonstrance or a tap of confession; my father, who was all sensibilities from head to foot, class'd it right;—Conscience redoubled her blow,—he turn'd his face suddenly the other way, and my mother, supposing his body was about to turn with it, in order to move homewards, by a cross-movement of her right leg, keeping her left as its centre, brought herself so far in front, that, as he turned his head, he met her eye: —Confusion again! he saw a thousand reasons to wipe out the reproach, and as many to reproach himself:—a thin, blue, chill, pellucid crystal, with all its humors so at rest, the least mote or speck of desire might have been seen at the bottom of it, had it existed;—it did not:—and how I happen to be so lewd myself, particularly a little before the vernal and autumnal equinoxes,—Heaven above knows;—my mother, Madam, was so at no time, either by nature, by institution, or example.

A temperate current of blood ran orderly through her veins in all months of the year, and in all critical moments both of the day and night alike; nor did she superinduce the least heat into her humors from the manual effervescences of devotional tracts, which, having little or no meaning in them, nature is oftentimes obliged to find one; and, as for my father's example! 'twas so far from being either aiding or abetting thereunto, that 'twas the whole business of his life to keep all fancies of that kind out of her head;—Nature had done her part to have spared him this trouble; and, what was not a little inconsistent, my father knew it. —And here am I sitting, this 12th day of August, 1766, in a purple jerkin and yellow pair of slippers, without either wig or cap on, a most tragi-comical completion of his prediction, "That I should neither think nor "act like any other man's child, upon that "very account."

The mistake of my father was, in attacking my mother's motive instead of the act itself; for, certainly, key-holes were made for other purposes; and, considering the act as an act which interfered with a true proposition, and denied a key-hole to be what i was,—it became a violation of nature; and was so far, you see, criminal.

It is for this reason, an' please your Reverences, that key-holes are the occasions of more sin and wickedness than all the other holes in this world put together:

—Which leads me to my uncle Toby's amours.

CHAP. II.

Though the Corporal had been as good as his word in putting my uncle Toby's great ramillie-wig into pipes, yet the time was too short to produce any great effects from it: it had lain many years squeezed up in the corner of his old campaign-trunk; and as bad forms are not so easy to be got the better of, and the use of candle-ends not so well understood, it was not so pliable a business as one would have wished. The Corporal, with cheery eye and both arms extended, had fallen back perpendicular from it a score of times, to inspire it, if possible, with a better air:—had *Spleen* given a look at it, 'twould have cost her ladyship a smile; —it curl'd everywhere but where the Corporal would have it; and where a buckle or two, in his opinion, would have done it honor, he could as soon have raised the dead.

Such it was,—or, rather, such would it have seem'd upon any other brow;—but the sweet look of goodness which sat upon my uncle Toby's assimilated every thing around it so sovereignly to itself, and Nature had, moreover, wrote *Gentleman* with so fair a hand in every line of his countenance, that even his tarnish'd gold-lac'd hat and huge cockade of flimsy taffety became him; and, though not worth a button in themselves, yet the moment my uncle Toby put them on, they became serious objects, and, altogether, seem'd to have been picked up by the hand of Science to set him off to advantage.

Nothing in this world could have co-operated more powerfully towards this, than my uncle Toby's blue and gold,—*had not Quantity, in some measure, been necessary to Grace.* In a period of fifteen or sixteen years since they had been made, by a total inactivity in my uncle Toby's life (for he seldom went farther than the bowling-green) —his blue and gold had become so miserably too strait for him, that it was with the utmost difficulty the Corporal was able to get him into them; the taking them up at the sleeves was of no advantage: they were laced, however, down the back, and at the seams of the sides, &c. in the mode of King William's reign; and to shorten all description, they shone so bright against the sun that morning, and had so metallic and doughty an air with them, that, had my uncle Toby thought of attacking in armor, nothing could have so well imposed upon his imagination.

As for the thin scarlet breeches, they had been unripp'd by the taylor between the legs, and left at *sixes and sevens.*

—Yes, Madam; but let us govern our fancies. It is enough they were held impracticable the night before; and, as there was no alternative in my uncle Toby's wardrobe, he sallied forth in the red plush.

The Corporal had array'd himself in poor Le Fevre's regimental coat; and with his hair tuck'd up under his Montero-cap, which he had furbish'd up for the occasion, march'd three paces distant from his master: a whiff of military pride had puff'd out his shirt at the wrist; and upon that, in a black leather thong clipp'd into a tassel beyond the knot, hung the Corporal's stick.—My uncle Toby carried his cane like a pipe.

—It looks well, at least, quoth my father to himself.

CHAP. III.

My uncle Toby turned his head more than once behind him, to see how he was supported by the Corporal; and the Corporal, as oft as he did it, gave a slight flourish with his stick,—but not vaporingly; and with the sweetest accent of most respectful encouragement, bid his Honor "never fear."

Now my uncle Toby did fear, and grievously too; he knew not (as my father had reproach'd him) so much as the right end of a woman from the wrong, and therefore, was never altogether at his ease near any one of them,—unless in sorrow or distress: then infinite was his pity; nor would the most courteous knight of romance have gone further, at least upon one leg, to have wiped away a tear from a woman's eye; and yet, excepting once that he was beguiled into it by Mrs. Wadman, he had never looked stedfastly into one; and would often tell my father, in the simplicity of his heart, that it was almost (if not about) as bad as talking bawdy.

—And suppose it is? my father would say.

CHAP. IV.

SHE cannot, quoth my uncle Toby, halting, when they had march'd up to within twenty paces of Mrs. Wadman's door,—she cannot, Corporal, take it amiss.

—She will take it, an' please your Honor, said the Corporal, just as the Jew's widow at Lisbon took it of my brother Tom.

—And how was that? quoth my uncle Toby, facing quite about to the Corporal.

Your Honor, replied the Corporal, knows of Tom's misfortunes; but this affair has nothing to do with them any further than this, That if Tom had not married the widow,—or had it pleased God, after their marriage, that they had but put pork into their sausages,the honest soul had never been taken out of his warm bed, and dragg'd to the Inquisition;—'tis a cursed place, added the Corporal, shaking his head; when once a poor creature is in, he is in, an' please your Honor, for ever.

—'Tis very true, said my uncle Toby, looking gravely at Mrs. Wadman's house as he spoke.

—Nothing, continued the Corporal, can be so sad as confinement for life,—or so sweet, an' please your Honor, as liberty.

—Nothing, Trim, said my uncle Toby, musing.

—Whilst a man is free, cried the Corporal, giving a flourish with his stick thus:—

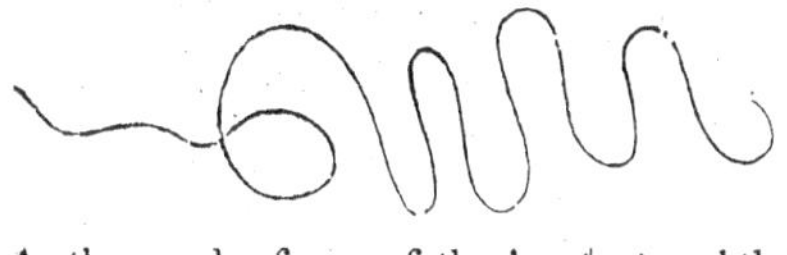

A thousand of my father's most subtle syllogisms could not have said more for celibacy.

My uncle Toby look'd earnestly towards his cottage and his bowling-green.

The Corporal had unwarily conjured up the Spirit of calculation with his wand; and he had nothing to do but to conjure him down again with his story; and in this form of exorcism, most unecclesiastically did the Corporal do it.

CHAP. V.

As Tom's place, an' please your Honor, was easy, and the weather warm, it put him upon thinking seriously of settling himself in the world, and as it fell out about that time, that a Jew, who kept a sausage-shop in the same street, had the ill-luck to die of a stranguary, and leave his widow in possession of a rousing trade,—Tom thought (as every body in Lisbon was doing the best he could devise for himself) there could be no harm in offering her his service to carry it on; so without any introduction to the widow, except that of buying a pound of sausages at her shop,—Tom set out,—counting the matter thus within himself as he walk'd along:—That, let the worst come of it that could, he should, at least, get a pound of sausages for their worth;—but, if things went well, he should be set up; inasmuch as he should get not only a pound of sausages,—but a wife and a sausage-shop, an' please your Honor, into the bargain.

Every servant in the family, from high to low, wish'd Tom success; and I can fancy, an' please your Honor, I see him this moment with his white dimity waistcoat and breeches, and hat a little o' one side, passing jollily along the street, swinging his stick, with a smile and a cheerful word for every body he met.—But, alas! Tom! thou smilest no more, cried the Corporal, looking on one side of him upon the ground, as if he apostrophized him in his dungeon.

—Poor fellow! said my uncle Toby, feelingly.

—He was an honest, light-hearted lad, an' please your Honor, as ever blood warm'd.

—Then he resembled thee, Trim, said my uncle Toby, rapidly.

The Corporal blush'd down to his fingers' ends,—a tear of sentimental bashfulness,—another of gratitude to my uncle Toby,—and a tear of sorrow for his brother's misfortunes, started into his eye, and ran sweetly down his cheek together.—My uncle Toby's kindled as one lamp does at another; and taking hold of the breast of Trim's coat, (which had been that of Le Fevre's) as if to ease his lame leg, but in reality to gratify a finer feeling,—he stood silent for a minute and a half; at the end of which he took his hand away, and the Corporal, making a bow, went on with his story of his brother and the Jew's widow.

CHAP. VI.

When Tom, an' please your Honor, got to the shop, there was nobody in it but a poor negro girl, with a bunch of white feathers slightly tied to the end of a long cane, flapping away flies,—not killing them. —'Tis a pretty picture! said my uncle Toby;—she had suffered persecution, Trim, and had learnt mercy.

—She was good, an' please your Honor, from nature, as well as from hardships; and there are circumstances in the story of that poor friendless slut, that would melt a heart of stone, said Trim; and some dismal winter's evening, when your Honor is in the humor, they shall be told you with the rest of Tom's story, for it makes a part of it.

-Then do not forget, Trim, said my uncle Toby.

—A negro has a soul! an' please your Honor, said the Corporal (doubtingly).

—I am not much versed, Corporal, quoth my uncle Toby, in things of that kind; but I suppose, God would not leave him without one, any more than thee or me.

—It would be putting one sadly over the head of another, quoth the Corporal.

It would so, said my uncle Toby.—Why then, an' please your Honor, is a black wench to be used worse than a white one?

—I can give no reason, said my uncle Toby.

—Only, cried the Corporal, shaking his head, because she has no one to stand up for her.

—'Tis that very thing, Trim, quoth my uncle Toby,—which recommends her to protection,—and her brethren with her; 'tis the fortune of war which has put the whip into our hands *now;*—where it may be hereafter, Heaven knows! but be it where it will, the brave, Trim, will not use it unkindly.

—God forbid! said the Corporal.

—Amen, responded my uncle Toby, laying his hand upon his heart.

The Corporal returned to his story, and went on,—but with an embarrassment in doing it, which here and there a reader in this world will not be able to comprehend; for by the many sudden transitions all along, from one kind and cordial passion to another, in getting thus far on his way, he had lost the sportable key of his voice, which gave sense and spirit to his tale: he attempted twice to resume it, but could not please himself; so giving a stout *hem!* to rally back the retreating spirits, and aiding nature at the same time, with his left arm a-kimbo on one side, and with his right a little extended, supporting her on the other, —the Corporal got as near the note as he could;—and in that attitude continued his story.

CHAP. VII.

As Tom, an' please your Honor, had no business at that time with the Moorish girl, he passed on into the room beyond, to talk to the Jew's widow about love,—and his pound of sausages; and being, as I have told your Honor, an open cheery-hearted lad, with his character wrote in his looks and carriage, he took a chair, and without much apology, but with great civility at the same time, placed it close to her at the table, and sat down.

There is nothing so awkward as courting a woman, an' please your Honor, whilst she is making sausages.—So Tom began a discourse upon them: First, gravely,—"As "how they were made;—with what meats, "herbs, and spices:"—then a little gaily,—as, "With what skins,—and if they never "burst?—Whether the largest were not "the best?" and so on,—taking care only as he went along, to season what he had to say upon sausages, rather under than over,—that he might have room to act in.—

It was owing to the neglect of that very precaution, said my uncle Toby, laying his hand upon Trim's shoulder, that Count de la Motte lost the battle of Wynnendale: he pressed too speedily into the wood: which if he had not done, Lisle had not fallen into our hands, nor Ghent and Bruges; which both followed her example.—It was so late in the year, continued my uncle Toby, and so terrible a season came on, that if things had not fallen out as they did, our troops must have perish'd in the open field.

—Why, therefore, may not battles, an' please your Honor, as well as marriages, be made in Heaven?—My uncle Toby mused.—Religion inclined him to say one thing, and his high idea of military skill tempted him to say another: so, not being able to frame a reply exactly to his mind,—my uncle Toby said nothing at all; and the Corporal finished his story.

As Tom perceived, an' please your Honor, that he gained ground, and that all he had said upon the subject of sausages was kindly taken, he went on to help her a little in making them.—First, by taking hold of the ring of the sausage whilst she stroked the forced meat down with her hand;—then by cutting the strings into proper lengths, and holding them in his hand, whilst she took them out, one by one;—then by putting them across her mouth, that she might take them out as she wanted them,—and so on from little to more, till at last he adventured to tie the sausage himself, whilst she held the snout.

Now a widow, an' please your Honor, always chooses a second husband as unlike the first as she can: so the affair was more than half settled in her mind before Tom mentioned it.

She made a feint, however, of defending herself by snatching up a sausage.—Tom instantly laid hold of another.—

But seeing Tom's had more gristle in it,—

She signed the capitulation,—and Tom sealed it; and there was an end of the matter.

CHAP. VIII.

All womankind, continued Trim (commenting upon his story) from the highest to the lowest, an' please your Honor, love jokes; the difficulty is to know how they choose to have them cut; and there is no knowing that but by trying, as we do with our artillery in the field, by raising or letting down their breeches, till we hit the mark.

—I like the comparison, said my uncle Toby, better than the thing itself.

—Because your Honor, quoth the Corporal, loves glory more than pleasure.

—I hope, Trim, answered my uncle Toby, I love mankind more than either; and as the knowledge of arms tends so apparently to the good and quiet of the world,—and particularly that branch of it which we have practised together in our bowling-green, has no object but to shorten the strides of *Ambition*, and intrench the lives and fortunes of the *few* from the plunderings of the *many*;—whenever that drum beats in our ears, I trust, Corporal, we shall neither of us want so much humanity and fellow-feeling as to face about and march.

In pronouncing this, my uncle Toby faced about and march'd firmly as at the head of his company;—and the faithful Corporal, shouldering his stick, and striking his hand upon his coat-skirt as he took his first step,—march'd close behind him down the avenue.

—Now what can their two noddles be about? cried my father to my mother.—By all that's strange, they are besieging Mrs. Wadman in form, and are marching round her house to mark out the lines of circum vallation!

—I dare say, quoth my mother,—But stop, dear Sir,—for what my mother dared to say upon the occasion,—and what my father did say upon it,—with her replies and his rejoinders, shall be read, perused, paraphrased, commented, and descanted upon,—or to say it all in a word, shall be thumb'd over by Posterity in a chapter apart; I say, by Posterity,—and care not, if I repeat the word again,—for what has this book done more than the Legation of Moses, or the

Tale of a Tub, that it may not swim down the gutter of Time along with them?

I will not argue the matter: Time wastes too fast: every letter I trace tells me with what rapidity Life follows my pen; the days and hours of it, more precious,—my dear Jenny,—than the rubies about thy neck, are flying over our heads like light clouds of a windy day, never to return more;—every thing presses on,—whilst thou art twisting that lock,—see! it grows grey; and every time I kiss thy hand to bid adieu, and every absence which follows it, are preludes to that eternal separation which we are shortly to make.—

Heaven have mercy upon us both!

CHAP. IX.

Now for what the world thinks of that ejaculation,—I would not give a groat.

CHAP. X.

My mother had gone with her left arm twisted in my father's right, till they had got to the fatal angle of the old garden-wall, where Doctor Slop was overthrown by Obadiah on the coach-horse. As this was directly opposite to the front of Mrs. Wadman's house, when my father came to it, he gave a look across; and seeing my uncle Toby and the Corporal within ten paces of the door, he turn'd about,—"Let us just stop a "moment," quoth my father, "and see with "what ceremonies my brother Toby and his "man Trim make their first entry;—it will "not detain us," added my father, "a sin- "gle minute."

—No matter if it be ten minutes, quoth my mother.

—It will not detain us half a one, said my father.

The Corporal was just then setting in with the story of his brother Tom and the Jew's widow: the story went on,—and on; —it had episodes in it,—it came back and went on,—and on again; there was no end of it:—the reader found it very long.

G— help my father! he *pish'd* fifty times at every new attitude, and gave the Corporal's stick, with all its flourishings and danglings, to as many Devils as chose to accept of them.

When issues of events like these my father is waiting for, are hanging in the scales of fate, the mind has the advantage of changing the principle of expectation three times, without which it would not have power to see it out.

Curiosity governs the *first moment;* and the second moment is all economy to justify the expense of the first;—and for the third, fourth, fifth, and sixth moments, and so on to the day of judgment,—'tis a point of *Honor.*

I need not be told, that the ethic writers have assigned this all to Patience; but that *Virtue,* methinks, has extent of dominion sufficient of her own, and enough to do in it, without invading the few dismantled castles which *Honor* has left him upon the earth.

My father stood it out as well as he could with these three auxiliaries, to the end of Trim's story; and from thence to the end of my uncle Toby's panegyric upon arms, in the chapter following it; when seeing that, instead of marching up to Mrs. Wadman's door, they both faced about and march'd down the avenue diametrically opposite to his expectation,—he broke out at once with that little subacid sourness of humor, which, in certain situations, distinguished his character from that of all other men.

CHAP. XI.

"Now what can their two noddles be about?" cried my father, - - &c. - - - -

—I dare say, said my mother, they are making fortifications.

—Not on Mrs. Wadman's premises! cried my father, stepping back.

—I suppose not, quoth my mother.

—I wish, said my father, raising his voice, the whole science of fortification at the Devil, with all its trumpery of saps, mines, blinds, gabions, faussebrays, and cuvettes.

—They are foolish things, said my mother.

Now she had a way, which, by the bye, I would this moment give away my purple jerkin, and my yellow slippers into the bargain, if some of your Reverences would imitate,—and that was, never to refuse her assent and consent to any proposition my father laid before her, merely because she did not understand it, or had no ideas of the principal word or term of art upon which the tenet or proposition rolled. She contented herself with doing all that her godfathers and godmothers promised for her,—but no more; and so would go on using a hard word for twenty years together,—and replying to it too, if it was a verb, in all its moods and tenses, without giving herself any trouble to inquire about it.

This was an eternal source of misery to my father, and broke the neck, at the first setting out, of more good dialogues between them, than could have done the most petulant contradiction;—the few that survived were the better for the *cuvettes*.

"They are foolish things," said my mother.

—Particularly the *cuvettes*, replied my father.

It was enough;—he tasted the sweet of triumph,—and went on.

—Not that they are, properly speaking, Mrs. Wadman's premises, said my father, partly correcting himself,—because she is but tenant for life.

—That makes a great difference—said my mother.

In a fool's head, replied my father.

—Unless she should happen to have a child, said my mother.

—But she must persuade my brother Toby first to get her one.

—To be sure, Mr. Shandy, quoth my mother.

—Though if it comes to persuasion, said my father,—Lord have mercy upon them!

—Amen, said my mother, *piano*.

Amen, cried my father, *fortissimò*.

—Amen, said my mother again,—but with such a sighing cadence of personal pity at the end of it, as discomfited every fibre about my father;—he instantly took out his almanac;—but before he could untie it, Yorick's congregation coming out of church, became a full answer to one half of his business with it,—and my mother telling him it was a sacrament day,—left him as little in doubt, as to the other part. He put his almanac into his pocket.

The First Lord of the Treasury, thinking of *ways and means*, could not have returned home with a more embarrassed look.

CHAP. XII.

Upon looking back from the end of the last chapter, and surveying the texture of what has been wrote, it is necessary, that upon this page and the five following, a good quantity of heterogeneous matter be inserted, to keep up that just balance betwixt wisdom and folly, without which, a book would not hold together a single year; nor is it a poor creeping digression (which, but for the name of, a man might continue as well going on in the King's highway) which will do the business.—No, if it is to be a digression, it must be a good frisky one, and upon a frisky subject too, where neither the horse nor his rider are to be caught but by rebound.

The only difficulty is, raising powers suitable to the nature of the service: *Fancy* is capricious,—*Wit* must not be searched for,—and *Pleasantry* (good-natured slut as she is) will not come in at a call, was an empire to be laid at her feet.

—The best way for a man is, to say his prayers.

Only, if it puts him in mind of his infirmities and defects, as well ghostly as bodily,—for that purpose, he will find himself rather worse after he has said them than before;—for other purposes better.

For my own part, there is not a way, either moral or mechanical, under Heaven, that I could think of, which I have not taken with myself in this case; sometimes by addressing myself directly to the soul herself, and arguing the point over and over again with her, upon the extent of her own faculties.

—I never could make them an inch the wider.

Then by changing my system, and trying what could be made of it upon the body, by temperance, soberness, and chastity These are good, quoth I, in themselves,—

they are good, absolutely;—they are good, relatively; — they are good for health,— they are good for happiness in this world,— they are good for happiness in the next.

In short, they are good for every thing but the thing wanted; and there they are good for nothing, but to leave the soul just as Heaven made it. As for the theological virtues of Faith and Hope, they give it courage; but then, that snivelling virtue of Meekness (as my father would always call it) takes it quite away again, so you are exactly where you started.

Now, in all common and ordinary cases, there is nothing which I have found to answer so well as this.—

Certainly, if there is any dependence upon Logic, and that I am not blinded by self-love, there must be something of true genius about me, merely upon this symptom of it, That I do not know what Envy is: for never do I hit upon any invention or device which tendeth to the furtherance of good writing, but I instantly make it public; willing that all mankind should write as well as myself:

—Which they certainly will, when they think as little.

CHAP. XIII.

Now, in ordinary cases, that is, when I am only stupid, and the thoughts rise heavily and pass gummous through my pen,—

Or that I am got, I know not how, into a cold unmetaphorical vein of infamous writing, and cannot take a plumb-lift out of it *for my soul;* so must be obliged to go on writing like a Dutch commentator to the end of the chapter, unless something be done,—

I never stand conferring with pen and ink one moment; for if a pinch of snuff, or a stride or two across the room, will not do the business for me,—I take a razor at once; and having tried the edge of it upon the palm of my hand, without further ceremony, except that of first lathering my beard, I shave it off; taking care only, if I do leave a hair, that it be not a grey one; this done, I change my shirt, put on a better coat,— send for my last wig,—put my topaz-ring upon my finger; and, in a word, dress myself from one end to the other of me, after my best fashion.

Now the Devil in hell must be in it, if this does not do: for, consider, Sir, as every man chooses to be present at the shaving of his own beard (though there is no rule without an exception), and unavoidably sits over-against himself the whole time it is doing, in case he has a hand in it, — the Situation, like all others, has notions of her own to put into the brain.

I maintain it, the conceits of a rough-bearded man are seven years more terse and juvenile for one single operation, and if they did not run a risk of being quite shaved away, might be carried up, by continual shavings, to the highest pitch of sublimity.—How Homer could write with so long a beard, I don't know; — and as it makes against my hypothesis, I as little care:—but let us return to the Toilet.

Ludovicus Sorbonensis makes this entirely an affair of the body (εξωτερικη πραξις) as he calls it,—but he is deceived: the soul and body are joint-sharers in every thing they get: a man cannot dress, but his ideas get cloth'd at the same time: and if he dresses like a gentleman, every one of them stands presented to his imagination, genteelized along with him; — so that he has nothing to do but take his pen, and write like himself.

For this cause, when your Honors and Reverences would know whether I write clean, and fit to be read, you will be able to judge full as well by looking into my laundress's bill, as my book: there was one single month, in which I can make it appear, that I dirtied one-and-thirty shirts with clean writing; and after all, was more abused, cursed, criticis'd, and confounded, and had more mystic heads shaken at me, for what I had wrote in that one month, than in all the other months of that year put together.

But their Honors and Reverences had not seen my bills.

CHAP. XIV.

As I never had any intention of beginning the Digression I am making all this preparation for, till I come to the 15th chapter,—I have this chapter to put to whatever use I think proper.—I have twenty this moment ready for it.—I could write my chapter of *Button-holes* in it,—

Or my chapter of *Pishes*, which should follow them,—

Or my chapter of *Knots*, in case their Reverences have done with them:—they might lead me into mischief. The safest way is, to follow the track of the learned, and raise objections against what I have been writing, though I declare beforehand, I know no more than my heels how to answer them.

And first, it may be said, there is a pelting kind of *Thersitical* satire, as black as the very ink 'tis wrote with—(and by the bye, whoever says so, is indebted to the Muster-master General of the Grecian army, for suffering the name of so ugly and foul-mouth'd a man as Thersites to continue upon his roll,—for it has furnish'd him with an epithet)—in these productions, he will urge, all the personal washings and scrubbings upon earth do a sinking genius no sort of good,—but just the contrary, inasmuch as the dirtier the fellow is, the better generally he succeeds in it.

To this I have no other answer,—at least ready,—but that the Archbishop of Benevento wrote his *nasty* Romance of the Galatea, as all the world knows, in a purple coat, waistcoat, and purple pair of breeches; and that the penance set him of writing a commentary upon the book of the Revelations, as severe as it was look'd upon by one part of the world, was far from being deem'd so by the other, upon the single account of that *Investment*.

Another objection to all this remedy, is its want of universality; forasmuch as the shaving part of it, upon which so much stress is laid, by an unalterable law of nature excludes one half of the species entirely from its use,—all I can say, is, that female writers, whether of England, or of France, must e'en go without it.

As for the Spanish ladies,—I am in no sort of distress.

CHAP XV.

The fifteenth chapter is come at last; and brings nothing with it but a sad signature of "How our pleasures slip from under "us in this world!"

For in talking of my Digression,—I declare before Heaven, I have made it! What a strange creature is mortal man! said she.

—'Tis very true, said I;—but 'twere better to get all these things out of our heads, and return to my uncle Toby.

CHAP. XVI.

When my uncle Toby and the Corporal had marched down to the bottom of the avenue, they recollected their business lay the other way; so they faced about, and marched up straight to Mrs. Wadman's door.

I warrant your Honor, said the Corporal, touching his Montero-cap with his hand as he passed him, in order to give a knock at the door.—My uncle Toby, contrary to his invariable way of treating his faithful servant, said nothing good or bad: the truth was, he had not altogether marshall'd his ideas; he wish'd for another conference, and, as the Corporal was mounting up the three steps before the door, he *hem'd* twice; a portion of my uncle Toby's most modest spirits fled, at each expulsion, towards the Corporal; he stood with the rapper of the door suspended for a full minute in his hand, he scarce knew why. Bridget stood perdue within, with her finger and her thumb upon the latch, benumb'd with expectation; and Mrs. Wadman, with an eye ready to be deflowered again, sat breathless behind the window-curtain of her bed-chamber, watching their approach.

—Trim! said my uncle Toby;—but, as he articulated the word, the minute expired, and Trim let fall the rapper.

My uncle Toby, perceiving that all hopes of a conference were knock'd on the head by it, whistled Lillibullero.

CHAP. XVII.

As Mrs. Bridget's finger and thumb were upon the latch, the Corporal did not knock as often as perchance your Honor's taylor.

—I might have taken my example something nearer home; for I owe mine some five-and-twenty pounds at least, and wonder at the man's patience.

—But this is nothing at all to the world: only 'tis a cursed thing to be in debt; and there seems to be a fatality in the exchequers of some poor princes, particularly those of our house, which no economy can bind down in irons. For my own part, I'm persuaded there is not any one prince, prelate, pope, or potentate, great or small, upon earth, more desirous in his heart of keeping straight with the world than I am,—or who takes more likely means for it. I never give above half a guinea,—nor walk with boots,—nor cheapen toothpicks, nor lay out a shilling upon a band-box, the year round; and, for the six months I'm in the country, I'm upon so small a scale, that with all the good temper in the world, I outdo Rousseau a bar-length!—for I keep neither man nor boy, nor horse, nor cow, nor dog, nor cat, nor any thing that can eat or drink, except a thin poor piece of a vestal (to keep my fire in) and who has generally as bad an appetite as myself:—but, if you think this makes a philosopher of me,—I would not, my good people, give a rush for your judgments.

True philosophy;—but there is no treating the subject whilst my uncle is whistling Lillibullero.

—Let us go into the house.

CHAP. XVIII.

CHAP. XIX.

CHAP. XX.

—You shall see the very place, Madam, said my uncle Toby.

Mrs. Wadman blush'd,—look'd towards the door,—turn'd pale,—blush'd slightly again,—recover'd her natural color,—blush'd worse than ever; which, for the sake of the unlearned reader, I translate thus:

"*L—d! I cannot look at it!*
"*What would the world say if I look'd at it?*
"*I should drop down if I look'd at it!*
"*I wish I could look at it.*
"*There can be no sin in looking at it*
—"*I will look at it.*"

Whilst all this was running through Mrs. Wadman's imagination, my uncle Toby had risen from the sofa, and got to the other side of the parlor-door, to give Trim an order about it in the passage——

* * * * * * * *
* * * ——I believe it is in the garret, said my uncle Toby.—I saw it there, an' please your Honor, this morning, answered Trim.—Then prithee step directly for it, Trim, said my uncle Toby, and bring it into the parlor.

The Corporal did not approve of the orders; but most cheerfully obeyed them. The first was not an act of his will;—the second was; so he put on his Montero-cap, and went as fast as his lame knee would let him. My uncle Toby returned into the parlor, and sat himself down again upon the sofa.

—You shall lay your finger upon the place, said my uncle Toby.—I will not touch it, however, quoth Mrs. Wadman to herself.

This requires a second translation:—it shows what little knowledge is got by mere words;—we must go up to the first springs.

Now, in order to clear up the mist which hangs upon these three pages, I must endeavor to be as clear as possible myself.

Rub your hands thrice across your foreheads,—blow your noses,—cleanse your emunctories,—sneeze, my good people;—God bless you.

Now give me all the help you can.

CHAP. XXI.

As there are fifty different ends (counting all ends in,—as well civil as religious) for which a woman takes a husband, she first sets about and carefully weighs, then separates and distinguishes, in her mind, which of all that number of ends is hers; then, by discourse, inquiry, argumentation, and inference, she investigates and finds out whether she has got hold of the right one;—and, if she has,—then, by pulling it gently this way and that way, she further forms a judgment, whether it will not break in the drawing.

The imagery under which Slawkenbergius impresses this upon his reader's fancy, in the beginning of his third Decade, is so ludicrous, that the honor I bear the sex will not suffer me to quote it,—otherwise, it is not destitute of humor.

"She first, saith Slawkenbergius, stops the ass; and holding his halter in her left hand (lest he should get away) she thrusts her right hand into the very bottom of his pannier, to search for it.—For what?—You'll not know the sooner, quoth Slawkenbergius, for interrupting me.

"I have nothing, good Lady, but empty bottles," says the ass.

—"I'm loaded with tripes," says the second.

—And thou art little better, quoth she to the third; for nothing is there in thy panniers but trunk-hose and pantofles;—and so to the fourth and fifth, going on, one by one, through the whole string, till coming to the ass which carries it, she turns the pannier upside-down, looks at it,—considers it,—samples it,—measures it,—stretches it,—wets it,—dries it,—then takes her teeth with to the warp and weft of it.

Of what? for the love of Christ!

—I am determined answered Slawkenbergius, that all the powers upon earth shall never wring that secret from my breast

CHAP. XXII.

We live in a world beset on all sides with mysteries and riddles,—and so 'tis no matter;—else it seems strange, that Nature, who makes every thing so well to answer its destination, and seldom or never errs, unless for pastime, in giving such forms and aptitudes to whatever passes through her hands, that, whether she designs for the plow, the caravan, the cart,—or whatever other creature she models, be it but an ass's foal, you are sure to have the thing you wanted; and yet, at the same time, should so eternally bungle it as she does, in making so simple a thing as a married man.

Whether it is in the choice of the clay—or that it is frequently spoil'd in the baking (by an excess of which a husband may turn out too crusty, you know, on one hand,—or not enough so, through defect of heat, on the other;)—or whether this great artificer is not so attentive to the little Platonic exigencies *of that part* of the species, for whose use she is fabricating *this*;—or that her Ladyship sometimes scarce knows what sort of a husband will do,—I know not: we will discourse about it after supper.

It is enough, that neither the observation itself, nor the reasoning upon it, are at all to the purpose—but rather against it; since, with regard to my uncle Toby's fitness for the marriage state, nothing was ever better: she had formed him of the best and kindliest clay, had temper'd it with her own milk, and breathed into it the sweetest spirit;—she had made him all gentle, generous, and humane;—she had filled his heart with trust and confidence, and disposed every passage which led to it for the communication of the tenderest offices; she had, moreover, considered the other causes for which matrimony was ordained—

And, accordingly, * * * *
* * * * * * * *
* * * * * * * *
* * * *

The *Donation* was not defeated by my uncle Toby's wound.

Now, this last article was somewhat apocryphal; and the Devil, who is the great disturber of our faiths in this world, had raised scruples in Mrs. Wadman's brain about it; and, like a true Devil as he was, had done his own work at the same time, by turning my uncle Toby's virtue thereupon into nothing but *empty bottles, tripes, trunk-hose,* and *pantofles.*

CHAP. XXIII.

Mrs. Bridget had pawn'd all the little stock of honor a poor chambermaid was worth in the world, that she would get to the bottom of the affair in ten days; and it was built upon one of the most concessible *postulata* in nature; namely, that, whilst my uncle Toby was making love to her mistress, the Corporal could find nothing better to do than to make love to her;—"*And I'll let him, as much as he will,*" said Bridget, "*to get it out of him.*"

Friendship has two garments, an outer and an under one. Bridget was serving her mistress's interests in the one,—and doing the thing which most pleased herself in the other; so had as many stakes depending upon my uncle Toby's wound as the Devil himself.—Mrs. Wadman had but one,—and as it possibly might be her last (without discouraging Mrs. Bridget, or discrediting her talents) was determined to play her cards herself.

She wanted not encouragement: a child might have look'd into his hand;—there was such a plainness and simplicity in his playing out what trumps he had,—with such an unmistrusting ignorance of the *ten-ace,*—and so naked and defenceless did he sit upon the same sofa with Widow Wadman, that a generous heart would have wept to have won the game of him

Let us drop the metaphor.

CHAP. XXIV.

—And the story too, if you please; for though I have all along been hastening towards this part of it, with so much earnest desire, as well knowing it to be the choicest morsel of what I had to offer to the world, yet now that I am got to it, any one is welcome to take my pen and go on with the story for me that will,—I see the difficulties of the descriptions I am going to give,—and feel my want of powers.

It is one comfort at least to me, that I lost some fourscore ounces of blood this week in a most uncritical fever which attacked me at the beginning of this chapter: so that I have still some hopes remaining it may be more in the serous or globular parts of the blood, than in the subtle *aura* of the brain:—be it which it will,—an Invocation can do no hurt;—and I leave the affair entirely to the *invoked,* to inspire or to inject me according as he sees good.

THE INVOCATION.

Gentle Spirit of sweetest humor, who erst did sit upon the easy pen of my beloved Cervantes! Thou who glided'st daily through his lattice, and turned'st the twilight of his prison into noon-day brightness by thy presence,—tinged'st his little urn of water with heaven-sent nectar, and, all the time he wrote of Sancho and his master, didst cast thy mystic mantle o'er his wither'd stump,* and wide extended it to all the evils of his life,—

—Turn in hither, I beseech thee!—behold these breeches!—they are all I have in the world;—that piteous rent was given them at Lyons.

My shirts! see what a deadly schism has happen'd amongst 'em;—for the laps are in Lombardy, and the rest of 'em here.—I never had but six, and a cunning gipsy of a laundress at Milan cut me off the *fore*-laps of five.—To do her justice, she did it with some consideration,—for I was returning out of Italy.

And yet, notwithstanding all this, and a pistol tinder-box, which was, moreover, filch'd from me at Sienna, and twice that I paid five Pauls for two hard eggs, once at Raddicofini, and a second time at Capua,—I do not think a journey through France and Italy, provided a man keeps his temper all the way, so bad a thing as some people

* He lost his hand at the battle of Lepanto.

would make you believe; there must be *ups* and *downs*, or how the deuce should we get into valleys where Nature spreads so many tables of entertainment?—'Tis nonsense to imagine they will lend you their voitures to be shaken to pieces for nothing; and, unless you pay twelve sous for greasing your wheels, how should the poor peasant get butter to his bread?—We really expect too much,—and, for the livre or two above par for your supper and bed, at the most they are but one shilling and ninepence halfpenny,—who would embroil their philosophy for it? for Heaven's and for your own sake, pay it,—pay it with both hands open, rather than leave *Disappointment* sitting drooping upon the eyes of your fair hostess and her damsels in the gateway, at your departure;—and besides, my dear Sir, you get a sisterly kiss of each of 'em, worth a pound:—at least I did;—

—For my uncle Toby's amours running all the way in my head, they had the same effect upon me as if they had been my own. —I was in the most perfect state of bounty and good-will, and felt the kindliest harmony vibrating within me; with every oscillation of the chaise alike; so that, whether the roads were rough or smooth, it made no difference; every thing I saw, or had to do with, touch'd upon some secret spring, either of sentiment or rapture.

—They were the sweetest notes I ever heard; and I instantly let down the fore-glass to hear them more distinctly.—'Tis Maria, said the postilion, observing I was listening. Poor Maria, continued he (leaning his body on one side to let me see her, for he was in a line betwixt us) is sitting upon a bank, playing her vespers upon her pipe, with her little goat beside her.

The young fellow utter'd this with an accent and a look so perfectly in tune to a feeling heart, that I instantly made a vow I would give him a four-and-twenty sous piece when I got to Moulins.

—And who is *poor* Maria? said I.

—The love and pity of all the villages around us, said the postilion: it is but three years ago that the sun did not shine upon so fair, so quick-witted and amiable a maid; and better fate did Maria deserve than to have her bans forbid by the intrigues of the curate of the parish who publish'd them.

He was going on, when Maria, who had made a short pause, put the pipe to her mouth and began the air again;—they were the same notes,—yet were ten times sweeter. —It is the evening service to the Virgin, said the young man;—but who has taught her to play it, or how she came by her pipe, no one knows: we think that Heaven has assisted her in both; for, ever since she has been unsettled in her mind, it seems her only consolation; she has never once had the pipe out of her hand, but plays that *service* upon it almost day and night.

The postilion delivered this with so much discretion and natural eloquence, that I could not help deciphering something in his face above his condition, and should have sifted out his history, had not poor Maria's taken such full possession of me.

We had got up by this time almost to the bank where Maria was sitting: she was in a thin white jacket, with her hair, all but two tresses, drawn up into a silk net, with a few olive-leaves twisted a little fantastically on one side;—she was beautiful; and, if ever I felt the full force of an honest heart-ache, it was the moment I saw her.

—God help her! poor damsel! above a hundred masses, said the postilion, have been said, in the several parish-churches and convents around, for her,—but without effect; we have still hopes, as she is sensible for short intervals, that the Virgin at last will restore her to herself; but her parents, who know her best, are hopeless upon that score, and think her senses are lost for ever.

As the postilion spoke this, Maria made a cadence so melancholy, so tender and querulous, that I sprung out of the chaise to help her, and found myself sitting betwixt her and her goat before I relapsed from my enthusiasm.

Maria look'd wistfully for some time at me, and then at her goat,—and then at me, —and then at her goat again, and so on, alternately.

—Well, Maria, said I softly, what resemblance do you find?

I do entreat the candid reader to believe me, that it was from the humblest conviction of what a *beast* man is,—that I asked the question; and that I would not have let fall an unseasonable pleasantry in the venerable presence of Misery, to be entitled to all the wit that ever Rabelais scatter'd,—and yet I own my heart smote me, and that I so smarted at the very idea of it, that I swore I would set up for Wisdom, and utter grave sentences the rest of my days;—and never,—never attempt again to commit mirth with man, woman, or child, the longest day I had to live.

As for writing nonsense to them,—I believe there was a reserve;—but that I leave to the world.

Adieu, Maria!—adieu, poor hapless damsel!—some time, but not *now*, I may hear thy sorrows from thy own lips,—but I was deceived; for that moment she took her pipe and told me such a tale of woe with it, that I rose up, and with broken and irregular steps walk'd softly to my chaise.

—What an excellent inn at Moulins!

CHAP. XXV.

When we have got to the end of this chapter (but not before) we must all turn back to the two blank chapters; on the account of which my honor has lain bleeding this half hour,—I stop it, by pulling off one of my yellow slippers, and throwing it, with all my violence, to the opposite side of my room, with a declaration at the heel of it,—

That whatever resemblance it may bear to half the chapters which are written in the world, or, for aught I know, may be now writing in it,—that it was as casual as the foam of Zeuxis his horse; besides, I look upon a chapter which has *only nothing in it*, with respect; and considering what worse things there are in the world,—that it is no way a proper subject for satire.

—Why then was it left so? And here, without staying for my reply, shall I be called as many blockheads, numskulls, doddypoles, dunderheads, ninnyhammers, goosecaps, joltheads, nincompoops, and sh-t-a-beds,—and other unsavory appellations as ever the cake-bakers of Lerne cast in the teeth of King Gargantua's shepherds;—and I'll let them do it, as Bridget said, as much as they please: for how was it possible they should foresee the necessity I was under of writing the 25th chapter of my book before the 18th? &c.

—So I don't take it amiss.—All I wish is, That it may be a lesson to the world, "*to* "*let people tell their stories their own way.*"

The Eighteenth Chapter.

As Mrs. Bridget opened the door before the Corporal had well given the rap, the interval betwixt that and my uncle Toby's introduction into the parlor was so short, that Mrs. Wadman had but just time to get from behind the curtain,—lay a Bible upon the table, and advance a step or two towards the door to receive him.

My uncle Toby saluted Mrs. Wadman, after the manner in which women were saluted by men in the year of our Lord God one thousand seven hundred and thirteen;—then facing about, he march'd up abreast with her to the sofa, and in three plain words, though not before he was sat down,—nor after he was sat down,—but as he was sitting down, told her, "*he was in love*;" so that my uncle Toby strained himself more in the declaration than he needed.

Mrs. Wadman naturally looked down upon a slit she had been darning up in her apron, in expectation every moment that my uncle Toby would go on; but having no talents for amplification, and love, moreover, of all others, being a subject of which he was the least a master,—when he had told Mrs. Wadman once that he loved her, he let it alone, and left the matter to work after its own way.

My father was always in raptures with this system of my uncle Toby's, as he falsely called it, and would often say, That could his brother Toby to his process have added but a pipe of tobacco,—he had wherewithal to have found his way, if there was faith in a Spanish proverb, towards the hearts of half the women upon the globe.

My uncle Toby never understood what my father meant: nor will I presume to extract more from it than a condemnation of an error which the bulk of the world lie under;—but the French, every one of 'em to a man, who believe in it almost as much as the *real presence*, "*That talking* "*of love is making it.*"

—I would as soon set about making a black-pudding by the same receipt.

Let us go on:—Mrs. Wadman sat in expectation my uncle Toby would do so, to almost the first pulsation of that minute, wherein silence on one side or the other generally becomes indecent: so edging herself a little more towards him, and raising up her eyes, sub-blushing, as she did it,—she took up the gauntlet,—or the discourse (if you like it the better) and communed with my uncle Toby thus—

The cares and disquietudes of the marriage-state, quoth Mrs. Wadman, are very great.—I suppose so, said my uncle Toby. —And therefore when a person, continued Mrs. Wadman, is so much at his ease as you are,—so happy, Captain Shandy, in yourself, your friends, and your amusements,—I wonder what reasons can incline you to the state!

—They are written, quoth my uncle Toby, in the Common-Prayer Book.

Thus far my uncle Toby went on warily, and kept within his depth, leaving Mrs. Wadman to sail upon the gulf as she pleased.

As for children, said Mrs. Wadman, though a principal end, perhaps, of the institution, and the natural wish, I suppose, of every parent,—yet do not we all find, they are certain sorrows, and very uncertain comforts? — and what is there, dear Sir, to pay for the heart-aches! — what compensation for the many tender and disquieting apprehensions of a suffering and defenceless mother, who brings them into life?—I declare, said my uncle Toby, smit with pity, I know of none; unless it be the pleasure which it has pleased God—

—A fiddle-stick! quoth she.

Chapter the Nineteenth.

Now there are such an infinitude of notes, tunes, cants, chants, airs, looks, and accents with which the word *fiddlestick* may be pronounced in all such cases as this. every one of 'em impressing a sense and meaning as different from the other as *dirt* from *cleanliness*,—that casuists (for it is an affair of conscience upon that score) reckon up no less than fourteen thousand in which you may do either right or wrong.

Mrs. Wadman hit upon the *fiddlestick* which summoned up all my uncle Toby's modest blood into his cheeks;—so feeling within himself that he had somehow or other got beyond his depth, he stopped short; and without entering further either into the pains or pleasures of matrimony, he laid his hand upon his heart, and made an offer to take them as they were, and share them along with her.

When my uncle Toby had said this, he did not care to say it again; so casting his eye upon the Bible, which Mrs. Wadman had laid upon the table, he took it up; and popping, dear soul! upon a passage in it, of all others the most interesting to him,—which was the siege of Jericho, — he set himself to read it over,—leaving his proposal of marriage, as he had done his declaration of love, to work with her after its own way. Now it wrought neither as an astringent nor a loosener; nor like opium, nor bark, nor mercury, nor buckthorn, nor any one drug which Nature had bestowed upon the world;—in short, it work'd not at all in her; and the cause of that was, that there was something working there before. —Babbler that I am! I have anticipated what it was a dozen times; but there is fire still in the subject.—*Allons!*

CHAP. XXVI.

It is natural for a perfect stranger who is going from London to Edinburgh, to inquire, before he sets out, how many miles to York? which is about the half-way:—nor does any body wonder, if he goes on and asks about the corporation, &c.

It was just as natural for Mrs. Wadman, whose first husband was all his time afflicted with a sciatica, to wish to know how far from the hip to the groin; and how far she was likely to suffer more or less in her feelings, in the one case than in the other.

She had accordingly read Drake's Anato

my from one end to the other. She had peep'd into Wharton upon the Brain, and borrowed *Graaf upon the Bones and Muscles; but could make nothing of it.

She had reason'd likewise from her own powers,—laid down theorems,—drawn consequences, and come to no conclusion.

To clear up all, she had twice asked Doctor Slop, "If poor Captain Shandy was "ever likely to recover of his wound——?"

—He is recovered, Doctor Slop would say.—

What, quite?

—Quite, Madam.

—But what do you mean by a recovery? Mrs. Wadman would say.

Doctor Slop was the worst man alive at definitions; and so Mrs. Wadman could get no knowledge. In short, there was no way to extract it, but from my uncle Toby himself.

There is an accent of humanity in an inquiry of this kind, which lulls *Suspicion* to rest;—and I am half persuaded the serpent got pretty near it, in his discourse with Eve; for the propensity in the sex to be deceived could not be so great, that she should have boldness to hold chat with the Devil without it.—But there is an accent of humanity:—how shall I describe it?—'tis an accent which covers the part with a garment, and gives the inquirer a right to be as particular with it as your body-surgeon.

"—Was it without remission?

"—Was it more tolerable in bed?

"—Could he lie on both sides alike with it?

"—Was he able to mount a horse?

"—Was motion bad for it?" *et cætera*, were so tenderly spoke to, and so directed towards my uncle Toby's heart, that every item of them sunk ten times deeper into it than the evils themselves;—but when Mrs. Wadman went round about by Namur to get at my uncle Toby's groin; and engaged him to attack the point of the advanced counterscarp, and *pêle mêle* with the Dutch, to take the counter-guard of St. Roch sword-in-hand,—and then, with tender notes laying upon his ear, led him, all bleeding, by the hand out of the trench, wiping her eye as he was carried to his tent,—Heaven! Earth! Sea!—all was lifted up,—the springs of nature rose above their levels,—an angel of mercy sat beside him on the sofa,—his heart glow'd with fire;—and had he been worth a thousand, he had lost every heart of them to Mrs. Wadman.

—And whereabouts, dear Sir, quoth Mrs. Wadman, a little categorically, did you receive this sad blow?—In asking this question, Mrs. Wadman gave a slight glance towards the waistband of my uncle Toby's red plush breeches, expecting naturally, as the shortest reply to it, that my uncle Toby would lay his fore-finger upon the place.—It fell out otherwise,—for my uncle Toby having got his wound before the gate of St Nicholas, in one of the traverses of the trench opposite to the salient angle of the demi-bastion of St. Roch, he could at any time stick a pin upon the identical spot of ground where he was standing when the stone struck him. This struck instantly upon my uncle Toby's sensorium;—and with it, struck his large map of the town and citadel of Namur, and its environs, which he had purchased and pasted down upon a board, by the Corporal's aid, during his long illness:—it had lain, with other military lumber, in the garret ever since; and accordingly the Corporal was detached to the garret to fetch it.

My uncle Toby measured off thirty toises, with Mrs. Wadman's scissars, from the returning angle before the gate of St. Nicholas; and with such a virgin modesty laid her finger upon the place, that the Goddess of Decency, if then in being,—if not, 'twas her shade,—shook her head, and with a finger wavering across her eyes, forbade her to explain the mistake.

Unhappy Mrs. Wadman!

—For nothing can make this chapter go off with spirit but an apostrophe to thee:—but my heart tells me, that in such a crisis an apostrophe is but an insult in disguise; and ere I would offer one to a woman in distress,—let the chapter go to the Devil; provided any damn'd critic *in keeping* will be but at the trouble to take it with him.

* This must be a mistake in Mr. Shandy; for Graaf wrote upon the pancreatic juice, and the parts of generation.

CHAP. XXVII.

My uncle Toby's map is carried down into the kitchen.

CHAP. XXVIII.

—And here is the Maes,—and this is the Sambre, said the Corporal, pointing with his right hand extended a little towards the map, and his left upon Mrs. Bridget's shoulder,—but not the shoulder next him;—and this, said he, is the town of Namur,—and this the citadel,—and there lay the French, and here lay his Honor and myself;—and in this cursed trench, Mrs. Bridget, quoth the Corporal, taking her by the hand, did he receive the wound which crush'd him so miserably *here*.—In pronouncing which, he slightly press'd the back of her hand towards the part he felt for,—and let it fall.

—We thought, Mr. Trim, it had been more in the middle, said Mrs. Bridget.

—That would have undone us for ever, said the Corporal.

—And left my poor mistress undone too, said Bridget.

The Corporal made no reply to the repartee, but by giving Mrs. Bridget a kiss.

—Come, come, said Bridget, holding the palm of her left hand parallel to the plane of the horizon, and sliding the fingers of the other over it, in a way which could not have been done, had there been the least wart or protuberance,'—Tis every syllable of it false, cried the Corporal, before she had half finished the sentence.

—I know it to be a fact, said Bridget, from credible witnesses.

—Upon my honor, said the Corporal, laying his hand upon his heart, and blushing as he spoke, with honest resentment,—'tis a story, Mrs. Bridget, as false as Hell,—Not, said Bridget, interrupting him, that either I or my mistress care a halfpenny about it, whether it is so or no;—only that when one is married, one would choose to have such a thing by one at least,—

It was somewhat unfortunate for Mrs. Bridget, that she had begun the attack with her manual exercise; for the Corporal instantly * * * * * *
* * * * * * * *
* * * * * * * *

CHAP. XXIX.

It was like the momentary contest in the moist eyelids of an April morning, "Wheth-"er Bridget should laugh or cry."

She snatch'd up a rolling-pin,—'twas ten to one she had laugh'd.—

She laid it down,—she cried: and had one single tear of 'em but tasted of bitterness, full sorrowful would the Corporal's heart have been that he had used the argument; but the Corporal understood the sex, a *quart major to a terce* at least, better than my uncle Toby, and accordingly he assailed Mrs. Bridget after this manner:—

I know, Mrs. Bridget, said the Corporal, giving her a most respectful kiss, that thou art good and modest by nature; and art withal so generous a girl in thyself, that, if I know thee rightly, thou would'st not wound an insect, much less the honor of so gallant and worthy a soul as my master, wast thou sure to be made a Countess of; but thou hast been set on, and deluded, dear Bridget, as is often a woman's case, "to please others "more than themselves——"

Bridget's eyes poured down at the sensations the Corporal excited.

—Tell me,—tell me, then, my dear Bridget, continued the Corporal, taking hold of her hand, which hung down dead by her side,—and giving a second kiss,—whose suspicion has misled thee?

Bridget sobb'd a sob or two,—then open'd her eyes;—the Corporal wiped 'em with the bottom of her apron;—she then open'd her heart and told him all.

CHAP. XXX.

My uncle Toby and the Corporal had gone on separately with their operations the greatest part of the campaign, and as effectually cut off from all communication of what either the one or the other had been doing, as if they had been separated from each other by the Maes or the Sambre.

My uncle Toby, on his side, had presented himself every afternoon in his red and silver, and blue and gold, alternately, and sustained an infinity of attacks in them, without knowing them to be attacks; and so had nothing to communicate.

The Corporal, on his side, in taking Bridget, by it gain'd considerable advantages,—and consequently had much to communicate;—but what were the advantages,—as well as what was the manner by which he had seiz'd them, required so nice an historian, that the Corporal durst not venture upon it; and, as sensible as he was of glory, would rather have been contented to have gone bare-headed and without laurels for ever, than torture his master's modesty for a single moment.

—Best of honest and gallant servants!—But I have apostrophiz'd thee, Trim, once before;—and could I apotheosize thee also (that is to say) with good company,—I would do it *without ceremony* in the very next page.

CHAP. XXXI.

Now my uncle Toby had one evening laid down his pipe upon the table, and was counting over to himself, upon his fingers' ends (beginning at his thumb) all Mrs. Wadman's perfections, one by one; and happening two or three times together, either by omitting some, or counting others twice over, to puzzle himself sadly before he could get beyond his middle-finger,—Prithee, Trim, said he, taking up his pipe again, bring me a pen and ink.—Trim brought paper also.

—Take a full sheet, Trim! said my uncle Toby, making a sign with his pipe at the same time to take a chair and sit down close by him at the table. The Corporal obeyed,—placed the paper directly before him,—took a pen, and dipp'd it in the ink.

—She has a thousand virtues, Trim! said my uncle Toby.

—Am I to set them down, 'an please your Honor? quoth the Corporal.

—But they must be taken in their ranks, replied my uncle Toby; for of them all, Trim, that which wins me most, and which is a security for all the rest, is the compassionate turn and singular humanity of her character.—I protest, added my uncle Toby, looking up, as he protested it, towards the top of the ceiling,—that was I her brother, Trim, a thousand-fold, she could not make more constant or more tender inquiries after my sufferings,—though now no more.

The Corporal made no reply to my uncle Toby's protestation, but by a short cough:—he dipp'd the pen a second time into the inkhorn; and my uncle Toby, pointing with the end of his pipe as close to the top of the sheet at the left-hand corner of it as he could get it,—the Corporal wrote down the word Humanity - - - - thus.

—Prithee, Corporal, said my uncle Toby, as soon as Trim had done it,—how often does Mrs. Bridget inquire after the wound on the cap of thy knee, which thou received'st at the battle of Landen?

—She never, an' please your Honor, inquires after it at all.

—That, Corporal, said my uncle Toby, with all the triumph the goodness of his nature would permit,—that shows the difference in the character of the mistress and maid.—Had the fortune of war allotted the same mischance to me, Mrs. Wadman would have inquired into every circumstance relating to it a hundred times.—She would have inquired, an' please your Honor, ten times as often about your Honor's groin.—The pain, Trim, is equally excruciating,—and Compassion has as much to do with the one as the other.

—God bless your Honor, cried the Corporal,—what has a woman's compassion to do with a wound upon the cap of a man's knee? Had your Honor's been shot into ten thousand splinters at the affair of Landen, Mrs. Wadman would have troubled her head as little about it as Bridget; because, added the Corporal, lowering his voice, and speaking very distinctly, as he assigned his reason,—

"The knee is such a distance from the "main body,—Whereas the groin, your "Honor knows, is upon the very *curtain* of "the *place*."

My uncle Toby gave a long whistle;—but in a note which could scarce be heard across the table.

The Corporal had advanced too far to retire;—in three words he told the rest.

My uncle Toby laid down his pipe as gently upon the fender as if it had been spun from the unravelling of a spider's web.

—Let us go to my brother Shandy's, said he.

CHAP. XXXII.

THERE will be just time, whilst my uncle Toby and Trim are walking to my father's, to inform you that Mrs. Wadman had, some moons before this, made a confidant of my mother; and that Mrs. Bridget, who had the burden of her own, as well as her mistress's secret to carry, had got happily delivered of both to Susannah, behind the garden-wall.

As for my mother, she saw nothing at all in it, to make the least bustle about;—but Susannah was sufficient by herself for all the ends and purposes you could possibly have, in exporting a family secret; for she instantly imparted it by signs to Jonathan; —and Jonathan by tokens to the cook, as she was basting a loin of mutton; the cook sold it with some kitchen-fat to the postilion for a groat; who truck'd it with the dairy-maid for something of about the same value; —and though whispered in the hay-loft, *Fame* caught the notes with her brazen trumpet, and sounded them upon the house-top.—In a word, not an old woman in the village, or five miles round, who did not understand the difficulties of my uncle Toby's siege, and what were the secret articles which had delayed the surrender.

My father, whose way was to force every event in nature into an hypothesis, by which means, never man crucified *Truth* at the rate he did,—had but just heard of the report as my uncle Toby set out; and catching fire suddenly at the trespass done his brother by it, was demonstrating to Yorick, notwithstanding my mother was sitting by,— not only, "That the Devil was in women, "and that the whole of the affair was lust;" but that every evil and disorder in the world, of what kind or nature soever, from the first fall of Adam, down to my uncle Toby's (inclusive) was owing, one way or other, to the same unruly appetite.

Yorick was just bringing my father's hypothesis to some temper, when my uncle Toby entering the room with marks of infinite benevolence and forgiveness in his looks, my father's eloquence rekindled against the passion;—and as he was not very nice in the choice of his words when he was wroth, —as soon as my uncle Toby was seated by the fire, and had filled his pipe, my father broke out in this manner:

CHAP. XXXIII.

—THAT provision should be made for continuing the race of so great, so exalted, and godlike a being as man,—I am far from denying; — but philosophy speaks freely of every thing; and therefore I still think, and do maintain it to be a pity, that it should be done by means of a passion, which bends down the faculties, and turns all the wisdom, contemplations and operations of the soul backwards;—a passion, my dear, continued my father, addressing himself to my mother, which couples and equals wise men with fools, and makes us come out of our caverns and hiding-places more like satyrs and four-footed beasts than men.

I know it will be said, continued my father, (availing himself of the *Prolepsis*) that, in itself, and simply taken,—like hunger, or thirst, or sleep,—'tis an affair neither good nor bad, — nor shameful, nor otherwise. Why then did the delicacy of Diogenes and Plato so recalcitrate against it? and wherefore, when we go about to make and plant a man, do we put out the candle? and for what reason is it, that all the parts thereof, — the congredients, — the preparations, — the instruments, and whatever serves thereto, are so held as to be conveyed to a cleanly mind by no language, translation, or periphrasis whatever?

—The act of killing and destroying a man, continued my father, raising his voice, —and turning to my uncle Toby,—you see is glorious,—and the weapons by which we do it are honorable;—we march with them upon our shoulders;—we strut with them by our sides;—we gild them;—we carve them;—we inlay them;—we enrich them; —nay, if it be but a *scoundrel* cannon, we cast an ornament upon the breech of it.

—My uncle Toby laid down his pipe to intercede for a better epithet;—and Yorick was rising up to batter the whole hypothesis to pieces,—

When Obadiah broke into the middle of the room with a complaint, which cried out for an immediate hearing.

The case was this:—

My father, whether by ancient custom of the manor, or as impropriator of the great tythes, was obliged to keep a Bull for the service of the parish; and Obadiah had led his cow upon a *pop-visit* to him one day or other the preceding summer;--I say, one day or other,—because, as chance would have it, it was the day on which he was married to my father's house-maid;—so one was a reckoning to the other. Therefore, when Obadiah's wife was brought to bed,—Obadiah thanked God.—

Now, said Obadiah, I shall have a calf; so Obadiah went daily to visit his cow.

She'll calve on Monday,—or Tuesday, or Wednesday at the farthest.

The cow did not calve;—no, she'll not calve till next week;—the cow put it off terribly,—till at the end of the sixth week, Obadiah's suspicions (like a good man's) fell upon the Bull.

Now the parish being very large, my father's Bull, to speak the truth of him, was no way equal to the department; he had, however, got himself, somehow or other, thrust into employment,—and as he went through the business with a grave face, my father had a high opinion of him.

—Most of the townsmen, an' please your Worships, quoth Obadiah, believe that 'tis all the Bull's fault.

But may not a cow be barren? replied my father, turning to Doctor Slop.

—It never happens, said Doctor Slop; but the man's wife may have come before her time, naturally enough.—Prithee, has the child hair upon his head? added Doctor Slop.

—It is as hairy as I am, said Obadiah.—Obadiah had not been shaved for three weeks.—Wheu - - u - - - - u - - - - - - -, cried my father, beginning the sentence with an exclamatory whistle;—and so, brother Toby, this poor Bull of mine, who is as good a Bull as ever p–ss'd, and might have done for Europa herself in purer times,—had he but two legs less, might have been driven into Doctors' Commons, and lost his character;—which to a Town-Bull, brother Toby, is the very same thing as his life.

—L—d! said my mother, what is all this story about?

A *Cock* and a *Bull*, said Yorick;—and one of the best of its kind I ever heard.

END OF TRISTRAM SHANDY

A
SENTIMENTAL JOURNEY
THROUGH
France and Italy.

THEY order, said I, this matter better in France.

—You have been in France? said my gentleman, turning quick upon me, with the most civil triumph in the world.—Strange! quoth I, debating the matter with myself, That one-and-twenty miles' sailing, for 'tis absolutely no further from Dover to Calais, should give a man these rights:—I'll look into them: so giving up the argument,—I went straight to my lodgings, put up half a dozen shirts and a black pair of silk breeches;—"the coat I have on," said I, looking at the sleeve, "will do,"—took a place in the Dover stage; and, the packet sailing at nine the next morning,—by three I had got set down to my dinner upon a fricaseed chicken, so incontestibly in France, that, had I died that night of an indigestion, the whole world could not have suspended the effects of the *droits d'aubaine*;*—my shirts, and black pair of silk breeches,—portmanteau and all, must have gone to the King of France;—even the little picture which I have so long worn, and so often told thee, Eliza, I would carry with me into my grave, would have been torn from my neck!—Ungenerous! to seize upon the wreck of an unwary passenger, whom your subjects had beckoned to their coast!—by Heaven! Sire! it is not well done; and much does it grieve me 'tis the monarch of a people so civilized and courteous, and so renowned for sentiment and fine feelings, that I have to reason with!—

But I have scarce set a foot in your dominions—

* All the effects of strangers (Swiss and Scots excepted) dying in France are seized, by virtue of this law, though the heir be upon the spot;—the profit of these contingencies being farmed, there is no redress.

CALAIS.

WHEN I had finished my dinner, and drank the King of France's health, to satisfy my mind that I bore him no spleen, but, on the contrary, high honor for the humanity of his temper,—I rose up an inch taller for the accommodation.

—No, said I, the Bourbon is by no means a cruel race; they may be misled, like other people, but there is a mildness in their blood. As I acknowledged this, I felt a suffusion of a finer kind upon my cheek, more warm and friendly to man than what Burgundy (at least of two livres a bottle, which was such as I had been drinking) could have produced.

—Just God! said I, kicking my portmanteau aside, what is there in this world's goods which should sharpen our spirits, and make so many kind-hearted brethren of us fall out so cruelly as we do by the way?

When man is at peace with man, how much lighter than a feather is the heaviest of metals in his hand! he pulls out his purse, and holding it airily and uncompress'd, looks round him, as if he sought for an object to share it with.—In doing this, I felt every vessel in my frame dilate,—the arteries beat all cheerly together, and every power which sustained life performed it with so little friction, that 'twould have confounded the most *physical precieuse* in France: with all her materialism, she could scarce have called me a machine.

I'm confident, said I to myself, I should have overset her creed.

The accession of that idea carried Nature, at that time, as high as she could go.—I was at peace with the world before, and this finish'd the treaty with myself

—Now, was I a King of France, cried I, what a moment for an orphan to have begg'd his father's portmanteau of me!

THE MONK.

CALAIS.

I HAD scarce uttered the words, when a poor monk, of the order of St. Francis, came into the room, to beg something for his convent. No man cares to have his virtues the sport of contingencies,—or one man may be generous, as another man is puissant;—*sed non quoad hanc*,—or be it as it may,—for there is no regular reasoning upon the ebbs and flows of our humors: they may depend upon the same causes, for aught I know, which influence the tides themselves;—'twould oft be no discredit to us to suppose it was so: I'm sure, at least for myself, that in many a case I should be more highly satisfied to have it said by the world—"I had had an affair with the moon, in which there was neither sin nor shame," than have it pass altogether as my own act and deed, wherein there was so much of both.

—But be this as it may,—the moment I cast my eyes upon him, I was predetermined not to give him a single sous; and, accordingly, I put my purse into my pocket, button'd it up, set myself a little more upon my centre, and advanced up gravely to him. There was something, I fear, forbidding in my look: I have his figure this moment before my eyes, and think there was that in it which deserved better.

The monk, as I judged from the break in his tonsure, a few scatter'd white hairs upon his temples being all that remained of it, might be about seventy; but from his eyes, and that sort of fire which was in them, which seemed more tempered by courtesy than years, could be no more than sixty:—truth might lie between,—he was certainly sixty-five; and the general air of his countenance, notwithstanding something seem'd to have been planting wrinkles in it before their time, agreed to the account.

It was one of those heads which Guido has often painted,—mild, pale, penetrating, free from all commonplace ideas of fat contented ignorance looking downwards upon the earth;—it look'd forwards, but look'd as if it look'd at something beyond this world. How one of his order came by it, Heaven above, who let it fall upon a monk's shoulders, best knows; but it would have suited a Brahmin, and, had I met it upon the plains of Indostan, I had reverenced it.

The rest of his outline may be given in a few strokes; one might put it into the hands of any one to design, for 'twas neither elegant nor otherwise, but as character and expression made it so: it was a thin, spare form, something above the common size, if it lost not the distinction by a bend forward in the figure,—but it was the attitude of entreaty: and, as it now stands presented to my imagination, it gained more than it lost by it.

When he had entered the room three paces, he stood still; and laying his left hand upon his breast (a slender white staff with which he journeyed being in his right) —when I had got close up to him, he introduced himself with the little story of the wants of his convent, and the poverty of his order;—and did it with so simple a grace,—and such an air of deprecation was there in the whole cast of his look and figure,—I was bewitch'd not to have been struck with it.—

—A better reason was, I had predetermined not to give him a single sous.

THE MONK.

CALAIS.

'TIS very true, said I, replying to a cast upwards with his eyes, with which he had concluded his address;—'tis very true,—and Heaven be their resource who have no other but the charity of the world! the stock of which, I fear, is no way sufficient for the many *great claims* which are hourly made upon it.

As I pronounced the words *great claims*, he gave a slight glance with his eye downwards upon the sleeve of his tunic:—I felt the full force of the appeal;—I acknowledge it, said I:—a coarse habit, and that but once in three years, with meagre diet,—are no great matters; and the true point of pity is, as they can be earn'd in the world with so little industry, that your order should wish to procure them by pressing upon a fund which is the property of the lame, the blind, the aged, and the infirm!—the captive, who lies down counting over and over again the days of his afflictions, languishes also for his share of it; and had you been of the *order of Mercy*, instead of the order of St. Francis, poor as I am, continued I, pointing at my portmanteau, full cheerfully should it have been opened to you, for the ransom of the unfortunate.—The monk made me a bow.—But of all others, resum'd I, the unfortunate of our own country, surely, have the first rights; and I have left thousands in distress upon our own shore.—The monk gave a cordial wave with his head,—as much as to say, No doubt, there is misery enough in every corner of the world, as well as within our convent.—But we distinguish, said I, laying my hand upon the sleeve of his tunic, in return for his appeal,—we distinguish, my good father, betwixt those who wish only to eat the bread of their own labor—and those who eat the bread of other people's, and have no other plan in life but to get through it in sloth and ignorance, *for the love of God*.

The poor Franciscan made no reply: a hectic of a moment pass'd across his cheek, but could not tarry:—Nature seemed to have had done with her resentments in him; he showed none:—but letting his staff fall within his arm, he press'd both his hands with resignation upon his breast, and retired.

THE MONK.

CALAIS.

My heart smote me the moment he shut the door.—Psha! said I, with an air of carelessness, three several times,—but it would not do; every ungracious syllable I had uttered crowded back into my imagination: I reflected I had no right over the poor Franciscan but to deny him; and that the punishment of that was enough to the disappointed, without the addition of unkind language.—I considered his grey hairs:—his courteous figure seem'd to re-enter, and gently ask me what injury he had done me?—and why I could use him thus?—I would have given twenty livres for an advocate.—I have behaved very ill, said I, within myself; but I have only just set out upon my travels, and shall learn better manners as I get along.

THE DESOBLIGEANT.

CALAIS.

When a man is discontented with himself, it has one advantage, however, that it puts him into an excellent frame of mind for making a bargain. Now, there being no travelling through France and Italy without a chaise, and nature generally prompting us to the thing we are fittest for, I walked out into the coach-yard to buy or hire something of that kind to my purpose: an old *desobligeant*,* the furthest corner of the court,—hit my fancy at first sight; so I instantly got into it, and finding it in tolerable harmony with my feelings, I ordered the waiter to call Monsieur Dessein, the master of the hotel;—but Monsieur Dessein being gone to vespers, and not caring to face the Franciscan, whom I saw on the opposite side of the court, in conference with a lady just arrived at the inn,—I drew the taffeta-curtain betwixt us, and, being determined to write my journey, I took out my pen and ink, and wrote the preface to it in the *desobligeant*.

PREFACE.

IN THE DESOBLIGEANT.

It must have been observed, by many a peripatetic philosopher, That Nature has set up, by her own unquestionable authority, certain boundaries and fences to circumscribe the discontent of man; she has effected her purpose in the quietest and easiest manner, by laying him under almost insuperable obligations to work out his ease, and to sustain his sufferings at home. It is there only that she has provided him with the most suitable objects to partake of his

* A chaise, so called in France, from its holding but one person.

happiness, and bear a part of the burden which, in all countries and ages, has ever been too heavy for one pair of shoulders. 'Tis true, we are endued with an imperfect power of spreading our happiness sometimes beyond *her* limits; but 'tis so ordered, that, from the want of languages, connexions, and dependencies, and, from the difference in educations, customs, and habits, we lie under so many impediments in communicating our sensations out of our own sphere, as often amount to a total impossibility.

It will always follow from hence, that the balance of sentimental commerce is always against the expatriated adventurer: he must buy what he has little occasion for, at their own price;—his conversation will seldom be taken in exchange for theirs without a large discount,—and this, by the bye, eternally driving him into the hands of more equitable brokers, for such conversation as he can find, it requires no great spirit of divination to guess at his party.

This brings me to my point, and naturally leads me (if the see-saw of this *desobligeant* will but let me get on) into the efficient as well as final causes of travelling.

Your idle people that leave their native country, and go abroad for some reason or reasons which may be derived from one of these general causes:—

Infirmity of body,
Imbecility of mind, or
Inevitable necessity.

The two first include all those who travel by land or by water, laboring with pride, curiosity, vanity, or spleen, subdivided and combined *in infinitum.*

The third class includes the whole army of peregrine martyrs; more especially those travellers who set out upon their travels with the benefit of the clergy, either as delinquents, travelling under the direction of governors recommended by the magistrate;—or young gentlemen, transported by the cruelty of parents and guardians, and travelling under the direction of governors recommended by Oxford, Aberdeen, and Glasgow.

There is a fourth class, but their number is so small, that they would not deserve a distinction, were it not necessary, in a work of this nature, to observe the greatest precision and nicety, to avoid a confusion of character: and these men I speak of are such as cross the seas, and sojourn in a land of strangers, with a view of saving money, for various reasons, and upon various pretences; but, as they might also save themselves and others a great deal of unnecessary trouble by saving their money at home,—and, as their reasons for travelling are the least complex of any other species of emigrants, I shall distinguish these gentlemen by the name of

Simple Travellers.

Thus the whole circle of travellers may be reduced to the following heads:—

Idle Travellers,
Inquisitive Travellers,
Lying Travellers,
Proud Travellers,
Vain Travellers;
Splenetic Travellers:

then follow

The Travellers of Necessity,
The Delinquent and Felonious Traveller,
The Unfortunate and Innocent Traveller,
The Simple Traveller,

And last of all (if you please) The Sentimental Traveller (meaning thereby myself) who have travell'd, and of which I am now sitting down to give an account,—as much out of *Necessity*, and the *besoin de Voyager*, as any one in the class.

I am well aware, at the same time, as both my travels and observations will be altogether of a different cast from any of my forerunners, that I might have insisted upon a whole niche entirely to myself;—but I should break in upon the confines of the *Vain* Traveller, in wishing to draw attention towards me, till I have some better grounds for it than the mere *Novelty of my Vehicle.* It is sufficient for my reader, if he has been a Traveller himself, that with study and reflection hereupon, he may be able to determine his own place and rank in the catalogue;—it will be one step towards knowing himself, as it is great odds but he retains some tincture and resemblance of what he imbibed or carried out, to the present hour.

The man who first transplanted the grape of Burgundy to the Cape of Good Hope (observe he was a Dutchman) never dreamt of drinking the same wine at the Cape that the same grape produced upon the French mountains,—he was too phlegmatic for that; —but, undoubtedly, he expected to drink some sort of vinous liquor; but whether good, bad, or indifferent,—he knew enough of this world to know that it did not depend upon his choice, but that what is generally called *chance* was to decide his success: however, he hoped for the best; and in these hopes, by an intemperate confidence in the fortitude of his head, and the depth of his discretion, *Mynheer* might possibly overset both in his new vineyard; and, by discovering his nakedness, become a laughing-stock to his people.

Even so it fares with the poor Traveller sailing and posting through the politer kingdoms of the globe, in pursuit of knowledge and improvements.

Knowledge and improvements are to be got by sailing and posting for that purpose; but whether useful knowledge and real improvements are all a lottery;—and, even where the adventurer is successful, the acquired stock must be used with caution and sobriety, to turn to any profit:—but, as the chances run prodigiously the other way, both as to the acquisition and application, I am of opinion, That a man would act as wisely, if he could prevail upon himself to live contented without foreign knowledge or foreign improvements, especially if he lives in a country that has no absolute want of either; and indeed much grief of heart has it oft and many a time cost me, when I have observed how many a foul step the Inquisitive Traveller has measured, to see sights and look into discoveries, all which, as Sancho Pança said to Don Quixote, they might have seen dry-shod at home. It is an age so full of light, that there is scarce a country or corner of Europe, whose beams are not crossed and interchanged with others.—Knowledge, in most of its branches, and in most affairs, is like music in an Italian street, whereof those may partake who pay nothing.—But there is no nation under Heaven,—and God is my record (before whose tribunal I must one day come and give an account of this work) —that I do not speak it vauntingly,—But there is no nation under Heaven abounding with more variety of learning,—where the sciences may be more fitly woo'd, or more surely won, than here,—where Art is encouraged, and will soon rise high,—where Nature (take her altogether) has so little to answer for,—and, to close all, where there is more wit and variety of character to feed the mind with:—Where, then, my dear countrymen, are you going?—

We are only looking at this chaise, said they.—Your most obedient servant, said I, skipping out of it, and pulling off my hat. —We were wondering, said one of them, who, I found, was an *Inquisitive Traveller*, —what could occasion its motion.—'Twas the agitation, said I, coolly, of writing a preface.—I never heard, said the other, who was a *Simple Traveller*, of a preface wrote in a *desobligeant*.—It would have been better, said I, in a *vis-a-vis*.

As an Englishman does not travel to see Englishmen, I retired to my room.

CALAIS.

I PERCEIVED that something darken'd the passage more than myself, as I stepp'd along it to my room; it was effectually Mons. Dessein, the master of the hotel, who had just returned from vespers, and, with his hat under his arm, was most complaisantly following me, to put me in mind of my wants. I had wrote myself pretty well out of conceit with the *desobligeant*; and Mons. Dessein speaking of it with a shrug, as if it would no way suit me, it immediately struck my fancy that it belonged to some *Innocent Traveller*, who, on his return home, had left it to Mons. Dessein's honor to make the most of. Four months had elapsed since it had finished its career of Europe in the corner of Mons. Dessein's coach-yard: and having sallied out from thence but a vampt-up business at the first, though it had been twice taken to pieces on Mount Sennis, it had not profited much by its adventures,—but by none so little as the standing so many months unpitied in the corner of Mons. Dessein's coach-yard. Much, indeed, was not to be said for it,—but something might,—and, when a few words will rescue Misery out of her Distress. I hate the man who can be a churl of them.

—Now, was I the master of this hotel, said I, laying the point of my fore-finger on

Mons. Dessein's breast, I would inevitably make a point of getting rid of this unfortunate *desobligeant;* it stands swinging reproaches at you every time you pass by it.

Mon Dieu! said Mons. Dessein,—I have no interest.—Except the interest, said I, which men of a certain turn of mind take, Mons. Dessein, in their own sensations.—I'm persuaded, to a man who feels for others as well as for himself, every rainy night, disguise it as you will, must cast a damp upon your spirits. You suffer, Mons. Dessein, as much as the machine.

I have always observed, when there is as much *sour* as *sweet* in a compliment, that an Englishman is eternally at a loss within himself whether to take it or let it alone; a Frenchman never is; Mons. Dessein made me a bow.

C'est bien vrai, said he.—But in this case, I should only exchange one disquietude for another, and with loss. Figure to yourself, my dear Sir, that in giving you a chaise which would fall to pieces before you had got half-way to Paris,—figure to yourself how much I should suffer, in giving an ill impression of myself to a man of honor, and lying at the mercy, as I must do, *d'un homme d'esprit.*

The dose was made up exactly after my own prescription; so I could not help taking it,—and returning Mons. Dessein his bow, without more casuistry we walked together towards his remise, to take a view of his magazine of chaises.

IN THE STREET.

CALAIS.

It must needs be a hostile kind of a world when the buyer (if it be but of a sorry post-chaise) cannot go forth with the seller thereof into the street, to terminate the difference betwixt them, but he instantly falls into the same frame of mind, and views his conventionist with the same sort of eye, as if he was going along with him to Hyde Park Corner to fight a duel. For my own part, being but a poor swordsman, and no way a match for Mons. Dessein, I felt the rotation of all the movements within me, to which the situation is incident;—I looked at Monsieur Dessein through and through, —eyed him as he walked along in profile,—then *en face;*—thought he looked like a Jew,—then a Turk,—disliked his wig, cursed him by my gods,—wished him at the Devil!

—And is all this to be lighted up in the heart for a beggarly account of three or four Louis d'ors, which is the most I can be overreached in?—Base passion! said I, turning myself about, as a man naturally does upon a sudden reverse of sentiment,—base, ungentle passion! thy hand is against every man, and every man's hand against thee.—Heaven forbid! said she, raising her hand up to her forehead, for I had turned full in front upon the lady whom I had seen in conference with the monk;—she had followed us unperceived.—Heaven forbid, indeed! said I, offering her my own;—she had a black pair of silk gloves, open only at the thumb and two fore-fingers, so accepted it without reserve,—and I led her up to the door of the remise.

Monsieur Dessein had *diabled* the key above fifty times, before he found out he had come with a wrong one in his hand: we were as impatient as himself to have it open'd; and so attentive to the obstacle, that I continued holding her hand almost without knowing it; so that Mons. Dessein left us together, with her hand in mine, and with our faces turned towards the door of the remise, and said he would be back in five minutes.

Now, a colloquy of five minutes, in such a situation, is worth one of as many ages, with your faces turned towards the street. In the latter case, 'tis drawn from the objects and occurrences without;—when your eyes are fixed upon a dead blank,—you draw purely from yourselves. A silence of a single moment, upon Mons. Dessein's leaving us, had been fatal to the situation,—she had infallibly turned about;—so I began the conversation instantly.

—But what were the temptations (as I write not to apologize for the weaknesses of my heart in this tour,—but to give an account of them)—shall be described with the same simplicity with which I felt them

THE REMISE DOOR.

CALAIS.

When I told the reader that I did not care to get out of the *desobligeant*, because I saw the monk in close conference with the lady just arrived at the inn, I told him the truth; but I did not tell him the whole truth; for I was full as much restrained by the appearance and figure of the lady he was talking to. Suspicion crossed my brain, and said, he was telling her what had passed: something jarred upon it within me, — I wished him at his convent.

When the heart flies out before the understanding, it saves the judgment a world of pains.—I was certain she was of a better order of beings;—however, I thought no more of her, but went on and wrote my preface.

The impression returned, upon my encounter with her in the street; a guarded frankness with which she gave me her hand, showed, I thought, her good education and her good sense; and, as I led her on, I felt a pleasurable ductility about her, which spread a calmness over all my spirits.

—Good God! how a man might lead such a creature as this round the world with him!

I had not yet seen her face,—'twas not material: for the drawing was instantly set about, and, long before we had got to the door of the remise, *Fancy* had finish'd the whole head, and pleased herself as much with its fitting her goddess, as if she had dived into the Tiber for it;—but thou art seduced, and a seducing slut; and albeit thou cheatest us seven times a day with thy pictures and images, yet with so many charms dost thou do it, and thou deckest out thy pictures in the shapes of so many angels of light, 'tis a shame to break with thee.

When we had got to the door of the remise, she withdrew her hand from across her forehead, and let me see the original: —it was a face of about six-and-twenty,—of a clear transparent brown, simply set off without rouge or powder;—it was not critically handsome, but there was that in it which, in the frame of mind I was in, attached me much more to it,—it was interesting; I fancied it wore the characters of a widow'd look, and in that state of its declension which had passed the two first paroxysms of sorrow, and was quietly beginning to reconcile itself to its loss;—but a thousand other distresses might have traced the same lines; I wish'd to know what they had been,—and was ready to inquire (had the same *bon ton* of conversation permitted as in the days of Esdras)— "*What aileth* " *thee? and why art thou disquieted? and* " *why is thy understanding troubled?*"— In a word, I felt benevolence for her, and resolv'd, some way or other, to throw in my mite of courtesy,—if not of service.

Such were my temptations; and in this disposition to give way to them, was I left alone with the lady, with her hand in mine, and with our faces both turned closer to the door of the remise than what was absolutely necessary.

THE REMISE DOOR.

CALAIS.

This certainly, fair lady, said I, raising her hand up a little lightly as I began, must be one of Fortune's whimsical doings; to take two utter strangers by their hands,—of different sexes, and, perhaps, from different corners of the globe, and in one moment place them together in such a cordial situation as Friendship herself could scarce have achieved for them, had she projected it for a month.

—And your reflection upon it shows how much, Monsieur, she has embarrassed you by the adventure.

When the situation is what we would wish, nothing is so ill-timed as to hint at the circumstances which make it so. — You thank Fortune, continued she—you had reason,—the heart knew it, and was satisfied; and who but an English philosopher would have sent notice of it to the brain to reverse the judgment?

In saying this, she disengaged her hand, with a look which I thought a sufficient commentary upon the text.

It is a miserable picture which I am going to give of the weakness of my heart, by owning that it suffered a pain, which worthier occasions could not have inflicted.— I was mortified with the loss of her hand; and the manner in which I had lost it, carried neither oil nor wine to the wound; I never felt the pain of a peevish inferiority so miserably in my life.

The triumphs of a true feminine heart are short upon these discomfitures. In a very few seconds she laid her hand upon the cuff of my coat, in order to finish her reply; so, some way or other, God knows how, I regained my situation.

—She had nothing to add.

I forthwith began to model a different conversation for the lady, thinking, from the spirit as well as moral of this, that I had been mistaken in her character; but, upon turning her face towards me, the spirit which had animated the reply was fled,—the muscles relaxed, and I saw the same unprotected look of distress which first won me to her interest: — melancholy! to see such sprightliness the prey of sorrow,—I pitied her from my soul; and, though it may seem ridiculous enough to a torpid heart, — I could have taken her into my arms, and cherished her, though it was in the open street, without blushing.

The pulsations of the arteries along my fingers pressing across hers, told her what was passing within me. She looked down: —a silence of some moments followed.

I fear, in this interval, I must have made some slight efforts towards a closer compression of her hand, from a subtle sensation I felt in the palm of my own,—not as if she was going to withdraw hers,—but as if she thought about it;—and I had infallibly lost it a second time, had not instinct, more than reason, directed me to the last resource in these dangers,—to hold it loosely, and in a manner as if I was every moment going to release it of myself: so she let it continue till Mons. Dessein returned with the key; and, in the mean time, I set myself to consider how I should undo the ill impressions which the poor monk's story, in case he had told it her, must have planted in her breast against me.

THE SNUFF-BOX.

CALAIS.

The good old monk was within six paces of us as the idea of him cross'd my mind; he was advancing towards us a little out of the line, as if uncertain whether he should break in upon us or no.—He stopp'd, however, as soon as he came up to us, with a world of frankness, and having a horn snuff-box in his hand, he presented it open to me.—You shall taste mine, said I, pulling out my box (which was a small tortoise one), and putting it into his hand. — 'Tis most excellent, said the monk.—Then do me the favor, I replied, to accept of the box and all; and when you take a pinch out of it, sometimes recollect it was the peace-offering of a man who once used you unkindly, but not from his heart.

The poor monk blush'd as red as scarlet. *Mon Dieu!* said he, pressing his hands together,—you never used me unkindly.—I should think, said the lady, he is not likely. —I blush'd in my turn; but from what movements, I leave to the few who feel, to analyze.—Excuse me, Madam, replied I,—I treated him most unkindly; and from no provocations. — 'Tis impossible, said the lady. — My God! cried the monk, with a warmth of asseveration which seemed not to belong to him,—the fault was in me, and in the indiscretion of my zeal.—The lady opposed it: and I joined with her,—in maintaining it was impossible that a spirit so regulated as his could give offence to any.

I knew not that contention could be rendered so sweet and pleasurable a thing to the nerves as I then felt it. We remained silent, without any sensation of that foolish pain which takes place, when, in such a circle, you look for ten minutes in one another's faces without saying a word. Whilst this lasted, the monk rubb'd his horn-box upon the sleeve of his tunic: and as soon as it had acquired a little air of brightness by the friction, he made a low bow, and said, 'Twas too late to say whether it was the weakness or goodness of our tempers which had involved us in this contest;—but, be it as it would,—he begged we might exchange boxes.—In saying this, he presented his to me with one hand, as he took mine from me in the other; and having kissed it,—with a stream of good-nature in his eyes, he put it into his bosom, — and took his leave.

I guard this box as I would the instrumental parts of my religion, to help my mind on to something better. In truth, I seldom go abroad without it;—and oft and many a time have I called up by it the courteous spirit of its owner to regulate my own, in the justlings of the world: they had found full employment for his, as I learnt from his story, till about the forty-fifth year of his age, when, upon some military services ill requited, and meeting at the same time with a disappointment in the tenderest of passions, he abandoned the sword and the sex together, and took sanctuary, not so much in his convent as in himself.

I feel a damp upon my spirits as I am going to add, that in my last return through Calais, upon inquiring after Father Lorenzo, I heard he had been dead near three months; and was buried, not in his convent, but according to his desire, in a little cemetery belonging to it, about two leagues off. I had a strong desire to see where they had laid him,—when upon pulling out his little horn-box, as I sat by his grave, and plucking up a nettle or two at the head of it, which had no business to grow there, they all struck together so forcibly upon my affections, that I burst into a flood of tears; —but I am as weak as a woman; and I beg the world not to smile, but pity me.

THE REMISE DOOR.

CALAIS.

I HAD never quitted the lady's hand all this time; and had held it so long, that it would have been indecent to have let it go, without first pressing it to my lips: the blood and spirits, which had suffered a revulsion from her, crowded back to her as I did it.

Now the two travellers, who had spoke to me in the coach-yard, happened at the crisis to be passing by, and, observing our communications, naturally took it into their heads that we must be *man and wife* at least; and so stopping as soon as they came up to the door of the remise, the one of them, who was the Inquisitive Traveller, ask'd us if we set out for Paris the next morning?—I could only answer for myself, I said;—and the lady added, she was for Amiens.—We dined there yesterday, said the Simple Traveller. — You go directly through the town, added the other, in your road to Paris. — I was going to return a thousand thanks for the intelligence *that Amiens was in the road to Paris;* but upon pulling out my poor monk's little horn-box to take a pinch of snuff, I made them a quiet bow, and wished them a good passage to Dover.—They left us alone.

Now where would be the harm, said I to myself, if I was to beg of this distressed lady to accept of half of my chaise?—and what mighty mischief would ensue?

Every dirty passion and bad propensity in my nature took the alarm as I stated the proposition;—It will oblige you to have a third horse, said *Avarice,* which will put twenty livres out of your pocket. — You know not what she is, said *Caution;* or what scrapes the affair may draw you into, whisper'd *Cowardice.*

—Depend upon it, Yorick, said *Discretion,* 'twill be said you went off with a mistress; and came, by assignation, to Calais for that purpose.

—You can never after, cried *Hypocrisy,* aloud, show your face in the world;—nor rise, quoth *Meanness,* in the church;—nor be any thing in it, said *Pride,* but a lousy prebendary.

But 'tis a civil thing, said I;—and as I generally act from the first impulse, and therefore seldom listen to these cabals, which serve no purpose that I know of, but to encompass the heart with adamant,—I turn'd instantly about to the lady,—

But she had glided off unperceived, as the cause was pleading, and had made ten or a dozen paces down the street by the time I had made the determination; so I set off after her with a long stride, to make her the proposal with the best address I was master of; but observing she walk'd with her cheek half resting upon the palm of her hand,—with the slow, short-measur'd step of thoughtfulness, and with her eyes, as she went step by step, fixed upon the ground, it struck me she was trying the same case herself.—God help her! said I, she has some mother-in-law, or tartufish aunt, or nonsensical old woman, to consult upon the occasion, as well as myself: so not caring to interrupt the process, and deeming it more gallant to take her at discretion than surprise, I faced about, and took a short turn or two before the door of the remise, whilst she walk'd musing on one side.

IN THE STREET.

CALAIS.

Having, on first sight of the lady, setled the affair in my fancy, "that she was of the better order of beings;"—and then laid it down as a second axiom, as indisputable as the first, That she was a widow, and wore a character of distress,—I went no further; I got ground enough for the situation which pleased me;—and had she remained close beside my elbow till midnight, I should have held true to my system, and considered her only under that general idea.

She had scarce got twenty paces distant from me, ere something within me called out for a more particular inquiry; — it brought on the idea of a further separation: —I might possibly never see her more:—the heart is for saving what it can; and I wanted the traces through which my wishes might find their way to her, in case I should never rejoin her myself. In a word, I wish'd to know her name,—her family,—her condition;—and as I knew the place to which she was going, I wanted to know from whence she came: but there was no coming at all this intelligence: a hundred little delicacies stood in the way. I form'd a score different plans. — There was no such thing as a man's asking her directly; —the thing was impossible.

A little French *debonnaire* captain, who came dancing down the street, showed me it was the easiest thing in the world;—for, popping in betwixt us, just as the lady was returning back to the door of the remise, he introduced himself to my acquaintance, and before he had well got announced, begg'd I would do him the honor to present him to the lady.—I had not been presented myself;—so turning about to her, he did it just as well, by asking her if she had come from Paris? — No; she was going that route. she said.— *Vous n'ètes pas de Londres?*--She was not, she replied.—Then Madame must have come through Flanders. —*Apparemment vous ètes Flammande?* said the French captain.—The lady answered, she was. — *Peut-être de Lisle?* added he.—She answered, she was not of Lisle.—Nor Arras?—nor Cambray?—nor Ghent? — nor Brussels? — She answered, she was of Brussels.

—He had had the honor, he said, to be at the bombardment of it last war;—that it was finely situated, *pour cela*,—and full of noblesse when the Imperialists were driven out by the French (the lady made a slight curtsey;)—so giving her an account of the affair, and of the share he had had in it,—he begg'd the honor to know her name,—so made his bow.

—*Et Madame a son Mari?* said he, looking back when he had made two steps, —and, without staying for an answer,—danced down the street.

Had I served seven years' apprenticeship to good-breeding, I could not have done as much.

THE REMISE.

CALAIS.

As the little French captain left us, Mons. Dessein came up with the key of the remise in his hand, and forthwith let us into his magazine of chaises.

The first object which caught my eye, as Mons. Dessein open'd the door of the remise, was another old tatter'd *desobligeant;* and, notwithstanding it was the exact picture of that which had hit my fancy so much in the coach-yard but an hour before,—the very sight of it stirr'd up a disagreeable sensation within me now; and I thought 'twas a churlish beast into whose heart the idea could first enter to construct such a machine; nor had I much more charity for the man who could think of using it.

I observed the lady was as little taken with it as myself: so Mons. Dessein led us on to a couple of chaises which stood abreast, telling us, as he recommended them, that they had been purchased by my Lord A. and B. to go the *grand tour,* but had gone no further than Paris; so were, in all respects, as good as new.—They were too good;—so I pass'd on to a third, which stood behind, and forthwith began to chaffer for the price.—But 'twill scarce hold two, said I, opening the door and getting in.—Have the goodness, Madam, said Mons. Dessein, offering his arm, to step in. —The lady hesitated half a second, and stepp'd in; and the waiter that moment beckoning to speak to Mons. Dessein, he shut the door of the chaise upon us, and left us.

THE REMISE DOOR.

CALAIS.

C'est bien comique, 'tis very droll, said the lady smiling, from the reflection that this was the second time we had been left together by a parcel of nonsensical contingencies,—*c'est bien comique*, said she.

—There wants nothing, said I, to make it so, but the comic use which the gallantry of a Frenchman would put it to,—to make love the first moment,—and an offer of his person the second.

—'Tis their *fort*, replied the lady.

—It is supposed so at least;—and how it has come to pass, continued I, I know not; but they have certainly got the credit of understanding more of love, and making it better, than any other nation upon earth; but for my own part, I think them arrant bunglers; and, in truth, the worst set of marksmen that ever tried Cupid's patience.

—To think of making love by *sentiments!*

I should as soon think of making a genteel suit of clothes out of remnants;—and to do it,—pop,—at first sight by declaration, — is submitting the offer, and themselves with it, to be sifted with all their *pours* and *contres*, by an unheated mind.

The lady attended as if she expected I should go on.

— Consider then, Madam, continued I, laying my hand upon hers,—

That grave people hate Love for the name's sake,—

That selfish people hate it for their own,—

Hypocrites for Heaven's,—

And that all of us, both old and young, being ten times worse frightened than hurt by the very *report*,

What a want of knowledge in this branch of commerce a man betrays, who ever lets the word come out of his lips till an hour or two at least after the time that his silence upon it becomes tormenting! A course of small, quiet attentions, not so pointed as to alarm, — nor so vague as to be misunderstood,—with now and then a look of kindness, and little or nothing said upon it,—leaves Nature for your mistress, and she fashions it to her mind.

—Then I solemnly declare, said the lady, blushing,—you have been making love to me all this while.

THE REMISE.

CALAIS.

Monsieur Dessein came back to let us out of the chaise, and acquaint the lady that Count de L——, her brother, was just arrived at the hotel. Though I had infinite good-will for the lady, I cannot say that I rejoiced in my heart at the event, — and could not help telling her so;—for it is fatal to a proposal, Madam, said I, that I was going to make to you.

—You need not tell me what the proposal was, said she, laying her hand upon both mine, as she interrupted me.—A man, my good Sir, has seldom an offer of kindness to make to a woman, but she has a presentiment of it some moments before.

—Nature arms her with it, said I, for immediate preservation.—But I think, said she, looking in my face, I had no evil to apprehend;—and, to deal frankly with you, had determined to accept it. — If I had—(she stopped a moment)—I believe your good-will would have drawn a story from me, which would have made pity the only dangerous thing in the journey.

In saying this, she suffered me to kiss her hand twice; and, with a look of sensibility mixed with concern, she got out of the chaise,—and bid adieu.

IN THE STREET.

CALAIS.

I never finished a twelve-guinea bargain so expeditiously in my life. My time seemed heavy upon the loss of the lady; and knowing every moment of it would be as two, till I put myself into motion, — I ordered post-horses directly, and walked towards the hotel.

Lord! said I, hearing the town-clock strike four, and recollecting that I had been little more than a single hour in Calais,—

What a large volume of adventures may be grasped within this little span of life, by him who interests his heart in every thing, and who, having eyes to see what time and chance are perpetually holding out to him as he journeyeth on his way, misses nothing he can *fairly* lay his hands on!

—If this won't turn out something,—another will;—no matter,—'tis an essay upon human nature;—I get my labor for my pains,—'tis enough;—the pleasure of the experiment has kept my senses and the best part of my blood awake, and laid the gross to sleep.

I pity the man who can travel from Dan to Beersheba, and cry, 'Tis all barren;—and so it is: and so is all the world to him who will not cultivate the fruits it offers. I declare, said I, clapping my hands cheerily together, that was I in a desert, I would find out wherewith in it to call forth my affections:—if I could not do better, I would fasten them upon some sweet myrtle, or seek some melancholy cypress to connect myself to;—I would court their shade, and greet them kindly for their protection;—I would cut my name upon them, and swear they were the loveliest trees throughout the desert;—if their leaves withered, I would teach myself to mourn:—and when they rejoiced, I would rejoice along with them.

The learned Smelfungus travelled from Boulogne to Paris,—from Paris to Rome,—and so on;—but he set out with the spleen and jaundice; and every object he pass'd by was discolored or distorted.—He wrote an account of them; but 'twas nothing but the account of his miserable feelings.

I met Smelfungus in the grand portico of the Pantheon:—he was just coming out of it.—'*Tis nothing but a huge cock-pit*,* said he.—I wish you had said nothing worse of the Venus of Medicis, replied I;—for in passing through Florence, I had heard he had fallen foul upon the goddess, and used her worse than a common strumpet, without the least provocation in nature.

I popp'd upon Smelfungus again at Turin, in his return home; and a sad tale of sorrowful adventures he had to tell, "wherein "he spoke of moving accidents by flood and "field, and of the cannibals who each other "eat: the Anthropophagi."—He had been flay'd alive, and bedevil'd, and used worse than St. Bartholomew, at every stage he had come at.—

I'll tell it, cried Smelfungus, to the world. —You had better tell it, said I, to your physician.

Mundungus, with an immense fortune, made the whole tour; going on from Rome to Naples,—from Naples to Venice,—from Venice to Vienna,—to Dresden, to Berlin, without one generous connexion or pleasurable anecdote to tell of; but he had travell'd straight on, looking neither to his right hand nor his left, lest Love or Pity should seduce him out of his road.

Peace be to them, if it is to be found; but Heaven itself, was it possible to get there with such tempers, would want objects to give it;—every gentle spirit would come flying upon the wings of Love to hail their arrival.—Nothing would the souls of Smelfungus and Mundungus hear of, but fresh anthems of joy, fresh raptures of love, and fresh congratulations of their common felicity.—I heartily pity them: they have brought up no faculties for this work: and was the happiest mansion in Heaven to be allotted to Smelfungus and Mundungus, they would be so far from being happy, that the souls of Smelfungus and Mundungus would do penance there to all eternity!

MONTRIUL.

I HAD once lost my portmanteau from behind my chaise, and twice got out in the rain, and one of the times up to the knees in dirt, to help the postilion to tie it on, without being able to find out what was wanting.—Nor was it till I got to Montriul, upon the landlord's asking me if I wanted not a servant, that it occurred to me that *that* was the very thing.

* Vide S——'s Travels.

A servant! that I do, most sadly, quoth I.—Because, Monsieur, said the landlord, there is a clever young fellow, who would be very proud of the honor to serve an Englishman.—But why an English one more than any other?—They are so generous, said the landlord.—I'll be shot if this is not a livre out of my pocket, quoth I to myself, this very night.—But they have wherewithal to be so, Monsieur, added he.—Set down one livre more for that, quoth I.—It was but last night, said the landlord, *qu'un my Lord Anglois presentoit un ecu à la fille de chambre.—Tant pis, pour Mademoiselle Janatone*, said I.

Now Janatone being the landlord's daughter, and the landlord supposing I was young in French, took the liberty to inform me, I should not have said *tant pis;*—but *tant mieux.—Tant mieux, toujours, Monsieur*, said he, when there is any thing to be got; —*tant pis*, when there is nothing.—It comes to the same thing, said I.—*Pardonnez moi*, said the landlord.

I cannot take a fitter opportunity to observe, once for all, that *tant pis* and *tant mieux* being two of the great hinges in French conversation, a stranger would do well to set himself right in the use of them, before he gets to Paris.

A prompt French Marquis at our Ambassador's table, demanded of Mr. H——, if he was H—— the poet?—No, said Mr. H——, mildly.—*Tant pis*, replied the Marquis.

—It is H—— the historian, said another.—*Tant mieux*, said the Marquis.—And Mr. H——, who is a man of an excellent heart, return'd thanks for both.

When the landlord had set me right in this matter, he called in La Fleur, which was the name of the young man he had spoke of,—saying only first, That as for his talents, he would presume to say nothing—Monsieur was the best judge what would suit him; but for the fidelity of La Fleur, he would stand responsible in all he was worth.

The landlord delivered this in a manner which instantly set my mind to the business I was upon;—and La Fleur, who stood waiting without, in that breathless expectation which every son of Nature of us have felt in our turns, came in.

MONTRIUL.

I AM apt to be taken with all kinds of people at first sight; but never more so than when a poor Devil comes to offer his service to so poor a Devil as myself; and as I know this weakness, I always suffer my judgment to draw back something on that very account,—and this more or less, according to the mood I am in, and the case;—and, I may add, the gender too of the person I am to govern.

When La Fleur entered the room, after every discount I could make for my soul, the genuine look and air of the fellow determined the matter at once in his favor, so I hired him at first,—and then began to inquire what he could do.—But I shall find out his talents, quoth I, as I want them;—besides, a Frenchman can do every thing.

Now poor La Fleur could do nothing in the world but beat a drum, and play a march or two upon the fife. I was determined to make his talents do; and can't say my weakness was ever so insulted by my wisdom as in the attempt.

La Fleur had set out early in life, as gallantly as most Frenchmen do, with *serving* for a few years: at the end of which, having satisfied the sentiment, and found, moreover, that the honor of beating a drum was likely to be its own reward, as it open'd no further track of glory to him, he retired *à ses terres*, and lived *comme il plaisoit à Dieu;*—that is to say, upon nothing.

—And so, quoth Wisdom, you have hired a drummer to attend you in this tour of yours through France and Italy!—Pshaw! said I, and do not one half of our gentry go with a humdrum *compagnon du voyage* the same round, and have the piper and the Devil and all to pay besides? When a man can extricate himself with an *equivoque* in such an unequal match,—he is not ill off.—But you can do something else, La Fleur? said I.—*O qu'oui!* he could make spatterdashes, and play a little upon the fiddle.—Bravo! said Wisdom.—Why I play a bass myself, said I;—we shall do very well. You can shave and dress a wig a little, La Fleur?—He had all the dispositions in the world.—It is enough for Heaven, said I, interrupting him,—and ought to be enough for me.—So supper coming in, and having a frisky English spaniel on one side of my chair, and a French valet, with as much hilarity in his countenance as ever Nature painted in one, on the other,—I was satisfied to my heart's content with my empire; and if monarchs knew what they would be at, they might be as satisfied as I was.

MONTRIUL.

As La Fleur went the whole tour of France and Italy with me, and will be often upon the stage, I must interest the reader a little further in his behalf, by saying, that I had never less reason to repent of the impulses which generally do determine me, than in regard to this fellow;—he was a faithful, affectionate, simple soul as ever trudged after the heels of a philosopher; and notwithstanding his talents of drum-beating and spatterdash-making, which, though very good in themselves, happened to be of no great service to me, yet was I hourly recompensed by the festivity of his temper;—it supplied all defects:—I had a constant resource in his looks, in all difficulties and distresses of my own—(I was going to have added, of his too;) but La Fleur was out of the reach of every thing; for whether it was hunger or thirst, or cold or nakedness, or watchings, or whatever stripes of ill-luck La Fleur met with in our journeyings, there was no index in his physiognomy to point them out by,—he was eternally the same; so that if I am a piece of a philosopher, which Satan now and then puts it into my head I am,—it always mortifies the pride of the conceit by reflecting how much I owe to the complexional philosophy of this poor fellow, for shaming me into one of a better kind. With all this, La Fleur had a small cast of the coxcomb;—but he seemed, at first sight, to be more a coxcomb of nature than of art; and before I had been three days in Paris with him,—he seemed to be no coxcomb at all.

MONTRIUL.

The next morning, La Fleur entering upon his employment, I delivered to him the key of my portmanteau, with an inventory of my half a dozen shirts and a silk pair of breeches; and bid him fasten all upon the chaise,—get the horses put to,—and desire the landlord to come in with his bill.

—*C'est un garcon de bonne fortune*, said the landlord, pointing through the window to half a dozen wenches who had got round about La Fleur, and were most kindly taking leave of him as the postilion was leading out the horses. La Fleur kissed all their hands round and round again, and thrice he wiped his eyes, and thrice he promised he would bring them all pardons from Rome.

—The young fellow, said the landlord, is beloved by all the town; and there is scarce a corner in Montriul where the want of him will not be felt. He has but one misfortune in the world, continued he, "He is always in love."—I am heartily glad of it, said I; 'twill save me the trouble every night of putting my breeches under my head. In saying this, I was making not so much La Fleur's eloge as my own, having been in love with one Princess or other almost all my life, and I hope I shall go on so till I die, being firmly persuaded, that if ever I do a mean action, it must be in some interval betwixt one passion and another: whilst this interregnum lasts, I always perceive my heart locked up,—I can scarce find in it to give misery a sixpence: and therefore I always get out of it as fast as I can; and the moment I am rekindled, I am all generosity and good-will again; and would do any thing in the world, either for or with any one, if they will but satisfy me there is no sin in it.

—But in saying this,—sure I am commending the passion,—not myself.

A FRAGMENT.

—The town of Abdera, notwithstanding Democritus lived there, trying all the powers of irony and laughter to reclaim it, was the vilest and most profligate town in all Thrace. What for poisons, conspiracies, and assassinations,—libels, pasquinades, and tumults, there was no going there by day;—'twas worse by night.

Now, when things were at the worst, it came to pass, that Andromeda of Euripides being represented at Abdera, the whole orchestra was delighted with it; but of all the passages which delighted them, nothing operated more upon their imaginations than the tender strokes of nature which the poet had wrought up in that pathetic speech of Perseus, *O Cupid, prince of Gods and men,* &c. Every man almost spoke pure iambics the next day, and talk'd of nothing but Perseus, his pathetic address,—" O Cupid, " prince of Gods and men !" in every street of Abdera, in every house, — " O Cupid ! " Cupid !" in every mouth, like the natural notes of some sweet melody which drop from it, whether it will or no,—nothing but "Cupid ! Cupid ! prince of Gods and men !" —The fire caught,—and the whole city, like the heart of one man, open'd itself to Love.

No pharmacopolist could sell one grain of hellebore,—not a single armorer had a heart to forge one instrument of death;—Friendship and Virtue met together and kiss'd each other in the street;—the golden age returned, and hung over the town of Abdera; — every Abderite took his oaten pipe; and every Abderitish woman left her purple web, and chastely sat her down, and listened to the song.

—'Twas only in the power, says the Fragment, of the God whose empire extendeth from Heaven to earth, and even to the depths of the sea, to have done this.

MONTRIUL.

When all this is ready and every article is disputed and paid for at the inn, unless you are a little soured by the adventure, there is always a matter to compound at the door, before you can get into your chaise, and that is, with the sons and daughters of poverty who surround you. Let no man say, " Let them go to the Devil !"—'tis a cruel journey to send a few miserables; and they have had sufferings enow without it. I always think it better to take a few sous out in my hand; and I would counsel every gentle traveller to do so likewise; he need not be so exact in setting down his motives for giving them;—they will be register'd elsewhere.

For my own part, there is no man gives so little as I do; for few, that I know, have so little to give: but as this was the first public act of my charity in France, I took the more notice of it.

—A well-a-way ! said I,—I have but eight sous in the world, showing them in my hand, and there are eight poor men and eight poor women for 'em.

A poor tatter'd soul, without a shirt on, instantly withdrew his claim, by retiring two steps out of the circle, and making a disqualifying bow on his part. Had the whole *parterre* cried out, *Place aux dames,* with one voice, it would not have conveyed the sentiment of a deference for the sex with half the effect.

Just Heaven ! for what wise reasons hast thou ordered it, that beggary and urbanity, which are at such variance in other countries, should find a way to be at unity in this?

I insisted upon presenting him with a single sous, merely for his *politesse.*

A poor little dwarfish brisk fellow, who stood over-against me in the circle, putting something first under his arm, which had once been a hat, took his snuff-box out of his pocket, and generously offer'd a pinch on both sides of him: it was a gift of consequence, and modestly declined.—The poor little fellow press'd it upon them with a nod of welcomeness.—*Prenez-en,—prenez,* said he, looking another way; so they each took a pinch.—Pity thy box should ever want one, said I to myself; so I put a couple of sous into it,—taking a small pinch out of his box to enhance their value, as I did it.—He felt the weight of the second obligation more than of the first,—'twas doing him an honor,—the other was only doing him a charity;—and he made me a bow to the ground for it.

—Here ! said I to an old soldier with one hand, who had been campaign'd and worn out to death in the service,—here's a couple of sous for thee.— *Vive le Roi !* said the old soldier.

I had then but three sous left: so I gave one, simply *pour l'amour de Dieu,* which was the footing on which it was begg'd.

The poor woman had a dislocated hip; so it could not be well upon any other motive.

Mon cher et très-charitable, Monsieur. —There's no opposing this, said I.

My Lord Anglois ;—the very sound was worth the money:—so I gave *my last sous for it.* But, in the eagerness of giving, I had overlooked a *pauvre honteux*, who had no one to ask a sous for him, and who, I believe, would have perish'd ere he could have ask'd one for himself; he stood by the chaise, a little without the circle, and wiped a tear from a face which I thought had seen better days. Good God! said I, and I have not one single sous left to give him.—But you have a thousand! cried all the powers of Nature, stirring within me;—so gave him—no matter what,—I am ashamed to say *how much* now,—and was ashamed to think how little then; so if the reader can form any conjecture of my disposition, as these two fixed points are given him, he may judge within a livre or two what was the precise sum.

I could afford nothing for the rest, but *Dieu vous benisse.—Et le bon Dieu vous benisse encore*, said the old soldier, the dwarf, &c. The *pauvre honteux* could say nothing,—he pull'd out a little handkerchief, and wiped his face as he turned away;—and I thought he thanked me more than them all.

THE BIDET.

Having settled all these little matters, I got into my post-chaise with more ease than ever I got into a post-chaise in my life; and La Fleur having got one large jack-boot on the far side of a little *bidet*,* and another on this (for I count nothing of his legs) he canter'd before me as happy and as perpendicular as a prince.

—But what is happiness? what is grandeur in this painted scene of life?—A dead ass, before we got a league, put a sudden stop to La Fleur's career; his bidet would not pass by it,—a contention arose betwixt them, and the poor fellow was kick'd out of his jack-boots the very first kick.

La Fleur bore his fall like a French Christian, saying neither more nor less upon it than *Diable!* so presently got up, and came to the charge again astride his bidet, beating him up to it as he would have beat his drum.

The bidet flew from one side of the road to the other, then back again, then this way, then that way, and, in short, every way but by the dead ass:—La Fleur insisted upon the thing,—and the bidet threw him.

—What's the matter, La Fleur, said I, with this bidet of thine?—*Monsieur*, said he, *c'est un cheval le plus opiniatre du monde.*—Nay, if he is a conceited beast, he must go his own way, replied I.—So La Fleur got off him, and giving him a good sound lash, the bidet took me at my word, and away he scampered back to Montriul.—*Peste!* said La Fleur.

It is not *mal-à-propos* to take notice here, that though La Fleur availed himself but of two different terms of exclamation in this encounter,—namely, *Diable!* and *Peste!* that there are, nevertheless, three in the French language, like the positive, comparative, and superlative, one or the other of which serve for every unexpected throw of the dice in life.

Le Diable! which is the first and positive degree, is generally used in ordinary emotions of the mind, where small things only fall out contrary to your expectations,—such as—the throwing one's doublets,—La Fleur's being kick'd off his horse, and so forth.—Cuckoldom, for the same reason, is always *Le Diable!*

But in cases where the cast has something provoking in it, as in that of the Bidet's running away after, and leaving La Fleur aground in jack-boots,—'tis the second degree.

'Tis then *Peste!*

And for the third—

—But here my heart is wrung with pity and fellow-feeling, when I reflect what miseries must have been their lot, and how bitterly so refined a people must have smarted, to have forced them upon the use of it.

—Grant me, O ye powers which touch the tongue with eloquence in distress!—whatever is my *cast*, grant me but decent words to exclaim in, and I will give my nature way.

—But as these were not to be had in France, I resolved to take every evil just

* Post-horse.

as it befell me, without any exclamation at all.

La Fleur, who had made no such covenant with himself, followed the Bidet with his eyes till it was got out of sight,—and then, you may imagine, if you please, with what word he closed the whole affair.

As there was no hunting down a fright-en'd horse in jack-boots, there remained no alternative but taking La Fleur either behind the chaise or into it.—

I preferred the latter, and, in half an hour, we got to the post-house at Nampont.

NAMPONT.

THE DEAD ASS.

—And this, said he, putting the remains of a crust into his wallet,—and this should have been thy portion, said he, hadst thou been alive to have shared it with me.—I thought, by the accent, it had been an apostrophe to his child; but 'twas to his ass, and to the very ass we had seen dead in the road, which had occasioned La Fleur's misadventure. The man seemed to lament it much; and it instantly brought into my mind Sancho's lamentation for his; but he did it with more true touches of nature.

The mourner was sitting upon a stone bench at the door, with the ass's pannel and ts bridle on one side, which he took up from time to time,—then laid them down,—look'd at them, and shook his head. He then took his crust of bread out of his wallet again, as if to eat it, held it some time in his hand,—then laid it upon the bit of his ass's bridle,—look'd wistfully at the little arrangement he had made,—and then gave a sigh.

The simplicity of his grief drew numbers about him, and La Fleur among the rest, whilst the horses were getting ready: as I continued sitting in the post-chaise, I could see and hear over their heads.

—He said he had come last from Spain, where he had been from the furthest borders of Franconia; and had got so far on his return home when his ass died. Every one seemed desirous to know what business could have taken so old and poor a man so far a journey from his own home.

—It had pleased Heaven, he said, to bless him with three sons, the finest lads in all Germany; but having, in one week, lost two of the eldest of them by the small-pox, and the youngest falling ill of the same distemper, he was afraid of being bereft of them all; and made a vow, if Heaven would not take him from him also, he would go, in gratitude, to St. Iago in Spain.

When the mourner got thus far on his story, he stopp'd to pay Nature his tribute,—and wept bitterly.

He said, Heaven had accepted the conditions, and that he had set out from his cottage with this poor creature, who had been a patient partner of his journey;—that it had eat the same bread with him all the way, and was unto him as a friend.

Every body who stood about, heard the poor fellow with concern.—La Fleur offered him money.—The mourner said he did not want it;—it was not the value of the ass, but the loss of him. The ass, he said, he was assured, loved him;—and, upon this, told them a long story of mischance upon their passage over the Pyrenean Mountains, which had separated them from each other three days; during which time the ass had sought him as much as he had sought the ass; and that they had scarce either eat or drunk till they met.

—Thou hast one comfort, friend, said I, at least, in the loss of thy poor beast,—I'm sure thou hast been a merciful master to him.—Alas! said the mourner, I thought so when he was alive; but now that he is dead, I think otherwise.—I fear the weight of myself and my afflictions together, have been too much for him,—they have shortened the poor creature's days, and I fear I have them to answer for.—Shame on the world! said I to myself.—Did we but love each other as this poor soul loved his ass,—'twould be something.

NAMPONT.

THE POSTILION.

The concern which the poor fellow's story threw me into, required some attention: the postilion paid not the least to it, but set off upon the *pavé* in a full gallop.

The thirstiest soul in the most sandy desert of Arabia could not have wished more for a cup of cold water than mine did for grave and quiet movements; and I should have had an high opinion of the postilion, had he but stolen off with me in something like a pensive pace. On the contrary, as the mourner finished his lamentation, the fellow gave an unfeeling lash to each of his beasts, and set off clattering like a thousand Devils.

I called to him as loud as I could, for Heaven's sake to go slower:—and the louder I called, the more unmercifully he galloped.—The deuce take him and his galloping too, said I, he'll go on tearing my nerves to pieces till he has worked me into a foolish passion, and then he'll go slow, that I may enjoy the sweets of it.

The postilion managed the point to a miracle: by the time he had got to the foot of a steep hill, about half a league from Nampont,—he had put me out of temper with him,—and then with myself for being so.

My case then required a different treatment: and a good rattling gallop would have been of real service to me.

—Then, prithee, get on,—get on, my good lad, said I.

—The postilion pointed to the hill.—I then tried to return back to the story of the poor German and his ass;—but I had broke the clue, and could no more get into it again than the postilion could into a trot.

—The deuce go, said I, with it all! Here am I, sitting as candidly disposed to make the best of the worst as ever wight was, and all runs counter.

There is one sweet lenitive at least for evils, which Nature holds out to us: so I took it kindly at her hands, and fell asleep; and the first word which roused me was Amiens.

—Bless me, said I, rubbing my eyes,—this is the very town where my poor lady is to come.

AMIENS.

The words were scarce out of my mouth, when the Count de L***'s post-chaise with his sister in it, drove hastily by: she had just time to make me a bow of recognition,—and of that particular kind of it which told me she had not yet done with me. She was as good as her look; for, before I quite finished my supper, her brother's servant came into the room with a billet, in which she said she had taken the liberty to charge me with a letter, which I was to present myself to Madame R*** the first morning I had nothing to do at Paris. There was only added, she was sorry, but from what *penchant* she had not considered, that she had been prevented telling me her story,—that she still owed it me; and if my route should ever lay through Brussels, and I had not by then forgot the name of Madame de L***,—that Madame de L*** would be glad to discharge her obligation.

—Then I will meet thee, said I, fair spirit! at Brussels;—'tis only returning from Italy, through Germany to Holland, by the route of Flanders, home;—'twill scarce be ten posts out of my way: but were it ten thousand! with what a moral delight will it crown my journey, in sharing in the sickening incidents of a tale of misery told to me by such a sufferer! To see her weep, and, though I cannot dry up the fountain of her tears, what an exquisite sensation is there still left, in wiping them away from off the cheeks of the first and fairest of women, as I'm sitting with my handkerchief in my hand in silence the whole night beside her!

There was nothing wrong in the sentiment; and yet I instantly reproached my heart with it in the bitterest and most reprobate of expressions.

It had ever, as I told the reader, been one of the singular blessings of my life, to be almost every hour of it miserably in love with some one: and my last flame happening to be blown out by a whiff of jealousy on the sudden turn of a corner, I had lighted it up afresh at the pure taper of Eliza but about three months before,—swearing, as I did it, that it should last me through the whole journey.—Why should I dissemble the matter? I had sworn to her eternal fidelity;—she had a right to my whole heart:—to divide my affections was to lessen them,—to expose them, was to risk them; where there is risk, there may be loss:—and what wilt thou have, Yorick, to answer to a heart so full of trust and confidence,—so good, so gentle, and unreproaching!

—I will not go to Brussels, replied I, interrupting myself;—but my imagination went on,—I recalled her looks at that crisis of our separation, when neither of us had power to say adieu! I look'd at the picture she had tied in a black riband about my neck,—and blush'd as I look'd at it.—I would have given the world to have kiss'd it,—but was ashamed;—and shall this tender flower, said I, pressing it between my hands,—shall it be smitten to its very root,—and smitten, Yorick! by thee, who hast promised to shelter it in thy breast?

Eternal Fountain of Happiness! said I, kneeling down upon the ground,—be thou my witness,—and every pure spirit which tastes it, be my witness also, that I would not travel to Brussels, unless Eliza went along with me, did the road lead me towards Heaven!

In transports of this kind, the heart, in spite of the understanding, will always say too much.

THE LETTER.

AMIENS.

Fortune had not smiled upon La Fleur; for he had been unsuccessful in his feats of chivalry,—and not one thing had offered to signalize his zeal for my service from the time he had entered into it, which was almost four-and-twenty hours. The poor soul burn'd with impatience; and the Count de L——'s servant coming with the letter, being the first practicable occasion which offered, La Fleur had laid hold of it, and, in order to do honor to his master, had taken him into a back-parlor in the *auberge*, and treated him with a cup or two of the best wine in Picardy; and the Count de L——'s servant, in return, and not to be behind-hand in politeness with La Fleur, had taken him back with him to the Count's hotel. La Fleur's *prevenancy* (for there was a passport in his very looks) soon set every servant in the kitchen at ease with him; and as a Frenchman, whatever be his talents, has no sort of prudery in showing them, La Fleur, in less than five minutes, had pulled out his fife, and, leading off the dance himself with the first note, set the *fille de chambre*, the *maitre d' hotel*, the cook, the scullion, and all the household, dogs and cats, besides an old monkey, a-dancing! I suppose there never was a merrier kitchen since the flood.

Madame de L——, in passing from her brother's apartments to her own, hearing so much jollity below stairs, rung up her *fille de chambre* to ask about it; and hearing it was the English gentleman's servant who had set the whole house merry with his pipe, she ordered him up.

As the poor fellow could not present himself empty, he had loaden'd himself in going up stairs with a thousand compliments to Madame de L——, in the part of his master,—added a long apocrypha of inquiries after Madame de L——'s health, told her that Monsieur his master was *au desespoire* for her re-establishment from the fatigues of her journey,—and, to close all, that Monsieur had received the letter which Madame had done him the honor —And he has done me the honor, said Madame de L——, interrupting La Fleur, to send a billet in return.

Madame de L—— had said this with such a tone of reliance upon the fact, that La Fleur had not power to disappoint her expectations;—he trembled for my honor, —and, possibly, might not altogether be unconcerned for his own, as a man capable of being attached to a master who could be wanting *en egards vis à vis d'une femme!* so that, when Madame de L—— asked La Fleur if he had brought a letter,—*O qu'oui* said La Fleur; so laying down his hat upon the ground, and taking hold of the flap of his right side-pocket with his left hand, he began to search for the letter with his right;—then contrariwise.—*Diable!*—then sought every pocket, pocket by pocket round, not forgetting his fob;—*Peste!*—then La Fleur emptied them upon the floor,—pulled out a dirty cravat,—a handkerchief,—a comb,—a whip-lash,—a night-cap,—then gave a peep into his hat,—*Quelle etourderie!* He had left the letter upon the table in the *auberge*;—he would run for it, and be back with it in three minutes.

I had just finished my supper when La Fleur came in to give me an account of his adventure: he told the whole story simply as it was; and only added that if Monsieur had forgot (*par hazard*) to answer Madame's letter, the arrangement gave him an opportunity to recover the *faux pas;*—and if not, that things were only as they were.

Now, I was not altogether sure of my *etiquette*, whether I ought to have wrote or no; but if I had,—a Devil himself could not have been angry: 'twas but the officious zeal of a well-meaning creature for my honor; and however he might have mistook the road, or embarrassed me in so doing,—his heart was in no fault,—I was under no necessity to write;—and, what weighed more than all,—he did not look as if he had done amiss.

'Tis all very well, La Fleur, said I.—'Twas sufficient. La Fleur flew out of the room like lightning, and return'd, with pen, ink, and paper, in his hand; and coming up to the table, laid them close before me, with such a delight in his countenance, that I could not help taking up the pen.

I began, and began again; and though I had nothing to say, and that nothing might have been expressed in half a dozen lines, I made half a dozen different beginnings, and could no way please myself.

In short, I was in no mood to write.

La Fleur stepp'd out and brought a little water in a glass to dilute my ink,—then fetch'd sand and seal-wax.—It was all one; I wrote, and blotted, and tore off, and burnt, and wrote again.—*Le Diable l'emporte*, said I half to myself,—I cannot write this self-same letter, throwing the pen down despairingly as I said it.

As soon as I had cast down my pen, La Fleur advanced with the most respectful carriage up to the table, and making a thousand apologies for the liberty he was going to take, told me he had a letter in his pocket, wrote by a drummer in his regiment to a corporal's wife, which, he durst say, would suit the occasion.

I had a mind to let the poor fellow have his humor.—Then prithee, said I, let me see it.

La Fleur instantly pulled out a little dirty pocket-book, cramm'd full of small letters and billet-doux in a sad condition, and laying it upon the table, and then untying the string which held them all altogether, ran them over, one by one, till he came to the letter in question,—*La voila*, said he, clapping his hands; so unfolding it first, he laid it before me, and retired three steps from the table whilst I read it.

THE LETTER.

Madame,

Je suis penetré de la douleur la plus vive, et reduit en même temps au desespoir par ce retour imprevû du Corporal, qui rend notre entrevue de ce soir la chose du monde la plus impossible.

Mais vive la joie! et toute la mienne sera de penser à vous.

L'amour n'est *rien* sans sentiment.

Et le sentiment est encore *moins* sans amour.

On dit qu'on ne doit jamais se desesperer,

On dit aussi que Monsieur le Corporal monte le garde Mercredi: alors ce sera mon tour.

Chacun à son tour.

En attendant,—vive l'amour! et vive la bagatelle!

Je suis, Madame,
Avec toutes les sentiments
les plus respectueux et les
tendres, tout á vous,
Jaques Roque

It was but changing the Corporal into the Count—and saying nothing about mounting guard on Wednesday,—and the letter was neither right nor wrong;—so to gratify the poor fellow, who stood trembling for my honor, his own, and the honor of his letter,—I took the cream gently off it,—and whipping it up in my own way,—seal'd it up, and sent it to Madame de L——; and the next morning we pursued our journey to Paris.

PARIS.

When a man can contest the point by dint of equipage, and carry on all floundering before him with half a dozen lackeys and a couple of cooks,—'tis very well in such a place as Paris,—he may drive in at which end of a street he will.

A poor prince, who is weak in cavalry, and whose whole infantry does not exceed a single man, had best quit the field, and signalize himself in the cabinet, if he can get up into it,—I say *up into it*,—for there is no descending perpendicularly amongst 'em with a "*Me voici, mes enfans*,"—here I am,—whatever many may think.

I own, my first sensations, as soon as I was left solitary and alone in my own chamber in the hotel, were far from being so flattering as I had prefigured them. I walked up gravely to the window in my dusty black coat, and looking through the glass, saw all the world in yellow, blue, and green, running at the ring of pleasure.—The old with broken lances, and in helmets which had lost their visors, — the young, in armor bright, which shone like gold, beplumed with each gay feather of the east,—all—all—tilting at it like fascinated knights in tournaments of yore for fame and love.

—Alas, poor Yorick! cried I, what art thou doing here? On the very first onset of all this glittering clatter, thou art reduced to an atom; — seek, — seek some winding alley, with a tourniquet at the end of it, where chariot never rolled, nor flambeau shot its rays;—there thou mayest solace thy soul in converse sweet with some kind *grisette* of a barber's wife, and get into such coteries!—

—May I perish! if I do, said I, pulling out a letter which I had to present to Madame de R***. —I'll wait upon this lady the very first thing I do. So I called La Fleur to go seek me a barber directly,—and come back and brush my coat.

THE WIG.

PARIS.

When the barber came, he absolutely refused to have any thing to do with my wig: 'twas either above or below his art: I had nothing to do but to take one ready-made of his own recommendation.

—But I fear, friend, said I, this buckle won't stand.—You may immerge it, replied he, into the ocean, and it will stand.

What a great scale is every thing upon in this city! thought I.—The utmost stretch of an English periwig-maker's ideas could have gone no further than to have "dipped "it into a pail of water."—What difference! 'tis like time to eternity!

I confess I do hate all cold conceptions as I do the puny ideas which engender them; and am generally so struck with the great works of Nature, that, for my own part, if I could help it, I never would make a comparison less than a mountain at least. All that can be said against the French sublime in this instance of it, is this:—that the grandeur is *more* in the *word*, and *less* in the *thing*. No doubt the ocean fills the mind with vast ideas; but Paris being so far inland, it was not likely I should run post a hundred miles out of it to try the experiment:—the Parisian barber meant nothing.

The pail of water standing beside the great deep, makes certainly but a sorry figure in speech;—but 'twill be said,—it has one advantage—'tis in the next room, and the truth of the buckle may be tried in it, without more ado, in a single moment.

In honest truth, and upon a more candid revision of the matter, *the French expression professes more than it performs.*

I think I can see the precise and distinguishing marks of national characters more in these nonsensical *minutiæ*, than in the most important matters of state; where great men of all nations talk and talk so much alike, that I would not give ninepence to choose among them.

I was so long in getting from under my barber's hands, that it was too late to think of going with my letter to Madame R—— that night: but, when a man is once dressed at all points for going out, his reflections turn to little account; so taking down the name of the Hotel de Modene, where I lodged, I walked forth, without any determination where to go; I shall consider of that, said I, as I walk along.

THE PULSE.

PARIS.

Hail, ye small sweet courtesies of life, for smooth do you make the road of it! like grace and beauty, which beget inclinations to love at first sight: 'tis ye who open this door, and let the stranger in.

—Pray, Madame, said I, have the goodness to tell me which way I must turn to go to the *Opera Comique*.—Most willingly, Monsieur, said she, laying aside her work.

I had given a cast with my eye into half a dozen shops as I came along, in search of a face not likely to be disordered by such an interruption; till, at last, this hitting my fancy, I had walked in.

She was working a pair of ruffles as she sat in a low chair on the far side of the shop facing the door.

—*Tres volontiers;* most willingly, said she, laying her work down upon a chair next her, and rising up from the low chair she was sitting in, with so cheerful a movement and so cheerful a look, that, had I been laying out fifty Louis d'ors with her, I should have said—"This woman is grateful."

You must turn, Monsieur, said she, going with me to the door of the shop, and pointing the way down the street I was to take, —you must turn first to your left hand,—*mais prenez garde*,—there are two turns; and be so good as to take the second,—then go down a little way, and you'll see a church, and when you are past it, give yourself the trouble to turn directly to the right, and that will lead you to the foot of the *Pont Neuf*, which you must cross, and there any one will do himself the pleasure to show you.

She repeated her instructions three times over to me, with the same good-natur'd patience the third time as the first;—and if *tones and manners* have a meaning, which certainly they have, unless to hearts which shut them out,—she seemed really interested that I should not lose myself.

I will not suppose it was the woman's beauty, notwithstanding she was the handsomest *grisette*, I think, I ever saw, which had much to do with the sense I had of her courtesy, only I remember, when I told her how much I was obliged to her, that I looked very full in her eyes,—and that I repeated my thanks as often as she had done her instructions.

I had not got ten paces from the door, before I found I had forgot every tittle of what she had said:—so looking back, and seeing her still standing in the door of the shop, as if to look whether I went right or not,—I returned back, to ask her whether the first turn was to my right or left, for that I had absolutely forgot.—Is it possible! said she, half laughing.—'Tis very possible, replied I, when a man is thinking more of a woman than of her good advice.

As this was the real truth, she took it, as every woman takes a matter of right, with a slight curtsey.

—*Attendez*, said she, laying her hand upon my arm to detain me, whilst she called a lad out of the back-shop to get ready a parcel of gloves. I am just going to send him, said she, with a packet into that quarter; and if you will have the complaisance to step in, it will be ready in a moment, and he shall attend you to the place. So I walked in with her to the far side of the shop; and taking up the ruffle in my hands which she laid upon the chair, as if I had a mind to sit, she sat down herself in her low chair, and I instantly sat myself down beside her.

He will be ready, Monsieur, said she, in a moment.—And in that moment, replied I, most willingly would I say something very civil to you for all these courtesies. Any one may do a casual act of good-nature, but a continuation of them shows it is a part of the temperature; and, certainly, added I, if it is the same blood which comes from the heart, which descends to the extremes (touching her wrist) I am sure you must have one of the best pulses of any woman in the world.—Feel it, said she, holding out her arm. So laying down my hat, I took hold of her fingers in one hand, and applied the two fore-fingers of my other to the artery.—

Would to Heaven! my dear Eugenius, thou hadst passed by, and beheld me sitting in my black coat, and in my lack-a-day-sical manner, counting the throbs of it, one by one, with as much true devotion as if I had been watching the critical ebb or flow of her fever! How wouldst thou have laughed and moralized upon my new profession!—and thou shouldst have laughed and moralized on.—Trust me, my dear Eugenius, I should have said "there are worse occupa-" tions in this world *than feeling a woman's* "*pulse*."—But a *grisette's!* thou wouldst have said,—and in an open shop, Yorick!—

THE WIDOW.

"I am sure you must have one of the best pulses of any woman in the world."—p. 294.

(Josh)

—So much the better: for when my views are direct, Eugenius, I care not if all the world saw me feel it.

THE HUSBAND.

PARIS.

I HAD counted twenty pulsations, and was going on fast towards the fortieth, when her husband coming unexpected from a back-parlor into the shop, put me a little out in my reckoning.—'Twas nobody but her husband, she said—so I began a fresh score.—Monsieur is so good, quoth she, as he passed by us, as to give himself the trouble of feeling my pulse.—The husband took off his hat, and making me a bow, said, I did him too much honor; and having said that, he put on his hat and walked out.

Good God! said I to myself, as he went out,—and can this man be the husband of this woman!

Let it not torment the few who know what must have been the grounds of this exclamation, if I explain it to those who do not.

In London, a shopkeeper and a shopkeeper's wife seem to be one bone and one flesh. In the several endowments of mind and body, sometimes the one, sometimes the other, has it, so as in general to be upon a par, and to tally with each other as nearly as a man and wife need to do.

In Paris, there are scarce two orders of beings more different; for the legislative and executive powers of the shop not resting in the husband, he seldom comes there: —in some dark and dismal room behind, he sits commerceless in his thrum night-cap, the same rough son of Nature that Nature left him.

The genius of a people where nothing but the monarchy is salique, having ceded this department, with sundry others, totally to the women—by a continual higgling with customers of all ranks and sizes from morning to night, like so many rough pebbles shook long together in a bag, by amicable collisions, they have worn down their asperities and sharp angles, and not only become round and smooth, but will receive, some of them, a polish like a brilliant—Monsieur *le Marli* is little better than the stone under your foot.

—Surely,—surely, man! it is not good for thee to sit alone; thou wast made for social intercourse and gentle greetings; and this improvement of our natures from it, I appeal to, as my evidence.

—And how does it beat, Monsieur? said she.—With all the benignity, said I, looking quietly in her eyes, that I expected.—She was going to say something civil in return, but the lad came into the shop with the gloves.—*Apròpos*, said I, I want a couple of pairs myself.

THE GLOVES.

PARIS.

THE beautiful *grisette* rose up when I said this, and, going behind the counter, reached down a parcel, and untied it: I advanced to the side over-against her: but they were all too large. The beautiful *grisette* measured them one by one across my hand.—It would not alter the dimensions.—She begged I would try a single pair, which seemed to be the least.—She held it open;—my hand slipped into it at once.—It will not do, said I, shaking my head a little.—No, said she, doing the same thing.

There are certain combined looks of simple subtlety, — where whim, and sense, and seriousness, and nonsense, are so blended, that all the languages of Babel set loose together, could not express them: — they are communicated and caught so instantaneously, that you can scarce say which party is the infector. I leave it to your men of words to swell pages about it,—it is enough in the present to say again, the gloves would not do; so folding our hands within our arms, we both loll'd upon the counter;—it was narrow, and there was just room for the parcel to lay between us.

The beautiful *grisette* looked sometimes at the gloves, then sideways to the window, then at the gloves,—and then at me. I was not disposed to break silence;—I followed her example: so I looked at the gloves, then to the window, then at the gloves, and then at her—and so on alternately.

I found I lost considerably in every attack:—she had a quick black eye, and shot through two such long and silken eye-lashes with such penetration, that she looked into my very heart and reins.—It may seem strange; but I could actually feel she did.

It is no matter, said I, taking up a couple of the pairs next me, and putting them into my pocket.

I was sensible the beautiful *grisette* had not asked a single livre above the price. I wished she had asked a livre more; and was puzzling my brains how to bring the matter about.—Do you think, my dear Sir, said she, mistaking my embarrassment, that I could ask a sous too much of a stranger—and of a stranger whose politeness, more than his want of gloves, has done me the honor to lay himself at my mercy!—*M'en croyez capable?*—Faith! not I, said I; and if you were, you are welcome. So counting the money into her hand, and with a lower bow than one generally makes to a shopkeeper's wife, I went out; and her lad with his parcel followed me.

THE TRANSLATION.

PARIS.

THERE was nobody in the box I was let into, but a kindly old French officer. I love the character, not only because I honor the man whose manners are softened by a profession which makes bad men worse, but that I once knew one,—for he is no more,—and why should I not rescue one page from violation by writing his name in it, and telling the world it was Captain Tobias Shandy, the dearest of my flock and friends, whose philanthropy I never think of at this long distance from his death, but my eyes gush out with tears. For his sake, I have a predilection for the whole corps of veterans; and so I strode over the two back rows of benches, and placed myself beside him.

The old officer was reading attentively a small pamphlet (it might be the book of the opera) with a large pair of spectacles. As soon as I sat down, he took his spectacles off, and putting them into a shagreen case, returned them and the book into his pocket together. I half rose up, and made him a bow

Translate this into any civilized language in the world, the sense is this:—

"Here's a poor stranger come into the "box; he seems as if he knew nobody; and "is never likely, was he to be seven years "in Paris, if every man he comes near "keeps his spectacles upon his nose:—'tis "shutting the door of conversation abso-"lutely in his face, and using him worse "than a German."

The French officer might as well have said it all aloud: and if he had, I should in course have put the bow I made him into French too, and told him, "I was sensible "of his attention, and returned him a thou-"sand thanks for it."

There is not a secret so aiding to the progress of sociality, as to get master of this *short-hand*, and to be quick in rendering the several turns of looks and limbs, with all their inflections and delineations, into plain words. For my own part, by long habitude, I do it so mechanically, that when I walk the streets of London, I go translating all the way; and have more than once stood behind the circle, where not three words have been said, and have brought off twenty different dialogues with me, which I could have fairly wrote down and sworn to.

I was going one evening to Martini's concert at Milan, and was just entering the door of the hall, when the Marquisina de F*** was coming out, in a sort of a hurry:—she was almost upon me before I saw her: so I gave a spring to one side to let her pass. She had done the same, and on the same side too: so we ran our heads together: she instantly got to the other side to get out; I was just as unfortunate as she had been; for I had sprung to that side, and opposed her passage again. We both flew together to the other side, and then back,—and so on:—it was ridiculous; we both blushed intolerably; so I did at last the thing I should have done at first;—I stood stock still, and the Marquisina had no more difficulty. I had no power to go into the room till I had made her so much reparation as to wait and follow her with my eye to the end of the passage. She looked back twice, and walked along it rather sideways, as if she would make room for any one coming up stairs to pass her.—No, said I, that's a vile translation: the Marquisina has a right to the best apology I can make her; and that opening is left for me to do it in:—so I ran and begged pardon for the embarrassment I had given her, saying it was my intention to have made her way. She answered she was guided by the same intention towards me;—so we reciprocally thanked each other. She was at the top of the stairs; and seeing no *cicisbeo* near her, I begged to hand her to her coach; so we went down the stairs, stopping at every third step to talk of the concert and the adventure.—Upon my word, Madam, said I, when I had handed her in, I made six different efforts to let you go out.—And I made six efforts, replied she, to let you enter.—I wish to Heaven you would make a seventh, said I.—With all my heart, said she, making room.—Life is too short to be long about the forms of it;—so I instantly stepped in, and she carried me home with her.—And what became of the concert? St. Cecilia, who, I suppose, was at it, knows more than I.

I will only add, that the connexion which arose out of the translation, gave me more pleasure than any one I had the honor to make in Italy.

THE DWARF.

PARIS.

I HAD never heard the remark made by any one in my life, except by one; and who that was, will probably come out in this chapter; so that being pretty much unprepossessed, there must have been grounds for what struck me the moment I cast my eye over the *parterre*,—and that was, the unaccountable sport of Nature in forming such numbers of dwarfs.—No doubt, she sports at certain times in almost every corner of the world; but in Paris, there is no end to her amusements.—The Goddess seems almost as merry as she is wise.

As I carried my idea out of the *Opera Comique* with me, I measured every body I saw walking in the streets by it.—Melancholy application! especially where the size was extremely little,—the face extremely dark,—the eyes quick,—the nose long,—the teeth white,—the jaw prominent,—to see so many miserables, by force of accidents, driven out of their own proper class into the very verge of another, which it gives me pain to write down:—every third man a pigmy!—some by rickety heads and hump-backs;—others by bandy-legs;—a third set arrested by the hand of Nature in the sixth and seventh years of their growth;—a fourth, in their perfect and natural state, like dwarf apple-trees; from the first rudiments and stamina of their existence, never meant to grow higher.

A Medical Traveller might say, 'tis owing to undue bandages;—a Splenetic one, to want of air;—and an Inquisitive Traveller to fortify the system, may measure the height of their houses,—the narrowness of their streets, and in how few feet square in the sixth and seventh stories such numbers of the *Bourgeoisie* eat and sleep together. But I remember, Mr. Shandy the Elder, who accounted for nothing like any body else, in speaking one evening of these matters, averred, That children, like other animals, might be increased almost to any size, provided they came right into the world; but the misery was, the citizens of Paris were so coop'd up, that they had not actually room enough to get them.—I do not call it getting any thing said he;—'tis getting nothing.—Nay, continued he, rising in his argument, 'tis getting worse than nothing, when all you have got, after twenty or twenty-five years of the tenderest care and most nutritious aliment bestowed upon it, shall not at last be as high as my leg. Now Mr. Shandy being very short, there could be nothing more said of it.

As this is not a work of reasoning, I leave the solution as I found it, and content myself with the truth only of the remark, which is verified in every lane and by-lane of Paris. I was walking down that which leads from the Carousal to the Palais Royal, and observing a little boy in some distress at the side of the gutter which ran down the middle of it, I took hold of his hand and help'd him over. Upon turning up his face to look at him after, I perceived he was about forty.—Never mind, said I, some good body will do as much for me when I am ninety.

I feel some little principles within me, which incline me to be merciful towards this poor blighted part of my species, who have neither size nor strength to get on in the world. — I cannot bear to see one of them trod upon; and had scarce got seated behind my old French officer ere the disgust was exercised, by seeing the very thing happen under the box we sat in.

At the end of the orchestra, and betwixt that and the first side-box, there is a small esplanade left, where, when the house is full, numbers of all ranks take sanctuary. Though you stand, as in the *parterre*, you pay the same price as in the orchestra. A poor defenceless being of this order had got thrust, somehow or other, into this luckless place;—the night was hot, and he was surrounded by beings two feet and a half higher than himself. The dwarf suffered inexpressibly on all sides; but the thing which incommoded him most, was a tall, corpulent German, near seven feet high, who stood directly betwixt him and all possibility of his seeing either the stage or the actors. The poor dwarf did all he could to get a peep at what was going forwards, by seeking for some little opening betwixt the German's arm and his body, trying first on one side, then on the other; but the German stood square in the most unaccommodating posture that can be imagined:—the dwarf might as well have been placed at the bottom of the deepest draw-well in Paris; so he civilly reach'd up his hand to the German's sleeve, and told him his distress.—The German turn'd his head back, look'd down upon him as Goliah did upon David,—and unfeelingly resumed his posture.

I was just then taking a pinch of snuff out of my monk's little horn-box.—And how would thy meek and courteous spirit, my dear monk! so temper'd to *bear and forbear!*—how sweetly would it have lent an ear to this poor soul's complaint.

The old French officer seeing me lift up my eyes with an emotion, as I made the apostrophe, took the liberty to ask me what was the matter?—I told him the story in three words, and added, how inhuman it was.

By this time the dwarf was driven to extremes, and in his first transports, which are generally unreasonable, had told the German he would cut off his long queue with his knife.—The German look'd back coolly, and told him he was welcome, if he could reach it.

An injury sharpened by an insult, be it to whom it will, makes every man of sentiment a party: I could have leap'd out of the box to have redressed it. — The old French officer did it with much less confusion; for leaning a little over, and nodding to a sentinel, and pointing at the same time with his finger at the distress,—the sentinel made his way to it.—There was no occasion to tell the grievance—the thing told itself; so thrusting back the German instantly with his musket,—he took the poor dwarf by the hand, and placed him before him.—This is noble! said I, clapping my hands together.—And yet you would not permit this, said the old officer, in England.

—In England, dear Sir, said I, *we sit all at our ease.*

The old French officer would have set me at unity with myself, in case I had been at variance,—by saying it was a *bon mot;* —and as a *bon mot* is always worth something in Paris, he offered me a pinch of snuff.

THE ROSE.

PARIS.

It was now my turn to ask the old French officer, "What was the matter?" for a cry of "*Haussez les mains, Monsieur l'Abbé,*" re-echoed from a dozen different parts of the *parterre*, was as unintelligible to me as my apostrophe to the monk had been to him.

He told me it was some poor Abbé in one of the upper *loges*, who he supposed had got planted *perdu* behind a couple of *grisettes*, in order to see the opera, and that the *parterre* espying him, were insisting upon his holding up both his hands during the representation.—And can it be supposed, said I, that an ecclesiastic would pick the *grisettes*' pockets?—The old French officer smiled, and whispering in my ear, opened a door of knowledge which I had no idea of.

—Good God! said I, turning pale with astonishment, is it possible, that a people so smit with sentiment should at the same time be so unclean, and so unlike themselves.—*Quelle grossierté!* added I.

—The French officer told me it was an illiberal sarcasm at the church, which had begun in the theatre about the time the Tartuffe was given in it, by Moliere:—but, like other remains of Gothic manners, was declining.—Every nation, continued he, have their refinements and *grossiertés*, in which they take the lead, and lose it of one another by turns;—that he had been in most countries, but never in one where he found not some delicacies, which others seemed to want. *Le pour et le contre se trouvant en chaque nation;* there is a balance, said he, of good and bad everywhere; and nothing but the knowing it is so, can emancipate one half of the world from the prepossession which it holds against the other:—that the advantage of travel, as it regarded the *scavoir vivre*, was by seeing a great deal both of men and manners; it taught us mutual toleration; and mutual toleration, concluded he, making me a bow, taught us mutual love.

The old French officer delivered this with an air of such candor and good sense, as coincided with my first favorable impressions of his character:—I thought I loved the man; but I fear I mistook the object:—'twas my own way of thinking,—the difference was, I could not have expressed it half so well.

It is alike troublesome to both the rider and his beast,—if the latter goes pricking up his ears, and starting all the way at every object which he never saw before.—I have as little torment of this kind as any creature alive; and yet I honestly confess, that many a thing gave me pain, and that I blush'd at many a word the first month,—which I found inconsequent and perfectly innocent the second.

Madame de Rambouilet, after an acquaintance of about six weeks with her, had done me the honor to take me in her coach about two leagues out of town.—Of all women, Madame de Rambouilet is the most correct;—and I never wish to see one of more virtues and purity of heart.—In our return back, Madame de Rambouilet desired me to pull the cord.—I asked her if she wanted any thing?—*Rien que pour pisser*, said Madame de Rambouilet.

Grieve not, gentle traveller, to let Madame de Rambouilet p—ss on.—And ye fair mystic nymphs, go each one *pluck your rose*, and scatter them in your path,—for Madame de Rambouilet did no more.—I handed Madame de Rambouilet out of the coach; and had I been the priest of the chaste *Castalia*, I could not have served at her fountain with a more respectful decorum.

A

SENTIMENTAL JOURNEY

THROUGH

France and Italy.

THE FILLE DE CHAMBRE.

PARIS.

WHAT the old French officer had delivered upon travelling, bringing Polonius's advice to his son, upon the same subject, into my head,—and that bringing in Hamlet,—and Hamlet the rest of Shakspeare's Works, I stopt at the Quai de Conti, in my return home, to purchase the whole set.

The bookseller said he had not a set in the world.—*Comment!* said I, taking one up out of a set which lay upon the counter betwixt us.—He said, they were sent him only to be got bound; and were to be sent back to Versailles in the morning to the Count de B****.

—And does the Count de B****, said I, read Shakspeare?—*C'est un Esprit fort,* replied the bookseller.—He loves English books; and, what is more to his honor, Monsieur, he loves the English too.—You speak this so civilly, said I, that it is enough to oblige an Englishman to lay out a Louis d'or or two at your shop.—The bookseller made a bow, and was going to say something, when a young decent girl, about twenty, who by her air and dress seemed to be *fille de chambre* to some devout woman of fashion, came into the shop and asked for *Les Egarements du Cœur & de l'Esprit.* The bookseller gave her the book directly; she pulled out a little green satin purse run round with a riband of the same color and putting her finger and thumb into it, she took out the money and paid for it. As I had nothing more to stay me in the shop, we both walk'd out of the door together.

—And what have you to do, my dear, said I, with *The Wanderings of the Heart,* who scarce know yet you have one? nor till Love has first told you it, or some faithless shepherd has made it ache, canst thou ever be sure it is so.—*Le Dieu m'en garde!* said the girl.—With reason, said I; for if it is a good one, 'tis a pity it should be stolen; 'tis a little treasure to thee, and gives a better air to your face, than if it was dress'd out with pearls.

The young girl listened with a submissive attention, holding her satin purse by its riband in her hand all the time.—'Tis a very small one, said I, taking hold of the bottom of it—(she held it towards me)—and there is very little in it, my dear, said I; but be but as good as thou art handsome, and Heaven will fill it. I had a parcel of crowns in my hand to pay for Shakspeare; and as she had let go the purse entirely, I put a single one in; and tying up the riband in a bow-knot, returned it to her.

The young girl made me more an humble curtsey than a low one;—'twas one of those quiet, thankful sinkings, where the spirit bows itself down,—the body does no more than tell it. I never gave a girl a crown in my life which gave me half the pleasure.

My advice, my dear, would not have been worth a pin to you, said I, if I had not given this along with it: but now, when you see the crown, you'll remember it;—so don't, my dear, lay it out in ribands.

—Upon my word, Sir, said the girl, earnestly, I am incapable;—in saying which, as is usual in little bargains of honor, she gave me her hand: *En verité, Monsieur, je mettrai cet argent apart,* said she.

When a virtuous convention is made betwixt man and woman, it sanctifies their most private walks; so notwithstanding it was dusky, yet as both our roads lay the same way, we made no scruple of walking along the Quai de Conti together.

She made me a second curtsey in setting off; and before we got twenty yards from the door, as if she had not done enough before, she made a sort of a little stop, to tell me again—she thank'd me.

—It was a small tribute, I told her, which I could not avoid paying to virtue, and would not be mistaken in the person I had been rendering it to for the world; but I see innocence, my dear, in your face,—and foul befall the man who ever lays a snare in its way!

The girl seem'd affected, some way or other, with what I said;—she gave a low sigh:—I found I was not empowered to inquire at all after it,—so said nothing more till I got to the corner of the Rue de Nevers, where we were to part.

—But is this the way, my dear, said I, to the Hotel de Modene?—She told me it was;—or that I might go by the Rue de Guenegault, which was the next turn.—Then I'll go, my dear, by the Rue de Guenegault, said I, for two reasons: first, I shall please myself; and next, I shall give you the protection of my company as far on your way as I can.—The girl was sensible I was civil,—and said, She wish'd the Hotel de Modene was in the Rue de St. Pierre.—You live there! said I.—She told me she was *fille de chambre* to Madame R****. Good God! said I, 'tis the very lady for whom I have brought a letter from Amiens.—The girl told me that Madame R****, she believed, expected a stranger with a letter, and was impatient to see him.—So I desired the girl to present my compliments to Madame R****, and say I would certainly wait upon her in the morning.

We stood still at the corner of the Rue de Nevers whilst this pass'd.—We then stopped a moment whilst she disposed of her *Egarements du Cœur*, &c. more commodiously than carrying them in her hand:—they were two volumes;—so I held the second for her whilst she put the first into her pocket; and then she held her pocket, and I put in the other after it.

'Tis sweet to feel by what fine-spun threads our affections are drawn together!

We set off afresh; and as she took her third step, the girl put her hand within my arm.—I was just bidding her,—but she did it of herself, with that undeliberating simplicity, which show'd it was out of her head that she had never seen me before. For my own part, I felt the conviction of consanguinity so strongly, that I could not help turning half round to look in her face, and see if I could trace out any thing in it of a family-likeness.—Tut! said I, are we not all relations?

When we arrived at the turning up of the Rue de Guenegault, I stopp'd to bid her adieu for good and all; the girl would thank me again for my company and kindness.—She bid me adieu twice;—I repeated it as often; and so cordial was the parting between us, that had it happened anywhere else, I'm not sure but I should have signed it with a kiss of charity, as warm and holy as an apostle.

But in Paris, as none kiss each other but the men,—I did what amounted to the same thing,—

I bid God bless her!

THE PASSPORT.

PARIS.

When I got home to my hotel, La Fleur told me I had been inquired after by the Lieutenant de Police.—The deuce take it, said I,—I know the reason. It is time the reader should know it; for in the order of things in which it happened, it was omitted; not that it was out of my head; but, that had I told it then, it might have been forgot now;—and now is the time I want it.

I had left London with so much precipitation, that it never entered my mind that we were at war with France; and had reached Dover, and looked through my glass at the hills beyond Boulogne, before the idea presented itself; and with this in its train, that there was no getting there without a passport. Go but to the end of a street, I have a mortal aversion for returning back no wiser than I set out; and as this was one of the greatest efforts I had ever made for knowledge, I could less bear the thoughts of it; so hearing the Count de **** had hired the packet, I begg'd he would take me in his *suite*. The Count had some little knowledge of me, so made little or no difficulty,—only said, his inclination to serve me could reach no farther than Calais, as he was to return by way of Brussels to Paris; however, when I had once pass'd there, I might get to Paris without interruption; but that in Paris I must make friends and shift for myself.—Let me get to Paris, Monsieur le Count, said I,—and I shall do very well. So I embarked, and never thought more of the matter.

When La Fleur told me the Lieutenant de Police had been inquiring after me,—the thing instantly recurred;—and by the time La Fleur had well told me, the master of the hotel came into my room to tell me the same thing, with this addition to it, that my passport had been particularly asked after: the master of the hotel concluded with saying he hoped I had one.—Not I, faith! said I.

The master of the hotel retired three steps from me, as from an infected person, as I declared this;—and poor La Fleur advanced three steps towards me, and with that sort of movement which a good soul makes to succor a distress'd one: the fellow won my heart by it; and from that single trait, I knew his character as perfectly, and could rely upon it as firmly, as if he had served me with fidelity for seven years.

Mon Seigneur! cried the master of the hotel:—but recollecting himself as he made the exclamation, he instantly changed the tone of it.—If Monsieur, said he, has not a passport (*apparemment*) in all likelihood he has friends in Paris who can procure him one.—Not that I know of, quoth I, with an air of indifference.—Then certes, replied he, you'll be sent to the Bastile, or the Chatelet, *au moins.*—Poo! said I, the King of France is a good-natured soul,—he'll hurt nobody.—*Cela n'empeche pas*, said he,—you will certainly be sent to the Bastile to-morrow morning. But I've taken your lodgings for a month, answered I, and I'll not quit them a day before the time for all the Kings of France in the world.—La Fleur whispered in my ear,—That nobody could oppose the King of France.

Pardi, said my host, *ces Messieurs Anglois sont des gens tres extraordinaires;*—and having both said and sworn it,—he went out.

THE PASSPORT.

THE HOTEL AT PARIS.

I COULD not find in my heart to torture La Fleur's with a serious look upon the subject of my embarrassment, which was the reason I had treated it so cavalierly; and to show him how light it lay upon my mind, I dropped the subject entirely; and whilst he waited upon me at supper, talk'd to him with more than usual gaiety about Paris, and of the *Opera Comique.*—La Fleur had been there himself, and had followed me through the streets as far as the bookseller's shop; but seeing me come out with the young *fille de chambre*, and that we walk'd down the Quai de Conti together, La Fleur deem'd it unnecessary to follow me a step further,—so making his own reflections upon it, he took a shorter cut,—and got to the hotel in time to be inform'd of the affair of the police against my arrival.

As soon as the honest creature had taken away, and gone down to sup himself, I then began to think a little seriously about my situation.

—And here, I know, Eugenius, thou wilt smile at the remembrance of a short dialogue which pass'd betwixt us the moment I was going to set out:—I must tell it here.

Eugenius, knowing that I was as little subject to be overburthen'd with money as thought, had drawn me aside to interrogate me how much I had taken care for. Upon telling him the exact sum, Eugenius shook his head, and said, it would not do; so pull'd out his purse, in order to empty it into mine.—I've enough, in conscience, Eugenius, said I.—Indeed, Yorick, you have not, replied Eugenius,—I know France and Italy better than you.—But you don't consider, Eugenius, said I, refusing his offer, that before I have been three days in Paris, I shall take care to say or do something or other for which I shall get clapp'd up into the Bastile, and that I shall live there a couple of months entirely at the King of France's expense.—I beg pardon, said Eugenius, drily: really, I had forgot that resource.

Now the event I treated gaily, came seriously to my door.

Is it folly, or *nonchalance*, or philosophy, or pertinacity:—or what is it in me, that after all, when La Fleur had gone down stairs, and I was quite alone, I could not bring down my mind to think of it otherwise than I had then spoken of it to Eugenius?

—And as for the Bastile,—the terror is in the word.—Make the most of it you can, said I to myself, the Bastile is but another word for a tower;—and a tower is but another word for a house you can't get out of.—Mercy on the gouty! for they are in it twice a year.—But with nine livres a day, and pen and ink and paper and patience, albeit a man can't get out, he may do very well within,—at least for a month or six weeks; at the end of which, if he is a harmless fellow, his innocence appears, and he comes out a better and wiser man than he went in.

I had some occasion, (I forget what) to step into the court-yard, as I settled this account; and remember I walked down stairs in no small triumph with the conceit of my reasoning.—Beshrew the *sombre* pencil! said I, vauntingly,—for I envy not its power, which paints the evils of life with so hard and deadly a coloring.—The mind sits terrified at the objects she has magnified herself, and blackened: reduce them to their proper size and hue, she overlooks them.—'Tis true, said I, correcting the proposition,—the Bastile is not an evil to be despised.—But strip it of its towers, —fill up the fossé,—unbarricade the doors, —call it simply a confinement, and suppose tis some tyrant of a distemper,—and not of a man, which holds you in it,—the evil vanishes, and you bear the other half without complaint.

I was interrupted in the hey-day of this soliloquy, with a voice which I took to be of a child, which complained "it could not "get out."—I look'd up and down the passage, and seeing neither man, woman, nor child, I went out without further attention.

In my return back through the passage, I heard the same words repeated twice over; and looking up, I saw it was a starling hung in a little cage.—"I can't get "out,—I can't get out," said the starling.

I stood looking at the bird: and to every person who came through the passage, it ran fluttering to the side towards which they approach'd it, with the same lamentation of its captivity,—"I can't get out," said the starling.—God help thee! said I,—but I'll let thee out, cost what it will; so I turned about the cage to get the door: it was twisted and double twisted so fast with wire, there was no getting it open without pulling the cage to pieces.—I took both hands to it.

The bird flew to the place where I was attempting his deliverance, and thrusting his head through the trellis, pressed his breast against it, as if impatient.—I fear, poor creature, said I, I cannot set thee at liberty.—"No," said the starling; "I can't "get out,—I can't get out," said the starling.

I vow I never had my affections more tenderly awakened; nor do I remember an incident in my life where the dissipated spirits to which my reason had been a bubble, were so suddenly call'd home. Mechanical as the notes were, yet so true in tune to nature were they chanted, that in one moment they overthrew all my systematic reasonings upon the Bastile; and I heavily walk'd up stairs, unsaying every word I had said in going down them.

Disguise thyself as thou wilt, still, Slavery, said I,—still thou art a bitter draught! and though thousands in all ages have been made to drink of thee, thou art no less bitter on that account.—'Tis thou, thrice sweet and gracious goddess, addressing myself to *Liberty*, whom all in public or in private worship, whose taste is grateful, and ever will be so, till Nature herself shall change. No *tint* of words can spot thy snowy mantle, or chymic power turn thy sceptre into iron;—with thee to smile upon him as he eats his crust, the swain is happier than his monarch, from whose court thou art exiled.—Gracious Heaven! cried I, kneeling down upon the last step but one in my ascent, grant me but health, thou great Bestower of it, and give me but this fair goddess as my companion,—and shower down thy mitres, if it seems good unto thy Divine Providence, upon those heads which are aching for them.

THE CAPTIVE

PARIS.

The bird in his cage pursued me into my room. I sat down close by my table, and, leaning my head upon my hand, I began to figure to myself the miseries of confinement. I was in a right frame for it, and so I gave full scope to my imagination.

I was going to begin with the millions of my fellow-creatures born to no inheritance but slavery: but finding, however affecting the picture was, that I could not bring it near me, and that the multitude of sad groups in it did but distract me,

—I took a single captive; and having first shut him up in his dungeon, I then look'd through the twilight of his grated door to take his picture.

I beheld his body half wasted away with long expectation and confinement, and felt what kind of sickness of the heart it was which arises from hope deferred. Upon looking nearer, I saw him pale and feverish; in thirty years the western breeze had not once fanned his blood;—he had seen no sun, no moon, in all that time;—nor had the voice of friend or kinsman breathed through his lattice!—His children!—

But here my heart began to bleed; and I was forced to go on with another part of the portrait.

He was sitting upon the ground upon a little straw, in the furthest corner of his dungeon, which was alternately his chair and bed: a little calendar of small sticks were laid at the head, notched all over with the dismal days and nights he had passed there:—he had one of these little sticks in his hand, and, with a rusty nail, he was etching another day of misery to add to the heap. As I darkened the little light he had, he lifted up a hopeless eye towards the door, then cast it down,—shook his head, and went on with his work of affliction. I heard his chains upon his legs, as he turned his body to lay his little stick upon the bundle. —He gave a deep sigh.—I saw the iron enter into his soul!—I burst into tears. I could not sustain the picture of confinement which my fancy had drawn.—I started up from my chair, and, calling La Fleur,—I bid him bespeak me a remise, and have it ready at the door of the hotel by nine in the morning.

—I'll go directly, said I to myself, to Monsieur le Duc de Choiseul.

La Fleur would have put me to bed; but not willing he should see any thing upon my cheek which would cost the honest fellow a heart-ache,—I told him I would go to bed by myself,—and bid him go do the same.

THE STARLING.

ROAD TO VERSAILLES.

I got into my remise the hour I proposed. La Fleur got up behind, and I bid the coachman make the best of his way to Versailles.

As there was nothing in this road or rather nothing which I look for in travelling, I cannot fill up the blank better than with a short history of this self-same bird, which became the subject of the last chapter.

Whilst the Honorable Mr. **** was waiting for a wind at Dover, it had been caught upon the cliffs, before it could well fly, by an English lad who was his groom; who, not caring to destroy it, had taken it in his breast into the packet;—and, by course of feeding it, and taking it once under his protection, in a day or two grew fond of it, and got it safe along with him to Paris.

At Paris, the lad had laid out a livre in a little cage for the starling; and as he had little to do better the five months his master staid there, he taught it, in his mother's tongue, the four simple words—(and no more)—to which I owned myself so much its debtor.

Upon his master's going on for Italy, the lad had given it to the master of the hotel. But his little song for liberty being in an *unknown* language at Paris, the bird had little or no store set by him;—so La Fleur bought both him and his cage for me, for a bottle of Burgundy.

In my return from Italy, I brought him with me to the country in whose language he had learned his notes; and telling the story of him to Lord A—, Lord A. begged the bird of me; in a week Lord A. gave him to Lord B—; Lord B. made a present of him to Lord C—; and Lord C.'s gentleman sold him to Lord D.'s for a shilling:—Lord D. gave him to Lord E. and so on, half round the alphabet. From that rank he passed into the lower house, and passed the hands of as many commoners.—But as all these wanted to get in, and my bird wanted to get out, he had almost as little store set by him in London as in Paris.

It is impossible but many of my readers must have heard of him; and if any by mere chance have ever seen him,—I beg leave to inform them that that bird was my bird,—or some vile copy set up to represent him.

I have nothing farther to add upon him, but that from that time to this, I have borne this poor starling as the crest to my arms. —And let the herald's officers twist his neck, about if they dare.

THE ADDRESS.

VERSAILLES.

I SHOULD not like to have my enemy take a view of my mind when I am going to ask protection of any man; for which reason I generally endeavor to protect myself: but this going to Monsieur le Duc de C——, was an act of compulsion;—had it been an act of choice, I should have done it, I suppose, like other people.

How many mean plans of dirty address, as I went along, did my servile heart form! I deserved the Bastile for every one of them.

Then nothing would serve me, when I got within sight of Versailles, but putting words and sentences together, and conceiving attitudes and tones to writhe myself into Monsieur le Duc de C——'s good grace. —This will do, said I.—Just as well, retorted I again, as a coat carried up to him by an adventurous taylor, without taking his measure.—Fool! continued I,—see Monsieur le Duc's face first;—observe what character is written in it;—take notice in what posture he stands to hear you;—mark the turns and expressions of his body and limbs;—and for the tone,—the first sound which comes from his lips will give you it; and from all these together you'll compound an address at once upon the spot, which cannot disgust the Duke;—the ingredients are his own, and most likely to go down.

Well! said I, I wish it well over.—Coward again! as if man to man was not equal throughout the whole surface of the globe; and if in the field, why not face to face in the cabinet too? and trust me, Yorick, whenever it is not so, man is false to himself, and betrays his own succors ten times where nature does it once. Go to the Duc de C—— with the Bastile in thy looks;—my life for it, thou wilt be sent back to Paris in half an hour with an escort.

I believe so, said I.—Then I'll go to the Duke, by Heaven! with all the gaiety and debonnairness in the world.

—And there you are wrong again, replied I.—A heart at ease, Yorick, flies into no extremes,—'tis ever on its centre.—Well! well! cried I, as the coachman turned in at the gates, I find I shall do very well: and by the time he had wheeled round the court, and brought me up to the door, I found myself so much the better for my own lecture, that I neither ascended the steps like a victim to justice, who was to part with life upon the topmast,—nor did I mount them with a skip and a couple of strides, as I do when I fly up, Eliza! to thee, to meet it.

As I entered the door of the saloon, I was met by a person who possibly might be the *maitre d'hotel*, but had more the air of one of the under-secretaries, who told me the Duc de C—— was busy.—I am utterly ignorant, said I, of the forms of obtaining an audience, being an absolute stranger, and, what is worse in the present conjuncture of affairs, being an Englishman too.—He replied, that did not increase the difficulty.—I made him a slight bow, and told him, I had something of importance to say to Monsieur le Duc. The secretary looked towards the stairs, as if he was about to leave me to carry up this account to some one.—But I must not mislead you, said I,—for what I have to say is of no manner of importance to Monsieur le Duc de C——, but of great importance to myself.—*C'est une autre affaire*, replied he.—Not at all, said I, to a man of gallantry. But pray, good Sir, continued I when can a stranger hope to have *accesse?*—In not less than two hours, said he, looking at his watch.—The number of equipages in the court-yard seemed to justify the calculation, that I could have no nearer prospect;—and as walking backwards and forwards in the saloon, without a soul to commune with, was for the time as bad as being in the Bastile itself, I instantly went back to my remise, and bid the coachman drive me to the *Cordon Bleu*, which was the nearest hotel.

I think there is a fatality in it;—I seldom go to the place I set out for.

LE PATISSER.

VERSAILLES.

Before I had got half-way down the street, I changed my mind: as I am at Versailles, thought I, I might as well take a view of the town; so I pulled the cord, and ordered the coachman to drive round some of the principal streets.—I suppose the town is not very large, said I.—The coachman begged pardon for setting me right, and told me it was very superb; and that numbers of the first dukes and marquisses and counts had hotels.—The Count de B——, of whom the bookseller at the Quai de Conti had spoke so handsomely the night before, came instantly into my mind. And why should I not go, thought I, to the Count de B——, who has so high an idea of English books and English men,—and tell him my story?—So I changed my mind a second time. In truth, it was the third; for I had intended that day for Madame de R——, in the Rue St. Pierre, and had devoutly sent her word by her *fille de chambre* that I would assuredly wait upon her;—but I am governed by circumstances:—I cannot govern them: so seeing a man standing with a basket on the other side of the street, as if he had something to sell, I bid La Fleur go up to him, and inquire for the Count's hotel.

La Fleur returned a little pale; and told me it was the Chevalier de St. Louis selling *pâtés*.—It is impossible, La Fleur, said I.—La Fleur could no more account for the phenomenon than myself; but persisted in his story; he had seen the croix set in gold, with its red riband, he said, tied to his button-hole; and had looked into the basket, and seen the *pâtés* which the Chevalier was selling; so could not be mistaken in that.

Such a reverse in a man's life awakes a better principle than curiosity: I could not help looking for some time at him as I sat in the remise. The more I looked at him, his croix and his basket, the stronger they wove themselves into my brain.—I got out of the remise, and went towards him.

He was begirt with a clean linen apron, which fell below his knees, and with a sort of a bib that went half-way up to his breast. Upon the top of this, but a little below the hem, hung his croix. His basket of little *pâtés* was covered over with a white damask napkin; another of the same kind was spread at the bottom; and there was such a look of *propreté* and neatness throughout, that one might have bought his *pâtés* of him as much from appetite as sentiment.

He made an offer of them to neither; but stood still with them at the corner of a hotel, for those to buy who chose it, without solicitation.

He was about forty-eight;—of a sedate look, something approaching to gravity. I did not wonder.—I went up rather to the basket than him, and having lifted up the napkin, and taken one of his *pâtés* into my hand,—I begged he would explain the appearance which affected me.

He told me in a few words, that the best part of his life had passed in the service; in which, after spending a small patrimony, he had obtained a company and the croix with it; but that, at the conclusion of the last peace, his regiment being reformed, and the whole corps, with those of some other regiments, left without any provision, he found himself in a wide world without friends, without a livre;—and indeed, said he, without any thing but this:—(pointing, as he said it, to his croix.)—The poor Chevalier won my pity; and he finished the scene by winning my esteem too.

The King, he said, was the most generous of princes; but his generosity could neither relieve nor reward every one; and it was only his misfortune to be amongst the number. He had a little wife, he said, whom he loved, who did the *patisserie;* and added, he felt no dishonor in defending her and himself from want in this way,—unless Providence had offered him a better.

It would be wicked to withhold a pleasure from the good, in passing over what happened to this poor Chevalier of St. Louis about nine months after.

It seems he usually took his stand near the iron gates which lead up to the palace; and as his croix had caught the eye of numbers, numbers had made the same inquiry which I had done.—He had told the same story, and always with so much modesty and good sense, that it had reached at last the King's ears; —who hearing the Chevalier had been a gallant officer, and respected by the whole regiment as a man of honor and integrity,—he broke up his little trade by a pension of fifteen hundred livres a-year.

As I have told this to please the reader, I beg he will allow me to relate another, out of its order, to please myself;—the two stories reflect light upon each other,—and 'tis a pity they should be parted.

THE SWORD.

RENNES.

When states and empires have their periods of declension, and feel in their turns what distress and poverty is,—I stop not to tell the causes which gradually brought the house of d'E—— in Britanny into decay. The Marquis d'E—— had fought up against his condition with great firmness; wishing to preserve and still show to the world some little fragments of what his ancestors had been; their indiscretions had put it out of his power. There was enough left for the little exigencies of obscurity.—But he had two boys who looked up to him for light;—he thought they deserved it. He had tried his sword,—it could not open the way,—the mounting was too expensive,—and simple economy was not a match for it:—there was no resource but commerce.

In any other province in France save Britanny, this was smiting the root for ever of the little tree his pride and affection wished to see re-blossom.—But in Britanny, there being a provision for this, he availed himself of it; and taking an occasion when the States were assembled at Rennes, the Marquis, attended with his two boys, entered the court; and having pleaded the right of an ancient law of the duchy, which, though seldom claimed, he said, was no less in force, he took his sword from his side;—Here, said he, take it; and be trusty guardians of it till better times put me in condition to reclaim it.

The president accepted the Marquis's sword;—he staid a few minutes to see it deposited in the archives of his house, and departed.

The Marquis and his whole family embarked the next day for Martinico, and in about nineteen or twenty years of successful application to business, with some unlooked-for bequests from distant branches of his house, returned home to reclaim his nobility, and to support it.

It was an incident of good fortune which will never happen to any traveller but a sentimental one, that I should be at Rennes at the very time of this solemn requisition. I call it solemn;—it was so to me.

The Marquis entered the court with his whole family: he supported his lady;—his eldest son supported his sister, and his youngest was at the other extreme of the line next his mother;—he put his handkerchief to his face twice.—

There was a dead silence. When the Marquis had approached within six paces of the tribunal, he gave the Marchioness to his youngest son, and advancing three steps before his family,—he reclaimed his sword. His sword was given him: and the moment he got it into his hand, he drew it almost out of the scabbard:—'twas the shining face of a friend he had once given up:—he looked attentively along it, beginning at the hilt, as if to see whether it was the same,—when observing a little rust which it had contracted near the point, he brought it near his eye, and bending his head down over it,—I think I saw a tear fall upon the place: I could not be deceived by what followed.

"I shall find," said he, "some other way "to get it off."

When the Marquis had said this, he returned his sword into its scabbard, made a bow to the guardians of it,—and, with his wife and daughter, and his two sons following him, walked out.

O how I envied his feelings!

THE PASSPORT.

VERSAILLES.

I found no difficulty in getting admittance to Monsieur le Count de B——. The set of Shakspeare was laid upon the table, and he was tumbling them over. I walked up close to the table, and giving first such a look at the books as to make him conceive I knew what they were,—I told him I had come without any one to present me, knowing I should meet with a friend in his apartment, who, I trusted, would do it for me;—it is my countryman the great Shakspeare, said I, pointing to his works, *et ayez la bonté, mon cher ami*, apostrophizing his spirit, added I, *de me faire cet honneur-là*.—

The Count smiled at the singularity of the introduction; and seeing I looked a little pale and sickly, insisted upon my taking an arm-chair; so I sat down; and to save him conjectures upon a visit so out of all rule, I told him simply of the incident in the bookseller's shop, and how that had impelled me rather to go to him with the story of a little embarrassment I was under, than to any other man in France.—And what is your embarrassment? let me hear it, said the Count.—So I told him the story just as I have told it the reader.

—And the master of my hotel, said I, as I concluded it, will needs have it, Monsieur le Count, that I should be sent to the Bastile;—but I have no apprehensions, continued I,—for in falling into the hands of the most polished people in the world, and being conscious I was a true man, and not come to spy the nakedness of the land, I scarce thought I lay at their mercy.—It does not suit the gallantry of the French, Monsieur le Count, said I, to show it against invalids.

An animated blush came into the Count de B——'s cheeks as I spoke this.—*Ne craignez rien*—Don't fear, said he.—Indeed I don't, replied I again.—Besides, continued I, a little sportingly, I have come laughing all the way from London to Paris; and I do not think Monsieur le Duc de Choiseul is such an enemy to mirth, as to send me back crying for my pains.

—My application to you, Monsieur le Count de B—— (making him a low bow) is to desire he will not.

The Count heard me with great good-nature, or I had not said half as much,—and once or twice said,—*C'est bien dit.* So I rested my cause there,—and determined to say no more about it.

The Count led the discourse: we talked of indifferent things,—of books, and politics, and men; and then of women.—God bless them all! said I, after much discourse about them,—there is not a man upon earth who loves them so much as I do. After all the foibles I have seen, and all the satires I have read against them, still I love them; being firmly persuaded that a man who has not a sort of an affection for the whole sex, is incapable of ever loving a single one as he ought.

He bien! Monsieur l'Anglois, said the Count, gaily;—you are not come to spy the nakedness of the land;—I believe you;—*ni encore*, I dare say, *that* of our women: but permit me to conjecture,—if, *par hazard*, they fell into your way, that the prospect would not affect you.

I have something within me which cannot bear the shock of the least indecent insinuation; in the sportability of chit-chat I have often endeavored to conquer it, and with infinite pain have hazarded a thousand things to a dozen of the sex together,—the least of which I could not venture to a single one to gain Heaven.

Excuse me, Monsieur le Count, said I:—as for the nakedness of your land, if I saw it, I should cast my eyes over it with tears in them;—and for that of your women (blushing at the idea he had excited in me) I am so evangelical in this, and have such a fellow-feeling for whatever is *weak* about them, that I would cover it with a garment, if I knew how to throw it on;—but I could wish, continued I, to spy the *nakedness* of their hearts, and through the different disguises of customs, climates, and religion, find out what is good in them to fashion my own by;—and therefore am I come.

It is for this reason, Monsieur le Count, continued I, that I have not seen the Palais Royal, nor the Luxembourg,—nor the Façade of the Louvre,—nor have attempted to swell the catalogues we have of pictures, statues, and churches.—I conceive every fair being as a temple, and would rather enter in, and see the original drawings and loose sketches hung up in it, than the Transfiguration of Raphael itself.

The thirst of this, continued I, as impatient as that which inflames the breast of the connoisseur, has led me from my own home into France,—and from France will lead me through Italy;—'tis a quiet journey of the heart in pursuit of *Nature*, and those affections which arise out of her, which make us love each other,—and the world, better than we do.

The Count said a great many civil things to me upon the occasion; and added, very politely, how much he stood obliged to Shakspeare for making me known to him. —But *à-propos*, said he;—Shakspeare is full of great things:—he forgot the small punctilio of announcing your name:—it puts you under a necessity of doing it yourself.

THE PASSPORT.

VERSAILLES.

There is not a more perplexing affair in life to me, than to set about telling any one who I am,—for there is scarce any body I cannot give a better account of than myself; and I have often wish'd I could do it in a single word,—and have an end of it. It was the only time and occasion in my life I could accomplish this to any purpose;—for Shakspeare lying upon the table, and recollecting I was in his books, I took up Hamlet, and turning immediately to the gravediggers' scene in the fifth act, I laid my finger upon Yorick; and advancing the book to the Count, with my finger all the way over the name,—*Me voici!* said I.

Now, whether the idea of poor Yorick's skull was put out of the Count's mind by the reality of my own, or by what magic he could drop a period of seven or eight hundred years, makes nothing in this account: 'tis certain, the French conceive better than they combine;—I wonder at nothing in this world, and the less at this; inasmuch as one of the first of our own church, for whose candor and paternal sentiments I have the highest veneration, fell into the same mistake in the very same case;—"He could "not bear," he said, "to look into sermons "wrote by the King of Denmark's jester." —Good my Lord! said I; but there are two Yoricks. The Yorick your Lordship thinks of, has been dead and buried eight hundred years ago: he flourish'd in Horwendillus's court;—the other Yorick is myself, who have flourish'd, my Lord, in no court.—He shook his head.—Good God! said I, you might as well confound Alexander the Great with Alexander the Coppersmith, my Lord! —'Twas all one, he replied.

—If Alexander King of Macedon, could have translated your Lordship, said I, I'm sure your Lordship would not have said so.

The poor Count de B**** fell but into the same *error*.

—*Et, Monsieur, est il Yorick?* cried the Count.—*Je le suis*, said I.—*Vous?—Moi—moi qui ai l'honneur de vous parler, Monsieur le Comte.—Mon Dieu!* said he, embracing me,—*Vous êtes Yorick!*

The Count instantly put the Shakspeare into his pocket, and left me alone in his room.

THE PASSPORT.

VERSAILLES.

I could not conceive why the Count de B**** had gone so abruptly out of the room, any more than I could conceive why he had put the Shakspeare into his pocket.—*Mysteries which must explain themselves, are not worth the loss of time which a conjecture about them takes up:* 'twas better to read Shakspeare; so taking up "*Much Ado about* "*Nothing*," I transported myself instantly from the chair I sat in to Messina in Sicily, and got so busy with Don Pedro, and Benedict and Beatrice, that I thought not of Versailles, the Count, or the passport.

Sweet pliability of man's spirit, that can at once surrender itself to illusions which cheat expectation and sorrow of their weary moments!—Long,—long since had ye number'd out my days, had I not trod so great a part of them upon this enchanted ground. When my way is too rough for my feet, or too steep for my strength, I get off it, to some smooth velvet path which fancy has scatter'd over with rose-buds of delights and, having taken a few turns in it, come back strengthen'd and refresh'd. —When evils press sore upon me, and there is no retreat from them in this world, then I take a new course;—I leave it,—and, as I have a clearer idea of the Elysian Fields than I have of Heaven, I force myself, like Æneas, into them;—I see him meet the pensive shade of his forsaken Dido, and wish to recognize it;—I see the injured spirit wave her head, and turn off silent from the author of her miseries and dishonors;—I lose the feelings for myself in hers, and in those affections which were wont to make me mourn for her when I was at school.

Surely, this is not walking in a vain shadow,—nor does man disquiet himself in vain *by it:*—he oftener does so in trusting the issue of his commotions to reason only. —I can safely say for myself, I was never able to conquer any one single bad sensation in my heart so decisively, as by beating up as fast as I could for some kindly and gentle sensation to fight it upon its own ground.

When I had got to the end of the third act, the Count de B**** entered with my passport in his hand. Mons. le Duc de C——, said the Count, is as good a prophet, I dare say, as he is a statesman.—*Un homme qui rit*, said the Duke, *ne sera jamais dangereux.*—Had it been for any one but the King's jester, added the Count, I could not have got it these two hours.—*Pardonnez moi*, Mons. le Count, said I, I am not the King's jester.—But you are Yorick?—Yes. —*Et vous plaisantez?*—I answered, Indeed I did jest,—but was not paid for it;—'twas entirely at my own expense.

We have no jester at court, Mons. le Count, said I; the last we had was in the licentious reign of Charles II.;—since which time, our manners have been so gradually refining, that our court at present is so full of patriots, who wish for *nothing* but the honors and wealth of our country;—and our ladies are all so chaste, so spotless, so good, so devout,—there is nothing for a jester to make a jest of.

Voila un persiflage! cried the Count.

THE PASSPORT.

VERSAILLES.

As the passport was directed to all lieutenant-governors, governors, and commandants of cities, generals of armies, justiciaries, and all officers of justice, to let Mr. Yorick the King's jester, and his baggage, travel quietly along,—I own the triumph of obtaining the passport was not a little tarnish'd by the figure I cut in it.—But there is nothing unmix'd in this world; and some of the gravest of our divines have carried it so far as to affirm, that enjoyment itself was attended even with a sigh, and that the greatest *they knew of* terminated, *in a general way*, in little better than a convulsion.

I remember the grave and learned Bevoriskius, in his Commentary upon the Generations from Adam, very naturally breaks off in the middle of a note, to give an account to the world of a couple of sparrows upon the out-edge of his window, which had incommoded him all the time he wrote: and, at last, had entirely taken him off from his genealogy.

—'Tis strange! writes Bevoriskius, but the facts are certain; for I have had the curiosity to mark them down, one by one, with my pen;—but the cock-sparrow, during the little time that I could have finished the other half of this note, has actually interrupted me with the reiteration of his caresses three-and-twenty times and a half.

How merciful, adds Bevoriskius, is Heaven to his creatures!

Ill-fated Yorick! that the gravest of thy brethren should be able to write that to the world, which stains thy face with crimson to copy, even in thy study.

But this is nothing to my travels;—so I twice,—twice beg pardon for it.

CHARACTER.

VERSAILLES.

And how do you find the French? said the Count de B——, after he had given me the passport.

The reader may suppose, that, after so obliging a proof of courtesy, I could not be at a loss to say something handsome to the inquiry.

Mais passe pour cela.—Speak frankly said he: do you find all the urbanity in the French which the world give us the honor of?—I had found every thing, I said, which confirmed it.—*Vraiment*, said the Count, *les Francois sont polis.*—To an excess, replied I.

The Count took notice of the word *excesse;* and would have it I meant more than I said. I defended myself a long time, as well as I could, against it;—he insisted I had a reserve, and that I would speak my opinion frankly.

I believe, Mons. le Count, said I, that man has a certain compass, as well as an instrument; and that the social and other calls have occasion, by turns, for every key in him; so that, if you begin a note too high or too low, there must be a want either in the upper or under part, to fill up the system of harmony.—The Count de B—— did not understand music: so desired me to explain it some other way.—A polish'd nation, my dear Count, said I, makes every one its debtor; and besides, Urbanity itself, like the fair sex, has so many charms, it goes against the heart to say it can do ill; and yet, I believe, there is but a certain line of perfection that man, take him altogether, is empower'd to arrive at;—if he gets beyond, he rather exchanges qualities than gets them. I must not presume to say how far this has affected the French in the subject we are speaking of;—but should it ever be the case of the English, in the progress of their refinements, to arrive at the same polish which distinguishes the French, if we did not lose the *politesse du cœur*, which inclines men more to humane actions than courteous ones,—we should at least lose that distinct variety and originality of character, which distinguishes them not only from each other, but from all the world besides.

I had a few of King William's shillings, as smooth as glass, in my pocket, and foreseeing they would be of use in the illustration of my hypothesis, I had got them into my hand, when I had proceeded so far:—

See, Mons. le Count, said I, rising up, and laying them before him upon the table,—by jingling and rubbing one against another for seventy years together in one body's pocket or another's, they are become so much alike, you can scarce distinguish one shilling from another.

The English, like ancient medals, kept more apart, and passing but few people's hands, preserve the first sharpness which the fine hand of Nature has given them;—they are not so pleasant to feel,—but, in return, the legend is so visible, that, at the first look, you see whose image and superscription they bear. But the French, Mons. le Count, added I, (wishing to soften what I had said), have so many excellencies, they can the better spare this;—they are a loyal, a gallant, a generous, an ingenious, and a good-temper'd people as is under Heaven;—if they have a fault, they are too *serious*.

Mon Dieu! cried the Count, rising out of his chair.

Mais vous plaisantez, said he, correcting his exclamation.—I laid my hand upon my breast, and, with earnest gravity, assured him it was my most settled opinion.

—The Count said he was mortified, he could not stay to hear my reasons, being engaged to go that moment to dine with the Duc de C——.

But, if it is not too far to come to Versailles, to eat your soup with me, I beg, before you leave France, I may have the pleasure of knowing you retract your opinion,—or in what manner you support it.—But if you do support it, *Mons. Anglois*, said he, you must do it with all your powers, because you have the whole world against you.—I promised the Count I would do myself the honor of dining with him before I set out for Italy;—so took my leave.

THE TEMPTATION.

PARIS.

When I alighted at the hotel, the porter told me a young woman with a band-box had been that moment inquiring for me.—I do not know, said the porter, whether she is gone away or not.—I took the key of my chamber of him, and went up stairs; and, when I had got within ten steps of the top of the landing before my door, I met her coming easily down.

It was the fair *fille de chambre* I had walked along the Quai de Conti with: Madame de R**** had sent her upon some commission to a *marchande des modes* within a step or two of the hotel de Modene; and, as I had fail'd in waiting upon her, had bid her inquire if I had left Paris; and, if so, whether I had not left a letter addressed to her.

As the fair *fille de chambre* was so near my door, she returned back, and went into the room with me for a moment or two whilst I wrote a card.

It was a fine still evening in the latter end of the month of May,—the crimson window-curtains (which were of the same color as those of the bed) were drawn close,—the sun was setting, and reflected through them so warm a tint into the fair *fille de chambre's* face, — I thought she blush'd;—the idea of it made me blush myself;—we were quite alone, and that superinduced a second blush before the first could get off.

There is a sort of a pleasing half-guilty blush, where the blood is more in fault than the man; — 'tis sent impetuous from the heart, and virtue flies after it,—not to call it back, but to make the sensation of it more delicious to the nerves;—'tis associated.

But I'll not describe it;—I felt something at first within me which was not in strict unison with the lesson of virtue I had given her the night before;—I sought five minutes for a card; I knew I had not one. I took up a pen,—I laid it down again,—my hand trembled:—the Devil was in me.

I know as well as any one he is an adversary; whom, if we resist, he will fly from us; but I seldom resist him at all, from a terror that, though I may conquer, I may still get a hurt in the combat;—so I give up the triumph for security; and, instead of thinking to make him fly, I generally fly myself.

The fair *fille de chambre* came close up to the bureau, where I was looking for a card,—took up first the pen I cast down, then offer'd to hold me the ink; she offer'd it so sweetly, I was going to accept it, but I durst not;—I have nothing, my dear, said I, to write upon.—Write it, said she, simply, upon any thing.

—I was just going to cry out, Then I will write it, fair girl, upon thy lips.

—If I do, said I. I shall perish: so I took her by the hand, and led her to the door, and begg'd she would not forget the lesson I had given her. — She said, indeed she would not, and as she uttered it with some earnestness, she turn'd about, and gave me both her hands, closed together, into mine; —it was impossible not to compress them in that situation;—I wish'd to let them go; and, all the time I held them, I kept arguing within myself against it,—and still I held them on.—In two minutes I found I had all the battle to fight over again;—and I felt my legs and every limb about me tremble at the idea.

The foot of the bed was within a yard and a half of the place where we were standing, —I had still hold of her hands—(and how it happened, I can give no account;) but I neither asked her, nor drew her, nor did I think of the bed;—but so it did happen, we both sat down.

I'll just show you, said the fair *fille de chambre*, the little purse I have been making to-day to hold your crown. So she put her hand into her right pocket, which was next me, and felt for it some time;—then into the left. — "She had lost it." — I never bore expectation more quietly; — it was in her right pocket at last; she pull'd it out; it was of green taffeta, lined with a little bit of white quilted satin, and just big enough to hold the crown:—she put it into my hand; it was pretty, and I held it ten minutes, with the back of my hand resting upon her lap, looking sometimes at the purse, sometimes on one side of it.

A stitch or two had broke out in the gathers of my stock; the fair *fille de chambre*, without saying a word, took out her little housewife, threaded a small needle, and sewed it up. I foresaw it would hazard the glory of the day, and as she passed her hand in silence across and across my neck in the manœuvre, I felt the laurels shake which fancy had wreathed about my head.

A strap had given way in her walk, and the buckle of her shoe was just falling off. —See, said the *fille de chambre*, holding up her foot,—I could not from my soul but fasten the buckle in return; and, putting in the strap,—and lifting up the other foot with it, when I had done, to see both were right, in doing it so suddenly, it unavoidably threw the fair *fille de chambre* off her centre,— and then—

THE CONQUEST.

Yes,—and then——Ye, whose clay-cold heads and lukewarm hearts can argue down or mask your passions, tell me, what trespass is it that man should have them? or how his spirit stands answerable to the Father of spirits but for his conduct under them?

If Nature has so wove her web of kindness, that some threads of love and desire are entangled with the piece,—must the whole web be rent in drawing them out?—Whip me such stoics, great Governor of Nature! said I to myself:—wherever thy Providence shall place me for the trials of my virtue; whatever is my danger,—whatever is my situation,—let me feel the movements which rise out of it, and which belong to me as a man,—and, if I govern them as a good one, I will trust the issues to thy justice; for thou hast made us, and not we ourselves.

As I finished my address, I raised the fair *fille de chambre* up by the hand, and led her out of the room;—she stood by me till I locked the door and put the key in my pocket,—*and then*,—the victory being quite decisive,—and not till then, I pressed my lips to her cheek, and, taking her by the hand again, led her safe to the gate of the hotel.

THE MYSTERY.

PARIS.

If a man knows the heart, he will know it was impossible to go back instantly to my chamber;—it was touching a cold key with a flat third to it, upon the close of a piece of music, which had called forth my affections; therefore, when I let go the hand of the *fille de chambre*, I remain'd at the gate of the hotel for some time, looking at every one who pass'd by, and forming conjectures upon them, till my attention got fix'd upon a single object which confounded all kind of reasoning upon him.

It was a tall figure, of a philosophic, serious, adust look, which pass'd and repass'd sedately along the street, making a turn of about sixty paces on each side of the gate of the hotel.—The man was about fifty-two, had a small cane under his arm, was dress'd in a dark drab-colored coat, waistcoat, and breeches, which seem'd to have seen some years' service;—they were still clean, and there was a little air of frugal *propreté* throughout him. By his pulling off his hat, and his attitude of accosting a good many in his way, I saw he was asking charity; so I got a sous or two out of my pocket ready to give him, as he took me in his turn. He pass'd by me without asking any thing,—and yet did not go five steps farther before he ask'd charity of a little woman,—I was much more likely to have given of the two. He had scarce done with the woman, when he pull'd his hat off to another who was coming the same way. An ancient gentleman came slowly, and, after him, a young smart one. He let them both pass, and ask'd nothing; I stood observing him half-an-hour; in which time he had made a dozen turns backwards and forwards, and found that he invariably pursued the same plan.

There were two things very singular in this, which set my brain to work, and to no purpose;—the first was, Why the man should *only* tell his story to the sex;—and secondly, What kind of story it was, and what species of eloquence it could be, which soften'd the hearts of the women, which he knew 'twas to no purpose to practise upon the men.

There were two other circumstances which entangled this mystery:—the one was, He told every woman what he had to say in her ear, and in a way which had much more the air of a secret, than a petition;—the other was, It was always successful;—he never stopp'd a woman but she pull'd out her purse, and immediately gave him something.

I could form no system to explain the phenomenon.

I had got a riddle to amuse me for the rest of the evening; so I walk'd up stairs to my chamber.

THE CASE OF CONSCIENCE.

PARIS.

I was immediately followed up by the master of the hotel, who came into my room to tell me I must provide lodgings elsewhere.—How so, friend? said I.—He answer'd, I had a young woman lock'd up with me two hours that evening in my bedchamber, and 'twas against the rules of his house.—Very well, said I, we'll all part friends then,—for the girl is no worse,—and I am no worse,—and you will be just as I found you.—It was enough, he said, to overthrow the credit of his hotel.—*Voyez vous, Monsieur*, said he, pointing to the foot of the bed we had been sitting upon.—I own it had something of the appearance of an evidence; but my pride not suffering me to enter into any detail of the case, I exhorted him to let his soul sleep in peace, as I resolved to let mine do that night, and that I would discharge what I owed him at breakfast.

—I should not have minded, Monsieur, said he, if you had had twenty girls,—'Tis a score more, replied I, interrupting him, than I ever reckoned upon.—Provided, added he, it had been but in a morning.—And does the difference of the time of the day, at Paris, make a difference in the sin? —It made a difference, he said, in the scandal.—I like a good distinction in my heart; and cannot say I was intolerably out of temper with the man.—I own it necessary, resumed the master of the hotel, that a stranger at Paris should have the opportunities presented to him of buying lace and silk stockings, and ruffles, *et tout cela;*—and 'tis nothing if a woman comes with a band-box. —O' my conscience, said I, she had one; but I never look'd into it.—Then, Monsieur, said he, has bought nothing.—Not one earthly thing, replied I.—Because, said he, I could recommend you to one who would use you *en conscience*.—But I must see her this night, said I.—He made me a low bow, and walk'd down.

Now shall I triumph over this *maitre d'hotel*, cried I:—and what then? Then I shall let him see I know he is a dirty fellow. —And what then? What then!—I was too near myself to say it was for the sake of others.—I had no good answer left;—there was more of spleen than of principle in my project, and I was sick of it before the execution.

In a few minutes the *grisette* came in with her box of lace.—I'll buy nothing, however, said I, within myself.

The *grisette* would show me every thing. —I was hard to please: she would not seem to see it. She open'd her little magazine, and laid all her laces, one after another, before me;—unfolded and folded them up again, one by one, with the most patient sweetness.—I might buy,—or not;—she would let me have every thing at my own price:—the poor creature seem'd anxious to get a penny; and laid herself out to win me, and not so much in a manner which seem'd artful, as in one I felt simple and caressing.

If there is not a fund of honest cullibility in man, so much the worse;—my heart relented, and I gave up my second resolution as quietly as the first.—Why should I chastise one for the trespass of another? If thou art tributary to this tyrant of an host, thought I, looking up in her face, so much harder is thy bread.

If I had not had more than four Louis d'ors in my purse, there was no such thing as rising up and showing her the door till I had first laid three of them out in a pair of ruffles.

—The master of the hotel will share the profit with her;—no matter,—then I have only paid, as many a poor soul has *paid* before me, for an act he *could* not do, or think of.

THE RIDDLE.

PARIS.

When La Fleur came up to wait upon me at supper, he told me how sorry the master of the hotel was, for his affront to me in bidding me change my lodgings.

A man who values a good night's rest will not lie down with enmity in his heart, if he can help it.—So I bid La Fleur tell the master of the hotel, that I was sorry on my side for the occasion I had given him; —and you may tell him if you will, La Fleur, added I, that if the young woman should call again, I shall not see her.

This was a sacrifice not to him, but myself, having resolv'd, after so narrow an escape, to run no more risks, but to leave Paris, if it was possible, with all the virtue I entered it.

C'est deroger à noblèsse, Monsieur, said La Fleur, making me a bow down to the ground as he said it.—*Et encore, Monsieur*, said he, may change his sentiments;—and if (*par hazard*) he should like to amuse himself,—I find no amusement in it, said I, interrupting him.

—*Mon Dieu!* said La Fleur,—and took away.

In an hour's time he came to put me to bed, and was more than commonly officious;—something hung upon his lips to say to me, or ask me, which he could not get off: I could not conceive what it was; and indeed gave myself little trouble to find it out, as I had another riddle so much more interesting upon my mind, which was that of the man's asking charity before the door of the hotel.—I would have given any thing to have got to the bottom of it; and that not out of curiosity,—'tis so low a principle of inquiry, in general, I would not purchase the gratification of it with a two-sous piece;—but a secret, I thought, which so soon and so certainly soften'd the heart of every woman you came near, was a secret at least equal to the philosopher's stone: had I had both the Indies, I would have given up one to have been master of it.

I toss'd and turn'd it almost all night long in my brains, to no manner of purpose; and when I awoke in the morning, I found my spirits as much troubled with my *dreams*, as ever the King of Babylon had been with his; and I will not hesitate to affirm, it would have puzzled all the wise men of Paris as much as those of Chaldea, to have given its interpretation.

LE DIMANCHE.

PARIS.

It was Sunday; and when La Fleur came in, in the morning, with my coffee and roll and butter, he had got himself so gallantly array'd, I scarce knew him.

I had covenanted at Montriul to give him a new hat with a silver button and four Louis d'ors *pour s'adoniser*, when we got to Paris; and the poor fellow, to do him justice, had done wonders with it.

He had bought a bright, clean, good scarlet coat, and a pair of breeches of the same.—They were not a crown worse, he said, for the wearing.—I wish'd him hang'd for telling me.—They look'd so fresh, that though I knew the thing could not be done, yet I would rather have imposed upon my fancy with thinking I had bought them new for the fellow, than that they had come out of the Rue de Friperie.

This is a nicety which makes not the heart sore at Paris.

He had purchased, moreover, a handsome blue satin waistcoat, fancifully enough embroidered: — This was indeed something the worse for the service it had done, but 'twas clean scour'd,—the gold had been touch'd up, and, upon the whole, was rather showy than otherwise; — and as the blue was not violent, it suited with the coat and breeches very well: he had squeezed out of the money, moreover, a new bag and a *solitaire;* and had insisted with the *fripier* upon a gold pair of garters to his breeches' knees.— He had purchased muslin ruffles *bien brodées*, with four livres of his own money;—and a pair of white silk stockings for five more;—and, to top all, Nature had given him a handsome figure, without costing him a sous.

He entered the room thus set off, with his hair drest in the first style, and with a handsome *bouquet* in his breast.— In a word, there was that look of festivity in every thing about him, which at once put me in mind it was Sunday—and by combining both together, it instantly struck me, that the favor he wish'd to ask of me the night before, was to spend the day as every body in Paris spent it besides. I had scarce made the conjecture, when La Fleur, with infinite humility, but with a look of trust, as if I should not refuse him, begg'd I would grant him the day, *pour faire le galant vis-à-vis de sa maîtresse.*

Now it was the very thing I intended to do myself *vis-à-vis* Madame de R****.—I had retained the remise on purpose for it, and it would not have mortified my vanity to have had a servant so well dress'd as La

Fleur was, to have got up behind it: I never could have worse spared him.

But we must *feel*, not argue, in these embarrassments;—the sons and daughters of Service part with liberty, but not with nature, in their contracts; they are flesh and blood, and have their little vanities and wishes in the midst of the house of bondage, as well as their task-masters;—no doubt, they have set their self-denials at a price,—and their expectations are so unreasonable, that I would often disappoint them, but that their condition puts it so much in my power to do it.

Behold,—Behold, I am thy servant,—disarms me at once of the powers of a Master.

—Thou shalt go, La Fleur, said I.

—And what mistress, La Fleur, said I, canst thou have pick'd up in so little a time at Paris?—La Fleur laid his hand upon his breast, and said, 'Twas a *petit demoiselle*, at Monsieur le Count de B****'s. La Fleur had a heart made for society; and to speak the truth of him, let as few occasions slip him as his master,—so that, somehow or other,—but how,—Heaven knows,—he had connected himself with the *demoiselle* upon the landing of the staircase, during the time I was taken up with my passport; and as there was time enough for me to win the Count to my interest, La Fleur had contrived to make it do to win the maid to his. The family, it seems, was to be at Paris that day, and he had made a party with her, and two or three more of the Count's household, upon the *boulevards*.

Happy people! that once a week at least are sure to lay down all your cares together, and dance and sing, and sport away the weights of grievance, which bow down the spirit of other nations to the earth.

THE FRAGMENT.

PARIS.

La Fleur had left me something to amuse myself with for the day, more than I had bargained for, or could have entered either into his head or mine.

He had brought the little print of butter upon a currant-leaf; and, as the morning was warm, and he had a good step to bring it, he had begged a sheet of waste paper to put betwixt the currant-leaf and his hand.—As that was plate sufficient, I bade him lay it upon the table as it was; and as I resolved to stay within all day, I ordered him to call upon the *traiteur*, to bespeak my dinner, and leave me to breakfast by myself.

When I had finished the butter, I threw the currant-leaf out of the window, and was going to do the same by the waste paper;—but, stopping to read a line first, and that drawing me on to a second and a third,—I thought it better worth; so I shut the window, and drawing a chair up to it, I sat down to read it.

It was in the old French of Rabelais's time; and, for aught I know, might have been wrote by him: it was, moreover, in a Gothic letter, and that so faded and gone off by damps and length of time, it cost me infinite trouble to make any thing of it.—I threw it down; and then wrote a letter to Eugenius,—then I took it up again, and embroiled my patience with it afresh;—and then, to cure that, I wrote a letter to Eliza.—Still it kept hold of me; and the difficulty of understanding it, increased but the desire.

I got my dinner; and after I had enlightened my mind with a bottle of Burgundy, I at it again;—and after two or three hours' poring upon it, with almost as deep attention as ever Gruter or Jacob Spon did upon a nonsensical inscription, I thought I made sense of it; but to make sure of it, the best way, I imagined, was to turn it into English, and see how it would look then;—so I went on leisurely, as a trifling man does, sometimes writing a sentence,—then taking a turn or two,—and then looking how the world went, out of the window; so that it was nine o'clock at night before I had done it.—I then began, and read it as follows:—

THE FRAGMENT.

PARIS.

—Now as the Notary's wife disputed the point with the Notary with too much heat,—I wish, said the Notary (throwing down the parchment), that there was another Notary here, only to set down and attest all this.

—And what would you do then, Monsieur? said she, rising hastily up.—The Notary's wife was a little fume of a woman, and the Notary thought it well to avoid a hurricane by a mild reply.—I would go, answered he, to bed.—You may go to the Devil, answered the Notary's wife.

Now there happening to be but one bed in the house, the other two rooms being unfurnished, as is the custom at Paris, and the Notary not caring to lie in the same bed with a woman who had but that moment sent him pell-mell to the Devil, went forth with his hat and cane, and short cloak, the night being very windy, and walk'd out ill at ease towards the Pont Neuf.

Of all the bridges which ever were built, the whole world who have pass'd over the Pont Neuf must own, that it is the noblest, —the finest,—the grandest,—the lightest, —the longest,—the broadest, that ever conjoin'd land and land together upon the face of the terraqueous globe.—

By this it seems as if the author of the Fragment had not been a Frenchman.

The worst fault which Divines and the Doctors of the Sorbonne can allege against it, is, that if there is but a cap-full of wind in or about Paris, 'tis more blasphemously *sacre Dieu*'d there than in any other aperture of the whole city,—and with reason, good and cogent, Messieurs; for it comes against you without crying *garde d'eau*, and with such unpremeditable puffs, that of the few who cross it with their hats on, not one in fifty but hazards two livres and a half, which is its full worth.

The poor Notary, just as he was passing by the sentry, instinctively clapp'd his cane to the side of it; but in raising it up, the point of his cane catching hold of the sentinel's hat, hoisted it over the spikes of the balustrade clear into the Seine.

—*'Tis an ill wind*, said a boatman, who catch'd it, *which blows nobody any good.*

The sentry, being a Gascon, incontinently twirl'd up his whiskers, and levell'd his arquebuse.

Arquebuses in those days went off with matches; and an old woman's paper lantern at the end of the bridge happening to be blown out, she had borrowed the sentry's match to light it;—it gave a moment's time for the Gascon's blood to run cool, and turn the accident better to his advantage.—*'Tis an ill wind*, said he, catching off the Notary's castor, and legitimating the capture with the boatman's adage.

The poor Notary cross'd the bridge, and passing along the Rue de Dauphine into the Fauxbourg of St. Germain, lamented himself as he walked along in this manner:—

Luckless man that I am! said the Notary, to be the sport of hurricanes all my days!—to be born to have the storm of ill language levell'd against me and my profession wherever I go!—to be forced into marriage by the thunder of the church to a tempest of a woman!—to be driven forth out of my house by domestic winds, and despoil'd of my castor by pontific ones!—to be here, bare-headed, in a windy night, at the mercy of the ebbs and flows of accidents!—Where am I to lay my head!—Miserable man! what wind in the two-and-thirty points in the whole compass can blow unto thee, as it does the rest of thy fellow-creatures, good!

As the Notary was passing on by a dark passage, complaining in this sort, a voice called out to a girl, to bid her run for the next Notary.—Now the Notary being the next, and availing himself of his situation, walk'd up the passage to the door, and passing through an old sort of saloon, was ushered into a large chamber, dismantled of every thing but a long military pike,—a breast-plate,—a rusty old sword, and bandoleer, hung up equidistant in four different places against the wall.

An old personage, who had heretofore been a gentleman, and unless decay of fortune taints the blood along with it, was a gentleman at that time, lay supporting his head upon his hand, in his bed; a little table with a taper burning was set close beside it, and close by the table was placed a chair,—the Notary sat him down in it; and pulling out his inkhorn and a sheet or two of paper which he had in his pocket, he placed them before him, and dipping his pen in his ink, and leaning his breast over the table, he disposed every thing to make the gentleman's last will and testament.

—Alas! Monsieur le Notaire, said the gentleman, raising himself up a little, I have nothing to bequeath, which will pay the expense of bequeathing, except the history of myself, which I could not die in peace unless I left it as a legacy to the world; the profits arising out of it I bequeath to you for the pains of taking it from me.—It is a story so uncommon, it must be read by all mankind;—it will make the fortunes of your house.—The Notary dipp'd his pen into the inkhorn.—Almighty Director of every event in my life! said the old gentleman, looking up earnestly, and raising his hands towards Heaven,—Thou, whose hand has led me on through such a labyrinth of strange passages down into this scene of desolation, assist the decaying memory of an old, infirm, and broken-hearted man!—Direct my tongue by the spirit of thy eternal truth, that this stranger may set down nought but what is written in that *Book*, from whose records, said he, clasping his hands together, I am to be condemn'd or acquitted!—the Notary held up the point of his pen betwixt the taper and his eye.

—It is a story, Monsieur le Notaire, said the gentleman, which will rouse up every affection in Nature;—it will kill the humane, and touch the heart of Cruelty herself with pity.—

The Notary was inflamed with a desire to begin, and put his pen a third time into his inkhorn!—and the old gentleman, turning a little more towards the Notary, began to dictate his story in these words:—

—And where is the rest of it, La Fleur? said I,—as he just then enter'd the room.

THE FRAGMENT, AND THE BOUQUET.*

PARIS.

When La Fleur came close up to the table, and was made to comprehend what I wanted, he told me there were only two other sheets of it, which he had wrapped round the stalks of a *bouquet* to keep it together, which he had presented to the *demoiselle* upon the *boulevards*.—Then prithee, La Fleur, said I, step back to her, to the Count de B****'s hotel, and *see if thou canst get it*.—There is no doubt of it, said La Fleur;—and away he flew.

In a very little time the poor fellow came back, quite out of breath, with deeper marks of disappointment in his looks, than could arise from the simple irreparability of the fragment. *Juste ciel!* in less than two minutes that the poor fellow had taken his last tender farewell of her,—his faithless mistress had given his *gage d'amour* to one of the Count's footmen,—the footman to a young sempstress,—and the sempstress to a fiddler, with my fragment at the end of it.—Our misfortunes were involved together;—I gave a sigh,—and La Fleur echo'd it back again to my ear.

—How perfidious! cried La Fleur.—How unlucky! said I.

—I should not have been mortified, Monsieur, quoth La Fleur, if she had lost it.—Nor I, La Fleur, said I, had I found it.

Whether I did or no, will be seen hereafter.

THE ACT OF CHARITY.

PARIS.

The man who either disdains or fears to walk up a dark entry, may be an excellent good man, and fit for a hundred things; but he will not do to make a good Sentimental Traveller. I count little of the many things I see pass at broad noon-day, in large and open streets.—Nature is shy, and hates to act before spectators; but in such an unobserved corner you sometimes see a single short scene of hers, worth all the sentiments of a dozen French plays compounded together,—and yet they are *absolutely* fine;—and whenever I have a more brilliant affair upon my hands than common, as they suit a preacher just as well as a hero, I generally make my sermon out of 'em;—and for the text,—"Cappadocia, Pontus and "Asia, Phrygia and Pamphylia,"—is as good as any one in the Bible.

There is a long dark passage issuing out from the *Opera Comique* into a narrow

* Nosegay.

street; 'tis trod by a few who humbly wait for a *fiacre*,* or wish to get off quietly o'foot when the opera is done. At the end of it, towards the theatre, 'tis lighted by a small candle, the light of which is almost lost before you get half-way down, but near the door;—'tis more for ornament than use: you see it as a fix'd star of the least magnitude:—it burns,—but does little good to the world, that we know of.

In returning along this passage, I discern'd, as I approach'd within five or six paces of the door, two ladies standing, arm in arm, with their backs against the wall, waiting, as I imagined, for a *fiacre:*—as they were next the door, I thought they had a prior right; so edged myself up within a yard or little more of them, and quietly took my stand,—I was in black, and scarce seen.

The lady next me was a tall lean figure of a woman, of about thirty-six; the other, of the same size and make, of about forty: there was no mark of wife or widow in any one part of either of them,—they seem'd to be two upright vestal sisters, unsapp'd by caresses, unbroke in upon by tender salutations. I could have wish'd to have made them happy;—their happiness was destin'd, that night, to come from another quarter.

A low voice, with a good turn of expression, and sweet cadence at the end of it, begg'd for a twelve-sous piece betwixt them, for the love of Heaven. I thought it singular that a beggar should fix the quota of an alms,—and that the sum should be twelve times as much as what is usually given in the dark. They both seem'd astonish'd at it as much as myself.—Twelve sous! said one.—A twelve-sous piece! said the other,—and made no reply.

—The poor man said, he knew not how to ask less of ladies of their rank; and bow'd down his head to the ground.

—Poo! said they,—we have no money.

The beggar remained silent for a moment or two, and renew'd his supplication.

—Do not, my fair young ladies, said he, stop your good ears against me.—Upon my word, honest man! said the younger, we have no change.—Then God bless you! said the poor man, and multiply those joys which you can give to others, without change!—I observed the eldest sister put her hand into her pocket.—I'll see, said she, if I have a sous!—A sous! give twelve, said the supplicant; Nature has been bountifu to you; be bountiful to a poor man.

—I would, friend, with all my heart, said the younger, if I had it.

—My fair charitable! said he, addressing himself to the elder,—what is it but your goodness and humanity which makes your bright eyes so sweet, that they outshine the morning, even in this dark passage? and what was it which made the Marquis de Santerre and his brother say so much of you both as they just pass'd by?

The two ladies seemed much affected; and impulsively at the same time they both put their hands into their pocket, and each took out a twelve-sous piece.

The contest betwixt them and the poor supplicant was no more,—it was continued betwixt themselves, which of the two should give the twelve-sous piece in charity;—and, to end the dispute, they both gave it together, and the man went away.

THE RIDDLE EXPLAINED

PARIS.

I STEPPED hastily after him: it was the very man whose success in asking charity of the women before the door of the hotel had so puzzled me;—and I found at once his secret, or at least the basis of it:—'twas flattery.

Delicious essence! how refreshing art thou to Nature! how strongly are all its powers and all its weaknesses on thy side! how sweetly dost thou mix with the blood, and help it through the most difficult and tortuous passages to the heart!

The poor man, as he was not straiten d for time, had given it here in a larger dose: 'tis certain he had a way of bringing it into less form, for the many sudden cases he had to do with in the streets; but how he contrived to correct, sweeten, concentre, and qualify it,—I vex not my spirit with the inquiry;—it is enough, the beggar gained two twelve-sous pieces,—and they can best tell the rest who have gained much greater matters by it.

* Hackney-coach.

PARIS.

We get forwards in the world, not so much by doing services as receiving them: you take a withering twig, and put it in the ground; and then you water it, because you have planted it.

Mons. le Count de B****, merely because he had done me one kindness in the affair of my passport, would go on and do me another, the few days he was at Paris, in making me known to a few people of rank; and they were to present me to others, and so on.

I had got master of my *secret* just in time to turn these honors to some little account; otherwise, as is commonly the case, I should have din'd or supp'd a single time or two round; and then, by *translating* French looks and attitudes into plain English, I should presently have seen that I had gold out of the *couvert** of some more entertaining guest; and, in course, should have resigned all my places, one after another, merely upon the principle that I could not keep them.—As it was, things did not go much amiss.

I had the honor of being introduced to the old Marquis de B****. In days of yore he had signaliz'd himself by some small feats of chivalry in the *Cour d'Amour*, and had dress'd himself out to the idea of tilts and tournaments ever since.—The Marquis de B**** wish'd to have it thought the affair was somewhere else than in his brain. "He "could like to take a trip to England;" and ask'd much of the English ladies. — Stay where you are, I beseech you, Mons. le Marquis, said I.—*Les Messieurs Anglois* can scarce get a kind look from them as it is.—The Marquis invited me to supper.

Mons. P****, the farmer-general, was just as inquisitive about our taxes.—They were very considerable, he heard.—If we knew but how to collect them, said I, making him a low bow.

I could never have been invited to Mons. P****'s concerts upon any other terms.

I had been misrepresented to Madame de Q*** as an *esprit*.—Madame de Q*** was an *esprit* herself: she burnt with impatience to see me, and hear me talk. I had not taken my seat, before I saw she did not care a sous whether I had any wit or no.—I was let in to be convinced she had.—I call Heaven to witness, I never once open'd the door of my lips.

Madame de V*** vow'd to every creature she met, "She had never had a more improv-"ing conversation with a man in her life."

There are three epochas in the empire of a French woman:—She is coquette,—then Deist,—then *devoté:* the empire during these is never lost; — she only changes her subjects; when thirty-five years and more have unpeopled her dominions of the slaves of love, she repeoples it with the slaves of infidelity, and then with the slaves of the church.

Madame de V*** was vibrating betwixt the first of these epochas: the color of the rose was fading fast away;—she ought to have been a Deist five years before the time I had the honor to pay my first visit.

She placed me upon the same sofa with her, for the sake of disputing the point of religion more closely.—In short, Madame de V*** told me she believed nothing.—I told Madame de V*** it might be her principle; but I was sure it could not be her interest to level the outworks, without which I could not conceive how such a citadel as hers could be defended; — that there was not a more dangerous thing in the world than for a beauty to be a Deist;—that it was a debt I owed my creed, not to conceal it from her;—that I had not been five minutes sat upon the sofa beside her, but I had begun to form designs;—and what is it but the sentiments of religion, and the persuasion they had excited in her breast, which could have check'd them as they rose up?

—We are not adamant, said I, taking hold of her hand;—and there is need of all restraints, till Age in her own time steals in and lays them on us.—But, my dear lady, said I, kissing her hand,—'tis too—too soon.

I declare I had the credit all over Paris of unperverting Madame de V***. — She affirmed to Mons. D*** and the Abbé M*** that in one half hour I had said more for revealed religion than all their Encyclopedia had said against it.—I was listed directly into Madame de V***'s *coterie;*—and she put off the epocha of Deism for two years.

I remember it was in this *coterie*, in the middle of a discourse, in which I was show-

* Plate, napkin, knife, fork, and spoon.

MARIA.

ing the necessity of a *first cause*, that the young Count de Faineant took me by the hand to the farthest corner of the room, to tell me my *solitaire* was pinn'd too strait about my neck.—It should be *plus badinant*, said the Count, looking down upon his own; —but a word, Mons. Yorick, *to the wise*,—

—And *from the wise*, Mons. le Count, replied I, making him a bow,—*is enough*.

The Count de Faineant embraced me with more ardor than ever I was embraced by mortal man.

For three weeks together, I was of every man's opinion I met.—*Pardi? ce Mons. Yorick a autant d'esprit que nous autres.* —*Il raisonne bien*, said another.—*C'est un bon enfant*, said a third.—And at this price I could have eaten and drunk and been merry all the days of my life at Paris; but 'twas a dishonest *reckoning*;—I grew ashamed of it.—It was the gain of a slave—every sentiment of honor revolted against it;—the higher I got, the more was I forced upon my *beggarly system*;—the better the *coterie*,—the more children of Art,—I languish'd for those of Nature; and one night, after a most vile prostitution of myself to half a dozen different people, I grew sick, —went to bed,—ordered La Fleur to get me horses in the morning to set out for Italy.

MARIA.

MOULINES.

I NEVER felt what the distress of plenty was in any one shape till now,—to travel it through the Bourbonnois, the sweetest part of France,—in the hey-day of the vintage, when Nature is pouring her abundance into every one's lap, and every eye is lifted up,—a journey through each step of which music beats time to *Labor*, and all her children are rejoicing as they carry in their clusters;—to pass through this with my affections flying out, and kindling at every group before me,—and every one of them was pregnant with adventures.—

Just Heaven!—it would fill up twenty volumes;—and alas! I have but a few small pages left of this to crowd it into,—and half of these must be taken up with the poor Maria my friend Mr. Shandy met with near Moulines.

The story he had told of that disordered maid affected me not a little in the reading; but when I got within the neighborhood where she lived, it returned so strong into my mind, that I could not resist an impulse which prompted me to go half a league out of the road, to the village where her parents dwelt, to inquire after her.

'Tis going, I own, like the knight of the Woful Countenance, in quest of melancholy adventures;—I know not how it is, but I am never so perfectly conscious of the existence of a soul within me, as when I am entangled in them.

The old mother came to the door; her looks told me the story before she opened her mouth.—She had lost her husband; he had died, she said, of anguish, for the loss of Maria's senses, about a month before.—She had feared at first, she added, that it would have plundered her poor girl of what little understanding was left;—but, on the contrary, it had brought her more to herself; —still she could not rest.—Her poor daughter, she said, crying, was wandering somewhere about the road.

—Why does my pulse beat languid as I write this? and what made La Fleur, whose heart seem'd only to be tuned to joy, to pass the back of his hand twice across his eyes, as the woman stood and told it? I beckoned to the postilion to turn back into the road.

When we had got within half a league of Moulines, at the little opening in the road, leading to a thicket, I discovered poor Maria sitting under a poplar.—She was sitting with her elbow in her lap, and her head leaning on one side within her hand —a small brook ran at the foot of the tree

I bid the postilion go on with the chaise to Moulines;—and La Fleur to bespeak my supper;—and that I would walk after him.

She was dressed in white, and much as my friend described her, except that her hair hung loose, which before was twisted with a silken net.—She had superadded likewise to her jacket, a pale green riband, which fell across her shoulder to the waist; at the end of which hung her pipe.—Her goat had been as faithless as her lover, and she had got a little dog in lieu of him, which she kept tied by a string to her [illegible] As I looked at her dog, she drew [illegible] wards her with the string.—"Thou shalt not leave me, Sylvio," said she. I looked in Maria's eyes, and saw she was thinking more of her father, than of her lover, or her little goat; for as she uttered them, the tears trickled down her cheeks.

I sat down close by her; and Maria let me wipe them away as they fell, with my handkerchief.—I then steeped it in my own, —and then in hers,—and then in mine,—and then I wiped hers again;—and as I did it, I felt such undescribable emotions within me, as I am sure could not be accounted for from any combinations of matter and motion.

I am positive I have a soul; nor can all the books with which materialists have pestered the world, ever convince me to the contrary.

MARIA.

When Maria had come a little to herself, I ask'd her if she remembered a pale thin person of a man, who had sat down betwixt her and her goat about two years before? —She said, she was unsettled much at that time, but remembered it upon two accounts: —That, ill as she was, she saw the person pitied her; and next, That her goat had stolen his handkerchief, and she had beat him for the theft;—she had washed it, she said, in the brook, and kept it ever since in her pocket, to restore it to him, in case she should see him again; which, she added, he had half-promised her. As she told me this, she took the handkerchief out of her pocket, to let me see it; she had folded it up neatly in a couple of vine-leaves, tied round with a tendril.—On opening it, I saw an *S* marked in one of the corners.

—She had, since that, she told me, strayed as far as Rome, and walked round St. Peter's once,—and returned back:—that she found her way alone across the Apennines,—had travelled over all Lombardy without money,—and through the flinty roads of Savoy without shoes:—how she had borne it, and how she had got supported, she could not tell;—but *God tempers the winds*, said Maria, *to the shorn lamb*.

—Shorn indeed! and to the quick, said I:—and wast thou in my own land, where I have a cottage, I would take thee to it, and shelter thee; thou should'st eat of my own bread, and drink of my own cup;—I would be kind to thy Sylvio;—in all thy weaknesses and wanderings I would seek after thee, and bring thee back;—when the sun went down, I would say my prayers, and when I had done, thou should'st play thy evening-song upon thy pipe: nor would the incense of my sacrifice be worse accepted for entering Heaven along with that of a broken heart!

Nature melted within me as I uttered this; and Maria observing, as I took out my handkerchief, that it was steeped too much already to be of use, would needs go wash it in the stream.—And where will you dry it, Maria? said I.—I'll dry it in my bosom, said she;—'twill do me good.

—And is your heart still so warm, Maria? said I.

I touched upon the string on which hung all her sorrows;—she looked with wistful disorder for some time in my face; and then, without saying any thing, took her pipe, and played her service to the Virgin. —The string I had touched ceased to vibrate;—in a moment or two Maria returned to herself,—let her pipe fall,—and rose up.

And where are you going, Maria, said I. —She said, to Moulines.—Let us go, said I, together.—Maria put her arm within mine and lengthening the string to let the dog follow,—in that order we enter'd Moulines.

MARIA.

MONTRIUL.

Though I hate salutations and greetings in the market-place, yet when we got into the middle of this, I stopped to take my last look and last farewell of Maria.

Maria, though not tall, was nevertheless of the first order of fine forms:—affliction had touched her looks with something that was scarce earthly;—still she was feminine;—and so much was there about her of all that the heart wishes, or the eye looks for in woman, that could the traces be ever worn out of her brain, and those of Eliza out of mine, she should not only *eat of my bread and drink of my own cup*, but Maria should lie in my bosom, and be unto me as a daughter.

Adieu, poor luckless maiden! — Imbibe the oil and wine which the compassion of a stranger, as he journeyeth on his way, now pours into thy wounds; — the Being who has twice bruised thee can only bind them up for ever.

THE BOURBONNOIS.

THERE was nothing from which I had painted out for myself so joyous a riot of the affections, as in this journey in the vintage, through this part of France; but pressing through this gate of sorrow to it, my sufferings have totally unfitted me. In every scene of festivity I saw Maria in the back-ground of the piece, sitting pensive under her poplar: and I had got almost to Lyons before I was able to cast a shade across her.

—Dear Sensibility! source inexhausted of all that's precious in our joys, or costly in our sorrows,—thou chainest thy martyr down upon his bed of straw,—and 'tis thou who lift'st him up to Heaven! — Eternal fountain of our feeling!—'tis here I trace thee,—and this is thy "*divinity which stirs* "*within me*;"—not that, in some sad and sickening moments, "*my soul shrinks back* "*upon herself, and startles at destruction!*" —mere pomp of words! — but that I feel some generous joys and generous cares beyond myself;—all comes from thee, great —great *Sensorium* of the world! which vibrates, if a hair of our heads but falls upon the ground, in the remotest desert of thy creation. — Touch'd with thee, Eugenius draws my curtain when I languish,—hears my tale of symptoms, and blames the weather for the disorder of his nerves. Thou giv'st a portion of it sometimes to the roughest peasant who traverses the bleakest mountains;—he finds the lacerated lamb of another's flock.—This moment I behold him leaning with his head against his crook, with piteous inclination looking down upon it!—Oh! had I come one moment sooner! — it bleeds to death! — his gentle heart bleeds with it!

Peace to thee, generous swain!—I see thou walkest off with anguish, — but thy joys shall balance it;—for happy is thy cottage,—and happy is the sharer of it,—and happy are the lambs which sport about you.

THE SUPPER.

A SHOE coming loose from the fore-foot of the thill-horse, at the beginning of the ascent of Mount Taurira, the postilion dismounted, twisted the shoe off, and put it in his pocket. As the ascent was of five or six miles, and that horse our main dependence, I made a point of having the shoe fasten'd on again as well as we could; but the postilion had thrown away the nails; and the hammer in the chaise-box being of no great use without them, I submitted to go on.

He had not mounted half a mile higher, when coming to a flinty piece of road, the poor Devil lost a second shoe, and from off his other fore-foot. I then got out of the chaise in good earnest; and seeing a house about a quarter of a mile to the left hand, with a great deal to do I prevailed upon the postilion to turn up to it. The look of the house, and of every thing about it, as we drew nearer, soon reconciled me to the disaster.—It was a little farm-house, surrounded with about twenty acres of vineyard, about as much corn;—and close to the house, on one side, was a *potagerie* of an acre and a half, full of every thing which could make plenty in a French peasant's house;—and, on the other side, was a little wood, which furnished wherewithal to dress it. It was about eight in the evening when I got to the house,—so I left the postilion to manage his point as he could; and, for mine, I walk'd directly into the house.

The family consisted of an old grey-headed man and his wife, with five or six sons and sons-in-law, and their several wives, and a joyous genealogy out of them.

They were all sitting down together to their lentil-soup; a large wheaten loaf was in the middle of the table; and a flagon of wine at each end of it promised joy through the stages of the repast:—'twas a feast of love.

The old man rose up to meet me, and, with a respectful cordiality, would have me sit down at the table; my heart was set down the moment I entered the room: so I sat down at once, like a son of the family; and, to invest myself in the character as speedily as I could, I instantly borrowed the old man's knife, and taking up the loaf, cut myself a hearty luncheon; and, as I did it, I saw a testimony in every eye, not only of an honest welcome, but of a welcome mix'd with thanks that I had not seem'd to doubt it.

Was it this? or tell me, Nature, what else it was that made this morsel so sweet, —and to what magic I owe it, that the draught I took of their flagon was so delicious with it, that they remain upon my palate to this hour?

If the supper was to my taste,—the grace which followed it was much more so.

THE GRACE.

When supper was over, the old man gave a knock upon the table with the haft of his knife, to bid them prepare for the dance; the moment the signal was given, the women and girls ran all together into a back apartment to tie up their hair,—and the young men to the door to wash their faces, and change their *sabots;* and, in three minutes, every soul was ready upon a little esplanade before the house to begin. —The old man and his wife came out last, and, placing me betwixt them, sat down upon a sofa of turf by the door.

The old man had some fifty years ago been no mean performer upon the *vielle*,—and, at the age he was then of, touch'd it well enough for the purpose. His wife sung now and then a little to the tune,—then intermitted,—and join'd her old man again as their children and grand-children danced before them.

It was not till the middle of the second dance, when, for some pauses in the movement wherein they all seem'd to look up, I fancied I could distinguish an elevation of spirit different from that which is the cause or the effect of simple jollity. In a word, I thought I beheld Religion mixing in the dance,—but, as I had never seen her so engaged, I should have look'd upon it now as one of the illusions of an imagination which is eternally misleading me, had not the old man, as soon as the dance ended, said that this was their constant way; and that all his life long he had made it a rule, after supper was over, to call out his family to dance and rejoice; believing, he said that a cheerful and contented mind was the best sort of thanks to Heaven that an illiterate peasant could pay.—

—Or a learned prelate either, said I.

THE CASE OF DELICACY.

When you have gain'd the top of Mount Taurira, you run presently down to Lyons· —adieu, then, to all rapid movements!— 'tis a journey of caution; and it fares better with sentiments, not to be in a hurry with them: so I contracted with a *voiturin* to take his time with a couple of mules, and convey me in my own chaise safe to Turin, through Savoy.

Poor, patient, quiet, honest people! fear not; your poverty, the treasury of your simple virtues, will not be envied you by the world, nor will your valleys be invaded by it.—Nature! in the midst of thy disorders, thou art still friendly to the scantiness thou hast created: with all thy great works about thee, little hast thou left to give, either to the scythe or to the sickle—but to that little thou grantest safety and protection; and sweet are the dwellings which stand so shelter'd!

Let the wayworn traveller vent his complaints upon the sudden turns and dangers of your roads, your rocks, your precipices; the difficulties of getting up, the horrors of getting down, mountains impracticable,—and cataracts, which roll down great stones from their summits, and block up his road. The peasants had been all day at work in removing a fragment of this kind between St. Michael and Madane: and, by the time my *voiturin* got to the place, it wanted full two hours of completing, before a passage could any how be gain'd. There was nothing but to wait with patience;—'twas a wet and tempestuous night; so that by the delay and that together, the *voiturin* found himself obliged to put up five miles short of his stage, at a little decent kind of an inn by the road-side.

I forthwith took possession of my bed-chamber, got a good fire, order'd supper, and was thanking Heaven it was no worse, when a *voiturin* arrived with a lady in it, and her servant-maid.

As there was no other bed-chamber in the house, the hostess, without much nicety, led them into mine, telling them, as she usher'd them in, that there was nobody in it but an English gentleman;—that there were two good beds in it, and a closet within the room which held another. The accent in which she spoke of this third bed, did not say much for it; — however, she said there were three beds, and but three people,—and she durst say the gentleman would do any thing to accommodate matters.—I left not the lady a moment to make a conjecture about it, so instantly made a declaration that I would do any thing in my power.

As this did not amount to an absolute surrender of my bed-chamber, I still felt myself so much the proprietor, as to have a right to do the honors of it;—so I desired the lady to sit down, pressed her into the warmest seat, call'd for more wood, desired the hostess to enlarge the plan of the supper, and to favor us with the very best wine.

The lady had scarce warm'd herself five minutes at the fire, before she began to turn her head back, and to give a look at the beds: and the oftener she cast her eyes that way, the more they return'd perplex'd. —I felt for her—and for myself; for in a few minutes, what by her looks, and the case itself, I found myself as much embarrassed as it was possible the lady could be herself.

That the beds we were to lie in were in one and the same room, was enough simply by itself to have excited all this;—but the position of them (for they stood parallel, and so very close to each other, as only to allow a space for a small wicker-chair betwixt them) rendered the affair still more oppressive to us; — they were fixed up, moreover, near the fire, and the projection of the chimney on one side; and a large beam which cross'd the room on the other, form'd a kind of recess for them that was no way favorable to the nicety of our sensations: — if any thing could have added to it, it was that the two beds were both of them so very small, as to cut us off from every idea of the lady and the maid lying together, which in either of them, could it have been feasible, my lying beside them, though a thing not to be wish'd, yet there was nothing in it so terrible which the imagination might not have pass'd over without torment.

As for the little room within, it offer'd little or no consolation to us: 'twas a damp, cold closet, with a half-dismantled window-shutter, and with a window which had neither glass nor oil-paper in it to keep out the tempest of the night. I did not endeavor to stifle my cough when the lady gave a peep into it; so it reduced the case in course to this alternative, — That the lady should sacrifice her health to her feelings, and take up with the closet herself, and abandon the bed next mine to her maid, —or, that the girl should take the closet, &c.

The lady was a Piedmontese of about thirty, with a glow of health in her cheeks. The maid was a Lyonoise of twenty, and as brisk and lively a French girl as ever moved. There were difficulties every way, and the obstacle of the stone in the road, which brought us into the distress, great as it appeared whilst the peasants were removing it, was but a pebble to what lay in our way now.—I have only to add, that it did not lessen the weight which hung upon our spirits, that we were both too delicate to communicate what we felt to each other upon the occasion.

We sat down to supper; and, had we not had more generous wine to it than a little inn in Savoy could have furnish'd, our tongues had been tied up till necessity herself had set them at liberty;—but the lady having a few bottles of Burgundy in her voiture, sent down her *fille de chambre* for a couple of them; so that by the time supper was over, and we were left alone, we felt ourselves inspired with a strength of mind sufficient to talk, at least, without reserve, upon our situation. We turn'd it every way, and debated and considered it in all kinds of lights, in the course of a two hours' negotiation; at the end of which the articles were settled finally betwixt us. and stipulated for in form and manner of a treaty of peace,—and, I believe, with as much religion and good faith on both sides, as in any treaty which has yet had the honor of being handed down to posterity.

They were as follow:—

First, As the right of the bed-chamber is in Monsieur,—and he thinking the bed next to the fire to be the warmest, he insists upon the concession on the lady's side of taking up with it.

Granted on the part of Madame; with a proviso, That as the curtains of that bed are of a flimsy transparent cotton, and appear likewise too scanty to draw close, that the *fille de chambre* shall fasten up the opening, either by corking-pins or needle and thread, in such manner as shall be deem'd a sufficient barrier on the side of Monsieur.

2dly, It is required on the part of Madame, that Monsieur shall lie the whole night through in his *robe de chambre.*

Rejected: inasmuch as Monsieur is not worth a *robe de chambre,* he having nothing in his portmanteau but six shirts and a black silk pair of breeches.

The mentioning the silk pair of breeches made an entire change of the article,—for the breeches were accepted as an equivalent for the *robe de chambre;* and so it was stipulated and agreed upon, what I should lie in my black silk breeches all night.

3dly. It was insisted upon, and stipulated for by the lady, that after Monsieur was got to bed, and the candle and fire extinguished, that Monsieur should not speak one single word the whole night.

Granted, provided Monsieur's saying his prayers might not be deem'd an infraction of the treaty.

There was but one point forgot in this treaty, and that was the manner in which the lady and myself should be obliged to undress and get to bed;—there was one way of doing it, and that I leave to the reader to devise, protesting as I do it, if it is not the most delicate in nature,—'tis the fault of his own imagination,—against which this is not my first complaint.

Now, when we were got to bed, whether it was the novelty of the situation, or what it was, I know not, but so it was, I could not shut my eyes; I tried this side and that, and turn'd and turn'd again, till a full hour after midnight, when Nature and Patience both wearing out,—O my God! said I.

—You have broke the treaty, Monsieur, said the lady, who had no more sleep than myself. I begg'd a thousand pardons; but insisted it was no more than an ejaculation. —She maintain'd it was an entire infraction of the treaty; I maintained it was provided for in the clause of the third article.

The lady would by no means give up the point, though she weaken'd her barrier by it; for, in the warmth of the dispute, I could hear two or three corking-pins fall out of the curtain to the ground.

—Upon my word and honor, Madame, said I, stretching my arm out of bed by way of asseveration,—

(I was going to have added, that I would not have trespass'd against the remotest idea of decorum for the world)—

But the *fille de chambre* hearing there were words between us, and fearing that hostilities would ensue in course, had crept silently out of her closet; and it being totally dark, had stolen so close to our beds, that she had got herself into the narrow passage which separated them, and had advanced so far up as to be in a line betwixt her mistress and me;—

So that when I stretch'd out my hand, I caught hold of the *fille de chambre's*—

END OF THE SENTIMENTAL JOURNEY.

Letters

BY

LAURENCE STERNE, A. M.

LETTER I.*

TO MISS L——.

YES! I will steal from the world, and not a babbling tongue shall tell where I am,—Echo shall not so much as whisper my hiding place, — suffer thy imagination to paint it at a little sun-gilt cottage, on the side of a romantic hill;—dost thou think I will leave love and friendship behind me? No! they shall be my companions in solitude, for they will sit down and rise up with me in the amiable form of my L——. We will be as merry and as innocent as our first parents in Paradise, before the arch-fiend entered that undescribable scene.

The kindest affections will have room to shoot and expand in our retirement, and produce such fruit as madness, and envy, and ambition, have always killed in the bud. —Let the human tempest and hurricane rage at a distance, the desolation is beyond the horizon of peace.——My L. has seen a polyanthus blow in December, — some friendly wall has sheltered it from the biting wind.—No planetary influence shall reach us, but that which presides and cherishes the sweetest flowers.—God preserve us! how delightful this prospect in idea! We will build and we will plant in our own way,—simplicity shall not be tortured by art,—we will learn of Nature how to live,—she shall be our alchymist to mingle all the good of life into one salubrious draught.—The gloomy family of care and distrust shall be banished from our dwelling, guarded by thy kind and tutelary deity;—we will sing our choral songs of gratitude, and rejoice to the end of our pilgrimage.

Adieu, my L. Return to one who languishes for thy society.

L. STERNE.

LETTER II.

TO THE SAME.

You bid me tell you, my dear L., how I bore your departure for S——, and whether the valley where D'Estella stands, retains still its looks,—or if I think the roses or jessamines smell as sweet, as when you left it.—Alas! every thing has now lost its relish and look! The hour you left D'Estella, I took to my bed.—I was worn out with fevers of all kinds, but most by that fever of the heart with which thou knowest well I have been wasting these two years —and shall continue wasting till you quit S——. The good Miss S——, from the forebodings of the best of hearts, thinking I was ill, insisted upon my going to her. — What can be the cause, my dear L., that I have never been able to see the face of this mutual friend, but I feel myself rent to pieces? She made me stay an hour with her, and in that short space, I burst into tears a dozen different times—and in such affectionate gusts of passion, that she was constrained to leave the room,—and sympathize in her dressing-room.—I have been weeping for you both, said she, in a tone of the sweetest pity,—for poor L.'s heart, I have long known it—her anguish is as sharp as yours,—her heart as tender, —her constancy as great,—her virtues as heroic;—Heaven brought you not together to be tormented. I could only answer her with a kind look, and a heavy sigh,—and returned home to your lodgings (which I have hired till your return) to resign myself to misery.—Fanny had prepared me a

* This, and the three subsequent letters, were written by Mr. Sterne to his wife, while she resided in Staffordshire, before their marriage.

supper,—she is all attention to me;—but I sat over it with tears; a bitter sauce, my L., but I could eat with no other:—for the moment she began to spread my little table, my heart fainted within me.—One solitary plate, one knife, one fork, one glass!—I gave a thousand pensive penetrating looks at the chair thou hadst so often graced, in those quiet and sentimental repasts,—then laid down my knife and fork, and took out my handkerchief, and clapped it across my face, and wept like a child.—I do so this very moment, my L.; for, as I take up my pen, my poor pulse quickens, my pale face glows, and tears are trickling down upon the paper, as I trace the word L——. O thou blessed in thyself, and in thy virtues,—blessed to all that know thee,—to me most so, because more do I know of thee than all thy sex.—This is the philtre, my L., by which thou hast charmed me, and by which thou wilt hold me thine, whilst virtue and faith hold this world together.—This, my friend, is the plain and simple magic by which I told Miss —— I have won a place in that heart of thine, on which I depend so satisfied, that time or distance, or change of every thing which might alarm the hearts of little men, create no uneasy suspense in mine.—Wast thou to stay in S—— these seven years, thy friend, though he would grieve, scorns to doubt or to be doubted;—'tis the only exception where security is not the parent of danger.—I told you poor Fanny was all attention to me since your departure—contrives every day bringing in the name of L. She told me last night (upon giving me some hartshorn), she had observed my illness began the very day of your departure for S——; that I had never held up my head, had seldom or scarce ever smiled, had fled from all society,—that she verily believed I was broken-hearted, for she had never entered the room, or passed by the door, but she heard me sigh heavily,—that I neither eat, or slept, or took pleasure in any thing as before;—judge then, my L., can the valley look so well,—or the roses and jessamines smell so sweet as heretofore? Ah me!—but adieu,—the vesper-bell calls me from thee to my God.

L. STERNE.

LETTER III.

TO THE SAME.

Before now my L. has lodged an indictment against me in the high court of Friendship;—I plead guilty to the charge, and entirely submit to the mercy of that amiable tribunal.—Let this mitigate my punishment, if it will not expiate my transgression,—do not say that I shall offend again in the same manner, though a too easy pardon sometimes occasions a repetition of the same fault.—A miser says, Though I do no good with my money to-day, to-morrow shall be marked with some deed of beneficence.—The Libertine says, Let me enjoy this week in forbidden and luxurious pleasures, and the next I will dedicate to serious thought and reflection.—The Gamester says, Let me have one more chance with the dice, and I will never touch them more.—The Knave of every profession wishes to obtain but independency, and he will become an honest man.—The female Coquette triumphs in tormenting her enamorato, for fear, after marriage, he should not pity her.

The apparition of the fifth instant (for letters may almost be called so) proved more welcome, as I did not expect it. Oh! my L. thou art kind, indeed, to make an apology for me, and thou never wilt assuredly repent of one act of kindness—for being thy debtor, I will pay thee with interest.—Why does my L. complain of the desertion of friends?—Where does the human being live that will not join in this complaint?—It is a common observation, and perhaps too true, that married people seldom extend their regards beyond their own fire-side.—There is such a thing as parsimony in esteem, as well as money—yet as one costs nothing, it might be bestowed with more liberality. We cannot gather grapes from thorns, so we must not expect kind attachments from persons who are wholly folded up in selfish schemes. I do not know whether I must despise or pity such characters—Nature never made an unkind creature—ill-usage, and bad habits, have deformed a fair and lovely creation.

My L.!—thou art surrounded by all the melancholy gloom of winter! wert thou alone, the retirement would be agreeable,

—disappointed ambition might envy such a retreat, and disappointed love would seek it out.—Crowded towns, and busy societies, may delight the unthinking and gay—but solitude is the best nurse of wisdom.—Methinks I see my contemplative girl now in the garden, watching the gradual approaches of spring.—Dost not thou mark with delight the first vernal buds of the snow-drop and primrose, these early and welcome visitors, spring beneath thy feet.—Flora and Pomona already consider thee as their handmaid, and a little time will load thee with their sweetest blessing.—The feathered race are all thy own, and with them, untaught harmony will soon begin to cheer thy morning and evening walks.—Sweet as this may be, return—return—the birds of Yorkshire will tune their pipes, and sing as melodiously as those of Staffordshire.

Adieu, my beloved L.; thine too much for my *peace*.

L. STERNE.

LETTER IV.

TO THE SAME.

I HAVE offended her whom I so tenderly love!—what could tempt me to it! but if a beggar was to knock at thy gate, would'st thou not open the door, and be melted with compassion?—I know thou would'st, for Pity has erected a temple in thy bosom.—Sweetest and best of all human passions! let thy web of tenderness cover the pensive form of affliction, and soften the darkest shades of misery!—I have reconsidered this apology, and, alas! what will it accomplish? Arguments, however finely spun, can never change the nature of things—very true—so a truce with them.

I have lost a very valuable friend by a sad accident, and what is worse, he has left a widow and five young children to lament this sudden stroke.—If real usefulness and integrity of heart could have secured him from this, his friends would not now be mourning his untimely fate.—These dark and seemingly cruel dispensations of Providence, often make the best of human hearts complain.—Who can paint the distress of an affectionate mother, made a widow in a moment, weeping in bitterness over a numerous, helpless, and fatherless offspring!—God! these are thy chastisements, and require (hard task!) a pious acquiescence.

Forgive me this digression, and allow me to drop a tear over a departed friend; and, what is more excellent, an honest man. My L.! thou wilt feel all that kindness can inspire in the death of ——. The event was sudden, and thy gentle spirit would be more alarmed on that account.—But, my L., thou hast less to lament, as old age was creeping on, and her period of doing good, and being useful, was nearly over.—At sixty years of age the tenement gets fast out of repair, and the lodger with anxiety thinks of a discharge.—In such a situation, the poet might well say,

"The soul uneasy," &c.

My L. talks of leaving the country—may a kind angel guide thy steps hither!—Solitude at length grows tiresome.—Thou sayest thou wilt quit the place with regret—I think so too.—Does not something uneasy mingle with the very reflection of leaving it? It is like parting with an old friend, whose temper and company one has long been acquainted with—I think I see you looking twenty times a day at the house—almost counting every brick and pane of glass, and telling them at the same time, with a sigh, you are going to leave them.—Oh, happy modification of matter! they will remain insensible of thy loss.—But how wilt thou be able to part with thy garden?—The recollection of so many pleasing walks must have endeared it to you. The trees, the shrubs, the flowers, which thou reared with thy own hands—will they not droop and fade away sooner upon thy departure?—Who will be thy successor to nurse them in thy absence?—Thou wilt leave thy name upon the myrtle-tree.—If trees, and shrubs, and flowers, could compose an elegy, I should expect a very plaintive one upon this subject.

Adieu, adieu! Believe me, ever, ever thine.

L. STERNE.

LETTER V.

TO MRS. F——.

York, Tuesday, Nov. 19. 1759.

Dear Madam,

Your kind inquiries after my health, deserve my best thanks.—What can give one more pleasure than the good wishes of those we value?—I am sorry you give so bad an account of your own health, but hope you will find benefit from tar-water—it has been of infinite service to me.—I suppose, my good lady, by what you say in your letter, "that I am busy writing an extraordinary "book," that your intelligence comes from York—the fountain-head of all chit-chat news—and—no matter.—Now for your desire of knowing the reason of my turning author? why truly I am tired of employing my brains for other people's advantage.—'Tis a foolish sacrifice I have made for some years to an ungrateful person.—I depend much upon the candor of the public, but I shall not pick out a jury to try the merit of my book amongst ********,—and, till you read my Tristram, do not, like some people, condemn it.—Laugh I am sure you will at some passages.—I have hired a small house in the Minster Yard for my wife and daughter—the latter is to begin dancing, &c.: if I cannot leave her a fortune, I will at least give her an education.—As I shall publish my works very soon, I shall be in town by March, and shall have the pleasure of meeting with you.—All your friends are well, and ever hold you in the same estimation that your sincere friend does.

Adieu, dear lady: believe me, with every wish for your happiness, your most faithful, &c.

LAURENCE STERNE.

LETTER VI.

TO DR. ******.

Jan. 30, 1760.

Dear Sir,

—*De mortuis nil nisi bonum*, is a maxim which you have so often of late urged in conversation, and in your letters (but in your last especially,) with such seriousness and severity against me, as the supposed transgressor of the rule;—that you have made me at length as serious and severe as yourself:—but that the humors you have stirred up might not work too potently within me, I have waited four days to cool myself, before I would set pen to paper to answer you, "*de mortuis nil nisi bonum.*" I declare I have considered the wisdom and foundation of it over and over again, as dispassionately and charitably as a good Christian can, and, after all, I can find nothing in it, or make more of it than a nonsensical lullaby of some nurse, put into Latin by some pedant to be chanted by some hypocrite to the end of the world, for the consolation of departing lechers.—'Tis, I own, Latin; and I think that is all the weight it has—for, in plain English, 'tis a loose and futile position below a dispute—"*you are not to speak any thing of the* "*dead but what is good.*" Why so?—Who says so?—neither reason nor scripture.—Inspired authors have done otherwise—and reason and common sense tell me, that if the characters of past ages and men are to be drawn at all, they are to be drawn like themselves; that is, with their excellencies, and with their foibles—and it is as much a piece of justice to the world, and to virtue too, to do the one as the other.—The ruling passion, *et les egaremens du cœur*, are the very things which mark and distinguish a man's character;—in which I would as soon leave out a man's head as his hobby-horse.—However, if, like the poor devil of a painter, we must conform to this pious canon, *de mortuis*, &c. which I own has a spice of piety in the *sound* of it, and be obliged to paint both our angels and our devils out of the same pot—I then infer that our Sydenhams, and Sangrados, our Lucretius, and Messalinas, our Somers, and our Bolingbrokes, are alike entitled to statues, and all the historians or satirists who have said otherwise since they departed this life, from Sallust to S——, are guilty of the crimes you charge me with, "cowardice and injustice."

But why cowardice? "because 'tis not "courage to attack a dead man who can't "defend himself."—But why do you doctors of the faculty attack such a one with your incision-knife? Oh! for the good of the living.—'Tis my plea.—But I have something more to say in my behalf—and it is this—I am not guilty of the charge—though defensible. I have not cut up Doctor Kunastrokius at all.—I have just scratch'd him—and that scarce skin-deep.—I do him first all honor—speak of Kunastrokius as a great man—(be he whom he will) and then most distantly hint at a droll foible in his character—and that not first reported (to the few who can even understand the hint) by me—but known before by every chamber-maid and footman within the bills of mortality—but Kunastrokius, you say, was a great man—'tis that very circumstance which makes the pleasantry—for I could name at this instant a score of honest gentlemen who might have done the very thing which Kunastrokius did, and seen no joke in it at all—as to the failing of Kunastrokius, which you say can only be imputed to his friends as a misfortune—I see nothing like a misfortune in it to any friend or relation of Kunastrokius, that Kunastrokius upon occasion should sit with ****** and ******—I have put these stars not *to hurt your worship's delicacy.*—If Kunastrokius after all is too sacred a character to be even smiled at (which is all I have done,) he has had better luck than his betters. In the same page (without imputation of cowardice) I have said as much of a man of twice his wisdom—and that is Solomon, of whom I have made the same remark, "That they were both great men "—and like all mortal men had each their "ruling passion."

—The consolation you give me, "That "my book, however, will be read enough "to answer my design of raising a tax upon "the public"—is very unconsolatory—to say nothing how very mortifying! by h——n! an author is worse treated than a common ***** at this rate—"*You will get a* "*penny by your sins, and that's enough.*" Upon this chapter let me comment.—That I proposed laying the world under contribution when I set pen to paper,—is what I own, and I suppose I may be allow'd to have that view in my head, in common with every other writer, to make my labor of advantage to myself.

Do you not do the same? but I beg I may add, that whatever views I had of that kind, I had other views—the first of which was, the hopes of doing the world good, by ridiculing what I thought deserving of it—or of disservice to sound learning, &c.—how I have succeeded, my book must show—and this I leave entirely to the world—but not to that little world of *your acquaintance*, whose opinion and sentiments you call the general opinion of the best judges *without exception*, who all affirm (you say) that my book cannot be put into the hands of any woman of *character*. (I hope you except widows, doctor—for they are not *all* so squeamish, but I am told they are all really of my party, in return for some good offices done their interests in the 274th page of my first volume.) But for the chaste married, and chaste unmarried part of the sex—they must not read my book! Heaven forbid the stock of chastity should be lessened by the Life and Opinions of Tristram Shandy—yes, his Opinions—it would certainly debauch 'em! God take them under his protection in this fiery trial, and send us plenty of Duennas to watch the workings of their humors till they have safely got through the whole work. If this will not be sufficient, may we have plenty of Sangrados to pour in plenty of cold water, till this terrible fermentation is over—as for the *nummum in loculo*, which you mention to me a second time, I fear you think me very poor, or in debt—I thank God, though I don't abound—that I have enough for a clean shirt every day—and a mutton chop—and my contentment, with this, has thus far (and I hope ever will) put me above stooping an inch for it, even for ——'s estate. Curse on it, I like it not to that degree, nor envy (*you may be sure*) any man who kneels in the dirt for it—so that howsoever I may fall short of the ends proposed in commencing author—I enter this *protest*, first, that my end was *honest;* and, secondly, that I wrote not to be *fed*, but to be *famous.* I am much obliged to Mr. Garrick for his very favorable opinion—but why, dear Sir, had he done better in finding fault with it than in commending it? to humble me! an author is not so soon humbled as you imagine—no, but to make the book better by castrations—that is still *sub judice*, and I can assure you upon this chapter, that the very passages and descriptions you propose that I should sacrifice in my second edition, are what are best relished by men of wit, and some others whom I esteem sound critics — so that, upon the whole, I am still kept up, if not above fear, at least above despair, and have seen enough to show me the folly of an attempt of castrating my book to the prudish humors of particulars. I believe the short-cut would be to publish this letter at the beginning of the third volume, as an apology for the first and second. I was sorry to find a censure upon the insincerity of some of my friends — I have no reason myself to reproach any one man—my friends have continued in the same opinions of my books which they first gave me of them—many indeed have thought better of 'em, by considering them more, few worse.

I am, Sir,

Your humble servant,

LAURENCE STERNE.

LETTER VII.

TO DAVID GARRICK, ESQ.

[*About April*, 1760,
Thursday, 11 o'clock—Night.

DEAR SIR,

'TWAS for all the world like a cut across my finger with a sharp pen-knife. I saw the blood—gave it a suck—wrapt it up—and thought no more about it.

But there is more goes to the healing of a wound than this comes to:—a wound (unless it is a wound not worth talking of,—but, by the bye, mine is) must give you some pain after. Nature will take her own way with it — it must ferment — it must digest.

The story you told me of Tristram's pretended tutor this morning — My letter by right should have set out with this sentence, and then the simile would not have kept you a moment in suspense.

This vile story, I say—though I then saw both how and where it wounded — I felt little from it at first — or, to speak more honestly (though it ruins my simile,) I felt a great deal of pain from it, but affected an air usual on such accidents, of less feeling than I had.

I have now got home to my lodgings, since the play (you astonished me in it,) and have been unwrapping this self-same wound of mine, and shaking my head over it this half-hour.

What the devil!—is there no one learned blockhead throughout the many schools of misapplied science in the Christian world, to make a *tutor* of for my Tristram? —*ex quovis ligno non fit*—Are we so run out of stock, that there is no one lumber-headed, muddle-headed, mortar-headed, pudding-headed *chap* amongst our doctors?—Is there no one single wight of much reading and no learning, amongst the many children in my *mother's* nursery, who bid high for this charge — but I must disable my judgment by choosing a Warburton? Vengeance! have I so little concern for the honor of my hero! Am I a wretch so void of sense, so bereft of feeling for the figure he is to make in story, that I should choose a preceptor to rob him of all the immortality I intended him? O! dear Mr. Garrick!

Malice is ingenious—unless where the excess of it outwits itself—I have two comforts in this stroke of it; the first is, that this one is partly of this kind; and secondly, that it is one of the number of those which so unfairly brought poor Yorick to his grave. The report might draw blood of the author of Tristram Shandy—but could not harm such a man as the author of the Divine Legation—God bless him! though (by the bye, and according to the natural course of descents) the blessing should come from him to me.

Pray have you no interest, lateral or collateral, to get me introduced to his Lordship.

Why do you ask?

My dear Sir, I have no claim to such an honor, but what arises from the honor and respect which, in the progress of my work, will be shown the world I owe to so great a man.

Whilst I am talking of owing—I wish, my dear Sir, that any body would tell you, how much I am indebted to you. I am determined never to do it myself, or say more upon the subject than this, that I am yours,

L. STERNE

LETTER VIII.

TO S—— C——, ESQ.

May, 1760.

DEAR SIR,

I RETURN you ten thousand thanks for the favor of your letter—and the account you give me of my wife and girl. I saw Mr. Ch——y to-night at Ranelagh, who tells me you have inoculated my friend Bobby. I heartily wish him well through, and hope in God all goes right.

On Monday we set out with a *grand retinue of Lord Rockingham's (in whose suite I move) for Windsor—they have contracted for fourteen hundred pounds for the dinner, to some general undertaker, of which the K. has bargained to pay one third. Lord George Sackville was last Saturday at the opera, some say with great effrontery,—others, with great dejection.

I have little news to add. There is a shilling pamphlet † wrote against Tristram. I wish they would write a hundred such.

Mrs. Sterne says her purse is light: will you, dear Sir, be so good as to pay her ten guineas, and I will reckon with you, when I have the pleasure of meeting you. My best compliments to Mrs. C. and all friends. Believe me, dear Sir, your obliged and faithful

LAU. STERNE.

LETTER IX.

TO THE SAME.

May, 1760.

DEAR SIR,

I THIS moment received the favor of your kind letter:—the letter in the Ladies' Magazine,‡ about me, was wrote by the noted Dr. Hill, who wrote the Inspector, and undertakes that magazine;—the people of York are very uncharitable to suppose any man so gross a beast as to pen such a character of himself.—In this great town, no soul ever suspected it, for a thousand reasons;—could they suppose I should be such a fool as to fall foul upon Dr. Warburton, my best friend, by representing him so weak a man,—or by telling such a lie of him,—as his giving me a purse, to buy off his tutorship for Tristram!—or I should be fool enough to own I had taken his purse for that purpose!

You must know there is a quarrel between Dr. Hill and Dr. M——y, who was the physician meant at Mr. Charles Stanhope's, and Dr. Hill has changed the place on purpose to give M——y a lick.—Now that conversation (though perhaps true,) yet happened at another place,* and with another physician; which I have contradicted in this city, for the honor of my friend M——y: all which shows the absurdity of

* Prince Ferdinand, the Marquis of Rockingham, and Earl Temple, were installed Knights of the Garter, on Tuesday, May 6th, 1760, at Windsor.

† "The Clock-maker's outcry against the author of Tristram Shandy." 8vo.

‡ The Royal Female Magazine, for April, 1760.

* As the truth of this anecdote is not denied, it may gratify curiosity to communicate it in Dr. Hill's own words.—"At the last dinner that the late lost amiable "Charles Stanhope gave to genius, Yorick was pres- "ent. The good old man was vexed to see a pedantic "medicine-monger take the lead, and prevent that "pleasantry which good wit and good wine might "have occasioned, by a discourse in the unintelligible "language of his profession, concerning the difference "between the phrenitis and the paraphrenitis, and "the concomitant categories of the mediastinum and "pleura.

"Good-humored Yorick saw the sense of the master "of the feast, and fell into the cant and jargon of "physic, as if he had been one of Radcliffe's travellers. "'The vulgar practice,' says he, 'savors too much of "mechanical principles; the venerable ancients were "all empirics, and the profession will never regain its "ancient credit, till practice falls into the old track "again. I am myself an instance; I caught cold by "leaning on a damp cushion, and, after sneezing and "sniveling a fortnight, it fell upon my breast. They "blooded me, blistered me, and gave me robs and bobs "and lohocks, and eclegmata; but I grew worse; for "I was treated according to the exact rules of the "College. In short, from an inflammation it came to "an ADHESION, and all was over with me. They "advised me to go to Bristol, that I might not do them "the scandal of dying under their hands; and the "Bristol people for the same reason consigned me over "to Lisbon. But what do I? why I considered an "adhesion is, in plain English, only a sticking of two "things together, and that force enough would pull "them asunder. I bought a good ash-pole, and began "leaping over all the walls and ditches in the coun- "try. From the height of the pole I used to come souse "down upon my feet, like an ass, when he tramples "upon a bull-dog: but it did not do. At last—when "I had raised myself perpendicularly over a wall, I "used to fall exactly across the ridge of it upon the "side opposite to the adhesion. This tore it off at "once, and I am as you see. Come, fill a glass to the "memory of the empiric medicine.' If he had been "asked elsewhere about this disorder (for he really "had a consumptive disorder), he would have an- "swered, that he was cured by Huxham's decoction "of the bark, and elixir of vitriol."

York credulity and nonsense. Besides, the account is full of falsehoods,—first, with regard to the place of my birth, which was at Clonmel, in Ireland,—the story of a hundred pounds to Mrs. W——,* not true, or of a *pension promised;* the merit of which I disclaimed,—and indeed there are so many other things so untrue, and unlikely to come from me, that the worst enemy I have here never had a suspicion,—and, to end all, Dr. Hill owns the paper.

I shall be down before May is out;—I preach before the judges on Sunday;—my Sermons come out on Thursday after;—and I purpose, the Monday, at furthest, after that, to set out for York;—I have bought a pair of horses for that purpose:—my best respects to your Lady ———.

I am, Dear Sir,
Your most obliged and faithful
L. STERNE.

P. S. I beg pardon for this hasty scrawl, having just come from a concert where the D. of York performed.—I have received great notice from him, and last week had the honor of supping with him.

LETTER X.

TO DR. WARBURTON, BISHOP OF GLOUCESTER.

York, June 9, 1760.

MY LORD,

NOT knowing where to send two sets of my Sermons, I could think of no better expedient than to order them into Mr. Berrenger's hands, who has promised me that he will wait upon your Lordship with them, the first moment he hears you are in town. The truest and humblest thanks I return to your Lordship, for the generosity of your protection, and advice to me; by making a good use of the one, I will hope to deserve the other: I wish your Lordship all the health and happiness in this world, for I am

Your Lordship's
Most obliged and
Most grateful Servant,
L. STERNE.

P. S. I am just sitting down to go on with Tristram, &c.—the scribblers use me ill, but they have used my betters much worse, for which may God forgive them.

LETTER XI.

TO MY WITTY WIDOW, MRS. F———.

Coxwould, Aug. 3, 1760.

MADAM,

WHEN a man's brains are as dry as a squeez'd orange,—and he feels he has no more conceit in him than a mallet, 'tis in vain to think of sitting down, and writing a letter to a lady of your wit, unless in the honest John-Trot style of *yours of the 15th instant came safe to hand, &c.*, which, by the bye, looks like a letter of business; and you know very well, from the first letter I had the honor to write to you, I am a man of no business at all. This vile plight I found my genius in was the reason I have told Mr. ——, I would not write to you till the next post,—hoping by that time to get some small recruit, at least of vivacity, if not wit, to set out with;—but upon second thoughts, thinking a bad letter in season,—to be better than a good one out of it,—this scrawl is the consequence, which if you will burn the moment you get it—I promise to send you a fine set essay in the style of your female epistolizers, cut and trimm'd at all points.—God defend me from such, who never yet knew what it was to say or write one premeditated word in my whole life;—for this reason I send you this with pleasure, because wrote with the careless irregularity of an easy heart.——Who told you, Garrick wrote the medley for Beard?—'Twas wrote in his house, however, and before I left town.—I deny it,—I was not lost two days before I left town.—I was lost all the time I was there, and never found till I got to this Shandy-castle of mine.—Next winter I intend to sojourn amongst you with more decorum, and will neither be lost or found anywhere.

Now I wish to God, I was at your elbow,—I have just finished one volume of Shandy, and I want to read it to some one who I know can taste and relish humor;—this, by the way, is a little impudent in me,—for I

* The widow of Mr. Sterne's predecessor in the living of Coxwould.

take the thing for granted, which their high mightinesses the world have yet to determine,—but I mean no such thing,—I could wish only to have your opinion;—shall I, in truth, give you mine?—I dare not,—but I will; provided you keep it to yourself;—know then, that I think there is more laughable humor,—with an equal degree of Cervantic satire, if not more,—than in the last;—but we are bad judges of the merit of our children.

I return you a thousand thanks for your friendly congratulations upon my habitation,—and I will take care, you shall never wish me but well, for I am, Madam,

With great esteem and truth,

Your most obliged,

L. STERNE.

P. S. I have wrote this so vilely and so precipitately, I fear you must carry it to a decipherer.—I beg you'll do me the honor to write,—otherwise you draw *me* in, instead of Mr.—— drawing *you* into a scrape;—for I should sorrow to have a *taste* of so agreeable a correspondent,—and *no more.*

Adieu.

LETTER XII.

TO S—— C——, ESQ.

London, Christmas Day, 1760.

MY DEAR FRIEND,

I HAVE been in such a continual hurry since the moment I arrived here,—what with my books, and what with visitors and visitings, that it was not in my power sooner to sit down and acknowledge the favor of your obliging letter; and to thank you for the most friendly motives which led you to write it.—I am not much in pain upon what gives my kind friends at Stillington so much on the chapter of Noses; because, as the principal satire throughout that part is levelled at those learned blockheads who, in all ages, have wasted their time and much learning upon points as foolish,—it shifts off the idea of what you fear, to another point:—and 'tis thought here very good;—'twill pass muster,—I mean not with all:—no, no! I shall be attacked and pelted, either from cellars or garrets, write what I will; and besides, must expect to have a party against me of many hundreds.—who either do not, or will not laugh.——'Tis enough if I divide the world;—at least, I will rest contented with it.—I wish you was here to see what changes of looks and political reasoning have taken place in every company and coffee-house since last year. We shall be soon Prussians and Anti-Prussians, B——s and Anti-B——s; and those distinctions will just do as well as Whig and Tory,—and, for aught I know, serve the same ends.——The King seems resolved to bring all things back to their original principles, and to stop the torrent of corruption and laziness. He rises every morning at six, to do business,—rides out at eight to a minute,—returns at nine, to give himself up to his people.—By persisting, 'tis thought he will oblige his ministers and dependants to dispatch affairs with him many hours sooner than of late;—and 'tis much to be questioned whether they will not be enabled to wait upon him sooner, by being freed from long levees of their own, and applications; which will in all likelihood be transferred from them directly to himself,—the present system being to remove that phalanx of great people which stood betwixt the throne and the subjects, and suffer them to have immediate access without the intervention of a cabal—(this is the language of others):—however, the King gives every thing himself, knows every thing, and weighs every thing maturely, and then is inflexible.—This puts old stagers off their game.—How it will end, we are all in the dark.

'Tis feared the war is quite over in Germany. Never was known such havoc amongst troops.—I was told yesterday by a Colonel from Germany, that out of two battalions of nine hundred men, to which he belonged, but seventy-one are left!—Prince Ferdinand has sent word, 'tis said, that he must have forty thousand men directly to take the field,—and with provisions for them too; for he can but subsist them for a fortnight.—I hope this will find you all got to York.—I beg my compliments to the amiable Mrs. Croft, &c. &c.

Though I purposed going first to Golden Square, yet Fate has thus long disposed o me,—so I have never been able to set a foot towards that quarter.

I am, dear Sir,

Yours affectionately,

L. STERNE.

LETTER XIII.

TO THE SAME.

[About Jan. 1, 1761.

MY DEAR DEAR SIR,

I HAVE just time to acknowledge the favor of yours; but not to get the two prints you mention, which shall be sent you by the next post. I have bought them, and lent them to Miss Gilbert, but will assuredly send for them, and inclose them to you. I will take care to get your pictures well copied, and at a moderate price: and if I can be of further use, I beseech you to employ me; and, from time to time, will send you an account of whatever may be worth transmitting. — The stream now sets in strong against the German war. Loud complaints of ——— ——— ——— making a trade of the war, &c.—much expected from Ld. Granby's evidence to these matters, who is expected every hour. The king wins every day upon the people, shows himself much at the play (but at no opera); rides out with his brothers every morning, half an hour after seven till nine; returns with them; spends an hour with them at breakfast and chat, and then sits down to business. I never dined at home once since I arrived: and fourteen dinners deep engaged just now; and fear matters will be worse with me in that point than better. As to the main points in view, at which you hint, all I can say is, that I see my way, and, unless Old Nick throws the dice, shall, in due time, come off winner.—Tristram will be out the 20th.—There is a great rout made about him before he enters the stage:—whether this will be of use or no, I can't say.—Some wits of the first magnitude here, both as to wit and station, engage me success;—time will show

Adieu.

LETTER XIV.

TO THE SAME.

March, 1761.

DEAR SIR,

SINCE I had the favor of your obliging letter, nothing has happened, or been said one day, which has not been contradicted the next: so having little certain to write, I have forborne writing at all, in hopes every day of something worth filling up a letter. We had the greatest expectations yesterday that ever were raised, of a pitched battle in the House of Commons; wherein Mr. Pitt was to have entered and thrown down the gauntlet, in defence of the German war.—There never was so full a house: —the gallery full to the top;—I was there all the day,—when lo! a political fit of the gout seized the great combatant:—he entered not the lists. — Beckford got up, and begged the House, as he saw not his Right Honorable friend there, to put off the debate. —It could not be done: so Beckford rose up, and made a most long, passionate incoherent speech, in defence of the Germanic war,—but very severe upon the unfrugal manner it was carried on;—in which he addressed himself principally to the Chancellor of the Exchequer; and laid on him terribly. — It seems the chancery of Hanover had laid out 350,000 pounds on account, and brought in our Treasury debtor; — and the grand debate was, for an honest examination of the particulars of this extravagant account, and for vouchers to authenticate it.—Legge answered Beckford very rationally and coolly.—Lord N. spoke long.—Sir F. Dashwood maintained, the German war was most pernicious.—Mr. C——, of Surrey, spoke well against the account, with some others.—L. Barrington at last got up, and spoke half an hour with great plainness and temper,—explained a great many hidden springs relating to these accounts, in favor of the late King, and told two or three conversations relative to these expenses; — which cast great honor upon the King's character. This was with regard to the money the King had secretly furnished out of his pocket, to lessen the account of the Hanover-score brought us to discharge.

Beckford and Barrington abused all who sought for peace, and joined in the cry for it; and Beckford added, that the reasons of wishing a peace now, were the same as the peace of Utrecht; that the people behind the curtain could not both maintain the war and their places too; so were for making another sacrifice of the nation to their own interests. After all, the cry for a peace is so general, that it will certainly end in one. —Now for myself.

One half of the town abuse my book as bitterly as the other half cry it up to the skies: the best is, they abuse it and buy it, and at such a rate, that we are going on with a second edition as fast as possible.

I am going down, for a day or two, with Mr. Spencer, to Wimbleton. On Wednesday there is to be a grand assembly at Lady N——. I have inquired everywhere about Stephen's affair; and can hear nothing. My friend Mr. Charles Townshend, will be now Secretary of War;* he bid me wish him joy of it, though not in possession. I will ask him; and depend, my most worthy friend, that you shall not be ignorant of what I learn from him. Believe me ever, ever,

Yours,

L. S.

LETTER XV.

TO THE SAME.

April, 1761.

My Dear Sir,

A strain which I got in my wrist by a terrible fall, prevented my acknowledging the favor of your obliging letter. I went yesterday morning to breakfast with Mr. V——, who is a kind of right-hand man to the Secretary, on purpose to inquire about the propriety, or feasibility, of doing what you wish me;—and he has told me an anecdote which, had you been here, would, I think, have made it wiser to have deferred speaking about the affair a month hence than now. It is this:—You must know that the numbers of officers who have left their regiments in Germany for the pleasures of the town, have been long a topic of merriment; as you see them in St. James's Coffee-house, and the Park, every hour, inquiring, open mouth, how things go on in Germany, and what news,—when they should have been there to have furnished news themselves:—but the worst part has been, that many of them have left their brother officers on their duty, and in all the fatigues of it, and have come with no end but to make friends, to be put unfairly over the *heads of those* who were left risking *their lives.*—In this attempt, there have been some but too successful, which has justly raised ill-blood and complaints from the officers who staid behind: the upshot has been, that they have every soul been ordered off: and woe be to him ('tis said) who shall be found listening! Now, just to mention our friend's case whilst this cry is on foot, I think, would be doing more hurt than good: but, if you think otherwise, I will go with all my heart, and mention it to Mr. Townshend; for, to do more, I am too inconsiderable a person to pretend to.—You made me and my friends here very merry with the accounts current at York, of my being forbid the court;—but they do not consider what a considerable person they make of me, when they suppose either my going, or my not going there, is a point that ever enters the King's head;—and, for those about him, I have the honor either to stand so personally well known to them, or to be so well represented by those of the first rank, as to fear no accident of that kind.

I thank God (B——'s excepted) I have never yet made a friend or connexion I have forfeited, or done aught to forfeit;—but, on the contrary, my true character is better understood; and where I had one friend last year who did me honor, I have three now.—If my enemies knew that, by this rage of abuse and ill-will, they were effectually serving the interests both of myself and works, they would be more quiet;—but it has been the fate of my betters; who have found, that the way to fame is, like the way to Heaven,—through much tribulation;—and, till I shall have the honor to be as much maltreated as Rabelais and Swift were, I must continue humble;—f r

* He was appointed Secretary at War the 24th of March, 1761.

I have not filled up the measure of half their *persecutions.*

The court is turning topsy-turvy. Lord Bute *le premier*;*—Lord Talbot to be Groom of the Chambers,† in room of the D. of R——d;—Lord Halifax to Ireland;‡—Sir F. Dashwood in Talbot's place;—Pitt seems unmoved;—a peace inevitable;—stocks rise;—the peers this moment kissing hands, &c. &c. (this week may be christened the kiss-hands week) for a hundred changes will happen in consequence of these. Pray present my compliments to Mrs. C. and all friends, and believe me, with the greatest fidelity,

Your ever obliged

L. STERNE.

P. S. Is it not strange that Lord Talbot should have power to remove the Duke of R——d?

Pray, when you have read this, send the news to Mrs. Sterne.

* Lord Bute was appointed Secretary of State on the 25th of March 1761.

† Lord Talbot was appointed Steward of the Household on the same day.

‡ Lord Halifax was appointed Lord-Lieutenant of Ireland on the 20th of March, 1761.

LETTER XVI.

TO J—— H—— S——, ESQ.

Coxwould, July 28, 1761.

DEAR H——,

I SYMPATHIZED for, or with you, on the detail you give me of your late agitations,—and would willingly have taken my horse, and trotted to the oracle to have inquired into the etymology of all your sufferings, had I not been assured, that all that evacuation of bilious matter, with all that abdominal motion attending it (both which are equal to a month's purgation and exercise) will have left you better than it found you.—Need one go to D——, to be told that all kind of mild (mark, I am going to talk more foolishly than your apothecary) opening, saponaceous, dirty-shirt, and washing liquors are proper for you; and, consequently, all styptical potations death and destruction.—If you had not shut up your gall-ducts by these, the glauber-salts could not have hurt:—as it was, 'twas like a match to the gunpowder, by raising a fresh combustion, as all physic does at first: so that you have been let off,—nitre, brimstone, and charcoal (which is blackness itself) all at one blast.—'Twas well the piece did not burst; for I think it underwent great violence, and, as it is proof, will, I hope, do much service in this militating world.—*Panty is mistaken; I quarrel with no one.—There was that coxcomb of —— in the house, who lost temper with me for no other reason upon earth but that I could not fall down and worship a brazen image of learning and eloquence which he set up, to the persecution of all true believers.—I sat down upon *his altar*, and whistled in the time of his divine service,—and broke down his carved work, and kicked his incense-pot to the D——; so he retreated, *sed non sine felle in corde suo.*—I have wrote a *clerum*, whether I shall take my doctor's degrees or not.—I am much in doubt, but I trow not.—I go on with Tristram.—I have bought seven hundred books at a purchase, dog-cheap,—and many good;—and I have been a week getting them set up in my best room here:—Why do not you transport yours to town? but I talk like a fool.—This will just catch you at your spaw. I wish you *incolumem apud Londinum.*—Do you go there for good and all,—or ill?—I am, dear cousin,

Yours affectionately,

L. STERNE.

LETTER XVII.

TO THE SAME.

Coxwould [about August] 1761.

DEAR H——,

I REJOICE you are in London;—rest you there in peace:—here 'tis the Devil.—You was a good prophet.—I wish myself back again, as you told me I should;—but not because a thin, death-doing, pestiferous, north-east wind blows in a line directly from Crazy Castle turret full upon me, in this cuckoldy retreat (for I value the north-east wind and all its powers not a straw)—but the transition from rapid motion to ab

* The Rev. Mr. R— L—.

solute rest was too violent.—I should have walked about the streets of York ten days, as a proper medium to have passed through, before I entered upon my rest.—I staid but a moment, and I have been here but a few, to satisfy me I have not managed my miseries like a wise man;—and if God, for my consolation under them, had not poured forth the spirit of Shandeism into me, which will not suffer me to think two moments upon any grave subject, I would else just now lie down and die,—die;—and yet, in half an hour's time, I'll lay a guinea, I shall be as merry as a monkey,—and as mischievous too, and forget it all;—so that this is but a copy of the present train running across my brain.—And so you think this cursed stupid,—but that, my dear H——, depends much upon the *quotâ horâ* of your shabby clock; if the pointer of it is in any quarter between ten in the morning or four in the afternoon,—I give it up;—or, if the day is obscured by dark engendering clouds of either wet or dry weather, I am still lost.—But who knows but it may be five,—and the day as fine a day as ever shone upon the earth since the destruction of Sodom;—and, peradventure, your Honor may have got a good hearty dinner to-day, and eat and drunk your intellectuals into a placidulish and a blandulish amalgama,—to bear nonsense:—so much for that.

'Tis as cold and churlish just now, as (if God had not pleased it to be so) it ought to have been in bleak December; and therefore I am glad you are where you are, and where (I repeat it again) I wish I was also.—Curse of poverty, and absence from those we love!—they are two great evils which embitter all things;—and yet, with the first, I am not haunted much.—As to matrimony, I should be a beast to rail at it, for my wife is easy,—but the world is not;—and, had I staid from her a second longer, it would have been a burning shame, else she declares herself happier without one; but not in anger is this declaration made,—but in pure sober good sense built on sound experience.—She hopes you will be able to strike a bargain for me before this time twelve-month, to lead a bear round Europe: and, from this hope from you, I verily believe it is, that you are so high in her favor at present.--She swears you are a fellow of wit, though humorous: a funny, jolly soul, though somewhat splenetic; and (bating the love of women) as honest as *gold*;—how do you like the simile?—Oh, Lord! now you are going to Ranelagh to-night, and I am sitting, sorrowful as the prophet was, when the voice cried out to him, and said, "What doest thou here, Elijah?"—'Tis well the spirit does not make the same at Coxwould;—for, unless for the few sheep left me to take care of in this wilderness, I might as well, nay better, be at Mecca.—When we find we can, by a shifting of places, run away from ourselves, what think you of a jaunt there, before we finally pay a visit to the *Vale of Jehosaphat?*—as ill a fame as we have, I trust I shall one day or other see you face to face.—So tell the two Colonels, if they love good company, to live righteously and soberly as *you do*, and then they will have no doubts or dangers within or without them.—Present my best and warmest wishes to them, and advise the eldest to prop up his spirits, and get a rich Dowager before the conclusion of the peace:—why will not the advice suit both *par nobile fratrum?*

To-morrow morning (if Heaven permit) I begin the fifth volume* of Shandy:—I care not a curse for the critics.—I'll load my vehicle with what goods *he* sends me, and they may take 'em off my hands, or let them alone.—I am very valorous:—and 'tis in proportion as we retire from the world, and see it in its true dimensions, that we despise it.—No bad rant!—God above bless you! You know I am

Your affectionate cousin,

LAURENCE STERNE.

What few remain of the Demoniacs, greet;—and write me a letter, if you are able, as foolish as this.

LETTER XVIII.

TO LADY ——.

Coxwould, Sept. 21, 1761.

I RETURN to my new habitation, fully determined to write as hard as can be, and thank you most cordially, my dear lady, for your letter of congratulation upon my Lord

* Alluding to the first edition.

Fauconberg's having presented me with the curacy of this place, — though your congratulation comes somewhat of the latest, as I have been possessed of it some time. —I hope I have been of some service to his Lordship; and he has sufficiently requited me. —'Tis seventy guineas a year in my pocket, though worth a hundred;— but it obliges me to have a curate to officiate at Sutton and Stillington.—'Tis within a mile of his Lordship's seat and park. 'Tis a very agreeable ride out in the chaise I purchased for my wife.—Lyd has a poney, which she delights in.—Whilst they take these diversions, I am scribbling away at my Tristram. These two volumes are, I think, the best.—I shall write as long as I live; 'tis, in fact, my hobby-horse, and so much am I delighted with my uncle Toby's imaginary character, that I am become an enthusiast. —My Lydia helps to copy for me;—and my wife knits, and listens as I read her chapters.—The coronation of his Majesty (whom God preserve!) has cost me the value of an ox, which is to be roasted whole in the middle of the town; and my parishioners will, I suppose, be very merry upon the occasion.—You will then be in town,— and feast your eyes with a sight which, 'tis to be hoped, will not be in either of our powers to see again;—for, in point of age, we have about twenty years the start of his majesty. —And now, my dear friend, I must finish this,—and, with every wish for your happiness, conclude myself your most sincere well-wisher and friend,

L. STERNE.

LETTER XIX.

TO DAVID GARRICK, ESQ.

Paris, Jan. 31, 1762.

My Dear Friend,

Think not, because I have been a fortnight in this metropolis without writing to you, that therefore I have not had you and Mrs. Garrick a hundred times in my head and heart.—Heart! yes, yes, say you;—but I must not waste paper in *badinage* this post, whatever I do the next. Well! here I am, my friend, as much improved in my health, for the time, as ever your friendship could wish, or, at least, your faith give credit to. —By the bye, I am somewhat worse in my intellectuals; for my head is turned round with what I see, and the unexpected honors I have met with here. Tristram was almost as much known here as in London, at least among your men of condition and learning, and has got me introduced into so many circles ('tis *comme à Londres.*) I have just now a fortnight's dinners and suppers upon my hands.—My application to the Count de Choiseul goes on swimmingly; for not only Mr. Telletiere (who, by the bye, sends ten thousand civilities to you and Mrs. Garrick) has undertaken my affair, but the Count de Limbourgh.—The Baron d'Holbach has offered any security for the inoffensiveness of my behavior in France:—'tis more, you rogue, than you will do!—This Baron is one of the most learned noblemen here, the great protector of wits, and the *Scavans*, who are no wits;—keeps open house three days a week. —His house is now, as yours was to me, my own.—He lives at great expense.—'Twas an odd incident when I was introduced to the Count de Bissie, which I was at his desire,—I found him reading Tristram.—This grandee does me great honors, and gives me leave to go a private way through his apartments into the Palais Royal, to view the Duke of Orleans's collections, every day I have time.—I have been at the doctors of Sorbonne.—I hope in a fortnight to break through, or rather from, the delights of this place, which, in the *Scavoir Vivre*, exceeds all the places, I believe, in this section of the globe.

I am going, when this letter is wrote, with Mr. Fox and Mr. Macartney to Versailles. The next morning I wait upon Mons. Titon, in company with Mr. Macartney, who is known to him, to deliver your commands.—I have bought you the pamphlet upon theatrical, or rather tragical declamation. I have bought another in verse, worth reading; and you will receive them, with what I can pick up this week, by a servant of Mr. Hodges, whom he is sending back to England.

I was last night with Mr. Fox to see Mademoiselle Clairon, in *Iphigene;*—she is extremely great:—would to God you had one or two like her! What a luxury, to see you with one of such powers in the same interesting scene! — but 'tis too much, — Ah!

Preville! thou art Mercury himself.—By virtue of taking a couple of boxes, we have bespoke, this week, *The Frenchman in London*, in which Preville is to send us home to supper *all happy*,—I mean about fifteen or sixteen English of distinction, who are now here, and live well with each other.

I am under great obligations to Mr. Pitt, who has behaved in every respect to me like a man of good-breeding and good-nature.—In a post or two I will write again.—Foley is an honest soul.—I could write six volumes of what has passed comically in this great scene, since these last fourteen days; but more of this hereafter.—We are all going into mourning; neither you nor Mrs. Garrick would know me, if you met me in my [illegible]. Bless you both! Service to Mrs. [illegible]. Adieu, adieu!

L. S.

LETTER XX.

TO LADY D——.

London,* Feb. 1. 1762.

Your Ladyship's kind inquiries after my health are indeed kind, and of a piece with the rest of your character. Indeed I am very ill, having broke a vessel in my lungs. —Hard writing in the summer, together with preaching, which I have not strength for, is ever fatal to me;—but I cannot avoid the latter yet; and the former is too pleasurable to be given up.—I believe I shall try if the south of France will not be of service to me: his G. of Y. has most humanely given me the permission for a year or two.—I shall set off with great hopes of its efficacy, and shall write to my wife and daughter to come and join me at Paris, else my stay could not be so long.—"Le Fevre's story has beguiled "your Ladyship of your tears;" and the thought of the accusing spirit flying up to Heaven's chancery with the oath, you are kind enough to say, is sublime. My friend Mr. Garrick thinks so too, and I am most vain of his approbation. Your Ladyship's opinion adds not a little to my vanity.

I wish I had time to take a little excursion to Bath, were it only to thank you for all the obliging things you say in your letter:—but 'tis impossible:—accept, at least, my warmest thanks.—If I could tempt my friend Mr. H—— to come to France, I should be truly happy.—If I can be of any service to you at Paris, command him who is, and ever will be,

Your Ladyship's faithful

L. STERNE.

* This letter, though dated from London, was evidently written at Paris.

LETTER XXI.

TO DAVID GARRICK, ESQ.

Paris, March 19, 1762.

Dear Garrick,

This will be put into your hands by Dr. Shippen, a physician who has been here some time with Miss Poyntz, and is this moment setting off for your metropolis: so I snatch the opportunity of writing to you and my kind friend Mrs. Garrick.—I see nothing like her here, and yet I have been introduced to one half of their best goddesses; and, in a month more, shall be admitted to the shrines of the other half;—but I neither worship nor fall (much) upon my knees before them; but, on the contrary, have converted many unto Shandeism;—for be it known, I Shandy it away fifty times more than I ever was wont, talk more nonsense than ever you heard me talk in your days, and to all sorts of people. *Qui le diable est cet homme-là*, said Choiseul, t'other day, *ce Chevalier Shandy*.—You'll think me as vain as a Devil, was I to tell you the rest of the dialogue:—whether the bearer knows it or not, I know not.—'Twill serve up after supper, in Southampton-street, amongst other small dishes, after the fatigues of Richard the Third.—O God! they have nothing here which gives the nerves so smart a blow as those great characters in the hands of Garrick!—but I forgot I am writing to the man himself.—The Devil take (as he will) these transports of enthusiasm! *Apropos*:—The whole city of Paris is *bewitch'd* with the comic opera; and if it was not for the affair of the Jesuits, which takes up one half of our talk, the comic opera would have it all. It is a tragical nuisance in all companies as it is; and, was it not for some sudden starts and dashes of Shandeism, which now and then either break the thread, or entangle it so, that the Devil himself would be puzzled in winding it off,—I should die a martyr:—this, by the way, I never will.

I send you over some of these comic operas by the bearer, with the *Sallon*, a satire.—The French comedy, I seldom visit it;—they act scarce any thing but tragedies;—and the Clairon is great, and Mademoiselle Dumesnil, in some places, still greater than her;—yet I cannot bear preaching: I fancy I got a surfeit of it in my younger days.—There is a tragedy to be damned to-night; peace be with it, and the gentle brain which made it! I have ten thousand things to tell you I cannot write. I do a thousand things which cut no figure *but in the doing*;—and, as in London, I have the honor of having done and said a thousand things I never did or dreamt of,—and yet I dream abundantly.—If the Devil stood behind me in the shape of a courier, I could not write faster than I do, having five letters more to dispatch by the same gentleman; he is going into another section of the globe; and when he has seen you, he will depart in peace.

The Duke of Orleans has suffered my portrait to be added to the number of some odd men in his collection; and a gentleman, who lives with him, has taken it most expressively at full length. I purpose to obtain an etching of it, and to send it you. Your prayer for me, of *rosy health*, is heard. If I stay here for three or four months, I shall return more than reinstated.—My love to Mrs. Garrick.

I am, my dear Garrick,
Your most humble servant,
L. STERNE.

LETTER XXII.

TO THE SAME.

Paris, April 10, 1762.

MY DEAR GARRICK,

I SNATCH the occasion of Mr. Wilcox (the late Bishop of Rochester's son) leaving this place for England, to write to you: and I inclose it to Hall, who will put it into your hand, possibly behind the scenes. I hear no news of you or your *empire;* I would have said *kingdom*, but here every thing is hyperbolized;—and if a woman is but simply pleased,—'tis *Je suis charmé;*—and if she is charmed, 'tis nothing less than that she is *ravi*-sh'd;—and when ravish'd (which may happen), there is nothing left for her but to fly to the other world for a metaphor, and swear, *Qu'elle étoit tout extasiée;*—which mode of speaking is, by the bye, here creeping into use; and there is scarce a woman who understands the *bon ton*, but is seven times in a day in downright ecstacy;—that is, the Devil's in her,—by a small mistake of one word for the other.—Now, where am I got?

I have been these two days reading a tragedy, given me by a lady of talent to read; and conjecture if it would do for you:—'Tis from the plan of Diderot; and possibly half a translation of it:—The Natural Son, or the Triumph of Virtue, in five acts.—It has too much sentiment in it, (at least for me), the speeches too long, and savor too much of *preaching;*—this may be a second reason it is not to my taste.—'Tis all love, love, love, throughout, without much separation in the characters; so I fear it would not do for your stage, and perhaps for the very reasons which recommend it to a French one.—After a vile suspension of three weeks, we are beginning with our comedies and operas again:—yours, I hear, never flourished more;—here, the comic actors were never so low;—the tragedians hold up their heads, in all senses. I have known *one little man* support the theatrical world, like a David Atlas, upon his shoulders; but Preville can't do half as much here, though Mademoiselle Clairon stands by him, and sets her back to his:—she is very great, however, and highly improved since you saw her;—she also supports her dignity at table, and has her public day every Thursday, when she *gives to eat* (as they say here) to all that are hungry and dry.

You are much talked of here, and much expected, as soon as the peace will let you.—These two last days you have happened to engross the whole conversation at two great houses where I was at dinner.—'Tis the greatest problem in nature, in this meridian, that one and the same man should possess such tragic and comic powers, and in such an equilibrio, as to divide the world for which of the two Nature intended him.

Crebillion has made a convention with me, which, if he is not too lazy, will be no bad *persiflage*:—As soon as I get to Toulouse, he has agreed to write me an expostulatory letter upon the indecorums of T. Shandy;—which is to be answered by recrimination upon the liberties in his own works:—these are to be printed together,—Crebillion against Sterne;—Sterne against Crebillion:—the copy to be sold, and the money equally divided.—This is good Swiss-policy.

I am recovered greatly; and if I could spend one whole winter at Toulouse, I should be fortified, *in my inner man*, beyond all danger of relapsing.—A sad asthma my daughter has been martyr'd with these three winters (but mostly this last), makes it, I fear, necessary she should try the last remedy of a warmer and softer air; so I am going this week to Versailles, to wait upon Count Choiseul to solicit passports for them.—If this system takes place, they join me here;—and, after a month's stay, we all decamp for the south of France:—if not, I shall see you in June next. Mr. Fox and Mr. Macartney having left Paris, I live altogether in French families.—I laugh till I cry, and, in the same tender moments, *cry till I laugh.* I Shandy it more than ever; and verily do believe, that by mere Shandeism, sublimated by a laughter-loving people, I fence as much against infirmities as I do by the benefit of air and climate. Adieu, dear Garrick:—present ten thousand of my best respects and wishes to and for my friend Mrs. Garrick;—had she been last night upon the Thuilleries, she would have annihilated a thousand French goddesses *in one single turn.*

I am, most truly,
My dear friend,
L. STERNE.

LETTER XXIII.

TO MRS. STERNE, YORK.

Paris, May 16, 1762.

My Dear,

It is a thousand to one that this reaches you before you have set out;—however, I take the chance.—You will receive one wrote last night, the moment you get to Mr. E. and to wish you joy of your arrival in town.—To that letter, which you will find in town, I have nothing to add that I can think on, for I have almost drain'd my brains dry upon the subject. For God's sake, rise early and gallop away in the cool;—and always see that you have not forgot your baggage in changing post-chaises.—You will find good tea upon the road from York to Dover;—only bring a little to carry you from Calais to Paris.—Give the custom-house officers what I told you;—at Calais give more, if you have much Scotch snuff;—but as tobacco is good here, you had best bring a Scotch-mill and make it yourself; that is, order your valet to manufacture it;—'twill keep him out of mischief.—I would advise you to take three days in coming up, for fear of heating yourselves.—See that they do not give you a bad vehicle, when a better is in the yard; but you will look sharp.—Drink small Rhenish, to keep you cool (that is, if you like it). Live well, and deny yourselves nothing your hearts wish. So God in Heaven prosper and go along with you!—kiss my Lydia, and believe me both affectionately,

Yours,
L. STERNE.

LETTER XXIV.

TO THE SAME.

Paris, May 31, 1762.

My Dear,

There have no mails arrived here till this morning, for three posts; so I expected, with great impatience, a letter from you and Lydia;—and lo! it is arrived. You are as busy as Throp's wife; and by the time you receive this, you will be busier still.—I have exhausted all my ideas about your journey,—and what is needful for you to do before and during it;—so I write only to tell you I am well.—Mr. Colebrooks, the minister of Swisserland's secretary, I got this morning to write a letter for you to the governor of the custom-house office, at Calais: it shall be sent you next post.—You must be cautious about Scotch snuff;—take half a pound in your pocket, and make Lyd do the same. 'Tis well I bought you a chaise;—there is no getting one in Paris now, but at an enormous price,—for they are all sent to the army; and such a one as yours we have not been able to match for forty guineas, for a friend of mine who is going from hence to Italy.—The weather was never known to have set in so hot as it has done the latter end of this month; so he and his party are to get into his chaise by four in the morning, and travel till nine,—and not stir out again till six;—but I hope this severe heat will abate by the time you come here:—however, I beg of you once more to take special care of heating your blood in travelling, and come *tout doucement* when you find the heat too much. I shall look impatiently for intelligence from you, and hope to hear all goes well; that you conquer all difficulties, that you have received your passport, my picture, &c. Write, and tell me something of every thing. I long to see you both, you may be assured, my dear wife and child, after so long a separation;—and write me a line directly, that I may have all the notice you can give me,—that I may have apartments ready and fit for you when you arrive.—For my own part, I shall continue writing to you a fortnight longer.—Present my respects to all friends.—You have bid Mr. C. get my visitations at P. done for me, &c. &c. If any offers are made about the inclosure at Rascal, they must be inclosed to me;—nothing that is fairly proposed shall stand still on my score. Do all for the best, as He who guides all things will, I hope, do for us!—so Heaven preserve you both!—believe me

Your affectionate

L. STERNE.

Love to my Lydia.—I have bought her a gold watch, to present to her when she comes.

LETTER XXV.

TO THE SAME.

Paris, June 7, 1762.

MY DEAR,

I KEEP my promise, and write to you again.—I am sorry the bureau must be open'd for the deeds;—but you will see it done.—I imagine you are convinced of the necessity of bringing three hundred pounds in your pocket.—If you consider, Lydia must have two slight negligees:—you will want a new gown or two.—As for painted linens, buy them in town—they will be more admired because English than French.—Mrs. H. writes me word that I am mistaken about buying silk cheaper at Toulouse than Paris; that she advises you to buy what you want here,—where they are very beautiful and cheap, as well as blonds, gauzes, &c.—These, I say, will all cost you sixty guineas;—and you must have them;—for in this country nothing must be spared for the back:—and if you dine on an onion, and lie in a garret seven stories high, you must not betray it in your clothes: according to which, you are well or ill look'd on.—When we are got to Toulouse, we must begin to turn the penny; and we may (if you do not game much) live very cheap.—I think that expression will divert you;—and now, God knows, I have not a wish but for your health, comfort, and safe arrival here.—Write to me every other post, that I may know how you go on.—You will be in raptures with your chariot:—Mr. R. a gentleman of fortune, who is going to Italy, and has seen it, has offered me thirty guineas for my bargain. You will wonder all the way, how I am to find room in it for a third. To ease you of this wonder, 'tis by what the coachmakers here call a Cave; which is a second bottom added to that you set your feet upon, which lets the person (who sits over-against you) down with his knees to your ancles; and by which you have all more room,—and, what is more, less heat,—because his head does not intercept the fore-glass,—little or nothing.—Lyd and I will enjoy this by turns; sometimes I shall take a *bidet* (a little post-horse) and scamper before:—at other times I shall sit *in fresco* upon the arm-chair without doors! and one way or other will do very well.—I am under infinite obligations to Mr. Thornhill, for accommodating me thus; and so genteelly, for 'tis like making a present of it.—Mr. T—— will send you an order to receive it at Calais:—and now, my dear girls, have I forgot any thing?

Adieu! adieu!

Yours, most affectionately,

L. STERNE.

A week or ten days wi'l enable you to see every thing;—and so long you must stay to rest your bones.

LETTER XXVI.

TO THE SAME.

Paris, June 14, 1762.

My Dearest,

Having an opportunity of writing by a friend who is setting out this morning for London, I write again, in case the two last letters I have wrote this week to you, should be detained by contrary winds at Calais.—I have wrote to Mr. E——, by the same hand, to thank him for his kindness to you, in the handsomest manner I could; —and have told him, his good heart, and his wife's, have made them overlook the trouble of having you at his house; but that if he takes you apartments near him, they will have occasion still enough left to show their friendship to us.—I have begged him to assist you, and stand by you as if he was in my place, with regard to the sale of the Shandys;—and then the copyright. —Mark to keep these things distinct in your head:—but Becket, I have ever found to be a man of probity, and, I dare say, you will have very little trouble in finishing matters with him: and I would rather wish you to treat with him than with another man;—but whoever buys the fifth and sixth volumes of the Shandys, must have the nay-say of the seventh and eighth.* — I wish, when you come here, in case the weather is too hot to travel, you could think it pleasant to go to the Spa for four or six weeks, where we could live for half the money we should spend at Paris:—after that, we should take the sweetest season of the vintage to go to the south of France; but we will put our heads together, and you shall just do as you please in this, and in every thing which depends on me,—for I am a being perfectly contented when others are pleased;—to bear and forbear will ever be my maxim, — only I fear the heats through a journey of five hundred miles for you and my Lydia, more than for myself. — Do not forget the watch-chains; bring a couple for a gentleman's watch likewise: we shall lie under great obligations to the Abbé M., and must make him such a small acknowledgment:—according to my way of flourishing, 'twill be a present worth a kingdom to him.—They have bad pins and vile needles here; — bring for yourself, and some for presents;—as also a strong bottle-screw for whatever scrub we may hire as butler, coachman, &c. to uncork us our Frontiniac.—You will find a letter for you at the Lyon d'Argent.— Send for your chaise into the court-yard, and see all is right.—Buy a chain at Calais, strong enough not to be cut off; and let your portmanteau be tied on the fore-part of your chaise, for fear of a dog's trick:— so God bless you both, and remember me to my Lydia.

I am yours affectionately,

L. STERNE

* Alluding to the first edition.

LETTER XXVII.

TO THE SAME.

Paris, June 17, 1762.

My Dearest,

Probably you will receive another letter with this, by the same post;—if so, read this the last.—It will be the last you can possibly receive at York; for I hope it will catch you just as you are upon the wing:—if that should happen, I suppose, in course, you have executed the contents of it, in all things which relate to pecuniary matters; and when these are settled to your mind, you will have got through your last difficulty:—every thing else will be a step of pleasure; and by the time you have got half a dozen stages, you will set up your pipes and sing Te Deum together, as you whisk it along.—Desire Mr. C—— to send me a proper letter of attorney by you: he will receive it back by return of post. You have done every thing well with regard to our Sutton and Stillington affairs, and left things in the best channel. —If I was not sure you must have long since got my picture, garnets, &c. I would write and scold Mr. T—— abominably,—he put them in Becket's hands, to be forwarded by the stage-coach to you, as soon as he got to town.—I long to hear from you, and that all my letters and things are come safe to you, and then you will say I have not been a bad lad; for you will find I have been writing continually, as I wished you to do. —Bring your silver coffee-pot: 'twill serve both to give water, lemonade, and orjead;—to say nothing of coffee and chocolate, which, by the bye, is both cheap and good at Toulouse, like other things.—I had like to have forgot a most necessary thing: —there are no copper tea-kettles to be had in France; and we shall find such a thing the most comfortable utensil in the house: —buy a good strong one, which will hold two quarts:—a dish of tea will be of comfort to us in our journey south.—I have a bronze tea-pot, which we will carry also: —as china cannot be brought over from England, we must make up a villanous party-colored tea equipage, to regale ourselves, and our English friends, whilst we are at Toulouse.—I hope you have got your bill from Becket.—There is a good-natured kind of a trader I have just heard of, at Mr. Foley's, who they think will be coming off from England to France, with horses, the latter end of June. He happened to come over with a lady, who is sister to Mr. Foley's partner; and I have got her to write a letter to him in London, this post, to beg he will seek you out at Mr. E——'s; and, in case a cartel-ship does not go off before he goes, to take you under his care. He was infinitely friendly, in the same office, last year, to the lady who now writes to him, and nursed her on shipboard, and defended her by land with great good-will.—Do not say I forget you, or whatever can be conducive to your ease of mind in this journey. —I wish I was with you, to do these offices myself, and to strew roses on your way; but I shall have time and occasion to show you I am not wanting. — Now, my dears, once more pluck up your spirits,—trust in God,—in me,—and in yourselves; — with this, was you put to it, you would encounter all these difficulties ten times told.—Write instantly, and tell me you triumph over all fears; tell me Lydia is better, and a helpmate to you.—You say she grows like me: let her snow me she does so in her contempt of small dangers, and fighting against tne apprehensions of them, which is better still.—As I will not have F.'s share of the books, you will inform him so.—Give my love to Mr. Fothergill, and to those true friends which envy has spared me; — and for the rest, *laissez passer*.—You will find I speak French tolerably; but I only wish to be understood. — You will soon speak better; a month's play with a French Demoiselle will make Lyd chatter like a magpie. Mrs. —— understood not a word of it when she got here; and writes me word she begins to prate apace: — you will do the same in a fortnight.—Dear Bess, I have a thousand wishes; but have a hope for every one of them;—you shall chant the same *jubilate*, my dears: so God bless you! My duty to Lydia, which implies my love too. Adieu. Believe me

Your affectionate

L. STERNE

Memorandum.—Bring watch-chains, tea-kettle, knives, cookery-book, &c.

You will smile at this last article — so adieu.—At Dover, the Cross Keys; at Calais, the Lyon d'Argent,—the master, a Turk in grain.

LETTER XXVIII.

TO LADY D

Paris, July 9, 1762.

I WILL not send your Ladyship the trifles you bid me purchase, without a line. I am very well pleased with Paris. Indeed I meet with so many civilities amongst the people here, that I must sing their praises: —the French have a great deal of urbanity in their composition; and to stay a little time amongst them will be agreeable.—I splutter French so as to be understood;—but I have had a droll adventure here, in which my Latin was of some service to me;—I had hired a chaise and a horse to go about seven miles into the country, but *Shandean-like*, did not take notice that the horse was almost dead when I took him.—Before I got half-way, the poor animal dropped down dead;—so I was forced to appear before the police, and began to tell my story in French, which was that the poor beast had to do with a worse beast than himself, namely, *his master*, who had driven him all the day before (Jehu-like)—and that he had neither had corn or hay, therefore I was not to pay for the horse;—but I might as well have whistled as have spoke French; and I believe my Latin was equal to my uncle Toby's Lillibullero,—being not understood, because of its purity; but by dint of words I forced my judge to do me justice:—no common thing, by the way, in France. My wife and daughter are arrived: the latter does nothing but look out of the window, and complain of the torment of being frizzled.—I wish she may ever remain a child of Nature:—I hate children of Art.

I hope this will find your Ladyship well;—and that you will be kind enough to direct to me at Toulouse; which place I shall set out for very soon.

I am, with truth and sincerity,
Your Ladyship's
Most faithful
L. STERNE.

LETTER XXIX.

TO MR. E.

Paris, July 12, 1762.

DEAR SIR,

MY wife and daughter arrived here safe and sound on Thursday, and are in high raptures with the speed and pleasantness of their journey; and, particularly, of all they see and meet with here. But in their journey from York to Paris, nothing has given them a more sensible and lasting pleasure than the marks of kindness they received from you and Mrs. E.—The friendship, good-will, and politeness of my two friends, I never doubted to me or mine; and I return you both all a grateful man is capable of, which is merely my thanks.—I have taken, however, the liberty of sending an Indian taffety, which Mrs. E. must do me the honor to wear for my wife's sake; who would have got it made up, but that Mr. Stanhope, the Consul of Algiers, who sets off to-morrow morning for London, has been so kind (I mean his lady) as to take charge of it; and we had but just time to procure it: and had we missed that opportunity, as we should have been obliged to have left it behind us at Paris, we knew not when or how to get it to our friend.—I wish it had been better worth a paragraph. If there is any thing we can buy or procure for you here (intelligence included) you have a right to command me,—for I am yours, with my wife and girl's kind love to you and Mrs. E.

L. STERNE.

LETTER XXX.

TO J—— H—— S——, ESQ.

Toulouse, August 12, 1762.

MY DEAR H.

BY the time you have got to the end of this long letter, you will perceive that I have not been able to answer your last till now:—I have had the intention of doing it almost as often as my prayers in my head:—'tis thus we use our best friends.—What an infamous story is that you have told me!—After some little remarks on it, the rest of my letter will go on like silk. ****—is a good-natured old easy fool, and has been deceived by the most artful of her sex; and she must have abundance of impudence and charlatanry, to have carried on such a farce. I pity the old man for being taken in for so much money;—a man of sense I should have laughed at.—My wife saw her when in town, and she had not the appearance of poverty; but when she wants to melt ****'s heart, she puts her gold-watch and diamond rings in her drawer.—But he might have been aware of her.—I could not have been mistaken in her character;—and 'tis odd she should talk of her wealth to one, and tell another the reverse;—so good-night to her.—About a week or ten days before my wife arrived at Paris, I had the same accident I had at Cambridge, of breaking a vessel in my lungs. It happened in the night,—and I bled the bed full; and finding in the morning I was likely to bleed to death, I sent immediately for a surgeon to bleed me at both arms:—this saved me, and with lying speechless three days, I recovered upon my back in bed; the breach healed, and, in a week after, I got out.—This, with my weakness and hurrying about, made me think it high time to haste to Toulouse. We have had four months of such heats, that the oldest Frenchman never remembers the like:—'twas as hot as *Nebuchadnezzar's oven*, and never has relaxed one hour:—in the height of this, 'twas our destiny (or rather destruction) to set out by way of Lyons, Montpellier, &c. to shorten, I trow, our sufferings.—Good God!—but 'tis over;—and here I am in my own house, quite settled by M—'s aid and good-natured offices; for which I owe him more than I can express, or know how to pay at present. 'Tis in the prettiest situation in Toulouse, with near two acres of garden;—the house too good by half for us,—well furnished; for which I pay thirty pounds a year.—I have got a good cook,—my wife a decent *femme de chambre*, — and a good-looking *laquais.* The Abbé has planned our expenses, and set us in such a train, we cannot easily go wrong;—though, by the bye, the D——l is seldom found sleeping under a hedge. Mr. Trotter dined with me the day before I left Paris.—I took care to see all executed according to your directions; but Trotter, I dare say, by this, has wrote to you. I made him happy beyond expression with your Crazy Tales; and more so with its frontispiece.—I am in spirits, writing a crazy chapter, with my face turned towards thy turret.—'Tis now I wish all warmer climates, countries, and every thing else, at ——, that separates me from our paternal seat;—*ce sera là où reposera ma cendre,—et ce sera là où mon cousin viendra repondre les pleurs dues à notre amitié.*—I am taking asses' milk three times a day, and cows' milk as often. I long to see thy face again once more.—Greet the Colonel kindly in my name; and thank him cordially from me, for his many civilities to Madame and Mademoiselle Shandy at York, who send all due acknowledgments. The humor is over for France and Frenchmen; but that is not enough for your affectionate cousin,

L. S.

(A year will tire us all out, I trow) but, thank Heaven, the post brings me a letter from my Anthony.—I felicitate you upon what Messrs. the Reviewers allow you; they have too much judgment themselves not to allow you what you are actually possessed of, "talents. wit, and humor."—Well, write on, my dear cousin, and be guided by thy own fancy.—Oh! how I envy you all at Crazy Castle!—I could like to spend a month with you; and should return back again for the vintage.—I honor the man that has given the world an idea of our parental seat; 'tis well done.—I look at it ten times a day with a *quando te aspiciam?*—Now farewell!—remember me to my beloved Colonel;—greet Panty most lovingly on my behalf; and, if Mrs. C—— and Miss C——, &c. are at G—, greet them likewise with a holy kiss;—so God bless you!

L. S.

LETTER XXXI.

TO MR. FOLEY, AT PARIS.

Toulouse, Aug. 14, 1762.

My Dear Foley,

After many turnings (*alias* digressions) to say nothing of downright overthrows, stops, and delays, we have arrived in three weeks at Toulouse, and are now settled in our house with servants, &c. about us, and look as composed as if we had been here seven years.—In our journey we suffered so much from the heats, it gives me pain to remember it:—I never saw a cloud from Paris to Nismes half as broad as a twenty-four sols piece.—Good God! we were toasted, roasted, grill'd, stew'd, and carbonaded on one side or other all the way;—and being all done enough (*assez cuits*) in the day, we were eat up at night by bugs, and other unswept-out vermin; the legal inhabitants (if length of possession gives right) of every inn we lay at.—Can you conceive a worse accident than that in such a journey, in the hottest day and hour of it, four miles from either tree or shrub which could cast a shade of the size of one of Eve's fig-leaves,—that we should break a hind-wheel into ten thousand pieces, and be obliged in consequence to sit five hours on a gravelly road, without one drop of water, or possibility of getting any!—To mend the matter, my two postilions were two dough-hearted fools, and fell a-crying.—Nothing was to be done! By Heaven, quoth I, pulling off my coat and waistcoat, something shall be done, for I'll thrash you both within an inch of your lives,—and then make you take each of you a horse, and ride like two devils to the next post for a cart to carry my baggage, and a wheel to carry ourselves!—Our luggage weighed ten quintals.—'Twas the fair of Baucaire:—all the world was going or returning:—we were ask'd by every soul who pass'd by us, If we were going to the fair of Baucaire?—No wonder, quoth I, we have goods enough! *Vous avez raison, mes amis.*

Well, here we are, after all, my dear friend,—and most deliciously placed at the extremity of the town, in an excellent house, well furnish'd, and elegant beyond any thing I look'd for.—'Tis built in the form of a hotel, with a pretty court towards the town;—and behind, the best garden in Toulouse, laid out in serpentine walks; and so large, that the company in our quarter usually come to walk there in the evening, for which they have my consent:—"the "more the merrier." The house consists of a good *salle à manger* above stairs, joining to the very great *salle à compagnie* as large as the Baron d'Holbach's; three handsome bed-chambers, with dressing-rooms to them;—below stairs, two very good rooms for myself; one to study in, the other to see company.—I have moreover cellars round the court, and all other offices.—Of the same landlord, I have bargained to have the use of a country-house, which he has two miles out of town; so that myself and all my family have nothing more to do than to take our hats and remove from the one to the other.—My landlord is moreover to keep the gardens in order:—and what do you think I am to pay for all this? Neither more nor less than thirty pounds a year! All things are cheap in proportion:—so we shall live for very little.—I dined yesterday with Mr. H——: he is most pleasantly situated; and they are all well.—As for the books you have received for D——, the bookseller was a fool not to send the bill along with them,—I will write to him about it.—I wish you was with me for two months; it would cure you of all evils, ghostly and bodily: but this, like many other wishes both for you and myself, must have its completion elsewhere.—Adieu, my kind friend, and believe that I love you as much from inclination as reason, for

I am most truly yours,

L. STERNE.

My wife and girl join in compliments to you.—My best respects to my worthy Baron d'Holbach, and all that society.—Remember me to my friend Mr. Panchaud.

LETTER XXXII.

TO J—— H—— S——, ESQ.

Toulouse, Oct. 19, 1762.

MY DEAR H——,

I RECEIVED your letter yesterday;—so has been travelling from Crazy Castle to Toulouse full eighteen days:—if I had nothing to stop me, I would engage to set out this morning, and knock at Crazy Castle gates in three days less time;—by which time, I should find you and the Colonel, Panty, &c. all alone;—the season I most wish and like to be with you.—I rejoice from my heart, down to my reins, that you have snatch'd so many happy and sunshiny days out of the hands of the blue devils.—If we live to meet and join our forces as heretofore, we will give these gentry a drubbing, and turn them for ever out of their usurped citadel:—some legions of them have been put to flight already by your operations this last campaign, and I hope to have a hand in dispersing the remainder, the first time my dear cousin sets up his banners again under the square tower.—But what art thou meditating with axes and hammers?—"I know the pride and the "naughtiness of thy heart," and thou lovest the sweet visions of architraves, friezes, and pediments with their tympanums; and thou hast found out a pretence *à raison de cinq cent livres sterling*, to be laid out in four years, &c. &c. (so as not to be felt, which is always added by the D——l as a bait) to justify thyself unto thyself.—It may be very wise to do this;—but it is wiser to keep one's money in one's pocket, whilst there are wars without, and rumors of wars within. St. —— advises his disciples to sell both coat and waistcoat,—and go rather without shirt or sword, than leave no money in their scrip to go to Jerusalem with. —Now those *quatre ans consecutifs*, my dear Anthony, are the most precious morsels of thy life to come (in this world;) and thou wilt do well to enjoy that morsel without cares, calculations, and curses, and damns, and debts;—for as sure as stone is stone, and mortar is mortar, &c. 'twill be one of the many works of thy repentance. —But after all, "if the Fates have decreed "it," as you and I have sometimes supposed it,—on account of your generosity, "that "you are never to be a moneyed man," the decree will be fulfilled whether you adorn your castle, and line it with cedar, and paint it withinside and withoutside with vermilion, or not,—*et cele étant* (having a bottle of Frontiniac and glass at my right hand) I drink, dear Anthony, to thy health and happiness, and to the final accomplishments of all thy lunary and sublunary projects. For six weeks together, after I wrote my last letter to you, my projects were many stories higher; for I was all that time, as I thought, journeying on to the other world. —I fell ill of an epidemic vile fever, which killed hundreds about me.—The physicians here are the errantest charlatans in Europe, or the most ignorant of all pretending fools. —I withdrew what was left of me out of their hands, and recommended my affair entirely to Dame Nature: she (dear goddess) has saved me in fifty different pinching bouts; and I begin to have a kind of enthusiasm now in her favor, and in my own, that one or two more escapes will make me believe I shall leave you all at last by translation, and not by fair death. I am now stout and foolish again as a happy man can wish to be; and am busy playing the fool with my uncle Toby, whom I have got soused over head and ears in love;—I have many hints and projects for other works: all will go on I trust as I wish in this matter.— When I have reaped the benefit of this winter at Toulouse, I cannot see I have any thing more to do with it; therefore, after having gone with my wife and girl to Bagnieres, I shall return from whence I came. —Now my wife wants to stay another year to save money; and this opposition of wishes, though it will not be as sour as lemon, yet 'twill not be as sweet as sugar-candy.—I wish T— would lead Sir Charles to Toulouse; 'tis as good as any town in the south of France.—For my own part,—'tis not to my taste;—but I believe, the groundwork of my *ennui* is more to the eternal *platitude* of the French character:—little variety, no originality in it at all,—than to any other cause, for they are very civil; but civility itself, in that uniform, wearies and bothers one to death.—If I don't mind, I shall grow most stupid and sententious.—Miss Shandy is hard at it with music, dancing, and French speaking; in the last of which she does *à merveille*, and speaks it with an excellent accent, considering she practises within sight of the Pyrenean Mountains.—If the snows will suffer me, I propose to spend two or three months at Barege, or Bagnieres, but my dear wife is against all schemes of additional expenses; which wicked propensity (though not of despotic power) yet I cannot suffer,—though, by the bye, laudable enough.—But she may talk;—I will do my own way; and she will acquiesce without a word of debate on the subject.—Who can say so much in praise of his wife? Few, I trow.—M—— is out of town, vintaging;— so write me, *Monsieur Sterne, gentilhomme Anglois:*—'twill find me.—We are as much out of the road of all intelligence here, as at the Cape of Good Hope;—so write a long nonsensical letter like this, now and then, to me;—in which, say nothing but what may be shown (though I love every paragraph and spirited stroke of your pen, others might not); for you must know, a letter no sooner arrives from England, but Curiosity is upon her knees to know the contents.— Adieu, dear H. believe me

Your affectionate

L. STERNE.

We have had bitter cold weather here these fourteen days,—which has obliged us to sit with whole pagells of wood lighted up to our noses;—'tis a dear article;—but every thing else being extreme cheap, Madame keeps an excellent good house, with *soupe, bouilli, roti*,—&c. &c. for two hundred and fifty pounds a year.

LETTER XXXIII.

TO MR. FOLEY, AT PARIS.

Toulouse, Nov. 9, 1762.

My Dear Foley,

I have this week your letter on my table, and hope you will forgive my not answering it sooner;—and even to-day I can but write you ten lines, being engaged at Mrs. M—'s. I would not omit one post more acknowledging the favor.—In a few posts I will write you a long one gratis; that is, for love.—Thank you for having done what I desired you;—and for the future direct to me under cover at Monsieur Brousse's:—I receive all letters through him, more punctual and sooner than when left at the post-house.—

H——'s family greet you with mine;—we are much together, and never forget you.—Forget me not to the Baron, and all the circle;—nor to your domestic circle.

I am got pretty well, and sport much with my uncle Toby in the volume I am now fabricating for the laughing part of the world; for the melancholy part of it, I have nothing but my prayers; so God help them. I shall hear from you in a post or two at least after you receive this. In the mean time, dear Foley, adieu, and believe no man wishes or esteems you more than your

L. STERNE.

LETTER XXXIV.

TO THE SAME.

Toulouse, Wednesday, Dec. 3, 1762.

Dear Foley,

I have for this last fortnight, every post-day, gone to Messrs. B—— and Sons, in expectation of the pleasure of a letter from you, with the remittance I desired you to send me here.—When a man has no more than half a dozen guineas in his pocket, and a thousand miles from home,—and in a country where he can as soon raise the D——l as a six-livre piece to go to market with, in case he has changed his last guinea, --you will not envy my situation. God bless you, remit me the balance due upon the receipt of this.—We are all at H——'s, practising a play we are to act here this Christmas holidays;—all the *dramatis personæ* are of the English, of which we have a happy society, living together like brothers and sisters.—Your banker here has just sent me word, the tea Mr. H—— wrote for, is to be delivered into my hands;—'tis all one into whose hands the treasure falls; we shall pay Brousse for it the day we get it.—We join in our most friendly respects, and believe me, dear Foley, truly yours,

L. STERNE.

LETTER XXXV.

TO THE SAME.

Toulouse, Dec. 17, 1762.

My Dear Foley,

The post after I wrote last, I received yours, with the inclosed draught upon the receiver; for which I return you all thanks. I have received this day likewise the box and tea, all safe and sound;—so we shall all of us be in our cups this Christmas, and drink without fear or stint.—We begin to live extremely happy, and are all together every night,—fiddling, laughing, and singing, and cracking jokes. You will scarce believe the news I tell you. There is a company of English strollers arrived here, who are to act comedies all the Christmas; and are now busy in making dresses, and preparing some of our best comedies.—Your wonder will cease, when I inform you these strollers are your friends with the rest of our society, to whom I proposed this scheme *soulagement;*—and I assure you we do well.—The next week, with a grand orchestra, we play the Busy Body,—and the Journey to London the week after; but I have some thoughts of adapting it to our situation and making it the Journey to Toulouse, which, with the change of half a dozen scenes, may be easily done.—Thus, my dear F—, for want of something better, we have recourse to ourselves, and strike out the best amusements we can from such materials.—My kind love and friendship to all my true friends; my service to the rest. H——'s family have just left me, having been this last week with us;—they will be with me all the holidays.—In summer we shall visit them, and so balance hospitalities. Adieu.

Yours most truly,

L. STERNE.

LETTER XXXVI.

TO THE SAME.

Toulouse, March 29, 1763

Dear Foley,

Though that's a mistake (I mean the date of the place); for I write at Mr. H——'s in the country, and have been there with my people all the week.—"How "does Tristram do?" you say in yours to him; —faith, but so so. —The worst of human maladies is poverty; —though that's a second lie; for poverty of spirit is worse than poverty of purse by ten thousand per cent.—I inclose you a remedy for the one, a draught of a hundred and thirty pounds, for which I insist upon a rescription by the very return, or I will send you and all your commissaries to the D——l.—I do not hear they have tasted of one fleshy banquet all this lent. You will make an excellent *grillé*. P——, they can make nothing of him but *bouillon*.—I mean my other two friends no ill; so shall send them a reprieve, as they acted out of necessity,—not choice. My kind respects to Baron d'Holbach, and all his household. Say all that's kind for me to my other friends. You know how much, dear Foley, I am yours,

L. STERNE.

I have not five Louis to vapor with in this land of coxcombs. My wife's compliments.

LETTER XXXVII.

TO THE SAME.

Toulouse, April 18, 1763.

Dear Foley,

I thank you for your punctuality in sending me the rescription, and for your box by the courier, which came safe by last post. I was not surprised much with your account of Lord ***** being obliged to give way;—and for the rest, all follows in course. I suppose you will endeavor to fish and catch something for yourself in these troubled waters; at least I wish you all a reasonable man can wish for himself, which is wishing enough for you: all the rest is in the brain. Mr. Woodhouse (whom you know) is also here; he is a most amiable worthy man; and I have the pleasure of having him much with me. In a short time he proceeds to Italy. The first week in June I decamp like a patriarch with my whole household, to pitch our tents for three months at the foot of the Pyrenean Hills at Bangieres, where I expect much health and much amusement from the concourse of adventurers from all corners of the earth. Mrs. M—— sets out, at the same time, for another part of the Pyrenean Hills, at Courtray: from whence to Italy. This is the general plan of operation here, except that I have some thoughts of spending the winter at Florence, and crossing over with my family to Leghorn by water; and in April of returning, by way of Paris, home.—But this is a sketch only; for in all things I am governed by circumstances; so that what is fit to be done on Monday may be very unwise on Saturday. On all days of the week believe me yours,

With unfeigned truth,

L. STERNE.

P. S. All compliments to my Parisian friends.

LETTER XXXVIII.

TO THE SAME.

Toulouse, April 29, 1763.

My Dear Foley.

Last post my agent wrote me word, he would send up from York a bill for fourscore guineas, with orders to be paid into Mr. Selwin's hands for me. This, he said, he would expedite immediately; so 'tis possible you may have had advice of it;—and 'tis possible also the money may not be paid this fortnight; therefore, as I set out for Bagnieres in that time, be so good as to give me credit for the money for a few posts or so, and send me either a rescription for the money, or a draught for it;—at the receipt of which, we shall decamp for ten or twelve weeks.—You will receive twenty pounds more on my account; which ser also:—so much for that. As for pleasure, you have it all amongst you at Paris: we have nothing here which deserves the name. —I shall scarce be tempted to sojourn another winter in Toulouse; for I cannot say it suits my health as I hoped: 'tis too moist, —and I cannot keep clear of agues here; —so that, if I stay the next winter on this side of the water, 'twill be either at Nice or Florence;—and I shall return to England in April.—Wherever I am, believe me, dear Foley, that I am

Yours faithfully,

L. STERNE.

Madame and Mademoiselle present their best compliments. Remember me to all I regard, particularly Messrs. Panchaud, and the rest of your *household.*

LETTER XXXIX.

TO THE SAME.

Toulouse, May 21, 1763.

I took the liberty, three weeks ago, to desire you would be so kind as to send me fourscore pounds, having received a letter the same post from my agent, that he would order the money to be paid to your correspondent in London in a fortnight.—It is some disappointment to me that you have taken no notice of my letter, especially as I told you we waited for the money before we set out for Bagnieres;—and so little distrust had I that such a civility would be refused me, that we have actually had all our things packed up these eight days, in hourly expectation of receiving a letter.—Perhaps my good friend has waited till he heard the money was paid in London;—but you might have trusted to my honor, that all the cash in your iron-box (and all the bankers in Europe put together) could not have tempted me to say the thing *that is not.*—I hope, before this, you will have received an account of the money being paid in London. But it would have been taken kindly, if you had wrote me word you would transmit me the money when you had received it, but no sooner; for Mr. R——, of Montpellier, though I know him not, yet knows enough of me to have given me credit for a fortnight for ten times the sum.

I am, dear F——, your friend
and hearty well-wisher,

L. STERNE

I saw the family of the H—— yesterday, and asked them if you was in the land of the living.—They said, Yea; for they had just received a letter from you.—After all, I heartily forgive you; for you have done me a signal service in mortifying me, and it is this:—I am determined to grow rich upon it.

Adieu, and God send you wealth and happiness. All compliments to —— Before April next, I am obliged to revisit your metropolis, in my way to England.

LETTER XL.

TO THE SAME.

Toulouse, June 9, 1763.

My Dear Foley,

I this moment received yours; consequently, the moment I got it, I sat down to answer it.—So much for a logical inference.

Now, believe me, I had never wrote you so testy a letter, had I not both loved and esteemed you;—and it was merely in vindication of the rights of friendship that I wrote in a way as if I was hurt;—for neglect me in your heart, I knew you could not, without cause; which my heart told me I never had—nor will ever give you.—I was the best friend with you that ever I was in my life, before my letter had got a league, and pleaded the true excuse for my friend, "That he was oppressed with a "multitude of business." Go on, my dear F——, and have but that excuse (so much do I regard your interest) that I would be content to suffer a *real evil* without future murmuring:—but, in truth, my disappointment was partly chimerical at the bottom, having a letter of credit for two hundred pounds from a person I never saw, by me, —but which, out of a nicety of temper, I would not make any use of.—I set out in two days for Bagnieres; but direct to me to Brousse, who will forward all my letters.—Dear F——, adieu. Believe me

Yours affectionately,

L. STERNE

LETTER XLI

TO THE SAME.

Toulouse, June 12, 1763.

Dear Foley,

Luckily, just before I was stepping into my chaise for Bagnieres, has a strayed fifty pound bill found its way to me; so I have sent it to its lawful owner inclosed.—My noodle of an agent, instead of getting Mr. Selwin to advise you he had received the money (which would have been enough) has got a bill for it, and sent it rambling to the farthest part of France after me: and, if it had not caught me just now, it might have followed me into Spain; for I shall cross the Pyreneans, and spend a week in that kingdom, which is enough for a fertile brain to write a volume upon.—When I write the history of my travels,—Memorandum! I am not to forget how honest a man I have for a banker at Paris.—But, my dear friend, when you say you dare trust me for what little occasions I may have, you have as much faith as honesty,—and more of both than of good policy.—I thank you however ten thousand times;—and, except such liberty as I have lately taken with you,—and that too at a pinch,—I say, beyond that I will not trespass upon your good-nature or friendliness to serve me.—God bless you, dear F——.

I am yours whilst

L. STERNE.

LETTER XLII.

TO THE SAME.

Montpellier, Oct. 5, 1763.

Dear Foley,

I am ashamed I have not taken an opportunity of thanking you before now, for your friendly act of civility, in ordering Brousse, your correspondent at Toulouse, in case I should have occasion, to pay me fifteen hundred livres;—which, as I knew the offer came from your heart, I made no difficulty of accepting.—In my way through Toulouse to Marseilles, where we have been,—but neither liking the place nor Aix (particularly the latter, it being a parliament town, of which Toulouse has given me a surfeit) we have returned here, where we shall reside the winter.—My wife and daughter purpose to stay a year at least behind me, and, when winter is over, to return to Toulouse, or go to Montauban, where they will stay till they return, or I fetch them.—For myself, I shall set out in February for England, where my heart has been fled these six months:—but I shall stay a fortnight with my friends at Paris; though I verily believe, if it was not for the pleasure of seeing and chattering with you, I should pass on directly to Brussels, and so on to Rotterdam, for the sake of seeing Holland, and embark from thence to London.—But I must stay a little with those I love and have so many reasons to regard:—you cannot place too much of this to your own score.—I have had an offer of going to Italy a fortnight ago;—but I must like my subject as well as the terms; neither of which were to my mind.—Pray what English have you at Paris?—where is my young friend Mr. F——? We hear of three or four English families coming to us here.—If I can be serviceable to any you would serve, you have but to write.—Mr. H—— has sent my friend W——'s picture.—You have seen the original, or I would have sent it you.—I believe I shall beg leave to get a copy of my own from yours, when I come *in propria persona;*—till when, God bless you, my dear friend, and believe me

Most faithfully yours,

L. STERNE.

LETTER XLIII.

TO THE SAME.

Montpellier, Jan. 5, 1764.

My Dear Friend,

You see I cannot pass over the fifth of the month without thinking of you, and writing to you.—The last is a periodical habit;—the first is from my heart; and I do it oftener than I remember:—however, from both motives together, I maintain I have a right to the pleasure of a single line,—be it only to tell me how your watch goes. — You know how much happier it would make me to know that all things belonging to you went on well.—You are going to have them all to yourself, I hear; and that Mr. S—— is true to his first intention of leaving business.—I hope this will enable you to accomplish yours in a shorter time, that you may get to your long-wished-for retreat of tranquillity and silence.—When you have got to your fire-side, and into your arm-chair, (and, by the bye, have another to spare for a friend) and are so much a sovereign as to sit in your furred cap, if you like it, though I should not (for a man's ideas are at least the cleaner for being dressed decently) why then it will be a miracle if I do not glide in like a ghost upon you, — and, in a very unghostlike fashion, help you off with a bottle of your best wine.

January 15.—It does not happen every day that a letter begun in the most perfect health, should be concluded in the greatest weakness.—I wish the vulgar, high and low, do not say it was a judgment upon me, for taking all this liberty with ghosts.—Be it as it may, I took a ride, when the first part of this was wrote, towards Perenas, — and returned home in a shivering fit, though I ought to have been in a fever, for I had tired my beast; and he was as unmovable as Don Quixote's wooden horse; and my arm was half dislocated in whipping him. —This, quoth I, is inhuman.—No, says a peasant on foot behind me, I'll drive him home; so he laid on his posteriors; but 'twas needless: as his face was turn'd towards Montpellier, he began to trot. But to return .—This fever has confined me ten days in my bed ; — I have suffered in this scuffle with death terribly ;—but unless the spirit of prophecy deceive me,—I shall not die but live.—In the mean time, dear F., let us live as merrily, but as innocently as we can.—It has ever been as good, if not better, than a bishopric to me ;—and I desire no other.—Adieu, my dear friend, and believe me yours,

L. STERNE.

Please to give the inclosed to Mr. T., and tell him I thank him cordially from my heart for his great good-will.

LETTER XLIV.

TO THE SAME

Montpellier, Jan. 20, 1764

My Dear Friend,

Hearing by Lord Rochford (who in passing through here in his way to Madrid has given me a call) that my worthy friend Mr. Fox was now at Paris,—I have inclosed a letter to him, which you will present in course, or direct to him. I suppose you are full of English ;—but in short, we are here as if in another world, where, unless some strayed soul arrives, we know nothing of what is going on in yours.—Lord G——r, I suppose, is gone from Paris, or I had wrote also to him. I know you are as busy as a bee, and have few moments to yourself; —nevertheless bestow one of them upon an old friend, and write me a line ;—and if Mr. F. is too idle, and has aught to say to me, pray write a second line for him.—We had a letter from Miss P—— this week, who it seems has decamped for ever from Paris.—All is for the best ;—which is my general reflection upon many things in this world. — Well, I shall shortly come and shake you by the hand in St. Sauveur, if still you are there. My wife returns to Toulouse, and purposes to spend the summer at Bagnieres ;—I, on the contrary, go and visit my wife, the church, in Yorkshire.—We all live the longer,—at least the happier, for having things our own way.—This is my conjugal maxim :—I own 'tis not the best of maxims; — but I maintain 'tis not the worst. Adieu, dear F., and believe me

Yours with truth,

L. STERNE

LETTER XLV.

TO MRS. F.

Montpellier, Feb. 1, 1764

I am preparing, my dear Mrs. F., to leave France, for I am heartily tired of it.—That insipidity there is in French characters has disgusted your friend Yorick.—I have been dangerously ill, and cannot think that the sharp air of Montpellier has been of service to me; and so my physicians told me when they had me under their hands for above a month:—"If you stay any longer here, Sir, "it will be fatal to you."—And why, good people, were you not kind enough to tell me this sooner?—After having discharged them, I told Mrs. Sterne that I should set out for England very soon;—but as she chooses to remain in France for two or three years, I have no objection, except that I wish my girl in England.—The States of Languedoc are met;—'tis a fine raree-show, with the usual accompaniments of fiddles, bears, and puppet-shows. I believe I shall step into my post-chaise with more alacrity to fly from these sights, than a Frenchman would to fly to them;—and, except a tear at parting with my little slut, I shall be in high spirits; and every step I take that brings me nearer England, will, I think, help to set this poor frame to rights. Now pray write to me, directed to Mr. F. at Paris, and tell me what I am to bring you over. How do I long to greet all my friends! few do I value more than yourself.—My wife chooses to go to Montauban, rather than stay here; in which I am truly passive.—If this should not find you at Bath, I hope it will be forwarded to you, as I wish to fulfil your commissions;—and so adieu.—Accept every warm wish for your health, and believe me ever yours,

L. STERNE.

P. S. My physicians have almost poisoned me with what they call *bouillons refraichissants*:—'tis a cock flayed alive, and boiled with poppy-seeds, then pounded in a mortar, afterwards passed through a sieve.—There is to be one craw-fish in it; and I was gravely told it must be a male one,—a female would do me more hurt than good!

LETTER XLVI.

TO MISS STERNE.

Paris, May 15, 1764.

My Dear Lydia,

By this time I suppose your mother and self are fixed at Montauban, and I therefore direct to your banker, to be delivered to you.—I acquiesced in your staying in France: likewise it was your mother's wish:—but I must tell you both (that unless your health had not been a plea made use of) I should have wished you both to return with me.—I have sent you the Spectators, and other books, particularly Metastasio; but I beg my girl to read the former, and only make the latter her amusement.—I hope you have not forgot my last request, to make no friendships with the French women;—not that I think ill of them all; but sometimes women of the best principles are the most *insinuating*;—nay, I am so jealous of you, that I should be miserable to see you had the least grain of coquetry in your composition.—You have enough to do;—for I have also sent you a guitar;—and as you have no genius for drawing (though you never could be made to believe it), pray waste not your time about it.—Remember to write to me as to a friend:—in short, whatever comes into your little head; and then it will be natural. If your mother's rheumatism continues, and she chooses to go to Bagnieres, tell her not to be stopped for want of money, for my purse shall be as open as my heart. I have preached at the Ambassador's chapel.—Hezekiah.*—(An odd subject, your mother will say.) There was a concourse of all nations, and religions too.—I shall leave Paris in a few days. I am lodged in the same hotel with Mr. T——: they are good and generous souls.—Tell your mother that I hope she will write to me; and that when she does so, I may also receive a letter from my Lydia.

Kiss your mother from me, and believe me

Your affectionate

L. STERNE.

LETTER XLVII.

TO MR. FOLEY.

York, August 6, 1764

My Dear Foley,

There is a young lady with whom I have sent a letter to you, who will arrive at Paris, in her way to Italy;—her name is Miss Tuting: a lady known and loved by

* See Sermon XVII.

the whole kingdom:—if you can be of any aid to her in your advice, &c. as to her journey, &c. your good-nature and politeness I am sure need no spur from me to do it. I was sorry we were like the two buckets of a well, whilst in London, for we were never able to be both resident together the month I continued in and about the environs. If I get a cough this winter which holds me three days, you will certainly see me at Paris the week following; for now I abandon every thing in this world to health and to my friends;—for the last sermon that I shall ever preach, was preached at Paris;—so I am altogether an idle man, or rather a free one, which is better. I sent, last post, twenty pounds to Mrs. Sterne; which makes a hundred pounds remitted since I got here. You must pay yourself what I owe you out of it,—and place the rest to account. Betwixt this and Lady-day next, Mrs. Sterne will draw, from time to time, upon you to about the amount of a hundred Louis,—but not more,—(I think) I having left her a hundred in her pocket.—But you shall always have money beforehand of mine;—and she purposes to spend no farther than five thousand livres in the year;—but twenty pounds this way or that, makes no difference between us.—Give my kindest compliments to Mr. P——. I have a thousand things to say to you; and would go half-way to Paris to tell them you in your ear. The Messrs. T——, H——, &c. and many more of your friends with whom I now am, send their services.—Mine to all friends.—Yours, dear F., most truly,

L. STERNE.

LETTER XLVIII.

TO J—— H—— S——, ESQ.

September 4. 1764.

Now, my dear, dear Anthony, I do not think a week or ten days playing the good fellow (at this very time) at Scarborough so abominable a thing; but if a man could get there cleverly, and every soul in his house in the mind to try what could be done in furtherance thereof, I have no one to consult in this affair:—therefore, as a man may do worse things, the English of all which is this,—That I am going to leave a few poor sheep here in the wilderness for fourteen days;—and, from pride and naughtiness of heart, to go and see what is doing at Scarborough,—stedfastly meaning afterwards to lead a new life and strengthen my faith.—Now some folk say there is much company there; and some say not; and I believe there is neither the one nor the other:—but will be both, if the world will have but a month's patience or so.—No, my dear H——, I did not delay sending your letter directly to the post.—As there are critical times, or rather turns and revolutions in *** humors, I knew not what the delay of an hour might hazard.—I will answer for him he has seventy times seven forgiven you,—and as often wish'd you at the D——l. After many oscillations, the pendulum will rest as firm as ever.

I send all compliments to Sir C. D— and G—s. I love them from my soul.—If G—t is with you, him also.—I go on, not rapidly, but well enough, with my uncle Toby's amours. There is no sitting and cudgelling one's brains whilst the sun shines bright;—'twill be all over in six or seven weeks; and there are dismal months enow after, to endure suffocation by a brimstone fireside.—If you can get to Scarborough, do.—A man who makes six tons of alum a week, may do any thing.—Lord Granby is to be there.—What a temptation!

Yours, affectionately,

L. STERNE.

LETTER XLIX.

TO THE SAME.

Coxwould, Thursday, Sept. 1764.

My Dear Cousin,

I am but this moment returned from Scarborough, where I have been drinking the waters ever since the races; and have received marvellous strength, had I not debilitated it as fast as I got it, by playing the good fellow with Lord Granby and Co. too much. I rejoice you have been encamp'd at Harrowgate; from which, by now, I suppose you are decamp'd;—otherwise, as idle a beast as I have been, I would have sacrificed a few days to the God of Laughter with you and your jolly set.—I have done nothing good that I know of, since I left you, except paying off your guinea and a half to K——, in my way through York hither.—I must try now and do better. Go on and prosper for a month.

Your affectionate,

L. STERNE.

LETTER L.

TO MR. FOLEY, AT PARIS.

York, Sept. 29, 1764.

My Dear Friend,

I having just had the honor of a letter from Miss Tuting, full of the acknowledgments of your attention and kind services to her,—I will not believe these arose from the D. of A———'s letters, nor mine. Surely, *she needed no recommendation;*—the truest and most honest compliment I can pay you, is to say they came from your own good heart, only you was introduced to the object;—for the rest follow'd in course. —However, let me cast in my mite of thanks to the treasury which belongs to good-natured actions. I have been with Lord G—y these three weeks at Scarborough;—the pleasures of which I found somewhat more exalted than those of Bagnieres last year.—I am now returned to my Philosophical Hut to finish Tristram, which I calculate will be ready for the world about Christmas; at which time I decamp from hence, and fix my head-quarters at London for the winter,—unless my cough pushes me forwards to your metropolis,—or that I can persuade some *gros* my Lord to take a trip to you.—I'll try if I can make him relish the joys of the *Thuilleries, Opera Comique, &c.*

I had this week a letter from Mrs. Sterne, from Montauban; in which she tells me she has occasion for fifty pounds immediately.—Will you send an order to your correspondent at Montauban to pay her so much cash? —and I will, in three weeks, send as much to Becket.—But as her purse is low, for God's sake write directly.—Now you must do something equally essential,—to rectify a mistake in the mind of your correspondent there, who it seems gave her a hint, not long ago, *that she was separated from me for life.* Now as this is not true in the first place, and may give a disadvantageous impression of her to those she lives amongst, —'twould be unmerciful to let her, or my daughter, suffer by it;—so do be so good as to undeceive him;—for, in a year or two she proposes (and indeed I expect it with impatience from her) to rejoin me;—and tell them I have all the confidence in the world she will not spend more than I can afford; and I only mentioned two hundred guineas a year,—because 'twas right to name some certain sum; for which I begged you to give her credit.—I write to you of all my most intimate concerns, as to a brother; so excuse me, dear Foley. God bless you!—Believe me

Yours affectionately,

L. STERNE.

Compliments to Mr. Panchaud, d'Holbach, &c.

LETTER LI.

TO THE SAME.

York, November 11, 1774

My Dear Friend,

I sent, ten days ago, a bank-bill of thirty pounds to Mr. Becket; and, this post, one of sixty.—When I get to London, which will be in five weeks, you will receive what shall always keep you in bank for Mrs. Sterne; in the mean time I have desired Becket to send you fourscore pounds; and if my wife, before I get to London, should have occasion for fifty Louis, let her not wait a minute; and if I have not paid it, a week or a fortnight, I know, will break no squares with a good and worthy friend. I will contrive to send you these two new volumes of Tristram, as soon as ever I get them from the press.—You will read as odd a tour through France as ever was projected or executed by traveller, or travel-writer, since the world began.—'Tis a laughing, good-tempered satire against travelling (as *puppies* travel); Panchaud will enjoy it.—I am quite civil to your Parisians,—*et pour cause*, you know:—'tis likely I may see them in spring. —Is it possible for you to get me over a copy of my picture any how? If so, I would write to Mademoiselle N—— to make as good a copy from it as she possibly could,—with a view to do her service here;—and I would remit her the price.—I really believe it would be the parent of a dozen portraits to her, if she executes it with the spirit of the original in your hands,—for it will be seen by many;—and as my phiz is as remarkable as myself, if she preserves the true character of both, it will do her honor and service too.—Write me a line about this, and tell me you are well and happy.—Will you present my kind respects to the worthy Baron?—I shall send him one of the best impressions of my picture from Mr. Reynolds's;—another to Monsieur P———.

My love to Mr. S——n and P——d.

I am most truly yours,

L. STERNE.

LETTER LII.

TO—— H—— S——, ESQ.

Nov. 13, 1764.

DEAR DEAR COUSIN,

'TIS a church militant week with me, full of marches and counter-marches,—and treaties about Stillington common, which we are going to inclose,—otherwise I would have obeyed your summons;—and yet I could not well have done it this week neither, having received a letter from C—, who has been very ill; and is coming down to stay a week or ten days with me.—Now I know he is ambitious of being better acquainted with you; and longs from his soul for a sight of you in your own castle.—I cannot do otherwise than bring him with me;—nor can I gallop away and leave him in an empty house to pay a visit to from London, as he comes half express to see me.—I thank you for the care of my northern vintage.—I fear, after all, I must give it a fermentation on the other side of the Alps, which is better than being on the lees with it; but *nous verrons:*—yet I fear, as it has got such hold of my brain, and comes upon it like an armed man at nights,—I must give way, for quietness sake, or be hag-ridden with the conceit of it all my life long.—I have been *Miss-ridden* this last week by a couple of romping girls (*bien mises et comme il faut*) who might as well have been in the house with me (though perhaps not, my retreat here is too quiet for them) but they have taken up all my time, and have given my judgment and fancy more airings than they wanted.—These things accord not well with sermon-making:—but 'tis my vile errantry, as Sancho says, and that is all that can be made of it.—I trust all goes swimmingly on with your alum; that the works amuse you, and call you twice out (at least) a day.—I shall see them, I trust, in ten days, or thereabouts.—If it was any way possible, I would set out this moment, though I have no cavalry (*except a she-ass.*) Give all friendly respects to Mrs. C. and to Col. H—s and the garrison, both of Guisbro and Skelton. I am, dear Anthony,

Affectionately yours,

L. STERNE.

LETTER LIII.

TO MR. FOLEY, AT PARIS.

York, Nov. 16, 1764.

MY DEAR FRIEND,

THREE posts before I had the favor of yours (which is come to hand this moment) I had wrote to set Mrs. Sterne right in her mistake,—that you had any money of mine in your hands;—being very sensible that the hundred pounds I had sent you, through Becket's hands, was but about what would balance with you. The reason of her error was owing to my writing her word I would send you a bill, in a post or two, for fifty pounds; which, my finances falling short just then, I deferred; so that I had paid nothing to any one,—but was, however, come to York this day; and I have sent you a draught for a hundred pounds. In honest truth, a fortnight ago I had not the cash;—but I am as honest as the king (as Sancho Pança says,) *only not so rich.*

Therefore, if Mrs. Sterne should want thirty Louis more, let her have them; and I will balance all (which will not be much) with honor at Christmas, when I shall be in London, having now just finished my two volumes of Tristram.—I have some thoughts of going to Italy this year; at least I shall not defer it above another,—I nave been with Lord Granby, and with Lord Shelburne; but am now sat down till December in my sweet retirement. I wish you was sat down as happily, and as free of all worldly cares.—In a few years, my dear F., I hope to see you a real country gentleman, though not altogether exiled from your friends in London: there I shall spend every winter of my life, in the same lap of contentment where I enjoy myself now, and wherever I go,—we must bring three parts in four of the treat along with us. In short, we must be happy within, and then few things without us make much difference. This is my Shandean philosophy.—You will read a comic account of my journey from Calais, through Paris, to the Garonne, in these volumes: my friends tell me they are done with spirit:—it must speak for itself. Give my kind respects to Mr. Selwin and my friend Panchaud.—When you see Baron d'Holbach, present him my respects, and believe me, dear F.,

Yours cordially,

L. STERNE.

LETTER LIV.

TO DAVID GARRICK, ESQ.

London, March 16, 1765.

DEAR GARRICK,

I THREATENED you with a letter in one I wrote a few weeks ago to Foley; but (to my shame be it spoken) I lead such a life of dissipation, I have never had a moment to myself which has not been broke in upon, by one engagement or impertinence or another; and as plots thicken towards the latter end of a piece, I find, unless I take pen and ink just now, I shall not be aole to do it till either I am got into the country, or you to the city. You are teased and tormented too much by your correspondents, to return to us; and with accounts how much your friends, and how much your theatre, wants you;—so that I will not magnify either our loss or yours, but hope cordially to see you soon.—Since I wrote .ast, I have frequently stepped into your nouse; that is as frequently as I could take the whole party, where I dined, along with me.—This was but justice to you, as I walked in as a Wit; but with regard to myself, I balanced the account thus:—I am sometimes in my friend ——'s house; but he is always in Tristram Shandy's; where my friends say he will continue (and, I hope, the prophecy is true for my own immortality) even when he himself is no more.

I have had a lucrative winter's campaign here.—Shandy sells well.—I am taxing the public with two more volumes of Sermons, which will more than double the gains of Shandy.—It goes into the world with a prancing list *de toute la noblesse;* which will bring me in three hundred pounds, exclusive of the sale of the copy;—so that, with all the contempt of money which *ma facon de penser* has ever impressed on me, I shall be rich in spite of myself; but I scorn, you must know, in the high *ton* I take at present, to pocket all this trash.—I set out to lay a portion of it out in the service of the world, in a tour round Italy; where I shall spring game, or the deuce is in the dice!—In the beginning of September I quit England, that I may avail myself of the time of vintage, when all Nature is joyous; and so saunter, philosophically, for a year or so, on the other side the Alps.—I hope your pilgrimages have brought Mrs. Garrick and yourself back *à la fleur de jeunesse.*—May you both long feel the sweets of it, and your friends with you!—Do, dear friend, make my kindest wishes and compliments acceptable to the best and wisest of the daughters of Eve!—You shall ever believe, and ever find me affectionately yours,

L. STERNE.

LETTER LV.

TO THE SAME.

Bath, April 6, 1775.

I SCALP you! my dear Garrick! my dear friend!—Foul befall the man who hurts a hair of your head!—and so full was I of that very sentiment, that my letter had not been put into the post-office ten minutes, before my heart smote me; and I sent to recall it,—but failed.—You are sadly to blame, Shandy, for this, quoth I, leaning with my head on my hand as I recriminated upon my false delicacy in the affair:—Garrick's nerves (if he has any left) are as fine and as delicately spun as thy own!—his sentiments as honest and friendly!—Thou knowest, Shandy, that he loves thee,—why wilt thou hazard him a moment's pain? Puppy, fool, coxcomb, jack-ass, &c. &c.—and so I balanced the account to your favor, before I received it drawn up in *your way*. —I say *your way*, for it is not stated so much to your honor and credit as I had passed the account before;—for it was a most lamented truth, that I never received one of the letters your friendship meant me, except whilst in Paris.—Oh! how I congratulate you for the anxiety the world has, and continues to be under, for your return! —Return, return to the few who love you, and the thousands who admire you!—The moment you set your foot upon your stage, —mark, I tell it you,—by some magic irresisted power, every fibre about your heart will vibrate afresh, and as strong and as feelingly as ever;—Nature, with Glory at her back, will light up the torch within you; and there is enough of it left to heat and enlighten the world these many, many years!

Heaven be praised! (I utter it from my soul) that your Lady, and my Minerva, is in a condition to walk to Windsor!—full rapturously will I lead the graceful pilgrim to the temple; where I will sacrifice with the purest incense to her;—but you may worship with me or not,—'twill make no difference either in the truth or warmth of my devotion;—still (after all I have seen) I still maintain her peerless!

Powell, good Heaven!—give me some one with less smoke and more fire!—There are who, like the Pharisees, still think they shall be heard for *much* speaking. Come, come away, my dear Garrick, and teach us another lesson.

Adieu!—I love you dearly, and your Lady better;—not hobby-horsically,—but most sentimentally and affectionately;—for I am yours (that is, if you never say another word about ——) with all the sentiments of love and friendship you deserve from me,

L. STERNE.

LETTER LVI.

TO MR. FOLEY.

Bath, April 15, 1765.

MY DEAR FOLEY,

MY wife tells me she has drawn for one hundred pounds;—and 'tis fit that you should be paid it that minute:—the money is now in Becket's hands. Send me, my dear Foley, my account, that I may discharge the balance to this time, and know what to leave in your hands.—I have made a good campaign of it this year in the field of the *literati*;—my two volumes of Tristram, and two of Sermons, which I shall print very soon, will bring me a considerable sum. Almost all the nobility in England honor me with their names; and 'tis thought it will be the largest and most splendid list which ever pranced before a book since subscriptions came into fashion. —Pray present my most sincere compliments to Lady H——; whose name I hope to insert with many others. As so many men of genius favor me with their names also, I will quarrel with Mr. Hume, and call him Deist, and what not, unless I have his name too.—My love to Lord W—— Your name, Foley, I have put in as a free-will offering of my labors. Your list of subscribers you will send:—'tis but a crown for sixteen sermons.—Dog-cheap! but I am in quest of honor, not money.—Adieu, adieu! Believe me, dear Foley,

Yours truly,
L. STERNE.

LETTER LVII.

TO MR. W.

Coxwould, May 23, 1765.

AT this moment I am sitting in my summer-house with my head and heart full, not of my uncle Toby's amours with the Widow Wadman, but my sermons; and your letter has drawn me out of a pensive mood:—the spirit of it *pleaseth me*;—but, in this solitude, what can I tell or write to you but about myself?—I am glad that you are in love;—'twill cure the spleen, at least, which has a bad effect on both man and woman.—I myself must ever have some

Dulcinea in my head; it harmonizes the soul;—and in those cases I first endeavor to make the lady believe so; or rather, I begin first to make myself believe that I am in love: — but I carry on my affairs quite in the French way, sentimentally,— *L'amour* (say they) *n'est rien sans sentiment.*—Now, notwithstanding they make such a pother about the *word*, they have no precise idea annex'd to it:—and so much for that same subject called Love.—I must tell you how I have just treated a French gentleman of fortune in France, who took a liking to my daughter: — Without any ceremony (having got my direction from my wife's banker) he wrote me word that he was in love with my daughter; and desired to know what *fortune* I would give her at present, and how much at my *death:* —by the bye, I think there was very little *sentiment* on *his side.* — My answer was, "Sir, I shall give her ten thousand pounds the day of marriage. My calculation is as follows:—She is not eighteen, you are sixty-two;—there goes five thousand pounds:— tnen, Sir, you at least think her not ugly; she has many accomplishments,—speaks Italian, French, plays upon the guitar; and as I fear you play upon no instrument whatever, I think you will be happy to take her at my terms; for here finishes the account of the ten thousand pounds." — I do not suppose but he will take this as I mean; that is, a flat refusal.—I have had a parsonage-house burnt down by the carelessness of my curate's wife.—As soon as I can, I must rebuild it, I trow;—but I lack the means at present; yet I am never happier than when I have not a shilling in my pocket: for when I have, I can never call it my own.— Adieu, my dear friend: — may you enjoy better health than me, though not better spirits, for that is impossible.

Yours sincerely,

L. STERNE.

My compliments to the Colonel.

LETTER LVIII.

TO MR. FOLEY, AT PARIS.

York, July 13, 1775.

My Dear Sir,

I wrote some time in spring, to beg you would favor me with my account. I believe you was set out from Paris, and that M. Garrick brought the letter with him; which, possibly, he gave you. In the hurry of your business you might forget the contents of it; and in the hurry of mine in town (though I called once) I could not get to see you. I decamp for Italy in September; and shall see your face at Paris, you may be sure: but I shall see it with more pleasure when I am out of debt;—which is your own fault, for Becket has had money left in his hands for that purpose.—Do send Mrs. Sterne her two last volumes of Tristram; they arrived with yours in spring, and she complains she has not got them.—My best services to Mr. Panchaud.—I am busy composing two volumes of Sermons; they will be printed in September, though I fear not time enough to bring them with me. Your name is amongst the list of a few of my honorary subscribers, who subscribe for love.—If you see Baron d'Holbach and Diderot, present my respects to them.—If the Baron wants any English books, he will let me know, and I will bring them with me.—Adieu.

I am truly yours,

L. STERNE.

LETTER LIX.

TO THE SAME.

London, October 7, 1765.

Dear Sir,

It is a terrible thing to be in Paris without a periwig on a man's head! In seven days from the date of this, I should be in that case, unless you tell your neighbor, Madame Requiere, to get her *bon mari de me faire un peruque à bourse, au mieux— c'est-à-dire—une la plus extraordinaire— la plus jolie—la plus gentille—et la plus— Mais qu'importe? j'ai l'honneur d'être grand critique—et bien difficile encore dans les affaires de peruques;* — and, in one word, that he gets it done in five days after notice.—

I beg pardon for this liberty, my dear friend, and for the trouble of forwarding this by the very next post. If my friend Mr. F. is in Paris, my kind love to him and respects to all others.—In sad haste.—

Yours, truly,

L STERNE.

I have paid into Mr. Becket's hands six hundred pounds; which you may draw upon at sight, according as either Mrs. Sterne or myself make it expedient.

LETTER LX.

TO MR. PANCHAUD, AT PARIS

Beau Point Voisin, Nov. 7, 1765.

DEAR SIR,

I FORGOT to desire you to forward whatever letters came to your hand, to your banker at Rome, to wait for me against I get there, as it is uncertain how long I may stay at Turin, &c. &c.: at present, I am held a prisoner in this town by the sudden swelling of two pitiful rivulets, from the snows melting on the Alps; so that we cannot either advance to them, nor retire back again to Lyons:—for how long the gentlemen, who are my fellow-travellers, and myself, shall languish in this state of vexatious captivity, Heaven and Earth surely know; for it rains as if they were coming together to settle the matter;—I had an agreeable journey to Lyons; and a joyous time there,—dining and supping every day at the Commandant's. — Lord F. W. I left there, and about a dozen English.—If you see Lord Ossory, Lord William Gordon, and my friend Mr. Crawford, remember me to them. If Wilkes is at Paris yet, I send him all kind wishes.—Present my compliments, as well as thanks, to my good friend Miss P——; and believe me, dear Sir, with all truth, yours,

L. STERNE.

LETTER LXI.

TO THE SAME.

Turin, Nov. 28, 1765.

DEAR SIR,

AFTER many difficulties I have got here safe and sound,—though eight days in passing the mountains of Savoy.—I am stopped here for ten days, by the whole country betwixt here and Milan being laid under water by continual rains;—but I am very happy, and have found my way into a dozen houses already.—To-morrow I am to be presented to the King; and when that ceremony is over, I shall have my hands full of engagements.—No English here, but Sir James Macdonald, who meets with much respect, and Mr. Ogilby.—We are all together, and shall depart in peace together.— My kind services to all. Pray forward the inclosed.

Yours, most truly,

L. STERNE.

LETTER LXII.

TO THE SAME.

Turin, Nov. 28, 1765.

DEAR SIR,

I AM just leaving this place with Sir James Macdonald for Milan, &c. — We have spent a joyous fortnight here, and met with all kinds of honors; and with regret do we both bid adieu:—but health on my side,—and good sense on his,—say 'tis better to be at Rome;—you say at Paris;—but you put variety out of the question.—I entreat you to forward the inclosed to Mrs. Sterne. — My compliments to all friends; more particularly to those I most value (that includes Mr. F., if he is in Paris.)

I am yours, most truly,

L. STERNE.

LETTER LXIII.

TO THE SAME.

Florence, Dec. 18, 1765.

DEAR SIR,

I HAVE been a month passing the plains of Lombardy, stopping in my way at Milan, Parma, Placenza, and Bologna,—with weather as delicious as a kindly April in England;—and have been three days in crossing a part of the Apennines, covered with thick snow. — Sad transition! — I stay here three days to dine with our Plenipo Lords T——d and C——r; and in five days shall tread the Vatican, and be introduced to all the Saints in the Pantheon.—I stay but fourteen days to pay these civilities, and then decamp for Naples.—Pray send the inclosed to my wife, and Becket's letter to London.

Yours, truly,

L. STERNE.

LETTER LXIV.

TO MISS STERNE.

Naples, February 3, 1766.

MY DEAR GIRL,

YOUR letter, my Lydia, has made me both laugh and cry. Sorry am I that you are both so afflicted with the ague; and by all means I wish you both to fly from Tours; because, I remember, it is situated between two rivers, la Loire and le Cher, which must occasion fogs, and damp unwholesome weather; therefore, for the same reason, go not to Bourges en Bresse; 'tis as vile a place for agues.—I find myself infinitely better than I was, and hope to have added at least ten years to my life, by this journey to Italy; the climate is heavenly, and I find new principles of health in me, which I have been long a stranger to; but trust me, my Lydia, I will find you out, wherever you are, in May. Therefore, I beg you to direct to me at Belloni's at Rome, that I may have some idea where you will be then.—The account you give me of Mrs. C—— is truly amiable; I shall ever honor her.—Mr. C. is a diverting companion:—what he said of your little French admirer, was truly droll. The Marquis de ——— is an impostor, and not worthy of your acquaintance; he only pretended to know me, to get introduced to your mother.——I desire you will get your mother to write to Mr. C., that I may discharge every debt; and then, my Lydia, if I live, the produce of my pen shall be yours: if Fate reserves me not that, the humane and good (part for thy father's sake, part for thy own) will never abandon thee!—If your mother's health will permit her to return with me to England, your summers I will render as agreeable as I can at Coxwould; your winters at York.—You know my publications call me to London.—If Mr. and Mrs. C—— are still at Tours, thank them from me for their cordiality to my wife and daughter. I have purchased you some little trifles, which I shall give you when we meet, as proofs of affection from

Your fond father,

L. STERNE

LETTER LXV.

TO J—— H—— S——, ESQ.

Naples, February 5, 1767.

MY DEAR H.,

'TIS an age since I have heard from you;—but as I read the London Chronicle, and find no tidings of your death, or that you are even at the point of it, I take it as I wish it, that you have got over thus much of the winter, free from the damps both of climate and spirits:—and here I am, as happy as a king after all, growing fat, sleek, and well liking; not improving in stature, but in breadth.—We have a jolly carnival of it; nothing but operas, punchinelloes, festinoes, and masquerades. We (that is, *nous autres*) are all dressing out for one this night at the Princess Francavivalla's, which is to be superb. The English dine with her (exclusively): and so much for small chat,—except that I saw a little comedy last week, with more expression and spirit, and true character, than I shall see one hastily again.—I stay here till the Holy Week, which I shall pass at Rome, where I occupy myself a month:—my plan was to have gone from thence for a fortnight to Florence, and then by Leghorn to Marseilles directly home; but am diverted from this by the repeated proposals of accompanying a gentleman who is returning by Venice, Vienna, Saxony, Berlin, and so by the Spa, and thence through Holland to England:—'tis with Mr. E. I have known him these three years, and have been with him ever since I reached Rome: and as I know him to be a good-hearted young gentleman, I have no doubt of making it answer both his views and mine; at least I am persuaded we shall return home together (as we set out) with friendship and good-will.—Write your next letter to me at Rome, and do me the following favor, if it lies in your way, which I think it does, to get me a letter of recommendation to our Ambassador (Lord Stormont) at Vienna. I have not the honor to be known to his Lordship; but Lords P——, or H——, or twenty you better know, would write a certificate for me; importing, that I am not fallen out of the clouds. If this will cost my cousin little trouble, do inclose it in your next letter to me at Belloni's.—You have left Skelton I trow a month, and I fear have had a most sharp winter, if one may judge of it from the severity of the weather here, and all over Italy, which exceeded any thing known, till within these three weeks, that the sun has been as hot as we could bear it. Give my kind services to my friends; especially to the household of faith:—my dear Garland,—to Gilbert,—to the worthy Colonel,—to Cardinal S——, — to my fellow-laborer Pantagruel.—Dear cousin Anthony, receive my kindest love and wishes.

Yours affectionately,

L. STERNE.

P. S. Upon second thoughts, direct your next to me at Mr. W.'s, banker at Venice.

LETTER LXVI.

TO MR. FOLEY, AT PARIS.

Naples, February 8, 1766.

Dear Sir,

I desire Mrs. Sterne may have what cash she wants,—if she has not received it before now: she sends me word she has been in want of cash these three weeks: be so kind as to prevent this uneasiness to her; which is doubly so to me. I have made very little use of your letters of credit, having, since I left Paris, taken up no more money than about fifty Louis at Turin, as much at Rome, and a few ducats here; and as I now travel from hence to Rome, Venice, through Vienna to Berlin, &c. with a gentleman of fortune, I shall draw for little more till my return; so you will have always enough to spare for my wife. The beginning of March be so kind as to let her have a hundred pounds to begin her year with.

There are a good many English here, very few in Rome, or other parts of Italy. The air of Naples agrees very well with me;—I shall return fat.—My friendship to all who honor me with theirs.—Adieu, my dear friend:—I am ever yours,

L. STERNE.

LETTER LXVII.

TO MR. PANCHAUD, AT PARIS.

Naples, February 14, 1766.

Dear Sir,

I wrote last week to you, to desire you would let Mrs. Sterne have what money she wanted.—It may happen, as that letter went inclosed in one to her at Tours, that you will receive this first. I have made little use of your letters of credit, as you will see by that letter: nor shall I want much (if any) till you see me, as I travel now in company with a gentleman:—however, as we return by Venice, Vienna, Berlin, &c. to the Spa, I should be glad if you will draw me a letter of credit upon some one at Venice, to the extent of fifty Louis; —but I am persuaded I shall not want half of them: however, in case of sickness or accidents, one would not go so long a route without money in one's pocket.—The bankers here are not so conscientious as my friend P.; they would make me pay twelve per cent. if I was to get a letter here. I beg your letters, &c. may be inclosed to Mr. Watson at Venice,—where we shall be in the Ascension. I have received much benefit from the air of Naples;—but quit it to be at Rome before the Holy Week. There are about five-and-twenty English here;—but most of them will be decamped in two months:—there are scarce a third of the number at Rome; I suppose, therefore, that Paris is full.—My warmest wishes attend you,—with my love to Mr. F., and compliments to all.—I am, dear Sir, very faithfully, yours,

L. STERNE.

Sir James Macdonald is in the house with me, and is just recovering from a long and most cruel fit of the rheumatism.

LETTER LXVIII.

TO J—— H—— S——, ESQ.

May 25, near Dijon, [1766.]

Dear Anthony,

My desire of seeing both my wife and girl, has turned me out of my road towards a delicious chateau of the Countess of M——, where I have been patriarching it these seven days with her Ladyship, and half a dozen of very handsome and agreeable ladies. — Her Ladyship has the best of hearts:—a valuable present, not given to every one. To-morrow, with regret, I shall quit this agreeable circle, and post it night and day to Paris, where I shall arrive in two days, and just wind myself up, when I am there, enough to roll on to Calais;—so I hope to sup with you the King's birth-day, according to a plan of sixteen days' standing. Never man has been such a wildgoose chase after a wife as I have been.—After having sought her in five or six different towns, I found her at last in *Franche Compté*.—Poor woman! she was very cordial, &c. and begs to stay another year or two.—My Lydia pleases me much.—I found her greatly improved in every thing I wished her.—I am most unaccountably well, and most unaccountably nonsensical;—'tis at least a proof of good spirits; which is a sign and token given me in these latter days, that I must take up again the pen. In faith, I think I shall die with it in my hand; but I shall live these ten years, my Anthony, notwithstanding the fears of my wife, whom I left most melancholy on that account. This is a delicious part of the world; most celestial weather, and we lie all day, without damps, upon the grass,—and that is the whole of it, except the inner man (for her Ladyship is not stingy of her wine) is inspired twice a day with the best Burgundy that grows upon the mountains which terminate our lands here. Surely, you will not have decamped to Crazy Castle before I reach town. The summer here is set in in good earnest:—'tis more than we can say for Yorkshire. I hope to hear a good tale of your alum-works. Have you no other works in hand? I do not expect to hear from you; so God prosper you, and all your undertakings.—I am, my dear cousin,

Most affectionately yours,

L. STERNE.

Remember me to Mr. G——, Cardinal S——, the Colonel, &c.

LETTER LXIX.

TO MR. PANCHAUD, AT PARIS.

York, June 28, 1766

Dear Sir,

I wrote last week to Mr. Becket to discharge the balance due to you;—and I have received a letter from him, telling me, that if you will draw upon him for one hundred and sixty pounds, he will punctually pay it to your order;—so send the draughts when you please.—Mrs. Sterne writes me word, she wants fifty pounds; which I desire you will let her have: I will take care to remit it to your correspondent. I have such an entire confidence in my wife, that she spends as little as she can, though she is confined to no particular sum:—her expenses will not exceed three hundred pounds a year, unless by ill-health or a journey,—and I am very willing she should have it;—and you may rely, in case it ever happens that she should draw for fifty or a hundred pounds extraordinary, that it and every demand shall be punctually paid,—and with proper thanks; and for this the whole Shandean family are ready to stand security. 'Tis impossible to tell you how sorry I was that my affairs hurried me so quick through Paris, as to deprive me of seeing my old friend Mr. Foley, and of the pleasure I proposed in being made known to his better half;—but I have a probability of seeing him this winter. Adieu, dear Sir, and believe me

Most cordially yours,

L. STERNE.

LETTER LXX.

TO MR. S.

Coxwould, July 23, 1766.

Dear Sir,

One might be led to think that there is a fatality regarding us:—we make appointments to meet; and for these two years have not seen each other's face but twice;—we must try and do better for the future. Having sought you with more zeal than

C—— sought the Lord, in order to deliver you the books you bade me purchase for you at Paris,—I was forced to pay carriage for them from London down to York;—but as I shall neither charge you the books nor the carriage,—'tis not worth talking about. Never man, my dear Sir, has had a more agreeable tour than your Yorick;—and at present I am in my peaceful retreat, writing the ninth volume* of Tristram. I shall publish but one this year; and the next I shall begin a new work of four volumes, which when finished, I shall continue Tristram with fresh spirit. What a difference of scene here! But, with a disposition to be happy, 'tis neither this place nor t'other that renders us the reverse. In short, each man's happiness depends upon himself:—he is a fool if he does not enjoy it.

What are you about, dear S——? Give me some account of your pleasures.—You had better come to me for a fortnight, and I will show, or give you (if needful) a practical dose of my philosophy; but I hope you do not want it;—if you did, 'twould be the office of a friend to give it. Will not even our races tempt you? You see I use all arguments.—Believe me yours most truly,

L. STERNE.

LETTER LXXI.

TO MR. PANCHAUD, AT PARIS.

Coxwould, Sept. 21, 1766.

My Dear Friend,

If Mrs. Sterne should draw upon you for fifty Louis d'ors, be so kind as to remit her the money;—and pray be so good as not to draw upon Mr. Becket for it (as he owes me nothing) but favor me with the draught, which I will pay to Mr. Selwin. A young nobleman is now negotiating a jaunt with me for six weeks, about Christmas, to the Fauxbourg de St. Germain.—I should like much to be with you for so long; and if my wife should grow worse (having had a very poor account of her in my daughter's last) I cannot think of her being without me:—and however expensive the journey would be, I would fly to Avignon to administer consolation to both her and my poor girl.—Wherever I am, believe me, dear Sir,

Yours,

L. STERNE.

My kind compliments to Mr. Foley. Though I have not the honor of knowing his rib, I see no reason why I may not present all due respects to the better half of so old a friend, which I do by these presents—with my friendliest wishes to Miss P.

LETTER LXXII.

TO MR. FOLEY, AT PARIS.

Coxwould, Oct. 25, 1766.

My Dear Foley,

I desired you would be so good as to remit to Mrs. Sterne fifty Louis, a month ago.—I dare say you have done it;—but her illness must have cost her a good deal:—therefore, having paid the last fifty pounds into Mr. Selwin's hands, I beg you to send her thirty guineas more,—for which I send a bank-bill to Mr. Becket by this post;—but surely, had I not done so, you would not stick at it;—for be assured, my dear Foley that the First Lord of the Treasury is neither more able nor more willing (nor perhaps half so punctual) in repaying with honor all I ever can be in your books.—My daughter says her mother is very ill,—and I fear, going fast down, by all accounts:—'tis melancholy in her situation to want any aid that is in my power to give.—Do write to her;—and believe me, with all compliments to your Hotel,

Yours very truly,

L. STERNE.

LETTER LXXIII.

TO MR. PANCHAUD.

York, November 25, 1766.

Dear Sir,

I just received yours; and am glad that the balance of accounts is now paid to you.—Thus far all goes well.—I have received a letter from my daughter with the pleasing tidings that she thinks her mother out of

* Alluding to the first edition.

danger,—and that the air of the country is delightful (excepting the winds); but the description of the chateau my wife has hired is really pretty:—on the side of the Fountain of Vaucluse,—with seven rooms of a floor, half furnished with tapestry, half with blue taffety, the permission to fish, and to have game; so many partridges a week, &c.; and the price——guess! Sixteen guineas a year!—there's for you, P. About the latter end of next month, my wife will have occasion for a hundred guineas;—and pray be so good, my dear Sir, as to give orders that she may not be disappointed:—she is going to spend the Carnival at Marseilles at Christmas.—I shall be in London by Christmas-week, and then shall balance this remittance to Mrs. S. with Mr. S——. I am going to lie-in of another child of the Shandaic procreation, in town.—I hope you wish me a safe delivery.—I fear my friend Mr. F. will have left town before I get there.—Adieu, dear Sir.—I wish you every thing in this world which will do you good, for I am, with unfeigned truth,

Yours,

L. STERNE.

Make my compliments acceptable to the good and worthy Baron d'Holbach,—Miss P. &c. &c.

LETTER LXXIV.

FROM IGNATIUS SANCHO

TO MR. STERNE.

[1766.]

Reverend Sir,

It would be an insult on your humanity (or, perhaps, look like it) to apologize for the liberty I am taking.—I am one of those people whom the vulgar and illiberal call Negroes.—The first part of my life was rather unlucky, as I was placed in a family who judged ignorance the best and only security for obedience. A little reading and writing I got by unwearied application.—The latter part of my life has been, through God's blessing, truly fortunate,—having spent it in the service of one of the best and greatest families in the kingdom.—My chief pleasure has been books:—Philanthropy I adore—How very much, good Sir, am I (amongst millions) indebted to you for the character of your amiable uncle Toby.—I declare I would walk ten miles in the dog-days, to shake hands with the honest Corporal.—Your sermons have touched me to the heart, and, I hope, have amended it; which brings me to the point.—In your tenth discourse, is this very affecting passage:—"Consider how great a part of our "species, in all ages down to this, have been "trod under the feet of cruel and capricious "tyrants, who would neither hear their "cries, nor pity their distresses!—Consider "slavery,—what it is,—how bitter a draught, "and how many millions are made to drink "of it!"—Of all my favorite authors, not one has drawn a tear in favor of my miserable black brethren,—excepting yourself, and the humane author of Sir Geo. Ellison.—I think you will forgive me,—I am sure you will applaud me,—for beseeching you to give one half-hour's attention to slavery, as it is this day practised in our West Indies.—That subject handled in your striking manner, would ease the yoke (perhaps of many;) but if only of one,—gracious God! what a feast to a benevolent heart! and sure I am, you are an Epicurean in acts of charity.—You, who are universally read, and as universally admired,—you could not fail.—Dear Sir, think in me you behold the uplifted hands of thousands of my brother Moors. Grief (you pathetically observe) is eloquent: figure to yourself their attitudes, hear their supplicating addresses!—alas! you cannot refuse. Humanity must comply;—in which hope, I beg permission to subscribe myself,

Reverend Sir, &c.

I. S

LETTER LXXV.

FROM MR. STERNE

TO IGNATIUS SANCHO.

Coxwould, July 27, 1766.

There is a strange coincidence, Sancho, in the little events (as well as in the great ones) of this world; for I had been writing a tender tale of the sorrows of a friendless poor negro girl; and my eyes had scarce done smarting with it, when your letter of recommendation, in behalf of so many of ner brethren and sisters, came to me;—but why *her brethren?*—or yours, Sancho,—any more than mine? It is by the finest tints and most insensible gradations that Nature descends from the fairest face about St. James's to the sootiest complexion in Africa.—At which tint of these is it, that the ties of blood are to cease? and how many shades must we descend lower still in the scale, ere mercy is to vanish with them? But 'tis no uncommon thing, my good Sancho, for one half of the world to use the other half of it like brutes, and then endeavor to make them so. For my own part, I never look *westward* (when I am in a pensive mood at least) but I think of the burdens which our brothers and sisters are *there* carrying; and, could I ease their shoulders from one ounce of them, I declare I would set out this hour upon a pilgrimage to Mecca for their sakes;—which, by the bye, Sancho, exceeds your walk of ten miles in about the same proportion that a visit of humanity should one of mere form.—However, if you meant my uncle Toby more, he is your debtor.—If I can weave the tale I have wrote into the work I am about,—'tis at the service of the afflicted,—and a much greater matter: for, in serious truth, it casts a sad shade upon the world, that so great a part of it are, and have been so long, bound in chains of darkness, and in chains of misery; and I cannot but both respect and felicitate you, that, by so much laudable diligence, you have broke the one;—and that, by falling into the hands of so good and merciful a family, Providence has rescued you from the other.

And so, good-hearted Sancho, adieu! and, believe me, I will not forget your letter.

Yours,

L. STERNE.

LETTER LXXVI.

TO MR. W.

Coxwould, Dec. 23, 1766.

Thanks, my dear W——, for your letter. I am just preparing to come and greet you and many other friends in town.—I have drained my inkstandish to the bottom; and, after I have published, shall set my face, not towards Jerusalem, but towards the Alps.—I find I must once more fly from death whilst I have strength.—I shall go to Naples, and see whether the air of that place will not set this poor frame to rights.—As to the project of getting a bear to lead, I think I have enough to do to govern myself;—and however profitable it might be (according to your opinion) I am sure it would be unpleasurable.—Few are the minutes of life; and I do not think that I have any to throw away on any one being.—I shall spend nine or ten months in Italy, and call upon my wife and daughter in France, at my return;—so shall be back by the King's birth-day.—What a project!—and now, my dear friend, am I going to York; not for the sake of society, nor to walk by the side of the muddy Ouse, but to recruit myself of the most violent spitting of blood that ever mortal man experienced; because I had rather (in case it is ordained so) die there than in a post-chaise on the road.—If the amour of my uncle Toby do not please you, I am mistaken; and so with a droll story I will finish this letter.

A sensible friend of mine, with whom, not long ago, I spent some hours in conversation, met an apothecary (an acquaintance of ours).—The latter asked him how he did?—"Why ill, very ill: I have been with "Sterne, who has given me such a dose of "*Attic Salt*, that I am in a fever."—'Attic 'salt, Sir! Attic salt! I have Glauber salt, 'I have Epsom Salt in my shop, &c.—Oh! 'I suppose 'tis some French salt.—I wonder 'you would trust his report of the medicine; 'he cares not what he takes himself.'—I fancy I see you smile.—I long to be able to be in London, and embrace my friends there;—and shall enjoy myself a week or ten days at Paris with my friends, particularly the Baron d'Holbach, and the rest of the joyous set.—As to the females;—no, I will not say a word about them;—only I hate borrowed characters, taken up as a woman does her shift, for the purpose she intends to effectuate. Adieu, adieu.—I am yours, whilst

L. STERNE.

LETTER LXXVII.

TO MR. PANCHAUD, AT PARIS.

London, Feb. 13, 1767.

Dear P——,

I paid yesterday (by Mr. Becket) a hundred guineas, or pounds, I forget which, to Mr. Selwin:—but you must remit to Mrs. Sterne, at Marseilles, a hundred Louis before she leaves that place, which will be in less than three weeks. Have you got the ninth volume of Shandy?*—it is liked the best of all here.—I am going to publish a Sentimental Journey through France and Italy.—The undertaking is protected and highly encouraged by all our noblesse;—'tis subscribed for at a great rate;—'twill be an original, in large quarto; the subscription half a guinea.—If you can procure me the honor of a few names of men of science or fashion, I shall thank you;—they will appear in good company, as all the nobility here almost have honored me with their names.—My kindest remembrance to Mr. Foley.—Respects to Baron d'Holbach, and believe me ever, ever yours,

L. STERNE.

LETTER LXXVIII.

TO MISS STERNE.

Old Bond Street, Feb. 28, 1767.

And so, my Lydia, thy mother and thyself are returning back again from Marseilles to the banks of the Sorgue,—and there thou wilt sit and fish for trouts.—I envy you the sweet situation.—Petrarch's tomb I should like to pay a sentimental visit to.—The Fountain of Vaucluse, by thy description, must be delightful.—I am also much pleased with the account you give me of the Abbé de Sade;—you find great comfort in such a neighbor.—I am glad he is so good as to correct thy translation of my Sermons.—Dear girl, go on, and make me a present of thy work:—but why not the House of Mourning? 'tis one of the best. —I long to receive the Life of Petrarch and his Laura, by your Abbé; but I am out of all patience with the answer the Marquis made the Abbé; 'twas truly coarse; and I wonder he bore it with any Christian patience.—But to the subject of your letter. —I do not wish to know who was the busy fool who made your mother uneasy about Mrs. ——: 'tis true, I have a friendship for her, but not to infatuation.—I believe I have judgment enough to discern hers, and every woman's faults. I honor thy mother for her answer.—That she wished not to be informed; and begged him to drop the subject.—Why do you say that your mother wants money? Whilst I have a shilling, shall you not have ninepence out of it?—I think, if I have my enjoyments, I ought not to grudge you yours.—I shall not begin my Sentimental Journey till I get to Coxwould. —I have laid a plan for something new, quite out of the beaten track. I wish I had you with me, and I would introduce you to one of the most amiable and gentlest of beings, whom I have just been with;—not Mrs. ——, but a Mrs. J——, the wife of as worthy a man as I ever met with; I esteem them both. He possesses every manly virtue;—honor and bravery are his characteristics, which have distinguished him nobly in several instances. I shall make you better acquainted with his character, by sending Orme's History, with the books you desired,—and it is well worth your reading; for Orme is an elegant writer, and a just one; he pays no man a compliment at the expense of truth.—Mrs. J—— is kind and friendly; of a sentimental turn of mind, and so sweet a disposition, that she is too good for the world she lives in.—Just God! if all were like her, what a life would this be!—Heaven, my Lydia, for some wise purpose, has created different beings.—I wish my dear child knew her; thou art worthy of her friendship, and she already loves thee; for I sometimes tell her what I feel for thee.—This is a long letter.—Write soon, and never let your letters be studied ones; write naturally, and then you will write well.—I hope your mother has got quite well of her ague.—I have sent her some of Huxham's tincture of the bark.—I will order you a guitar, since the other is broke.—Believe me, my Lydia, that I am yours affectionately,

L. STERNE

* Alluding to the first edition.

LETTER LXXIX.

TO MR. PANCHAUD, AT PARIS.

London, Feb. 27, 1767.

DEAR SIR,

MY daughter begs a present of me, and you must know I can deny her nothing.—It must be strung with cat-gut and of five chords, *si chiama in Italiano la chitera di cinque corde*. She cannot get such a thing at Marseilles; at Paris one may have every thing. Will you be so good to my girl as to make her happy in this affair, by getting some musical body to buy one, and send it her to Avignon, directed to Monsieur Teste?—I wrote last week to desire you would remit Mrs. S—— a hundred Louis: 'twill be all, except the guitar, I shall owe you. Send me your account, and I will pay Mr. Selwin.—Direct to me at Mr. Becket's. All kind respects to my friend Mr. F. and your sister.

Yours cordially,

L. STERNE.

LETTER LXXX.*

TO ELIZA.†

ELIZA will receive my books with this. The sermons came all hot from the heart. I wish that I could give them any title to be offered to yours. The others came from the head: I am more indifferent about their reception.

I know not how it comes about, but I am half in love with you; I ought to be wholly so; for I never valued (or saw more good qualities to value) or thought more of one of your sex than of you; so adieu.

Yours faithfully,

If not affectionately,

L. STERNE.

LETTER LXXXI.

TO THE SAME.

I CANNOT rest, Eliza, though I shall call on you at half past twelve, till I know how you do.—May thy dear face smile, as thou risest like the sun of this morning. I was much grieved to hear of your alarming indisposition yesterday; and disappointed too, at not being let in.—Remember, my dear, that a friend has the same right as a physician. The etiquettes of this town (you'll say) say otherwise.—No matter. Delicacy and propriety do not always consist in observing their rigid doctrines.

I am going out to breakfast, but shall be at my lodgings by eleven: when I hope to read a single line under thy own hand, that thou art better, and wilt be glad to see thy Bramin.

9 o'clock.

---

* This and the nine following Letters have no dates to them, but were evidently written in the months of March and April, 1767. They are therefore here placed together.

† The Editor of the first publication of Mr. Sterne's Letters to Eliza, gives the following account of this Lady;—"Mrs. Elizabeth Draper, wife of Daniel Draper, Esq. Counsellor at Bombay, and at present (*i. e.* in 1775,) chief of the factory at Surat, a gentleman very much respected in that quarter of the globe.—She is by birth an East Indian; but the circumstance of being born in the country, not proving sufficient to defend her delicate frame against the heats of that burning climate, she came to England for the recovery of her health, when, by accident, she became acquainted with Mr. Sterne. He immediately discovered in her, a mind so congenial with his own, so enlightened, so refined, and so tender, that their mutual attraction presently joined them in the closest union that purity could possibly admit of: he loved her as his friend, and prided in her as his pupil: all her concerns became presently his; her health, her circumstances, her reputation, her children, were his; his fortune, his time, his country, were at her disposal, so far as the sacrifice of all or any of these might, in his opinion, contribute to her real happiness. If it is asked, whether the glowing heat of Mr. Sterne's affection never transported him to a flight beyond the limits of pure Platonism? the publisher will not take upon him absolutely to deny it: but this, he thinks, so far from leaving any stain upon that gentleman's memory, that it, perhaps, includes his fairest encomium; since to cherish the seeds of piety and chastity in a heart which the passions are interested to corrupt, must be allowed to be the noblest effort of a soul fraught and fortified with the justest sentiments of religion and virtue."

After reading these letters, the curiosity of the public will be naturally excited to inquire concerning the fate of the Lady to whom they are addressed. To this question, it will be sufficient to answer, that she has been dead some years, and that it might give pain to many worthy persons, if the circumstances which attended the latter part of her life were disclosed as they are generally said to have reflected no credit either on her prudence or discretion.

LETTER LXXXII.

TO THE SAME.

I GOT thy letter last night, Eliza, on my return from Lord Bathurst's, where I dined, and where I was heard (as I talked of thee an hour without intermission) with so much pleasure and attention, that the good old Lord toasted your health three different times; and now he is in his eighty-fifth year, says he hopes to live long enough to be introduced, as a friend, to my fair Indian disciple, and to see her eclipse all other Nabobesses as much in wealth as she does already in exterior and (what is far better) in interior merit. I hope so too. This nobleman is an old friend of mine. — You know he was always the protector of men of wit and genius; and has had those of the last century, Addison, Steele, Pope, Swift, Prior, &c. &c. always at his table. —The manner in which his notice began of me, was as singular as it was polite.— He came up to me, one day, as I was at the Princess of Wales's court. "I want to know you, Mr. Sterne; but it is fit you should know also, who it is that wishes this pleasure. You have heard, continued he, of an old Lord Bathurst, of whom your Popes and Swifts have sung and spoken so much. I have lived my life with geniuses of that cast; but have survived them; and despairing ever to find their equals, it is some years since I have closed my accounts, and shut up my books, with thoughts of never opening them again; but you have kindled a desire in me of opening them once more before . die; which I now do; so go home and dine with me."—This nobleman, I say, is a prodigy; for at eighty-five he has all the wit and promptness of a man of thirty,—a disposition to be pleased, and a power to please others beyond whatever I knew: added to which, a man of learning, courtesy, and feeling.

He heard me talk of thee, Eliza, with uncommon satisfaction;—for there was only a third person, and of sensibility, with us: —and a most sentimental afternoon, till nine o'clock, have we passed. But thou, Eliza, wert the star that conducted and enliven'd the discourse:—and when I talked not of thee, still didst thou fill my mind, and warmed every thought I uttered; for I am not ashamed to acknowledge, I greatly miss thee. — Best of all girls! the sufferings I have sustained the whole night on account of thine, Eliza, are beyond my power of words. — Assuredly does Heaven give strength proportioned to the weight he lays upon us! Thou hast been bowed down, my child, with every burden that sorrow of heart and pain of body could inflict upon a poor being; and still thou tellest me, thou art beginning to get ease; —thy fever gone, thy sickness, the pain in thy side vanishing also.—May every evil so vanish that thwarts Eliza's happiness, or but awakens thy fears for a moment!—Fear nothing, my dear! — hope every thing;— and the balm of this passion will shed its influence on thy health, and make thee enjoy a spring of youth and cheerfulness more than thou hast hardly yet tasted!

And so thou hast fixed thy Bramin's portrait over thy writing-desk; and wilt consult it in all doubts and difficulties.—Grateful and good girl! Yorick smiles contentedly over all thou dost: his picture does not do justice to his own complacency!

Thy sweet little plan and distribution of thy time, — how worthy of thee! Indeed, Eliza, thou leavest me nothing to direct thee in! thou leavest me nothing to require,— nothing to ask,—but a continuation of that conduct which won my esteem, and has made me thy friend for ever!

May the roses come quick back to thy cheeks, and the rubies to thy lips! But trust my declaration, Eliza, that thy husband (if he is the good feeling man I wish him) will press thee to him with more honest warmth and affection, and kiss thy pale, poor dejected face with more transport than he would be able to do in the best bloom of all thy beauty!—and so he ought, or I pity him. He must have strange feelings if he knows not the value of such a creature as thou art!

I am glad Miss Light* goes with you. She may relieve you from many anxious moments.—I am glad your ship-mates are friendly beings. You could least dispense with what is contrary to your own nature, —which is soft and gentle, Eliza.—It would

* Miss Light afterwards married George Stratton, Esq. late in the service of the East India Company at Madras. She is since dead.

civilize savages!—though pity were it thou should'st be tainted with the office! How canst thou make apologies for thy last letter? 'tis most delicious to me, for the very reason you excuse it. Write to me, my child, only such. Let them speak the easy carelessness of a heart that opens itself any how, and every how, to a man you ought to esteem and trust. Such, Eliza, I write to thee;—and so I should ever live with thee, most artlessly, most affectionately, if Providence permitted thy residence in the same section of the globe:—for I am, all that honor and affection can make me,

THY BRAMIN.

LETTER LXXXIII.

TO THE SAME.

I WRITE this, Eliza, at Mr. James's whilst he is dressing, and the dear girl, his wife, is writing beside me, to thee.—I got your melancholy billet before we sat down to dinner. 'Tis melancholy indeed, my dear, to hear so piteous an account of thy sickness! Thou art encountered with evils enow, without that additional weight! I fear it will sink thy poor soul, and body with it, past recovery:—Heaven supply thee with fortitude! We have talked of nothing but thee, Eliza, and of thy sweet virtues and endearing conduct, all the afternoon. Mrs. James and thy Bramin have mixed their tears a hundred times, in speaking of thy hardships, thy goodness, and thy graces.—The ****s, by heavens, are worthless! I have heard enough to tremble at the articulation of the name! How could you, Eliza, leave them (or suffer them to leave you rather) with impressions the least favorable? I have told thee enough to plant disgust against their treachery to thee, to the last hour of thy life! Yet still thou toldest Mrs. James at last, that thou believest they affectionately love thee.—Her delicacy to my Eliza, and true regard to her ease of mind, have saved thee from hearing more glaring proofs of their baseness. For God's sake, write not to them; nor foul thy fair character with such polluted hearts:—They love thee! what proof? Is it their actions that say so? or their zeal for those attachments, which do thee honor, and make thee happy? or their tenderness for thy fame? No; but they weep, and say tender things.—Adieu to all such for ever. Mrs. James's honest heart revolts against the idea of ever returning them one visit.—I honor her, and I honor thee, for almost every act of thy life, but this blind partiality for an unworthy being.

Forgive my zeal, dear girl, and allow me a right which arises only out of that fund of affection I have, and shall preserve for thee to the hour of my death! Reflect, Eliza, what are my motives for perpetually advising thee? think whether I can have any, but what proceed from the cause I have mentioned! I think you are a very deserving woman; and that you want nothing but firmness and a better opinion of yourself, to be the best female character I know. I wish I could inspire you with a share of that vanity your enemies lay to your charge (though to me it has never been visible) because I think, in a well-turned mind it will produce good effects.

I probably shall never see you more: yet I flatter myself, you'll sometimes think of me with pleasure! because you must be convinced I love you, and so interest myself in your rectitude, that I had rather hear of any evil befalling you, than your want of reverence for yourself. I had not power to keep this remonstrance in my breast.—It's now out; so adieu. Heaven watch over my Eliza!

Thine,

YORICK.

LETTER LXXXIV.

TO THE SAME.

To whom should Eliza apply in her distress, but to her friend who loves her? why then, my dear, do you apologize for employing me? Yorick would be offended, and with reason, if you ever sent commissions to another which he could execute. I have been with Zumps; and your piano-forte must be tuned from the brass middle string of your guitar, which is C.—I have got you a hammer too, and pair of pliers to twist your wire with; and may every one of them, my dear, vibrate sweet comfort to my hopes! I have bought you ten handsome brass screws, to hang your necessaries upon: I purchased twelve; but stole a couple from you to put up in my own cabin, at Coxwould: I shall never hang, nor take my hat off one of them, but I shall think of you. I have bought thee, moreover, a couple of iron screws, which are more to be depended on than brass, for the globes.

I have written also to Mr. Abraham Walker, pilot at Deal, that I had dispatched these in a packet directed to his care; which I desired he would seek after the moment the Deal machine arrived. I have, moreover, given him directions what sort of an arm-chair you would want, and have directed him to purchase the best that Deal could afford; and take it, with the parcel, in the first boat that went off. Would I could, Eliza, so supply all thy wants, and all thy wishes!—it would be a state of happiness to me.—The journal is as it should be, all but its contents. Poor, dear, patient being! I do more than pity you; for I think I lose both firmness and philosophy—as I figure to myself your distresses. Do not think I spoke last night with too much asperity of ****; there was cause; and besides, a good heart ought not to love a bad one; and, indeed, cannot. But, adieu to the ungrateful subject.

I have been this morning to see Mrs. James: she loves thee tenderly and unfeignedly. She is alarmed for thee:—she says thou looked'st most ill and melancholy on going away. She pities thee. I shall visit her every Sunday while I am in town.—As this may be my last letter, I earnestly bid thee farewell. May the God of kindness be kind to thee, and approve himself thy protector, now thou art defenceless! And, for thy daily comfort, bear in thy mind this truth, That whatever measure of sorrow and distress is thy portion, it will be repaid to thee in a full measure of happiness, by the Being thou hast wisely chosen for thy eternal friend.

Farewell, farewell, Eliza! Whilst I live, count upon me as the most warm and disinterested of earthly friends.

YORICK.

LETTER LXXXV.

TO THE SAME.

My Dearest Eliza,

I began a new journal this morning; you shall see it; for if I live not till your return to England, I will leave it you as a legacy. 'Tis a sorrowful page; but I will write cheerful ones; and could I write letters to thee, they should be cheerful ones too: but few, I fear, will reach thee! However, depend upon receiving something of the kind by every post; till then, thou wavest thy hand, and bid'st me write no more.

Tell me how you are; and what sort of fortitude Heaven inspires you with. How are you accommodated, my dear?—is all right? Scribble away, any thing and every thing to me. Depend upon seeing me at Deal, with the Jameses, should you be detained there by contrary winds.—Indeed, Eliza, I should with pleasure fly to you, could I be the means of rendering you any service, or doing you kindness. Gracious and merciful God! consider the anguish of a poor girl!—Strengthen and preserve her in all the shocks her frame must be exposed to! She is now without a protector, but thee! Save her from all accidents of a dangerous element, and give her comfort at the last!

My prayer, Eliza, I hope, is heard! for the sky seems to smile upon me, as I look up to it. I am just returned from our dear Mrs. James's, where I have been talking of thee for three hours.—She has got your picture, and likes it: but Marriot, and some other judges, agree that mine is the better, and expressive of a sweeter character.—But what is that to the original? yet I acknowledge that hers is a picture for the world, and mine is calculated only to please a very sincere friend, or sentimental philosopher. In the one, you are dressed in smiles, and with all the advantages of silks, pearls, and ermine;—in the other, simple as a vestal,—appearing the good girl Nature made you;—which, to me, conveys an idea of more unaffected sweetness than Mrs. Draper, habited for conquest in a birth-day suit, with her countenance animated, and her dimples visible. If I remember right, Eliza, you endeavored to collect every charm of your person into your face, with more than common care, the day you sat for Mrs. James. — Your color, too, brightened; and your eyes shone with more than usual brilliancy. I then requested you to come simple and unadorned when you sat for me; — knowing (as I see with unprejudiced eyes) that you could receive no addition from the silk-worm's aid, or jeweller's polish. Let me now tell you a truth, which I believe I have uttered before.—When I first saw you, I beheld you as an object of compassion, and as a very plain woman. The mode of your dress (though fashionable) disfigured you. —But nothing now could render you such, but the being solicitous to make yourself admired as a handsome one.—You are not handsome, Eliza, nor is yours a face that will please the tenth part of your beholders,—but are something more; for I scruple not to tell you, I never saw so intelligent, so animated, so good a countenance; nor ever was there, nor ever will be, that man of sense, tenderness, and feeling, in your company three hours, that was not, or will not be, your admirer or friend, in consequence of it; that is, if you assume, or assumed, no character foreign to your own, but appeared the artless being Nature designed you for. A something in your eyes and voice, you possess in a degree more persuasive than any woman I ever saw, read, or heard of. But it is that bewitching sort of nameless excellence, that men of nice sensibility alone can be touched with.

Were your husband in England, I would freely give him five hundred pounds, if money could purchase the acquisition, to let you only sit by me two hours in a day, while I wrote my Sentimental Journey. I am sure the work would sell so much the better for it, that I should be reimbursed the sum more than seven times told. — I would not give nine-pence for the picture of you the Newnhams have got executed: —it is the resemblance of a conceited, made-up coquette. Your eyes, and the shape of your face (the latter the most perfect oval I ever saw) which are perfections that must strike the most indifferent judge, because they are equal to any of God's works in a similar way, and finer than any I beheld in all my travels, are manifestly injured by the affected leer of the one, and strange appearance of the other; owing to the attitude of the head, which is a proof of the artist's or your friend's false taste. The ****s, who verify the character I once gave of teasing, or sticking like pitch or bird-lime, sent a card that they would wait on Mrs. **** on Friday. — She sent back she was engaged.—Then to meet at Ranelagh to-night.—She answered, she did not go.—She says, if she allows the least footing, she never shall get rid of the acquaintance; which she is resolved to drop at once. She knows them:—she knows they are not her friends, nor yours;—and the first use they would make of being with her, would be to sacrifice you to her, if they could, a second time. Let her not then; let her not, my dear, be a greater friend to thee than thou art to thyself. She begs I will reiterate my request to you, that you will not write to them. It will give her, and thy Bramin, inexpressible pain. Be assured, all this is not without reason on her side. I have my reasons too; the first of which is, that I should grieve to excess, if Eliza wanted that fortitude her Yorick has built so high upon. I said I never more would mention the name to thee; and had I not received it as a kind of charge from a dear woman that loves you, I should not have broke my word. I will write again to-morrow to thee, thou best and most endearing of girls! A peaceful night to thee.—My spirit will be with thee through every watch of it.—Adieu.

LETTER LXXXVI.

TO THE SAME.

I THINK you could act no otherwise than you did with the young soldier. There was no shutting the door against him either in politeness or humanity. Thou tellest me he seems susceptible of tender impressions; and that before Miss Light has sailed a fortnight, he will be in love with her.—Now I think it a thousand times more likely that he attaches himself to thee Eliza; because thou art a thousand times more amiable. Five months with Eliza,—and in the same room,—and an amorous son of Mars besides!—"*It can no be, Mas-*"*ser.*"—The sun, if he could avoid it, would not shine upon a dunghill; but his rays are so pure, Eliza, and celestial,—I never heard that they were polluted by it.—Just such will thine be, dearest child, in this, and every such situation you will be exposed to, till thou art fixed for life.—But thy discretion, thy wisdom, thy honor, the spirit of thy Yorick, and thy own spirit, which is equal to it, will be thy ablest counsellors.

Surely, by this time, something is doing for thy accommodation.—But why may not clean washing and rubbing do instead of painting your cabin, as it is to be hung? Paint is so pernicious, both to your nerves and lungs, and will keep you so much longer, too, out of your apartment; where, I hope, you will pass some of your happiest hours.

I fear the best of your ship-mates are only genteel by comparison with the contrasted crew, with which thou must behold them. So was—you know who!—from the same fallacy that was put upon the judgment, when—but I will not mortify you. If they are decent and distant, it is enough; and as much as is to be expected. If any of them are more, I rejoice;—thou wilt want every aid; and 'tis thy due to have them. Be cautious only, my dear, of intimacies. Good hearts are open, and fall naturally into them. Heaven inspire thine with fortitude in this, and every deadly trial. Best of God's works, farewell! Love me, I beseech thee; and remember me for ever!

I am, my Eliza, and will ever be, in the most comprehensive sense,

Thy friend,

YORICK.

P. S. Probably you will have an opportunity of writing to me by some Dutch or French ship, or from the Cape de Verd Islands.—It will reach me somehow.

LETTER LXXXVII.

TO THE SAME.

My Dear Eliza,

Oh! I grieve for your cabin:—and the resh painting will be enough to destroy every nerve about thee. Nothing so pernicious as white lead. Take care of yourself, dear girl; and sleep not in it too soon: it will be enough to give you a stroke of an epilepsy. I hope you will have left the ship; and that my letters may meet and greet you, as you get out of your post-chaise, at Deal. When you have got them all, put them, my dear, into some order.—The first eight or nine are numbered; but I wrote the rest without that direction to thee; but thou wilt find them out by the day or hour, which, I hope, I have generally prefixed to them. When they are got together, in chronological order, sew them together under a cover. I trust they will be a perpetual refuge to thee, from time to time; and that thou wilt (when weary of fools and uninteresting discourse) retire and converse an hour with them and me.

I have not had power, or the heart, to aim at enlivening any one of them with a single stroke of wit or humor; but they contain something better: and what you will feel more suited to your situation;—a long detail of much advice, truth, and knowledge. I hope, too, you will perceive loose touches of an honest heart in every one of them; which speaks more than the most studied periods; and will give thee more ground of trust and reliance upon Yorick, than all that labored eloquence could supply. Lean then thy whole weight, Eliza, upon them and upon me. "May poverty, distress, an-"guish, and shame, be my portion, if ever "I give thee reason to repent the know-"ledge of me!"—With this asseveration, made in the presence of a just God, I pray to him, that so it may speed with me, as I deal candidly and honorably with thee! I would not mislead thee, Eliza: I would not injure thee, in the opinion of a single individual, for the richest crown the proudest monarch wears.

Remember, that while I have life and power, whatever is mine, you may style and think yours,—though sorry should I be, if ever my friendship was put to the test thus, for your own delicacy's sake.—Money and counters are of equal use, in my opinion; they both serve to set up with.

I hope you will answer me this letter. but if thou art debarred by the elements, which hurry thee away, I will write one for thee; and knowing it is such a one as thou would'st have written, I will regard it as my Eliza's.

Honor, and happiness, and health, and comforts of every kind, sail along with thee, thou most worthy of girls! I will live for thee, and my Lydia;—be rich for the dear children of my heart;—gain wisdom, gain fame, and happiness, to share with them,—with thee,—and her, in my old age.—Once for all, adieu.—Preserve thy life; steadily pursue the ends we proposed; and let nothing rob thee of those powers Heaven has given thee for thy well-being.

What can I add more, in the agitation of mind I am in, and within five minutes of the last postman's bell, but recommend thee to Heaven, and recommend myself to Heaven with thee, in the same fervent ejaculation, "That we may be happy, and meet "again; if not in this world, in the next." —Adieu.—I am thine, Eliza, affectionately and everlastingly,

YORICK.

LETTER LXXXVIII.

TO THE SAME.

I wish to God, Eliza, it was possible to postpone the voyage to India for another year;—for I am firmly persuaded within my own heart, that thy husband could never limit thee with regard to time.

I fear that Mr. B—— has exaggerated matters.—I like not his countenance. It is absolutely killing.—Should evil befall thee, what will he not have to answer for? I know not the being that will be deserving of so much pity, or that I shall hate more. He will be an outcast, alien,—in which case I will be a father to thy children, my good girl!—therefore take no thought about them.—

But, Eliza, if thou art so very ill, still put off all thoughts of returning to India this year.—Write to your husband:—tell him the truth of your case.—If he is the generous, humane man you describe him to be, he cannot but applaud your conduct.—I am credibly informed, that his repugnance to your living in England arises only from the dread, which has entered his brain, that thou mayest run him in debt beyond thy appointments, and that he must discharge them.—That such a creature should be sacrificed for the paltry consideration of a few hundreds, is too, too hard! Oh! my child! that I could, with propriety, indemnify him for every charge, even to the last mite, that thou hast been of to him! With joy would I give him my whole subsistence;—nay, sequester my livings, and trust the treasures Heaven has furnished my head with, for a future subsistence.

You owe much, I allow, to your husband,—you owe something to appearances, and the opinion of the world; but, trust me, my dear, you owe much likewise to yourself.——Return therefore from Deal, if you continue ill.—I will prescribe for you, gratis.—You are not the first woman, by many, I have done so for, with success.—I will send for my wife and daughter, and they shall carry you in pursuit of health, to Montpellier, the wells of Bançois, the Spa, or whither thou wilt. Thou shalt direct them, and make parties of pleasure in what corner of the world fancy points out to thee. We shall fish upon the banks of Arno, and lose ourselves in the sweet labyrinths of its valleys.—And then thou should'st warble to us, as I have once or twice heard thee,—"I'm lost, I'm lost!"—but we should find thee again, my Eliza.—Of a similar nature to this was you physician's prescription:—"Use gentle exercise, the pure southern air "of France, or milder Naples, with the so-"ciety of friendly, gentle beings." Sensible man! He certainly entered into your feelings. He knew the fallacy of medicine to a creature whose illness has arisen from the affliction of her mind. Time only, my dear, I fear you must trust to, and have your reliance on; may it give you the health so enthusiastic a votary to the charming goddess deserves!

I honor you, Eliza, for keeping secret some things, which, if explained, had been a panegyric on yourself. There is a dignity in venerable affliction which will not allow it to appeal to the world, for pity or redress Well have you supported that character, my amiable, philosophic friend! And, indeed, I begin to think you have as many virtues as my uncle Toby's Widow.—I don't mean to insinuate, hussy, that my opinion is no better founded than his was of Mrs. Wadman; nor do I conceive it possible for any Trim to convince me it is equally fallacious.—I am sure, while I have my reason, it is not.—Talking of widows:—Pray, Eliza, if ever you are such, do not think of giving yourself to some wealthy nabob,—because I design to marry you myself.—My wife cannot live long,—she has sold all the provinces in France already;—and I know not the woman I should like so well for her substitute as yourself. — 'Tis true, I am ninety-five in constitution, and you but twenty-five;—rather too great a disparity this!—but what I want in youth, I will make up in wit and good-humor. — Not Swift so loved his Stella, Scarron his Maintenon, or Waller his Sacharissa, as I will love and sing thee, my wife elect! All those names, eminent as they were, shall give place to thine, Eliza. Tell me, in answer to this, that you approve and honor the proposal, and that you would (like the Spectator's mistress) have more joy in putting on an old man's slipper, than associating with the gay, the voluptuous, and the young.—

—Adieu, my Simplicia!

Yours,

TRISTRAM.

LETTER LXXXIX.

TO THE SAME.

My Dear Eliza,

I have been within the verge of the gates of death.—I was ill the last time I wrote to you, and apprehensive of what would be the consequence.—My fears were but too well founded; for, in ten minutes after I dispatched my letter, this poor, fine-spun frame of Yorick's gave way, and I broke a vessel in my breast, and could not stop the loss of blood till four this morning. I have filled all thy India handkerchiefs with it. — It came, I think, from my heart; I fell asleep through weakness. At six I awoke, with the bosom of my shirt steeped in tears. I dreamt I was sitting under the canopy of Indolence, and that thou camest into the room with a shawl in thy hand, and told me, my spirit had flown to thee in the Downs, with tidings of my fate; and that you were come to administer what consolation filial affection could bestow, and to receive my parting breath and blessing. — With that you folded the shawl about my waist, and, kneeling, supplicated my attention. I awoke; but in what a frame! Oh! my God! "But "thou wilt number my tears, and put them "all into thy bottle." — Dear girl! I see thee; — thou art for ever present to my fancy, — embracing my feeble knees, and raising thy fine eyes to bid me be of comfort: and, when I talk to Lydia, the words of Esau, as uttered by thee, perpetually ring in my ears. — "Bless *me* even also, "my father!"—Blessings attend thee, thou child of my heart!

My bleeding is quite stopped, and I feel the principle of life strong within me; so be not alarmed, Eliza;—I know I shall do well. I have eat my breakfast with hunger; and I write to thee with a pleasure arising from that prophetic impression in my imagination, that "all will terminate to our "hearts' contents." Comfort thyself eternally with this persuasion,—"That the best "of Beings (as thou hast sweetly expressed it) "could not, by a combination of acci-"dents, produce such a chain of events, "merely to be the source of misery to the "leading person engaged in them."—The observation was very applicable, very good, and very elegantly expressed. I wish my memory did justice to the wording of it.—Who taught you the art of writing so sweetly, Eliza? — You have absolutely exalted it to a science.—When I am in want of ready cash, and ill-health will not permit my genius to exert itself, I shall print your letters, as finished essays, "by an un-"fortunate Indian Lady." The style is new; and would almost be a sufficient recommendation for their selling well, without merit;—but their sense, natural ease, and spirit, is not to be equalled, I believe, in this section of the globe; nor, I will answer for it, by any of your countrywomen in yours.—I have shown your letter to Mrs. B——, and to half the *literati* in town.—You shall not be angry with me for it, because I meant to do you honor by it.—You cannot imagine how many admirers your epistolary productions have gained you, that never viewed your external merits. I only wonder where thou could'st acquire thy graces, thy goodness, thy accomplishments, —so connected! so educated! Nature has surely studied to make thee her peculiar care;—for thou art (and not in my eyes alone) the best and fairest of all her works.

And so this is the last letter thou art to receive from me; because the Earl of Chatham* (I read in the papers) is got to the Downs; and the wind, I find, is fair. If so, —blessed woman! take my last, last farewell!—Cherish the remembrance of me; think how I esteem, nay, how affectionately I love thee, and what a price I set upon thee! Adieu, adieu! and with my adieu, let me give thee one straight rule of conduct, that thou hast heard from my lips in a thousand forms,—but I concentre it in one word,

REVERENCE THYSELF.

Adieu once more, Eliza! May no anguish of heart plant a wrinkle upon thy face, till I behold it again! May no doubt or misgivings disturb the serenity of thy mind, or awaken a painful thought about thy children;—for they are Yorick's,—and Yorick is thy friend for ever!—Adieu, adieu, adieu!

P. S. Remember that Hope shortens all journeys, by sweetening them;—so sing my little stanza on the subject, with the devotion of an hymn, every morning when thou arisest, and thou wilt eat thy breakfast with more comfort for it.

Blessings rest, and Hygeia go with thee! —May'st thou soon return, in peace and affluence, to illume my night! I am, and shall be, the last to deplore thy loss, and will be the first to congratulate and hail thy return.

Fare thee well.

LETTER XC.

TO MISS STERNE.

Bond-street, April 9, 1767.

THIS letter, my dear Lydia, will distress thy good heart; for, from the beginning, thou wilt perceive no entertaining strokes of humor in it.—I cannot be cheerful when a thousand melancholy ideas surround me. —I have met with a loss of near fifty pounds, which I was taken in for, in an extraordinary manner:—but what is that loss in comparison of one I may experience? —Friendship is the balm and cordial of life, and, without it, 'tis a heavy load not worth sustaining.—I am unhappy,—thy mother and thyself at a distance from me; and what can compensate for such destitution?—For God's sake, persuade her to come and fix in England, for life is too short to waste in separation; and, whilst she lives in one country, and I in another, many people will suppose it proceeds from choice;—besides, I want thee near me, thou child and darling of my heart!—I am in a melancholy mood, and my Lydia's eyes will smart with weeping, when I tell her the cause that now affects me.—I am apprehensive the dear friend I mentioned in my last letter is going into a decline.—I was with her a few days ago, and I never beheld a being so altered; —she has a tender frame, and looks like a drooping lily, for the roses are fled from her cheeks.—I can never see or talk to this incomparable woman without bursting into tears.—I have a thousand obligations to her, and I owe her more than her whole sex, if not all the world put together.—She has a delicacy in her way of thinking that few possess.—Our conversations are of the most interesting nature; and she talks to me of quitting this world with more composure than others think of living in it.—I have wrote an epitaph, of which I send thee a copy;—'tis expressive of her modest worth; —but may Heaven restore her;—and may she live to write mine!

Columns and labor'd urns but vainly show
An idle scene of decorated woe.
The sweet companion, and the friend sincere,
Need no mechanic help to force the tear.
In heartfelt numbers, never meant to shine,
'Twill flow eternal o'er a hearse like thine
'Twill flow whilst gentle goodness has one friend,
Or kindred tempers have a tear to lend.

Say all that is kind of me to thy mother, and believe me, my Lydia, that I love thee most truly.—So adieu.—I am what I ever was, and hope ever shall be,

Thy affectionate Father,

L. STERNE.

* By the newspapers of the times, it appears that the Earl of Chatham East Indiaman sailed from Deal April 3, 1767.

As tc Mr. M——, by your description he is a fat fool. I beg you will not give up your time to such a being.—Send me some *batons pour les dents;*—there are none good here.

LETTER XCI.

TO LADY P——.

Mount Coffee-house, Tuesday, 3 o'clock.

THERE is a strange mechanical effect produced in writing a *billet-doux* within a stone-cast of the Lady who engrosses the heart and soul of an *enamorato;*—for this cause (but mostly because I am to dine in this neighborhood) have I, Tristram Shandy, come forth from my lodgings to a coffee-house, the nearest I could find to my dear Lady ——'s house, and have called for a sheet of gilt paper, to try the truth of this article of my creed.—Now for it.

O my dear Lady, what a dish-clout of a soul hast thou made of me!—I think, by the bye, this is a little too familiar an introduction for so unfamiliar a situation as I stand in with yon,—where, Heaven knows, I am kept at a distance,—and despair of getting one inch nearer you, with all the steps and windings I can think of to recommend myself to you.—Would not any man in his senses run diametrically from you,—and as far as his legs would carry him, rather than thus causelessly, foolishly, and fool-hardily expose himself afresh,—and afresh, where his heart and his reason tell him he shall be sure to come off loser, if not totally undone?—Why should you tell me you would be glad to see me?—Does it give you pleasure to make me more unhappy?—or does it add to your triumph, that your eyes and lips have turned a man into a fool, whom the rest of the town is courting as a wit?—I am a fool,—the weakest, the most ductile, the most tender fool,—that ever woman tried the weakness of;—and the most unsettled in my purposes and resolutions of recovering my right mind.—It is but an hour ago that I kneeled down and swore I never would come near you;—and, after saying my Lord's Prayer for the sake of the close, *of not being led into temptation*,—out I sallied like any Christian hero, ready to take the field against the world, the flesh, and the Devil; not doubting but I should finally trample them all down under my feet;—and now I am got so near you,—within this vile stone's cast of your house,—I feel myself drawn into a vortex, that has turned my brain upside downwards; and, though I had purchased a box-ticket to carry me to Miss *******'s benefit, yet I know very well, that was a single line directed to me to let me know Lady —— would be alone at seven, and suffer me to spend the evening with her, she would infallibly see every thing verified I have told her.—I dine at Mr. C——r's, in Wigmore-street, in this neighborhood, where I shall stay till seven, in hopes you purpose to put me to this proof. If I hear nothing by that time, shall conclude you are better disposed of,—and shall take a sorry hack, and sorrily jog on to the play.—Curse on the world! I know nothing but sorrow, except this one thing, that I love you (perhaps foolishly, but)

Most sincerely,

L. STERNE.

LETTER XCII.

TO MR. AND MRS. J——.

Old Bond-street, April 21, 1767.

I AM sincerely affected, my dear Mr. and Mrs. J——, by your friendly inquiry, and the interest you are so good to take in my health. God knows I am not able to give a good account myself, having passed a bad night in much feverish agitation.—My physician ordered me to bed, and to keep therein till some favorable change.—I fell ill the moment I got to my lodgings:—he says it is owing to my taking James's Powder, and venturing out on so cold a day as Sunday;—but he is mistaken, for I am certain whatever bears the name must have efficacy with me.—I was bled yesterday, and again to-day, and have been almost dead; but this friendly inquiry from Gerrard-street has poured balm into what blood I have left.—I hope still, and (next to the sense of what I owe my friends) it shall be the last pleasurable sensation I will part with;—if I continue mending, it will yet be some time before I shall have strength enough to get out in a carriage.—My first visit will be a visit of true gratitude.—I leave my kind friends to guess where.—A thousand blessings go along with this; and may Heaven preserve you both!—Adieu, my dear Sir, and dear Lady.

I am your ever obliged,

L. STERNE.

LETTER XCIII.

TO IGNATIUS SANCHO.

Bond-street, Saturday, [April 25, 1767.]

I WAS very sorry, my good Sancho, that I was not at home, to return my compliments by you for the great courtesy of the Duke of M—g—'s family to me, in honoring my list of subscribers with their names;—for which I bear them all thanks.—But you have something to add, Sancho, to what I owe your good-will also on this account, and that is to send me the subscription-money, which I find a necessity of dunning my best friends for before I leave town,—to avoid the perplexities of both keeping pecuniary accounts (for which I have very slender talents) and collecting them (for which I have neither strength of body or mind;) and so, good Sancho, dun the Duke of M——, the Duchess of M——, and Lord M——, for their subscriptions; and lay the sin, and money with it too, at my door.—I wish so good a family every blessing they merit, along with my humblest compliments. You know, Sancho, that I am your friend and well-wisher,

L. STERNE.

P. S. I leave town on Friday morning,—and should on Thursday, but that I stay to dine with Lord and Lady S——.

LETTER XCIV.

TO THE EARL OF S——.

Old Bond-street. May 1, 1767.

MY LORD,

I WAS yesterday taking leave of all the town, with an intention of leaving it this day: but I am detained by the kindness of Lord and Lady S——, who have made a party to dine and sup, on my account.—I am impatient to set out for my solitude, for there the mind gains strength, and learns to lean upon herself.—In the world it seeks or accepts of a few treacherous supports;—the feigned compassion of one,—the flattery of a second,—the civilities of a third,—the friendship of a fourth,—they all deceive, and bring the mind back to where mine is retreating, to retirement, reflection, and books. My departure is fixed for to-morrow morning; but I could not think of quitting a place where I have received such numberless and unmerited civilities from your Lordship, without returning my most grateful thanks, as well as my hearty acknowledgments for your friendly inquiry from Bath. Illness, my Lord, has occasioned my silence.—Death knocked at my door, but I would not admit him;—the call was both unexpected and unpleasant;—and I am seriously worn down to a shadow,—and still very weak:—but, weak as I am, I have as whimsical a story to tell you as ever befell one of my family;—Shandy's nose, his name, his sash-window, are fools to it;—it will serve at least to amuse you.—The injury I did myself last month in catching cold upon James's powder,—fell, you must know, upon the worst part it could,—the most painful and most dangerous of any in the human body. It was on this crisis I called in an able surgeon, and with him an able physician (both my friends) to inspect my disaster.—'Tis a venereal case, cried my two scientific friends.—'Tis impossible, however, to be that, replied I;—for I have had no commerce whatever with the sex,—not even with my wife, added I, these fifteen years.—You are, however, my good friend, said the surgeon, or there is no such case in the world.—What the Devil, said I, without knowing woman?—We will not reason about it, said the physician, but you must undergo a course of mercury.—I will lose my life first, said I: and trust to nature, to time, or, at the worst, to death.—So I put an end, with some indignation, to the conference,—and determined to bear all the torments I underwent, and ten times more, rather than submit to be treated like a *sinner*, in a point where I had acted like a *saint*.—Now as the father of mischief would have it, who has no pleasure like that of dishonoring the righteous, it so fell out that from the moment I dismissed my doctors, my pains began to rage with a violence not to be expressed, or supported. Every hour became more intolerable.—I was got to bed, cried out, and raved the whole night, and was got up so near dead, that my friends insisted upon my sending again for my physician and surgeon. I told them, upon the word of a man of honor, they were both mistaken as to my case;—but, though they had reasoned wrong, they might act right: but that, sharp as my sufferings were, I felt them not so sharp as the imputation which a venereal treatment of my case laid me under.—They answered, that these taints of the blood lie dormant twenty years; but they would not reason with me in a point wherein I was so delicate, but would do all the offices for which they were called in, namely to put an end to my torment, which otherwise would put an end to me;—and so I have been compelled to surrender myself: —and thus, my dear Lord, has your poor friend, with all his sensibilities, been suffering the chastisement of the grossest sensualist!—Was it not as ridiculous an embarrassment as ever Yorick's spirit was involved in?—Nothing but the purest conscience of innocence could have tempted me to write this story to my wife, which, by the bye, would make no bad anecdote in Tristram Shandy's Life.—I have mentioned it in my journal to Mrs. ——. In some respects, there is no difference between my wife and herself:—when they fare alike, neither can reasonably complain.—I have just received letters from France, with some hints that Mrs. Sterne and my Lydia are coming to England, to pay me a visit.—If your time is not better employed, Yorick flatters himself he shall receive a letter from your Lordship, *en attendant*.—I am, with the greatest regard, my Lord,

Your Lordship's

Most faithful humble servant,

L. STERNE.

LETTER XCV.

TO J—— D——N, ESQ.

Old Bond-street, Friday morning.

I WAS going, my dear D——n, to bed before I received your kind inquiry; and now my chaise stands at my door, to take and convey this poor body to its legal settlement. —I am ill, very ill;—I languish most affectingly.—I am sick both soul and body.—It is a cordial to me to hear it is different with you;—no man interests himself more in your happiness; and I am glad you are in so fair a road to it:—enjoy it long, my D——; whilst I—no matter what,—but my feelings are too nice for the world I live in:—things will mend.—I dined yesterday with Lord and Lady S——: we talked much of you and your goings on; for every one knows why Sunbury Hill is so pleasant a situation! —You rogue! you have lock'd up my boots, —and I go bootless home:—and I fear I shall go bootless all my life.—Adieu, gentlest and best of souls,—adieu.

I am yours, most affectionately,

L. STERNE.

LETTER XCVI.

TO J—— H—— S——, ESQ.

Newark, Monday,
Ten o'clock in the morn

MY DEAR COUSIN,

I HAVE got conveyed thus far, like a bale of cadaverous goods, consigned to Pluto and company,—lying in the bottom of my chaise most of the route, upon a large pillow, which I had the *prevoyance* to purchase before I set out.—I am worn out;—but press on to Barnby Moor to-night, and, if possible, to York the next.—I know not what is the matter with me,—but some *derangement* presses hard upon this machine:—still, I think, it will not be overset this bout.—My love to G——. We shall all meet from the east, and from the south, and (as at the last) be happy together. My kind respects to a few.—I am, dear H——,

Truly yours,

L. STERNE.

LETTER XCVII.

TO A. L——E, ESQ.

Coxwould, June 7, 1767.

DEAR L——E,

I HAD not been many days at this peaceful cottage before your letter greeted me with the seal of friendship: and most cordially do I thank you for so kind a proof of your good-will. I was truly anxious to hear of the recovery of my sentimental friend,—but I would not write to inquire after her, unless I could have sent her the testimony without the tax; even how d'yes to invalids, or those that have lately been so, either call to mind what is past or what may return; at least I find it so. I am as happy as a prince, at Coxwould; and I wish you could see in how princely a manner I live: 'tis a land of plenty. I sit down alone to venison, fish, and wild fowl, or a couple of fowls or ducks, with curds, and strawberries, and cream, and all the simple plenty which a rich valley (under Hamilton Hills) can produce; with a clean cloth on my table, and a bottle of wine on my right hand to drink your health. I have a hundred hens and chickens about my yard, and not a parishioner catches a hare, or a rabbit, or a trout, but he brings it as an offering to me. If solitude would cure a love-sick heart, I would give you an invitation; but absence and time lessen no attachment which virtue inspires. I am in high spirits; care never enters this cottage. —I take the air every day in my post-chaise, with two long-tailed horses,—they turn out good ones; and as to myself, I think I am better upon the whole for the medicines and regimen I submitted to in town.—May you, dear L——, want neither the one nor the other!

Yours, truly,

L. STERNE.

LETTER XCVIII.

TO THE SAME.

Coxwould, June 30, 1767.

I AM in still better health, my dear L——e, than when I wrote last to you, owing I believe to my riding out every day with my friend H——, whose castle lies near the sea; and there is a beach as even as a mirror, of five miles in length, before it, where we daily run races in our chaises, with one wheel in the sea, and the other on land. D—— has obtained his fair Indian, and has this post sent a letter of inquiries after Yorick and his Bramin. He is a good soul, and interests himself much in our fate.—I cannot forgive you, L——e, for your folly in saying you intend to get introduced to the ——. I despise them; and I shall hold your understanding much cheaper than I now do, if you persist in a resolution so unworthy of you.—I suppose Mrs. J—— telling you they were sensible, is the groundwork you go upon. By —— they are not clever; though what is commonly called wit, may pass for literature on the other side of Temple-Bar.—You say Mrs. J—— thinks them amiable:—she judges too favorably: but I have put a stop to her intentions of visiting them. They are bitter enemies of mine; and I am even with them. La Bramine assured me they used their endeavors with her to break off her friendship with me, for reasons I will not write, but tell you.—I said enough of them before she left England; and though she yielded to me in every other point, yet in this she obstinately persisted.—Strange infatuation!—but I think I have effected my purpose by a falsity, which Yorick's friendship to the Bramine can only justify. —I wrote her word that the most amiable of women reiterated my request, that she would not write to them. I said, too, she had concealed many things for the sake of her peace of mind, when, in fact, L——, this was merely a child of my own brain, made Mrs. J——'s by adoption, to enforce the argument I had before urged so strongly. —Do not mention this circumstance to Mrs. J——; 'twould displease her; and I had no design in it but for the Bramine to be a friend to herself.—I ought now to be busy from sun-rise to sun-set, for I have a book to write,—a wife to receive,—an estate to sell,—a parish to superintend,—and, what is worst of all, a disquieted heart to reason with: these are continual calls upon me.—I have received half a dozen letters to press me to join my friends at Scarborough, but I am at present deaf to them all. I perhaps may pass a few days there something later in the season, not at present;—and so, dear L——, adieu.

I am most cordially yours,

L. STERNE

LETTER XCIX.

TO IGNATIUS SANCHO.

Coxwould, June 30, 1767.

I MUST acknowledge the courtesy of my good friend Sancho's letter, were I ten times busier than I am; and must thank him too for the many expressions of his good-will and good opinion:—'tis all affectation to say a man is not gratified with being praised; we only want it to be sincere: and then it will be taken, Sancho, as kindly as yours. I left town very poorly, and with an idea I was taking leave of it for ever; but good air, a quiet retreat, and quiet reflections along with it, with an ass to milk, and another to ride upon (if I choose it), all together do wonders. I shall live this year at least, I hope, be it but to give the world, before I quit it, as good impressions of me, as you have, Sancho. I would only covenant for just so much health and spirits as are sufficient to carry my pen through the task I have set it this summer. But I am a resigned being, Sancho, and take health and sickness as I do light and darkness, or the vicissitudes of seasons; that is, just as it pleases God to send them, and accommodate myself to their periodical returns as well as I can; only taking care, whatever befalls me in this silly world, not to lose my temper at it. This I believe, friend Sancho, to be the truest philosophy; for this we must be indebted to ourselves, but not to our fortunes. Farewell.—I hope you will not forget your custom of giving me a call at my lodgings next winter. In the mean time, I am, very cordially,

My honest friend Sancho,

Yours,

L. STERNE.

LETTER C.

TO MR. AND MRS. J——.

Coxwould, July 6, 1767.

IT is with as much true gratitude as ever heart felt, that I sit down to thank my dear friends, Mr. and Mrs. J——, for the continuation of their attention to me; but for this last instance of their humanity and politeness to me, I must ever be their debtor. I never can thank you enough, my dear friends, and yet I thank you from my soul; and for the single day's happiness your goodness would have sent me, I wish I could send you back thousands:—I cannot, but they will come of themselves; and so God bless you.—I have had twenty times my pen in my hand since I came down, to write a letter to you both in Gerrard-street; but I am a shy kind of a soul at the bottom, and have a jealousy about troubling my friends,—especially about myself. I am now got perfectly well; but was, a month after my arrival in the country, in but a poor state: my body has got the start, and is at present more at ease than my mind;—but this world is a school of trials, and so Heaven's will be done!—I hope that you have enjoyed all that I have wanted; and to complete your joy, that your little lady flourishes like a vine at your table; to which I hope to see her preferred by next winter.—I am now beginning to be truly busy at my Sentimental Journey;—the pains and sorrows of this life having retarded its progress; but I shall make up my lee-way, and overtake every body in a very short time.

What can I send you that Yorkshire produces? Tell me; I want to be of use to you, for I am, my dear friends, with the truest value and esteem,

Your ever obliged

L. STERNE.

LETTER CI.

TO MR. PANCHAUD, AT PARIS.

York, July 20, 1767.

MY DEAR PANCHAUD,

BE so kind as to forward what letters are arrived for Mrs. Sterne, at your office, by to-day's post, or the next; and she will receive them before she quits Avignon, for England. She wants to lay out a little money in an annuity for her daughter:—advise her to get her life insured in London, lest my Lydia should die before her.—If there are any packets, send them with the ninth volume* of Shandy; which she has

* Alluding to the first edition.

failed of getting. She says, she has drawn for fifty Louis. When she leaves Paris, send by her my account.—Have you got me any French subscriptions? or subscriptions in France?—Present my kindest service to Miss P. I know, her politeness and good-nature will incline her to give Mrs. J. her advice about what she may venture to bring over. — I hope every thing goes on well, though never half so well as I wish.—God prosper you, my dear friend!—Believe me most warmly

Yours,

L. STERNE.

The sooner you send me the gold snuff-box, the better: — 'tis a present from my best friend.

LETTER CII.

TO MR. AND MRS. J.

Coxwould, Aug. 2, 1767.

My dear friends, Mr. and Mrs. J—, are infinitely kind to me, in sending now and then a letter to inquire after me; and to acquaint me how they are. — You cannot conceive, my dear Lady, how truly I bear a part in your illness.—I wish Mr. J— would carry you to the south of France, in pursuit of health:—but why need I wish it, when I know his affection will make him do that and ten times as much, to prevent a return of those symptoms which alarmed him so much in the spring?—Your politeness and humanity are always contriving to treat me agreeably; and what you promise next winter, will be perfectly so:—but you must get well; and your little dear girl must be of the party, with her parents and friends, to give it a relish.—I am sure you show no partiality but what is natural and praiseworthy, in behalf of your daughter; but I wonder my friends will not find her a play-fellow: and I both hope and advise them not to venture along, through this warfare of life, without two strings at least to their bow.—I had letters from France by last night's post; by which (by some fatality) I find not one of my letters has reached Mrs. Sterne. This gives me concern, as it wears the aspect of unkindness, which she by no means merits from me.—My wife and dear girl are coming to pay me a visit for a few months:—I wish I may prevail with them to tarry longer.—You must permit me, dear Mrs. J., to make my Lydia known to you, if I can prevail with my wife to come and spend a little time in London, as she returns to France. I expect a small parcel: — may I trouble you, before you write next, to send to my lodgings to ask if there is any thing directed to me that you can inclose under cover?—I have but one excuse for this freedom, which I am prompted to use, from a persuasion that it is doing you pleasure to give you an opportunity of doing an obliging thing;—and, as to myself, I rest satisfied; for 'tis only scoring up another debt of thanks to the millions I owe you both already.—Receive a thousand and a thousand thanks! yes, and with them ten thousand friendly wishes for all you wish in this world!—May my friend Mr. J. continue blessed with good health! and may his good Lady get perfectly well! there being no woman's health or comfort I so ardently pray for.—Adieu, my dear friends. — Believe me most truly and faithfully yours,

L. STERNE.

P. S. In Eliza's last letter, dated from St. Jago, she tells me, as she does you, that she is extremely ill. — God protect her! — By this time surely she has set foot upon dry land at Madras.—I heartily wish her well; and if Yorick was with her, he would tell her so;—but he is cut off from this by bodily absence:—I am present with her in spirit, however—but what is that? you will say.

LETTER CIII.

TO J—— H—— S——, ESQ.

Coxwould, August 11, 1767.

My Dear H.

I am glad all has passed with so much amity, *inter te et filium Marcun tuum*, and that Madame has found grace in thy sight.—All is well that ends well;—and so much for moralizing upon it. I wish you could or would take up your parable, and prophesy as much good concerning me and my affairs.—Not one of my letters has got to Mrs. Sterne since the notification of ne-

intentions; which has a pitiful air on my side, though I have wrote her six or seven. —I imagine she will be here the latter end of September; though I have no date for it but her impatience;—which, having suffered by my supposed silence, I am persuaded will make her fear the worst;—if that is the case, she will fly to England:—a most natural conclusion.—You did well to discontinue all commerce with James's powders,—as you are so well; rejoice, therefore, and let your heart be merry; mine ought upon the same score;—for I never have been so well since I left college; and should be a marvellous happy man, but for some reflections which bow down my spirits; but if I live but even three or four years, I will acquit myself with honor; and, no matter, we will talk this over when we meet.—If all ends as temperately as with you, and that I find grace, &c. &c., I will come and sing *Te Deum*, or drink *poculum elevatum*, or do any thing with you in the world.—I should depend upon G—'s critic upon my head, as much as Moliere's old woman upon his comedies. When you do not want her society, let it be carried into your bed-chamber to flay her, or clap it upon her bum, —to ——, and give her my blessing as you do it.

My postilion has set me aground for a week, by one of my pistols bursting in his hand; which he taking for granted to be quite shot off,—he instantly fell upon his knees, and said (Our Father, which art in Heaven, hallowed be thy Name); at which like a good Christian he stopped, not remembering any more of it. The affair was not so bad as he at first thought; for it has only *bursten* two of his fingers, he says.—I long to return to you; but I sit here alone as solitary and sad as a Tom-cat; which, by the bye, is all the company I keep:—he follows me from the parlor to the kitchen, into the garden, and every place. I wish I had a dog;—my daughter will bring me one;—and so God be about you, and strengthen your faith.—I am affectionately, dear cousin, yours,

L. STERNE.

My service to the C——s, though they are from home; and to Panty.

LETTER CIV.

TO MR. AND MRS. J.

Coxwould, Aug. 13. 1767.

My Dear Friends,

I but copy your great civility to me in writing you word, that I have this moment received another letter, wrote eighteen days after the date of the last, from St. Jago.—If our poor friend could have wrote another letter to England, you would, in course, have had it; but, I fear, from the circumstances of great hurry and bodily disorder in which she was when she dispatched this, she might not have time.—In case it has so fallen out, I send you the contents of what I have received:—and that is a melancholy history of herself and sufferings since they left St. Jago;—continual and most violent rheumatism all the time; —a fever, brought on with fits, and attended with delirium, and every terrifying symptom:—the recovery from this left her low and emaciated to a skeleton.—I give you the pain of this detail with a bleeding heart, knowing how much, at the same time, it will affect yours.—The three or four last days of our journal leave us with hopes she will do well at last, for she is more cheerful,—and seems to be getting into better spirits; and health will follow in course. They have crossed the Line:—are much becalmed; by which, with other delays, she fears they will lose their passage to Madras,—and be some months sooner for it at Bombay.—Heaven protect her! for she suffers much, and with uncommon fortitude.—She writes much to me about her dear friend Mrs. J——, in her last packet.—In truth, my good Lady, she loves and honors you from her heart; but, if she did not, I should not esteem her, or wish her so well as I do.—Adieu, my dear friends:—you have few in the world more truly and cordially

Yours,

L. STERNE.

P. S. I have just received, as a present from a man I shall ever love, a most elegant gold snuff-box, fabricated for me at Paris; —'tis not the first pledge I have received of his friendship.—May I presume to inclose you a letter of chit-chat which I shall write to Eliza. I know you will write yourself; and my letter may have the honor to *chaperon* yours to India:—they will neither of them be the worse received for going together in company; but I fear they will get late in the year to their destined port, as they go first to Bengal.

LETTER CV.

TO MISS STERNE.

Coxwould, Aug. 24, 1767.

I AM truly surprised, my dear Lydia, that my last letter has not reached thy mother, and thyself;—it looks most unkind on my part, after your having wrote me word of your mother's intention of coming to England, that she has not received my letter to welcome you both;—and though in that I said I wished you would defer your journey till March (for before that time I should have published my sentimental work, and should be in town to receive you)—yet I will show you more real *politesses* than any you have met with in France, as mine will come warm from the heart.—I am sorry you are not here at the races; but *les fêtes champêtres* of the Marquis de Sade have made you amends.—I know B—— very well; and he is what in France would be called Admirable,—that would be but *so so* here.—You are right;—he studies Nature more than any, or rather most of the French comedians.—If the Empress of Russia pays him and his wife a pension of twenty thousand livres a year, I think he is very well off.—The folly of staying till after twelve for supper,—that you two excommunicated beings might have meat!—"his conscience would not let it be served "before."—Surely the Marquis thought you both, being English, could not be satisfied without it.—I would have given, not my gown and cassock (for I have but one) but my topaz ring, to have seen the *petits maîtres et maîtresses* go to mass, after having spent the night in dancing.—As to my pleasures, they are few in compass.—My poor cat sits purring beside me. Your lively French dog shall have his place on the other side of my fire;—but if he is as devilish as when I last saw him, I must tutor him; for I will not have my cat abused.—In short, I will have nothing devilish about me:—a combustion will spoil a sentimental thought.

Another thing I must desire:—do not be alarmed;—'tis to throw all your *rouge*-pots into the Sorgue before you set out.—I will have no *rouge* put on in England;—and do not bewail them as —— —— did her silver *seringue*, or glister-equipage, which she lost in a certain river; but take a wise resolution of doing without *rouge*.—I have been three days ago bad again, with a spitting of blood:—and that unfeeling brute ******* came and drew my curtains, and with a voice like a trumpet, halloo'd in my ear,—"Z——ds, what a fine kettle of fish "have you brought yourself to, Mr. S——!" In a faint voice, I bade him leave me; for comfort sure was never administered in so rough a manner.—Tell your mother, I hope she will purchase what either of you may want at Paris,—'tis an occasion not to be lost,—so write to me from Paris, that I may come and meet you in my post-chaise, with my long-tailed horses;—and the moment you have both put your feet in it, call it hereafter yours.—Adieu, dear Lydia. Believe me, what I ever shall be,

Your affectionate father,

L. STERNE.

I think I shall not write to Avignon any more; but you will find one for you at Paris.—Once more, adieu.

LETTER CVI.

TO SIR W.

Sept. 19, 1767

MY DEAR SIR,

You are perhaps the drollest being in the universe.—Why do you banter me so about what I wrote to you?—Though I told you, every morning I jump'd into Venus's lap (meaning thereby the sea) was you to infer from that, that I leaped into the ladies' beds afterwards?—The body guides you,—the mind me.—I have wrote the most whimsical letter to a Lady that was ever read, and talked of body and soul too.—I said she had made me vain, by saying she was mine more than ever woman was; but she is not the Lady of Bond-street; nor —— square: nor the Lady who supp'd with me, in Bond-street, on scollop'd oysters, and other such things;—nor did she ever go *tête-à-tête* with me to Salt Hill.—Enough of such nonsense; the past is over, and I can justify myself unto myself.—Can you do as much?—No, faith!—"You can "feel!" Ay, so can my cat, when he hears a female caterwauling on the house-top;—but caterwauling disgusts me. I had rather raise a gentle flame, than have a different one raised in me. Now, I take Heaven to witness, after all this *badinage*, my heart is innocent;—and the sporting of my pen is equal, just equal, to what I did in boyish days, when I got astride of a stick, and gallop'd away.—The truth is this,—That my pen governs me;—not me my pen.—You are much to blame if you dig for marl, unless you are sure of it. I was once such a puppy myself, as to pare, and burn, and had my labor for my pains, and two hundred pounds out of my pocket. Curse on farming (said I) I will try if the pen will not succeed better than the spade. The following up of that affair (I mean farming) made me lose my temper: and a cart-load of turnips was (I thought) very dear at two hundred pounds.

In all your operations, may your own good sense guide you! Bought experience is the Devil.—Adieu, adieu.—Believe me

Yours, most truly,

L. STERNE.

LETTER CVII.

TO THE SAME.

Coxwould, Sept. 27, 1767.

DEAR SIR,

You are arrived at Scarborough when all the world has left it; but you are an unaccountable being; and so there is nothing more to be said on the matter.—You wish me to come to Scarborough, and join you to read a work that is not yet finished; besides, I have other things in my head.—My wife will be here in three or four days, and I must not be found straying in the wilderness; but I have been there. As for meeting you at Bluit's, with all my heart.—I will laugh and drink my barley-water with you. As soon as I have greeted my wife and daughter, and hired them a house at York, I shall go to London; where you generally are in spring:—and then my Sentimental Journey will, I dare say, convince you that my feelings are from the heart; and that that heart is not of the worst of moulds.—Praised be God for my sensibility! Though it has often made me wretched, yet I would not exchange it for all the pleasures the grossest sensualist ever felt. Write to me the day you will be at York;—'tis ten to one but I may introduce you to my wife and daughter. Believe me, my good Sir,

Ever yours,

L. STERNE.

LETTER CVIII.

TO MR. PANCHAUD, AT PARIS.

York, Oct. 1, 1767

DEAR SIR,

I HAVE ordered my friend Becket to advance, for two months, your account, which my wife this day delivered: she is in raptures with all your civilities.—This is to give you notice to draw upon your correspondent;—and Becket will deduct out of my publication. To morrow morning I repair with her to Coxwould; and my Lydia seems transported with the sight of me.—Nature, dear P——, breathes in all her composition; and, except a little vivacity, which is a fault in the world we live in, I am fully content with her mother's care of her.—Pardon this digression from business;—but 'tis natural to speak of those we love. As to the subscriptions which your friendship has procured me, I must have them to incorporate with my lists, which are to be prefix'd to the first volume.—My wife and daughter join in millions of thanks:—they will leave me the first of December.—Adieu, adieu.—Believe me

Yours, most truly,

L. STERNE

LETTER CIX.

TO MR. AND MRS. J.

Coxwould, Oct. 3, 1767.

I HAVE suffered under a strong desire, for above this fortnight, to send a letter of inquiries after the health and the well-being of my dear friends, Mr. and Mrs. J——; and I do assure you both, 'twas merely owing to a little modesty in my temper, not to make my good-will troublesome, where I have so much, and to those I never think of but with ideas of sensibility and obligation, that I have refrain'd.—Good God! to think I could be in town, and not go, the first step I made, to Gerrard-street!—My mind and body must be at sad variance with each other, should it ever fall out that it is not both the first and last place also where I shall betake myself, were it only to say, "God "bless you!"—May you have every blessing he can send you! 'tis a part of my litany; where you will always have a place whilst I have a tongue to repeat it. And so you heard I had left Scarborough; which you would no more credit, than the reasons assign'd for it:—I thank you for it kindly: though you have not told me what they were; being a shrewd divine, I think I can guess.—I was ten days at Scarborough, in September; and was hospitably entertained by one of the best of our bishops; who, as he kept house there, press'd me to be with him; and his household consisted of a gentleman and two ladies;—which, with the good bishop and myself, made so good a party, that we kept much to ourselves.—I made in this time a connexion of great friendship with my mitred host; who would gladly have taken me with him back to Ireland.—However, we all left Scarborough together, and lay fifteen miles off, where we kindly parted.—Now it was supposed (and I have since heard) that I e'en went on with the party to London; and this, I suppose, was the reason assign'd for my being there.—I dare say, Charity would add a little to the account, and give out that 'twas on the score of one, and perhaps both of the ladies,—and I will excuse Charity on that head, for a heart disengaged could not well have done better.—I have been hard writing ever since;—and hope, by Christmas, I shall be able to give a gentle rap at your door,—and tell you how happy I am to see my two good friends.—I assure you I spur on my Pegasus more violently upon that account, and am now determined not to draw bit till I have finished this Sentimental Journey;—which I hope to lay at your feet, as a small (but very honest) testimony of the constant truth with which I am,

My dear friends,
Your ever obliged
And grateful

L. STERNE.

P. S. My wife and daughter arrived here last night from France.—My girl has return'd an elegant, accomplished little slut.—My wife,—but I hate to praise my wife:—'tis as much as decency will allow, to praise my daughter. I suppose they will return next summer to France.—They leave me in a month, to reside at York for the winter;—and I stay at Coxwould till the first of January.

LETTER CX.

TO MRS. F——.

Coxwould, Friday

DEAR MADAM,

I RETURN you a thousand thanks for your obliging inquiry after me.—I got down last summer, very much worn out,—and much worse at the end of my journey.—I was forced to call at his Grace's house (the Archbishop of York) to refresh myself a couple of days upon the road near Doncaster.—Since I got home to quietness, and temperance, and good books, and good hours, I have mended; and am now very stout;—and, in a fortnight's time, shall perhaps be as well as you yourself could wish me.—I have the pleasure to acquaint you that my wife and daughter are arrived from France.—I shall be in town to greet my friends by the first of January.—Adieu, dear Madam.—Believe me

Yours, sincerely,

L. STERNE

LETTER CXI.

TO MRS. H.

Coxwould, October 12, 1767.

Ever since my dear H. wrote me word she was mine more than ever woman was, I have been racking my memory to inform me where it was that you and I had that affair together.—People think that I have had many (some in body, some in mind); but as I told you before, you have had me more than any woman; therefore, you must have had me, H——, both in mind and in body.—Now I cannot recollect where it was, nor exactly when:—it could not be the Lady in Bond-street, or Grosvenor-street, or —— Square, or Pall-mall.—We shall make it out, H——, when we meet; I emphatically long for it; 'tis no matter; I cannot now stand writing to you to-day:—I will make it up next post,—for dinner is upon table; and if I make Lord F—— stay, he will not frank this.—How do you do? Which parts of Tristram do you like best?—God bless you.

Yours
L. STERNE.

LETTER CXII.

TO MR. AND MRS. J.

Coxwould, November 12, 1767.

Forgive me, dear Mrs. J——, if I am troublesome in writing something betwixt a letter and a card, to inquire after you and my good friend Mr. J——, whom 'tis an age since I have heard a syllable of.—I think so, however; and never more felt the want of a house I esteem so much, as I do now, when I can hear tidings of it so seldom;—and have nothing to recompense my desire of seeing its kind possessors, but the hopes before me of doing it by Christmas.—I long sadly to see you,—and my friend Mr. J——. I am still at Coxwould;—my wife and girl * here.—She is a dear good creature,—affectionate, and most elegant in body and mind;—she is all Heaven could give me in a daughter;—but, like other blessings, not given, but lent; for her mother loves France;—and this dear part of me must be torn from my arms to follow her mother, who seems inclined to establish her in France, where she has had many advantageous offers.—Do not smile at my weakness, when I say I don't wonder at it, for she is as accomplished a slut as France can produce.—You shall excuse all this;—if you won't, I desire Mr. J—— to be my advocate;—but I know I don't want one.—With what pleasure shall I embrace your dear little pledge,—whom I hope to see every hour increasing in stature, and in favor, both with God and man!—I kiss all your hands with a most devout and friendly heart.—No man can wish you more good than your meagre friend does; few so much;—for I am, with infinite cordiality, gratitude, and honest affection,

My dear Mrs. J——,
Your ever faithful
L. STERNE.

P. S. My Sentimental Journey will please Mrs. S—— and my Lydia.—I can answer for those two. It is a subject which works well, and suits the frame of mind I have been in for some time past.—I told you my design in it was to teach us to love the world and our fellow-creatures better than we do:—so it runs most upon those gentler passions and affections, which aid so much to it. Adieu; and may you and my worthy friend Mr. J—— continue examples of the doctrine I teach!

* Mrs. Medalle thinks an apology may be necessary for publishing this letter;—the best she can offer is,—That it was written by a fond parent (whose commendation she is proud of) to a very sincere friend.

LETTER CXIII.

TO MRS. H.

Coxwould, Nov. 15, 1767.

Now be a good dear woman, my H——, and execute these commissions well;—and when I see you, I will give you a kiss:—there's for you!—But I have something else for you, which I am fabricating at a great rate, and that is my Sentimental Journey, which shall make you cry as much as it has affected me,—or I will give up the business of sentimental writing,—and write to the body;—that is, H——, what I am doing in writing to you:—but you are a *good body*, which is worth half a score mean souls.

I am yours, &c.

L. SHANDY.

LETTER CXIV.

TO A. L——E, ESQ.

Coxwould, Nov. 19, 1767.

You make yourself unhappy, dear L——, by imaginary ills,—which you might shun, instead of putting yourself in the way of. —Would not any man in his senses fly from the object he adores, and not waste his time and his health in increasing his misery by so vain a pursuit?—The idol of your heart is one of ten thousand.—The Duke of—— has long sighed in vain:—and can you suppose a woman will listen to you, that is proof against titles, stars, and red ribands?—Her heart (believe me, L——e) will not be taken by fine men, or fine speeches;—if it should ever feel a preference, it will choose an object for itself; and it must be a singular character that can make an impression on such a being:—she has a Platonic way of thinking, and knows love only by name.—The natural reserve of her character, which you complain of, proceeds not from pride, but from a superiority of understanding which makes her despise every man that turns himself into a fool. —Take my advice, and pay your addresses to Miss——: she esteems you; and time will wear off an attachment which has taken so deep a root in your heart.—I pity you from my soul;—but we are all born with passions which ebb and flow (else they would play the Devil with us) to different objects;—and the best advice I can give you, L——e, is to turn the tide of yours another way.—I know not whether I shall write again while I stay at Coxwould.—I am in earnest at my sentimental work,—and intend being in town soon after Christmas. In the mean time, adieu.—Let me hear from you, and believe me, dear L.,

Yours, &c.

L. STERNE.

LETTER CXV.

TO THE EARL OF ——.

Coxwould, November 28, 1767

My Lord,

'Tis with the greatest pleasure I take my pen to thank your Lordship for your letter of inquiry about Yorick;—he has worn out both his spirits and body with the Sentimental Journey:—'tis true that an author must feel himself, or his reader will not;—but I have torn my whole frame into pieces by my feelings.—I believe the brain stands as much in need of recruiting as the body,—therefore I shall set out for town the 20th of next month, after having recruited myself a week at York. I might indeed solace myself with my wife (who is come from France) but in fact I have long been a sentimental being,—whatever your Lordship may think to the contrary. The world has imagined, because I wrote Tristram Shandy, that I was myself more Shandean than I really ever was.—'Tis a good-natured world we live in; and we are often painted in divers colors, according to the ideas each one frames in his head.—A very agreeable lady arrived three years ago at York, in her road to Scarborough.—I had the honor of being acquainted with her, and was her *chaperon*.—All the females were very inquisitive to know who she was.—"Do not tell, ladies; 'tis a mistress my "wife has recommended to me!—nay, "moreover, has sent her from France!"

I hope my book will please you, my Lord, and then my labor will not be totally in vain. If it is not thought a chaste book, mercy on them that read it, for they must have warm imaginations indeed!—Can your Lordship forgive my not making this a longer epistle?—In short, I can but add this, which you already know, that I am, with gratitude and friendship,

My Lord,

Your obedient, faithful

L. STERNE.

If your Lordship is in town in Spring, I should be happy if you became acquainted with my friends in Gerrard-street;—you would esteem the husband, and honor the wife;—she is the reverse of most of her sex;—they have various pursuits,—she but one,—that of pleasing her husband.

LETTER CXVI.

TO HIS EXCELLENCY SIR G. M.

Coxwould, Dec. 3, 1767.

My Dear Friend,

For though you are His Excellency, and I still but Parson Yorick,—I still must call you so;—and were you to be next Emperor of Russia, I could not write to you, or speak of you, under any other relation.—I felicitate you,—I don't say how much, because I can't.—I always had something like a kind of revelation within me, which pointed out this track for you, in which you are so happily advanced:—it was not only my wishes for you, which were ever ardent enough to impose upon a visionary brain, but I thought I actually saw you just where you now are;—and that is just, my dear Macartney, where you should be.—I should long, long ago, have acknowledged the kindness of a letter of yours from Petersburgh; but hearing daily accounts you was leaving it,—this is the first time I knew well *where* my thanks would find you:—how they will find you, I know well;—that is, the same I ever knew you. In three weeks I shall kiss your hand;—and sooner, if I can finish my Sentimental Journey.—The deuce take all sentiments!—I wish there was not one in the world!—My wife is come to pay me a sentimental visit as far as from Avignon;—and the *politesse* arising from such a proof of her urbanity, has robbed me of a month's writing, or I had been in town now.—I am going to *lie-in*, being at Christmas at my full reckoning;—and unless what I shall bring forth is not *press'd* to death by these devils of printers, I shall have the honor of presenting to you *a couple of as clean brats* as ever chaste brain conceived;—they are frolicksome too, *mais cela n'empeche pas.*—I put your name down with many wrong and right *honorables*, knowing you would take it not well if I did not make myself happy with it. Adieu, my dear friend.

Believe me yours, &c.

L. STERNE.

P. S. If you see Mr. Crawford, tell him greet him kindly.

LETTER CXVII.

TO A. L——E, ESQ.

Coxwould, Dec. 7, 1767

Dear L.,

I said I would not perhaps write any more; but it would be unkind not to reply to so interesting a letter as yours.—I am certain you may depend upon Lord ——'s promises;—he will take care of you in the best manner he can; and your knowledge of the world, and of languages in particular, will make you useful in any department.—If his Lordship's scheme does not succeed, leave the kingdom;—go to the east, or the west, for travelling would be of infinite service to both your body and mind.—But more of this when we meet:—now to my own affairs.—I have had an offer of exchanging two pieces of preferment I hold here, for a living of three hundred and fifty pounds a year in Surrey, about thirty miles from London, and retaining Coxwould, and my prebendaryship;—the country also is sweet;—but I will not, cannot come to any determination, till I have consulted with you, and my other friends.—I have great offers too in Ireland;—the Bishops of C—— and R—— are both my friends;—but I have rejected every proposal, unless Mrs. S—— and my Lydia could accompany me thither.—I live for the sake of my girl, and with her sweet light burthen in my arms, I could get fast up the hill of preferment, if I chose it;—but without my Lydia, if a mitre was offered me, it would sit uneasy upon my brow.—Mrs. S——'s health is insupportable in England.—She must return to France; and justice and humanity forbid me to oppose it.—I will allow her enough to live comfortably, until she can rejoin me.—My heart bleeds, L——, when I think of parting with my child;—'twill be like the separation of soul and body,—and equal to nothing but what passes at that tremendous moment; and like it in one respect, for she will be in one kingdom, whilst I am in another.—You will laugh at my weakness,—but I cannot help it;—for she is a dear disinterested girl.—As a proof of it,—when she left Coxwould, and I bade her adieu, I pulled out my purse and offered her ten guineas for her private pleasures:—her answer was pretty, and affected me too much·

—'No, my dear papa, our expenses of coming from France may have straitened 'you';—I would rather put an hundred 'guineas into your pocket than take ten 'out of it.'—I burst into tears:—but why do I practise on your feelings,—by dwelling on a subject that will touch your heart?—It is too much melted already by its own sufferings, L——, for me to add a pang, or cause a single sigh.—God bless you!—I shall hope to greet you by New-year's-day in perfect health.—Adieu, my dear friend. --I am most truly and cordially yours,

L. STERNE.

LETTER CXVIII.

TO J—— H—— S——, ESQ.

December, 1767.

Literas vestras lepidissimas, mi consobrine, consobrinis meis omnibus carior, accepi die Veneris; sed posta non rediebat versus Aquilonem eo die, aliter scripsissem prout desiderabas. Nescio quid est materia cum me, sed sum fatigatus & ægrotus de meâ uxore plus quam unquam,—& sum possessus cum diabolo qui pellet me in urbem,—& tu es possessus cum eodem malo spiritu qui te tenet in deserto esse tentatum ancillis tuis, et perturbatum uxore tuâ,—crede mihi, mi Antoni, quod isthæc non est via ad salutem sive hodiernam, sive eternam; num tu incipis cogitare de pecuniâ, quæ, ut ait Sanctus Paulus, est radix omnium malorum, & non satis dicis in corde tuo, ego Antonius de Castello Infirmo, sum jam quadraginta & plus annos natus, & explevi octavum meum lustrum, et tempus est me curare, & meipsum Antonium facere hominem felicem & liberum, et mihimet ipsi benefacere, ut exhortatur Solomon, qui dicit quòd nihil est melius in hâc vitâ, quàm quòd homo vivat festivè & quòd edat et bibat, & bono fruatur, quia hoc est sua portio & dos in hoc mundo.

Nunc te scire vellemus, quòd non debeo esse reprehendi pro festinando eundo ad Londinum, quia Deus est testis, quòd non propero præ gloria, & pro me ostendere; nam diabolus iste qui me intravit, non est diabolus vanus, aut consobrinus suus Lucifer,—sed est diabolus amabundus, qui non vult sinere me esse solum; nam cùm non cumbendo cum uxore meâ, sum mentulatior quàm par est,—& sum mortaliter in amore,—& sum fatuus;—ergo tu me, mi care Antoni, excusabis, quoniam tu fuisti in amore, & per mare & per terras ivisti & festinâsti sicut diabolus eodem te propellente diabolo. Habeo multa ad te scribere,—sed scribo hanc epistolam in domo coffeatariâ & plenâ sociorum strepitosorum, qui non permittent me cogitare unam cogitationem.

Saluta amicum Panty meum, cujus literis respondebo,—saluta amicos in domo Gisbrosensi, & oro, credas me vinculo consobrinitatis & amoris ad te, mi Antoni, devinctissimum,

L. STERNE.

LETTER CXIX.

TO MR. AND MRS. J——.

York, December 23, 1767.

I WAS afraid that either Mr. or Mrs. J—, or their little blossom, was drooping, or that some of you were ill, by not having the pleasure of a line from you; and was thinking of writing again to inquire after you all,—when I was cast down myself with a fever, and bleeding at my lungs, which had confined me to my room near three weeks; when I had the favor of yours, which till to-day I have not been able to thank you both kindly for, as I most cordially now do, as well as for all your professions and proofs of good-will to me. I will not say I have not balanced accounts with you in this; all I know is, that I honor and value you more than I do any good creatures upon earth; and that I could not wish your happiness, and the success of whatever conduces to it, more than I do, was I your brother:—but, good God! are we not all brothers and sisters, who are friendly, virtuous, and good? Surely, my dear friends, my illness has been a sort of sympathy for your afflictions, upon the score of your dear little one.—I am worn down to a shadow; but, as my fever has left me, I set off the latter end of next week with my friend Mr. Hall for town.—I need not tell my friends in Gerrard-street.

shall do myself the honor to visit them, before either Lord —— or Lord ——, &c.—I thank you, my dear friend, for what you say so kindly about my daughter: it shows your good heart; for as she is a stranger, 'tis a free gift in you; but when she is known to you, she shall win it fairly: but, alas! when this event is to happen, is in the clouds.—Mrs. S—— has hired a house ready furnished at York, till she returns to France; and my Lydia must not leave her.

What a sad scratch of a letter!—but I am weak, my dear friends, both in body and mind; so God bless you! you will see me enter like a ghost; so I tell you beforehand not to be frightened.—I am, my dear friends, with the truest attachment and esteem, ever yours,

L. STERNE.

LETTER CXX.

TO THE SAME.

Old Bond-street, Jan. 1, 1768.

Not knowing whether the moisture of the weather will permit me to give my kind friends in Gerrard-street a call this morning for five minutes,—I beg leave to send them all the good wishes, compliments, and respects I owe them. I continue to mend; and doubt not but this, with all other evils and uncertainties of life, will end for the best. I send all compliments to your firesides this Sunday night:—Miss Ascough the wise, Miss Pigot the witty, your daughter the pretty, and so on.—If Lord O—— is with you, I beg my dear Mrs. J—— will present the inclosed to him;—'twill add to the millions of obligations I already owe you.—I am sorry that I am no subscriber to Soho this season; it deprives me of a pleasure worth twice the subscription; but I am just going to send about this quarter of the town, to see if it is not too late to procure a ticket, undisposed of, from some of my Soho friends; and if I can succeed, I will either send or wait upon you with it by half an hour after three to-morrow: if not, my friend will do me the justice to believe me truly miserable.—I am half engaged, or more, for dinner on Sunday next; but will try to get disengaged, in order to be with my friends. If I cannot, I will glide like a shadow uninvited to Gerrard-street some day this week, that we may eat our bread and meat in love and peace together.—God bless you both! I am, with the most sincere regard,

Your ever obliged,

L. STERNE.

LETTER CXXI.

TO THE SAME.

Old Bond-street, Monday.

My Dear Friends,

I have never been a moment at rest since I wrote yesterday about this Soho ticket.—I have been at the Secretary of State to get one;—have been upon one knee to my friends Sir G—— M——, Mr. Lascelles, and Mr. Fitzmaurice;—without mentioning five more.—I believe I could as soon get you a place at court, for every body is going: but I will go out and try a new circle; and if you do not hear from me by a quarter after three, you may conclude I have been unfortunate in my supplications.—I send you this state of the affair, lest my silence should make you think I had neglected what I promised;—but no;—Mrs. J— knows me better, and would never suppose it would be out of the head of one who is with so much truth

Her faithful friend,

L. STERNE.

LETTER CXXII.

TO THE SAME.

Thursday, Old Bond-street.

A thousand thanks, and as many excuses, my dear friends, for the trouble my blunder has given you. By a second note, I am astonished I could read Saturday for Sunday, or make any mistake in a card wrote by Mrs. J—-s, in which my friend is as unrivalled as in a hundred greater excellencies.

I am now tied down neck and heels (twice over) by engagements every day this week, or most joyfully would have trod the old pleasing road from Bond to Gerrard-street.—My books will be to be had on Thursday, but possibly on Wednesday in the afternoon.—I am quite well, but exhausted with a room full of company every morning till dinner.—How do I lament I cannot eat my morsel (which is always sweet) with such kind friends. The Sunday following I will assuredly wait upon you both, and will come a quarter before four, that I may have both a little time and a little daylight, to see Mrs. J——'s picture. I beg leave to assure my friends of my gratitude for all their favors, with my sentimental thanks for every token of their good-will.—Adieu, my dear friends.

I am truly yours,

L. STERNE.

LETTER CXXIII.

TO DR. EUSTACE, IN AMERICA.

London, Feb. 9, 1768.

SIR,

I THIS moment received your obliging letter, and Shandean piece of sculpture along with it: of both which testimonies of your regard I have the justest sense, and return you, dear Sir, my best thanks and acknowledgment. Your walking-stick is in no sense more Shandaic than in that of its having more handles than one; the parallel breaks only in this, that in using the stick, every one will take the handle which suits his convenience. In Tristram Shandy, the handle is taken which suits the passions, their ignorance, or their sensibility. There is so little true feeling in the herd of the world, that I wish I could have got an act of parliament, when the books first appeared, that none but wise men should look into them. It is too much to write books, and find heads to understand them: the world, however, seems to come into a better temper about them, the people of genius here being to a man on its side; and the reception it has met with in France, Italy, and Germany, has engaged one part of the world to give it a second reading. The other, in order to be on the strongest side, has at length agreed to speak well of it too. A few hypocrites and Tartuffes, whose approbation could do it nothing but dishonor, remain unconverted.

I am very proud, Sir, to have had a man like you on my side from the beginning; but it is not in the power of every one to taste humor, however he may wish it; it is the gift of God; and, besides, a true feeler always brings half the entertainment along with him; his own ideas are only called forth by what he reads; and the vibrations within him entirely correspond with those excited —'Tis like reading himself, and not the book.

In a week's time I shall be delivered of two volumes of the Sentimental Travels of Mr. Yorick through France and Italy; but alas! the ship sails three days too soon, and I have but to lament it deprives me of the pleasure of presenting them to you.

Believe me, dear Sir, with great thanks for the honor you have done me, with true esteem,

Your obliged humble servant,

L. STERNE.

LETTER CXXIV.

TO L. S——N, ESQ.

Old Bond-street, Wednesday.

DEAR SIR,

YOUR commendations are very flattering; I know no one whose judgment I think more highly of; but your partiality for me is the only instance in which I can call it in question.—Thanks, my good Sir, for the prints;—I am much your debtor for them. —If I recover from my ill state of health and live to revisit Coxwould this summer, I will decorate my study with them, along with six beautiful pictures I have already of the sculptures on poor Ovid's tomb, which were executed on marble at Rome.—It grieves one to think such a man should have died in exile, who wrote so well on the art of love.—Do not think me encroaching if I solicit a favor;—'tis either to borrow, or beg (to beg, if you please) some of those touched with chalk which you brought from Italy.—I believe you have three sets and if you can spare the imperfect one of cattle on colored paper, 'twill answer my purpose, which is namely this, to give a friend of ours.—You may be ignorant she has a genius for drawing; and whatever she excels in she conceals; and her humility adds lustre to her accomplishments.—I presented her last year with colors, and an apparatus for painting, and gave her several lessons before I left town.—I wish her to follow this art, to be a complete mistress of it; and it is singular enough, but not more singular than true, that she does not know how to make a cow or a sheep, though she draws figures and landscapes perfectly well; which makes me wish her to copy from good prints.—If you come to town next week, and dine where I am engaged next Sunday, call upon me and take me with you.—I breakfast with Mr. Beauclerc, and am engaged for an hour afterwards with Lord O——; so let our meeting be either at your house or my lodgings:—do not be late, for we will go half an hour before dinner, to see a picture executed by West, most admirably;—he has caught the character of our friend:—such goodness is painted in that face, that when one looks at it, let the soul be ever so much unharmonized, it is impossible it should remain so.—I will send you a set of my books;—they will take with the generality:—the women will read this book in the parlor, and Tristram in the bed-chamber.—Good-night, dear Sir;—I am going to take my whey, and then to bed. Believe me

Yours most truly,

L. STERNE.

LETTER CXXV.

TO MISS STERNE.

Feb. 20, Old Bond-street.

My Dearest Lydia,

My Sentimental Journey, you say, is admired in York by every one:—and 'tis not vanity in me to tell you that it is no less admired here:—but what is the gratification of my feelings on this occasion?—The want of health bows me down, and vanity harbors not in thy father's breast.—This vile influenza!—be not alarmed! I think I shall get the better of it;—and I shall be with you both the first of May; and, if I escape, 'twill not be for a long period, my child,—unless a quiet retreat and peace of mind can restore me.—The subject of thy letter has astonished me.—She could but know little of my feelings, to tell thee that, under the supposition I should survive thy mother, I should bequeath thee as a legacy to——! No, my Lydia! 'tis a Lady, whose virtues I wish thee to imitate, that I shall intrust my girl to; I mean that friend whom I have so often talked and wrote about. From her you will learn to be an affectionate wife, a tender mother, and a sincere friend;—and you cannot be intimate with her without her pouring some part of the milk of human kindness into your breast, which will serve to check the heat of your own temper, which you partake in a small degree of.—Nor will that amiable woman put my Lydia under the painful necessity to fly to India for protection whilst it is in her power to grant her a more powerful one in England.—But I think, my Lydia, that thy mother will survive me. Do not deject her spirits with thy apprehensions on my account. I have sent you a necklace, buckles, and the same to your mother.—My girl cannot form a wish that is in the power of her father, that he will not gratify her in;—and I cannot, in justice, be less to thy mother.—I am never alone.—The kindness of my friends is ever the same.—I wish, though, I had thee to nurse me; but I am denied that.—Write to me twice a week, at least.—God bless thee, my child, and believe me ever, ever, thy

Affectionate father,

L. STERNE.

LETTER CXXVI.

TO MRS. J.

Tuesday.

Your poor friend is scarce able to write; he has been at Death's door this week with a pleurisy.—I was bled three times on Thursday, and blistered on Friday.—The physician says I am better.—God knows, for I feel myself sadly wrong, and shall, if I recover, be a long while of gaining strength.—Before I have gone through half this letter, I must stop to rest my weak hand above a dozen times.—Mr. J—— was so good as to call upon me yesterday. I felt emotions not to be described at the sight of him: and he overjoyed me by talking a great deal of you.—Do, dear Mrs. J——, entreat him to come to-morrow, or next day, for perhaps I have not many days or hours to live.—I want to ask a favor of him, if I find myself worse,—that I shall beg of you, if in this wrestling I come off conqueror.—My spirits are fled;—'tis a bad omen.—Do not weep, my dear Lady;—your tears are too precious to shed for me;—bottle them up, and may the cork never be drawn!—Dearest, kindest, gentlest, and best of women! may health, peace, and happiness, prove your handmaids!—If I die, cherish the remembrance of me, and forget the follies which you so often condemned,—which my heart, not my head, betrayed me into. Should my child, my Lydia, want a mother, may I hope you will (if she is left parentless) take her to your bosom?—You are the only woman on earth I can depend upon for such a benevolent action.—I wrote to her a fortnight ago,* and told her what, I trust, she will find in you.—Mr. J—— will be a father to her;—he will protect her from every insult; for he wears a sword which he has served his country with, and which he would know how to draw out of the scabbard in defence of innocence. Commend me to him, as I now commend you to that Being who takes under his care the good and kind part of the world.—Adieu.—All grateful thanks to you and Mr. J——.

Your poor affectionate friend,

L. STERNE.

* From this circumstance it may be conjectured, that this letter was written on Tuesday, the eighth of March, 1768, ten days before Mr. Sterne died.

LETTER CXXVII.

TO *********.

——I BEHELD her tender look;—her pathetic eye petrified my fluids;—the liquid dissolution drowned those once-bright orbs; the late sympathetic features, so pleasing in their harmony, are now blasted, withered, and are dead;—her charms are dwindled into a melancholy which demands my pity.—Yes, my friend, our once sprightly and vivacious Harriot is that very object that must thrill your soul.—How abandoned is that heart which bulges the tear of innocence, and is the cause,—the fatal cause of overwhelming the spotless soul, and plunging the yet untainted mind into a sea of sorrow and repentance!—Though born to protect the fair, does not man act the part of a demon?—first alluring by his temptations, and then triumphing in his victory.—When villany gets the ascendency, it seldom leaves the wretch till it has thoroughly polluted him.—T*******, once the joyous companion of our juvenile extravagancies, by a deep-laid scheme, so far ingratiated himself into the good graces of the old man,—that even he, with all his penetration and experience (of which old folks generally pique themselves) could not perceive his drift, and, like the goodness of his own heart, believed him honorable!—Had I known his pretensions,—I would have flown on the wings of friendship,—of regard,—of affection,—and rescued the lovely innocent from the hands of the spoiler.—Be not alarmed at my declaration:—I have been long bound to her in the reciprocal bonds of affection; but it is of a more delicate stamp than the gross materials Nature has planted in us for procreation.—I hope ever to retain the idea of innocence, and love her still.—I would love the whole sex, were they equally deserving.

—— —— taking her by the hand,—the other thrown round her waist,—after an intimacy allowing such freedoms, — with a look deceitfully pleasing, the villain poured out a torrent of protestations,—and, though oaths are sacred,—swore with all the fortitude of a conscientious man—the depth of his love,—the height of his esteem,—the strength of his attachment.—By these, and other artful means to answer his abandoned purpose (for which, you know, he is but too well qualified)—gained on the open inexperienced heart of the generous Harriot, and robbed her of her brightest jewel. — Oh, England! where are your senators?—where are your laws?—Ye Heavens! where rests your deadly thunder?—why are your bolts restrained from overwhelming with vengeance this vile seducer?—I, my friend, I was the minister sent by justice to revenge her wrongs.—Revenge!—I disclaim it:—to redress her wrongs.—The news of affliction flies;—I heard it, and posted to ****, where, forgetting my character, — this is the style of the enthusiast,—it most became my character,—I saw him in his retreat;—I flew out of the chaise, caught him by the collar, and, in a tumult of passion, demanded,—sure, if anger is excusable, it must be when it is excited by a detestation of vice,—I demanded him to restore,—alas! what was not in his power to return.—Vengeance! and shall these vermin, these spoilers of the fair, these murderers of the mind, lurk and creep about in dens, secure to themselves, and pillage all around them?—Distracted with my rage, — I charged him with his crime,—exploded his baseness,—condemned his villany;—while coward-guilt sat on his sullen brow, and, like a criminal conscious of his deed, tremblingly pronounced his fear.—He hoped means might be found for a sufficient atonement,—offered a tender of his hand as a satisfaction, and a life devoted to her service, as a recompense for his error. His humiliation struck me;—'twas the only means he could have contrived to assuage my anger. — I hesitated, paused, thought, and still must think on so important a concern. — Assist me;—I am half afraid of trusting my Harriot in the hands of a man, whose character I too well know to be the antipodes of Harriot.—He is all fire and dissipation;—she all meekness and sentiment!—nor can I think there is any hopes of reformation:—the offer proceeds more from surprise or fear, than justice and sincerity.—The world, the world will exclaim, and my Harriot be a cast-off from society!—Let her;—I had rather see her thus, than miserably linked for life to a lump of vice.—She shall retire to some corner of the world, and there weep out the remainder of her days in sorrow,—forgetting the wretch who has abused her confidence, but ever remembering the friend who consoles her in retirement.—You, my dear Charles, shall bear a part with me in the delightful task of whispering "peace to 'those who are in trouble, and healing the 'broken in spirit."

Adieu.

L. STERNE.

LETTER CXXVIII.

TO THE SAME.

SIR,

I FEEL the weight of obligation which your friendship has laid upon me; and if it should never be in my power to make you a recompense, I hope you will be recompensed at the "resurrection of the just."—I hope, Sir, we shall both be found in that catalogue; and we are encouraged to hope, by the example of Abraham's faith, even "against hope."—I think there is, at least, as much probability of our reaching, and rejoicing in the "haven where we would "be," as there was of the old patriarch's having a child by his old wife.—There is not any person, living or dead, whom I have so strong a desire to see and converse with as yourself:—indeed, I have no inclination to visit, or say a syllable to, but a few persons in this lower vale of vanity and tears, beside you;—but I often derive a peculiar satisfaction in conversing with the ancient and modern dead, who yet live and speak excellently in their works.—My neighbors think me *often alone*;—and yet, at such times, I am in company with more than five hundred mutes, — each of whom, at my pleasure, communicates his ideas to me by dumb signs,—quite as intelligibly as any person living can do by *uttering* of words.—They always keep the distance from me which I direct;—and, with a motion of my hand, I can bring them as near to me as I please.—I lay hands on fifty of them sometimes in an evening, and handle them as I like:—they never complain of ill-usage, — and, when dismissed from my presence,—though ever so abruptly,—take no offence.—Such convenience is not to be enjoyed,—nor such liberty to be taken,—with the living:—we are bound, in point of good manners, to admit all our pretended friends when they knock for an entrance; and dispense with all the nonsense or impertinence which they broach, till they think proper to withdraw: nor can we take the liberty of humbly and decently opposing their sentiments, without exciting their disgust, and being in danger of their splenetic representation after they have left us.

I am weary of talking to the *many*,—who, though quick of hearing,—are so "slow "of heart to believe"—propositions which are next to self-evident.—You and I were not cast in *one mould*,—corporeal comparison will attest it;—and yet we are fashioned so much alike, that we may pass for twins:—were it possible to take an inventory of all our sentiments and feelings,—just and unjust,—holy and impure,—there would appear as little difference between them as there is between instinct and reason,—or, wit and madness. The barriers which separate these,—like the real essence of bodies, —escape the piercing eye of metaphysics, and cannot be pointed out more clearly than geometricians define a straight line, which is said to have length without breadth.—O ye learned anatomical aggregates! be as candid as the sage whom ye pretend to revere;—and tell them that all you know is, that you know nothing!

——I have a *mort* to communicate to you on different subjects;—my mountain will be in labor till I see you,—and then,—what then?—why you must expect to see it bring forth—a mouse!—I therefore beseech you to have a watchful eye to the cats!—but it is said that mice were designed to be killed by cats,—cats to be worried by dogs, &c. &c.—This may be true;—and I think I am made to be killed by my cough, which is a perpetual plague to me. What in the name of sound lungs, has my cough to do with you, or you with my cough?

I am, Sir, with the most perfect affection and esteem,

Your humble servant,

L. STERNE.

LETTER CXXIX.

TO * * * *.

DEAR SIR,

I HAVE received your kind letter of critical, and I will add, of parental advice, which, contrary to my natural humor, set me upon looking gravely for half a day together: sometimes I concluded you had not spoke out, but had stronger grounds for your hints and cautions than what your good-nature knew how to tell me, especially with regard to prudence, as a divine; and that you thought, in your heart, the vein of humor too free for the solemn color of my coat. A meditation upon Death had been a more suitable trimming to it, I own; but then it could not have been set on by me. Mr. F——, whom I regard in the class I do you, as my best of critics and well-wishers, preaches daily to me on the same text: "Get your preferment first, Lory," he says "and then write and welcome." But suppose preferment is long a-coming,—and, for aught I know, I may not be preferred till the resurrection of the just;—and all that time in labor, how must I bear my pains? Like pious divines? or, rather, like able philosophers, knowing that one passion is only to be combated with another? But to be serious (if I can) I will use all reasonable caution,—only with this caution along with it, not to spoil my book; that is, the air and originality of it, which must resemble the author; and I fear it is the number of these slighter touches which make the resemblance, and identify it from all others of the same stamp, which this understrapping virtue of Prudence would oblige me to strike out.—A very able critic, and one of my color too, who has read over Tristram, made answer, upon my saying I would consider the color of my coat as I corrected it,—that that idea in my head would render my book not worth a groat.—Still I promise to be cautious; but deny I have gone as far as Swift: he keeps a due distance from Rabelais; I keep a due distance from him. Swift has said a hundred things I durst not say, unless I was Dean of St. Patrick's.

I like your caution, *ambitiosa recides ornamenta.* As I revise my book, I will shrive my conscience upon that sin; and whatever ornaments are of that kind, shall be defaced without mercy. Ovid is justly censured for being *ingenii sui amator;* and it is a reasonable hint to me, as I am not sure I am clear of it. To sport too much with your wit, or the game that Wit has pointed out, is surfeiting; like toying with a man's mistress, it may be very delightful solacement to the enamorato, but little to the bystander

Though I plead guilty to part of the charge, yet it would greatly alleviate the crime, if my readers knew how much I have suppressed of this device. I have burnt more wit than I have published, on that very account, since I began to avoid the fault I fear I may yet have given proofs of.—I will reconsider Slop's fall, and my too minute description of it; but, in general, I am persuaded that the happiness of the Cervantic humor arises from this very thing:—of describing silly and trifling events with the circumstantial pomp of great ones. Perhaps this is overloaded, and I can ease it.—I have a project of getting Tristram put into the hands of the Archbishop, if he comes down this autumn; which will ease my mind of all trouble upon the topic of discretion.

I am, &c.

L. STERNE

AN IMPROMPTU.

TO MR. B.

Exeter, July, 1775.

Sir,

This was quite an *impromptu* of Yorick's after he had been thoroughly *soused.*—He drew it up in a few moments, without stopping his pen. I should be glad to see it in your intended collection of Mr. Sterne's Memoirs, &c. If you should have a copy of it, you will be able to rectify a misapplication of a term that Mr. Sterne could never be guilty of; as one great excellence of his writing lies in the most happy choice of metaphors and allusions,—such as showed his philosophic judgment, at the same time that they display his wit and genius;—but it is not for me to comment on, or correct so great an original. I should have sent this fragment as soon as I saw Mrs. Medalle's advertisement, had I not been at a distance from my papers. I expect much entertainment from this posthumous work of a man to whom no one is more indebted for amusement and instruction than,

Sir,

Your humble servant,

S. P.

AN IMPROMPTU.

No;—not one farthing would I give for such a coat, in wet weather or dry.—If the sun shines, you are sure of being melted because it closes so tight about one;—if it rains, it is no more a defence than a cobweb;—a very sieve, o' my conscience, that lets through every drop! and, like many other things that are put on only for a cover, mortifies you with disappointment, and makes you curse the imposture, when it is too late to avail one's-self of the discovery. Had I been wise, I should have examined the claim the coat had to the title of "Defender of the Body,"—before I had trusted my body in it.—I should have held it up to the light, like other suspicious matters, to have seen how much it was likely to admit of that which I wanted to keep out:—whether it was no more than such a frail, flimsy contexture of flesh and blood, as I am fated to carry about with me through every tract of this dirty world, could have comfortably and safely dispensed with in so short a journey,—taking into my account the chance of spreading trees,—thick hedges o'erhanging the road,—with twenty other coverts that a man may thrust his head under, if he is not violently pushed on by that d——d stimulus,—you know where,—that will not let a man sit still in one place for half a minute together;—but, like a young nettlesome tit, is eternally on the fret, and is for pushing on still farther:—or, if the poor scared devil is not haunted tantivy by a hue and cry, with gyves and a halter dangling before his eyes.—Now, in either case, he has not a minute to throw away in standing still, but, like King Lear, must brave "the peltings of a pitiless "storm," and give Heaven leave to "rumble "its belly-full,—spit fire,—or spout rain," —as spitefully as it pleaseth, without finding the inclination or the resolution to slacken his pace, lest something should be lost that might have been gained; or more gotten than he well knows how to get rid of.—Now had I acted with as much prudence as some other good folks,—I could name many of them who have been made B—ps within my remembrance, for having been hooded and muffled up in a larger quantity of this dark drab of mental manufacture than ever fell to my share,—and absolutely for nothing else; as will be seen when they are undressed another day.—Had I but as much as might have been taken out of their cloth, without lessening much of the size, or injuring in the least the shape, or contracting aught of the doublings and foldings, or confining to a less circumference the superb sweep of any one cloak that any one B— ever wrapt himself up in,—I should never have given this coat a place upon my shoulders. I should have seen by the light, at one glance, how little it would keep out of rain, by how little it would keep in of darkness.—This a coat for a rainy day! Do pray, Madam, hold it up to that window.—Did you ever see such an *illustrious* coat since the day you could distinguish between a coat and a pair of breeches?—My Lady did not understand derivatives, and so she could not see quite through my splendid pun. Pope Sixtus would have blinded her with the same "darkness of excessive light." What a flood of it breaks in through this rent!—what an irradiation beams through that!—what twinklings!—what sparklings as you wave it before your eyes in the broad face of the sun!—Make a fan out of it for the Ladies, to look at their gallants with at church.—It has not served me for one purpose;—it will serve them for two. This is coarse stuff,—of worse manufacture than the cloth;—put it to its proper use, for I love when things sort and join well:—make a philtre* of it while there is a drop to be extracted.—I know but one thing in the world that will draw, drain, or suck like it; and that is, neither wool nor flax;—make, make any thing of it but a vile, hypocritical coat for me;—for I never can say *sub Jove* (whatever Juno might) that "it is a pleasure to "be wet."

L. STERNE.

* This allusion is improper. A philtre originally signifies a love-potion;—and as it is used as a noun from the verb *philtrate*, it must signify a *strainer*, not a *sucker*.—Cloth is sometimes used for the purpose of *draining*, by means of its pores or capillary tubes; but its action is contrary to philtration. His meaning is obvious enough; but as he drew up this fragment without stopping his pen, as I was informed, it is no wonder he erred in the application of some of his terms.

THE FRAGMENT.

CHAP. I.

Showing two Things; first, what a Rabelaic Fellow LONGINUS RABELAICUS *is: and, secondly, how cavalierly he begins his Book.*

MY dear and thrice-reverend brethren, as well Archbishops and Bishops, as the *rest* of the inferior clergy! would it not be a glorious thing, if any man of genius and capacity amongst us for such a work, was fully bent within himself to sit down immediately and compose a thorough-stitched system of the KERUKOPAEDIA, fairly setting forth to the best of his wit and memory, and collecting for that purpose all that is needful to be known and understood of that art?——Of what art? cried PANURGE.—Good God! answered LONGINUS (making an exclamation, but taking care at the same time to moderate his voice,) why, of the art of making all kinds of your theological, hebdodomical, rostrummical, humdrummical what-d'ye-call-ems—I will be shot, quoth EPISTEMON, if all this story of thine of a roasted horse, is simply no more than S—— Sausages! quoth PANURGE. Thou hast fallen twelve feet and about five inches below the mark, answered EPISTEMON, for I hold them to be *Sermons*—which said word (as I take the matter) being but a word of low degree, for a book of high rhetoric—LONGINUS RABELAICUS was fore-minded to usher and lead in his dissertation, with as much pomp and parade as he could afford;—and for my own part, either I know no more of Latin than my horse, or the KERUKOPAEDIA is nothing but the art of making of 'em.—And why not, quoth GYMNAST, of preaching them when we have done?—Believe me, dear souls, this is half in half—and if some skilful body would but put us in a way to do this to some *tune*—Thou would'st not have them *chanted* surely? quoth TRIBOULET, laughing.—No, nor *canted* neither! quoth GYMNAST, crying—But what I mean, my friends, says LONGINUS RABELAICUS (who is certainly one of the greatest critics in the western world, and as Rabelaic a fellow as ever existed)—what I mean, says he, interrupting them both, and resuming his discourse, is this, that if all the scatter'd rules of the KERUKOPAEDIA could be but once carefully collected into one code, as thick as PANURGE'S head, and the whole *cleanly* digested—(pooh, says PANURGE, who felt himself aggrieved)—and bound up, continued LONGINUS, by way of a regular institute, and then put into the hands of every licensed preacher in Great Britain and Ireland, just before he began to compose, I maintain it—I deny it flatly, quoth PANURGE.—What? answered LONGINUS RABELAICUS with all the temper in the world.

CHAP. II.

In which the Reader will begin to form a Judgment of what an Historical, Dramatical, Anecdotical, Allegorical, and Comical Kind of a Work he has got hold of.

HOMENAS, who had to preach next Sunday (before God knows whom,) knowing nothing at all of the matter—was all this while at it as hard as he could drive in the very next room:—for, having fouled two clean sheets of his own, and being quite stuck fast in the entrance upon his third general *division*, and finding himself unable to get either forwards or backwards with any grace—"Curse it," says he (thereby xcommunicating every mother's son who should think differently,) "why may not a "man lawfully call in for help in this, as "well as any other human emergency?"—So without any more argumentation, except starting up and nimming down from the top shelf but one, the second volume of CLARK—though without any felonious intention in so doing, he had begun to clap me in (making a joint first) five whole pages, nine round paragraphs, and a dozen and a half of good thoughts, all of a row; and because there was a confounded high gallery—was transcribing it away like a little devil.—Now—quoth HOMENAS to himself, "though I hold all this to be fair "and square, yet, if I am found out, there "will be the deuce and all to pay."—*Why are the bells ringing backwards, you lad? what is all that crowd about, honest man?* HOMENAS *was got upon* DOCTOR CLARK'S *back, Sir.—And what of that, my lad? Why, an' please you, he has broke his neck, and fractured his skull, and befouled himself into the bargain, by a fall from the pulpit two stories high.* Alas! poor HOMENAS! HOMENAS has done his business!—HOMENAS will never preach more while breath is in his body.—No, faith, I shall never again be able to tickle it off as I have done. I may sit up whole winter nights baking my blood with hectic watchings, and write as solid as a FATHER of the church—or I may sit down whole summer days, evaporating my spirits into the finest thoughts, and write as florid as a MOTHER of it.—In a word, I may compose myself off my legs, and preach till I burst—and when I have done, it will be worse than if not done at all.—*Pray Mr. Such-a-one, who held forth last Sunday? Doctor* CLARK, *I trow, says one. Pray what Doctor* CLARK? *says a second. Why,* HOMENAS'S *Doctor* CLARK, *quoth a third.* O rare HOMENAS! cries a fourth; your *servant*, Mr. HOMENAS, quoth a *fifth.*—'Twill be all over with me, by Heaven—I may as well put the book from whence I took it.—Here HOMENAS burst into a flood of tears, which falling down helter-skelter, ding dong, without any kind of intermission for six minutes and almost twenty-five seconds, had a marvellous effect upon his discourse; for the aforesaid tears, do you mind, did so temper the wind that was rising upon the aforesaid discourse, but falling for the most part perpendicularly, and hitting the spirits at right angles, which were mounting horizontally all over the surface of his harangue, they not only played the devil and all with the sublimity—but moreover the said tears, by their nitrous quality, did so refrigerate, precipitate, and hurry down to the bottom of his soul, all the unsavory particles which lay fermenting (as you saw) in the middle of his conception, that he went on in the coolest and chastest style (for a *soliloquy*, I think) that ever mortal man uttered.

"This is really and truly a very hard "case," continued HOMENAS to himself.—PANURGE, by the bye, and all the company in the next room, hearing all along every syllable he spoke: for you must know, that notwithstanding PANURGE had opened his mouth as wide as he could for his blood, in order to give a round answer to LONGINUS RABELAICUS'S interrogation, which concluded the last chapter—yet HOMENAS'S rhetoric had poured in so like a torrent, slapdash through the wainscot amongst them, and happening at that *uncritical* crisis when PANURGE had just put his ugly face into the above-said posture of defence—that he stopt short—he did indeed, and, though his head was full of matter, and he had screwed up every nerve and muscle belonging to it, till all cried *crack* again, in order to give a due projectile force to what he was going to let fly full in LONGINUS RABELAICUS'S teeth, who sat over-against him—Yet for all that, he had the continence to contain himself, for he stopt short, I say, without uttering one word except Z——ds.—Many reasons may be assigned for this, but the most true, the most strong, the most hydrostatical, and the most philosophical reason, why PANURGE did not go on, was—that the fore-mentioned *torrent* did so *drown* his voice that he had none left to go on with.—God help him, poor fellow! so he stopt short (as I have told you before,) and all the time HOMENAS was speaking, he said not another word, good or bad, but stood gaping and staring, like what you please—so that the break, marked thus—which Homenas's grief had made in the middle of his discourse, which he could no more help than he could fly—produced no other change in the room where LONGINUS RABELAICUS, EPISTEMON, GYMNAST, TRIBOULET, and nine or ten more honest blades, had got Kerukopaedizing together, but that it gave time to GYMNAST to give PANURGE a good squashing chuck under his double chin; which PANURGE taking in good part, and just as it was meant by GYMNAST, he forthwith shut his mouth—and gently sitting down upon a stool, though somewhat eccentrically and out of neighbor's row, but listening as all the rest did with might and main, they plainly and distinctly heard every syllable of what you will find recorded in the very next chapter

INTRODUCTION TO THE HISTORY

OF

A GOOD WARM WATCH-COAT.

As the following piece was suppressed during the lifetime of Mr. Sterne, and as there are some grounds to believe that it was not intended by him for publication, an apology may be deemed necessary for inserting it in the present edition of his works. It must be acknowledged, that a mere *jeu d'esprit* relating to a private dispute, which could interest only a few, and which was intended to divert a small circle of friends, was, with great propriety, concealed while it might tend to revive departed animosities, or give pain to any of the persons who were concerned in so trifling a contest. And these considerations seem to have had weight with those to whom the MS. was intrusted, it not having been made public until many years after it was written, nor until most of the gentlemen mentioned in it were dead. After the lapse of more than twenty years, it may be presumed that there can be no impropriety in giving one of the earliest of Mr. Sterne's *bagatelles* a place among his more important performances. The slightest sketches of a genius are too valuable to be neglected; and the present edition would be incomplete, if this composition, written immediately before Tristram Shandy, and which may be considered as the precursor of it, was omitted. As the whole of it alludes to facts and circumstances confined to the city of York, it will be necessary to observe, that it was occasioned by a controversy between Dr. Fountayne and Dr. Topham, in the year 1758, on a charge made by the latter against the former, of a breach of promise, in withholding from him some preferment, which he had reason to expect. For the better illustration of this little satire, a few notes are added, from the pamphlets which appeared while this insignificant difference was agitating.

THE HISTORY

OF

A good warm Watch-Coat.

Sir,

In my last, for want of something better to write about, I told you what a world of fending and proving we have had of late in this village* of ours, about an old cast pair of black plush breeches,† which John,‡ our parish-clerk, about ten years ago, it seems, had made a promise of to one Trim,§ who is our sexton and dog-whipper.—To this you write me word, that you have had more than either one or two occasions to know a great deal of the shifty behavior of the said master Trim,—and that you are astonished, nor can you for your soul conceive, how so worthless a fellow, and so worthless a thing into the bargain, could become the occasion of so much racket as I have represented.

Now, though you do not say expressly you could wish to hear any more about it, yet I see plainly enough I have raised your curiosity; and therefore, from the same motive that I slightly mentioned it at all in my last letter, I will in this give you a full

* York.

† The Commissaryship of Pickering and Pocklington.

‡ Dr. John Fountayne, Dean of York.

§ Dr. Topham.

and very circumstantial account of the whole affair.

But, before I begin, I must first set you right in one very material point, in which I have misled you, as to the true cause of all this uproar amongst us,—which does not take its rise, as I then told you, from the affair of the breeches; but, on the contrary, the whole affair of the breeches has taken its rise from it.—To understand which, you must know, that the first beginning of the squabble was not betwixt John the parish-clerk and Trim the sexton, but betwixt the parson* of the parish and the said master Trim, about an old *watch-coat*,† that had hung up many years in the church, which Trim had set his heart upon; and nothing would serve Trim but he must take it home, in order to have it converted into a *warm under-petticoat* for his wife, and a *jerkin* for himself against winter; which, in a plaintive tone, he most humbly begged his Reverence would consent to.

I need not tell you, Sir, who have so often felt it, that a principle of strong compassion transports a generous mind sometimes beyond what is strictly right;—the parson was within an ace of being an honorable example of this very crime; for no sooner did the distinct words—*petticoat,—poor,—life,—warm,—winter*, strike upon his ear, but his heart warmed; and, before Trim had well got to the end of his petition (being a gentleman of a frank open temper) he told him he was welcome to it with all his heart and soul. But Trim, says he, as you see I am but just got down to my living, and am an utter stranger to all parish-matters, knowing nothing about this old watch-coat you beg of me, having never seen it in my life, and, therefore, cannot be a judge whether 'tis fit for such a purpose; or, if it is, in truth, know not whether 'tis mine to bestow upon you or not,—you must have a week or ten days' patience, till I can make some inquiries about it;—and if I find it is in my power, I tell you again, man, your wife is heartily welcome to an under-petticoat out of it, and you to a jerkin, was the thing as good again as you represent it.

It is necessary to inform you, Sir, in this place, that the parson was earnestly bent to serve Trim in this affair, not only from the motive of generosity, which I have just ascribed to him, but likewise from another motive, and that was by making some sort of recompense for a multitude of small services which Trim had occasionally done, and indeed was continually doing (as he was much about the house) when his own man was out of the way.—For all these reasons together, I say, the parson of the parish intended to serve Trim in this matter to the utmost of his power. All that was wanting, was, previously to inquire if any one had a *claim* to it; or whether, as it had time immemorial hung up in the church, the taking it down might not raise a clamor in the parish. These inquiries were the things that Trim dreaded in his heart: he knew very well, that, if the parson should but say one word to the churchwardens about it, there would be an end of the whole affair. For this, and some other reasons not necessary to be told you at present, Trim was for allowing no time in this matter,—but on the contrary, doubled his diligence and importunity at the vicarage-house,—plagued the whole family to death,—prest his suit morning, noon, and night; and, to shorten my story, teased the poor gentleman, who was but in an ill state of health, almost out of his life about it.

You will not wonder when I tell you, that all this hurry and precipitation on the side of master Trim, produced its natural effect on the side of the parson; and that was, a suspicion that all was not right at the bottom.

He was one evening sitting alone in his study, weighing and turning this doubt every way in his mind, and, after an hour and a half's serious deliberation upon the affair, and running over Trim's behavior throughout, he was just saying to himself —*it must be so*,—when a sudden rap at the door put an end to his soliloquy, and, in a few minutes, to his doubts too, for a laborer in the town, who deemed himself past his fifty-second year, had been returned by the constables in the militia-list, and he had

* Dr. Hutton, Archbishop of York.

† A patent place in the gift of the Archbishop, which had been given to Dr. Topham for his life, and which in 1758, he solicited to have granted to one of his family after his death.

come with a groat in his hand to search the parish-register for his age. The parson bid the poor fellow put the groat into his pocket, and go into the kitchen,—then shutting the study-door, and taking down the parish-register,—*who knows*, says he, *but I may find something here about this self-same watch-coat?* He had scarce unclasped the book in saying this, when he popped on the very thing he wanted, fairly wrote in the first page, pasted to the inside of one of the covers, whereon was a memorandum about the very thing in question, in these express words—"*Memorandum:* The great watch- "coat was purchased and given, above two "hundred years ago, by the lord of the manor, "to this parish-church, to the sole use and be- "hoof of the poor sextons thereof, and their "successors for ever, to be worn by them re- "spectively in winterly cold nights in ring- "ing *complines, passing-bells, &c.* which "the said lord of the manor had done in "piety, to keep the poor wretches warm, "and for the good of his own soul, for which "they were directed to pray," &c.—*Just Heaven!* said the parson to himself, looking upwards, *what an escape have I had! Give this for an under-petticoat to Trim's wife! I would not have consented to such a desecration to be primate of all England;—nay, I would not have disturbed a single button of it for all my tythes.*

Scarce were the words out of his mouth, when in pops Trim with the whole subject of the exclamation under both his arms,—I say under both his arms, for he had actually got it ript and cut out ready (his own jerkin under one arm, and the petticoat under the other) in order to carry to the taylor to be made up; and had just stepped in, in high spirits, to show the parson how cleverly it had held out.

There are many good similies subsisting in the world, but which I have time neither to recollect nor look for, which would give you a strong conception of the astonishment and honest indignation which this unexpected stroke of Trim's impudence impressed upon the parson's looks;—let it suffice to say, that it exceeded all fair description,—as well as all power of proper resentment,—except this, that Trim was ordered, in a stern voice, to lay the bundles down upon the table,—to go about his business, and wait upon him, at his peril, the next morning, at eleven precisely.—Against this hour, like a wise man, the parson had sent to desire John the parish-clerk, who bore an exceeding good character, as a man of truth, and who having, moreover, a pretty freehold of about eighteen pounds a year in the township, was a leading man in it; and, upon the whole, was such a one, of whom it might be said, that he rather did honor to his office than that his office did honor to him;—him he sends for, with the churchwardens, and one of the sidesmen, a grave knowing old man, to be present;—for, as Trim had withheld the whole truth from the parson touching the watch-coat, he thought it probable he would as certainly do the same thing to others. Though this, I said, was wise, the trouble of the precaution might have been spared,—because the parson's character was unblemished,—and he had ever been held by the world in the estimation of a man of honor and integrity.—Trim's character, on the contrary, was as well known, if not in the world, at least in all the parish, to be that of a little dirty, pimping, pettifogging, ambidextrous fellow,—who neither cared what he did or said of any, provided he could get a penny by it. This might, I said, have made any precaution needless;—but you must know, as the parson had in a manner but just got down to his living, he dreaded the consequences of the least ill-impression on his first entrance among his parishioners, which would have disabled him from doing them the good he wished:—so that, out of regard to his flock, more than the necessary care due to himself,—he was resolved not to lie at the mercy of what resentment might vent, or malice lend an ear to.

Accordingly the whole matter was rehearsed, from first to last, by the parson, in the manner I've told you, in the hearing of John, the parish-clerk, and in the presence of Trim.

Trim had little to say for himself, except "that the parson had absolutely promised to befriend him and his wife in the affair, to the utmost of his power; that the watch coat was certainly in his power, and that he might still give it him, if he pleased."

To this the parson's reply was short, but strong: "That nothing was in his *power* to do, but what he could do *honestly*;—that, in giving the coat to him and his wife, he should do a manifest wrong to the *next* sexton, the great watch-coat being the most comfortable part of the place;—that he should, moreover, injure the right of his own successor, who would be just so much a worse patron as the worth of the coat amounted to; and, in a word, he declared, that his whole intent in promising that coat, was charity to Trim, but *wrong* to no man;—that was a reserve, he said, made in all cases of this kind: and he declared solemnly, *in verbo sacerdotis*, that this was his meaning, and was so understood by Trim himself."

With the weight of this truth, and the great good sense and strong reason which accompanied all the parson said on the subject,—poor Trim was driven to his last shift, and begged he might be suffered to plead his right and title to the watch-coat, if not by *promise*, at least by *servitude*;—it was well known how much he was entitled to it upon these scores: That he had blacked the parson's shoes without count, and greased his boots above fifty times: that he had run for eggs in the town upon all occasions,—whetted the knives at all hours, catched his horse, and rubbed him down:—that, for his wife, she had been ready upon all occasions to char for them; and neither he nor she, to the best of his remembrance, ever took a farthing, or any thing beyond a mug of ale.——To this account of his services, he begged leave to add those of his wishes, which, he said, had been equally great.—He affirmed, and was ready, he said, to make it appear, by a number of witnesses, "he had drunk his Reverence's health a thousand times (by the bye, he did not add out of the parson's own ale)—that he had not only drunk his own health, but wished it, and never came to the house but asked his man kindly how he did; that, in particular, about half a year ago, when his Reverence cut his finger in paring an apple, he went half a mile* to ask a cunning woman what was good to staunch blood; and actually returned with a cobweb in his breeches' pocket. Nay, says Trim, it was not a fortnight ago, when your Reverence took that strong purge, that I went to the far end of the whole town to borrow you a close-stool, and came back, as the neighbors who flouted me will all bear witness, with the pan upon my head, and never thought it too much." Trim concluded this pathetic remonstrance with saying, "he hoped his Reverence's heart would not suffer him to requite so many faithful services by so unkind a return: that if it was so, as he was the first, so he hoped he should be the last example of a man of his condition so treated."—This plan of Trim's defence, which Trim had put himself upon, could admit of no other reply than a general smile.—Upon the whole, let me inform you, that all that could be said *pro* and *con*, on both sides, being fairly heard, it was plain that Trim in every part of this affair had behaved very ill;—and one thing, which was never expected to be known of him, happened, in the course of this debate, to come out against him, namely, that he had gone and told the parson, before he had ever set foot in his parish,* that John, his parish-clerk, his churchwardens, and some of the heads of the parish, were a parcel of scoundrels.—Upon the upshot, Trim was kick'd out of doors, and told, at his peril, never to come there again.

At first, Trim huff'd and bounced most terribly,—swore he would get a warrant,—that nothing would serve him but he would call a by-law, and tell the whole parish how the parson had misused him; but cooling of that, as fearing the parson might possibly bind him over to his good behavior, and, for aught he knew, might send him to the house of correction, he lets the parson alone, and, to revenge himself, falls foul upon the clerk, who has no more to do in the quarrel than you or I,—rips up the promise of the old—cast pair of black—plush—breeches; and raises an uproar in the town about it, notwithstanding it had slept ten

* "Long before any thing of my patent was thought "of, I not only most sincerely lamented the Arch-"bishop's illness, but made it my business to inquire "after every place and remedy that might help his 'Grace in his complaints." *Extract of a Letter from Dr. Topham, p. 26 of Dr. Fountayne's Answer.*

* In Dr. Fountayne's pamphlet, p. 18 and 19, Dr Topham is charged with having assured Archbishop Hutton, before he came into the diocese, that the Dean and Chapter of York were a set of *strange people*; and that he would find it *very difficult*, if *not impossible*, to live upon good terms with them.

years; — but all this, you must know, is looked upon in no other light but as an artful stroke of generalship in Trim to raise a dust, and cover himself under the disgraceful chastisement he has undergone.

If your curiosity is not yet satisfied,—I will now proceed to relate the *Battle of the Breeches*, in the same exact manner I have done that of the Watch-Coat.

Be it known then, that about ten years ago, when John was appointed parish-clerk of this church, this said Trim took no small pains to get into John's good graces, in order, as it afterwards appeared, to coax a promise out of him of a pair of breeches, which John had then by him, of black plush, not much the worse for wearing. — Trim only begged for God's sake to have them bestowed upon him when John should think fit to cast them.

Trim was one of those kind of men who loved a bit of finery in his heart; and would rather have a tatter'd rag of a better body's, than the best plain whole thing his wife could spin him.

John, who was naturally unsuspicious, made no more difficulty of promising the breeches than the parson had done in promising the great coat; and indeed with something less reserve,—because the breeches were John's *own;* and he could give them, without wrong, to whom he thought fit.

It happened, I was going to say unluckily, but I should rather say most luckily for Trim, for he was the only gainer by it, that a quarrel, about some six or eight weeks after this, broke out betwixt *the* late* parson of the parish and John the clerk. Somebody (and it was thought to be nobody but Trim) had put it into the parson's head, "that John's † desk, in the church, was at "the least four inches higher than it should "be;—that the thing gave offence, and was "indecorous, inasmuch as it approached too "near upon a level with the parson's desk "itself."—This hardship the parson complained of loudly; and told John one day after prayers, "he could bear it no longer; "and would have it altered, and brought "down as it should be."—John made no other reply, but "that the desk was not of "his raising; — that 'twas not one hair-"breadth higher than he found it;—and "that as he found it, so he would leave it. "In short, he would neither make an en-"croachment, neither would he suffer one." —The *late* parson might have his virtues, but the leading part of his character was not *humility;*—so that John's stiffness in this point was not likely to reconcile matters.——This was Trim's harvest.

After a friendly hint to John to stand his ground, away hies Trim to make his market at the vicarage.—What passed there I will not say, intending not to be uncharitable; so shall content myself with only guessing at it from the sudden change that appeared in Trim's dress for the better;—for he had left his old ragged coat, hat, and wig, in the stable, and was come forth strutting across the churchyard, yclad in a good charitable cast coat, large hat, and wig, which the parson had just given him. ——"Ho! ho! hollo! John," cries Trim, in an insolent bravo, as loud as ever he could bawl,—"see here, my lad, how fine "I am!"—The more shame for you, answered John, seriously. — Do you think, Trim, says he, such finery, gained by such services, becomes you, or can wear well? —Fy upon it, Trim, I could not have expected this from you, considering what friendship you pretended, and how kind I have ever been to you; how many shillings and sixpences I have generously lent you in your distresses.—Nay, it was but the other day that I promised you these black plush breeches I have on. —— Rot your breeches, quoth Trim (for Trim's brain was half-turned with his new finery), rot your breeches, says he,—I would not take them up were they laid at my door;—give them, and be d——d to you, to whom you like:—I would have you to know, I can have a better pair of the parson's any day in the week. —— John told him plainly, as his word had once passed him, he had a spirit above taking advantage of his insolence, in giving them away to another;—but to tell him his mind freely, he thought he had got so many favors of that kind, and was so likely to get many more for the same services, of the parson, that he had better give

* Archbishop Herring.

† This alludes to the right of appointing preachers for the vacant stalls, which Dr. Fountayne, as Dean of York, claimed against the Archbishop.

up the breeches, with good-nature, to some one who would be more thankful for them.

Here John mentioned Mark * Slender (who it seems the day before had asked John for them) not knowing they were under promise to Trim.——"Come, Trim, says he, let poor Mark have them,—you know he has not a pair to his a—; besides, you see he is just of my size, and they will fit to a T: whereas, if I give 'em to you, look ye, they are not worth much; and, besides, you could not get your backside into them, if you had them, without tearing them all to pieces."—Every tittle of this was most undoubtedly true; for Trim, you must know, by foul-feeding, and playing the good-fellow at the parson's, was grown somewhat gross about the lower parts, *if not higher;* so that, as all John said upon the occasion was fact, Trim, with much ado, and after a hundred *hums* and *hahs*, at last, out of mere compassion to Mark, *signs*,† *seals, and delivers up* ALL RIGHT, *interest, and pretensions whatsoever, in and to the said Breeches, thereby binding his heirs, executors, administrators, and assigns, never more to call the said claim in* QUESTION.—All this renunciation was set forth in an ample manner, to be in pure pity to Mark's nakedness;—but the secret was, Trim had an eye to, and firmly expected in his own mind, the great green pulpit-cloth,‡ and old velvet cushion, which were that year to be taken down;—which, by the bye, could he have wheedled John a second time, as he had hoped, would have made up the loss of the breeches sevenfold.

Now you must know, this pulpit-cloth and cushion were not in John's gift, but in the churchwardens',§ &c. However, as I said above, that John was a leading man in the parish, Trim knew he could help him to 'em if he would;—but John had got a surfeit of him,—so when the pulpit-cloth, &c. were taken down, they were immediately given (John having a great say in it) to William Doe,* who understood very well what use to make of them.

As for the old breeches, poor Mark lived to wear them but a short time; and they got into the possession of Lorry Slim,† an unlucky wight, by whom they are still worn:—in truth, as you will guess, they are very thin by this time.

But Lorry has a light heart; and what recommends them to him is this,—That, as thin as they are, he knows that Trim, let him say what he will to the contrary, still envies the *possessor* of them; and, with all his pride, would be very glad to wear them after *him*.

Upon this footing have these affairs slept quietly for near ten years;—and would have slept for ever, but for the unlucky kick-bout, which, as I said, has ripp'd this squabble up afresh; so that it was no longer ago than last week, that Trim met and insulted John in the public town-way, before a hundred people;‡—tax'd him with the promise of the old cast pair of black breeches, notwithstanding Trim's solemn renunciation;—twitted him with the pulpit-cloth and velvet cushion;—as good as told him he was ignorant of the common duties of his clerkship; adding, very insolently, that he knew not so much as to give out a common psalm in tune.

John contented himself by giving a plain answer to every article that Trim had laid to his charge, and appealed to his neighbors, who remembered the whole affair;—and, as he knew there was never any thing to be got by wrestling with a chimney-sweeper, he was going to take his leave of Trim for ever. But hold,—the mob by this time had got round them, and their high mightinesses insisted upon having Trim tried upon the spot.

Trim was accordingly tried; and after a full hearing, was convicted a second time, and handled more roughly by one or more of them than even at the parson's.

* Dr. Braithwaite.

† Extract of a letter from Dr. Topham to Dr. Fountayne:—"As Dr. Ward has proposed to resign the "jurisdiction of Pickering and Pocklington to Dr. "Braithwaite, if you have not any other objection, I "shall very readily give up what *interest* arises to "me in these jurisdictions from your friendship and "regard."—*P. 5. of Dr. Fountayne's Answer to Dr. Topham.*

‡ The Commissaryship of the Dean of York, and the Commissaryship of the Dean and Chapter of York.

§ The members of the Chapter.

* Mr. Stables.

† Mr. Sterne himself.

‡ At the Sessions-dinner, where Dr. Topham charges Dr. Fountayne with the breach of his promise, in giving the Commissaryship of Pocklington and Pickering to another person.

—Trim, says one, are you not ashamed of yourself, to make all this rout and disturbance in the town, and set neighbors together by the ears, about an old,—worn-out,—pair of cast—breeches, not worth half a crown? Is there a cast coat, or a place in the whole town, that will bring you in a shilling, but what you have snapped up like a greedy hound as you are?

In the first place, are you not sexton and dog-whipper,* worth three pounds a year? Then you begged the churchwardens to let your wife have the washing and darning of the church-linen, which brings you in thirteen shillings and four-pence:—then you have six shillings and eight-pence for oiling and winding up the clock; both paid you at Easter:—the pounder's place, which is worth forty shillings a year, you have got that too:—you are the bailiff, which the late parson got you, which brings you in forty shillings more.

Besides all this, you have six pounds a year paid you quarterly, for being mole-catcher to the parish.—Ay, says the luckless wight above-mentioned (who was standing close by him with the plush breeches on), "you are not only mole-catcher, Trim, "but you catch STRAY CONIES too in the *dark*, "and you pretend a license for it; which, "I trow, will be looked into at the next "quarter-sessions."—I maintain it, I have a license, says Trim, blushing as red as scarlet,—I have a license; and, as I farm a warren in the next parish, I will catch conies every hour in the night.—*You catch conies!* says a toothless old woman just passing by.

This set the mob a-laughing, and sent every man home in perfect good-humor, except Trim, who waddled very slowly off, with that kind of inflexible gravity only to be equalled by one animal in the creation and surpassed by none.

I am, Sir,
Yours, &c. &c.

POSTSCRIPT.

I HAVE broke open my letter to inform you, that I missed the opportunity of sending it by the messenger, who, I expected, would have called upon me in his return through this village to York; so it has lain a week or ten days by me.—I am not sorry for the disappointment, because something has since happened, in continuation of this affair, which I am thereby enabled to transmit to you, all under one trouble.

When I finished the above account, I thought (as did every soul in the parish) Trim had met with so thorough a rebuff from John the parish-clerk, and the town's-folks, who all took against him, that Trim would be glad to be quiet, and let the matter rest.

But it seems it is not half an hour ago since Trim* sallied forth again; and, having borrowed a sow-gelder's horn—with hard blowing he got the whole town round him, and endeavored to raise a disturbance, and fight the whole battle over again;—alleged, That he had been used in the last fray worse than the dog; not by John the parish-clerk, for I should not, quoth Trim, have valued him a rush single hands;—but all the town sided with him; and twelve men in *buckram*† set upon me, all at once, and kept me in play at sword's-point for three hours together.

Besides, quoth Trim, there were two misbegotten knaves in Kendal-green, who lay all the while in ambush in John's own house; and they, all sixteen, came upon my back, and let drive at me all together:—a plague, says Trim, of all cowards.

Trim repeated his story above a dozen times, which made some of the neighbors pity him, thinking the poor fellow crack-

* "In the first place, would any one imagine that "Dr. Topham, who was now Master of the Faculties, "—Commissary to the Archbishop of York,—Official "to the Archdeacon of York,—Official to the Arch-"deacon of the East Riding,—Official to the Arch-"deacon of Cleveland,—Official to the peculiar juris-"diction of Howdenshire,—Official to the Precentor.—"Official to the Chancellor of the Church of York,—"and Official to several of the Prebendaries thereof, "could accept of so poor an addition as a Commissary-"ship of five guineas per annum?"—*P. S. of Dr. Fountayne's Answer to Dr. Topham.*

* Alluding to Dr. Topham's Reply to Dr. Fountayne's Answer.

† In Dr. Topham's Reply, he asserts, that Dr. Fountayne's Answer was *the child and offspring of many parents*, p. 1.

brain'd, and that he actually believed what he said.

After this Trim dropped the affair of the breeches, and began a fresh dispute about the reading-desk; which I told you had occasioned some small dispute between the *late* parson and John some years ago.— This reading-desk, as you will observe, was but an episode wove into the main story by the bye; for the main affair was *the battle of the breeches and the great coat.*

However, Trim being at last driven out of these two citadels,—he has seized hold, in his retreat, of this reading-desk, with a view, as it seems, to take shelter behind it.

I cannot say but the man has fought it out obstinately enough; and, had his cause been good, I should have really pitied him. For, when he was *driven out of the great watch-coat*, you see he did not run away. No;—he retreated *behind the breeches;* and when he could make nothing of it behind the breeches, he got *behind the reading-desk.* To what other hold Trim will next retreat, the politicians of this village are not agreed. Some think his next move will be towards the rear of *the parson's boot:* but as it is thought he cannot make a long stand there, others are of opinion, That Trim will once more in his life get hold of *the parson's horse*, and charge upon him, or perhaps behind him; but as the horse is not easy to be caught, the more general opinion is, That, when he is driven out of the reading-desk, he will make his last retreat in such a manner, as, if possible, to gain the *close-stool*, and defend himself behind it to the very last drop.

If Trim should make this movement, by my advice, he should be left, besides his citadel, in full possession of the field of battle, where 'tis certain he will keep every body a league off, and may hop by himself till he is weary. Besides, as Trim seems bent upon *purging* himself, and may have abundance of foul humors to work off, I think he cannot be better placed.

But this is all matter of speculation.— Let me carry you back to matter-of-fact, and tell you what kind of stand Trim has actually made behind the said desk:— "Neighbors and townsmen all, I will be sworn before my Lord Mayor, that John and his nineteen men in *buckram* have abused me worse than a dog, for they told you that I play'd fast-and-go-loose with the *late* parson and him in that old dispute of theirs about the *reading-desk;* and that I made matters worse between them, and not better."

Of this charge, Trim declared he was as innocent as the child that was unborn;— than he would be book-sworn, he had no hand in it.

He produced a strong witness, and moreover insinuated, that John himself, instead of being angry for what he had done in it, had actually thanked him.—Ay, Trim, says the wight in the plush breeches, but that was, Trim, the day before John found thee out. Besides, Trim, there is nothing in that; for the very year that you was made town's pounder, thou knowest well that I both thanked thee myself, and moreover gave thee a good warm supper for turning John Lund's cows and horses out of my hard corn-close, which if thou hadst not done (as thou told'st me) I should have lost my whole crop; whereas John Lund and Thomas Patt, who are both here to testify, and are both willing to take their oaths on't, that thou thyself wast the very first man who set the gate open;—and after all it was not thee, Trim, 'twas the blacksmith's poor lad who turned them out;—so that a man may be thanked and rewarded too for a good turn which he never did, nor ever did intend.

Trim could not sustain this unexpected stroke—so Trim marched off the field without colors flying, or his horn sounding, or any other ensigns of honor whatever.— Whether, after this, Trim intends to rally a second time,—or whether he may not take it into his head to claim the victory,— none but Trim himself can inform you.

However, the general opinion upon the whole is this, That, in three several pitch'd battles, Trim has been so *trimm'd*, as never disastrous hero was *trimm'd* before.

THE END OF STERNE'S WORKS.

CONTENTS

OF

STERNE'S WORKS.

THE LIFE AND OPINIONS OF TRISTRAM SHANDY, GENTLEMAN.

COMPRISING THE HUMOROUS ADVENTURES OF

UNCLE TOBY AND CORPORAL TRIM.

BY L. STERNE.

Beautifully Illustrated by Darley. Stitched.

A SENTIMENTAL JOURNEY.

BY L. STERNE.

Illustrated as above by Darley. Stitched.

The beauties of this author are so well known, and his errors in style and expression so few and far between, that one reads with renewed delight his delicate turns, &c.

THE LIFE OF GENERAL JACKSON,

WITH A LIKENESS OF THE OLD HERO.

One volume, 18mo.

LIFE OF PAUL JONES.

In one volume, 12mo.

WITH ONE HUNDRED ILLUSTRATIONS.

BY JAMES HAMILTON.

The work is compiled from his original journals and correspondence, and includes an account of his services in the American Revolution, and in the war between the Russians and Turks in the Black Sea. There is scarcely any Naval Hero, of any age, who combined in his character so much of the adventurous, skilful and daring, as Paul Jones. The incidents of his life are almost as startling and absorbing as those of romance. His achievements during the American Revolution—the fight between the Bon Homme Richard and Serapis, the most desperate naval action on record—and the alarm into which, with so small a force, he threw the coasts of England and Scotland—are matters comparatively well known to Americans; but the incidents of his subsequent career have been veiled in obscurity, which is dissipated by this biography. A book like this, narrating the actions of such a man, ought to meet with an extensive sale, and become as popular as Robinson Crusoe in fiction, or Weems's Life of Marion and Washington, and similar books, in fact. It contains 400 pages, has a handsome portrait and medallion likeness of Jones, and is illustrated with numerous original wood engravings of naval scenes and distinguished men with whom he was familiar.

THE GREEK EXILE;

Or, A Narrative of the Captivity and Escape of Christophorus Plato Castanis,

DURING THE MASSACRE ON THE ISLAND OF SCIO BY THE TURKS.

TOGETHER WITH VARIOUS ADVENTURES IN GREECE AND AMERICA.

WRITTEN BY HIMSELF,

Author of an Essay on the Ancient and Modern Greek Languages; Interpretation of the Attributes of the Principal Fabulous Deities; The Jewish Maiden of Scio's Citadel; and the Greek Boy in the Sunday-School.

One volume, 12mo.

THE YOUNG CHORISTER;

A Collection of New and Beautiful Tunes, adapted to the use of Sabbath-Schools, from some of the most distinguished composers; together with many of the author's compositions.

EDITED BY MINARD W. WILSON.

CAMP LIFE OF A VOLUNTEER.

A Campaign in Mexico; Or, A Glimpse at Life in Camp.

BY "ONE WHO HAS SEEN THE ELEPHANT."

Life of General Zachary Taylor,

COMPRISING A NARRATIVE OF EVENTS CONNECTED WITH HIS PROFESSIONAL CAREER, AND AUTHENTIC INCIDENTS OF HIS EARLY YEARS.

BY J. REESE FRY AND R. T. CONRAD.

With an original and accurate Portrait, and eleven elegant Illustrations, by Darley.

In one handsome 12mo. volume.

"It is by far the fullest and most interesting biography of General Taylor that we have ever seen." —*Richmond (Whig) Chronicle.*

"On the whole, we are satisfied that this volume is the most correct and comprehensive one yet published." —*Hunt's Merchants' Magazine.*

"The superiority of this edition over the ephemeral publications of the day consists in fuller and more authentic accounts of his family, his early life, and Indian wars. The narrative of his proceedings in Mexico is drawn partly from reliable private letters, but chiefly from his own official correspondence."

"It forms a cheap, substantial, and attractive volume, and one which should be read at the fireside of every family who desire a faithful and true life of the Old General."

GENERAL TAYLOR AND HIS STAFF:

Comprising Memoirs of Generals Taylor, Worth, Wool, and Butler; Cols. May, Cross, Clay, Hardin, Yell, Hays, and other distinguished Officers attached to General Taylor's Army. Interspersed with

NUMEROUS ANECDOTES OF THE MEXICAN WAR,

and Personal Adventures of the Officers. Compiled from Public Documents and Private Correspondence. With

ACCURATE PORTRAITS, AND OTHER BEAUTIFUL ILLUSTRATIONS.

In one volume, 12mo.

GENERAL SCOTT AND HIS STAFF:

Comprising Memoirs of Generals Scott, Twiggs, Smith, Quitman, Shields, Pillow, Lane, Cadwalader, Patterson, and Pierce; Cols. Childs, Riley, Harney, and Butler; and other distinguished officers attached to General Scott's Army.

TOGETHER WITH

Notices of General Kearny, Col. Doniphan, Col. Fremont, and other officers distinguished in the Conquest of California and New Mexico; and Personal Adventures of the Officers. Compiled from Public Documents and Private Correspondence. With

ACCURATE PORTRAITS, AND OTHER BEAUTIFUL ILLUSTRATIONS.

In one volume, 12mo.

THE FAMILY DENTIST,

INCLUDING THE SURGICAL, MEDICAL AND MECHANICAL TREATMENT OF THE TEETH.

Illustrated with thirty-one Engravings.

By CHARLES A. DU BOUCHET, M. D., Dental Surgeon.

In one volume, 18mo.

SCHOOLCRAFTS GREAT NATIONAL WORK ON THE

Indian Tribes of the United States.

PART SECOND—QUARTO.

WITH EIGHTY BEAUTIFUL ILLUSTRATIONS ON STEEL,

Engraved in the first style of the art, from Drawings by Captain Eastman, U. S. A.

PRICE, FIFTEEN DOLLARS.

COCKBURN'S LIFE OF LORD JEFFREY.

LIFE OF LORD JEFFREY,

WITH A SELECTION FROM HIS CORRESPONDENCE,

BY LORD COCKBURN,

One of the Judges of the Court of Sessions in Scotland. Two volumes, demi-octavo.

"Those who know Lord Jeffrey only through the pages of the Edinburgh Review, get but a one-sided, and not the most pleasant view of his character."

"We advise our readers to obtain the book, and enjoy it to the full themselves. They will unite with us in saying that the self-drawn character portrayed in the letters of Lord Jeffrey, is one of the most delightful pictures that has ever been presented to them."—*Evening Bulletin.*

"Jeffrey was for a long period editor of the Review, and was admitted by all the other contributors to be the leading spirit in it. In addition to his political articles, he soon showed his wonderful powers of criticism in literature. He was equally at home whether censuring or applauding; in his onslaughts on the mediocrity of Southey, or the misused talents of Byron, or in his noble essays on Shakspeare, or Scott, or Burns."—*New York Express.*

PRICE, TWO DOLLARS AND A HALF.

ROMANCE OF NATURAL HISTORY;

OR, WILD SCENES AND WILD HUNTERS.

WITH NUMEROUS ILLUSTRATIONS, IN ONE VOLUME OCTAVO, CLOTH.

BY C. W. WEBBER.

"We have rarely read a volume so full of life and enthusiasm, so capable of transporting the reader into an actor among the scenes and persons described. The volume can hardly be opened at any page without arresting the attention, and the reader is borne along with the movement of a style whose elastic spring and life knows no weariness."—*Boston Courier and Transcript.*

PRICE, TWO DOLLARS.

THE LIFE OF WILLIAM PENN,

WITH SELECTIONS FROM HIS CORRESPONDENCE AND AUTOBIOGRAPHY,

BY SAMUEL M. JANNEY.

Second Edition, Revised.

"Our author has acquitted himself in a manner worthy of his subject. His style is easy, flowing, and yet sententious. Altogether, we consider it a highly valuable addition to the literature of our age, and a work that should find its way into the library of every Friend."—*Friends' Intelligencer, Philadelphia.*

"We regard this life of the great founder of Pennsylvania as a valuable addition to the literature of the country."—*Philadelphia Evening Bulletin.*

"We have no hesitation in pronouncing Mr. Janney's life of Penn the best, because the most satisfactory, that has yet been written. The author's style is clear and uninvolved, and well suited to the purposes of biographical narrative."—*Louisville Journal.*

PRICE, TWO DOLLARS.

LIPPINCOTT'S CABINET HISTORIES OF THE STATES,

CONSISTING OF A SERIES OF

Cabinet Histories of all the States of the Union,

TO EMBRACE A VOLUME FOR EACH STATE.

We have so far completed all our arrangements, as to be able to issue the whole series in the shortest possible time consistent with its careful literary production. SEVERAL VOLUMES ARE NOW READY FOR SALE. The talented authors who have engaged to write these Histories, are no strangers in the literary world.

NOTICES OF THE PRESS.

"These most tastefully printed and bound volumes form the first instalment of a series of State Histories, which, without superseding the bulkier and more expensive works of the same character, may enter household channels from which the others would be excluded by their cost and magnitude."

"In conciseness, clearness, skill of arrangement, and graphic interest, they are a most excellent earnest of those to come. They are eminently adapted both to interest and instruct, and should have a place in the family library of every American."—*N. Y. Courier and Enquirer.*

"The importance of a series of State History like those now in preparation, can scarcely be estimated. Being condensed as carefully as accuracy and interest of narrative will permit, the size and price of the volumes will bring them within the reach of every family in the country, thus making them home-reading books for old and young. Each individual will, in consequence, become familiar, not only with the history of his own State, but with that of the other States; thus mutual interests will be re-awakened, and old bonds cemented in a firmer re-union."—*Home Gazette.*

NEW THEMES FOR THE PROTESTANT CLERGY;

CREEDS WITHOUT CHARITY, THEOLOGY WITHOUT HUMANITY, AND PROTESTANTISM WITHOUT CHRISTIANITY:

With Notes by the Editor on the Literature of Charity, Population, Pauperism, Political Economy, and Protestantism.

"The great question which the book discusses is, whether the Church of this age is what the primitive Church was, and whether Christians—both pastors and people—are doing their duty. Our anthor believes not, and, to our mind, he has made out a strong case. He thinks there is abundant room for reform at the present time, and that it is needed almost as much as in the days of Luther. And why? Because, in his own words, 'While one portion of nominal Christians have busied themselves with forms and ceremonies and observances; with pictures, images, and processions; others have given to doctrines the supremacy, and have busied themselves in laying down the lines by which to enforce human belief—lines of interpretation by which to control human opinion —lines of discipline and restraint, by which to bring human minds to uniformity of faith and action. They have formed creeds and catechisms; they have spread themselves over the whole field of the sacred writings, and scratched up all the surface; they have gathered all the straws, and turned over all the pebbles, and detected the colour and determined the outline of every stone and tree and shrub; they have dwelt with rapture upon all that was beautiful and sublime; but they have trampled over mines of golden wisdom, of surpassing richness and depth, almost without a thought, and almost without an effort to fathom these priceless treasures, much less to take possession of them.'"

PRICE, ONE DOLLAR.

SIMPSON'S MILITARY JOURNAL.

JOURNAL OF A MILITARY RECONNOISSANCE FROM SANTA FE, NEW MEXICO, TO THE NAVAJO COUNTRY,

BY JAMES H. SIMPSON, A. M.,

FIRST LIEUTENANT CORPS OF TOPOGRAPHICAL ENGINEERS.

WITH SEVENTY-FIVE COLOURED ILLUSTRATIONS.

One volume, octavo. Price, Three Dollars.

TALES OF THE SOUTHERN BORDER.

BY C. W. WEBBER.

ONE VOLUME OCTAVO, HANDSOMELY ILLUSTRATED.

The Hunter Naturalist, a Romance of Sporting;

OR, WILD SCENES AND WILD HUNTERS,

BY C. W. WEBBER,

Author of "Shot in the Eye," "Old Hicks the Guide," "Gold Mines of the Gila," &c.

ONE VOLUME, ROYAL OCTAVO.

ILLUSTRATED WITH FORTY BEAUTIFUL ENGRAVINGS, FROM ORIGINAL DRAWINGS,

MANY OF WHICH ARE COLOURED.

Price, Five Dollars.

NIGHTS IN A BLOCK-HOUSE;

OR, SKETCHES OF BORDER LIFE,

Embracing Adventures among the Indians, Feats of the Wild Hunters, and Exploits of Boone, Brady, Kenton, Whetzel, Fleehart, and other Border Heroes of the West

BY HENRY C. WATSON,

Author of "Camp-Fires of the Revolution."

WITH NUMEROUS ILLUSTRATIONS.

One volume, 8vo. Price, $2 00.

HAMILTON, THE YOUNG ARTIST.

BY AUGUSTA BROWNE.

WITH

AN ESSAY ON SCULPTURE AND PAINTING,

BY HAMILTON A. C. BROWNE.

1 vol. 18mo. Price, 37 1-2 cents.

THE FISCAL HISTORY OF TEXAS:

EMBRACING AN ACCOUNT OF ITS REVENUES, DEBTS, AND CURRENCY, FROM THE COMMENCEMENT OF THE REVOLUTION IN 1834, TO 1851-2, WITH REMARKS ON AMERICAN DEBTS.

BY WM. M. GOUGE,

Author of "A Short History of Paper Money and Banking in the United States."

In one vol. 8vo., cloth. Price $1 50.

INGERSOLL'S HISTORY OF THE SECOND WAR:

A HISTORY OF THE SECOND WAR BETWEEN THE U. STATES AND GT. BRITAIN.

BY CHARLES J. INGERSOLL.

Second series. 2 volumes, 8vo. Price $4 00.

These two volumes, which embrace the hostile transactions between the United States and Great Britain during the years 1814 and '15, complete Mr. Ingersoll's able work on the Second or "Late War," as it has usually been called. A great deal of new and valuable matter has been collected by the author from original sources, and is now first introduced to the public.

In Press,

A NEW AND COMPLETE

GAZETTEER OF THE UNITED STATES.

It will furnish the fullest and most recent information respecting the Geography, Statistics, and present state of improvement, of every part of this great Republic, particularly of

TEXAS, CALIFORNIA, OREGON, NEW MEXICO,

&c. The work will be issued as soon as the complete official returns of the present Census are received.

THE ABOVE WORK WILL BE FOLLOWED BY

A UNIVERSAL GAZETTEER, OR GEOGRAPHICAL DICTIONARY,

of the most complete and comprehensive character. It will be compiled from the best English, French, and German authorities, and will be published the moment that the returns of the present census of Europe can be obtained.

History of the Mormons of Utah,

THEIR DOMESTIC POLITY AND THEOLOGY,

BY J. W. GUNNISON,

U. S. Corps Topographical Engineers.

WITH ILLUSTRATIONS, IN ONE VOLUME DEMI-OCTAVO.

PRICE FIFTY CENTS.

REPORT OF A GEOLOGICAL SURVEY

OF

WISCONSIN, IOWA, AND MINNESOTA,

AND INCIDENTALLY OF

A PORTION OF NEBRASKA TERRITORY,

MADE UNDER INSTRUCTIONS FROM THE U. S. TREASURY DEPARTMENT,

BY DAVID DALE OWEN,

United States' Geologist.

WITH OVER 150 ILLUSTRATIONS ON STEEL AND WOOD.

Two volumes, quarto. Price Ten Dollars.

MERCHANTS' MEMORANDUM BOOK,

CONTAINING LISTS OF ALL GOODS PURCHASED BY COUNTRY MERCHANTS, &c

One volume, 18mo., Leather cover. Price, 50 cents.

A REVIEW

OF

"NEW THEMES FOR THE PROTESTANT CLERGY."

ONE VOLUME 12mo.

Price, paper, 25 cents. Cloth, 50 cents.

THE BIBLE IN THE COUNTING-HOUSE.

BY H. A. BOARDMAN, D.D.,

AUTHOR OF "THE BIBLE IN THE FAMILY."

One vol. 12mo., cloth. Price One Dollar.

AUTOBIOGRAPHY OF A NEW CHURCHMAN.

BY JOHN A. LITTLE.

ONE VOLUME 12mo. PRICE 75 CENTS.

MILTON'S WORKS—NEW AND COMPLETE EDITION.

Milton's Poetical Works,

WITH A LIFE, DISSERTATION, INDEX, AND NOTES.

BY PROF. C. D. CLEVELAND.

ONE VOLUME ROYAL 12mo., CLOTH. PRICE $1 25.

UNIFORM AND DRESS

OF THE

ARMY OF THE UNITED STATES.

WITH COLOURED ILLUSTRATIONS.

QUARTO, CLOTH. PRICE FIVE DOLLARS.

UNIFORM AND DRESS

OF THE

NAVY OF THE UNITED STATES.

WITH COLOURED ILLUSTRATIONS.

QUARTO, CLOTH. PRICE FIVE DOLLARS.

SCHOOL BOOKS.

THE CHILD'S FIRST BOOK IN GEOGRAPHY, half bound... 25
SMITH'S NEW COMMON SCHOOL GEOGRAPHY... 50
WALKER'S SCHOOL DICTIONARY, new edition, well bound... 25
*** The above is the popular Philadelphia school edition, printed from new stereotype plates, on fine white paper, and well bound.
COMLY'S SPELLING AND READING BOOK, Bonsal's edition... 10
COMLY'S READER AND BOOK OF KNOWLEDGE, with Exercises on Spelling and Defining, 12mo... 37
EMERSON'S N. A. Arithmetic. Part First... 10
Do. do. do. Second 25
BENTLEY'S PICTORIAL DEFINER. Illustrated by 2000 engravings... 20
THE MANUAL OF ELOCUTION AND ORATORY, by John Walker, with Selections, by Richard Culver, 1 vol. 12mo... 75
THE COLUMBIAN ORATOR, by Caleb Bingham... 50
THE AMERICAN PRECEPTOR, by Caleb Bingham... 25
DILLAWAY'S LIBER PRIMUS... 75
DILLAWAY'S COLLOQUIES OF ERASMUS, 1 vol. 12mo... 38
FORSTER'S PENCILLED COPY-BOOKS, in 12 numbers, *per doz*... 1 00
FORSTER'S DOUBLE-ENTRY BOOKKEEPING, new edition... 1 00
FIRST BOOKS OF NATURAL HISTORY FOR SCHOOLS, COLLEGES, AND FAMILIES. BY W. S. RUSCHENBERGER, M. D.
Elements of Anatomy and Physiology... 37
Elements of Mammalogy... 37
Elements of Ornithology... 37
Elements of Herpetology and Ichthyology... 37
Elements of Conchology... 37
Elements of Entomology... 37
Elements of Botany... 37
Elements of Geology... 50
The whole Series, complete, with a new Glossary, bound in 2 vols., half Turkey mor... 3 00
GROVES' GREEK AND ENGLISH DICTIONARY, new ed., 1 vol. 8vo., well bound 2 00
TICKNOR'S MENSURATION, sheep... 50
KEY TO TICKNOR'S MENSURATION... 50
THE COLUMBIAN CALCULATOR, by A. Ticknor... 30
YOUTH'S COLUMBIAN CALCULATOR, by A. Ticknor... 18
KEY TO COLUMBIAN AND YOUTH'S CALCULATOR, in one vol... 50
TICKNOR'S COLUMBIAN SPELLING-BOOK... 10
TICKNOR'S ARITHMETICAL TABLES; designed for the use of Younger Classes... 3
LEXICON OF TERMS USED IN NATURAL HISTORY, by W. S. Ruschenberger, M. D., 12mo., half roan... 30
BALDWIN'S PRONOUNCING GAZETTEER, new ed., enlarged—census of 1850... 1 25
BALDWIN'S VOCABULARY OF ENGLISH PRONUNCIATION, 1 vol. 12mo., half b'd. 25
PEIRCE'S PRIMER, 16mo... 6
do. FIRST READER, " ... 10
do. SECOND do. " ... 20
do. THIRD do. 12mo... 37
HAZEN'S NEW SPELLER AND DEFINER, 1 vol. 12mo., half roan... 34
TRACY'S ELEMENTARY ARITHMETIC, 12mo., half roan... 25
TRACY'S SCIENTIFIC AND PRACTICAL ARITHMETIC, 12mo., half roan... 38
KEY to do... 38
TRACY'S COMMERCIAL AND MECHANICAL ARITHMETIC, sheep... 75
Key to do... 75
GRIGG AND ELLIOT'S COMMON SCHOOL READER, No. 1. 12
Do. do. do. No. 2. 20
Do. do. do. No. 3. 30
Do. do. do. No. 4. 50
Do. do. do. No. 5. 62
THE CHILD'S LITTLE THINKER; a Practical Spelling Book, by J. B. Burleigh. 12
THE THINKER, a Moral Reader, by J. B. Burleigh, A. M., 12mo., half roan... 25
THE AMERICAN MANUAL, by J. Bartlett Burleigh, A. M., new edition, with Census, 1851. In 1 vol. 12mo., half arabesque... 75
ENGLISH READER, new edition, 12mo., half roan, large type... 25
SMILEY'S TABLE-BOOK... 3
SMILEY'S ARITHMETIC... 25
Do. KEY to do... 37
BEAUTIES OF HISTORY, new edition... 50
THE YOUNG GENTLEMAN'S LEXICON... 37
THE YOUNG LADY'S LEXICON... 37
FULBORN'S GERMAN INSTRUCTOR, a new and natural method of learning to read and speak the German language, 1 vol. 12mo., half roan... 1 00
EPITOME OF GREEK AND ROMAN MYTHOLOGY, with Explanatory Notes and a Vocabulary. By John S. Hart, LL. D. 1 vol. 12mo... 50
CICERO DE OFFICIIS DE SENECTUTE and DE AMICITIÆ. New edition, with Valpy's Notes... 50
LARDNER'S KEIGHTLEY'S UNIVERSAL HISTORY, comprising a Concise History of the World from the Earliest Period. By Thomas Keightley, author of Mythology, Histories of Greece and Rome, England, &c. Revised and brought down to the present period; with Questions and Engravings. 1 vol. 12mo., cloth. emb'd... 1 00
JONES' CONVERSATIONS ON NATURAL PHILOSOPHY... 50
JONES' CONVERSATIONS ON CHEMISTRY... 62
CLEVELAND'S GRECIAN ANTIQUITIES, new edition, half arabesque... 62
GRIMSHAW'S HISTORY OF ENGLAND... 50
GRIMSHAW'S HISTORY OF ROME... 50
GRIMSHAW'S PICTORIAL HISTORY OF THE UNITED STATES, new edition, enlarged, with Questions in the Book... 75
GRIMSHAW'S HISTORY OF GREECE... 50
GRIMSHAW'S HISTORY OF FRANCE... 50
GRIMSHAW'S HISTORY OF NAPOLEON. 50
GRIMSHAW'S SOUTH AMERICA, new ed. 50
QUESTIONS and KEYS to all the above Histories, each... 10
BIGLAND'S NATURAL HISTORY, h'f roan 50
MURRAY'S EXERCISES, 12mo... 20
MURRAY'S KEY to do... 20
WEEMS' MARION, new edition, tinted pl's 75
WEEMS' WASHINGTON, do. do. 75
GRIMSHAW'S ETYMOLOGICAL DICTIONARY, in 1 vol. 12mo... 75
MOODEY'S BOOKKEEPING, Double Entry 1 00
ELEMENTS OF LITERATURE. By E. A. Ansley, A. M., half cloth... 75
ELEMENTS OF THE LAWS; or, Outlines of the System of Civil and Criminal Law in force in the United States, and the several States of the Union, designed for popular use. By the Hon. Thomas J. Smith, one of the Judges of the Supreme Court of the State of Indiana. In one handsome demi 8vo. volume... 1 00
VIRGIL DELPHINI, 1 vol. 8vo... 1 50

EBERLE'S NOTES FOR STUDENTS. new edition........ 1 00
EBERLE AND MITCHELL'S TREATISE ON THE DISEASES AND PHYSICAL EDUCATION OF CHILDREN. 1 vol. 8vo. 2 50
THE FAMILY DENTIST. 18mo.. cloth gilt.. 50
COSTILL'S TREATISE ON POISONS. 18mo. cloth........ 50

NEW PUBLICATIONS.

THE LIFE OF GEORGE FOX. By Samuel M. Janney. 1 vol. 8vo........ 1 75
CIVIL LIBERTY AND SELF-GOVERNMENT. By Francis Lieber, LL. D.. C. M. 2 vols. 12mo........ 2 25
THE AMERICAN ABORIGINAL PORTFOLIO. By Mrs. Mary H. Eastman. With 27 superb line engravings on steel. One vol. folio........ 6 00
THE WARS OF AMERICA. Containing a Complete History of the early Indian Wars, from the landing of the Pilgrims, the War of the Revolution, the Second War with Great Britain, and the Mexican War. With numerous illustrations. In 2 vols. 8vo.
GREAT TRUTHS BY GREAT AUTHORS. A Dictionary of Aids to Reflection, quotations of Maxims, Metaphors, Counsels, Cautions, Aphorisms, Proverbs, &c. &c., from writers of all ages and both hemispheres. 1 vol. demi octavo........ 1 50
A NEW AND COMPLETE GAZETTEER OF THE UNITED STATES. Edited by T. Baldwin and J. Thomas, M. D., with a new and superb map of the United States, engraved on steel. Complete in one large octavo volume........ 4 00
THE ABBOTSFORD EDITION OF THE WAVERLEY NOVELS, printed on fine white paper, with new and beautiful type, from the last English edition. Complete in twelve volumes, demi octavo, with illustrations........ 12 00
REPORT OF A GEOLOGICAL SURVEY OF WISCONSIN, IOWA, AND MINNESOTA. By David Dale Owen, United States Geologist. With nearly 300 illustrations, including maps, sections, &c. Two vols. quarto, cloth........ 10 00
STANSBURY'S EXPEDITION TO THE GREAT SALT LAKE, 2 vols. 8vo., cloth... 4 50
SCHOOLCRAFT'S GREAT NATIONAL WORK ON THE INDIAN TRIBES OF THE UNITED STATES. *Library edition.* With over 200 beautiful and accurate illustrations on steel. Three vols. 4to., cloth, *per volume*........ 7 50
PERSONAL NARRATIVE OF SCENES AND ADVENTURES in the Semi-Alpine Region of the Ozark Mountains of Missouri and Arkansas. By Henry R. Schoolcraft. One vol. demi 8vo........ 1 50
ELLET ON THE OHIO AND MISSISSIPPI RIVERS. With 12 illustrations, 1 vol. 8vo. 3 00
ROLAND TREVOR; or, The Pilot of Human Life. One vol. 12mo........ 1 00
FOOTPATH AND HIGHWAY. By Benjamin Moran. One vol. 12mo........ 1 25
HISTORY OF THE NATIONAL FLAG OF THE UNITED STATES, with colored illustrations........ 1 00
THE FISCAL HISTORY OF TEXAS. By William M. Gouge. In 1 vol. 8vo........ 1 50
A HISTORY OF THE SECOND WAR BETWEEN THE UNITED STATES OF AMERICA AND GREAT BRITAIN. By C. J. Ingersoll. 2 vols. 8vo., cloth........ 4 00
JOURNAL OF A MILITARY RECONNAISSANCE FROM SANTA FE, NEW MEXICO, TO THE NAVAJO COUNTRY. With 75 colored illustrations. 1 vol. 8vo........ 3 00
THE LIFE AND CORRESPONDENCE OF LORD JEFFREY. By Lord Cockburn, two vols. in one. demi 8vo........ 1 50
MILTON'S POETICAL WORKS, with a Life, Dissertations, Index, and Notes, by Prof. C. D. Cleveland, 1 vol. royal 12mo........ 1 25
THE BIBLE IN THE FAMILY, by H. A. Boardman, D. D., 1 vol. 12mo........ 75
THE BIBLE IN THE COUNTING-HOUSE. A Course of Lectures to Merchants, by H. A. Boardman, D. D. In one vol. 12mo..... 1 00
THE RACE FOR RICHES, AND SOME OF THE PITS INTO WHICH THE RUNNERS FALL. By William Arnot. With Preface and Notes, by Stephen Colwell.... 62
ANCIENT CHRISTIANITY EXEMPLIFIED. By Rev. Lyman Coleman, D. D., in 1 vol. octavo........ 2 50
HISTORY OF THE MORMONS OF UTAH. By J. W. Gunnison, U. S. A. With illustrations, in 1 vol. 12mo., cloth........ 50
THE LIFE OF WILLIAM PENN. By Samuel M. Janney, 2d edition, revised, cloth. 1 75
TRAVELS IN EGYPT AND PALESTINE, by J. Thomas, M. D.. 1 vol. 12mo........ 62
LIPPINCOTT'S CABINET HISTORIES OF THE STATES, edited by T. S. ARTHUR and WILLIAM H. CARPENTER.

THE HISTORY OF VIRGINIA, cap 8vo........	62
" " " KENTUCKY, " "	62
" " " GEORGIA, " "	62
" " " NEW YORK, " "	62
" " " MASSACHUSETTS, cap 8vo..	62
" " " VERMONT, " "	62
" " " OHIO, " "	62

YIEGER'S CABINET—SPIRITUAL VAMPIRISM. A History of Ethereal Softdown, and her friends of the New Light, by C. W. Webber, 1 vol. demi octavo........ 1 00
SIMON KENTON, or the Scout's Revenge. An Historical Romance, by James Weir, illustrated, cloth........ 62
MARIE DE BERNIERE, THE MAROON, AND OTHER TALES, by W. Gilmore Simms, 1 vol. 12mo., cloth........ 1 00
THE SWORD AND THE DISTAFF; OR, FAIR, FAT, AND FORTY. By W. Gilmore Simms. 1 vol. 12mo........ 1 25
THE WIGWAM AND THE CABIN. By W. Gilmore Simms. 2 vols. in one, 12mo. cloth........ 1 25
LIBRARY FOR TRAVELLERS AND THE FIRESIDE. THE BRITISH CABINET IN 1853........ 50
THE ANNALS OF TENNESSEE, from its Settlement to the End of 18th Century. By J. G. M. Ramsey, A. M., M. D. 1 vol. 8vo., cloth........ 3 00
COMPREHENSIVE COMMENTARY ON THE HOLY BIBLE. 6 vols., including Supplement, sheep, library style........ 12 00
AUTOBIOGRAPHY OF A NEW CHURCHMAN, by John A. Little, 1 vol. 12mo., cloth........ 75
THE UNITED STATES: ITS POWER AND PROGRESS. By Guillaume Tell Poussin. Translated from the French, 1 vol. 8vo.... 2 00
AUNT PHILLIS'S CABIN; or, Southern Life as it is. An answer to "Uncle Tom's Cabin." 1 vol. 12mo. illustrated, cloth, gilt........ 75
THE HUMAN BODY AND ITS CONNECTION WITH MAN. Illustrated by th principal Organs. By James John Garth Wilkinson, in one vol. 12mo........ 1 00

www.ingramcontent.com/pod-product-compliance
Lightning Source LLC
LaVergne TN
LVHW021140110826
845150LV00005B/1077

9781425549190